THE MAIL-ORDER CRAFTS CATALOGUE

THE MAIL-ORDER CRAFTS CATALOGUE
First Edition

Supplies, Kits, Finished Items, Publications, Home Study Courses, Organizations, Services

MARGARET A. BOYD

CHILTON BOOK COMPANY
Radnor, Pennsylvania

For FRANK, the other half of me.

Copyright © 1975 by Margaret A. Boyd
First Edition
All Rights Reserved
Published in Radnor, PA, by Chilton Book Company and simultaneously in Don Mills, Ontario, Canada, by Thomas Nelson & Sons, Ltd.
Designed by Carole L. DeCrescenzo
Manufactured in the United States of America

Library of Congress Catalog Card Number: 75-4190

For their time, patience, and encouragement, I am deeply grateful to all the companies and individuals who have contributed material to this catalogue. Never were the words "I couldn't have done it without you" more true than right here!

Among the many I wish to thank, I am especially indebted to: Tom Aegeson of Candle Mill Village for his help, Barbara Brabec of Artisian Crafts for her aid and enthusiasm, Earl Bagby of Textile Crafts for his encouraging words, Patrick Donahue of Handweaver & Craftsman, Inc, and a special acknowledgment to Raymond P. Wallace.

This compilation of information is copyrighted and, therefore, reproduction by any means, of any part or parts, for any purpose, is prohibited by law unless permission for such reproduction has been granted by Chilton Book Company. Mailing lists, broken out in various ways, are available from Chilton Book Company, Radnor, PA 19089.

Although the information in this catalogue is based on verified sources and is as complete as possible at the time of publication, the possibility exists that some of the suppliers listed may have changed their stock, address, phone number, etc. While striving for total accuracy, Chilton Book Company cannot assume responsibility for errors, changes, or omissions that may exist in the compilation of this data.

CONTENTS

Author's Preface, *vii*

Editor's Preface, *ix*

How to Use This Book, *xi*

List of Abbreviations, *xiii*

Company Listing, 1

This section is an alphabetical listing of the names, addresses, and phone numbers of all the suppliers. Each listing includes the following information: an alphabetical listing of the craft materials carried; whether or not a catalogue is available; the cost of the catalogue; the discounts offered, if any; and a listing of special services and items offered, such as kits, group packs, and custom-made articles.

Craft Item Index, 143

This index is made up of an alphabetical listing of specific craft supplies such as crepe paper, glass globs, kilns, self-hardening clay, shells, Styrofoam®, and pre-made wooden items. You would go to this index if you are looking for a specific item and it will refer you to the names of the companies listed in the book that carry this item.

Craft Category Index, 221

In this index, all the craft items and suppliers are listed alphabetically in their respective craft categories—such as beadery, books, candlemaking, ceramics, decoupage, jewelrymaking, kits, plaster craft, pottery making, string craft, and tools. If you are interested in a particular craft, as a whole, this index will refer you to the suppliers listed who carry the items you need.

Geographical Index, 415

This index is a state-by-state guide to all craft suppliers listed in this book. Within each state, companies are listed alphabetically by city. This enables you to locate and place orders with the companies closest to your home.

AUTHOR'S PREFACE

Working in handcrafts, provides an outlet for the creativity and energy that we don't use in our normal work-a-day activities, and also helps to alleviate the frustrations that build up in all of us. When you're working on a craft project, all other things seem to leave your mind as you cut, paste, pound, miter, mold, distress, sculpt, stitch, whittle, or perform any one of the many other techniques now pursued by craft enthusiasts all over the country. But, before you practice any of these, you must have supplies; and to buy supplies, you need money *and* a supplier.

How much money is presently being spent in the United States for craft supplies? Let's get an idea by looking at one company—a big one—Lee Wards. About seventeen years ago, this operation (store and mail order) was doing approximately $250,000 in business annually. By the end of 1971, this same company had an annual gross of over $30 million. Their goal is to establish stores in every major selling area of the country (from "The Story Behind the Story" by Jack Wax, *Profitable Craft Merchandising*, May 1972). They are planning "to open an average of one store per month throughout the year [1973]" with more in 1974 (from Jack Wax, *Profitable Craft Merchandising*, March 1973). And this is just *one company!*

It is logical to assume that new stores aren't opened or expansion undertaken unless it is felt that a definite, growing demand for craft supplies is present. This growing company is just one place a handcrafter may find supplies. How—and where else—do handcrafters locate the items they need?

The how of it is the craftsperson cribbing household money; figuratively pawning his trombone; haunting bargain barns, junk yards, flea markets, and other unlikely places; and harassing librarians, neighbors, and old instructors. He searches for elusive raw materials, often to the limits of frustration.

Ideally, the handcrafter's "studio" is right across the street from the shop that carries all the supplies he needs. But who knows such a paradise? Even if there is a craft outlet close by, chances are it doesn't stock the bantie shell, electric wax spatula tool, or the two-inch square mirror called for by the project in the magazine you grabbed off the

Author's Preface

supermarket shelf; or even some of the standard, always needed items. So the craftsperson may turn to mail-order suppliers for craft materials.

At last, then, with supplies in hand, this wizard-craftsperson will spill them into the pot of his imagination, pulling forth the utmost his straining creativity can conjure—an object bright in the sun, truly a glory to the eye.

This Catalogue, then, is a beginning. If it aids creative human beings in their search, solving at least one of their problems, I rest contented.

Margaret A. Boyd

EDITOR'S PREFACE

We have provided two pre-paid postcards with *The Mail-Order Crafts Catalogue* for your use. On one of these cards we ask you to evaluate the book. You can use the other card to let us know if you don't receive a reply from one of the companies you wrote to, if you can't find an item that you think we should list in the Catalogue, or if you would like to be listed in the next edition.

We have verified the material herein by both written questionnaire and telephone, prior to publication. We cannot be responsible if you don't receive a reply from one of the listed companies, but we will verify that listing again before we publish the next edition; and if we don't receive a reply, we will delete the listing.

We hope you enjoy using this Catalogue as much as we enjoyed preparing it.

C.E.L.

HOW TO USE THIS BOOK

The following is a sample company listing:

Corner Cupboard Crafts, Inc.
Box 368
Lilburn, GA   30247
404–921–2153
  Decoupage, tole painting, woodware.
  Catalog: general, $1; wood.
  Complete line of arts and crafts supplies, open stock and kits.
  Kits: string art.

In the Craft Item Index, the materials that this sample company carries appear in alphabetical order among all the materials carried by other companies listed in the Catalogue. For example:

tjanting tool
  Hazel Pearson Handi Craft.
tole painting
  ⇨ Corner Cupboard Crafts, Inc.; P. C. Herwig Co., Inc.; Kraft Korner; John & Susan Scheewe; Sunflower Crafts.
tole patterns
  Bernadette Decorative Art; Decorative Designs by Dare; John & Susan Scheewe; Transart.

How to use this book

In the Craft Category Index, the materials that this sample company carries are listed by craft item under the craft category or categories in which these supplies would be used. For example:

> **tole art**
> *paper tole*
>   John's Hardware & Decoupage Supplies
>   Make It Happen Craft Studio
> *tole painting*
> ▷ Corner Cupboard Crafts, Inc.
>   P. C. Herwig Co., Inc.
>   Kraft Korner
>   John & Susan Scheewe
>   Sunflower Crafts
> *tole patterns*
>   Bernadette Decorative Art
>   Decorative Designs by Dare
>   John & Susan Scheewe

In the Geographical Index, this sample company would be found under the name of the state in which it is located. Within each state, company names are listed alphabetically by city. For example:

> **Georgia**
>   H & A Mfg. Corp., Avondale Estates
>   House of Stitches, Bainbridge
>   Purcelli's Gems, Decatur
>   Trader South, Dunwoody
>   Argosy Products, Gainesville
>   Prospector's Pouch, Kennesaw
> ▷ Corner Cupboard Crafts, Inc., Lilburn
>   The Rev. Henry N. Thomas, Macon
>   Loosie Goosie Egg Craft Shop, Rome
>   Solartherm Co., Roswell

Therefore, if you are looking for a specific item, such as *tole painting supplies*, you would go to the Craft Item Index which would, in turn, refer you to the companies which carry that item; if you are interested in supplies for a specific craft, such as *tole art*, you would go to the Craft Category Index and under the name of the craft you would find all the supplies and suppliers listed in the Catalogue who carry those items; if you want to try to order your supplies from companies that are close by, you would go to the Geographical Index where you would find all the companies contained in the Catalogue listed under the state in which they are located (foreign companies are grouped together at the end of the Geographical Index).

You will also find in the upper outside corner of each page, the name of the book section. Below the section name, you will find key words for the first and last alphabetical entries on the page, following dictionary style.

LIST OF ABBREVIATIONS

BOOK	book or books	NEWL	newsletters
CLUB	club plans	NEWP	newspapers
GROU	group packs	ORGA	organizations
HOME	home study courses	SERV	special services
LEAF	leaflets	SUBS	subscriptions
MAGA	magazines		

STATE NAMES

AL	Alabama	MT	Montana
AK	Alaska	NE	Nebraska
AZ	Arizona	NV	Nevada
AR	Arkansas	NH	New Hampshire
CA	California	NJ	New Jersey
CO	Colorado	NM	New Mexico
CT	Connecticut	NY	New York
DE	Delaware	NC	North Carolina
DC	District of Columbia	ND	North Dakota
FL	Florida	OH	Ohio
GA	Georgia	OK	Oklahoma
HI	Hawaii	OR	Oregon
ID	Idaho	PA	Pennsylvania
IL	Illinois	RI	Rhode Island
IN	Indiana	SC	South Carolina
IA	Iowa	SD	South Dakota
KS	Kansas	TN	Tennessee
KY	Kentucky	TX	Texas
LA	Louisiana	UT	Utah
ME	Maine	VT	Vermont
MD	Maryland	VA	Virginia
MA	Massachusetts	WA	Washington
MI	Michigan	WV	West Virginia
MN	Minnesota	WI	Wisconsin
MS	Mississippi	WY	Wyoming
MO	Missouri		

THE MAIL-ORDER CRAFTS CATALOGUE

COMPANY LISTING

A 'N L's Hobbicraft, Inc.
50 Broadway, P.O. Box 7025
Asheville, NC 28807
704–253–4444

Aluminum, artist's supplies, basketry, cane, ceramic kilns, ceramic supplies, decoupage, dip film, egg stands, enameling, enameling kilns, miniatures, mosaics, toleware.
Books.
Catalog: $1.
Kits: leather.

Acme Dress Form Co., Inc.
380 Throop Ave.
Brooklyn, NY 11221
212–782–7110

Stretch dress forms.
Write for information.

Activa Products Inc.
582 Market St.
San Francisco, CA 94104
415–421–9630

Books: celluclay (instant papier mache), flower drying with silica gel, general arts & crafts series, porcelainizing fresh flowers with Ceramex.
Write for information.

Adhesive Products Corp.
1660 Boone Ave.
Bronx, NY 10460
212–542–4600

Additives, fiberglass, fillers, liquid latex (bonded bronze), polyurethane foam, rayon towels.
Catalog.

Adobe-Craft
18322 Carlwyn Dr.
Castro Valley, CA 94546
415–893–3546

Books: making water resistant adobes.
Catalog.

Adris Oriental Gem & Art Corp.
565 Fifth Avenue
New York, NY 10017
212–986–0720

Agate cabochons, beggar beads, bloodstone, emerald beads, emeralds, Indian stones, moss agate, rubies, sapphire, star ruby, star sapphires.
Catalog.

Advance Process Supply Co.
400 N. Noble St.
Chicago, IL 60622
312–829–1400

Company Listing
Advance—Allcraft

Inks, screen printing equipment.
Catalog: $1.
Kits: screen printing.
One of the world's largest manufacturer/supplier for screen printing materials and equipment.

Adventures In Crafts
218 East 81 St.
New York, NY 10028
212-628-8081

Decoupage, hardware, prints, tinware, trims, undecorated woodenware.
Books: decoupage.
Kits: decoupage.
Write for information.

Air Capitol Molds, Inc.
6352 North Hillside
Wichita, KS 67219
316-744-0351

Casting tables, ceramic industrial hand cream, ceramic molds, quick-slip pouring.
Catalog: $1.

Mrs. Marilyn G. Alabran
91 Spruce St.
Framingham, MA 01701
617-877-3427

Mini-pots.
Write for information.

Albert Findings, Inc.
66 W. 47th St.
New York, NY 10036
212-765-5385

Gold filled findings, gold findings, sterling silver findings.
Catalog.

Alberta's Molds Inc.
209 E. Foothill Blvd., P.O. Box 692
Monrovia, CA 91016
213-358-1831

Ceramic molds.
Catalog: $1.
Molds include vases, animals, planters, figurines, angels, Christmas and Easter items, lamps, ashtrays.

J. Alday
Box 310
Lucern Valley, CA 92356
714-248-6161

Preserved butterflies.
Write for information.

Alessi Lapidary Supplies
16 E. Central Blvd.
Villa Park, IL 60181
312-832-3424

Baroques, copper enameling supplies, lapidary equipment, mountings, rough cutting stones, slabs, sterling silver sheet, sterling silver wire.
Books.
Write for information or mountings catalog, $1 (refundable).

Aleta's Rock Shop
1515 Plainfield, N.E.
Grand Rapids, MI 49505
616-363-5394

Diamond powders, faceting units, gem findings, gem saws, grinding compounds, grinding units, lapidary supplies, lapidary tumblers, rocks.
Carries rocks from Mexico, America, Africa, Brazil, Australia and India for cutting and tumbling.
Catalog.

Allcraft Tool & Supply Co.
215 Park Ave.
Hicksville, NY 11801
516-433-1660

Casting equipment, casting tools, casting waxes, crafting equipment, enameling, engraving, gem making equipment, goldsmithing equipment, hand tools, jewelrymaking tools, kilns, lapidary supplies, polishing machines, power tools, sandblasting tools, scrimshaw scribers, silversmithing machinery, silversmithing tools, soldering tools, tools, vacuum casting, wax casting tools, welding unit, workshop power tools.
Books.
Carries workshop power tools called "unimat" that can be used for miniatures (metal, plastic or wood).

Catalogs: $1.
Discount: quantity purchases.

Mrs. Barbara Allen
Box 1158
Canyon Country, CA 91351
No phone orders.
    Turkey eggs.
    Books: egg decorating.

Herb Allen's Hole in One
3926 Kenosha
San Diego, CA 92117
714-276-0200
    Goose eggshells, ostrich eggs, precut eggs. Also has goose eggs with one mini-hole.
    Discount: quantity purchases.
    Write for information.

Alohalei Hawaii
Dept. M.
P.O. Box 10
Honolulu, HI 96816
808-847-0249
    Bead necklace kits contain pearls, supplies, instructions in various Polynesian designs.
    Catalog: 25¢ (refundable).
    Kits: bead lei necklace.

A. D. Alpine Inc.
353 Coral Cir.
El Segundo, CA 90245
213-322-2430
    Ceramic kilns, ceramic supplies, clay carts, electric lehrs, gas lehrs, glass blowing equipment, glass melting tanks, glory holes, potter's wheels, pug mills.
    Write for information.

Althor Products
202 Bay 46 St.
Brooklyn, NY 11214
212-373-7444
    Blank labels, plastic boxes.
    Write for information.

The Amber Lion
P.O. Box 686
Fulton, TX 78358
512-729-7046
    Hand-painted needlepoint canvas.
    Books: decorative patterns for tole and cutouts.
    Write for information.

America's Hobby Center Inc.
146 W. 22nd St.
New York, NY 10011
212-675-8922
    Decals, model accessories, model hand tools, model power tools.
    Books.
    Catalogs: complete set, $1.79.
    Kits: model aircraft, wood ship model ship.
    Separate model catalogs are available: airplane, boats, cars, 50¢; HO railroads, HO cars, motoring, 75¢; ships (wood hulls), 50¢; plastic displays (boats, planes, cars), 50¢; plastic airplanes, boats, cars, 10¢; also carries parts including miniature light bulbs, engines, mufflers, hand pumps, filters.

American Art Associates Publications, Inc.
P.O. Box 34263
Bethesda, MD 20034
301-229-5522
    Books: decoupage under glass.

American Art Clay Co. Inc.
4717 W. 16th St.
Indianapolis, IN 46222
317-244-6871
    Chalks, clays, firing clay, floral clay, furniture finishes, metal enameling equipment, Mexican pottery clay, modeling clay, modeling dough clay, nonfiring clay, plaster impregnated sculpture tape.
    Books: ceramic decoration, metal enameling, potter's wheel.
    Catalog: general; pottery and metal enameling.
    Write for local distributor.

American Butterfly Co.
3609 Glen Ave.
Baltimore, MD 21215
301-578-0017
    Preserved butterflies.
    Write for information.

Company Listing
American—American

The American Candlemaker
2010 Sunset
Pacific Grove, CA 93950
No phone orders.
  Magazines: candlemaking.
  Subscriptions: monthly copy 50¢, 1 year $3.50.
  Write for one free issue.

American Crafts Council
44 W. 53rd St.
New York, NY 10019
212-977-8980
  National spokesman for the crafts; annual directory of craft shops, galleries, supply sources; membership includes a bimonthly magazine "Craft Horizons" and slide rental service.
  Organizations: general arts and crafts.
  Write for information.

American Decorative Arts, Inc.
Box 117
Dorset, VT 05251
802-867-2235
  Paints, stencil brushes.
  Books: stencils.
  Catalog.
  Kits: home decorating stencils.

American Edestaal Inc.
Unimat Div.
1 Atwood Ave.
Tenafly, NJ 07670
201-871-3800
  Table top machining center.
  Catalog.
  Machining center used for miniature crafting--to machine small parts from metal, plastic and wood, converts from lathe to vertical mill to drill press, grinder and polisher.
  Write for local distributor.

American Handicrafts
National Office
1001 Foch St.
Fort Worth, TX 76107
817-335-4161
  Art metal, beadery, blockprinting, bottle cutters, candlemaking supplies, copper craft, copper enameling supplies, crochet jewelry, crushed glass, decoupage, dip film, felt, frames, jewelrymaking accessories, lacing, lampmaking, leather, macrame accessories, mini-easels, papier mache, patterns, prints, resin craft supplies, stained glass.
  Catalog: 25¢.
  Discount: quantity purchases.
  Group packs.
  Kits: antiquing, candlemaking, copper, decoupage, dip film, lamps, leather, resin, string, tooling.
  Write for nearest location.

American Home Crafts
641 Lexington Ave.
New York, NY 10022
212-935-4100
  Magazines: batik, beadcraft, decorative accessories, decoupage, jewelry making, macrame, needlecraft.
  Subscriptions: semi-annually at newsstand, $1.25.

American Indian Portrait Dolls
June Goodnow
Box 283, Dept 12
Armour, SD 57313
605-724-2105
  Rag doll patterns.
  Send SASE for information.

American Machine & Tool Co.
Royersford, PA 19468
215-948-3800
  Belt sanders, carpentry power tools, drill presses, joiner-planers, lathes, woodworking tools.
  Catalog.
  Kits: wood shaper.

American School
Drexel Ave. at 58th St.
Chicago, IL 60637
312-643-4700
  Home study courses: blacksmith, carpentry, cement masonry, graphic arts, machine shop, masonry, metallurgy, sheet metal, sheet metal working, upholstery, welding, woodworking.
  Write for information.

American Technical Society
848 E. 58th St.
Chicago, IL 60637
312-643-4700
  Books: basic graphic arts, cabinetmaking, carpentry

fundamentals, machine shop operations, masonry, metal work, metallurgy, millwork, oxyacetylene welding, plastering, sheet metal, upholstery.
Catalog.
Contact your nearest bookstore or write above.

Sonie Ames
P.O. Box 1076
Paradise, CA   95969
916-877-0909
  Books.
  Catalog.
  China painting instructions include flowers, plants, cherubs, female figures.
  Discount: quantity purchases for teachers, studios.
  Leaflets: china painting.

Amherst Press
Amherst, WI   54406
715-824-5890
  Books: silhouettes.
  Write for information.

Anne Amiot
4642 Southfield Rd.
Dearborn, MI   48125
No phone orders.
  Ceramic tools, patterns, soap cutting tools, wax cutting tools.
  Books.
  Write for information.
  Write for local distributor.

Amro
121 Lincolnway West
New Oxford, PA   17350
No phone orders.
  Foreign model railroad accessories, foreign model railroad trains.
  Carries models of all scales and gauges.
  Catalog.

The Amulet
1541 Kingston Rd.
Scarborough, Ontario, Canada
416-691-7641
  Books: jewelry wire.
  Catalog of wire supplies available.

Anchor Mold Co.
8500 So. State Rt. 202
Tipp City, OH   45371
513-667-1234
  Ceramic molds.
  Catalog: $1.
  Write for local distributor.

Anchor Tool & Supply Co.
Box 265
Chatham, NJ   07928
201-635-2094
  Copper, enameling supplies, jeweler's bronze, jeweler's circles, jeweler's tools, jeweler's wire, jewelry findings, kilns, pewter, silversmithing supplies, sterling silver sheet.
  Catalog: $1.50 (50¢ refundable).

P. S. Andrews Co.
603 So. Main St.
St. Charles, MO   63301
314-946-6095
  Beadery, bottle cutters, candlemaking supplies, cooking crystals, decoupage, felt, filigree paper lace, gold braids, gold leaf, hardware, lacing, leather, mosaic rock, prints, rhinestones, toleware, woodware.
  Catalog: $2 (refundable).

Rebecca Andrews
P.O. Box 390
Walnut Ridge, AR   72476
501-886-3160
  Rug cutters, rug frames, rug hooks, rug patterns.
  Books.
  Send SASE for information.

Angelo Bros. Co.
Lamparts Div.
10981 Decatur Rd.
Philadelphia, PA   19154
215-632-9600
  Brass lamp ornaments, candle covers, decorative lamp chain, lamp accessories, lamp ball ornaments, lamp bandings, lamp bases, lamp canopies, lamp filigrees, lamp finials, lamp finishes, lamp marble bases, lamp parts, lamp switchplates, lamp tassels,

Company Listing
Angelo—Arco

lampshade holders, light bulbs, teakite lamp bases, wood lamp bases.
> Carries unusual light bulbs: neon glow, glass flame, flickering, mod, sphere, torch, symbolic, star; carries lamp shades including tiffany, plastic, dome, glass, parchment; chimneys, prisms, crystal beads.
> Kits: lamp adapters, lamp converters, lamp shade, make-a-lamp, swag lamp, wired converter.
> Write for local distributor.
> Write for information.

Angora Diablo
805 La Gonda Way
Danville, CA   94526
415-837-6843
> Grease mohair wool.
> Write for information.

Anita of Calif.
10950 Longford St.
Lakeview Terrace, CA   91342
No phone orders.
> China painting supplies.
> Catalog: 25¢.
> Includes Dresden bisque designs.

Anne's Treasure Trove
P.O. Box 10705
Honolulu, HI   96816
808-988-6696
> American Indian seed beads, cowry shells, leather lacings, pearls.
> Carries kola, wiliwili, job's tears and other seeds from exotic Hawaiian plants.
> Catalog: 25¢ (refundable).
> Discount: quantity purchases.
> Kits: pits, seeds, tropical seeds.

Anozira Jewelers
4002 North Stone Ave.
Tucson, AZ   85705
602-888-0605
> Carnelian agate gemballs, cultured pearls, faceted garnets, gold filled findings, green agate gemballs.
> Catalog: $1 (refundable).

Antique Doll Reproductions
Box 103, Montevallo Route
Milo, MO   64767
417-876-4785
> China doll parts, doll parts, dressed dolls, Parian doll heads.
> Also carries doll parts "expertly copied" from rare antiques.
> Kits.
> Send 2 stamps for information.

Antoine's
112 E. Lexington St.
Independence, MO   64050
816-252-8860
> Catalog: 25¢.
> Kits: processing-your-own rose petals.

Archer's Hobby World
1852 North Trustin Ave.
Orange, CA   92665
714-998-1272
> Kits: British railroad model.
> Posters, postcards, tools, paints, all model supplies for the scale modeler of aircraft, ships, armor, military miniatures and railroad. Specializing in hard-to-get overseas items.
> Write for information, or railroads $1; aircraft and armor, $1.

Arco Publishing Co., Inc.
219 Park Ave. So.
New York, NY   10003
212-673-6600
> Books: boats, cabinetry, carpentry, children's projects, craft anthology, furniture refinishing, general arts & crafts series, metal working, model airplanes, model car handbook, needlework, Early American furniture making.
> Catalog.
> Contact your nearest bookstore or write above.

Arco Tools Inc.
421 W. 203rd St.
New York, NY   10034
212-942-1400
> Carpentry power tools, drill attachments, woodworking tools.
> Write for local distributor.
> Write for information.

ARE Creations Inc.
No. Montpelier Rd., Box 155N
Plainfield, VT 05667
802-454-8325
Jewelrymaking supplies, silver.
Write for information.

Argosy Products
Rt 1 Box 350B
Gainesville, GA 30501
404-887-9769
Catalog.
Kits: gem picture, gem tree.

Art Consultants
405 Lexington Ave.
New York, NY 10017
212-682-1881
Casting items, ceramic supplies, ceramic tools, kilns, melting equipment, metals, polyurethane foam, resins, sculpture supplies, sculpture tools, wax pens.
Catalog.

Art Decal Co.
1145 Loma Ave.
Long Beach, CA 90804
213-434-2711
Custom-made ceramic decals.
Write for information.

Art Mart, Inc.
31 N. Meramac
St. Louis, MO 63105
314-725-7858
Adhesives, blockprinting, carving tools, carving wood, ceramic supplies, enameling, etching supplies, felt pens, furniture finishes, jewelry findings, knives, marking pencils, mosaic tiles, paints, plaster, plastic casting, screen process supplies, sculpturing metal, sculpturing stone, stained glass paints, textile paints.
Books.
Catalog: 25¢.

Artcraft
Baldwin, MD 21013
301-877-8113
Books.
Catalog: 25¢.
Services: out-of-print book search.

Artis, Inc.
9123 E. Las Tunas, Box A
Temple City, CA 91780
213-287-6147
Cold water dyes, macrame accessories, papier mache, silica gel, synthetic raffia straw.
Books: painting.
Catalog.

Artisan Crafts
Star Route 4, Box 179-Mo
Reeds Spring, MO 65737
No phone orders.
Magazines: general arts and crafts.
Organization offers handcrafts registry service, sources of supplies, shops/galleries information and "The Eggers Directory".
Organizations: general arts and crafts.
Subscriptions: quarterly copy $1.50, 1 year $5, foreign $6.
Write for information.

Artistry In Wood
P.O. Box 131
Columbia, IL 62236
618-939-8808
Easels, paper strips, prints, quilling supplies, wood boxes, wood jewelry, wood plaques.
Books.
Catalog: $1.
Kits: filigree ornament.

Artists & Craftsman Guild
17 Eastman St.
Cranford, NJ 07016
201-276-1191
Cathedral glass, copper tape, lead came, stained glass supplies.
Catalog.
Kits: stained glass.

Artrox Rock of the Month Club
3901 Pershing
El Paso, TX 79903
915-566-1520
Club plans: lapidary.

Company Listing
Artrox—Atlantic

Membership includes monthly memos of new materials available, no purchase obligation. Write for information.

Arts and Crafts Unlimited
P. O. Box 572
Minneapolis, MN 55440
No phone orders.
Books: greeting card patterns.
Catalog: 50¢ includes free greeting card pattern.
Kits: birthday cards, note cards, Christmas cards.

Artweek
1305 Franklin St.
Oakland, CA 94612
415-763-0422
Discount: group rates.
Magazine features calendar of events in West Coast galleries and museums, and listings of regional, national and international festivals, sales and competitions.
Magazines: general arts and crafts.
Subscriptions: single copy 35¢, 45 times yearly, 1 year $8.

Ashford Handicrafts Ltd.
P.O. Box 12
Rakaia, Canterbury, New Zealand
No phone orders.
Catalog.
Kits: spinning wheels.

E. H. Ashley & Co., Inc.
200 Dean St.
Providence, RI 02903
401-421-3666
Flexible brass settings, glass stones, semi-precious stones.
Carries semi-precious stones from Germany and glass stones from Germany and Austria.
Kits: do-it-yourself, neckchains.
Write for information.

Aspen Lapidary
P.O. Box 6517
Denver, CO 80206
303-388-4666
Agates, amethyst, jewelry findings, lapidary abrasives, lapidary machinery, lapidary supplies, lapidary tools, rhodosite, thulite, tigereye, verdite, zebra stone.
Catalog.

Associated Book Sellers
147 McKinley Avenue
Bridgeport, CT 06606
203-366-5494
Books: general arts & crafts series.
Catalog.

Associated Hobby Manufacturers Inc.
623 E. Cayuga St.
Philadelphia, PA 19120
215-744-9820
Model railroad buildings, model railroad cars, model railroad equipment.
Catalog: parts and 'scratch' builders, $1; plastic kit, 50¢.
Kits.
Write for local distributor.

Association Press
291 Broadway
New York, NY 10007
212-349-0700
Books: clock repair, jewelrymaking, American Indian crafts.
Contact your nearest bookstore or write above.
Write for information.

Atlantic Mold Corp.
3660 Quaker Bridge Rd.
Trenton, NJ 08619
609-587-5151
Ceramic molds, clock movements, mold releases.
Catalog: $1.
Molds include modern, antique, novelty, classic and religious subjects. Specific molds include Kennedy half dollar bank, turkey, smilies, steins, pitcher, go-go boys and girls, Civil War soldiers, Easter and Christmas items.

Atlantic Upholstery Supply Co.
12 E. Camden St.
Hackensack, NJ 07601
201-489-2220
Basketry, bolsters, cane, drapery supplies, furniture legs, furniture parts, rods, rubber

cushions, rush, seagrass, slip cover supplies, splint seat weaving, table bases, upholstery cleaning, upholstery supplies, wheels.
  Send 25¢ and SASE for catalog.

Theodore Audel & Co.
4300 W. 62nd St.
Indianapolis, IN   46268
317-291-3100
  Books: bricklaying, building, carpentry, masonry.
  Write for information.

Audria's
538 Seminary South
Fort Worth, TX   76115
817-926-1191
  Kits: craft dog fur.
  Write for information.

Aunt Martha's Studios Inc.
1245 Swift
Kansas City, MO   64116
816-471-3313
  Quilt designs.
  Books: quilt patterns.
  Write for information.

M. B. Austin
138 W. 25th Ave.
San Mateo, CA   94403
415-341-5847
  Patches, sew-on railroad patches.
  Catalog: 50¢; plus sample patch, $1.

Australian Exports
10049 Alondra Blvd.
Bellflower, CA   90706
213-866-6581
  Australian opals, gemstones, Mexican fire agate, Mexican opal, opal chips, opal cutting pieces, opal practice pieces, opal triplets.
  Catalog.
  Kits.

Australian Gem Trading Co.
294 Little Collins St.
Melbourne, Australia 3000
No phone orders.
  Black opals, opals, sapphire.
  Books: gemstones of Australia.
  Write for information.

Australian Imports
3684 Fairmount Ave.
San Diego, CA   92105
714-282-1700
  Australian chrysoprase, Australian opals, bulk opals, gemstones, Mexican opal, opal carvings, opal specimens, opal triplets, opals.
  Write for information.

Auto Modeler
7950 Deering Ave.
Canoga Park, CA   91304
213-887-0550
  Magazine features coverage of racing, sports and stock cars; tips on painting and scratch building; information on new models and model kits.
  Magazines: modeling.
  Subscriptions: quarterly copy $1.25.

Auto Upholstery Institute
Box 64
Orange, CA   92669
714-997-1235
  Courses are VA approved and include renovating, repairing, and customizing vehicle interiors.
  Home study courses: upholstering.
  Write for information.

Auto World, Inc.
701 N. Keyser Ave.
Scranton, PA   18508
717-346-7495
  Model car accessories, model HO cars, model slot cars.
  Catalog: model car, 25¢.
  Kits: model car.

Robert Ayottes' Designery
P.O. Box 287
Center Sandwich, NH   03227
603-284-6915
  Hand weaving, looms, spinning accessories, yarns.
  Books.
  Club offers members lower than usual prices on yarns.
  Club plans: yarns.
  Send SASE for information.

Company Listing
B & J—Barnes

B & J Star Co.
P.O. Box 577
Westfield, NJ 07090
201–647–4575
Catalog.
Kits: Linde star jewelry.

B & M Yarn Co.
151 Essex St.
New York, NY 10002
212–475–6380
   Dutch yarn, French yarn, raffia, ribbon, yarns.
Catalog: 50¢; yarn color card available.

Bachmann
1400 E. Erie Ave.
Philadelphia, PA 19124
215–533–1600
   Model animals, model cars, model fencing, model freight load equipment, model railroad accessories, model railroad signs, model trees, model trucks.
Catalog: 50¢.
Kits: building lighting, model animals, model birds, model dogs, model planes, model ships, model tanks.

Badger Air-Brush Co.
9201 Gage Ave.
Franklin Park, IL 60131
312–678–3104
   Airbrushes, bench power tools.
Catalog.

R. C. Baker
3580 East Hampton
Tucson, AZ 85716
602–326–2744
   Cabochons, lapis lazuli.
Carries lapis lazuli in a vivid blue color with pyrite and some matrix; also has rough material for cutting.
Send SASE for sample and information.

Ball O' Yarn
146 Merchant
Decatur, IL 62523
217–428–6722
Catalog.
Kits: knitting poncho, mitten, Christmas bell.

Ballantine Books, Inc.
201 E. 50th St.
New York, NY 10022
212–751–2600
Books: clothing, fabric printing, general arts & crafts series, macrame, pottery, printing, sewing, tie-dye.

Barbara Bannister
Needlecraft Books
Alanson, MI 49706
616–529–6558
   Patterns.
Books: dolls, needlecrafts, quilts.
Catalog: 50¢ each craft.

Barb's Shoe Makings
15834 S.E. 10th St.
Bellevue, WA 98008
206–746–3468
   Handcrafted shoes supplies.
Price list available.

Barker Enterprises
15106 10th Ave. S.W.
Seattle, WA 98166
206–244–1870
   Bayberry wax, beeswax, candle additives, candle dyes, candle scents, candle waxes, candle wicks, candleholders, candlemaking supplies, carnauba wax, glassware, plastic candle molds, wooden candle molds.
Books.
Catalog: 25¢ (refundable).

Barnes & Blake
P.O. Box 2387
New York, NY 10001
No phone orders.
   Fabrics.
Also has canvas by the yard.
Kits: embroidery, needlepoint.
Write for information.

A. S. Barnes and Co., Inc.
Cranbury, NJ 08512
609–655–0190
Books: candlemaking, country crafts, decorating, general arts & crafts series, wood carving, wood crafts.

Contact your nearest bookstore or write above.
Write for information.

Barnstable Originals by H.W. Smith
50 Harden Ave.
Camden, ME   04843
207–236–8162
  Miniature furniture.
  Carries individual pieces or complete settings for the serious collector.
  Catalog: $1.

Bee Basch Designs
1525 Gulph Blvd.
Englewood, FL   33533
813–474–1402
  Mold patterns, plaster ceramic molds.
  Catalog: $2.
  Original designs and original patterns for molds.

Basic Crafts Co.
312 E. 23rd St.
New York, NY   10010
212–674–7220
  Adhesives, binders board, book cloths, book presses, gold foil, hand bookbinding equipment, tools.
  Catalog.

Baxwood Crafters
1141 Commercial Dr.
Lexington, KY   40505
606–266–8989
  Catalog.
  Kits: lamp, with wood bases.

Bay Country Woodcrafters
U. S. Rt 13
Oak Hall, VA   23416
804–824–3639
  Glass eyes, green wing teals, wood ducks, wood mallards.
  Catalog: 25¢.
  Kits: wood duck decoy.

Beacon
Box 117
Rothsay, MN   56579
218–867–2154
  Lapidary grinders, lapidary polishing equipment, lapidary saws, lapidary supplies.
  Catalog.
  Write for local distributor.

Beacon Chemical Co., Inc.
244 Lafayette St.
New York, NY   10012
212–226–6051
  Candle scents, candlemaking supplies, epoxy adhesives.
  Write for local distributor.

Bead Game
505 N. Fairfax Ave.
Los Angeles, CA   90036
213–653–3991
  Alphabet beads, bead looms, beadery, brass beads, clay beads, cow horn beads, evil-eye beads, feathers, gem beads, gemstones, glass beads, glazed beads, imported beads, ivory beads, jewelry chains, jewelry findings, jewelrymaking accessories, mache beads, mosaic beads, nuts, pearls, plastic beads, porcelain beads, pre-Columbian beads, seeds, shell beads, tortoise-shell beads, trade beads, wood beads.
  Catalog: 25¢.
  Discount: quantity purchases.

Beadcraft
24843 Blackmar
Warren, MI   48091
313–756–8148
  Kits: flower bead.
  Send SASE for information.

The Beadcraft Corner/Beadcraft Club
P.O. Box 5754
Augusta, GA   30906
404–798–3157
  American Indian seed beads, aurora borealis beads, bamboo beads, beadery, beadery accessories, doll parts, faceted beads, findings, key chains, metallic beads, pearls, pony beads, propellar (tri) beads, rocailles, rondelles, rosebeads, safety pins.
  Books.
  Catalog.

Company Listing
Beadcraft—Bell

Club offers discounts and periodically sends special bead lists.
Club plans: beadery.
Discount: quantity purchases.

Beadnik's Arts & Crafts
P.O. Box 212, Wyk. Sta.
New Rochelle, NY 10804
914–235–6827

Beadery, Christmas decorating items, tape, wire.
Catalog: 25¢.
Kits: beaded flower.

Bead-Weavers
526 Duncan St.
San Francisco, CA 94131
415–826–1869

Kit design are adapted from American Indian pottery, baskets, rugs, fabrics.
Kits: necklace bead-weaving.
Write for information.

Beagle Mfg. Co.
4377 No. Baldwin Ave.
El Monte, CA 91731
213–442–1168

Books: leaded stain glass.

Bear Cave
P.O. Box 94
West Roxbury, MA 02132
No phone orders.

Acrylics, casting epoxy, casting foam, electric tools, hand tools, plastic squeeze bottles, styrene.
Catalog: send 10¢ stamp.
Discount: quantity purchases.
Kits: acrylic restoring and creating finishes, birdhouse, boats, patchwork, sewing, wood boxes.

Beard's Art Needlework Studio
P.O. Box 5222
Lexington, KY 40505
606–254–4372

Coat-of-arms needlepoint, portraits of customer's home or pets.
Catalog.
Kits: monogrammed handbags, needlepoint.
Southwestern designs include cactus, blossoms, Pueblo mission, Navajo woman, chili peppers.

Beaver Canyon Campground
Box 849
Beaver, UT 84713
801–438–5654

Black agate nodules, blue agate, clear quartz, facet grade flourite, giant quartz, green flourite, green grossular garnets, red jasper, smoky quartz, snowflake obsidian, topaz, tourmaline XL'S, Transvaal jade, Utah red nodules.
Carries Utah red nodules up to 200 lb; also has gold sheen in golf-ball size pebbles for eyes, eggs, spheres.
Discount: 20% on $50+ Order on official letterhead.
Price list available.

Dorothy H. Becker
1378 E. 8 St.
Brooklyn, NY 11230
No phone orders.

Dressmakers pattern graph paper.
Write for information.

Bedford Lumber Co., Inc.
P.O. Box 65
Shelbyville, TN 37160
615–684–2825

Hardware, lumber, turned legs.
Carries 117 furniture making kits in red cedar and veneer.
Catalog: 25¢.
Kits: furniture making.

Behnsen Silk Screen Supply Ltd.
950 Richards St.
Vancouver 2, B.C., Canada
604–683–6951

Batik supplies, screen process supplies.
Also has frames, screens, tools, equipment, inks and dyes, papers, screen accessories.
Write for information.

Bell Studio
7061 8th Ave. N.W.
Seattle, WA 98117
206–784–5013

China painting designs, decoupage designs, glass designs, one stroke design.
Discounts: for teachers, studios.
Send SASE for information.

Company Listing
Belle—Berry's

Belle Craft
119 E. Oklahoma
Guthrie, OK 73044
405-282-0775
 Plaster craft, resin craft molds.
 Books.
 Catalog: $1.
 General arts and crafts supplies. Carries over 900 plaster craft and resin molds.

Belsaw Power Tools
994 Field Bldg.
Kansas City, MO 64111
816-561-9255
 Workshop power tools.
 Catalog.
 Power tool (saws to width, planes to thickness, and molds to desired pattern in one operation).

Charles A. Bennett Co., Inc.
809 West Detweiller Dr.
Peoria, IL 61614
309-691-4454
 Books: cabinetry, drafting, enameling, furniture making, industrial plastics, leather craft, metal working, millwork, sheet metal, tailoring, wood turning, woodworking.
 Catalog.

Dorothy Benson
8031 Pawnee
Prairie Village, KS 66208
913-383-3077
 Books.
 Has patterns and ideas for a variety of crafts, also helpful hints on tracing, papers, lettering with colored inks; and enlarging and reducing patterns.

Bruce Benziger
8701 Wilshire Blvd.
Beverly Hills, CA 90211
213-657-4800
 Books: general arts & crafts series, machine shop, operation of woodworking machines, sheet metal, upholstery, woodturning.
 Catalog.

Bergen Arts & Crafts, Inc.
Box 381
Marblehead, MA 01945
617-631-8440
 Artist's supplies, basketry, batik, block-printing, candlemaking supplies, ceramic glazes, ceramic kilns, clock movements, copper, decoupage, dip film, drawing paper, enameling, enameling kilns, engraving, engraving tools, glass chunks, glass gems, hand tools, jewelrymaking accessories, kilns, lamp parts, lighter inserts, macrame accessories, metal craft, mosaics, music boxes, porcelain flowers, potter's equipment, power tools, resins, rice paper, stained glass, textile paints, tissue paper, woodware.
 Books.
 Catalog: $1 (refundable; free on institution letterhead).

Bergsten Jade Co.
Box 2381
Castro Valley, CA 94546
415-538-7136
 Jade, nephrite jade.
 Also has jade from Alaska, British Columbia, Burma, California, Kazakstan, New Zealand, Rhodesia, Siberia, Taiwan and Wyoming.
 Price list available.

Bernadette Decorative Art
2400 S.W. Richardson St.
Portland, OR 97201
503-244-5798
 Decorative patterns, tole patterns, unfinished woodenware.
 Folk art patterns and brochure, $1.

Berry's of Maine
20-22 Main St.
Yarmouth, ME 04096
207-846-4112
 Braiders, burlap, dyes, patterns, rug braiding, rug frames, rug hooking supplies, rug hooking tools, rugmaking supplies, stands, swatches, tapestry wool.
 Books.
 Catalog: 10¢.
 Kits: embroidery, needlepoint.

Company Listing
Berryman—Birchwood

Dorothy Berryman Studio
4641 Valley Forge Lane
Virginia Beach, VA 23462
No phone orders.
   China painting supplies.
   Discount: quantity purchases.
   Scarf clips with unpainted china medallions.
   Write for information.

Bersted's
Box 40
Monmouth, IL 61462
309-734-7011
   Basketry, candle paints, candlemaking supplies, cane, liquid rubber, papier mache, plaster casting, reed.
   Books.
   Catalog: 25¢ (refundable).
   Kits: candlemaking, decoupage, reed.

Best Foods
A Division of CPC International Inc.
International Plaza
Englewood Cliffs, NJ 07632
No phone orders.
   Books: dye patterns and techniques, dye-craft.
   Write for information.

Bet-Roc Enterprises Inc.
5605 Noble Circle, S.E.
Huntsville, AL 35802
205-881-5058
   Casting equipment, lapidary supplies, lapidary tumblers, tree making.
   Books: gemology, lapidary, rockhounding.
   Catalog: $1 (refundable with $10 order).
   Kits: jewelrymaking.

Bethlehem Imports
5231 Cushman Place
San Diego, CA 92110
714-296-4591
   Beadery, carved beads, glass tubular beads, olivewood beads.
   Also has Blue Persian donkey, Turkish evil-eye, onyx, clay, venetian mosaic, glass chevrons and pony, bamboo, sea urchin spines and beads, shells, mother-of-pearl, camel bone, sandlewood, african traders, ambers, sand and ostrich eggshell.
   Catalog: plus samples, $1.

Better Homes & Gardens
P.O. Box 374
Des Moines, IA 50302
515-284-9011
   Patterns, yarns.
   Books.
   Kits: crewel, sampler.
   Write for information.

Better Homes & Gardens Books
1716 Locust St.
Des Moines, IA 50309
515-284-9011
   Books: bead craft, crewel embroidery, embroidery, general arts & crafts series, needlepoint, sewing.
   Contact your nearest bookstore or write above.
   Write for information.

Dorothy Biddle Service
Mail Order Dept.
Hawthorne, NY 10532
914-769-0240
   Corsage making supplies, flower arrangement supplies, flowermaking supplies, preserved butterflies.
   Catalog.

F. E. Biegert Co.
11232 Indian Trail
Dallas, TX 75209
214-526-2291
   Grout, grout colors, Italian glass mosaic tiles, nippers.
   Catalog: tile sample board, $1.50.

Bingaman Plans
Dept. 100, P.O. Box 74
Langhorne, PA 19047
215-945-8166
   Leaflets: plans for making wooden lanterns.
   Send SASE for information.

Birchwood Casey
7900 Fuller Rd.
Eden Prairie, MN 55343
612-941-1240
   Antiquing, metal finishing, wood finishing.
   Catalog.

Biship's House of Gems
Box 38481
Dallas, TX 75238
214–341–6426

Abalone, agates, amethyst, diamonds, faceted stones, garnet, Indian moonstone, jade, mother-of-pearl, peridot, polished gemstones, red cullet, rock crystal, rose quartz, tigereye, turquoise.
Catalog: 25¢.

Bitterroot Lapidary Supply
Rt. 5, Bitterroot Rd.
Missoula, MT 59801
406–549–1671

Green plume, Idaho tapestry agate, ivory plume, lapidary cutting materials, lava-talc, Montana moss.
Write for information.

Virginia Black Designs
P.O. Box 1712
Studio City, CA 91604
213–763–5808

Stuffed doll patterns.
Catalog: 25¢.
Whimsical doll patterns include ballerina, jesters, elves, Santa Claus, puppets.

Glen Black Handwoven Textiles
1414 Grant
San Francisco, CA 94133
415–982–1977

Acid dyes, batik tools, cold water dyes.
Write for information.

Dorothy Blake
1700 S. Bedford St.
Los Angeles, CA 90035
213–870–1926

Gem polishers, polishes.
Catalog.
Write for local distributor.

Blank-It Corp.
P.O. Box 569
Monroe, NC 28110
704–283–2125

No-slip frame.
Catalog.
No-slip frame has no steel tubing with aluminum clamps for frame-making, with brackets (produces perfectly mitered corner) adjustable for large and small size frames.

Dick Blick
Box 1267
Galesburg, IL 61401
309–343–6181

Acetate, airbrushes, art foam, artist's supplies, beadery, blockprinting, bunting, casting supplies, cellophane paper, ceramic supplies, chenille, cords, corrugated paper, crepe paper, felt pens, felt vinyl, flocking, foil paper, gummed paper, looms, magnifiers, paper cutters, rug hooking supplies, screen process supplies, small mirrors, stained glass, threads, tissue paper, velour paper, wood carving supplies, yarns.
Books.
Catalog.
Discount: quantity purchases.

James Bliss & Co. Inc.
Route 128
Dedham, MA 02026
617–329–2430

Electric model motors, model fittings, model steam engines, model tools.
Books: ship model building.
Catalog: 50¢.
Kits: ship model.
Leaflets: model ship building.

Blue Grass Art & Hobby Center
Box 206
Blue Grass, IA 52726
319–381–3111

Ceramic supplies, china painting supplies, rubber, stained glass supplies.
Instructive catalog $1.

Bluebird Manufacturing
C/O Judson Pottery
100 Gregory Rd.
Ft. Collins, CO 80521
303–484–3243

Ceramic supplies, clay mixers, potter's wheels, pug mills.
Catalog.

Company Listing
Bluejacket—Book

Bluejacket Ship Crafters
145 Water St.
So. Norwalk, CT 06854
203-853-3353
  Model fittings.
  Catalog: 50¢.
  Kits: ship model.
  Leaflets: model ship building.

Boat Builder
229 Park Ave. South
New York, NY 10003
212-673-1300
  Magazine features many types of boats and boat building projects, includes building materials and tools information.
  Magazines: boat building, features boat building projects, information on building materials and tools.
  Subscriptions: tri-annual copy at $1.

Bob's Arts & Crafts
11880 North Washington
Northglenn, CO 80233
303-451-1361
  Artist's supplies, balsa wood, beadery, bottle cutters, candlemaking supplies, chenille, clays, doll making, foil craft, jewelry findings, lampmaking, macrame accessories, magnets, marbles, miniatures, nylon net, plaster casting, resin casting, Styrofoam®, wood fibre.
  Books.
  Catalog: $2.

Boin Arts & Crafts
87 Morris St.
Morristown, NJ 07960
201-539-9040
  Accessories, American Indian crafts, art foam, artist's supplies, bamboo, basketry, batik, beadery, blockprinting, candlemaking supplies, clays, corrugated paper, crepe paper, decoupage, dip film, fabric paint, felt, fiber optics, firing enamel, flocking, foil, glass globs, hand tools, jewelrymaking accessories, kilns, leathercraft, looms, macrame accessories, metals, mosaic tiles, nonfiring enamel, paints, plaster casting, plastic foam, plastic mosaic tile, power tools, resins, sculpture supplies, self-hardening clays, shells, stained glass, Styrofoam®, tissue paper, weaving supplies, woodware.
  Books.
  Catalog: $1 (refundable).
  Discount: quantity purchases.
  Group packs: beads, games, leather, paper, toys, American Indian crafts.
  Kits: sculpture.

Nadja Bolio
R. F. D. 2 Box 62
Buckfield, ME 04220
207-388-2721
  Kits: key holder, wood jewelry.
  Send SASE for information.

Bon Bazar
149 Waverly Pl.
New York, NY 10014
212-255-8889
  Burlap.
  Carries burlap in 36 colors.
  Send 25¢ for color swatches and information kit.

Vivian Bonnema
Prinsburg, MN 56281
612-978-6155
  Also has doll clothes patterns selection of crochet clothes patterns for 8 in. dolls.
  Books.
  Send SASE for information.

Bonnie's Rock Shop
R.F.D. 2
Brigham, UT 84302
801-723-2635
  Laguna, lapidary mountings, lapidary supplies, petrified wood, rain forest jasper, red horn coral, snowflake obsidian, Utah ribbon agate, Wyoming jade.
  Write for information.

Book Barn
P.O. Box 256
Avon, CT 06001
203-678-1575
  Books: applique, batik, bead crafts, bird carving, blacksmithing, book binding, calligraphy, candlemaking, ceramics, crewel, crochet, decoupage, design, doll making, dyeing, embroidery, enamel, flower drying, general arts & crafts series,

handweaving, jewelry, knitting, lacemaking, lapidary, leather crafts, macrame, metalwork, mosaics, needlepoint, papier mache, patchwork, printing, puppetry, rug hooking, silk screen, spinning, symmography, tie-dye, toleware, woodworking.
Catalog: 50¢.
Services: information on craft courses, teachers and suppliers (particularly in Connecticut).

Bookful of Crochet
Box 39
Valley Park, MO   63088
314-825-2021
Magazine features out-of-print patterns, including some collectors' items.
Magazines: crochet patterns.
Subscriptions: bimonthly copy $1.

Bookpost
Box 2307F
Leucadia, CA   92024
714-753-3392
Books: old book values.
Services: appraisals by mail, free out-of-print book search.
Write for specific information.

Harry Bookstone
22 W. 48th St.
New York, NY   10036
212-586-6178
   Aquamarine, baroques, cabochons, cat's-eye, cut gemstones, norganite, rough faceting material, rough stones, rubellite, topaz, tourmaline, tumbling stones.
Write for information.

The Booted Sheepherder Inc.
Francestown, NH   03043
603-547-3456
   Sheepskin.
Catalog: 25¢.
Kits: jackets, sheepskin.

Frank Boothe
2516 N.E. 27th Ave.
Portland, OR   97212
503-284-3729
   China painting designs.
Designs include birds, animals, flowers.

Discount: quantity purchases for teachers.
Send SASE for information.

Bourget Bros. Gems & Minerals
1626-11th St.
Santa Monica, CA   90404
213-394-1233
   Gemstones, precious casting metals, precious metal findings, wax, wax pens, wax ring stands.
Catalog: $1 (refundable).

Bourget Bros. Gems & Minerals
12478 Washington Blvd.
Los Angeles, CA   90021
213-391-9693
See entry above.

Boutique Trims
P.O. Drawer P
So. Lyon, MI   48178
313-437-2017
   Beadery, braids, brass hinges, edgings, egg craft, egg stands, filigrees, jewelry findings, miniatures, rhinestone chain, rhinestones, sequins, silver hinges, velvet ribbons.
Carries over 200 miniatures in assorted subjects.
Catalog: $1.

Bovin Publishing
68-36 108th St.
Forest Hills, NY   11375
212-268-2292
Books: centrifugal or lost wax casting, jewelrymaking, silversmithing & art metal.

Bowersox Eggcraft Supplies
Box 61
Diamond City, AR   72644
501-422-7459
   Duck eggshells, goose eggshells.
Catalog.

Boxcar Ken
Box 4514-CB
Whittier, CA   90607
No phone orders.
   Model decals, model figures, model paints, model railroads, model scenery, model structures, model tools.
Send stamp for O model or HO model newsletter.

Company Listing
Boycan's—Bree

Boycan's Craft Supplies
1052 East State St.
Sharon, PA 16146
412-346-6181

Artificial foliage, beadery, cones, feathers, jewelry findings, miniatures, paints, preserved foliage, ribbon, Styrofoam®, wood fibre.

Books: advanced wood fibre, corsage designs, crocheted jewelry, foliage arrangements, marble jewelry, pine cones, plastic laminating, wood fibre, Christmas projects.
Catalog: 50¢.

C. R. Boylin
720-49th Ave.
No. St. Petersburg, FL 33703
No phone orders.

Miocene vertebrate fossils, polished Tampa Bay coral, shark's teeth.

Carries different varieties of shark teeth.
Send SASE for catalog of fossils.

Brad's Rock Shop
911 W. Nine Mile Rd.
Ferndale (Detroit), MI 48220
313-546-3085

Faceting supplies, grinding equipment, lapidary laps, lapidary machinery, polishing accessories, sanding machines, saws, trim saws.

Catalog.

Mrs. Ruby Brandon
4030 Minnich Ave.
Paducah, KY 42001
502-442-8053

Precut wood forms.

Limited supply of 12 in camels; heads and hands for wisemen and shepherds from bread dough.
Send SASE for information.

Yvonne Brandon
1620 Wayland Ave.
Sacramento, CA 95825
No phone orders.

Doll patterns.

Carries doll patterns for various sizes and types dolls: old fashioned, reversible.
Send 10¢ and SASE for information.

Ed Brandt Stone Co.
Route 2
Nampa, ID 83651
208-466-7533

Garnet, gemstones, jasper.
Send stamp for price list.

Brandywine Studies
2510 Deepwood Dr., Foulk Woods,
Wilmington, DE 19810
302-475-8796

Discounts: quantity purchases.
Leaflets: china painting.
Send SASE for information, or $1.25 for sample study.

Charles T. Branford Co.
28 Union St.
Newton Centre, MA 02159
617-244-6009

Books: bead embroidery, canvas work, creative stitchery, crochet, doll making, embroidery from English patterns, fabric printing, general arts & crafts series, patchwork, rug making.
Catalog: needlecraft 25¢.
Contact your nearest bookstore or write above.

Branson Cleaning Equipment
Parrott Drive
Shelton, CT 06484
203-929-5341

Ultrasonic cleaners.

Ultrasonic deep cleaning tool (cleans with high frequency sound waves).
Write for information.

N. S. Braverman
P.O. Box 20145
Cleveland, OH 44120
216-921-3602

Prints.

Antiquarian prints from the 18th and 19th century.
Catalog: plus sample $1.

Andria Bree Gem Co.
164 E. Main St.
El Cajon, CA 92020
714-447-5755

Cherry opals, gem rough material, gold mountings, matrix opals, silver mountings.
Catalog: $1 (refundable).

Bric-Mold Corp.
P.O. Box 178
Bethpage, NY 11714
516–433–6442
Plaster casting.
Catalog.
Molds come in decorator or Roman style bricks, also in fieldstone.

Brookhurst Hobbys
12741 Brookhurst Way
Garden Grove, CA 92640
714–539–4121
Books.
Carries over 6,000 scale model kits including figures, armor, aircraft, ships and hard-to-get models; imported kits from Japan and England.
Catalog: $1.
Kits: scale models.

Brooklyn Botanic Garden
Education Dept.
1000 Washington Ave.
Brooklyn, NY 11225
212–622–4433
Books: dye plants and dyeing.
Catalog: of 50 handbooks.

Brookstone Co.
Brookstone Bldg.
Peterborough, NH 03458
603–924–7181
Carpentry tools, glass cutters, glass scribing tools, hand tools, jewelrymaking tools, magnifiers, metal working tools, miniature power tools, power tools, soldering tools, surgical knives, surgical scissors, wood carving tools, woodworking tools.
Books: metal, woodworking.
Catalog: 50¢ for year's subscription (5 issues).

Brother International Corp.
680 Fifth Ave.
New York, NY 10019
212–581–6262
Automatic knitting machines, computerized knitting machine.
Course offers machine knitting in 12 lessons, includes yarns and patterns and offers certificate of achievement upon completion.
Home study courses: machine knitting.
Write for information or catalog.

Arthur Brown & Bro., Inc.
2 West 46th St.
New York, NY 10036
212–575–5555
Adhesives, airbrushes, artist's supplies, ballpoint paints, batik, blockprinting, butterflies, cellophane paper, cork, cutters, etching supplies, felt pens, ferns, firing clay, flexible curve ruler, flint paper, flocking, fluorescent paper, gold leaf, greeting card craft, hand tools, kilns, leathercraft, Lucite®, mache, macrocrystalline wax, magnifiers metal foil paper, nonfiring clay, nonhardening clay, parchment paper, plaster casting, potter's wheels, power tools, repeat glass, resin casting, rice paper, rock polishers, scaleograph proportional slide rule, scissors, screen process supplies, sculpture supplies, sculpture tools, stained glass paints, tape, textile paints, wax gold, wood carving tools.
Books.
Catalog.

Brown's Miniatures
P.O. Box 35
Cambridge, NY 12816
518–692–2931
Candlemaking supplies, honeycomb wax sheets, metal hand-painted miniatures, miniature animals.
Send SASE for information.

Brown's Rock & Lapidary Supplies
1107 So. 12th St.
Moorhead, MN 56560
218–233–3341
Lapidary grits, lapidary machinery, lapidary supplies, metal detectors, teredo wood slabs.
Catalog.

Company Listing
Brunswick—Cadillac

Brunswick Worsted Mills
P.O. Box 276
Pickens, SC 29671
803-878-6375
   Crochet patterns, knitting patterns, latch rug yarns, rug canvas.
   Catalog: needlepoint $1.25; fashions $1.50; latch rugs $1.
   Kits: latch rug, needlepoint.
   Write for local distributor.

Buck Hill Associates
Johnsburg, NY 12843
518-998-2743
   Decoupage prints, historic advertisements, historic handbills, historic posters, historic prints.
   Catalog: 25¢.

Budget Buddy Co.
11141 Orchard Rd., P.O. Box 9777
Kansas City, MO 64134
816-761-7657
   Ballpoint paints, paints, stencil paper, stencil tools, stencils, textile, transfers.
   Books.
   Catalog: stencil designs $1 (ref); transfer sample for SASE.
   Kits: crewel, needlepoint.

C. W. Bullock
290 Grandview Circle
Jackson, MS 39212
601-372-0205
   Clock dial cutters, kitchen clock glass, OG clock glass.
   Clock kits include 13th century wooden wheel, and 14th century iron wheel watchman's clocks; all OG clock glass are silk screened with/enamel and are photographically reproduced from original items.
   Kits: clock.
   Write for information.

Gary Bunting
435 N. Main
Cape Girardeau, MO 63701
314-334-0496
   Decoupage posters.
   Catalog: plus samples 50¢.

Karen Burrus
804 W. 36th Ave.
Albany, OR 97321
No phone orders.
   Books: tole designs.

Butterick Fashion Marketing Co.
P.O. Box 1914
Altoona, PA 16601
814-943-5281
   Books: sewing adjustments and alterations.

Butterick Home Catalog
P.O. Box 5000
Greenwich, CT 06830
212-620-2567
   Magazine features newest women's, men's, and children's clothing and patterns.
   Magazines: sewing fashions.
   Subscriptions: single copy 60¢, quarterly, 1 year $2.40, foreign $3.

Charles M. Butterworth
Box 3603
Philadelphia, PA 19125
215-844-7340
   Nylon, weaving yarns, wool.
   Discount: quantity purchases.
   Write for information.

The Cab-N-Facet, Inc.
932 West Columbia Street
Springfield, OH 45504
513-325-3972
   Natural gemstones.
   Carries 170 different varieties of slabbed rough, 120 different varieties of faceting rough; has two full time goldsmiths.
   Write for information.

Cadillac Plastic & Chemical Co.
P.O. Box 810
Detroit, MI 48232
313-869-9500
   Books: plastics craftsmanship.
   Catalog: $1.
   Has ready made or do-it-yourself plastic items for furniture, clocks, lamps, jewelry, accessories, decorations, games, for home and office use.

Cake Decorators & Craft Supplies
Blacklick, OH 43004
614-471-7757
   Cake decorating supplies, cake molds, cake tops, candle dyes, candle scents, candle waxes, candle wicks, candlemaking supplies, candy molding, metal molds, plastic molds.
   Books.
   Catalog: 50¢.
   Kits: soap making.

Cambridge Wools
16-22 Anzac Ave., P.O. Box 2572
Auckland, New Zealand
No phone orders.
   Spinning wheels, spinning yarns.
   Write for information.

The Camp Fire Co.
Box 205 200 N. Madison
Raymore, MO 64083
816-331-7112
   Silver, silversmithing supplies, silversmithing tools.
   Catalog: 25¢.
   Course includes discount on silver and tools.
   Home study courses: silversmithing.

D. M. Campana Co.
Hwy. 176 At 60, Box 740
Mundelein, IL 60060
No phone orders.
   Artist's supplies, china decals, china painting supplies, china studies, imported white china, jewelrymaking supplies, oil paints.
   Books.
   Catalog: decal 50¢; jewelry 50¢; general $1.

Gilmour Campbell
14258 Maiden
Detroit, MI 48213
313-527-4532
   Mold stands, potter's wheels, turntables.
   Write for information.

Campbell Scale Models
P.O. Box 121
Tustin, CA 92680
714-546-3380
   HO models, model accessories, model bridges, model coaling dock, model freight depots, model passenger depots, model produce docks, model saloons, model sand house, model scenery, model town buildings, model tressels, model water tank.
   Catalog: $1.50.
   Kits: model railroad trackside.

Campbell Tools Co.
1424 Barclay Rd.
Springfield, OH 45505
513-322-8562
   Lathes, metals, tools.
   Catalog: 50¢.

Canadian Aero-Supply
Box 20, Station 'O'
Toronto Canada
No phone orders.
   Model aircraft engines.
   Catalog: 75¢ for Canadians.
   Kits: model aircraft.

Candle Institute
1600 Cabrillo Ave.
Torrance, CA 90501
No phone orders.
   Course features candlemaking techniques and monthly candlecraft news; offers 42 lessons and includes basic molds and supplies; state approved certificate upon completion.
   Home study courses: candlemaking.
   Write for information.

Candle Kitchen
27 S. Union Ave.
Cranford, NJ 07016
201-272-5755
   Candle additives, candle dyes, candle molds, candle scents, candle waxes, candlemaking supplies.
   Catalog: 35¢ (refundable).

Candle Mill Village
100 Main St.
East Arlington, VT 05252
802-375-6068
   Candle dyes, candle molds, candle scents, candle waxes, candlemaking supplies.

Company Listing
Candle—Carver

Books: candlemaking.
Catalog: 25¢.

Candlewic Co.
P.O. Box 363
Warrington, PA 18976
215-343-3653

Candle dyes, candle molds, candle scents, candlemaking supplies.
Also carries clear mold with snap-away bases.
Write for information.

Candy & Cake Institute
1600 Cabrillo Ave.
Torrance, CA 90501
No phone orders.

Course offers instructions for candy and cakes for weddings; Christmas, Easter, anniversaries and other special events; state certification upon completion.
Home study courses: cake decorating, candy making.
Write for information.

Cane & Basket Supply Co.
1283 So. Cochran Ave.
Los Angeles, CA 90019
213-939-9644

Basketry, cane, rush.
Books.
Samples and price lists 50¢.

Carlbert Fabrics
2 York St.
Portland, ME 04112
207-773-0606

Wool, wool mill ends, wool remnant pieces.
Catalog.

Carnival Arts & Crafts
360 Shore Drive.
Hinsdale, IL 60521
312-654-8650

Aerosol finishes, antiquing, decoupage decals, decoupage finishes, decoupage fixatives, decoupage prints, egg hardware, foil prints, rub-on wax gilts, spray adhesives.
Write for information.
Write for local distributor.

Carson & Ellis, Inc.
1153 Warwick Ave.
Warwick, RI 02888
401-463-8822

Bronze powder, decoupage, dip film, furniture finishes, glues, gold leaf, hardware, metal boxes, metal sconces, metal trays, metal ware, paints, patterns, prints, small unfinished furniture, unfinished boxes, unfinished purse boxes, wood, woodware.
Also has many Early American decorations.
Books.
Catalog: 50¢.

Carstens Publications
P. O. Box 700
Newton, NJ 07860
201-383-3355

Magazine features calendar of events; newest railroad items, models and kits; diagrams of structures and scratch building.
Magazines: modeling.
Subscriptions: monthly copy 60¢, 1 year $6, foreign $7.

Carter Associates
P.O. Box 1477
New Iberia, LA 70560
318-369-3226

Folding precision scissors.
Kits: old fashioned monkey sock.
Send SASE for information.

Carter Craft Doll House
5505 42nd Ave.
Hyattsville, MD 20781
301-277-3051

Also has available list of dolls and doll dress patterns; send stamp.
Books: doll fashions.
Send stamp for information.

Donna Jean Carver
Box 41
New London, MN 56273
612-354-2381

Needlecraft designs, needlework dolls, needlework stuffed toys.
Catalog: 25¢.

Carver Co.
P.O. Box 95
Plympton, MA 02367
No phone orders.
> Colored sawdust.
> *Colored sawdust is used with clear cast resins and other crafts.*
> *Write for information.*

Castolite
P.O. Box 391
Woodstock, IL 60098
815-338-4670
> Accessories, additives, casting compounds, dyes, fiberglass cloth, fillers, molds.
> *Books.*
> *Catalog: 25¢.*
> *Discount: quantity purchases.*
> *Kits: casting.*
> *Simulated compounds for wood, ceramics, aluminum.*

Cavalier Handicrafts
1839 West Broad
Richmond, VA 23220
703-359-1345
> *Books.*
> *Catalog.*
> *Discount: quantity purchases.*
> *Group packs.*
> *Kits: leather craft, screen process.*

Celebrate
833 W. 115th St.
Chicago, IL 60643
312-785-1144
> *Magazines: cake & food decorating.*
> *Subscriptions: bimonthly.*

Celebration Candlemaking Supplies
P.O. Box 134, Dept B
Pentwater, MI 49449
616-869-8691
> Candle accessories, candle additives, candle dyes, candle molds, candlemaking supplies.
> *Catalog: 25¢.*
> *Discount: quantity purchases.*

The Cellar Ceramic Shop
111 E. Coover St.
Mechanicsburg, PA 17055
717-766-8017
> Ceramic plaques, decoupage plaques, wood plaques.
> *Send SASE for information.*

Century 21
3711 Mahoning Ave.
Youngstown, OH 44515
216-792-3893
> Basketry, decoupage, decoupage accessories, decoupage finishes, decoupage glues, decoupage prints, decoupage stains, woodware.
> *Write for information.*

Cerami Corner Inc.
607 N. San Gabriel Ave., P.O. Box 516
Azusa, CA 91702
213-334-0242
> Water-mount decals.
> *Catalog: $1.*
> *Decals for china, porcelain, ceramics, glass.*

Ceramic Coating Co.
P.O. Box 370
Newport, KY 41072
606-781-1915
> Aluminum enamels, copper enameling supplies, lead bearing enamels, lead free enamels.
> *Write for information.*

Ceramics
P.O. Box 8126
Fresno, CA 93727
209-291-2521
> *Magazine features teaching guides, newest trends and ideas.*
> *Magazines: ceramics.*
> *Subscriptions: monthly, copy 75¢ 1 year $7.50.*

Ceramics Monthly
Box 4548
Columbus, OH 43212
614-488-8236
> *Books: ceramics, enameling, pottery.*
> *Magazine features firing projects and techniques and new products.*

Company Listing
Ceramics—Chilton

Magazines: ceramics.
Subscriptions: monthly, 1 year $6.

Challenge Publications, Inc
7950 Deering Ave.
Canoga Park, CA   91304
213–887–0550
   Magazines: ceramics, foil, leather craft, macrame, needlepoint, resin, wood.
   Subscriptions: monthly copy $1, 1 year $11.

Champs Creative Materials Center
30 No. Franklin St.
Hempstead, NY   11550
516–538–1810
   Catalog.
   General arts and crafts supplies.
   Kits: "China" gloss floral arrangements, metal art sculpture.

Charbonneau's Lapidary Service
4020 Bow Trail S.W.
Calgary, Alberta, Canada
403–249–0322
   Gold, lapidary equipment, lapidary findings, lapidary tools, rocks, silver, silversmithing tools.
   Books.
   Catalog: for Canadians; $1 (refundable).

Charm Woven Labels
Box 14664
Portland, OR   97214
No phone orders.
   Woven labels.
   Catalog.

Muriel N. Charney
25 North Ave.
Rochester, NY   14626
716–225–5238
   Braids for Battenburg lace.
   Send SASE for information.

Chemical Additives Co.
2 Rice Dr.
Farmingville, NY   11738
516–698–7088
   Light stabilizer additive.
   Additive preserves beauty of color, prevents yellowing of white and fading of colors.
   Write for information.

Chemical Publishing Co., Inc.
200 Park Ave. So.
New York, NY   10003
212–677–1930
   Books: brickwork, inventor's reference book, technical devices handbook.
   Contact your nearest bookstore or write above.
   Technical device handbook is a reference guide of mechanical movements, devices, tools and elements to make machinery work: magnetics, electronics, light and optics, fluid.
   Write for information.

Polly Chester Inc.
205 E. Hartsdale Ave.
Hartsdale, NY   10530
914–725–3290
   Embroidery scissors, scissors, shears, trimming tools.
   Catalog.

Chestnut Hill Studio, Ltd.
Box 38
Churchville, NY   14428
716–293–1626
   Carries over 700 fine quality miniatures, 1 in. to 1 ft. scale, including furniture (18th century reproductions, Early American) and accessories (draperies, prints, ceramics).
   Catalog: $1.50 (50¢ refundable).

Chicago School of Interior Decoration
555 E. Lange St., Dept. 71100
Mundelein, IL   60060
312–566–5400
   Course includes practical basic training for professional or personal use.
   Home study courses: interior decorating.
   Write for information.

Chilton Book Co.
Chilton Way
Radnor, PA   19089
215–687–8200
   Patterns.
   Books: ceramics, cloth toys, collage, enameling,

flameworking, gemcraft, general arts & crafts series, glass craft, glassforming, jewelrymaking, kiln-fired glass, knitting & crocheting, leather, metalsmithing, nature crafts, needlepoint, papier mache, plastics, polystyrene foam craft, porcelain painting, potterymaking, quilting, rug making, sandcast candles, sculpting in steel, sculpture, selling handcrafts, shellcraft, stained glass, stained glass lamps, wax sculpture, wooden toys, Christmas creations.
Contact your nearest bookstore or write for local distributor.
Write for information.

The China Cottage
260 So. Pennsylvania
Casper, WY 82601
307-234-0801
China painting supplies.
Also has colored studies with painting instructions and line drawings.

China Decorator
P.O. Box 45375
Los Angeles, CA 90045
No phone orders.
Books: china painting.
Magazines: china decorating.
Subscriptions: monthly.
Write for sample copy, 50¢.

China Painter
3111 N.W. 19th
Oklahoma City, OK 73107
405-943-3841
Magazine features news of china painting programs and events, offers new and old reprints of china designs.
Magazines: china painting.
Subscriptions: bimonthly, 1 year $5.50; foreign $6.50.

Chrismon Committee
Lutheran Church of the Ascension
314 W. Main St.
Danville, VA 24541
804-792-5795
Books: Chrismon monograms and symbols.

Circus Hobby Hall
Freddie Daw
249 Catalonia Ave.
Coral Gables, FL 33134
305-446-3020
Model figures, old time circus wagons.
Catalog: $1.

J & H Clasgens Co.
610 High Street
New Richmond, OH 45157
513-553-4177
Hand weaving yarns, knitting yarns, synthetic yarn, wool yarn.
Write for information.

Classic Crafts
401 North Section St.
Fairhope, AL 36532
205-928-8955
Catalog: 25¢.
Furniture kits include footstools, pedestals, collector's tables and vanity table; also has parts milled in mahogany ready for assembly.
Kits: furniture.

Clay-Crafters Products
2606 Culverson Ave.
Evansville, IN 47714
812-477-3648
Ceramic kilns, ceramic molds.
Also has edition molds, blocks and cases; molds include: vases, pitcher, bowls, palm leaf, masks, goblets, jars, ash trays; custom mold for volume buyers.
Catalog: $1.

Vern Clements
P.O. Box 608
Caldwell, ID 83605
208-459-7608
Model airplanes.
Also carries plans for various model aircraft remote control and other models in several sizes including: in 2 in. 1 ft. scale--Gee Bee r-1 (also 1 1/2 in. 1 ft.), Gee Bee Z, Monocoupe 110 Clipwing; in 1 in. 1 ft. scale--1940 Culver Cadet; 1/2 in. 1 ft. scale--Hall Racer.
Send SASE for information.

Company Listing

Clems—Cole

Clems and Clems Spinning Wheels
665 San Pablo Ave.
Pinole, CA 94564
415-758-2036

Fibers, skein maker, spinning accessories, spinning wheels.
Catalog: plus samples, 50¢.
Kits: distaff for ashford wheel.

Cleve-Craft E-Z Loom
5512 N. Marshburn Ave.
Arcadia, CA 91006
213-448-3282

Inkle looms, peg looms, stick looms.
Write for information.

Cleveland Leather Co.
2824 Lorain Ave.
Cleveland, OH 44113
216-651-5404

Art foam, burlap, cork, crepe paper, dip film, dyes, enameling, felt, foil etching, glues, honeycomb candles, leather, mache, metal craft, mosaics, paints, plaster craft, raffia, reed, resins, shells, tools.
Books: American Indian crafts.
Catalog.
Discount: purchases.
Kits: decoupage, leather, wood, wood ware, American Indian crafts.

Cleveland Model & Supply Co.
10307 Detroit
Cleveland, OH 44102
216-961-3600

Also carries 600 plans for model aircraft building (antique, classics, contemporary, W.W. I, W.W. II, military, racers).
Catalog: 60¢.
Leaflets: plans for model aircraft.

The Clever Crafters
1795 Fall River Rd., Box 1126
Estes Park, CO 80517
303-586-3865

Nylon net, patterns, vinyl doll heads.
Books: art foam, egg, net, scrap craft.
Carries soft vinyl doll heads with hair, including girl, freckles, "miss with pucker", angel, wiseman (painted or unpainted), grandma and grandpa.
Kits: sewing doll.
Send SASE for information.

Cliveden Yarns
39 N. 8th St.
Philadelphia, PA 19107
215-925-8891

Crochet yarns, knitting yarns.
Catalog: yarns; $1 (refundable).

Cohasset Colonials
211 Ship St.
Cohasset, MA 02025
617-383-0110

Carries furniture kits of Early American reproduction, including child's chair with rush seat.
Catalog: 50¢.
Kits: furniture.

Coker Craft
P.O. Box 124
Charleston, SC 29402
803-723-3958

Miniature tanks, ship models.
Books: ships, tanks.
Catalog: 50¢.
Leaflets: plans for model military railway equipment.

H. A. Cole
P.O. Box 1911
Oakland, CA 94604
415-658-6480

Fine silver casting grains, precious casting metals, sterling silver casting grains, yellow gold casting grains.
Price list available.

Cole Ceramics Laboratories
Box 248, Gay St.
Sharon, CT 06069
203-364-5025

Ball mills, casting table racks, ceramic armatures, ceramic bead trees, ceramic chemicals, ceramic hardware, ceramic supplies, ceramic tools, clay containers, clays, drying cabinets, electric kilns, electric potter's wheels, gas kilns, glass melting furnaces, glaze formula tables, glazes, glory holes, kiln

shelves, lehrs, plaster, potter's kick wheels, potter's tools, pug mills, sculpture tools, sieves, spray booths, stains, ware trucks, wedging tables.
Catalog.
Kits: potter's wheels.

Collector Studies
5205 Holt
Los Angeles, CA 90056
213-645-1617
China painting supplies.
Carries 50 full color studies (many by C. Klein) of flowers birds, fruit, vase designs, scenes, Christmas, Thanksgiving, Dutch.
Send SASE for information.

The Collector's Cabinet
1000 Madison Ave.
New York, NY 10021
212-861-4133
Butterflies, coral, exotic minerals, fossils, seashells.
Catalog: 25¢.

The Collector's Cabinet
222 N. Federal Hwy., (U.S. Route 1)
Dania, FL 33004
305-922-6082
See entry above.

Colonial Decorations
7416 Sheffield Drive
Knoxville, TN 37919
No phone orders.
Wooden apple cone.
Write for information.

Colonial Printing Ink Co.
180 E. Union Ave.
E. Rutherford, NJ 07073
201-933-6100
Clamps, screen fabrics, screen nylon, screen polyester, screen process supplies, screen silk.
Catalog.

Colonial Textiles
82 Plants Dam Rd.
East Lyme, CT 06333
203-739-9900
Alpaca, camel hair, carders, cashmere, drop spindles, fleece, organic dyes, spinning wheels.
Catalog: samples, 25¢.

Colorado Geological Industries Inc.
5818 E. Colfax Ave.
Denver, CO 80220
303-388-6405
Fossils, lapidary equipment, lapidary supplies, mineral collections, mineral specimens, rock collections.
Books: geological.
Discount: quantity purchases.
Write for information.

Columbia Candlecraft
411 Front St.
Catasauqua, PA 18032
215-264-3281
Kits: candlemaking, cascading candles, foliating candles.
Price list available.

Commercial Mineral Corp.
22 W. 48th St.
New York, NY 10036
212-245-4734
Amethyst, andalusite, aquamarine, citrine, clear quartz, diamond crystals, gemstones, green quartz, iolite, kunzite, lazulite, mineral specimens, rough amethyst, rough aquamarine, rough citrine, rough tourmalines, rubies, sapphire, sphenes, spinel, tourmaline, zircon.
Write for information.

Commonwealth Felt Co.
211 Congress St.
Boston, MA 02110
617-423-3445
Felt, felt remnants.
Color chart 50¢.

Concrete Machinery Co.
Drawer 99
Hickory, NC 28601
704-322-7710
Aluminum molds for ornamental concrete.
Carries over 350 designs including flower pots and

Company Listing
Concrete—Cork

planters, bird baths, statuaries, animals, seats, tables, park bench ends, ornamental figures including Indian Chief.
Instruction manual-catalog: $3.

Wm. Condon & Sons Ltd.
Charlottetown
P.E. Island, Canada
902-894-8712
Wool yarn.
Color card and prices.

Conlin Yarns
P.O. Box 11812
Philadelphia, PA 19128
215-482-6443
Knitting yarns, weaving yarns.
Color card: 50¢.

Albert Constantine & Son Inc.
2050 Eastchester Rd.
Bronx, NY 10461
212-792-1600
Ash tray inserts, bottle cutters, cane, cane webbing, carved trims, carving blocks, carving tools, catches, clock motors, fraternal wood emblems, furniture finishes, furniture glues, furniture hardware, furniture polishes, furniture stains, hand tools, hardware, hinges, lamp parts, locks, lumber, marquetry items, molded plaques, moldings, music box movements, patterns, period hardware, power tools, salt and pepper shakers mechanisms, shop tools, sliding hardware, table legs, table lighter inserts, unfinished basswood boxes, unfinished plaques, upholstery tools, wagon wheels, wood veneers.
Books.
Catalog: 50¢; plus 20 rarewood samples, $1 (refundable).
Kits: chair caning, clocks, guitar making, marquetry, ship model, veneer, Appalachian dulcimer.

Contemporary Quilts
5305 Denwood Ave., Dept. 2B
Memphis, TN 38117
901-683-8654
Dacron® batting, quilt patterns.
Books: beginner quilting.
Catalog: $1.
Kits: crib quilts.

Contessa Yarns
P.O. Box 37
Lebanon, CT 06249
203-642-7630
Cottons, jute, linen, rayon yarn, silk, sisal, weaving yarns, wool, yarn mixture packages.
Catalog: plus samples 25¢.

Continental Hobbies Inc.
P.O. Box 116
Adelphia, NJ 07710
201-431-8555
Catalog: 25¢.
Kits: aircraft, imported model, military vehicles, trains.

Cooke Novelty Co.
18820 River Rd. 2
Milwaukee, OR 97222
503-655-4504
Books: cement casting, mold making, plaster casting.

Cookson & Thode
2960 S. Monroe St.
Denver, CO 80210
303-756-0945
Glass cutters.
Books: leaded stained glass designs.

Hallie Copeland
916 N. Alisos St., Apt. C
Santa Barbara, CA 93102
805-966-3833
Handcrafted bread dough miniatures, miniature birdhouses, miniature birds, miniature boys, miniature girls, miniature Japanese girls, miniature mice, miniature rabbits.
Send SASE for complete price list.

Cork Products Co. Inc.
239 Park Ave. So.
New York, NY 10003
212-254-6477
Corks.
Write for local distributor.

Corner Cupboard Crafts, Inc.
Box 368
Lilburn, GA 30247
404-921-2153
> Decoupage, tole painting, woodware.
> Catalog: general, $1; wood.
> Complete line of arts and crafts supplies, open stock and kits.
> Kits: string art.

The Corner Shop
P.O. Box 22
Wewoka, OK 74884
405-257-2345
> Catalog: 25¢.
> Kits: embroidery, felt needle art, needlepoint.

Corrado Cutlery Inc.
33 E. Adams St.
Chicago, IL 60603
312-332-2965
> Kits: jewelry repair, tool pack.
> Write for information.

Cottage Crafts
RFD 1
Pomfret Center, CT 06259
203-974-1479
> Stitchery, weaving yarns.
> Catalog: plus samples 25¢.

Cottage Crafts
149 Lancaster Pike
Malvern, PA 19355
215-647-5288
> Kits: tote bags, velvet mushrooms, velvet strawberries.
> Write for information.

Coulter Studios
138 E. 60th St.
New York, NY 10022
212-421-8085
> Backings for hangings, backings for rya rugs, linen yarns, rya yarn, tapestry yarn, weaving yarns, wool yarn.
> Catalog: $1; yarn cards, 50¢.

Country Crafts
Route 208
Maybrook, NY 12543
914-427-2718
> Braids, egg stands, glitter, gold findings, gold paper decorations, hinges, jewels, manzanita wood, miniature egg craft, miniature silk pictures, music boxes, plastic shapes, velvet flowers, velvet leaves, white jewelry findings, 3-D beading.
> Catalog: $1.
> Kits: boutique, egg, Christmas ornament.
> Over 200 unusual miniatures and landscaping materials.

The Country Craftsmen
Rt. 7, Box 7843
Bainbridge Island, WA 98110
206-842-4007
> Books: weaving with fur.
> Catalog: hand-made Christmas items, 50¢.

Country Woodcraft
Rt. 2, Box 233
Maple Plain, MN 55359
612-479-1405
> Basswood figures, soap blocks, tinware, wood carving tools, woodware.
> Books: carving, handmade soap, wood carving patterns.
> Catalog: 25¢.
> Kits: wood carving.
> Services: spinning wheels and wood carvings.

Countrywide Crafts
222 Park Ave. South
New York, NY 10003
212-777-4200
> Magazine features do-it-yourself projects; new trends, products and events; offers unusual uses of commonly found items.
> Magazines: general arts and crafts.
> Subscriptions: bimonthly, copy at newsstand $1.

Covington Engineering Corp.
112 First Street Box 35
Redlands, CA 92373
714-792-4611
> Belt sanders, diamond blades, facet heads, facet laps, gem shops, grinders, grinding wheels, grits, lapidary equipment, metal de-

Company Listing
Covington—Craft

tectors, polishes, slab polishers, slab saws, sphere makers, treasure detectors, trim saws.
> *Books: cabochons, facet cutting, gems, minerals, rocks.*
> *Catalog: $1.50.*
> *Kits: build-your-own equipment.*

Coward, McCann & Geogheagan
200 Madison Ave.
New York, NY 10016
212–883–5500
> *Books: fiberglass boat building.*
> *Contact your nearest bookstore or write above.*
> *Write for information.*

Lyman E. Cox, Scale Trains
1631 Arden Way
Sacramento, CA 95815
916–442–7796

Circus model equipment, model railroad equipment.
> *Also has HO brass locomotive lists, 50¢; O scale locomotive and equipment list, 50¢; circus model equipment catalog, HO & O scale, $1.*
> *Catalog: HO & O Scale, $1.*

Craft & Candle House
1417 Poplar St.
Terre Haute, IN 47807
812–234–6502

Candle dyes, candle molds, candle scents, candle wicks.
> *Catalog.*
> *Kits: candlemaking starter.*

The Craft Corner
P. O. Box 5754-C
Augusta, GA 30906
404–798–3157

Beadery, candlemaking supplies, felt, macrame accessories.
> *Books.*
> *Catalog: general; clay recipes, (30¢ SASE).*
> *Discount: quantity purchases.*
> *Kits: candlemaking, felt, macrame, nylon net, papier mache.*

Craft Course Publishers
P.O. Box 280
Rosemead, CA 91770
213–579–3630
> *Books: art foam, bead jewelry, bread dough, candlemaking, craft sticks, crepe paper flowers, decoupage, dip film, felt, figure draping, general arts & crafts series, macrame, nylon net, papier mache, resin craft, synthetic straw, tissue flowers, American Indian crafts.*
> *Catalog.*
> *Contact your local craft dealer or write above.*

Craft House
1091 N. Military Trail
West Palm Beach, FL 33406
305–686–0509

Cabochons, golden tiger's-eye, hobby workbench, honey cat's-eye, jewelry workbench.
> *Write for information.*

Craft Kits
P.O. Box 55563
Houston, TX 77055
713–461–9279
> *Catalog.*
> *Kits: decoupage.*

Craft/Midwest
Box 42
Northbrook, IL 60062
312–498–2250
> *Magazine features, new trends exhibits, events and supply sources in the Midwest.*
> *Magazines: general arts and crafts.*
> *Subscriptions: quarterly, copy $1.25; 1 year $4.*

Craft Patterns
North Ave. and Route 83
Elmhurst, IL 60126
312–832–6287

Woodworking patterns.
> *Catalog: 60¢.*

Craft Products
P.O. Box 206
Elmhurst, IL 60126
312–832–6287

Clock movements, clock patterns, hardware, moldings, music box movements.

Catalog: 25¢.
Kits: wood clock.
Wood clock kits include wooden wheel, circa 1300; steeple, grandmother clock parts.

Craft Service
337 341 University Ave.
Rochester, NY   14607
716-325-5547

American Indian crafts, art foam, artist's supplies, basketry, beadery, blockprinting, candle waxes, cane, clays, cork, dip film, enameling, enameling kilns, etching supplies, felt, flocking, flowermaking, glass paperweights, honeycomb, jewelry findings, lacing, leathercraft, mosaics, paints, papers, plaster casting, plastic boxes, reed, resin casting, stained glass supplies, Styrofoam®, synthetic straw, textile paints, wire, wood carving supplies, woodware.
Books.
Catalog.
Discounts: quantity purchases.

Craft Yarns of Rhode Island Inc.
P.O. Box 151
Harrisville, RI   02830
401-568-3066

Burlap, canvas, cotton yarn, homespun yarns, macrame cords, mesh cloth, mohair yarn, Persian needlepoint yarn, rayon yarn, rug backings, rug frames, rug hooks, rug yarn, rugmaking supplies, tapestry yarn, warp yarn, weaving yarns, yarns.
Catalog: information and yarn cards; 50¢.
Discount: quantity purchases.

Craft-Mark Products
Box 399
Syosset, NY   11791
No phone orders.

Cigarette lighter mechanisms.
Catalog.
Discount: quantity purchases.
Lighter mechanisms have brass plated inserts for inserting into various bases of wood, ceramics, plastics, leather, others (1 1/2 in. diameter, regular lighters--no butane).

Craftint Manufacturing Co.
18501 Euclid Ave.
Cleveland, OH   44112
216-486-4400

Kits: screen process starter.
Write for local distributor.
Write for information.

Craftool Co.
1421 W. 240th St.
Harbor City, CA   90710
213-325-9696

Batik, gem making equipment, lapidary supplies, potter's wheels, rug weaving accessories, spinning wheels, weaving supplies.
Books: canework, cardboard model making, glove making, lacemaking, lampshades, netting, terracotta, willow work, wood toymaking.
Catalog: $1.
Kits: batik, book binding, ceramics, etching, graphic arts, jewelrymaking, lapidary, papermaking, sculpture, stone carving, weaving, wood carving, woodworking.
Write for local distributor.

Craftplans
Rogers, MN   55374
612-428-4101

Patterns.
Catalog: 25¢.
Leaflets: action windmills, bars, birdhouses and feeders, fireplaces, flocking, garages, gem cutting, jigsaw projects, lawn novelties, looms, mirror silvering, mosaic designs, nursery pinups, Old English letters, plating baby shoes, spinning wheels, unusual alphabets, weathervanes, wire figures, wood lathe projects, work benches, Christmas decorations, Stradivarius violin.
Offers 2512 assorted plans for spinning wheels.

Crafts Manufacturing Co.
72 Massachusetts Ave.
Lunenburg, MA   01462
617-342-1717

Decorated tinware, undecorated tinware.
Catalog: 25¢.

Crafts Yarns & Gifts
8212 Menaul N.E.
Albuquerque, NM 87110
505-298-8920
> Also has special kits with "Eye of God" symbol.
> Books.
> Kits: crewel, needlepoint, Southwestern scenes designs.
> Write for information.

Crafts Yarns & Gifts Ltd.
1100 San Mateo, S.E.
Albuquerque, NM 87108
505-265-9250
> Books: safety pin jewelry, tri-bead jewelry, yarn winding.
> Kits: crewel in Southwestern theme designs.
> Write for information.

Craftsman Circle Book Club
220 Fifth Ave.
New York, NY 10001
212-679-2748
> Books: macrame, needlecraft, spinning, weaving.
> Catalog.
> Club offers 15% discount on any craft book in print; no purchase obligation.
> Club plans: craft book.

Craftsman Supply House
35 Brown's Ave.
Scottsville, NY 14546
716-889-3403
> Art foam, basketry, beadery, bottle cutters, burlap, candlemaking supplies, chenille, cork, dip film, doll parts, engraving, etching supplies, feather craft, felt, flower looms, flowermaking, foil, glues, hand tools, Hong Kong grass, jewelrymaking accessories, lacing, lampshades, mache, miniatures, mosaics, paints, papers, plaster casting, plastic domes, plastic frames, power tools, raffia, rattan, reed, resin craft supplies, rush, Styrofoam®, trims.
> Books.
> Catalog: 50¢.
> Kits: leather, rush.

Craftsman Wood Service Co.
2727 So. Mary St.
Chicago, IL 60608
312-842-0507
> Cabinet hardware, clock accessories, clock movements, domestic hardwoods, hand tools, imported hardwoods, lamp parts, moldings, music box accessories, music box movements, power tools, upholstery tools, veneers, zodiac inlay emblems.
> Carries over 3500 items.
> Catalog: 50¢.
> Kits: musical instruments, pictures, woodworking.

Crafty Ideas
409 South First St.
Evansville, WI 53536
608-882-4682
> Ceramic bisque, ceramic bisque sets, ceramic wisemen, decorating stains.
> Books: candlemaking, ceramics, decoupage, folk art painting, folk painting, glass and resin crafts, needlework, rosemaling, Christmas crafts.
> Catalog: $1.25; book circular, 10¢.
> Magazine features craft ideas and how-to articles.
> Magazines: general arts and crafts.
> Subscriptions: quarterly, 1 year, $4.

Crafty's Backroom
R.R. 1, Box 7
Augusta, NJ 07822
201-875-6891
> Egg craft.
> Also has egg-a-month designs, send SASE.
> Catalog: $1.

Craigle Studios
8316 N. Merrill St.
Niles, IL 60648
312-823-3602
> Kits: metal sculpture.
> Write for information.

Crain-Harmon
799 Broadway
New York, NY 10003
212-254-8170
> Catalog.
> Kits: astrological, crewel, designs, needlepoint, African.

Company Listing
Cramer—Creativity

Cramer Mold Shop
11139 Columbus Ave. West
Fostoria, OH 44830
419-435-8374
  Ceramic molds.
  Catalog: $1.

Create Your Own, Inc.
Box 84
Medham, NJ 07945
201-543-6113
  Kits: patchwork, patchwork aprons, patchwork crib quilts, patchwork pillows, patchwork place mats, patchwork tote bags.
  Write for information.

Creations by Julianna
11081 Riviera Rd.
New Buffalo, MI 49117
616-469-1152
  Kits: stain glass.
  Write for information.

Creations for the Artist
205 Loetscher Pl. B5
Princeton, NJ 08540
609-452-2057
  Jewelry patterns, porcelain in gold plated jewelry findings.
  Catalog: $1.
  Discount: quantity purchases.

Creative Craft House
Box 1386
Santa Barbara, CA 93102
805-966-5858
  Beadery, edgings, feather craft, jewelry findings, miniatures.
  Books: selling crafts.
  Catalog: 25¢.

Creative Crafts
P. O. Box 700
Newton, NJ 07860
201-383-3355
  Magazine features how-to projects, information on newest trends, list of supplies sources, notices of craft events throughout the U. S..
  Magazines: general arts and crafts.
  Subscriptions: single copy 60¢, 8 times yearly, 12 issues $6; foreign $7.

Creative Crafts Christmas Annual
P. O. Box 700
Newton, NJ 07860
201-383-3355
  Magazines: Christmas crafts.
  Subscriptions: annual copy 75¢.

Creative Hands Co., Inc.
4146 Library Rd.
Pittsburgh, PA 15234
412-563-6688
  Books.
  Catalog.
  Discount: quantity purchases.
  Group packs.
  Kits: leather craft, screen process.

Creative Industries
P.O. Box 343
La Mesa, CA 92041
714-469-5012
  Potter's wheels.
  Also has variable speed control from 0-250 rpm; full-size floor model wheel.
  Catalog.

Creative Metalcraft
1083 Bloomfield Ave.
W. Caldwell, NJ 07006
201-575-0822
  Catalog.
  Kits: wrought iron craft.

Creative Murals, Inc.
14707 Keswick St.
Van Nuys, CA 91405
213-781-3849
  Catalog: 25¢ postage/handling.
  Kits: mural, paint-by-number.

Creative Spoolcraft
252 So. Middletown Rd.
Pearl River, NY 10965
914-735-5357
  Kits: heirloom ornaments from spools.
  Write for information.

Creativity Needlepoint
3804 S. Ocean Dr.
Hollywood, FL 33020
305-925-0877

Company Listing
Creativity—Crown

Crewel, hand-painted needlepoint canvas.
Kits: latch hooking, needlepoint.
Write for information.

Creator's Corner
2140 W. 4th Ave.
Vancouver, B.C., Canada
604-732-0121

Candlemaking supplies, cold water dyes, cotton cord, flower drying agents, jute, nylon dyes, soapmaking, wool dyes.
Write for information.

Dr. David Crespi
Dan-Lin Art Sales
358 Jinny Hill Rd.
Cheshire, CT 06410
203-272-7184

Books: ceramic glazes, clay and glazes.

Crewel Elephant
Box 217
Silverton, CO 81433
303-387-5714

Embroidery transfer patterns.
Books: patterns for embroidered clothing.
Catalog: of pattern, 25¢.

Crewel World
Box 303
Huntingdon Valley, PA 19006
609-428-4575

Frames.
Catalog: 50¢.
Kits: crewel.

Crossroads
Creative Needlecrafts
P. O. Box 1372
Burbank, CA 91505
213-762-9500

Canvas, embroidery frames, embroidery hoops, embroidery threads, fabrics, needlepoint canvas, Persian yarn, quickstitch yarn, rug hooks, rug yarn, yarns.
Books: crewel, needlepoint.
Catalog: $1.
Kits: embroidery, needlepoint, Scandinavian rya.

Crowe & Coulter
Box 484CB
Cherokee, NC 28719
704-497-5588

American Indian bead corn, American Indian flower corn, beadery, cherry blocks, mahogany blocks, poplar blocks, walnut blocks, wood carving supplies.
Catalog: general; whittling 25¢.
Kits: fingerweaving, American Indian designs.

Crown Cultured Pearl Corp.
580 8th Ave.
New York, NY 10018
212-947-0540

Burma cabochons, Burma jade (jadeite) jewelry, cabochons, carvings, cultured pearls, jade, nephrite jade.
Price lists available.

Crown Gems Co.
Box 5536
Sherman Oaks, CA 91413
213-788-4367

Australian opals, blue Australian sapphires, cut amethyst, cut aquamarine, cut gemstones, cut opals, cut peridot, cut turquoise, fire agate, fire cut agate, gem rough material, gemstone accessories, gemstone solutions, Mexican opal, peridot, turquoise, ultrasonic cleaners.
Information and price lists available.

Crown Publishers
419 Park Ave. So.
New York, NY 10016
212-685-8550

Books: bargello, batik, bead design, bottle cutting, candlemaking, card weaving, casting, ceramics, crewel, crochet, decoupage, dye, found materials, gem cutting, general arts & crafts series, gold and silversmithing, gold leaf, hand weaving, macrame, metal enameling, metal sculpture, model aircraft, mosaics, paper, papier mache, plastics, sculpture casting, shell crafts, stone sculpture, string art, tie dye, tole designs, wall hanging, wood.
Contact your nearest bookstore or write above.
Write for information.

Cummings Wood Co.
P.O. Box 27
East Hartford, CT 06108
No phone orders.
  Hardwood blocks.
  Catalog.

Curio Ceramic Molds
5341 Ash Lane
Dallas, TX 75223
214-827-0193
  Ceramic molds.
  Catalog: $1.

Custom Drapery Institute
Box 899
Orange, CA 92669
714-997-1235
  Course offers custom decorating, slip-covers, bedspreads, ensembles; fabrics and decorator items available at wholesale.
  Home study courses: drapery making.
  Write for information.

The Custom House of Needle Arts & Design
76 Elm St.
W. Towsend, MA 01474
617-597-6639
  Crewel.
  Catalog: 50¢.
  Kits: embroidery.
  Services: needlework blocking, mounting and framing.

Custom Made Carvings & Miniatures
Hermania Anslinger
320 So. Ralph
Spokane, WA 99202
509-534-9206
  Custom-made miniatures, miniature animals, miniature furniture, miniatures.
  Send SASE for information.

Cutaway
Box 151
Weaubleau, MO 65774
No phone orders.
  Factory cutaway fabrics.
  Factory cutaway fabrics are sold by the pound for quilts, doll clothes, pillows, etc.
  Write for information.

D-Carol
Kear Rd., R.D. 5
Canandiagua, NY 11424
315-394-0873
  Patterns.
  Catalog: 50¢.
  Has patterns for 20 whimsical felt figures and animals, ornaments for Christmas, party favors, appliques, bazaar items.

D. M. C. Corporation
109 Trumbull St.
Elizabeth, NJ 07206
201-351-4550
  Kits: tapestry.
  Write for information.
  Write for local distributor.

Daddy's Mold Shop
147 Sloan Ave.
Trenton, NJ 08611
609-587-1244
  Ceramic molds.
  Catalog: 50¢.

Dairy Service, Inc.
Box 253
Bluffton, IN 46714
219-824-3305
  Milk bottles, milk cans, unfinished milk cans, wood barrels, wood kegs, wood milk cases, wood milk kegs.
  Catalog: 25¢.
  Discount: quantity purchases.

Danfield Threads Inc.
Winsted, CT 06098
203-379-2137
  Nylon thread.
  Write for information.

Mrs. Danner's Quilts
Box 650
Emporia, KS 66801
316-342-1033
  Books: basic quiltmaking.
  Send SASE for information; quilting pattern catalogs, $1.25.

Company Listing
Davault—Decorating

Davault Miniature Furniture
422 Livingston
Creston, IA 50801
515-782-7661
    Dollhouse furniture, furniture patterns.
    Catalog: 35¢.
    Leaflets: patterns for modern & period doll house furniture.

Davidson's Old Mill Yarn
Box 115
Eaton Rapids, MI 48827
517-663-2711
    Mill yarns.
    Send SASE for information and samples, $1.

Margaret Davis
1922 Lindell
San Angelo, TX 76901
915-944-3108
    Books: rugs from nylons and pantyhose.

Davis & Co.
Box 206
Concord, TN 37720
615-966-5352
    Patterns.
    Books: American folk art painting.
    Carries patterns for Pennsylvania Dutch, dolls and toys to stitch-and-stuff, stencils, decals, tole designs.
    Catalog.

Davis Publications, Inc.
50 Portland St.
Worcester, MA 01608
617-754-7201
    Books: batik dye, ceramics, clay, design, general arts & crafts series, mosaics, papier mache, puppetmaking, scrap art, screen, sculpture, stitchery, tie-dye, tissue paper, wall hangings, weaving without a loom, wire sculpture.
    Write for information.

Marquerite P. Davison
Box 163
Swarthmore, PA 19081
215-876-4191
    Books: handweaver's patterns.

J. W. Day Mfg. Co.
11309 Indianhead Dr.
Austin, TX 78753
512-836-3645
    Bolo tie slides.
    Bola tie slides has spring clasps (non-slipping with flat front for decorating--can be silver soldered).
    Write for information.

De Lapa Mining Inc.
Suite 313 Wilson Bldg.
Corpus Christi, TX 78401
512-884-4612
    Alexandrite, amethyst, andalusite, aquamarine, citrine, emeralds, faceted gemstones, morganite, opals.
    Write for information.

De Mallie Crafts
1654 Ridge Rd.
Webster, NY 14580
716-872-1485
    Jewel stone assortments.
    Write for information.

Deb Products
(Div. of Barker Enterprises)
15106 10th Avenue S.W.
Seattle, WA 98166
206-244-1870
    Driftwood polish.
    Driftwood polish is a finish for raw driftwood pieces.
    Write for information.

Alfred Decker
1637 N.W. Drake
Camas, WA 98607
206-834-4494
    Bobbins, lacemaking materials, wooden tatting shuttles.
    Send SASE for information.

Decorating & Craft Ideas Made Easy
P. O. Box 9737
Fort Worth, TX 76107
817-338-4401
    Magazine features how-to's for tole batik, candlemaking and other popular crafts; also decorating with crafts for limited budgets.

Magazines: general arts and crafts.
Subscriptions: single copy 75¢, 10 times yearly, 1 year $6, foreign $7.50.

Decorative Designs by Dare
8122 Meadow Lane
Munster, IN 46321
No phone orders.
   Tole patterns.
   Catalog: 25¢.

H. DeCovnick & Son
P.O. Box 68
Alamo, CA 94507
415-837-1244
   Clock accessories, clock movements.
   Catalog: 50¢.
   Kits: grandfather clocks, grandmother clocks.

Deep Flex Plastic Molds, Inc.
Box 11471
Ft. Worth, TX 76110
817-927-5337
   Candle molds, craft furs, decoupage, hobby optics, jewelry findings, pearls, plaster molds, resin craft molds, resin craft supplies, string art.
   Catalog.
   Kits: decoupage.

Deft
P.O. Box 3669
Torrance, CA 90503
213-320-2452
   Books: decoupage.

Dek-Co Manufacturing Co.
P.O. Box 1314
Amarillo, TX 79105
806-355-9781
   Clock accessories, decoupage, decoupage boxes, decoupage easels, decoupage frames, decoupage lap desks, decoupage plaques, decoupage purse handles, decoupage slat purses, decoupage stools, hardware, patterns, pine wood purse, prints.
   Catalog: $1 (refundable).
   Kits: clock.

Delco Craft Center, Inc.
30081 Stephenson Highway
Madison Heights, MI 48071
313-585-1678
   Alcohol lamps, aluminum foils, armatures, art foam, art paper, artist's supplies, batik wax, beadery, blockprinting, bottle cutters, burlap, candlemaking supplies, cane, canvas, casting stone, casting waxes, cements, ceramic kilns, ceramic supplies, chenille boutique trims, cold enameling, cold water dyes, cooking crystals, copper foil, dip film, dyes, ecology shadow boxes, enameling, felt, firing clay, flower looms, flowermaking, frames, glass gems, glass globs, glass marbles, glazes, hand tools, jewelry findings, kiln accessories, leathercraft, linen, looms, macrame accessories, macrame cords, metal compounds, metal etching, model making, modeling tools, mosaic forms, mosaic tiles, mosaic tools, mosaics, nonfiring clay, paints, paper dip dyes, papers, papier mache, pebble gems, plaster casting, plaster molds, potter's wheels, power tools, printmaking, raffia, reed, replacement parts for kilns, resin craft molds, resin craft supplies, rug hooks, rugmaking supplies, scales, screen process supplies, sculpture wax, soldering tools, squeeze bottles, stained glass, stained glass paints, stitchery mesh (2 gauges), Styrofoam®, synthetic straw loom, textile stencils, tools, turntables, urethane foam blocks, wiggle eyes, yarns.
   Books.
   Catalog.
   Discount: quantity purchases.
   Group packs.
   Kits: leather craft, screen process.

Delmar Publishers
a Div. of Litton Educational Publishing Inc.
50 Wols Rd.
Albany, NY 12205
518-459-1150
   Books: hand tools for woodworking.
   Catalog.
   Contact your nearest bookstore or write above.

Company Listing
Denison—Diamond-Pro

T. S. Denison & Co., Inc.
5100 W. 82nd St.
Minneapolis, MN 55437
612-831-1221
> Books: paper crafts, party decorations.
> Contact your nearest bookstore or write above.
> Write for information.

Derby Lane Shell Center
10515 Gandy Blvd.
St. Petersburg, FL 33702
813-576-1131
> Beadery, cut shells, marble craft, plastic disks, rhinestones, shells.
> Catalog: 50¢.
> Discount: quantity purchases.

Dersh Feather & Trading Corp.
494 Broadway
New York, NY 10012
212-226-6432
> Domestic feathers, fluffs feathers, imported feathers, marabou feathers, ostrich feathers, peacock feathers, pheasant feathers, turkey feathers.
> Write for information.
> Write for local distributor.

Design Magazine
1100 Waterway Blvd.
Indianapolis, IN 46202
317-634-1100
> Magazine features calendar of events, new product information and unusual crafts utilizing easily found raw materials.
> Magazines: general arts and crafts.
> Subscriptions: bimonthly, 1 year $7, Canada and foreign $7.50.

Designers Fabrics Buy-Mail
P.O. Box 569, 1948 Ridge Ave.
Evanston, IL 60204
312-869-3750
> Club offers seven swatchbooks yearly; offers fine quality fabrics from cottons to camel hair, including satin acetate for pillow cases and 60 inch fabrics (Dacron and others) for tablecloths.
> Club plans: fabrics.
> Discount: for club members.
> Write for information.

Determined Productions, Inc.
P.O. Box 2150
San Francisco, CA 94126
415-433-0667
> Also has Snoopy and Linus needlepoint designs.
> Kits: needlepoint, quickpoint, Joan Walsh Anglund designs.
> Write for information.

Dharma Trading Co.
P.O. Box 1288
Berkeley, CA 94701
415-841-7722
> Dyes, handspun yarns, macrame accessories, macrame cords, procion® dyes, vegetable dyes, yarns.
> Books.
> Catalog: 50¢; also free dye information sheet.

Dial-A-Glaze
Box 88
Davenport, CA 95017
408-423-0984
> Circular glaze calculator.
> This is device enabling the potter to easily design his own glaze recipes.
> Write for information.

The Dial Press Inc.
1 Dag Hammarskjöld Plaza, (245 E. 47th St.)
New York, NY 10017
212-832-7300
> Books: collage, needlepoint, sand sculpturing, slate sculpturing.
> Contact your nearest bookstore or write above.
> Write for information.

Diamond-Pro Unlimited
P.O. Box 25
Monterey Park, CA 91754
213-281-2277
> Balls, cones, diamond wheels, lapidary supplies.
> Diamond sintered wheels are not plated--straight cylinders, safe side, heavy duty, thin, flat saws, tapered cylinders.
> Write for information.
> Write for local distributor.

Diamond Sales Co.
117 N.E. 1st Ave.
Miami, FL 33132
305-379-4234
   Diamonds, emeralds, gemstones, rubies, sapphire.
   Write for information.

Diedricks Crafts
409 S. First
Evansville, WI 53536
608-882-4682
   Block bisque, ceramic supplies, clock movements, electric kilns, lamp parts, plastic objects, potter's wheels.
   Catalog: $1.25; send SASE and 25¢ for information.
   Kits: ceramic kilns.

Diffraction Co., Inc.
Box 151
Riderwood, MD 21139
301-296-4789
   Iridescent diffraction (polyester) foil, self-adhesive iridescent foil jewels.
   Catalog: plus samples.
   Kits.

Dildine's Arts & Crafts
5713 Calumet
Hammond, IN 46320
219-932-8885
   Complete line of arts and crafts supplies, open stock and kits.
   Kits: general.
   Write for information (SASE).

Dinky Molds
Smith Clove Rd.
Central Valley, NY 10917
914-928-2544
   Ceramic molds.
   Catalog: $1.25.

Distlefink Designs
718 Broadway
New York, NY 10003
212-477-7625
   Catalog: plus fabric swatches, 25¢.
   Kits: patchwork pillow, patchwork quilt.

Diversikit, Inc.
Box 4479
Philadelphia, PA 19140
215-457-1639
   Catalog: 25¢.
   Kits: crochet jute, hats, shoulder bags, suede leather purse.

William Dixon Co.
750 Washington Ave.
Carlstadt, NJ 07072
201-935-0100
   Chasing supplies, electroplating supplies, electroplating tools, enameling supplies, enameling tools, etching supplies, etching tools, hammered metal supplies, hammered metal work tools, jewelrymaking supplies, jewelrymaking tools, silversmithing supplies, silversmithing tools.
   Catalog: $2 (refundable).

Doll Castle News
Brass Castle Rd.
Washington, NJ 07882
201-689-7512
   Doll clothes patterns.
   Magazines: dolls and dollhouses.
   Subscriptions: bimonthly, copy 60¢ 1 year $3.50.

The Doll Cupboard
Box 458
Branson, MO 65616
417-334-4161
   Dollhouse miniatures, handcrafted miniatures.
   Carries over 350 doll house miniatures.
   Catalog: 60¢.

Doll Repair Parts, Inc.
9918 Lorain
Cleveland, OH 44102
216-961-3545
   China doll parts, doll accessories, doll parts.
   Books.
   Catalog: 25¢.
   Kits: doll repair.

Doll's Candle & Craft Supplies
633 W. Catella Ave.
Orange, CA 92667
714-639-3180
 Candle additives, candle dyes, candle scents, candle waxes, candle wicks, candle-making supplies, flower wax cutters, metal molds, rubber molds, 3-D plastic molds.
 Books.
 Kits: candle wax dye.

Dollspart Supply Co., Inc.
506 51st Ave.
Long Island City, NY 11101
212-784-5454
 Doll accessories, doll bisque, doll parts, doll repair items.
 Books.
 Catalog.

Dolly Darling Inc.
Box 3206, Norland St.
Miami, FL 33169
No phone orders.
 Doll patterns.
 Catalog: 25¢ (refundable).
 Kits: "Teen doll" clothing.

Don's Hobby Co.
424 So. Front
Mankato, MN 56001
507-387-1330
 Art foam patterns, chenille, flowermaking supplies, tri-beads.
 Catalog.
 Kits: flower making.

Dorothy Mae's Trunks
Box 536--M-B
Spearman, TX 79081
No phone orders.
 Trunk repair parts.
 Books: installing interiors, refinishing, repairing, restoring antique trunks.
 Send SASE for repair parts catalog.

The Dorr Mill Store
Guild, NH 03754
603-863-1197
 Braiding chair seats, braiding hangings, hand hooking, rug braiding, rug wool.
 Books.
 Catalog: 50¢.

Dorris Dolls
401 W. 36th St.
Riviera Beach, FL 33404
305-848-7774
 Cloth doll patterns, toy patterns.
 Catalog: 10¢ and long SASE.

Dot's Dollhouse
7309 Bergstrom Rd.
Rockford, IL 61103
815-633-8034
 Rag doll patterns.
 Catalog: send 10¢ and long SASE.
 Kits.

Douglas & Sturgess, Inc.
730 Bryant St.
San Francisco, CA 94107
415-421-4456
 Airbrushes, furniture finishes, modeling clay, moulage molding, plaster casting, resin craft supplies, rubber latex, sculpture wax.
 Catalog.

James L. Douthat
Box 233
Pikeville, TN 37367
615-447-2802
 Catalog.
 Kits: coat-of-arms, crewel, needlepoint, painting.
 Over 500,000 names on file for coat-of-arms.

Dover Publications Inc.
180 Varick St.
New York, NY 10014
212-255-3755
 Books: basketry, furniture making, general arts & crafts series, pottery, primitive, screen printing, sculpture, wood carving, Pueblo and other American Indian design.
 Contact your nearest bookstore or write above.
 Write for information.

Dover Scientific Co.
P.O. Box 6011
Long Island City, NY 11106
212-721-0136
 American Indian artifacts, cabochons, fa-

ceted gemstones, fossils, lapidary supplies, magnifiers, minerals, rocks.
Books.
Catalog: 25¢.

Down Under Opal
P. O. Box 30635
Seattle, WA 98103
206–634–3457
Opals, quartz tops.
Price lists available.

Evelyn Downing
1210 Park Ave.
Richmond, VA 23220
804–358–3075
Leaflets include instructions on cutting, hinging and decorating eggs.
Leaflets: eggery.

Downs
1014 Davis Street
Evanston, IL 60204
312–328–0500
Cookie stamp sets, doll stands, embossed pewter buttons, frames for hanging tiles, gay 90's newsprint sacks, glass display domes, miniature pewter dishes, plastic portrait balls, plate (dish) frames, plate holders, sticker prints, wood bookends.
Catalog.
General arts and crafts supplies.

Dowse's Lapidary Supply, Inc.
754 N. 300 West
Salt Lake City, UT 84103
801–322–1962
Bloodstone, crazy lace agate, dinosaur bone, gemstones, golden labradorite, green moss, green tree agates, hickoryite, lapidary equipment, lapidary supplies, Mexican fire agate, obsidian, pigeon blood agate, red horn coral, sagenite, topaz.
Books: table top making.
Write for information.

Walter Drake
4510 Edison Ave., Drake Bldg.
Colorado Springs, CO 80901
303–596–1882
Bottle cutters, daisy looms, decals, hand looms, magnifiers, miniature tools, nylon thread, plastic display domes, power tool attachments, scissors, sewing awls, woven labels.
Catalog.
General arts and crafts supplies.

Drake Publishers Inc.
381 Park Ave. So.
New York, NY 10016
212–679–4500
Books: cabinet making, carpenter's tools, china repairs and restoration, crochet, dried flower decorating, egg decorating, embroidery, fabric crafts, furnituremaking, general arts & crafts series, knitting, leather crafts, log sculpture, marquetry, masonry, mosaics, paper crafts, rag doll making, rug making, scratch board, smocking, toys and wood toys, upholstery, woodworking.
Contact your nearest bookstore or write above.
Write for information.

Dremel Creative Power Tools
Div. of Dremel Man. Co.
P.O. Box 518
Racine, WI 53401
414–637–8831
Bench top multiuse units, drill presses, engraving tools, hand grinder, jigsaw, power accessories, power tools.
Catalog.
Write for local distributor.

Driftwood House
Box 2247
Harbor, OR 97415
503–469–3850
Cones, driftwood, driftwood wax, pods, seeds.
Books: crafting, driftwood.
Carries numerous cones: gum balls, eucalyptus bell, jacaranda, Chinese fir, devil claw, deodor rose and rose spine, acorns, redwood.
Catalog: $1.
Kits: driftwood.

Drykiln Design
5121 Ygnacio
Oakland, CA 94601
415–534–2122

Company Listing
Drykiln—Easy

Cullets, furnaces, lehrs, pipes, pontils, precision glass blowing tools.
   Catalog: with guide to glass studio construction, $1.

The Ducketts
P.O. Box 969, 1410 W. 8th
Medford, OR 97501
503-772-8570
   Adhesives, belts, diamond abrasives, faceted stones, faceting supplies, jewelry findings, jewelry mountings, motors, polishes, pulleys, silicon carbide, silver ring castings.
   Books.
   Catalog.
   Kits: tumbler.

Dulcimer
Box 2
Simpsonville, MD 21150
301-465-0977
   Kits: dulcimer, musical instrument.
   Write for information.

R. S. Duncan & Co.
30 Chapel St.
Bradford, BD150P, West Yorkshire, England
No phone orders.
   Accessories, English yarns, knitting worsted, lambswool, patterns, rug wool, Shetland.
   Carries English yarns in over 500 colors.
   Catalog: plus yarn samples, $1.

E. P. Dutton & Co., Inc.
201 Park Ave. So.
New York, NY 10003
212-674-5900
   Books: candlemaking, classic guitar making and guitar repair, folding paper masks, general arts & crafts series, origami, puppet making, sewing.
   Contact your nearest bookstore or write above.
   Write for information.

Dye-Craft Ideas
Box 307
Coventry, CT 06238
No phone orders.
   Books: batik, dye craft, solid color dyeing, stitch dyeing, tie-dye.

Eagle Mill
Direct Discount Division
Box 21264
Dallas, TX 75211
214-339-2750
   Fabrics, sewing accessories, trims.
   Send SASE for information.

Earth Treasures
Box 1267
Galesburg, IL 61401
309-343-6181
   Diamond blades, gem cutting equipment, gem faceting supplies, gem polishing supplies, lapidary equipment, lapidary supplies, potter's wheels.
   Catalog.
   Kits: lapidary.
   Pottery wheel has 9 in. throwing wheel and complete accessories.

Earthworks
624 W. Willow
Chicago, IL 60614
312-642-7462
   Handcrafted stoneware beads.
   Carries large and small holed beads shapes and sizes.
   Catalog: plus samples, 50¢ (refundable).

East River Publications
30 Park Rd. Apt. 313
Hamden, CT 06511
203-777-1470
   Books: belt-weaving, loom building.

Eastern Mills
Box 154
Chelsea, MA 02150
617-846-3278
   Felt mill ends.
   Discount: quantity purchases.
   Mill ends are sold by the pound, yard or square for bazaar items, appliques, Christmas decorations, etc.
   Write for information.

Easy Street
10 Main St.
Chester, MA 01011
413-354-6330

Beadery, embroidery materials, porcupine quills, yarns.
Write for information.

Ebersole Lapidary Supply Inc.
11417 W. Hwy. 54, R.R. 8
Wichita, KS 67209
316-722-4771

Cabochons, findings, lapidary equipment, lapidary tools, mountings, rocks.
Catalog: 30¢.

Kristine Eckert
1430 Montrose
Dayton, OH 45414
513-276-5633

Unbleached cotton cord.
Catalog: plus samples, 50¢.

Economy Handicrafts, Inc.
50-21 69th St.
Woodside, NY 11377
212-426-1600

Art foam, art tape, basketry, beadery, blockprinting, candlemaking supplies, cellophane paper, ceramic supplies, ceramic tools, cork, dip film, enameling, etching supplies, fabrics, felt, foil, hand tools, jewelry findings, leathercraft, lost wax casting, mache, macrame accessories, metallic sculpture compound, modeling clay, mosaics, papers, plexiglass, power tools, resin craft supplies, screen process supplies, sculpture supplies, self-hardening clays, shells, stained glass, stencils, Styrofoam®, Styrofoam® cutter, wood carving supplies, woodware.
Catalog.
Discount: quantity purchases.
Kits: paper flower, sculpture, wood ware.

Edmund Scientific Co.
555 Edscorp Bldg.
Barrington, NJ 08007
609-547-3488

Bottle cutters, crystallizing paint, diffraction jewels, fiber optics, hand tools, lapidary supplies, magnets, mirrors, plastic display domes, power tools.
Books.

Catalog.
Kits: clay modeling, crystal growing, glass painting, lighting, sculpture, transfer process (print-to-cloth), wax sculpture.

Edwards Jewelry Co.
Whitewater, CO 81527
303-227-3917

Aventurine balls, belt buckles, cabochons, gold filled findings, goldstone balls, jewelry findings, onyx balls, sterling silver findings, tigereye balls.
Catalog of discount items.

Egg Album
87 Lewis St.
Phillipsburg, NJ 08865
201-859-4496

Magazines: eggery.
Subscriptions: quarterly, copy $1.50; 1 year $5.

The Egg Shell
P.O. Box F
South Lyon, MI 48178
No phone orders.

Egg marker.
Egg marker is used to draw lines to divide eggs.
Send SASE for information.

The Eggs-Aminer
C/O Barbara Allen
P.O. Box 1158
Saugus, CA 91350
No phone orders.

Newspaper features design, decorating tips, supply sources and directory.
Newspapers: eggery.
Subscriptions: quarterly, 1 year $10.

Electro Stylus Mfg. Co.
31 Cheyenne Blvd.
Colorado Springs, CO 80906
303-633-5969

Power etching instrument.
Power etching instrument can be used on glass, plastic, metals, film negatives, silk screen, leather, stencils.
Write for information.

Company Listing
Ells—Ensz

Dick Ells Co.
908 Venice Blvd.
Los Angeles, CA 90015
213-747-5129
>Casting equipment, casting supplies.
>Books: lost wax jewelry casting.
>Write for information.

Elvette Handbag Co.
164 Princess St.
Winnipeg, R3B1K9, Canada
204-942-5973
>Catalog.
>Services: needlepoint and petitpoint handbag mounting.

Elvin
P.O. Box 1096
Mountainside, NJ 07092
201-647-4575
>Cabochon preforms, Linde star boules.
>Kits: simulated diamond jewelry.
>Write for information.

Emberugs
P.O. Box 391
Syosset, NY 11791
516-921-2422
>Catalog: plus wool samples, 25¢.
>Kits: rya.

Embroiderer's Guild of America Inc.
120 E. 56th St.
New York, NY 10022
212-751-2539
>Organizations: embroidery.
>With over 25 chapters throughout the country, membership includes a quarterly publication "Needle Arts", use of reference library and slide rental service; offers over a hundred transfer designs for sale.
>Write for information.

Embroideries Unlimited
P.O. Box 162, Dept. X
Long Beach, NY 11561
516-431-6419
>Embroidered appliques.
>Catalog: 25¢.

Emerson Books Inc.
Reynolds Lane
Buchanan, NY 10511
914-739-3506
>Books: knotting, leather craft, mobiles, net making, paper crafts, watch and clock repair, woodworking.
>Contact your nearest bookstore or write above.
>Write for information.

Emperor Clock Co.
P.O. Drawer A-T
Fairhope, AL 36532
205-928-2316
>Clock movements.
>Catalog.
>Kits: grandfather clock.

The Enchanted Doll House
Manchester Center, VT 05255
802-362-1327
>Miniature Early American furniture, miniatures.
>Books: doll making.
>Catalog: 50¢.
>Kits: clock, macrame.

Ewanna England
P. O. Box 4301
Tulsa, OK 74104
918-939-9874
>Books: dimensional painting, reverso painting with foil.

English's Model Railroad Supply
21 Howard St.
Montoursville, PA 17754
717-368-2516
>Also has AHM general (HO, O, N scales), 75¢; Atlas, HO track and buildings, 25¢; Suydam building (HO scale), 50¢; Tyco trains catalog (HO scale), 50¢; and other catalogs available in HO, H, O and other scales.
>Catalog.

Luella Ensz
The Art Cellar
Inman, KS 67546
316-585-2187
>Books: patterns for tole painters.

Eric Martin Co.
Box 1072
Anderson, CA 96007
916–357–2654

Gold mountings, silver mountings, synthetic sapphire, synthetic spinel rough, wax ring patterns.
Catalog.
Services: custom faceting and jewelry design.

Ervins
120th Raytown Rd.
Kansas City, MO 64149
816–765–0805

Doll patterns, dough doll heads.
Kits: granny dolls.
Send 25¢ and SASE for information.

Essayons Studio, Hand Arts Center
8725 Big Bend Blvd.
St. Louis, MO 63119
314–962–9126

Batik, ceramic supplies, copper enameling supplies, hand spinning wool, jewelrymaking accessories, looms, macrame accessories, weaving supplies, yarns.
Books.
Write for information.

Ettl Studios Inc.
Studio 45, Ettl Lane
Greenwich, CT 06830
203–531–9000

Casting supplies, ceramic supplies, modeling supplies, sculpture supplies, wood carving supplies.
Catalog: $1 (refundable).

Eva Ann Dolls
9741 Crosby Ave.
Garden Grove, CA 92644
No phone orders.
Books: applehead dolls.
Patterns include "Miss Purr and Cousin Sue", kitty kat dolls, panda (19 in.), and "Jenny Doll and Wardrobe".
Send SASE for information on original patterns.

Eva Mae Doll Co.
Box 331X
San Pablo, CA 94806
415–235–3056
Catalog: 25¢.
Kits: china doll.

Exact Performance
200 Bloomfield Ave.
Bloomfield, NJ 07003
201–743–2248
Books: aviation, military.
Catalog: 35¢.
Kits: aircraft, domestic plastic model, figures, imported plastic model, ships.

Exactra-Craft Corp.
11729 Cardinal Circle
Garden Grove, CA 92643
714–636–2404

Cabbers, faceting instruments, jewelry casting supplies, jewelrymaking equipment, wax patterns.
Catalog: supplies; wax patterns; $1 (ref) foreign orders, $1.

Exotic Thai Silks
395 Main
Los Angeles, CA 94022
415–948–8611

China silk brocades, china silks, fabrics, Indian silks, Italian silks, Japanese pongee prints, Japanese silk, Thai cottons, Thai silks.
Catalog: 10¢.

Exposition Press
50 Jericho Tnpk.
Jericho, NY 11753
516–997–9050
Books: cornshuck crafts.
Contact your nearest bookstore or write above.
Write for information.

Fabricon Co.
2021 Montrose Ave.
Chicago, IL 60618
312–929–5700
Course offers reweaving of burns, tears and other damage to fabrics; also invisible reknitting for knit fabrics, wool and polyester.

Company Listing
Fabricon—Fashion

Home study courses: mending fabrics.
Write for information.

Fabrics 'Round the World Inc.
270 West 38th St.
New York, NY 10018
212–695–1380
  Club offers swatches every 2 weeks; includes cottons from Italy, India, Switzerland and France; silks from the Orient; polyester double knits from the U. S.; no purchase obligation.
  Club plans: fabrics.

Fabulous Holiday House
Hwy. 22 & 523
Whitehouse Station, NJ 08889
201–534–4400
  Boutique items, Christmas decorating items, Easter decorating items, findings, miniatures, trims.
  Catalog: 50¢.

Fairtex Distributing Co.
868 Sixth Ave.
New York, NY 10001
212–532–2145
  Yarn surprise boxes, yarns.
  Books.
  Carries both domestic and imported yarns.
  Catalog: general, 15¢; color chart, 50¢.
  Kits: knitting and crochet.

Family Circle Kits
P.O. Box 450
Teaneck, NJ 07666
No phone orders.
  Catalog: 25¢.
  Kits: needlecraft.

The Family Handyman
P.O. Box 537
Farmingdale, NY 11735
No phone orders.
  Books: carpentry, furniture antiquing and restoring, hand and power tools.
  Write for information.

The Family Handyman
P.O. Box 2897
Boulder, CO 80302
No phone orders.

  Magazines: how-to household projects.
  Subscriptions: 75¢ a copy, 9 times yearly, 1 year $5.75, foreign $6.75.

Fantastic Fit Products
1475 N. Broadway, Suite 306-B
Walnut Creek, CA 94596
415–933–1869
  Kits: 'fit and sew'.
  Write for information.

Mark Farmer Co., Inc.
Box 428 CBC
Point Richmond, CA 94807
415–234–4312
  Doll accessories, doll clothes patterns, dollhouse furniture.
  Catalog: $1.
  Kits: doll.

Farmers Gem and Rock Shop
10037 Cave Creek Rd.
Phoenix, AZ 85020
602–943–1301
  Diamond blades, faceting units, jewelry findings, lapidary combination units, lapidary machinery, lapidary supplies, lapidary templates, lapidary tools, lapidary tumblers, mountings.
  Catalog: $1 (refundable).
  Discount: quantity purchases.

The Farmhouse Craft Shoppe
7811 Belfort St.
Houston, TX 77017
713–643–4004
  Kits: "decaling".
  Turn announcements into plaques.
  Write for information.

Fashion Fabrics Club
122 Cuttermill Rd.
Great Neck, NY 11022
516–487–1559
  Club offers a home pattern publication with a monthly swatch kit of domestic and foreign fabrics; savings on fabrics.
  Club plans: fabrics.
  Write for information.

Company Listing
Fawcett—Fieldwood

Frederick J. Fawcett, Inc.
129 South St.
Boston, MA 02111
617-542-2370

Bobbin winders, cloth slitting machines, embroidery threads, flax line fiber, flax straw (retted), linen thread, looms, macrame yarn, needlepoint yarn, spinning wheels, weaving supplies, weaving yarns, wool carders, yarns, 2/20's handweaving worsted.
Catalog: plus samples, $1.
Discount: quantity purchases.
One of the world's largest collection of linen thread in all sizes and colors.

Fawcett Special Interest Magazines & Books
1515 Broadway
New York, NY 10036
212-869-3000

Books: decorating, general arts & crafts series, needlework, Christmas crafts.
Contact your nearest bookstore or write above.
Write for information.

Feather & Flower Craft
827 South 21st Ave.
Hollywood, FL 33020
305-929-2711

Beadery, findings.
Catalog.
Kits: bead, doll key chain.

Federal Smallwares
85 Fifth Ave.
New York, NY 10003
212-989-5162

Handcrafted miniatures, miniature antique replicas, miniature furniture.
Write for information.

Felts Manufacturing Co. Inc.
3801 Morrison Place
Indianapolis, IN 46204
317-923-9881

Porcelain findings.
Has hand decorated porcelain findings including florals, portraits, animals, birds, scenery designs.
Write for information; plaque sample, $1.

Mrs. C. Ference
Box 295, 10789 Jordan Rd.
Saline, MI 48176
313-429-4744

Books: Ukrainian Easter Eggs.

Fetty-Nielsen Macrame Loom
P.O. Box 15111, Wedgewood Station
Seattle, WA 98115
206-525-8996

Macrame cords, nylon braided cord, portable macrame looms.
Also has portable looms for blind or handicapped.
Kits: loom.
Send SASE for information.

Fezandie & Sperrle, Inc.
103 Lafayette St.
New York, NY 10013
212-226-7653

Alcohol dyes, aniline dyes, artist's dry colors, batik dyes, leather dyes, oil soluble dyes, wood stains.
Discount: quantity purchases.
Price list.

Fiber to Fabric
317 4th St.
Kirkland, WA 98033
206-827-5767

Knitting supplies, looms, macrame accessories, needlecraft supplies, spinning, weaving supplies.
Catalog.

Ficket
Whitneyville, ME 04692
No phone orders.
Books: resilvering mirrors, using sawdust 20 ways.

Betty Fielding
123 Donovan Ave.
Mogadore, OH 44260
216-628-4061

Handcrafted miniatures.
Send SASE for price list.

Fieldwood Co.
Box 223
Ho-Ho-Kus, NJ 07423
201-825-3174

Company Listing
Fieldwood—Florida

Ceramic greenware, dollhouse accessories, jewelry findings, miniatures.
Send 20¢ SASE for information.

Filature Lemieux Inc.
St. Ephrem De Beauce, Quebec, Canada
418–484–2169

Knitting yarns, rug yarn, tapestry yarn, weaving yarns, wool yarn.
Catalog: plus samples, 25¢.

Anne Fitch's Handicrafts
109 South Parrot Ave.
Okeechobee, FL 33472
813–763–7787
Catalog: handbag designs 25¢.

Flags Galore
6525 Swathmore Dr.
Memphis, TN 38138
No phone orders.

Miniature flags.
Also has miniature country and historical flags.
Discount: quantity purchases.
Free price list available.

Flair-Craft Inc.
Box 3494
Kimberling City, MO 65686
417–739–2180

Brass rings, color parchment posters.
Books: decoupage, tole painting.
Catalog.

N. Flayderman & Co.
Squash Hollow, R.F.D. 2
New Milford, CT 06776
203–354–5567
Books: scrimshaw.
Catalog.

Floyd Fleming
2041 S. 320th Space 159
Federal Way, WA 98002
206–838–1888

Bottle cutters, jug cutter.
Write for information.

Flemington Cut Glass Co.
156 Main St.
Flemington, NJ 08822
201–782–3017

Glass display domes.
Discount: quantity purchases.
Write for information.

J. P. Fliegel Co.
P.O. Box 505
Gloversville, NY 12078
518–725–4117

Double woven cotton accessories, leather skins.
Kits: leather glove.
Price list: plus color swatches 35¢.

Flint FBG Imports
P.O. Box 838
Royal Oak, MI 48067
313–542–5081

Hand-painted miniatures, miniature animals, miniature 19th century figures.
Catalog: plus price list, 25¢.

Floating Gem Co.
P.O. Box 478
Woodland Hills, CA 91364
313–347–5196

Glass bulbs, heart glass bulbs, long flat glass bulbs, round glass bulbs.
Catalog.
Glass bulbs used for displaying gemstones or pendants.

Floquil, Inc.
Cobleskill, NY 12043
518–234–2076

Painting fabrics, painting glass, painting wood, paints, printing ceramics.
Catalog.
Kits.

Florida Supply House, Inc.
P.O. Box 847
Bradenton, FL 33506
813–756–1831

Bolo tie cords, bolo tie tips, floral craft, glass jewel pendants, glass paperweights, jewelry findings, plastic beads, plastic boxes, plastic ornaments, plastic shapes, rhinestones, shark's teeth, shells, stones, wood beads.
Books.

Catalog.
Discount: quantity purchases.

The Fluorite Shop
811 So. Werner Ave.
Evansville, IN 47712
812-425-7986
Crystals, fossils, minerals, rock supplies.
Also has fossils from Indiana, Illinois and Kentucky including also nodular Pennsylvania plants.
Write for information or brochure.

Flying Models
Fredon-Springdale Rd., Fredon, P.O. Box 700
Newton, NJ 07860
201-383-3355
Magazine features newest innovations, products, plans and instructions.
Magazines: aircraft models.
Subscriptions: monthly copy 60¢, 1 year $6, foreign $7.

Foam Fantasy
1415 East Genessee
Saginaw, MI 48605
No phone orders.
Accessories, art foam, patterns, Styrofoam®.
Carries Styrofoam® balls, eggs, other shapes.
Catalog: 25¢.

Folbot Corp.
P.O. Box 7097
Charleston, SC 29405
803-744-3483
Dacron® sail rigs.
Catalog.
Kits: paddle boat.

Folkcrafts
952 Fairview Ave., P.O. Box 171
Bowling Green, KY 42101
502-842-6232
Construction paper, quilling paper.
Write for information.

Folklorico
P.O. Box 625
Palo Alto, CA 94302
415-327-6302

Austrian angora yarns, embroidery threads, Icelandic lopi, Mexican wool, wool yarn.
Carries angora yarns in 42 colors, woolen yarn in 7 natural colors and embroidery yarn in 56 colors.
Color card: 75¢.

Follett Publishing Co.
1010 W. Washington Blvd.
Chicago, IL 60607
312-666-5855
Books: model rocketry, taxidermy.
Contact your nearest bookstore or write above.
Write for information.

Foredom Electric Co.
Div. of Blackstone Industries, Inc.
Rt. 6
Bethel, CT 06801
203-748-3521
Abrasive disks, abrasive points, burrs, carbide cutters, carving drills, hand-piece accessories, miniature power tools, sanding bands, saw blades, vanadium steel cutters.
Carries miniature power tools in hangup or bench models for wood, leather, metal, plastic, stone.
Catalog.

Fotocut Lab
c/o Frederic Hultberg
222 Rucholme Rd.
Toronto Ontario M6H 2Y8, Canada
416-423-6503
Kits: photo-etching.
Offers custom parts in any modeling scale from customer's drawings or sketches.
Send SASE for information and rate card.

Fountains for the Home
2921 N. 24th St.
Arlington, VA 22207
703-525-5753
Books: ceramic fountain.
Leaflets: ceramic fountains.

Alice Fowler Originals
P.O. Box 787
Colorado Springs, CO 80901
No phone orders.

Company Listing
Fowler—Frye

Crochet designs for baby things, designs for baby things.
Catalog.

Framaway Co.
East Main St.
Roanoke, AL 36274
205-863-4916

Artist portfolios, canvas panels, easels, ready-stretched canvas, roll canvas, stretcher strips, wool velour panels.
Catalog.

Fran's Basket House
Rt. 10
Succasunna, NJ 07876
201-584-2230

Ready-made baskets.
Catalog: 25¢.
One of the largest importers of rattan and wicker furniture and accessories.

Frank's Jewelry & Gem Shop
9849 Kimker Lane
St. Louis, MO 63127
No phone orders.

Australian opals, Brazilian opal, lapidary cutting materials, opal chip cabochons.
Books: gem.
Catalog.
Kits: cabochons making.

Frankie's Twistcraft Jewelry
P. O. Box 408
La Pine, OR 97739
503-536-2327

Square gold filled wire, wire jewelrymaking tools.
Books: twistcraft jewelry.
Write for information.

Franzen Gifts
110 Franzen Bldg.
Flanagan, IL 61740
815-796-4407

Kits: rug braiding.
Write for information.

The Freed Co.
Box 394
Albuquerque, NM 87103
505-247-9311

Coral, glass beads, grease wool, hand cards, spinning supplies.
Write for information.

Bea Freeman Enterprises
Box 87
Bryn Mawr, PA 19010
215-525-7179

Knitting instructions, latch hook rugs, patterns, rug hooking guns, sweater wheels.
Also has knit instructions for over 360 sweaters on sweater wheel.
Catalog: 25¢.

Fres-O-Lone Mold Corp.
U.S. Rt. 1
Princeton, NJ 08540
609-452-8444

Plaster molds.
Catalog: $1.

The Fringe and Frame
732 Filber St.
Pittsburgh, PA 15232
412-621-6466

Looms, textile crafts, weaving accessories, yarns.
Price list available.

Sam Frost
Box 151
Lake George, NY 12845
518-668-2544

Rough faceting material.
Carries rare and unusual, as well as familiar varieties of rough faceting materials.
Catalog: send 32¢ stamps.

Frostline
1750 30th Street
Boulder, CO 80302
303-449-1180

Findings.
Catalog.
Kits: children's jackets, hunter's gear, parkas, ponchos, rain pants, sewing, ski apparel, sleeping bag.

E. B. Frye & Son, Inc.
Wilton, NH 03086
603-654-4811

Hand cards, weaving supplies.
Send SASE for information.

Furniture Designs
1425 Sherman Ave.
Evanston, IL 60201
312-475-3213
Catalog: $1 (refundable).
Leaflets: furniture making.
Offers over 150 plans in Early American, traditional, Danish modern, Mediterranean and English periods.

Mrs. G's
Hwy 12 West
Starkville, MS 39759
601-323-8212
Silk screened fraternity and sorority crests.
Write for information.

Gager's Handicrafts
3516 Beltline Blvd.
Minneapolis, MN 55416
612-929-2696
Books.
Catalog.
Discount: quantity purchases.
Group packs.
Kits: leather craft, screen process.

Gail's Decorative Arts Studio
9602 S.W. 57 St., P.O. Box 696, Olympia Heights Station
Miami, FL 33165
305-271-9502
Egg decorating supplies, egg stands, leaves, rhinestone bandings, rhinestones, roses.
Catalog: 25¢.

Helen Gallagher
Foster House
6523 N. Galena Rd.
Peoria, IL 61601
309-691-4610
Basket tote bags, glass display domes, metal mini-easels, miniature dolls, miniature furniture, specialty cake pans.
Catalog.
Kits: candlemaking, needlecraft.

Gladys Galloway
670 Gibbs St.
Caro, MI 48723
No phone orders.
China painting supplies, decoupage designs.
Also has color studies including flowers, fruits, pine cones, trees, birds, oriental.
Catalog: 25¢.

James A. Gardner
Box 214, 2235 W. 25th St.
San Pedro, CA 90732
213-831-8138
Kits: embroidery.

John E. Garrett Ltd.
New Glasgow
Nova Scotia, Canada
902-752-7161
Burlap rug patterns, mesh canvas rug patterns, rug hooks, yarns.
Catalog: 25¢.

Gay World of Dolls Museum
15403 So. Hatton Rd.
Oregon City, OR 97045
503-631-3146
Books: Doll Repair.
Send SASE for information.

Geecraft
Box 391-G
Blue Earth, MN 56013
507-526-3453
Rooster designs, silhouette designs.
Catalog: 25¢.
400 silhouettes on graph squares for enlarging; 72 rooster designs in detail on graph squares.

Gem Center, U.S.A.
4100 Alameda St.
El Paso, TX 79905
915-544-2271
Bloodstone rough material, lapidary cutting materials, lapidary supplies.
Price list available.

Gem-O-Rama, Inc.
400 Franklin St.
Braintree, MA 02184
617-843-3905

Amethyst, Australian opals, cut gemstones, green malachite, imperial chrysophrase, jewelry findings, lapis lazuli, mountings, polished gemstones, Taiwan jade, tigereye.
Discount: quantity purchases.
Write for catalog.

Gem Tec Diamond Tool Co.
7310 Melrose St.
Buena Park, CA 90620
714-521-1810

Diamond bar wheel dressers, diamond gem maker, diamond tools, diamond wheels.
Write for local distributor.
Write for information.

Gem Tool Specialties
P.O. Box 2386
Alhambra, CA 91803
No phone orders.

Diamond arbors, diamond blades, diamond burrs, diamond cores, diamond disks, diamond drills, diamond lapidaries, diamond machines, diamond pads, diamond points, diamond powders, diamond tools, diamond wheels.
Catalog.
Diamond tools for cabachon, faceting, lapping.
Kits.

Gemex Co.
P.O. Box 37, Los Vallecitos Blvd.
San Marcos, CA 92069
No phone orders.

Batik, beadery, cabochons, cameos, candlemaking supplies, decoupage, dip film, faceted stones, feathers, findings, gemballs, jewelry casting supplies, jewelrymaking supplies, macrame accessories, mountings, needlecraft supplies, prints, stained glass, 3-D flexible decoupage cut-outs.
Books.
Catalog.
Kits: bead flower, crochet jewelry, jewelry, leather beads, metal decor, needlepoint, pottery, stained glass, string art, weaving.

Gemological Institute of America
11940 San Vicente Blvd.
Los Angeles, CA 90049
213-826-3533

Eye loupes, gem detectors, gem graders, hand loupes, hot point testers, polariscopes, professional jeweler's instruments, refractometers.
Books: gem identification, gemstone carving and cutting, ivory, jewelry design and instructions, jewelry repair, stones.
Course teaches design elements and motifs for custom jewelry designing; classification and identification of gems; appraising and grading of pearls; a 2 to 3 year course; all stones and materials are included.
Home study courses: lapidary.
Write for information.

Gems & Minerals
P.O. Box 687, 1797 Capri Ave.
Mentone, CA 92359
714-794-1843

Books: gem cutting, jewelrymaking, lost wax casting, minerals, stone collecting, tumbling.
Magazine features gem cutting, jewelrymaking, carving, intorsias, silver working, new product information, gem and mineral locations; calendar of events.
Magazines.
Subscriptions: monthly copy 50¢, 1 year $4.75.

Gems Galore
240 Castro St.
Mountain View, CA 94040
415-968-8707

Casting equipment, casting supplies, corundum boules, findings, flexible shaft machines, gold, jewelrymaking tools, lapidary equipment, lapidary supplies, metal detectors, metals, mountings, silver, spinel boules.
Catalog: 50¢.

Gems International
P. O. Box 4463, Valley Village Stn.
No. Hollywood, CA 91607
805-492-2308

Blue star sapphire, cabbing amethyst, faceting amethyst, lapidary supplies, ruby cabochon rough, star ruby, turquoise rough.
Deals primarily in faceting rough and finished goods; also has amethyst from Brazil.
Write for information.

Gene's Rock Shop
1906 East F. Street
Oakdale, CA 95361
209-847-1697
Black nephrite, botryoidal jade, Clearcreek jadeite, green nephrite.
Price list available.

General Crafts Corp.
3031 James St.
Baltimore, MD 21230
301-644-6400
Crewel tapestry wall hangings.
Catalog.
Kits: by-number handbag, crewel, mosaic wall plaque.
Write for local distributor.

General Supplies Co.
P.O. Box 338
Fallbrook, CA 92028
714-728-8314
Cake decorating molds, cake decorating tools, candle accessories, candle molds, candlemaking supplies, candy decorating tools, candy making equipment, mill ends, professional sewing machines, upholstery fabrics, upholstery tools, wedding cake supplies.
Catalog: 50¢.
Kits: seasonal trim, upholstery, vinyl repair.

Genie
2320 N. Alameda
Compton, CA 90222
213-636-9777
Automatic knitting machines, machine attachments, pattern cards.
Catalog.

Geode Industries
106-108 W. Main, U.S. Hwy. 34
New London, IA 52645
319-367-2286
Black opals, diamond drills, faceting machines, lapidary supplies, lapidary tumblers, opals, smoky quartz, tektites, ultrasonic cleaners.
Carries over 2500 items for lapidary; over 1000 mountings, various types and styles; 3000 cut stones.
Catalog: $1.

Geological Enterprises
Box 996
Ardmore, OK 73401
405-223-8537
Animal fossils, plant fossils.
Catalog: $2.

Geophile International
Box 358
Appalachin, NY 13732
607-625-3703
Gem rough material, gemstones, jewelry mountings, jewelrymaking supplies, lapidary equipment, lapidary supplies, lapidary tumblers.
Catalog: 50¢ (refundable).

Gerhardt Macrame Studio
P.O. Box 221
Rock Island, IL 61201
No phone orders.
Bottle knotting looms, looms.
Books: square knotting.
Leaflets: build-it-yourself looms.
Write for information.

The Ghen Studio
203 Brimbal Ave.
Beverly, MA 01915
617-922-3258
Patterns.
Books: came method of making stained glass medallions, copper foil stained glass medallions.
Send SASE for pattern list.

Gibsons Creations
4733 W. Grace St.
Chicago, IL 60641
312-283-5232
Basketry, beadery, boutique supplies, filigrees, findings, foil paper, jewels, metallic braids, rhinestone bandings, rhinestones, silk wrap ornaments, tree skirts.

Company Listing
Gibsons—Glass

Catalog: $1.25.
Kits: holiday ornament.

Gift Craft
Handcraft Bldg.
Des Moines, IA 50301
515-288-8953

Catalog: 25¢.
Kits: dolls, macrame, nature crafts, needlecraft, planters, trivets, Christmas decorations, Christmas ornaments.

The Gift Shoppe
1438 Countrywood 42
Hacienda Heights, CA 91745
No phone orders.

Miniature bone china animals, miniature ceramic animals, miniature glass animals.
Send stamp for list.

Giles & Kendall Inc.
Box 188
Huntsville, AL 35804
205-776-2979

Furniture legs, furniture lumber, furniture parts, hardware.
Carries over 60 unfinished furniture making kits including cedar chests, bookcases, tables, gun racks, others.
Catalog: 25¢.
Kits: unfinished wood furniture making.

Gilliom Mfg. Co.
St. Charles, MO 63301
314-724-1812

Build-your-own kits include saws, band saws, sanders, lathes.
Catalog: 25¢.
Kits: build-your-own power tool.

Gilman's
Hellertown, PA 18055
215-838-8767

Alcohol burners, bead mills, belt sanders, blowpipes, cabochons, cutting machines, demagnetizer, dies, faceted stones, faceting units, findings, flat laps, gem makers, gem scales, gem vises, gemstones, horn anvils, jewelry mountings, lamps, lapidary equipment, lapidary tumblers, miniature power tools, pearls, polishes, polishing motor, ring blanks, scarabs, slab saws, solder, soldering tools, stamps, templates, trim saws, wax, wire.
Books.
Carries tools such as pliers and nippers, shears, scrapers, snips, drills, hammers, burnishers, files, stone setting burs, saws and sawframes, rock clamp, tongs.
Catalog.
Kits: grandfather clock, hand jewelry casting, polishing, sand casting.

Glass Art Magazine
Box 7527
Oakland, CA 94601
415-534-2122

Magazine is devoted to contemporary blown and stained glass on an international professional level; features calendar of events and new techniques.
Magazines: glass crafts.
Subscriptions: bimonthly copy $3, 1 year $15, foreign $16.

Glass Bottle Blowers Assn.
226 S. 16th St.
Philadelphia, PA 19102
215-545-0540

Books: making useful articles for the home from glass bottles.

Glass Creations
1251 Glenbrook Rd.
Huntingdon Valley, PA 19006
215-884-0429

Fused glass items, glass anchors, glass angels, glass fish, glass icicles, glass sailboats, glass snowflakes, glass stars.
Catalog.
Kits: mobile.
The glass is fused and tempered to be impact and heat resistant.

Glass House Studio
P.O. Box 3267
St. Paul, MN 55165
612-227-0749

Books: introducing stained glass.
Kits: leaded stained glass.
Write for information.

The Glass Workshop
P. O. Box 244
Norwood, NJ   07648
201-768-7055
> Magazine features articles for beginner and advanced loaded glass craftsmen.
> Magazines: stained glass crafts.
> Subscriptions: bimonthly, 1 year $4.

Glencraft Shop
Rt. 2, Box 360
Poulsbo, WA   98370
206-779-5701
> Wood, wood carving scraps, wood jewelry scraps.
> Send SASE for information.

Glo-Classics
24 Brighton 10th Path
Brooklyn, NY   11235
No phone orders.
> Unpainted miniatures.
> Carries miniature figures of Egyptians, slave girls, Greeks, Vikings, knights, colonial women, colonial soldiers, Civil War, W.W. II, Napoleanic, novelty girls, cannons.
> Catalog: 50¢.

Gloria
5 Amero Lane
Saugus, MA   01906
617-233-5319
> Patterns.
> Handicraft pattern list, 25¢; doll pattern list, 25¢.
> Has patterns for handicrafts including knitting, crochet, Christmas, scrap craft, bazaar items.

Gloria's Glass Garden
220 Santa Monica Blvd.
Santa Monica, CA   90401
213-393-4169
> Ceramic beads, glass beads, wood beads.
> Books: beadcraft, candlemaking, macrame.
> Catalog: 25¢.
> Kits: venetian glass bead.

The Golden Egg
210 Crain Hwy South, Severn Run Bldg.
Millersville, MD   21108
301-987-5150
> Goose eggshells, ostrich eggs, pheasant eggshells, quail eggshells.
> Catalog: $1.
> Complete quality line of trims for boutiquing eggs.

Good Housekeeping
P.O. Box 900
Teaneck, NJ   07666
No phone orders.
> Catalog: needlework 25¢.
> Kits: crewel, embroidery, needlecraft, needlepoint.

Good Housekeeping Needlecraft
959 Eighth Ave.
New York, NY   10019
212-262-6248
> Magazine features how-to articles on needlecrafts, crewel, crochet, knitting, macrame, needlepoint, bazaar and gift items, recycling throwaways.
> Magazines: needlecrafts.
> Subscriptions: semi-annual copy at newsstand, $1.

Goodhert-Willcox Co., Inc.
123 W. Taft Dr.
South Holland, IL   60473
312-333-7200
> Books: ceramics, industrial woodworking, metal projects, metal working, plastics, welding.
> Catalog.
> Contact your nearest bookstore or write above.

Irene Goodwin
3018 67th St.
Lubbock, TX   79413
806-795-4798
> China decorating, gold etching.
> Books: gold etching.
> Write for information.

Gordon's
1741 Cherry Ave., Box 4073
Long Beach, CA   90804
213-591-8956
> Findings, jewelrymaking supplies, mountings.
> Books.
> Catalog: $1 (refundable).
> Kits: metal casting.

Company Listing
Gorin's—Greentree

Gorin's Gem Arts & Rocks
4108 N. Piedras St.
El Paso, TX 79930
915-565-2666

Lapidary material, Mexican agates grab bag.
Send SASE for information.

Henry B. Graves Co.
1190 So. Old Dixie Hwy.
Delray Beach, FL 33444
305-278-4579

Faceting machines.
Write for information.
Write for local distributor.

Great Brook Miniatures
Box 148
Jackson, NH 03846
603-383-6673

Handcrafted miniatures, hand-painted miniatures, metal miniatures, miniature animals, wildlife miniatures.
Catalog: 25¢.

Great Central Fur Corp.
7912 W. Appleton Ave.
Milwaukee, WI 53218
414-462-9292

Dressed fur pelts, fur trimmings, miniature animals, mink, raccoon furs.
Catalog.

Great Outdoors Publishing Co.
4747 28th St. N.
St. Petersburg, FL 33714
813-525-6609

Books: cast net construction, general arts & crafts series, pine cone crafts, shells.
Contact your nearest bookstore or write above.
Write for information.

Great Western Equipment Co.
3444 Main St.
Chula Vista, CA 92011
714-422-4157

Lapidary belt sanders, lapidary combination units, lapidary equipment, lapidary grinders, lapidary polishing equipment, lapidary sanders, slab saws.
Catalog.

Units made to customer's specifications.
Write for local distributor.

Green Bay Exploration & Mining Co. Ltd.
44735 W. Yale Box 36
Chilliwack, B.C., Canada
604-792-2447

Nephrite jade from British Columbia in first & second grade gemstone material, also carving material (orders of 500 lb. or more only).
Write for information.

Green's Rock & Lapidary Ltd.
1603 Centre St. No.
Calgary, Alberta T2E 2S2, Canada
403-276-6447

Arbors, bolo tie slides, chains, crystals, diamond products, electric carver, electric wax spatula, findings, fossils, gem makers, gemstones, gold grain, gold sheet, gold wire, inlay casting wax, jeweler's sprue wax, jewelrymaking supplies, jewelrymaking tools, lapidary laps, lapidary machinery, lapidary supplies, lapidary tumblers, lost wax casting, metal stampings, mountings, resin craft accessories, resin craft molds, resin craft supplies, ring shapes, rough rock, sheet waxes, silver grain, slab saws, sterling silver sheet, sterling silver wire, sticky wax, synthetic faceting material, templates, trim saws.
Books.
Catalog: $1 (refundable).
Discount: quantity purchases.
Kits: tumbling.

Greentree Ranch Wools, Countryside Handweavers
163 N. Carter Lake Rd.
Loveland, CO 80537
303-667-6183

Acrylic items, alpaca, alpencarpet, Belgian linen, British tapestry wool, carpet round, Danish wool, flat chenille, fleece, fringe wool, German goathair, homespun wool, Japanese silk, linen, looms, mill products, round chenille, spindles, spinning accessories, spinning wheels, spinning yarns, worsted yarn, yarns, 2/7 wool.
Carries Danish wool in 75 colors, 2/7 wool in 94

colors, homespun wool in 37 colors, worsted in 44 colors, British tapestry wool in 25 colors, German goathair in 14 colors Rya yarn in 73 colors and cowhair in 43 colors.
Write for list of catalog yarn samples.

Grieger's Inc.
900 So. Arroyo Pkwy.
Pasedena, CA 91109
213-795-9775
Button backs, findings, imitation gemstones, jewelrymaking equipment, jewelrymaking supplies, mountings, natural gemstones.
Carries over 10,000 jewelry making supplies.
Catalog.

Griegers/B & M
2961 State St.
Carlsbad, CA 92008
704-729-1626
See entry above.

Grosset & Dunlap Inc.
51 Madison Ave.
New York, NY 10010
212-689-9200
Books: candlecraft, crewel, general arts & crafts series, needlepoint, quilting, sewing.
Contact your nearest bookstore or write above.
Write for information.

Grueny's Gift Center
17 West Second
Little Rock, AR 72201
501-376-0393
Miniature ceramic bowls, miniature ceramic figures, miniature ceramic pitchers, miniature ceramic vases, miniature French dolls, miniature furniture, miniatures.
Catalog: 75¢.

Guild of Strawberry Banks Inc.
93 State St.
Portsmouth, NH 03801
603-436-8032
Kits: sampler.
Write for information.

Paul K. Guillow Inc.
P.O. Box 229
Wakefield, MA 01880
617-245-5255
Balsa wood, ready-to-fly gliders.
Catalog: 10¢.
Kits: balsa model aircraft.

Guitar Center
Box 15444
Tulsa, OK 74115
918-835-4181
Carries supplies for making a guitar, banjo, mandolin.
Catalog: 25¢.

Beno J. Gundlach Co.
P.O. Box 544
Belleville, IL 62222
618-233-1781
Asbestos tile cutters, asphalt cutters, carpet knives, carpet tools, ceramic tile cutters, cutters, engraving tools, floor tile cutters, jamb, linoleum knives, nippers, notching tools, plastic laminate countertopping, plastic laminate tools, plastic wall tile cutters, power tools, propane equipment, saws, scribers, shears, tile cutters, tile saws, trimming tools, utility knives.
Catalog.

Gyro Lamp Supply Corp.
5218 N.W. 35th Ave.
Miami, FL 33142
305-635-5284
Lamp parts, lamp wiring diagrams, replacement burners for oil lamps.
Catalog: 50¢.

H & A Mfg. Corp.
2847 Franklin St.
Avondale Estates, GA 30002
404-294-5360
Diamonds, emeralds, gemstones, opals, rubies, sapphire.
Price list available.

T. B. Hagstoz & Son
709 Sansom St.
Philadelphia, PA 19106
215-922-1627

Company Listing
Hagstoz—Handweavers

Alloyed gold, brass, bronze model metal, centrifugal casting equipment, copper, cuttle bone, gold filled findings, jewelrymaking supplies, jewelrymaking tools, nickel silver, pewter, platinum, sand, sheet metal, sterling silver, wire.
Books.
Catalog.

Peg Hall Studios
113A Clapp Rd.
Scituate, MA 02066
617-545-3605

Bronze powder, brushes, gold leaf, metal trays, quill engravers, quill scrollers.
Books: designs, metal and wood ware decorating, patterns, stenciling.
Catalog 25¢.

B. T. Hallam
139 Lewis Ave.
Billings, MT 59102
406-248-6704

Montana agate rough forms, Montana agate slab, nephrite jade, tumble polished gems.
Catalog.

Handcraft House
110 W. Esplanade
North Vancouver, B.C., Canada
604-988-6912

Clays, dyes, kilns, looms, potter's wheels, weaving supplies, yarns.
Books.
Catalog: 50¢.

Handcraft Originals
1702 Cornwallis Pkwy.
Cape Coral, FL 33904
813-542-7369

Brass hinges, duck eggshells, goose eggshells, jewelry findings, metal miniatures, pee wee eggshells, plastic miniatures, quail eggshells, rhinestones, shell flowers, wood miniatures.
Send SASE for price list.

The Handcraft Supply Corp.
Dodge Center
Minneapolis, MN 55927
507-374-6552

Art foam, drying paper, flower press, frames, pressed flower craft, shadowboxes.
Write for information.
Write for local distributor.

The Handcrafters
1 West Brown St.
Waupun, WI 53963
414-324-2031

Ballpoint paints, beadery, bottle cutters, candlemaking supplies, cane, cork, craft furs, crushed glass, decoupage, embroidery, enameling, etching supplies, felt, foil, hand tools, knitting supplies, knitting yarns, leathercraft, looms, mache, mosaics, paints, patterns, plastic pellets, power tools, raffia, resin craft supplies, rug hooking supplies, rug yarn, stained glass paints, weaving yarns, wood carving supplies.
Books.
Catalog: 50¢.
Discount: quantity purchases.

Arlene Handley Rock Hobby Supplies
800 N.W. 72nd Way
Vancouver, WA 98665
206-693-1034

Jewel caps, tiny tumbled stones, tumbled stone tree materials.
Write for information.

Handweaver & Craftsman
220 Fifth Ave.
New York, NY 10001
212-679-2748

Discount: group rates.
Magazine features design techniques, yarns, new products, spinning and weaver's guild events.
Magazines: weaving.
Subscriptions: bimonthly copy $1.75, 1 year $8.

Handweavers Guild of America, Inc.
998 Farmington Ave.
West Hartford, CT 06107
203-233-7136

National nonprofit organization serves all individual and groups interesting in the weaving arts; membership includes "Shuttle Spindle & Dyepot" magazine.
Organizations: weaving.
Write for information.

Hanover House Industries, Inc.
340 Poplar St.
Hanover, PA 17331
717-637-2271
Awls, bottle cutters, display domes, flower looms, polyurethane foam, power tool attachments, small easels, $2 bills.
Catalog.
General arts and crafts supplies.

Happy Hobbies Magazine
Cherryvale, KS 67335
316-336-2077
Magazines: features instructions and patterns for quilting, quilting, stationery decorating, textile painting, tole.
Subscriptions: bimonthly, copy 50¢.

Harper & Row, Publishers Inc.
10 E. 53rd St.
New York, NY 10022
212-593-7000
Books: crochet, general arts & crafts series, knitting, model airplanes, needlework, pile rug making, pottery.
Contact your nearest bookstore or write above.
Write for information.

Harrison-Hoge Ind. Inc.
104 Arlington Ave.
St. James, NY 11780
516-724-8900
Dress form.
Write for information.

Harrisville Designs
P.O. Box 51
Harrisville, NH 03450
603-827-3334
Hand looms, wool yarn.
Catalog: plus samples 50¢.
Kits: handlooms.

Harrower House of Decoupage
37 Carpenter St.
Milford, NJ 08848
201-995-2310
Decoupage, decoupage boxes, decoupage foil papers, decoupage hardware, decoupage plaques, decoupage tools, gold lace frames, gold lace borders, gold lace ornaments, lining papers, prints, rice paper.
Books.
Catalog: $1.
Course offers decoupage by Dorothy Harrow on LP records, with instruction booklets and supplies.
Home study courses: decoupage.

John Hathaway
410 W. 6th St.
San Pedro, CA 90731
213-833-9853
Paper models.
Catalog: 25¢.
Kits: paper model aeroplanes, paper model castles, paper model chateaus, paper model churches, paper model miniature rooms, paper model moon rover, paper model palaces, paper model ships, paper model towns, paper model trains, paper model villages, paper model European buildings, paper model U.S. western 1883's mining town.

Hawthorne House, Inc.
P.O. Box 112
Bloomington, IL 61701
309-827-8714
Kits: soapmaking and candlemaking.
Write for information.

Hearth & Heather Ltd.
3904 1/2 Sauk Trail
Richton Park, IL 60471
312-718-7800
Wood carving supplies.
Also has carve-a-pipe (briar block with stem, whittle own design for bowl).
Write for information.

Hearthside Press
445 Northern Blvd.
Great Neck, NY 11021
516-466-6600
Books: bargello, beaded flower making, crochet, decoupage, egg decorating, general arts & crafts

Company Listing
Hearthside—Hidden

series, knitting, leather and fur sewing, macrame, needle made rug design, needlecraft, paper crafts, papier mache, pottery, preserved flower designs and decorating, quilting, shell craft, tole, Christmas decorations.
Contact your nearest bookstore or write above.
Write for information.

Heirloom Rugs
28 Harlem St
Rumford, RI 02916
401-438-5672
Rug patterns.
Catalog: $1.

Helmor Label Co.
5143 W. Diversey Ave.
Chicago, IL 60639
312-237-6163
Printed woven edge satin labels.
Catalog: plus samples.

The Hen House
920 Eastside Blvd.
Muskogee, OK 74401
918-683-1392
Kits: needlepoint.
Write for information.

Carl Hepp Mosaic Co.
3126 Nebraska
St. Louis, MO 63118
314-664-1645
Colored metal foils, cooking crystals, lead came, lead came soldering fluids, mosaic mirrors, mosaics, solder, stained glass.
Catalog.
Kits: tiffany shade.

HERE Inc.
410 Cedar Ave.
Minneapolis, MN 55404
612-338-1156
Custom wood, instrument bridge, instrument strings, instrument tuners, instrument nut.
Catalog.
Folk type instrument kits include dulcimers, psalteries, banjos, thumb pianos.
Kits: musical instrument.

Heritage Hill Patterns
Box 624
Westport, CT 06880
203-227-7321
Cutting machines, fabrics, rug frames, rug hooks, rug patterns, yarns.
Catalog: (with instructions) rug hooking $1; general info, 50¢.
Kits: embroidery, needlepoint.

Heritage Looms
1445 S. Mountain Ave.
Monrovia, CA 91016
213-358-0512
Handcrafted looms, shuttles, weaving supplies.
Catalog: 50¢.

Herter's, Inc.
R.R. 1
Waseca, MN 56093
507-835-4011
Bird feathers, curly maple wood, sew-and-stuff animals, sew-and-stuff dolls.
Catalog.
Kits: candlemaking, fishing, gunstock finishing, lamp, lure and rod, ships, taxidermy.

P. C. Herwig Co., Inc.
Rt. 2 Box 140
Milaca, MN 56353
612-369-4144
Beadery, candlemaking supplies, cords, decoupage, earthenware beads, glass beads, jute, macrame accessories, sisal, stoneware beads, tole painting, wood beads, woodware, yarns.
Books: beadery, candlemaking, decoupage, knitting, macrame, paper, weaving.
Catalog: cord and yarn samples, $1.
Kits: candlemaking, macrame.

The Hidden Village
215 Yale Ave.
Claremont, CA 91711
714-626-9511
Aida, alpaca, basketry, beadery, Belgian yarn, canvas, cashmere yarn, cottolin yarn, crewel wool, dyes, electric tufting, embroidery, fabrics, feathers, fleece, floor looms, frames, fur, handspun yarns, hardanger,

hertha, hoops, horsehair, Icelandic yarn, jute, latch hook rugs, leather, linen cord, linen thread, macrame accessories, manual tufting, metallic threads, Mexican heavy-spun yarn, mink scraps, mohair yarn, monk's cloth, natural yarn, navy cord, nylon, Persian yarn, pillows, primitive yarn, rattail, rug frames, rug patterns, rug punch, rug wool, rugmaking supplies, rya yarn, seine twine, silk thread, spinning, spinning wheels, table looms, tapestry wool, tapestry yarn, tarred marlin cord, transfers, waxed linen, weaving supplies, yarns.
Books: textile handicrafts.
Catalog: 50¢.
Special services include mounting needlepoint and blocking leather.
Services: custom design, needlepoint.

Elizabeth Hiddleson
121 9th St.
Vallejo, CA   94590
707–643–6102
Books: crochet.
Write for information.

High Strength Adhesives Corp.
1701 N. Damen Ave.
Chicago, IL   60647
312–278–3800
Epoxy glues, epoxy resins, fiberglass cloth, fiberglass mat, mold releases, polyester resins, polyurethane foam, resin craft accessories, resin craft supplies, silicone rubber, vinyl glues.
Catalog.
Kits: marble resin craft, resin crafts.

Highland Park Manufacturing
Div. of Mustro Industries Inc.
12600 Chadron Ave.
Hawthorne, CA   90250
213–679–1478
Belt sanders, diamond products, diamond saw blades, finishers, lapidary equipment, slab saws, trim saws.
Catalog.
Write for local distributor.

Alexandra Hill Needlepoint Studios Ltd.
215 Park Avenue South
New York, NY   10003
212–674–7520
Kits: needlepoint.
Write for information.
Write for local distributor.

C. R. Hill Co.
2734 W. 11 Mile Rd.
Berkley, MI   48072
313–543–1555
Casting supplies, plating accessories, enamels, findings, goldsmithing equipment, jewelrymaking supplies, silversmithing supplies.
Catalog: $1 (refundable).

Hillquist
1545 N.W. 49th
Seattle, WA   98107
206–784–1960
Lapidary equipment.
Catalog.
Write for local distributor.

Historic House
960 W. Henderson Rd.
Columbus, OH   43220
614–451–4778
Kits: cross stitch, sampler.
Write for information.

Historical Society of Early American Decoration, Inc.
511 Post Rd.
Darien, CT   06820
203–655–0810
Books: publishes semi-annual journal "The Decorator".
Organization promotes research of Early American decoration, preserves examples of this work, encourages appreciation of this work, encourages appreciation of this art and upholds standards of reproductions.
Organizations: Early American decor.

Hobbi-Carve
930 Duluth St.
St. Paul, MN 55106
612–774–8757
 Wood carving tools.
 Write for information.

The Hobby Bench
832 So. Grand Ave.
Glendora, CA 91740
213–963–3711
 Military miniatures, model airplanes, model HO railroad, model HON3 railroad, model N railroad, model ON3 railroad, model ships.
 Write for information.

Hobby Gallery
3414 El Caminoreal
Santa Clara, CA 95051
408–244–6267
 Decals, miniature lead figures, miniature soldiers, model paints.
 Books.
 Catalog: $1.
 Kits: model.

Hobby House Press
4701 Queensbury Rd.
Riverdale, MD 20840
301–779–6612
 Books: doll collecting, dollmaking.
 Catalog.

Hoff House Ceramic Supplies, Inc.
40 Essex St.
Rochelle Park, NY
212–843–9385
 No-fire stone-like flakes for ceramics.
 Write for information.
 Write for local distributor.

Hoffman Hatchery
Gratz, PA 17030
717–365–3407
 Duck eggshells, egg craft, goose eggshells, guinea eggs, turkey eggs, unfinished woodenware.

 Also has unfinished Pennsylvania Dutch style miniature furniture.
 Free price list available.

Holgate & Raynolds
601 Davis St.
Evanston, IL 60201
312–328–5190
 Metal miniature doll houses, model room castings, O gauge sheets plastic embossed, plastic embossed HO gauge sheets.
 Carries castings of bowls, plates, silver, candlesticks; has plastic embossed sheets of brick, stone, roofing, clapboard sidings.
 Catalog: general 10¢; doll house castings, 50¢.
 Kits: HO structure.

Holiday Craft
9 Main St.
Sparta, NJ 07871
201–729–3626
 Adhesives, beadery, Christmas boutique items, diamond dust, dimensional plastic shapes, egg craft, filigrees, flat plastic shapes, glass ornaments, gold paper trims, jewels, lichen, miniature angels, miniature creche figures, miniature flowers, miniature grass, miniature trees, miniatures, peps, porcelain, ribbon, tinsel sticks.
 Catalog: $1.

Holiday Handicrafts, Inc.
Box 470
Winsted, CT 06098
203–379–3374
 Art foam, boutique items, candlemaking supplies, decoupage, felt, flowermaking, glitter, leathercraft, miniatures, movable eyes, rattan, resin craft supplies, rosette winders, starched lace, Styrofoam®, three king heads, tissue beads, trims, wood boxes, wreaths.
 Books.
 Catalog.
 Kits: art foam, crochet jewelry, ornament, three kings.

Holland Mold Inc.
1040 Pennsylvania Ave.
Trenton, NJ 08638
609–392–7032

Ceramic molds.
Catalog: $1.

Holly Studio Inc
Box 32
Kilmarnock, VA 22482
804-435-6414

China painting supplies, decorative stamping items.
Catalog: $1 (refundable).
Kits: china painting.

Hollywood Fancy Feather Co.
512 So. Broadway
Los Angeles, CA 90013
213-625-8453

Domestic feathers, imported feathers, marabou feathers, ostrich feathers, quill feathers, satnet feathers.
Write for information.

Holmes-Corey Ltd.
1069 Jackson, P.O. Box 786
Marco Island, FL 33937
813-394-2412

Catalog and research data card (send name and origin): 35¢.
Kits: coat-of-arms, crewel embroidery.
Over 500,000 names on linen with research documents.

Home-Sew Inc.
Bethlehem, PA 18018
215-867-3833

Braids, buttons, cotton lace, elastics, felt appliques, fringes, interfacing, laces, magnets, metallic trims, movable eyes, nonmetallic trims, nylon lace, pearls, pins, polyester lace, rhinestones, ribbon, rickrack, sequins, Styrofoam®, threads, zippers.
Catalog.
Kits: soap decorating.

Homecraft Veneer
Box 3
Latrobe, PA 15650
412-537-3938

Finishing supplies, laminating supplies, marquetry items, tools, wood veneers.
Carries 25 varieties of wood veneers.
Veneering instructions and price list, 25¢.

Homespun Fabrics
10115 Washington Blvd.
Culver City, CA 90230
213-839-6984

Fabrics, needlecraft supplies.
Also has 8 ft to 10 ft wide cottons.
Catalog: plus samples, 50¢.

Cherie Hooper
c/o Hidden House Press
81 Encino
Palo Alto, CA 94301
408-476-5562

Books: candlemaking.

Wm. Hooper
1931 S.E. 155th Pl.
Portland, OR 97233
503-255-3027

Custom-made needlepoint patterns, needlepoint lace.
Send SASE.

House of Clay China Shop
1100 N.W. 30
Oklahoma City, OK 73118
405-524-5610

China blanks, china painting designs.
Catalog: $1.

House of Figurines
1713 Central
Dubuque, IA 52001
No phone orders.

Unpainted plaster figurines.
Figurines including busts, lamps, statuary, blanks, wall plaques.
Write for information.

House of Flowers
6875 46th Ave. North
St. Petersburg, FL 33709
813-546-3058

Art foam, artificial straw, beadery, bunka embroidery, chenille, craft furs, felt, findings, floral craft, needlepoint yarn, purse trimmings, quilling supplies, ribbon, yarns.
Books: quilling.
Catalog.
Kits: needlecraft.

Company Listing
House—House

House of Gould
1290 N.E. 135th St.
Miami, FL 33161
No phone orders.
    Clamps, cutting machines, dyes, lacers, needles, rug braiding, rug hooking supplies, rug hooks, rug patterns, transfer pencils.
    Books.
    Catalog.
    Kits: braiding.

House of Kleen
P.O. Box 265
Hope Valley, RI 02832
No phone orders.
    Cowhair yarns, rya pillow backings, rya rug backing, rya rug yarn, weaving yarns.
    Catalog: plus samples, 35¢.

House of Lines
P.O. Box 156
Kentfield, CA 94904
No phone orders.
    Cotton patchwork quilt squares, die-cuts, felt remnants, velvet patchwork quilt squares, wool patchwork quilt square patterns.
    Catalog: 50¢.
    Kits.

The House of Miniatures
P.O. Box 1816
Santa Fe, NM 87501
505-988-2062
    Miniature accessories, miniature furniture.
    Catalog: 50¢.

House of Orange
P.O. 1777
Victoria, B.C. Canada
604-382-7002
    Beadery, beadery accessories, glass mosaic crosses, glass mosaic pendants, glassware, macrame cords, seed beads.
    Also has other beads: bugle, crow, cylinder, glass, agate from India, sandlewood, ivory, glass tube, pearl, glass rings beads Hebron glass, African tribal, wood, bamboo and Egyptian paste beads, chevron, shale, Italian mosaic.
    Catalog: $1 (refundable).
    Discount: quantity purchases.

House of Patterns
Box 39
Valley Park, MO 63088
315-825-2021
    Candlemaking supplies, embroidery designs, fabric paint, patterns, plastic bottle craft, sewing, stationery decorating, toys.
    Catalog: 50¢.
    Has patterns for numerous applique & patchwork quilts including Little Women, zodiac, floral, Mother Goose, state bird and flower, medevial, Christmas decorations; crochet including 1930's and 1940's; old patterns dolls and doll clothes.

House of Stitches
Box 547
Bainbridge, GA 31717
912-246-3142
    Catalog: 25¢.
    Kits: linen, sampler.

House of Wood Candles
P.O. Box 2502
Allentown, PA 18001
215-749-2371
    Candle accessories, candle additives, candle molds, candle waxes, candlemaking supplies.
    Catalog.

House of Yarn & Crafts
Rt. 1, Lafayette Rd.
Seabrook, NH 03874
603-474-9601
    Floor looms, Irish fisherman yarn, knitting machines, knitting yarns, mohair yarn, table looms, weaving yarns.
    Books.
    Catalog: plus samples, $1.50.
    Newspapers: for machine knitters.

House of York
63 Oakleaf Dr.
Doylestown, PA 18901
215-345-1035
    Belt buckles, butterflies, buttons, glass

ladybug, metal squirrel, pewter buttons, porcelain.
Catalog: 15¢.

Howe Studio
P.O. Box 178
Lake Havasu City, AZ 86403
602-855-3274
Bisque eggs, egg stands, miniatures.
Books: designs for eggers and mini-crafts.
Catalog: 25¢ (refundable).

HTH Publishers
1607-A E. Edinger
Santa Ana, CA 92705
714-541-5704
Books: looms, tapestry, textiles, weaving.
Write for information.

W. D. Hudson, Jr.
4692 E. Ponce DeLeon Ave.
Stone Mt., GA 30083
404-939-7855
Andalusite, black star sapphire, cabbing rough, chrysoberyl, emeralds, garnet, rough faceting material, sapphire, star ruby, tourmaline, zircon, zoisite.
Catalog: 20¢.

Helen Humes Studio
611 E. Angeleno
Burbank, CA 91501
213-848-9259
China painting supplies.
Also has studies and patterns for flowers, fruit, jewelry scenes.
Write for information.

Immerman's Crafts
21668 Libby
Cleveland, OH 44137
216-475-3560
Catalog: general 50¢ (refundable); enameling 50¢ (refundable).
General arts and crafts supplies.

Industrial Diamond Tool Co. Inc.
P.O. Box 1824, 1803 2nd St. S.W.
Cedar Rapids, IA 52406
319-363-7845
Colored diamond, diamond powders, faceting units, lapidary carving tools, lapidary compounds, lapidary dressers, lapidary drills, lapidary historical scribes, lapidary laps, lapidary saw blades, lapidary saws, lapidary supplies, lapidary tumblers, lapidary vibrating laps, lapidary wheels, loose diamond-cut, uncut diamond.
Catalog.
Write for local distributor.

Industrial Press Inc.
200 Madison Ave.
New York, NY 10016
212-889-6330
Books: machine shop.
Catalog.
Contact your nearest bookstore or write above.

Inkle Looms
2406 W. 14th St
Panama City, FL 32401
No phone orders.
Kits: old English style inkle loom.
Write for information.

Inkodye
1199 E. 12th St.
Oakland, CA 94606
415-451-1048
Vat dyes.
Catalog.

Inter-Ocean Trade Co.
48 W. 48th St.
New York, NY 10036
212-246-9460
Amethyst, aquamarine, Brazilian gems, citrine, crystals, garnet, green beryl, kunzite, morganite, rose quartz, rough cuts, topaz.
Write for information.

Interlectric House of Fine Australian Opals
P.O. Box 36, Collingwood
Victoria, Australia
No phone orders.
Australian jade, Australian opals, cut chrysoprase, cut gemstones, rough chrysoprase.
Write for information.

Company Listing

International Bookfinders, Inc.
Box 1
Pacific Palisades, CA 90272
No phone orders.
Services: out-of-print books search.
Write for specific information.

International Correspondence Schools
Scranton, PA 18515
717-342-7701
Home study courses: interior design.
Write for information.

International Creations
Box 55
Great Neck, NY 11023
516-487-1950
Canvas, fabrics, hand knitting yarns, linen, needlepoint designs, rug canvas, rug designs.
Catalog: needlepoint, 50¢; rug, 50¢; sweater pattern, 25¢.
Kits: Icelandic sweater.

International Guild of Candle Artisans
721 Kimberley Dr.
Fort Collins, CO 80521
414-473-5154
Organization has over 800 menbers; has monthly publication "We Candlelighter", listing sources of supplies, regional workshops, conventions and competition.
Organizations: candlemaking.
Write for information.

International Import Co.
P.O. Box 747
Stone Mt., GA 30083
No phone orders.
Alexandrite, amethyst, andalusite, aquamarine, beryl zircon, beryls, black opals, cabochon gemstones, cat's-eye, chrysoberyl, citrine, coral, diamonds, diopside star, emeralds, faceted gemstones, fire opals, garnet, iolite, jade, kunzite, lapis lazuli, moonstone, morganite, opals, pearls, peridot, precious opals, precious stones, quartz, rare gems, rubies, sapphire, semi-precious stones, smoky quartz, spinel, topaz, tourmaline, turquoise, zircon.
Catalog.
Offers speakers for jeweler's conventions and professional gemologists' services.
Services: lapidary.

International Old Lacers
475 Chapin St.
Ludlow, MA 01056
413-583-2040
Organization for promoting an interest in lace, crochet hairpin Bottenburg, macrame; has bimonthly publication.
Organizations: lace making, tatting.
Write for information.

International Violin
414 E. Baltimore St.
Baltimore, MD 21202
301-727-3535
Instrument accessories, instrument wood.
Carries supplies for making a violin, guitar, cello, viola, bass, dulcimer and mandolin.
Write for information.

International Wood Collectors Society
3155 Edsel Dr.
Trenton, MI 48183
No phone orders.
Nonprofit organization devoted to advancement and understanding of wood and wood products; has monthly bulletin and regional and national meetings.
Organizations: wood and woodworking.
Write for information.

J. L. T.
P.O. Box 1112
Palos Verdes Estate, CA 90274
213-378-6403
Americana samplers, barrettes, coasters.
Catalog: $1.
Kits: belt, needlepoint, pillow, tote bag.

M. W. Jackson & Assoc.
270 Skyline
Pocatello, ID 83201
208-233-4663
Amber agate, banded agate, black agate,

blue agate, flourescent agate, Idaho agates, tube agate, wood agate.
Price list available.

Jade World/Wilderness Originals
7960 Uva Dr.
Redwood Valley, CA 95470
707–485–8407

Chloromelanite, gemstone supplies, glacier green jade, ivory jade, jade, jadeite, mosaic jade, nephrite jade, shimmering silk jade, storm scene jade, twilight blue jade.
Catalog.
Nephrite jades including alpine lichen, antique tapestry, blue sky, Chinese porcelain, damask royal, eldorado, golden green, green leaf, mountain mohogany, olive glow; also jade in jewel chips, sampler collections and end pieces.

Jamar, Inc.
279 Knollwood Ave.
Winston-Salem, NC 27103
919–723–1506

Tin buckets, tin candleholders, tin mini-water cans, tin pitchers, tin sconces, tin trays, tin wash tubs, tinware.
Catalog.
Discount: quantity purchases.
Kits: decoupage tin bucket.

Jamar-Mallory Inc.
6813-19 West Blvd.
Inglewood, CA 90302
213–674–4269

Ceramic molds.
Catalog: $1.

Betty James Originals
Box 774
Severna Park, MD 21146
No phone orders.

Rag doll patterns, teenage doll patterns.
Write for information.

Jane's Ceramic Molds
P.O. Box 1178
Athens, TX 75751
214–675–7282

Ceramic molds.
Catalog: $1.

Jans Jewels
P.O. Box 6159
San Mateo, CA 94403
No phone orders.
Catalog.
Kits: jewelry making.

Japan Publications Trading Co.
1255 Howard St.
San Francisco, CA
415–431–3394
Books: mobiles, origami, paper aircraft, Japanese kits.
Write for local distributor.
Write for information.

Jean's
P.O. Box 14341
Oklahoma City, OK 73114
No phone orders.
Decorative painting designs.
Catalog.
Patterns, Early American/prints.

Jeane's
300 Fairhope St.
Fairhope, AL 36532
205–928–7613

Beadery, crewel, decoupage, statuary.
Catalog: $2.
Kits.

Jenkins Lapidary Equipment
6226 S.E. 71st Ave.
Portland, OR 97206
503–774–8334

Blades, grinding wheels, lapidary supplies.
Catalog.
Kits: "build-it-yourself saw", saw, slab saw.

Jesop Co.
3700 S. 70th Pl.
Chicago, IL 60629
312–735–8389
Catalog.
Kits.
Leaflets: wax crafts.

Company Listing
Jewel—JMC

Jewel Creations
National Office
100 Washington St.
Newark, NJ 07102
201-642-8359
   Beadery, chains, jewelrymaking supplies.
   Catalog.
   Write for nearest location.

Jewelart Inc.
7753 Densmore Ave.
Van Nuys, CA 91406
213-786-4813
   African trading beads, alphabet beads, awls, beadery, beadery accessories, beadery tools, bells, boutique pendants, cameos, ceramic beads, colored safety pins, filigree beads, findings, garnet, gemstones, glass beads, glass cabochons, glass intaglios, glass jewels, gold coin replicas, gold finish mini-easels, ivory beads, jewelrymaking supplies, leather thongs, mountings, natural stone beads, painted porcelain cabochons, pearls, rubies, sandlewood beads, sapphire, silver finish mini-easels, sterling silver beads, Taiwan jade, tigereye, turquoise, whistles, wood beads.
   Books.
   Catalog: 10¢.
   Findings include (antique, chain, coins, lockets, bracelets, rings, hoops, religious items, brooches, other settings, filigree, 14 kt., men's items) printed porcelain cabochons include religious, animals, flowers, zodiac.
   Kits: jewelry, American Indian jewelry.

J. J. Jewelcraft
4959 York Blvd.
Los Angeles, CA 90042
213-255-1488
   Casting supplies, electroplated mountings, gemstones, gold filled mountings, gold mountings, hand tools, jewelrymaking supplies, lapidary supplies, machinery, rhodium mountings, sterling silver mountings, yellow gold mountings.
   Books.
   Catalog: $1.

Jeweler's Emporium
P.O. Box 27736
Los Angeles, CA 90027
213-665-4783
   African trading beads, beadery, bells, bolo parts, brooches, cameos, cast iron rings, chains, costume jewelrymaking, findings, glues, intaglios, jewels, limoges, macrame accessories, mosaic beads, neck rings, ornamental stampings, pearl strands, safety pins, seeds, stones, tools, wood jewelry scraps, zodiacs.
   Catalog: 50¢.

The Jewelry Mart
R.D. 1
Munnsville, NY 13409
315-495-6200
   Chrysocolla, diamonds, earring mountings, Linde stars, ring mountings, YAG, yellow gold earwires.
   Discount: quantity purchases.
   Write for information.

Jim's Rock Shop
5822 Sunland, N.E.
Louisville, OH 44641
216-453-7589
   Amazonite baroques, bloodstone baroques, cabochons, faceted stones, faceting equipment, findings, garnet, gemstone baroques, gemstones, jade, jade baroques, moonstone baroques, mountings, opal baroques, precious moonstone, rough faceting material, star ruby, tigereye baroques, tourmaline.
   Price list available.

JMC
5412 W. Diversey Ave.
Chicago, IL 60639
312-685-2664
   Model HO railroad, model N railroad, model O railroad, model railroad accessories, model trains.
   Catalog: N gauge, $2.50; NO gauge, $3.
   Kits: plastic building.
   Write for local distributor.

Jo's Doll Dressing Course
c/o Hobby House, Dept. C
413 Maryland Ave.
Bristol, TN 37620
615–968–1218
> Course offers miniature garments step-by-step instructions in 9 lessons; some materials included.
> Home study courses: doll clothes.
> Write for information.

Jo-El's Craft Co.
222 Santa Monica Blvd.
Santa Monica, CA 90401
213–393–4169
> Beadery, jewelry findings, macrame accessories, macrame cords.
> Catalog: $1 (refundable).

Walter E. Johansen
P.O. Box 907
Morgan Hill, CA 95037
408–779–3896
> Australian opals, cabochons, cat's-eye, chrysoprase, cutting laps, diamond compounds, diamond powders, dops, faceting machines, faceting supplies, firey astrilite, gemstones, polishes, polishing laps, spinel, star, synthetic corundum, white YAG, YAG.
> Books.
> Catalog: 40¢ U.S.; $1.20 foreign.

John's Hardware & Decoupage Supplies
4756 Tecumseh Rd. E.
Windsor 19, Ontario, Canada
519–945–5462
> Basketry, brass hardware, decoupage, decoupage brushes, decoupage finishes, decoupage frames, floral prints, Old Masters prints, oriental prints, paper tole, woodware, 18th century prints.
> Write for information.

Kathryn Johnson
R.D. 2
Easton, PA 18042
215–252–8651
> Goose eggshells, ostrich eggs.
> Books: eggery.
> Send SASE for information.

Barbara Jones China House
209 W. Niblick
Longview, TX 75601
214–759–4294
> Brushes, china painting designs, china painting supplies, decoupage designs, painting mediums.
> Discount: quantity purchases for teachers.
> Send SASE for information.

Sachiye Jones
Rt. 2 Box 123-D
Monroe, OR 97456
503–847–3392
> Handspun yarns.
> Catalog: plus samples, 50¢.

Journal of Contemporary Metalcraft, Casting, Related Arts
622 Western Ave.
Seattle, WA 98104
206–329–5308
> Magazines: metal crafts.
> Subscriptions: quarterly copy $1.50; 1 year $5.50.

JV Models
P.O. Box 44365
Panorama City, CA 91412
213–982–2070
> Model boat landings, model forest ranger station, model produce stands.
> Kits: metal castings, model dairy barn, wood castings.
> Write for information.

K & L Co.
P. O. Box 3781
Tulsa, OK 74152
918–299–9011
> HO gauge figures, metal miniature figures.
> Send stamp for information.

K42 Rock Shop
Box 118
Isabel, KS 67065
316–739–4324
> Costume jewelrymaking, findings, jewelry mountings, jewelrymaking equipment,

Company Listing
K42—Kaye

jewelrymaking supplies, semi-precious stones.
Catalog: 30¢.

Kachina Gem Co.
1830 E. 3rd St.
Tempe, AZ 85281
602-966-2702
Lapidary supplies, peridot baroques, peridot faceted stones, peridot faceting material, peridot gemstones, peridot rough.
Price list available.

Kaleidoscope Needleworks
2525 N. Reynolds
Toledo, OH 43560
419-531-7502
Needlepoint yarn.
Kits: needlepoint.
Write for information.

Kalico Kits
522 Wilshire Blvd.
Santa Monica, CA 90401
213-394-0786
Catalog: 50¢ (refundable).
Kits: needlepoint.

Kalmbach Publishing Co.
1027 N. 7th St.
Milwaukee, WI 53233
414-272-2060
Books: model railroading.
Catalog.
Contact your nearest bookstore or write above.

Kandel Knits, Inc.
4834 N. Interstate
Portland, OR 97217
503-288-6975
Perfect-measurement sewing patterns for knit fabrics.
Pattern catalog 50¢.

Joen Ellen Kanze
26 Palmer Ave.
North White Plains, NY 10603
914-948-0330
Dollhouse accessories, miniature accessories.
Send SASE for catalog.

Karlkraft Studio-Cheva
Severns Bridge Road
S. Merrimack, NH 03054
603-883-4429
Hooked rug patterns.
Books.
Catalog: 50¢.

KAY an EE Corp. of America
200 Fifth Ave.
New York, NY 10010
212-243-0964
Embroidery frames, embroidery hoops, floor hoops, floor looms, loom accessories, quilting frames, rug frames, table hoops, table looms, yarn winders.
Carries West German looms.
Catalog: 25¢.

Kaydee
P.O. Box 2789
Fort Myers, FL 33931
No phone orders.
Beadery, egg blowers, egg craft, jewelry findings, pearls.
Books.
Carries all general craft supplies.
Catalog: 25¢.
Kits.

Kaydee Craft Supplies
P.O. Box 8
Ft. Myers Beach, FL 33931
813-463-5938
Beadery, candlemaking supplies, findings, macrame accessories.
Catalog: 50¢ (refundable).

Jerry S. Kaye Assoc.
13358 Albers St.
Van Nuys, CA 91401
213-786-8839
Canvas, crewel, embroidery, embroidery linen, frames, hoops, needlepoint, needles, rugs, transfers, yarns.
Catalog: 50¢.
Kits: miniature needlepoint.

Kazari
Div. of Cronar Ltd.
7382 Pershing Ave.
St. Louis, MO 63130
314-721-4016
   Needlecraft supplies.
   Kits: punch needlecraft.
   Write for local distributor.
   Write for information.

KeeWai Krafts
Echo-In-Dell
Wells River, VT 05081
802-429-3552
   Bulky knit yarns, fleece wool, handspun wool, homespun crewel yarn, rug yarn, single ply for warp, spinning wheels, table size yarn winders, tapestry yarn.
   Caters to schools having crafts; write giving name of family clan for tartan.
   Send SASE for information; yarn or wool samples, $2.

Keller-Charles of Philadelphia
2413-27 Federal St.
Philadelphia, PA 19146
215-732-2614
   Tin basket shapes, tin boxes, tin buckets, tin coal hods, tin sconces, tin storage cans, tin trays, tin umbrella stands, tin urns, tin watering cans, unfinished tinware.
   Catalog.

Kerr Mfg. Co.
28200 Wick Rd.
Romulus, MI 48174
313-946-7800
   Casting accessories, casting investment molding material, lost wax jewelrymaking, wax.
   Catalog.
   Write for local distributor.

Kessenich Looms
7463 Harwood Ave.
Wauwatosa, WI 53213
414-258-2025
   Foot-operated looms, hand looms, looms for handicapped.
   Catalog.

Jim Kesterson
214 N. 3rd St.
Millville, NJ 08332
609-825-4970
   Cabochons, faceted beads, gemstones, jewelry findings, jewelrymaking machinery, jewelrymaking tools, rough rock.
   Catalog.

Kick-Shaw Inc.
3513 Hixson Pike
Cattanooga, TN 37415
615-875-6672
   Fiberglass cloth, fiberglass mat, polyurethane foam, resins.
   Catalog: 25¢.

Kieffer's Lingerie Fabric & Supplies
1625 Hennepin Ave.
Minneapolis, MN 55403
612-332-3395
   Elastics, laces, lingerie fabrics, notions, patterns.
   Also carries extra large 'queen size' patterns.
   Buyers guide.
   Books: lingerie construction.

Kile-Gore Designs
NATO P.O. Box 1418
Sarasota, FL 33578
No phone orders.
   Hairpin lace patterns.
   Write for information.

Miles Kimball
41 West East Ave.
Oshkosh, WI 54901
414-231-3800
   Engraving tools, mini vacuum-vise, miniature accessories, miniature furniture, miniatures, paint stripers.
   Catalog.
   Kits: needlecraft.
   Miniature furniture brass bed include butter churns, wood stoves, cobbler's benches, chests, cabinets and baby furniture, (most of Early American style); accessories include variety of lamps, preserves jars, washtubs, coffee grinders, cook and glass ware, rugs music books, pictures,

Company Listing
Kimball—Knitking

mirrors, bathtubs, toilets, fireplaces, animals, people.

Elizabeth R. King
352 Garnett St.
Wichita, KS 67206
316–684–4612
> Adz.
> Carries "circle-master" compass (works on any surface including rough).
> *Write for information.*

King's Studio
Box 412, R.D. 4
Quakertown, PA 18951
215–536–2595
> Custom crafted hand tools, fittings, frow, planes, scauper, shaving horses, tool handles, work benches.
> *Carries most tools that are hard or impossible to find.*
> *Send stamp for information.*

Kay Kinney-Contoured Glass
725 Laguna Canyon Rd.
Laguna Beach, CA 92651
714–494–6108
> Bead rods, bottle cutters, clay molds, collar molds, glass additives, glass crafts, glass enamels, glass mold coats, patterns, stained glass paints.
> *Books.*
> *Catalog: $1 or send SASE for information.*

Kit Kraft
12109 Ventura Pl.
Studio City, CA 91604
213–984–0780
> Bead flowermaking, beadery, candlemaking supplies, copper enameling supplies, findings, flowermaking, jewelrymaking accessories, jewels, macrame accessories, pearls, plaster casting, rhinestones, sequins, wood boxes.
> *Books.*
> *Catalog: 10¢.*

Kitsophrenia, Inc.
P.O. Box 5024
Glendale, CA 91201
No phone orders.

Mica mirrors.
> *Imported mica mirrors from Pakistan are sold by the pound.*
> *Kits: shisha "mirror".*
> *Send SASE for information.*

KM Yarn Co.
18691 Wyoming
Detroit, MI 48221
No phone orders.
> Alpaca, dyes, electric punch rug hook, fleece, goathair, hand weaving, karakul, looms, mesh cloth, monk's cloth, rug canvas, rug yarn, tapestry yarn, warp cloth.
> *Services: dyeing.*
> *Write for information.*

Knit Services, Inc.
3001 Indianola Ave.
Columbus, OH 43202
614–262–5341
> Bag handles, beadery, bells, braids, butcher's twine, cable cord, carpet warp, cements, cold water dyes, cotton blends, cotton ropes polished, handspun Greek yarns, inkle looms, jute, lame cord, leather lacings, linen, linen rope, linen twine, macrame accessories, macrame board, macrame cords, macrame pins, metal rings, metallic braids, navy cord, needles, nylon blends, nylon parachute cord, rayons, rug filler, seine twine, stoneware beads, Swedish fishnet, tubular braid, tubular tufting, twine, wood buckles, wood hoops.
> *Catalog: 25¢.*
> *Kits: belt.*

Knitking
1128 Crenshaw Blvd.
Los Angeles, CA 90019
213–938–2077
> Automatic knitting machines, overlock sewing machines, yarns.
> *Books: machine knitting.*
> *Catalog: general; yarn catalog, $1 (refundable).*

Knitking Magazine
1128 Crenshaw Blvd.
Los Angeles, CA 90019
213–938–2077
> Yarns.

Magazine features instructions and patterns for machine knitting; subscription includes bimonthly newsletter.
Magazines: machine knitting.
Subscriptions: bimonthly, 1 year $7.

Knit-O-Graf Pattern Co.
3536 Holmes Ave.
Minneapolis, MN 55408
612–823–7531
Children's knitting patterns.
Catalog: 35¢.

Knit-Sew Labels
Box 113
Hopedale, MA 01747
No phone orders.
Woven labels.
Write for information.

Knits'N That Yarn Shop
555 W. Michigan
Saline, MI 48176
313–429–7070
Accessories, needlecrafts, rug braiding.
Kits: rug hooking.
Write for information.

The Knittery
2040 Union St.
San Francisco, CA 94123
415–922–0887
Needlepoint designs, needlepoint supplies.
Write for information.

The Knitting Needle
P. O. Box 7162
Colorado Springs, CO 80933
303–635–4552
Patterns.
Catalog: 25¢.
Has patterns including rag doll, Wynken Blynken and Nod in shoe, mermaid, American Indian girl, skier, shepherd with drum, Eskimo, black girl and boy, grandma and grandpa, Hawaiian, Oriental, leprechaun, elves, astronaut, scarecrow, skaters--all 16" dolls, some with knitted sweaters; others knitting patterns including ponchos, baby sweaters, Christmas stocking.

M. Knopp
2105 W. 300 S.
Marion, IN 46952
317–674–4759
Kits: doll head for antique replica china & porcelain dolls.
Write for information.

Kodansha International, U.S.A.
10 East 53rd St.
New York, NY 10022
212–593–7050
Books: Japanese ceramics.
Contact your nearest bookstore or write above.
Write for information.

M. Koehler
P.O. Drawer 56160
Harwood Heights, IL 60656
No phone orders.
Leaflets: oriental colored lacquers & gold leaf methods.

Koehler's Craft Outlet
205 S. Boundary Ave.
Proctor, MN 55810
218–624–0743
Crepe paper, decorative foil, Dylite®, feathers, floral craft, glues, hutch boxes, jewelry findings, marble craft, miniatures, paints, pallettes, pearl parchment, plaster plaques, ribbon, ribbon straw, rosebud seashell craft, sequins, stained glass paints, Styrofoam®, velvet crepe papers, wood fibre.
Books.
Catalog: $1 (refundable).
Kits: art foam, beads, candlemaking, chenille, cooking crystals, craft fur, flower dip doll, pearls.

Mrs. Frieda Koudelka
10 Eastgate Dr.
Medina, OH 44256
216–723–8713
Leaflets: tatting.
Send SASE and 50¢.

Kraft Korner
5864 Mayfield Rd.
Cleveland, OH 44124
216–442–1020

Company Listing
Kraft—Ladies

Artist's supplies, beadery, decoupage, enameling, macrame accessories, silversmithing supplies, stained glass, tole painting.
Catalog: $2.
Discount: 10% on first $10 min. order.

Krick Kits
31 North Brentwood
St. Louis, MO   63105
314-862-3188
Catalog: $2.
Kits: needlepoint.

Kulch
127 N. Palm Dr.
Beverly Hills, CA   90210
No phone orders.
Hand-operated wool carding machine, heavy duty hand carders.
Write for information.

Harry Z. Kurs
55 East Washington St.
Chicago, IL   60602
312-332-1988
Brilliant cut diamonds, mountings.
Services: setting and sizing diamonds.
Write for information.

Ken Kyte
Rt. 4, Box 151
Asheville, NC   28806
704-253-8546
Ganoin ivory, gem rough material, moss agate, petrified woods agate, pompon agate, tumbling accessories, unusual agates.
Price list available.

L & L Stitchery
Box 550, Cooper Station
New York, NY   10003
No phone orders.
Personalized woven labels.
Write for information.

L & R Manufacturing Co.
577 Elm St.
Kearny, NJ   07032
201-991-5330
Lapidary cleaning accessories, lapidary ultrasonic cleaning systems.
Catalog.
Write for local distributor.

Frances La Monica
67 Pomona Ave.
Yonkers, NY   10703
914-968-7616
Doll accessories, dollhouse accessories.
Catalog: 25¢.

La Venta Corp.
R.R. 2, Box 103
Bloomington, IN   47401
812-336-2362
Buckles, carving leathers, latigo, leather dyes, leather tools, leathercraft, used leather machinery.
Carries 30 styles of buckles.
Free supplement or complete catalog, $1 (refundable).

Lace Lady
Box 662
St. Louis, MO   63101
No phone orders.
Braids, buttons, edgings, lace, trims, unwoven cotton, zippers.
Discount: quantity purchases.
Write for information.

Ladies Home Journal Needle & Craft
641 Lexington Ave.
New York, NY   10022
212-935-4100
Needlepoint, stitchery.
Kits: needlecraft.

Ladies Home Journal Needlecraft
641 Lexington Ave.
New York, NY   10022
212-935-4100
Magazine features crochet, doll making, embroidery and crewel, knitting, needlepoint, patchwork, puppetry, sewing, trapunto.
Magazines: needlecraft.
Subscriptions: semi-annual copy $1.25, 3 years $7.50.

Lakewood Lapidary
12305 Lake City Blvd.
Tacoma, WA 98498
206–584–4987
   Cut gemstones, gemstones, Oregon agate, steatite (soapstone), Washington opalized wood, Washington wood agate.
Write for information.

Virginia Lakin
P.O. Box 356
Loveland, CO 80537
No phone orders.
   Doll clothes crochet patterns, doll clothes knitting patterns.
Catalog: 25¢.

Lamonica
67 Pomona Ave.
Yonkers, NY 10703
914–968–7616
   Dollhouse miniatures, miniature bedding, miniature doll accessories, miniature furniture, miniature lamps, miniatures.
Catalog: 25¢.

Lane Magazine & Book Co.
Willow & Middlefield
Menlo Park, CA 94025
415–321–3600
   Books: ceramics, furniture finishing, furniture upholstery, general arts & crafts series, leather, macrame, needlepoint, outdoor construction, papier mache, quilting and patchwork, woodcarving, woodworking.
Contact your nearest bookstore or write above.
Write for information.

Lantern Press Inc.
354 Hussey Rd.
Mt. Vernon, NY 10552
914–668–9736
   Books: craft anthologies, holiday crafts, world-wide crafts.
Contact your nearest bookstore or write above.
Write for information.

Lapidabrade Inc.
8 E. Eagle Rd.
Havertown, PA 19083
215–789–4022
   Electric lapidary equipment, gold casting mountings, jewelry findings, jewelry mountings, jewelrymaking supplies, lapidary supplies, plated gold filled mountings, plated gold findings, sterling silver findings, sterling silver mountings, watch repair supplies.
Write for catalog information.

Lapidary Journal Book Dept.
P.O. Box 80937
San Diego, CA 92138
714–297–4841
   Books: carving, cutting, fluorescence, gem craft, gemology, gold and silversmithing, jewelry craft, jewelry repair, lost wax, minerals, precious and semi-precious stones, rocks, stones.
   Magazine features gems and stores, jewelry design, new product information, calendar of events in North America and April Buyers' Guide.
Magazines: lapidary.
Subscriptions: monthly copy 60¢, 1 year $5.75, foreign $6.25.

J. C. Larson Co.
7330 North Clark St.
Chicago, IL 60626
312–338–7220
Catalog.
Discount: quantity purchases.

Lashette Co., Inc.
Box 205
Natick, MA 01760
617–653–1420
   Carries eyelashes 6 in. wide--may be sewn, glued or stapled to toys, animals, puppets, whiskers.
Catalog.
Discount: quantity purchases.

Barbara Lawshe
Box 288
Franklin Lakes, NJ 07417
201–891–1344
   Flux, foil, lead came, patterns, solder.
Books.
Catalog: 25¢.
Kits: stained glass.

Company Listing
Leathercrafters—Leman

Leathercrafters Supply Co.
Div. of Roni Industries, Inc.
25 Great Jones (E. 3rd) St.
New York, NY 10012
212-673-5460

Belt buckles, brass snap closures, British buckles, bronze buckles, buckles, calf lacing, Canadian latigo, cast metal buckles in antique finishes, cements, chamois, cleaners, cobbler sandal supplies, cowhide, cowing leather, deerskin, dyes, English kip, findings, furniture finishes, garment leathers, goat lacing, hardware, hides, inks, leather, leather preservatives, leather rawhide lacing, leather tools, miniature animals, pewter buckles, round cowhide lacing, sole leather, solid brass buckles, speed rivets, stencils, suede, threads, tiffany glass buckles, tooling leather, western Latigo.
Books: leatherworking.
Catalog: $1.
One of the largest buckle selections.

Leclerc Corp.
P.O. Box 491
Plattsburg, NY 12901
518-561-7900

Bobbins, looms, shuttles, spinning wheels, weaving accessories.
Books: weaving.
Carries 42 types and sizes of looms.
Catalog.

Nilus Leclerc Inc.
P.O. Box 69
L'Islet, Quebec, Canada
418-247-3975
See entry above.

Leclerc West
2799A Del Monte St.
West Sacramento, CA 95691
916-372-0670
See entry above.

Lee Lapidaries
3425 W. 117th St.
Cleveland, OH 44111
216-941-7458

Facet preforms, facet units, lapidary equipment, lapidary laps.
Catalog.
Write for local distributor.

Lee Mountain
Pisgah, AL 35765
205-657-4333
Books: ceramics, rugmaking, used books silk screening.
Catalog: 10¢.
Home study courses: carpentry, needlecrafts.

The Left Hand Inc.
145 E. 27th St.
New York, NY 10016
212-689-7894

Left handed tools.
Catalog: 50¢.
Kits: geodesic dome model, omnistar (geodesic).
Left-handed tools include scissors, shears, knitting, crochet and needlepoint instructions rulers, fountain pens.

Leisure Hour Products
R.D. 3
Freeland, PA 18224
717-636-2370
Books: coathanger items, various crafts.
Catalog: 25¢.

Leisure Services
P.O. Box 2763
Kansas City, MO 64142
816-942-2230
Quilling paper.
Books: quilling.
Catalog.
Kits: quilling.

LeJeune, Inc.
1060 W. Evelyn
Sunnyvale, CA 94086
408-735-9911
Books: batik and dyeing, macrame.
Write for local distributors.
Write for information.

Leman Publications
Box 394
Wheatridge, CO 80033
303-423-8442

Appliques, patchwork techniques, quilting.

Company Listing
Leman—Lifetime

Books: quilting.
Catalog: 25¢.

LeMar's Decoupage Center
47th at Gilbert
La Grange, IL 60525
312–352–0362
Dollhouse accessories, miniature rooms accessories.
Send SASE for information.

Leonida Leatherdale's Embroidery Studio
East Gate
Winnipeg, Manitoba R3C 2C3, Canada
204–774–0217
Canvas, embroidery fabrics, embroidery threads, looms.
Catalog: information and swatched price list, 50¢

Darlene Lewis
5508 Terrace Q
Birmingham, AL 35208
No phone orders.
China painting supplies.
Also has studies by Darlene Lewis china jewelry blanks.
Discount: quantity purchases for teachers.
Send SASE for information.

Lewiscraft
284 King St. West
Toronto M5V 1J3, Canada
416–363–5206
Books: crafts for children.
Write for information.

Libby's Needlepoint
200 Hyne St.
Brighton, MI 48116
313–229–6558
Kits: handbag, needlepoint.
Write for information.

Liberty Gem & Supply
Box 229
Liberty, IL 62347
217–645–3474
Cultured pearls, gemstones, imitation gemstones, jewelry display cases, jewelry findings, jewelry mountings.
Catalog.

Libra Gems
51 David St.
Goderich, Ontario, Canada
519–524–9972
Blue lace agate, gemstones, gold filled mountings, golden tiger's-eye, green aventurine, opal quartz, smoky quartz, sterling silver.
Catalog.

The Library Corner
Box 1178
Marathon, FL 33050
305–743–3367
Books: ceramics.
Write for information.

Life-Like Products Inc.
1600 Union Ave.
Baltimore, MD 21211
301–889–1023
Do-it-yourself Christmas ornaments, lichen, lifelike grass, lifelike stone, model accessories, model cars, paper grass, paper sparkle.
Catalog.
Kits: historic sailing ships, model airplane, model motorcycles, model ship building, model steamboats, prehistoric man and animal anatomy, HO scale buildings.
Write for local distributor.

Lifetime Career Schools
2251 Barry Ave.
Los Angeles, CA 90064
213–478–0617
Course offers dressing, repairing and restoring dolls; designing and making flower arrangements for centerpieces, wreaths, bouquets; dressmaking repair, alterations and design; creating, decorating and selling decorative gifts.
Home study courses: decorative arts and crafts, doll craft, flower arranging, modern dressmaking.
Write for information.

Company Listing
Lightsaround — Loftons

Lightsaround, Inc.
Box A51M
Wantagh, NY 11793
516-579-9595
  Lampshades, lighting supplies.
  Catalog: 25¢.
  Write for local distributor.

Lillstina Inc.
50 Front St.
Binghamton, NY 13902
607-722-0123
  Spinning accessories, Swedish looms.
  Catalog.

Lily Mills Co.
P.O. Box 88
Shelby, NC 28150
704-487-6361
  Hand weaving yarns, inkle looms, loom equipment, looms, macrame cords.
  Books: needlecraft, weaving.
  Catalog: general weaving; yarn swatches, 50¢.

James F. Lincoln Arc Welding Foundation
Box 3035
Cleveland, OH 44117
216-481-8100
  Books: Arc Welding.

Lindell Industries
2689 S. 10th St.
Fresno, CA 93725
209-237-6171
  Arbors, gem drills, lapidary equipment, lapidary machinery, rock clamps, slab saws, trim saws.
  Write for local distributor.
  Write for information.

Lion Brand Yarn Co.
1270 Broadway
New York, NY 10001
212-736-7937
  Leaflets: crochet granny vest and cap.
  Write for local distributor.

J. B. Lippincott Co.
Trade Division
E. Washington Square
Philadelphia, PA 19105
215-925-4100
  Books: children's crafts, general arts & crafts series, nature crafts, Christmas decorations.
  Contact your nearest bookstore or write above.
  Write for information.

Ruth Little's Studio
3426 34th St.
Lubbock, TX 79410
806-792-1809
  China brushes, china painting designs, china painting supplies.
  Books: flower studies.
  Discount: quantity purchases.
  Write for information.

Liveright
386 Park Ave.
New York, NY 10016
212-683-2050
  Crocheting supplies, knitting machines, knitting patterns.
  Books: knitting.

Lochs
R.D. 1
Center Valley, PA 18034
215-967-3479
  Beryls, faceting equipment, garnet, quartz, rare fine facet rough, rough faceting material, tanzanite, topaz.
  Catalog: 40¢.

Locomotive Workshop
R. F. D. 1, Box 211 B-1
Englishtown, NJ 07726
201-536-6873
  Catalog: 50¢.
  Kits: aluminum casting, brass diesel locomotive, brass railroad car.

Loftons
6708 N.E. Roselawn
Portland, OR 97218
503-281-1839
  Rugmaking supplies.

Catalog: 50¢ each, rug or stitchery.
Kits: latch hook rug, stitchery.

The Loom Factory
Star Round
Marcola, OR 97454
503-933-2613
  Inkle looms.
  Catalog.
  Kits: floor loom.

The Loomery
3237 Eastlake Ave. E.
Seattle, WA 98102
206-329-2088
  Inkle looms, jute, looms.
  Carries jute in 40 colors.
  Send SASE for information.

The Loomery
3124 Harvard Ave. E.
Seattle, WA 98102
206-329-2088
  See entry above.

The Looming Arts
Box 233
Sedona, AZ 86336
602-282-3671
  Magazine gives detailed instructions for 4 and multiharness looms; features handwoven designs.
  Magazines: 4 harness & multiharness looms.
  Subscriptions: bimonthly, multiharness issues $5 & $6.50, foreign $6 and $7.50.

Edna Looney Originals
P.O. Box 1533
Wewoka, OK 74884
405-257-2639
  Catalog: 25¢.
  Kits: applique, bottle covers, calendars, needlecraft, wall hangings.
  Write for local distributor.

Loosie Goosie Egg Craft Shop
Rt. 7, Old Dalton Rd.
Rome, GA 30161
404-232-5213
  Egg cutter attachment, goose eggshells.
  Send SASE for information.

The egg cutter is an attachment for power tools (with 1/2 in. very thin diamond blade).

Loretta's Ceramic Studio
2006 St. 22
Scotch Plains, NJ 07076
201-322-8932
  Ceramic supplies, kilns, lamp parts.
  Catalog: $1 (refundable); free to institutions.

Lortone Inc.
2854 N.W. Market St.
Seattle, WA 98107
206-789-3100
  Arbors, grinders, lapidary equipment, lapidary laps, lapidary saws, lapidary tumblers, splash shields.
  Catalog.
  Write for local distributor.

Lothrop, Lee & Shephard
105 Madison Ave.
New York, NY 10016
212-889-3050
  Books: bread dough craft, general arts & crafts series, spoolcraft.
  Contact your nearest bookstore or write above.
  Write for information.

Lox-Seal Adhesives
P.O. Box 10127
Kansas City, MO 64111
816-561-5957
  Fluid solder, liquid cement.
  Send SASE for technique sheet and instructions.

LTA Products
15 William St.
Closter, NJ 07624
No phone orders.
  Leaflets: plans for model dirigible building.
  Write for information.

Luger
3800 W. Hwy. 13
Burnsville, MN 55337
612-890-3000
  Boat kits are fiberglass, assemble-it-yourself in 20 models including cruisers, runabouts, sailboats.
  Catalog.
  Kits: boat.

Company Listing
Lukasik—Macrame

Ruth Lukasik
3443 W. 53rd St.
Chicago, IL 60632
312-476-7329
  Crochet doll patterns.
  Catalog: plus sample pattern, 25¢.

Virgil V. Lundell
414 Glenarm Place
San Antonio, TX 78201
512-732-3971
  Cut gemstones, jade, semi-precious cabochons, YAG.

Lynchburg Hdwr. & General Store
Box 239
Lynchburg, TN 37352
615-759-7184
  Civil War prints, old barn wood picture frames, old time whiskey labels.
  Catalog: 25¢.
  Kits: whittling.

S. Lynds Patterns
71 Park Ave.
Natlick, MA 01760
No phone orders.
  Books: jig saw patterns.

M & M Distributors
3527 Wetmore
Everett, WA 98201
206-259-3773
  Cut stones, jewelry findings, jewelry mountings, pearls.
  Catalog: $1 (refundable).
  Over 2500 mountings and findings in 10, 14 and 18kt. gold.

M & M Hardwood
5344 Vineland
No. Hollywood, CA 91601
213-766-8325
  Boat building supplies, carving tools, hardwood, moldings.
  Catalog: $1.

MAC Enterprises
56 Norwood Ave.
Plainfield, NJ 07060
No phone orders.
  Books: refinishing and restoring antiques.

Mac Leather Co.
424 Broome St.
New York, NY 10013
212-964-0850
  Buckles, leather dyes, leather lacings, leather scraps, leather skins, leather tools.
  Write for information.

The Macmillan Publishing Co.
866 Third Ave.
New York, NY 10022
212-935-2000
  Books: candlemaking, ceramics, general arts & crafts series, leather craft, paper craft, plastics.
  Contact your nearest bookstore or write above.
  Write for information.

L. W. Macomber Ad-A Harness Looms
130 Neptune Blvd.
Lynn, MA 01905
617-581-5564
  Hand looms.
  Catalog.

The Macrame Studio
3001 Indianola Ave.
Columbus, OH 43202
614-262-5341
  Catalog: 25¢.
  See Knit Services, Inc.

Macrame and Weaving Supply Co.
63 East Adams St., Dept. MB
Chicago, IL 60603
312-922-3756
  Beadery, belt buckles, brass beads, camel bells, camel hair, ceramic beads, cords, crocheting supplies, glass beads, macrame accessories, mohair yarn, nylon, seed beads, weaving supplies, yarns.
  Books.
  Price list plus samples, 50¢.

Madewell Products Inc.
Box 7011
Oakland, CA 94601
415-532-6927
  14 kt gold castings.
  Catalog: $1 (refundable).

Magic Circle Corp.
622 Western Ave.
Seattle, WA 98104
206-329-5308
  Batik, goldsmithing equipment, jewelry casting supplies, metal alloys, sculpturing, silversmithing supplies.
  Books: construction of wax models.
  Catalog: $2 (refundable).
  Home study courses: jewelry casting and sculpting.
  Kits: stone setting.

Magic Needle
44 Green Bay Rd.
Winnetka, IL 60093
312-446-5141
  Catalog: $1.
  Kits: needlepoint, patchwork purse kit.
  Write for local distributor.

Magnolia Weaving
2635 29th Ave. West
Seattle, WA 98199
206-282-5114
  Looms, weaving supplies, yarns.
  Catalog.

Magnus Craft Materials, Inc.
109 Lafayette St.
New York, NY 10013
212-925-7220
  American Indian crafts, basketry, batik, beadery, candlemaking supplies, cork, decoupage, dyes, enameling, felt, glass globs, leathercraft, macrame accessories, mesh cloth, metal craft, metal ware, mosaics, paints, rush, shells, small mirrors, stained glass, stuffed animals, tiles, trims, wood, woodware.
  Catalog.
  Discount: quantity purchases.
  Kits: stencil, wood.

Dale Magnuson
Winter, WI 54896
No phone orders.
  Driftwood, stones, weathered decorative boards, white birch bark.
  Write for information.

Maharani Boutique
10 Quadrant Arcade, 80-82 Regent St.
London W1, England
No phone orders.
  Shisha glass.
  Write for information.

Maid of Scandinavia
3244 Raleigh Ave.
Minneapolis, MN 55416
612-927-7996
  Cake decorating supplies, cake decorating tools, specialty cake pans.
  Books.
  Catalog: 50¢.

Edith Maier
205 So. 5th St.
Mapleton, IA 51034
712-882-1940
  Ostrich eggs, silk finish eggshells.
  Send SASE for information.

The Mail Train
4007 Bellaire Blvd.
Houston, TX 77025
713-665-5599
  Cotton threads, embroidery threads, fabrics, huck, instant papier mache, needles, nonfiring enamel, rug hooking supplies.
  Books: Swedish weaving (crewel).
  Write for information; huck swatches, 25¢ SASE.

Main Service Co.
P.O. Box 777
Monroe, NY 10950
914-783-6604
  Lapidary equipment.
  Offers repair service for major makes of handpieces and lapidary equipment.
  Services: lapidary equipment.
  Write for information.

Company Listing
Maison—Maquire's

W. L. Maison Opals, Etc.
394 Mesa Road
Salinas, CA 93901
408–455–1765
  Chrysoprase, opals, rough triplets.

Make It Happen Craft Studio
2620 W. Chester Pk.
Broomall, PA 19008
215–356–4922
  Artist's supplies, candlemaking supplies, decoupage, dip film, looms, paper frames, paper tole, purse craft, stained glass, synthetic straw.
  Books.
  Catalog: candle 25¢; general, $1.
  Kits.

Make It With Leather
P.O. Box 1386
Fort Worth, TX 76101
817–335–4161
  Magazine features how-to crafting techniques for lacing, carving, tooling; how to buy, assemble, decorate and finish leather; offer new patterns and designs; gives notices of shows and events.
  Magazines: leathercraft.
  Subscriptions: bimonthly copy $1, 1 year $4.95, foreign $5.45.

The Makings
2001 University Ave.
Berkeley, CA 94704
415–548–5159
  Fleece, looms, spinning accessories, spinning wheels, yarns.
  Books.
  Samples of specific yarns or fibers on request.

Augusta Malle
1270B Argyll Circle
Lakewood, NJ 08701
201–477–8792
  Write for information.

Jean Malsada Inc.
P.O. Box 28182
Atlanta, GA 30328
404–993–8285
  Weaving yarns.
  Catalog: plus samples, 25¢.

Man-Pak, Inc.
1243 Blalock Rd., Dept. 25
Houston, TX 77055
713–467–4464
  Kits: "interior construction" items, canvas coat fronts, jackets women's, man's jackets, man's regular and deluxe pants, non-roll waistbands, sewing, shoulder pads, undercollar.
  Write for information.
  Write for local distributor.

Mangrove Feather Co., Inc.
468-470 Greenwich St.
New York, NY 10013
212–431–5806
  Feathers, goose feathers, hackle feathers, turkey flats feathers, turkey hip feathers, turkey marabou feathers.
  Write for information.

Manlove Originals
Box 157
New Smyrna, FL 32069
904–428–6988
  Teenage doll patterns.
  Patterns include boys and girls clothes, tuxedo, business, suits, western outfits, work clothes.
  Send SASE for information.

The Mannings Creative Crafts
R.D. 2
East Berlin, PA 17316
717–624–2223
  Beadery, looms, macrame accessories, macrame cords, spinning, spinning wheels, weaving cutters, weaving frames, weaving supplies, weaving yarns.
  Books.
  Leaflets.
  Write for information.

Thomas S. Maquire's
Dept. C, West 520 Euclid
Spokane, WA 99205
509–327–2645
  Patterns.
  Catalog: plus sample designs 15¢.
  Leaflets: instructions and designs for crafts.

Marcella's Ceramics Inc.
1150 Inman Pkwy.
Beloit, WI 53511
608-362-5056
> Ceramic power tool.
> Write for information.

Margaret's Egg Craft
17 Waushakum St.
Framingham, MA 01701
617-879-7039
> Books: egg craft.

Sal Marino Co.
48 Greenleaf Ave.
Staten Island, NY 10310
212-273-9699
> Model power tools.
> Kits: model accessories, model buildings, model railroad trains, structure.
> Newsletter available, send 12 large SASE for 1 year.

Maroon Bells Ind. Inc.
3400 Tejon St.
Denver, CO 80211
303-433-2283
> Jewelrymaking tools.
> Write for information.

The Marquetry Society of America
2050 Eastchester Rd.
Bronx, NY 10461
212-792-1600
> Dedicated to the development of marquetry and related wood crafts; membership includes quarterly publications.
> Organizations: marquetry.
> Write for information.

Mars Models
10420 Northfield Rd.
Northfield, OH 44067
216-467-0124
> Model accessories, model railroads, N gauge O scale traction equipment.
> HO scale building kits include furniture factory, "Black Bart" mine, warehouse, follies theatre, feed mill, coal mine, gas station, farm house, bridges, figures.
> Kits: HO scale building.
> Write for information.

George Marshall
5637 N.E. 16th Ave.
Portland, OR 97211
503-281-3023
> Write for information.

Marshall's Lapidary Co., Ltd.
2025 W. 41st Ave.
Vancouver, B.C., Canada
604-266-4949
> Lapidary supplies.
> Catalog: Canadians only.

Thelma Sutton Martin
Cherryvale, KS 67335
316-336-2077
> Stencils, textile brushes, textile paints, textile stencils.
> Books: decorative painting, textile designs, tole designs.
> Stencil catalog, 60¢; or send stamp for design list.

Martin Fabrics
111 W. 40th St.
New York, NY 10018
212-546-2020
> Books: sewing and caring for velvet.
> Write for local distributor.

Maryland Magnet Co.
Box 192
Randallstown, MD 21133
301-922-2272
> Bar magnets, disk magnets, flexible magnetic strips, magnets, stick magnets.
> Write for information.

Mason & Sullivan Co.
39 Blossom Ave.
Osterville, MA 02655
617-428-2963
> Carries clock kits in banjo, grandfather and grandmother, steeple and other styles.
> Catalog: 25¢.
> Kits: clock.

Max of Dallas
2512 Mahon St.
Dallas, TX 75201
214-744-0031

Coral, crystals, glass display domes, jewelry cutting materials, jewelry display cases, jewelry findings, lapidary machinery, metal stands, minerals, rocks, seashells.

Maxant Button & Supply Co.
117 South Morgan St.
Chicago, IL 60607
312-226-7545

Books: covered buttons.
Write for local distributor.

Mary Maxim Inc.
2001 Holland Ave.
Port Huron, MI 48060
313-987-2000

Beadery, canvas, embroidery frames, embroidery hoops, fabrics, felt, handbag frames, handbag handles, long separating zippers, needles, rosette winders, rug hooks, rug yarn, tatting, threads, weave-it looms, yarns.
Books.
Catalog: general; latch hook rugs.
Club offers fabrics, patterns, accessories and swatches for a great variety of needlecrafts; numbers receive six mailings annually.
Club plans: needlecraft.
Kits: candlemaking, crochet, knitting, latch hook rug, paper pottery, wood birdhouse, Indian bead loom.

May-Wal, Inc.
P.O. Box 2143, 2464 N.E. Andresen Rd.
Vancouver, WA 98661
206-694-7561

Candle accessories, candle additives, candle dyes, candle scents, candlemaking supplies.
Catalog.
Write for local distributor.

Maytex
P. O. Box 31069
El Paso, TX 79931
915-778-6175

Handspun yarns, hardtwist yarns.
Send SASE for information and samples.

A. D. McBurney
1610 Victory Blvd.
Glendale, CA 91201
213-245-5701

Dops, faceter's trim slab saw, lapidary machinery, rock vise.
Catalog.
Lapidary machinery include combination gem maker, large saw table size--grinds, sands, polishes without removing shaft; aluminum arbor complete self-contained, accommodates all 6 in. diameter wheels, drums, disks.
Write for local distributor.

McCall's Needlework & Crafts
615 McCall Rd.
Manhattan, KS 66502
913-776-4041

Magazine feature how-to instructions for knitting, crochet, needlepoint, batik, macrame, jewelrymaking, metal craft, papier mache, plaster crafts and other crafts; also lists sources of decorator items and calender of craft fairs in the U. S..
Magazines: needlecrafts.
Subscriptions: semi-annual copy $1.50, 2 years $6, Canada $7.

McCall's Pattern Fashions
615 McCall Rd.
Manhattan, KS 66502
913-776-4041

Magazine features new fashions and patterns; also discusses sewing and using fabrics; instructions given for batik, knitting, crochet, embroidery and needlepoint.
Magazines: sewing fashions.
Subscriptions: tri-annual copy $1, 1 year $1.80, foreign $2.10.

McCall's You-Do-It Home Decorating
615 McCall Rd.
Manhattan, KS 66502
913-776-4041

Magazines: decorating ideas.
Subscriptions: tri-annual $1.

McEnglevan Heat Treating & Mfg. Inc.
700-708 Griggs St., P.O. Box 31
Danville, IL 61832
217-446-0941
> Furnaces for bronze casting.
> Write for information.

McGraw-Hill Book Co.
1221 Avenue Of The Americas
New York, NY 10020
212-997-1221
> Books: building modern and built-in furniture, general arts & crafts series, machine metal working, making children's furniture, making children's furniture and play equipment, plywood projects, upholstered furniture making and design, woodworking and wood finishing.
> Catalog.
> Contact your nearest bookstore or write above.

Jean McIntosh Ltd.
1064 Valour Rd.
Winnipeg 10, Manitoba, Canada
204-772-6058
> Catalog: $1.35.
> Kits: needlecraft.

David McKay Co., Inc.
750 Third Ave.
New York, NY 10017
212-661-1700
> Books: general arts & crafts series, paper crafts, puppets.
> Catalog.
> Contact your nearest bookstore or write above.

McKnight Publishing Co.
301 Prospect Rd.
Bloomington, IL 61701
309-663-1341
> Books: general arts & crafts series, jewelrymaking, leather craft, metal working, plastics, upholstering, wood furniture making, wood laminating, woodworking.
> Catalog.
> Contact your nearest bookstore or write above.

MDR Mfg. Co., Inc.
4853 W. Jefferson Blvd.
Los Angeles, CA 90016
213-732-7889
> Faceting instruments, Gemmaster faceting laps, Gemmaster faceting systems, trim saws.
> Catalog.
> Write for local distributor.

Melbourn Gem Co.
P.O. Box 14042
Ft. Worth, TX 76117
817-284-0722
> Amethyst, lapidary rough material, opals, star quartz, star ruby.
> Write for information.

Melrose Yarn Co., Inc.
1305 Utica Ave.
Brooklyn, NY 11203
212-629-0200
> Knitting needles, knitting yarns, personalized woven labels.
> Catalog: plus yarn folio, 50¢ (refundable).
> Kits: afghan.

Menco Engineers Inc.
5520 Crebs Ave.
Tarzana, CA 91356
213-881-1167
> Potter's accessories, potter's wheels.
> Write for information.

Merribee
2904 W. Lancaster
Fort Worth, TX 76107
817-335-9413
> Accessories, afghans, canvas, crewel, crochet yarns, embroidery frames, embroidery hoops, embroidery threads, fabrics, felt, handbag frames, handbag handles, knitting supplies, needlecrafts, needlepoint, needles, rosette winders, rug hooks, rug yarn, stamped linens, tatting, transfer pencils.
> Catalog.
> Kits: knitting, tapestry rugs.
> Write for local distributor.

Company Listing
Metals—Miller

Metals Engineering Institute
American Society for Metals
Metals Park, OH 44073
216-338-5151
Courses offered in aluminum casting, principles and applications; arc welding designs and fundamentals, resistance and oxy-acetylene welding, design and fundamentals, metal working; stainless steel casting, melting, processing, cutting, joining and welding; electroplating and metal finishing; copper, brass and bronze metallurgy.
Home study courses: metal working, welding.
Write for information.

Metro Diamond Drill Co.
845 Masselin Ave.
Los Angeles, CA 90036
213-255-2463
Diamond carvers, diamond coated files, diamond impregnated core drills, lapidary supplies.
Catalog.

Mexiskeins
P.O. Box 1624
Missoula, MT 59801
406-728-3547
Handspun Mexican wool yarns.
Carries wool yarns in 80 colors and 3 weights.
Catalog: plus color cards $1.

Michigan Lapidary Supply Co.
8257 Joy Rd.
Detroit, MI 48204
313-933-0256
Brazilian fire agate, faceted stones, gem rock, jade, lapidary machinery, Mexican fire agate, opals, precious metals, rough stones, star ruby, tigereye.
Kits: jewelry casting.
Write for information.

Michigan Wool Products Co.
Benton Harbor, MI 49022
616-926-8262
Rug wool.
Catalog: plus samples 25¢.
Kits: rug braiding.

Midland Walnut
Box 262
Savannah, MO 64485
816-324-3612
Blank gun stocks, cherry wood, lumber, lumber squares, moldings, walnut wood, wood bowls, wood frames, wood legs.
Write for information.

Midwest Mail Service
P.O. Box 1148
Elkhart, IN 46514
219-293-5621
Catalog.
Kits: foil craft tape.

Midwest Wool Marketing Cooperative
125 E. 10th Ave.
S. Hutchinson, KS 67501
816-842-8581
Graded grease wool, spinning supplies.
Write for information.

Allegra Milano
Bear Path, R.D. 2
Guilford, ME 04443
207-997-3242
Bantam eggshells, buck eggshells, goose eggshells, wood spools.
Write for information.

Mill Ends Store
Box 14505
Portland, OR 97214
503-236-1234
Color cards: handweaving and knitting yarns, 35 each.
Sells yarn at mill-end prices.

Mill Store
Box 848J
Williamsport, PA 17701
717-326-9125
Braids, mill ends, trims.
Price list available.

Charles W. Miller
402 Emerson Ave.
Alliance, NE 69301
308-762-4379

Bobbins.
Write for information.

Mindy Molds
6812 Torresdale Ave.
Philadelphia, PA   19135
215-331-4440
Ceramic molds.
Write for information.

Minerals & Gems
P.O. Box 5351
Albany, NY   12205
No phone orders.
Blue fire flash moonstone, cabochons, faceted gemstones, garnet, New York Adirondack gem garnet rough.
Also has "grab bag" type gem garnets as mined with waste to wash and sort.
Write for information.

Minex Lapidary Supplies
306 Russell St.
Melbourne 3000, Australia
No phone orders.
Australian gem rough, cabochons, chrysoprase rough, foreign gem rough, lapidary machinery, mineral specimens, opal chips, opal specimens, rough opals, rough sapphires.
Also has opal and sapphire practice and cutting grades.
Books.
Write for information.

Miniature Aircraft
Box 26262
Indianapolis, IN   46226
No phone orders.
Model accessories, model airbrushes, model decals, model paints.
Catalog: 50¢.
Kits: balsa model airplane, plastic model airplane.
Leaflets: plans for models.

Miniature Figurines--USA, Inc.
4311 Lemmon Ave.
Dallas, TX   75219
214-522-0093
English war-game figures.
Books.
Catalog: $2.

The Miniature Mart-The Peddler's Shop
883 39th Ave.
San Francisco, CA
415-221-0724
Dollhouse miniatures, dollhouse wallpaper, egg craft, miniature accessories, miniature chandeliers, miniature El-Kru china, miniature furniture, miniature glass, miniature hardware, miniature ornaments, miniature pulls, miniature silver.
Catalog: $1.50.

Miniatures by Marty
388 Wildwood Dr.
Holland, MI   49423
No phone orders.
Dollhouse accessories, modern miniatures, Victorian miniatures.
Catalog: 10¢.

Minicraft Models Inc.
1510 W. 228th St.
Torrance, CA   90501
213-325-8383
Plastic scale models.
Catalog: 50¢.

Minnesota Clay
8001 Grand Ave. So.
Bloomington, MN   55420
612-884-9101
Bamboo handles, chemicals, clays, corks, glazes, kilns, potter's wheels.
Books.
Catalog: $1.

Minnesota Lapidary Supply Inc.
524 North 5th St.
Minneapolis, MN   55401
612-333-8281
Lapidary abrasives, lapidary equipment, lapidary machinery, lapidary supplies, lapidary tools.
Catalog.

Company Listing
Minnesota—Modern

Minnesota Woodworkers Supply Co.
Rogers, MN 55374
612–428–4101

Clock movements, craft plans, hardware wood, lamp parts, moldings, music box movements, plans, tools, upholstery supplies, veneers, wood finishing supplies, wood hardware, wood legs, wood parts, woodworking supplies.
Books.
Catalog: 50¢.
Discount: plan of up to 1/3.
Kits: clock.

Mission Rocks
Rt. 4, Box 24
San Angelo, TX 76901
915–653–2037

Barite of roses, cabochons, crinoids, moss agate, palm onions, petrified wood stumps, plume, soapstone, Texas cutting material, turritella.
Write for information.

Mississippi Petrified Forest
P.O. Box 98
Flora, MS 39071
601–879–2291

Agates, lapidary cutting materials, lapidary supplies, petrified wood.
Write for information.

Marie Mitchell's Decoupage Center
16111 Mack Ave.
Detroit, MI 48224
313–882–1755

Coasters, decoupage finishes, decoupage hardware, decoupage prints, gold leaf, rice paper, teak trays, wood frames, wood tables, wooden candle sconces, wooden clocks, wooden switch plates, woodware.
Books: crafts, decoupage, rice paper.
Catalog: 50¢.
Kits: decoupage.

Frank Mittermeier Inc.
3577 E. Tremont Ave.
Bronx, NY 10465
212–828–3843

Anvils, craft knives, engraving blocks, engraving chisels, oilstones, power tools, sculpture supplies, sculpture tools, soldering tools, stone carving tools, wood carving tools.
Books.
Catalog.

Model Craftsman Publishing Corp.
Reader Service Dept.
Box 700
Newton, NJ 07860
201–383–3355

Books: model aircraft, model railroad, model ship building.
Leaflets: model leaflets, plans for model trains.
Write for information.

Model Die Casting Inc.
3811 W. Rosecrans, Box 926
Hawthorne, CA 90250
213–678–3131

Carries over 200 plastic model railroad kits in old time to modern, including metal locomotives, box, passenger, flat and cattle cars, cabooses.
Catalog: $1.
Kits: plastic model railroad.

Model Railroad Equipment Corp.
23 W. 45th St.
New York, NY 10036
212–582–2760

Model accessories, model cements, model paints, model scratch building supplies, model tools, model trains.
Books.
Carries over 60,000 items for model railroading kits.
Kits: model railroading.
Write for information.

Modern Craft
Box 4796
Clearwater, FL 33518
No phone orders.

Beadery, jewelry findings, jewelrymaking supplies.
Catalog: 25¢.

Modern Needlepoint
11 W. 32nd St.
New York, NY 10001
212-279-3263

Handbag frames, handbag leather, needlepoint handbag linings, needlepoint mountings.
Also has accessory mountings including tennis racquets, book covers, bell pulls, wallets, eyeglass cases.
Catalog.

Modern Upholstery Institute
Box 899
Orange, CA 92669
714-997-1235

Course offers furniture upholstering, includes tools, chair frames and materials; VA approved.
Home study courses: furniture upholstering.
Write for information; sample lesson available.

Mohave Industries
3770 Hearne Ave.
Kingman, AZ 86401
602-757-2480

Gem drills, grinding equipment, lapidary supplies, lapidary tumblers, rock clamps, slab saws.
Catalog.
Kits: saw.

Mollica Stained Glass Press
1940-A Bonita
Berkeley, CA 94704
415-849-1591

Glass tools, stained glass supplies.
Books: leaded glass technique.
Catalog.

Mon Tricot
C/O Paris Match
22 E. 67th St.
New York, NY 10021
212-535-1313

Books: hairpin lace, jacquard, knitting dictionary, knitting stitches & patterns/crochet stitches & patterns, patchwork.
Magazine features Paris designs keyed to American yarns; French fashion trends for men, women, children, infants and home accessories.
Magazines: needlecrafts.
Subscriptions: 6 times yearly, 1 year $6.

Montana Assay Office
610 S.W. 2nd Ave.
Portland, OR 97204
503-222-3211

Cut stones, jewelry findings, jewelry mountings, jewelrymaking tools, metals.
Catalog.

Morang Balance Co.
28915 Harper St.
St. Clair Shores, MI 48081
313-779-3220

Gem scales.
Gem scales have equal arm balances and weights to measure in grams and carats.
Write for information.

Sid Morgan
13157 Ormond
Belleville, MI 48111
313-697-9325

Catalog: 25¢.
Leaflets: plans for building model aircraft.

Morgan Inkle Loom Factory
Railroad Engine House
Guilford, CT 06437
203-453-6341

Inkle looms.
Discount: quantity purchases.
Write for information.

William Morrow & Co.
105 Madison Ave.
New York, NY 10016
212-889-3050

Books: general arts & crafts series, string art.
Contact your nearest bookstore or write above.
Write for information.

Joan Moshimer
North St.
Kennebunkport, ME 04046
207-967-3711

Accessories, batik, batik tools, burlap, cutting machines, fabric dyes, frames, rug hooking supplies, rug hooks, rug patterns, wool swatches.
Books.

Company Listing
Moshimer—Natalie

Kits: rug.
Write for information.

Most Unusual Custom Needleworks Inc.
400 New York Ave.
Huntington, NY 11743
516-271-0409

Hand-painted needlepoint canvas.
Also has Don Quixote needlepoint designs.
Kits: needlepoint.
Services: custom painting.
Write for information.

Mountain Ceramic Crafts
R.R. 1, Box 241
Bethesda, OH 43719
614-782-1095

Ceramic supplies.
Books: ceramic project.

Mueller's
1000 E. Camelback
Phoenix, AZ 85014
602-274-4724

Cabochons, faceted stones, gemstones, lapidary material, lapidary mountings.
Price list available, 35¢.

Mrs. Carl F. Murray
713 Quaker Dr.
Friendswood, TX 77546
713-482-2077

Books: dyeing.

Murray American Corp.
15 Commerce St.
Chatham, NJ 07928
201-635-7373

Agate carnelian, amazonite, amethyst, aquamarine, Brazilianite, cabochons, chrysoprase, emeralds, enstatite, gem rough material, opals, ruby in zoisite, turquoise.
Price list available.

Museum Books Inc.
48 E. 43rd St.
New York, NY 10017
212-682-0430

Books: bead crafts, candlemaking, ceramics, crochet, decoupage, enameling, general arts & crafts series, gold leafing, jewelrymaking, knitting, macrame, metal, needlecrafts, pottery, rug making, sewing, stained glass, textile, weaving, wood carving and working.
Carries over 1,000 crafts books.
50¢.

Naakai Dine-E Biye
Box 69
Mexican Hat, UT 84531
No phone orders.

Navajo Indian yarns.
Catalog: plus samples $1.

Nantucket Needleworks
Nantucket, MA 02554
617-228-1913

Crewel embroidery design transfers, embroidery threads, fabrics, frames, hoops, linen, needlepoint yarn, needleweaving cloth, rug frames, rug yarn.
Books: needlecraft.
Catalog: $2.75; yarn color card, $3.00.
Kits: needlepoint crewel.

Nantucket School of Needlery
2 India St.
Nantucket Island, MA 02554
617-228-1909

Course includes meshwork, hardanger, blackwork, drown fabric or pulled work; materials included; 3-year course.
Home study courses: needlecrafts.
Write for information.

NASCO Arts & Crafts
901 Janesville Ave.
Ft. Atkinson, WI 53538
414-563-2446

Artist's supplies, basketry, ceramic supplies, cork, metals, wood.
Catalog.

Natalie Originals Studio
4271 Dewey Ave.
Rochester, NY 14616
716-663-6674

Egg bases, egg craft, European miniature figures, goose eggshells, jewels, pearls.
Catalog: 50¢.

Natcol Crafts, Inc.
P.O. Box 299
Redlands, CA 92373
714-795-2407

Candle additives, candle dyes, candle scents, candlemaking supplies, dough art mix, dough art patterns, dough art tools, jewelry findings, lamp parts, molding compound, plastic candle molds, resin craft accessories, resin craft additives, resin craft embediments, resin craft molds.
Books.
Catalog: general, $1; candle molds, free.
Discount: quantity purchases.
Kits: dough art.
Write for local distributor.

National Art Worker's Community
32 Union Square East
New York, NY 10003
212-533-0150

Organization is dedicated to improving living and work conditions for all visual artists and craftsmen; publishes "We Art Workers Newsletter" 10 times yearly, dealing with artists' housing, job and grant opportunities, alternatives to the galley system.
Organizations: general arts and crafts.
Write for information; 1st copy of newsletter free on request.

National Artcraft Supply Co.
23456 Mercantile Rd.
Beechwood, OH 44122
216-292-4944

Ceramic decals, cheese boards, clock movements, cotton lace, electrical parts, glass jewels, jewelry mountings, jewelrymaking accessories, lamp parts, lighter inserts, metal trivets, mosaics, music boxes, picture frames, resin craft supplies, rhinestones.
Catalog: $1 (refundable).

National Calendar of Indoor-Outdoor Art Fairs
5423 New Haven Ave.
Ft. Wayne, IN 46803
No phone orders.

Magazines: calendar of crafts and arts.
Subscriptions: quarterly 1 year $7.

National Camera Inc.
Englewood, CO 80110
303-789-1893
Catalog.

National Carvers Museum
7825 S. Claremont Ave.
Chicago, IL 60620
312-925-6696

Organization is dedicated to the preservation of carvings as an art and the furtherance of carving as a hobby; nonprofit foundation.
Organizations: wood carving.
Send 25¢ for information on wood carving.

National Craft & Hobby Co., Inc.
8311 Pillsbury Ave. So.
Minneapolis, MN 55420
612-888-7764

No-fire glazes, plaster ware finishes, stained glass.
Books: figurine, painting.
Kits: painting, paints, stained glass.
Write for information.

National Handcraft Society
Handcraft Bldg., 1425 Grand Ave.
Des Moines, IA 50309
515-288-8953

Club offers craft kits for decorative home items; free enrollment gift and a surprise package craft kit monthly; 6-month trial membership.
Club plans: decorative crafts.
Write for information.

National Hobby Inc.
5238 Ridge Rd.
Cleveland, OH 44129
216-749-2450

Model accessories, model airplanes, model boats, model railroads, model tools.
Books.
Catalog: $1 (refundable).
Kits: model airplane, model boats, model railroads.

National Quilting Association
P.O. Box 62
Greenbelt, MD 20770
No phone orders.

Company Listing
National—Nature's

Organization is open to quilters and interested persons throughout U. S. and foreign countries; newsletter "Patchwork Patter" is published quarterly and is distributed free to members and available to non-members for $1 each.
Organizations: quilting.
Write for information.

National School of Dress Design
555 E. Lange St., Dept. 71100
Mundelein, IL 60060
312-566-5400

Course offers foundamentals of designing, pattern making, droping, modern adapting of historical fashions, advanced sewing and finishing; dipoloma awarded upon completion.
Home study courses: sewing.
Write for information.

National Sculpture Review
75 Rockefeller Plaza
New York, NY 10019
212-582-5564

Magazine features events and exhibits; reviews materials, methods, techniques and public and privately owned sculpture pieces.
Magazines: sculpting.
Subscriptions: quarterly copy $1.25, 1 year $4, foreign $5.

National Standards Council of American Embroiderers
Correspondence School
Box 4594
Pittsburgh, PA 15205
No phone orders.

Course offers amateur and professional needlecrafts including design, color, applique, canvas work, drawn fabric, use of metallic threads, and crewel; has advanced courses for certification to teach. Organization promotes quality in embroidery and provides an exchange of ideas; publishes "We Flying Needle" for members.
Home study courses: embroidery.
Organizations: embroidery.
Write for information.

National Weavers Training School
1888 Century Park East
Century City, CA 90067
277-4646

Course offers reweaving and reknitting to repair burns and holes in various fabrics.
Home study courses: weaving.
Write for information.

National Wildlife Art Exchange
Drawer 3385, Beach Station
Vero Beach, FL 32960
305-567-7177

Prints.
Catalog.
Guaranteed limited editions of wildlife prints.

Nationwide Ceramic Enterprises
1406 Highland Ave., P.O. Box 1386
Melbourne, FL 32935
305-254-7932

Mini molds.
Write for information.
Write for local distributor.

Nationwide Plastics Co.
4140 Eagle Rock Blvd.
Los Angeles, CA 90065
213-254-9798

Liquid plastic casting equipment, plastic vacuum molding.
Catalog.

Nature's Fibers
Box 183
Woodstock, NY 12498
914-679-9287

Cording, Japanese filament, noil, rug yarn, silk yarn, tussah type yarn.
Catalog: plus 50¢.

Nature's Treasures
P.O. Box 982
Hawthorne, CA 90250
213-373-3601

Crystallized mineral specimens, decorative mounts, hobby lighting, jewelry display cases, specimen trimmers, ultraviolet lights.
Price list available, 10¢.

Naturegraph Publishers
8339 W. Dry Creek Rd.
Healdsburg, CA 95448
707-433-3232
> Books: preserving in clear plastic, sandpainting, American Indian basket weaving.
> Contact your nearest bookstore or write above.
> Write for information.

Nautique Arts
215 Thompson St.
New York, NY 10012
212-254-7315
> Kits: macrame.
> Write for information.

Needle-Ease
81 Uplands Dr.
West Hartford, CT 06107
203-521-7492
> Canvas tape, roll and stretch frame.
> Write for local distributor.
> Write for information.

The Needle Works
1123 Elm Ave.
Brooklyn, NY 11230
212-339-1300
> Antique dolls, bargello, dressmaking curves, dressmaking rulers, imported canvas, needlepoint, needlepoint cleaner, needles, patterns, Persian yarn, personalized woven labels, rug hooking supplies, scissors, seam steamers, sewing accessories, thread holders.
> Books: embroidery, needlepoint, quilting.
> Catalog: 50¢.
> Kits: crewel, handbag, needlepoint, quilting.

The Needlecase
c/o Farmside Country Store
Long Grove, IL 60047
312-634-3835
> Canvas, crewel embroidery, threads, yarns.
> Books.
> Services: custom designing.
> Write for information.

Needlecraft House
Main St.
West Townsend, MA 01474
617-597-2971
> Canvas, crewel wool, embroidery fabrics, embroidery hoops, embroidery threads, linen, needlepoint rods, patterns, rug wool, tapestry wool.
> Books: needlecraft.
> Catalog: $1.
> Kits: bargello, crewel, embroidery, needlepoint.

Needlecraft Shop Inc.
4501 Van Nuys Blvd.
Sherman Oaks, CA 91403
213-783-0559
> Aida, crewel, electric punch rug hook, embroidery, embroidery charts, frames, hand punch hooks, hardanger, hoops, iron-on transfers, latch hooks, needlepoint, needlepoint canvas, needlepoint charts, needles, rug patterns, rug yarn, rugs, tapestry threads, tapestry wool, transfer pencils, twill.
> Books.
> Catalog: 10¢.

Needles 'N Hoops
Box 165
Abington, PA 19001
215-884-2167
> Catalog: 25¢.
> Kits: needlecraft, sampler.

Needlewoman Shop
146-148 Regent St.
London, WIR6BA, England
No phone orders.
> Catalog: 75¢.
> Kits: crochet, embroidery, knitting, needlepoint, rugmaking, toymaking.

Nel-King Products
811 Wyandotte
Kansas City, MO 64105
816-842-2040
> Magnifying glasses.
> Carries 1/2 and full-frame magnifying glasses with impact-resistant lenses (non-prescription).
> Catalog.

Company Listing
Nelco—Newport

Nelco Sewing Machine Co. Inc.
164 W. 25th St.
New York, NY 10001
212-924-7604
> *Catalog.*
> *Machines feature giant stitches for decorative embroidery, non-tangle rotary honk, stretch stitches, free-arm models.*
> *Write for local distributor.*

Frank J. Nelson
2127 Kensington Ave.
Salt Lake City, UT 84108
801-581-9017
> Netting patterns.
> *Books.*
> *Kits: netting.*
> *Write for information.*

Robert Nelson
RR 2, Box 540
Newport, NH 03773
603-863-4394
> Backstrap (waist) loom, folding frame loom.
> *Also has a foot loom designed to help children learn to weave.*
> *Catalog.*

Nelson-Hall Co.
325 West Jackson Blvd.
Chicago, IL 60606
312-922-0856
> *Books: watch repairing.*
> *Contact your nearest bookstore or write above.*
> *Write for information.*

Netcraft
2101 Sylvania Avenue
Toledo, OH 43613
419-472-9826
> Twine, wire winder tool.
> *Catalog.*
> *Kits: net making.*

Harrison Neustadt
6480 N.W. 24th Court
Sunrise, FL 33313
305-739-7619
> Wood scraps.
> *Scraps of rare and exotic wood, seasoned and dry,* suitable for small carving, jewelrymaking, other crafts (minimum 5 lb.).
> *Send SASE for information.*

The New England Craftsman
Box 20
Elnora, NY 12065
No phone orders.
> Looms, weaving supplies, wood veneers.
> *Catalog.*
> *Kits: wood inlay (marquetry).*

New England Village Crafts
7 Front St.
Weymouth, MA 02188
617-337-1318
> *Kits: stained glass.*
> *Write for information.*

New Products Co.
Box 321
Maple Shade, NJ 08052
609-665-3492
> Beadery, candlemaking supplies, cooking crystals, custom rug templates, needlepoint templates, paint-by-number, pearls, stained glass.
> *Catalog.*
> *Kits: cooking crystals.*

New World Jade Co.
1696 W. 1st Ave.
Vancouver 9, B.C., Canada
604-732-7635
> Jade.
> *Carries jade from Ogden Mt., British Columbia and Canada in green and black.*
> *Write for information.*

Margaret Newman
1001 East Druid Rd.
Clearwater, FL 33516
813-447-1307
> *Catalog.*
> *Leaflets: hand weaving, instructions in weaving.*

Newport Enterprises
2309 W. Burbank Blvd.
Burbank, CA 91506
213-845-0555
> Clock movements.

Company Listing
Newport—Nowotny

Catalog: 25¢.
Kits: clock.

Newton's Potters Supply
96 Rumford Ave., P.O. Box 96
West Newton, MA   02165
617-244-1145
  Airbrushes, bisqued ceramic tiles, ceramic armatures, ceramic glazes, ceramic kilns, ceramic stands, ceramic supplies, ceramic tools, glazed ceramic tiles, high-fire clays, potter's wheels, self-hardening clays, stone carving tools, wood carving tools.
  Books.
  Catalog.

Nicole Bead & Craft Co., Inc.
1023 1/2 Arch St.
Philadelphia, PA   19107
No phone orders.
  American Indian seed beads, bead looms, beadery, beadery accessories, beading wax, mosaic mirrors, safety pin jewelry items.
  Kits: beaded flower, carpetbag.
  Write for information.

The Niddy Noddy
416 Albany Post Rd.
Croton-On-Hudson, NY   10520
914-271-9724
  Dyes, fleece, looms, textile crafts.
  Books.
  Catalog: 50¢.

Nimble Thimble
P.O. Box 713
Aptos, CA   95003
408-722-7755
  Canvas, needlecraft supplies, yarns.
  Books.
  Catalog.

Norlene Lapidary
320 Interstate North
Atlanta, GA   30339
404-436-0813
  Amethyst, apatite, aquamarine, citrine, garnet, gemstones, golden beryl, kunzite, peridot, rubies, sapphire, topaz, tourmaline, zircon.
  Offers custom designing and casting services.
  Price list available, 50¢ (refundable).
  Services: lapidary.

Northeastern Scale Models Inc.
Box 425
Methuen, MA   01844
617-688-6019
  Model building materials, model railroad car parts.
  Also carries siding, structural shapes, stripwood and sheetwood, for model building.
  Catalog: wood plus samples, 50¢.

Northwest Handcraft House
110 West Esplanade
North Vancouver, B.C., Canada
604-988-6912
  Americana samplers, batik dyes, looms, weaving accessories, weaving supplies, wool, wool dyes.
  Books.
  Catalog: 50¢.

Northwest Looms
Rt. 4, Box 4872
Bainbridge Island, WA   98110
206-842-3634
  Portable loom.
  Write for information.

Norwood Loom Co.
Box 272
Baldwin, MI   49304
616-745-3871
  Folding floor harness looms, weaving accessories.
  Catalog.

M. Nowotny
8823 Callaghan Rd.
San Antonio, TX   78230
512-342-2512
  Abalone, amethyst, aventurine, bloodstone, fire agate, gemstones, goldstones, jade, labradorite, malachite, moss agate, onyx, opals, rhodochrosite, rose quartz, sodalite, tektites, tigereye.
  Catalog.

Company Listing
Nucleus—Old

Nucleus
Box 670
Ossining, NY 10562
No phone orders.
   Nylon lace, velvet quilt pieces.
   Write for information.

O Scale Railroading
6710 Hampton Dr. East
Indianapolis, IN 46226
317-897-4466
   Magazines: features articles and diagrams, for O scale and tenplate models, instructions for railroad layouts, kits, models.
   Subscriptions: monthly, sample copy 60¢, 1 year $6.

O-P Craft Co., Inc.
Sandusky, OH 44870
419-626-5220
   Basswood boxes, music box movements, plastic domes, shadowboxes, wood bowls, wood buttons, wood chests, wood crosses, wood eggs, wood plaques, wood trays, wooden candleholders.
   Books.
   Catalog: 50¢.

H. Obodda
P.O. Box 51
Short Hills, NJ 07078
201-467-0212
   Rare cut gemstones.
   Specific inquiries invited.

O'Brien Lapidary Equipment Co.
1116 N. Wilcox Ave.
Hollywood, CA 90038
213-465-5424
   Jewelry casting lamps, jewelry casting supplies, jewelry casting tools, jewelry scales.
   Catalog: 25¢.

Oceanside Gem Imports, Inc.
P.O. Box 222, 426 Marion St.
Oceanside, NY 11572
516-678-3473
   Amethyst, andalusite, aquamarine, beryls, Brazilian gems, chrysoberyl, citrine, garnet, kunzite, rose quartz, smoky quartz, topaz, tourmaline.
   Price list available (gemstones only).

Odyssey Mineral and Fossil
147 N. 12th St.
Philadelphia, PA 19107
215-923-7888
   Mexican crystal, North American fossils, polished stones.
   Write for information.

Ohio Ceramic Supply Inc.
P.O. Box 630, 2861 State Rt. 59
Kent, OH 44240
216-296-3815
   Brushes, ceramic molds, ceramic supplies, clays, clock movements, glazes, kilns, lamp parts, potter's wheels, tools.
   Discount: quantity purchases.
   Free brochures or mold catalog, $1; supply catalog, $1.
   Write for local distributor.

Old Print Center
981 Second Ave.
New York, NY 10022
212-753-1441
   Decoupage prints, prints, reproduction prints.
   Also has Dali interpretations of Currier and Ives.
   Write for information, or Dali catalog: $1.

Old South Patterns
P.O. Box 11143
Charlotte, NC 28209
704-333-8242
   Catalog: 25¢.
   Leaflets: plans of Early American furniture.

Old Time Shop
Box 5126
Poland, OH 44514
No phone orders.
   Carries reproductions of antique clock dials and date strips, second hands, alarms, calendar dials, custom cut wheels.
   Send stamp for information.

Bob and Carol Oliver
P.O. Box 6275
Burbank, CA   91505
213-767-4601
  Bead making, copper enameling supplies, solderless jewelry.
  Books: solderless jewelry.
  Catalog.
  Kits: beading, jewelry, macrame, 12 kt. gold filled square wire.

1001 Decorating Ideas
149 Fifth Ave.
New York, NY   10010
212-677-0870
  Magazine features crafting of home accessories, decoupage, furniture refinishing, sewing and make-it-yourself items.
  Magazines: interior decorating.
  Subscriptions: quarterly 75¢, 1 year $3, Canada $3.50, foreign, $4.

1001 Fashion & Needlecraft Ideas
149 Fifth Ave.
New York, NY   10010
212-677-0870
  Magazine features patterns and instructions for sewing clothing, decorative accessories, crochet, knitting, batik and leathercraft.
  Magazines: needlecrafts.
  Subscriptions: semi-annual 75¢, 1 year $3, Canada $3.50, foreign $4.

1001 How-To Ideas
229 Park Ave. South
New York, NY   10003
212-673-1300
  Magazines features how-to articles and plans for home decorating, house alterations and maintenance projects.
  Magazines: home decorating.
  Subscriptions: semi-annual copy at newsstand $1.

J. Opal Stover Studio
Box 19, 1302 Carsen
Seminole, OK   74868
405-382-2714
  China painting designs, china painting supplies, frames for china.
  Discount: quantity purchases.
  Send SASE for information.

Open Door Co.
1249 Dell Ave.
Campbell, CA   95008
408-374-6868
  Catalog.
  Kits: geometric thread design.

The Oriental Rug Co.
P.O. Box 917
Lima, OH   45802
419-225-6731
  Carpet warp, looms, rug filler, weaving accessories.
  Send 25¢ for information.

Out of Print Bookfinder
Box 663
Seaside, CA   93955
408-394-8998
  Send stamp for specific information.
  Services: book search out-of-print.

Ima Ova
Box 605
Holland, MO   63853
No phone orders.
  Books: decorating eggs for Christmas, Easter and special occasions.
  Write for information.

Ovgem Craft Supply Co.
Dept. 21
236 Nepean St.
Ottawa, Canada K2POB8
613-234-3284
  Beadery, candlemaking supplies, copper enameling supplies, lapidary supplies, lost wax casting, macrame accessories, minerals, resin casting, silversmithing supplies.
  Catalog: available to Canadians only.

Virgil Owens
1213 Bel Aire
Tullahoma, TN   37388
615-455-2706
  Carnelian, lapidary supplies, Tennessee Mt. agate.
  Price list available.

Company Listing
Oxford—Paradise

Oxford Crafts
Box 469
Cortland, NY 13045
607–753–3858
> Kits: model historic buildings, model lighthouses, model planes, model ships, English and American card model.
> Send SASE for information.

Oxford University Press
200 Madison Ave.
New York, NY 10016
212–679–7300
> Books: mosaics.
> Contact your nearest bookstore or write above.
> Write for information.

Pacific Crafts
Dept. G., Box 1407
Fenndale, WA 98248
206–384–1504
> Potter's kick wheels.
> Carries wheels with wood frames and portable and professional electric with variable speed electronic control foot pedal; kick wheel easily dismantles for shipping and storing; has a variable weight kick 22 lb to 140 lb.
> Catalog.

Pacific Gemstones
Box 3417
Granada Hills, CA 91344
213–361–2927
> Pre-ringed baroques.
> Carries (gemstones fitted with gold filled jump rings).
> Sample and price list available.

Pack-O-Fun
14 Main St.
Park Ridge, IL 60068
312–825–2161
> Bamboo beads, craft sticks, looper looms, loopers, wood tiles.
> Books.
> Kits: basket, leathercraft, tissue picture, wood.
> Magazine features low-cost and scrap craft ideas, patterns and instructions.
> Magazines: general arts and crafts.
> Subscriptions: 10 times yearly, 1 year $5, foreign $6.

Paige Enterprises
400 Lee Terrace
Wilmington, DE 19803
302–738–7238
> HO railroad accessories, illuminated number boards, model tools, O gauge railroad accessories, passenger car drumheads, white metal castings.
> Catalog: send SASE.
> Illuminated number boards are available in most major road names, also has HO and O gauge trolley illuminated destination boards.
> Kits: freight and passenger car, structure, trackside detailing way, HO structure.
> Names, also has HO and O gauge trolley illuminated destination.
> Write for local distributor.

Palmloom Co.
P.O. Box 3333
New York, NY 10017
212–592–6990
> Hand fabric loom.
> Catalog.

Panther International Ltd.
P.O. Box P
Scottsdale, AZ 85252
No phone orders.
> American Indian jewelry supplies, Apache tears, bloodstone, blue calcite, carnelian, castings, Chatham emerald rough, coral, diamond crystals, epidote, fetishes heishe, flux, garnet, gemstones, hollow geodes, jewelrymaking supplies, Kingman turquoise, peridot rough, rose quartz, rough Russian emerald, sapphire, semi-precious stones, sodalite, solder, sterling silver, tigereye, white coral.
> Write for information.

Paradise Rocks
R.R. 3, Box 373
Warsaw, MO 65355
No phone orders.
> T'Caro material.
> Carries T'Caro material from N.C. for cabbing, carving, sphere-making, intarsia and tumbling; also custom sawing with great variety of hundreds of semi-precious materials.
> Write for information.

Paragon Industries Inc.
Box 10133
Dallas, TX 75207
214-942-6121
Ceramic kilns.
Catalog.

Paragon Needlecraft
367 Southern Blvd
Bronx, NY 10454
212-683-8000
Catalog: 10¢.
Kits: needlecraft.

Paramount Ceramic Inc.
220 No. State
Fairmont, MN 56031
507-235-3461
Bamboo handles, ceramic clays, ceramic glazes, ceramic kilns, ceramic supplies, ceramic tools, potter's wheels.
Books.
Catalog: $1.

George W. Park Seed Co., Inc.
Greenwood, SC 29646
803-374-3341
Brass stands, gourd seeds, seeds.
Catalog.

Parker Publishing Co., Inc.
West Nyack, NY 10994
914-358-8800
Books: batik, bottle items, foil etching, mobiles, nail design, paper crafts, pine cone decorating, plaster of Paris carvings, scenic oceans, sculpture, shell chimes, string printing, teaching arts and crafts, wall plaques.
Write for information.

Parkway Plastics Inc.
P.O. Box 4751
Piscataway, NJ 08854
201-752-3636
Stock threaded plastic jars.
Catalog.

Party Bazaar
390 Fifth Ave.
New York, NY 10018
212-695-6820
Craft tissue, crepe paper, decoupage, mirrors, rug hooking supplies, spray paints, Styrofoam®, wood plaques.
Kits: candlemaking.
Write for information.

Patterns for Pennies, Inc.
Box 209
Franklin Square, NY 11010
No phone orders.
Kits: instruction for perfectly fitting garments.
Write for information.

Hazel Pearson Handi Craft
P.O. Box 519, 4128 Temple City Blvd.
Rosemead, CA 91770
213-443-6136
Art foam, batik, batik wax, beadery, boutique ribbons, braids, butterflies, candlemaking supplies, chenille, clock movements, cooking crystal molds, cooking crystals, crepe paper, decoupage, decoupage finishes, doll parts, dough craft, fabrics, feathers, felt, figure draping, floral craft, floral tools, flower looms, furniture finishes, glues, gold leaf, gold paper laces, hardware, hat pins, jewelry findings, macrame accessories, magnets, metal tooling, miniatures, mirrors, paints, pearl parchment, pedestals, perforated ribbon, plaster casting, plastic domes, plastic heads, prints, scissors, tin can craft, tissue paper, tjanting tool, trims, velour paper, white foam shapes.
Books.
Catalog: $1.50 (refundable).
Kits: floral, macrame, synthetic straw.

The Pendleton Shop
Sedona, AZ 86336
602-282-3671
Harness looms, jack looms, Navajo Indian loom.
Write for information.

Penguin Books Inc.
7110 Ambassador Rd.
Baltimore, MD 21207
301-944-8600
Books: pottery, selling crafts.
Write for information.

Company Listing
Penney—Plantabbs

J. C. Penney Co., Inc.
National Office
P.O. Box 2056
Milwaukee, WI   53201
414-771-6000
   Bottle cutters, candlemaking supplies, crewel embroidery, crocheting supplies, decoupage, dip film, enameling, jewelrymaking accessories, leathercraft, macrame accessories, needlepoint, resin craft supplies.
   Catalog.
   Kits.
   Write for nearest location.

Peri's Homework
157 Larchmont Ave.
Larchmont, NY   10538
914-834-3444
   Canvas, grospoint yarn, tennis racquet covers.
   Kits: belt and bag, needlepoint, quickpoint.
   Write for information.

H. H. Perkins Co.
P.O. Box 1601
New Haven, CT   06506
203-389-9501
   Natural cane, plastic cane, rush, splint seat weaving.
   Catalog: 25¢ (refundable).

Phentex, Inc.
P.O. Box 99
Plattsburg, NY   12901
518-563-2510
   Books: knitting and crochet patterns.
   Write for local distributor.

Phentex, Inc.
U.S. Hwy 441, 1601 N. State Rd 7
Hollywood, FL   33021
305-983-7205
   See above entry.

Phentex, Inc.
St. Hyacinthe
Quebec, Canada
No phone orders.
   See above entry.

Reo N. Pickens, Jr.
610 N. Martin Ave.
Waukegan, IL   60085
312-623-2823
   Minerals.
   Carries minerals from world wide localities, color cards and framing prints, 35mm color slides.
   Price list available.

Pins & Needles
P.O. Box 2535
Hialeah, FL   33012
305-685-2698
   Carbon tracing paper, pattern paper.
   Books: patternmaking and designing.
   Kits: patchwork.
   Pattern paper is marked in inches, 44 in x 36 in.
      Clips for pre-tied ties.
   Write for information.

Pioneer Crafts
Box 128
Malvern, PA   19355
215-644-5812
   Kits: stitchery flower pillow.
   Write for information.

The Pirate's Cove
Box 152
Bayport, NY   11705
No phone orders.
   Irish oiled yarn.
   Color cards: 25¢.

Pitman Publishing Corp.
6 E. 43rd St.
New York, NY   10017
212-867-7400
   Books: basketry, general arts & crafts series, millinery, paper sculpture, screen process, welding.
   Contact your nearest bookstore or write above.
   Write for information.

Plantabbs Co.
Lutherville-Timonium, MD   21093
301-252-4620
   Silica gel.
   Write for local distributor.
   Write for information.

Plasco
P.O. Box 348
Alvord, TX 76225
817–427–3231

Clock movements, furniture finishes, iron table pedestals, molds, papier mache, plaques, spray paints, wax gilt.
Also has simulated plastic 'stone' materials, used and poured like plaster, but with properties of stone.
Books.
Catalog: 50¢.

Plastruct
1621 N. Indiana St.
Los Angeles, CA 90063
213–261–8174

Model piping components, plastic model structural components.
Catalog: 50¢.
Kits: railroad.

Platers Service Co.
1511 Esperanza Street
Los Angeles, CA 90023
213–264–1880

Portable plating equipment, used plating equipment.
Carries platers, liners, rectifier components, parts. Write for information.

Platypus
200 W. 82 St.
New York, NY 10024
212–874–0753

Doll patterns, stitch-and-stuff toys.
Catalog: plus sample pattern, 25¢.

Plaza Artists Materials, Inc.
210 E. 58th St.
New York, NY 10022
212–759–7550

Acetate, airbrushes, armatures, artist's supplies, bamboo brushes, blank greeting cards, brushes, cellophane paper, clays, cork, corrugated paper, double stick tape, firing clay, flint paper, gilding brushes, kilns, magnifiers, map pins, metallic tape, Mylar®, nonfiring clay, potter's wheels, push pins, repeat glass, scaleograph, screen process supplies, stained glass paints, tape, tools, tracing paper, wire bending jig.
Catalog.
Kits: screen processing.

Plexiglas
P.O. Box 4470
Philadelphia, PA 19140
No phone orders.
Books: plexiglas acrylic sheet.

Plush Point Patterns by Marcia Podell
233 East 69th St., Lenox Hill Station
New York, NY 10021
212–861–9390

Canvas, satin yarn.
Books.
Catalog: 35¢.
Kits: satin needlepoint.

Plycrete Mold Co.
Elk Rapids, MI 49629
616–264–8093

Fiberglass molds, fiberglass plaques, metallic latex paints.
Catalog: $2.

Polk's Hobby Dept. Store
314 Fifth Ave.
New York, NY 10001
212–279–9034

Military miniatures, model airplanes, model railroads, model ships.
Catalog: $2.95.

Pollack's Furrier's Supply Corp.
160 W. 29th St.
New York, NY 10001
212–524–2680

Buckles, leather belts, leather buttons, leather interlinings, leather linings, leather padding, leather skins.
Write for information.

Polyproducts Corp.
13810 Nelson Ave.
Detroit, MI 48227
313–931–1088

Batik (instant), epoxy resins, fiberglass,

Company Listing
Polyproducts—Praeger

metal powders, mold materials, polyester resins.
   Free brochure; catalogs, $2.

Forrest W. Pond
2904 East Coast Hwy
Corona, CA 91720
714-644-8857
   Books: gem carving tools, making.

Popular Ceramics
6011 Santa Monica Blvd.
Los Angeles, CA 90038
213-469-3942
   Magazine features techniques and projects, supply sources and news of shows and events.
   Magazines: ceramics.
   Subscriptions: monthly copy 75¢, 1 year $7.50.

Popular Library Inc.
600 Third Ave.
New York, NY 10017
212-661-4200
   Books: bottle cutting, general arts & crafts series, American Indian crafts.
   Contact your nearest bookstore or write above.
   Write for information.

Popular Mechanics Press
224 W. 57th St.
New York, NY 10019
212-765-6850
   Books: furniture refinishing, upholstery.
   Leaflets: aircushions vechicle plans, billiard table plans, boat plans, houseboat plans, model ship plans, sailboat plans, travel trailer plans, two-man submarine plans.
   Photocopies of articles are available on a wide variety of subjects, including antiquing, annealing, arc welding, electronic banjo, clocks, chess sets, dollhouses, drill press, fireplace construction, glass blowing and cutting, gunstock checkering, kayak building, kilns, table lamps, lathes, linoleum block press, log projects, marble working, metal craft, plastics, power shop.
   Write for information.

Popular Science Book Club
44 Hillside Ave.
Manhasset, NY 11030
516-365-9696

   Club offers one or more free books to new members, must purchase at least one book per year at discount; may include workshops on home improvements.
   Club plans: books.
   Write for information.

Port Lobster Co.
Ocean Ave.
Kennebunk, ME 04046
207-967-2081
   Kits: authentic oak lobster trap.
   Write for information.

Portfolio of Egg Artistry
2704 Boyd St.
Bethlehem, PA 18017
No phone orders.
   Magazine features instructions in the art of egg decorating by Glenroy Dankel and Salley LeVan.
   Magazines: eggery.
   Subscriptions: bimonthly, 1 year $31.50.

Pourette Mfg. Co.
6818 Roosevelt Way, N.E.
Seattle, WA 98115
206-525-4488
   Candle additives, candle dyes, candle molds, candle scents, candle wicks, candle-making supplies.
   Catalog: 35¢.
   Magazines: candlemaking.
   Subscriptions: monthly, 1 year $2.
   Write for local distributor.

Powell
Box 218-Mason St.
E. Pepperell, MA 01437
617-433-6228
   Books: knitting.

Praeger Publishers
111 4th Ave.
New York, NY 10003
212-254-4100
   Books: craftsman's manual, general arts & crafts series.
   Contact your nearest dealer or write above.
   Craft anthology features many crafts including weaving, pottery, macrame, beading, leather

craft, batik, candlemaking, bronze work, sandlemaking.
Write for information.

Ken Prag
Box 431
Hawthorne, CA   90250
213-973-7562

Decoupage mining prints, decoupage oil company prints, decoupage railroad prints, decoupage stock certificates prints.
Catalog.

Prentice-Hall Inc.
Route 9-W
Englewood Cliffs, NJ   07632
201-947-1000

Books: general arts & crafts series, industrial arts for the shop, metal working, model railroading, sculpture, seriography, textiles, woodworking for industrial arts.
Contact your nearest bookstore or write above.
Write for information.

Mrs. Mell Prescott
Box 177
Warrenville, CT   06278
203-429-1586

Miniature accessories, miniature furniture.
Also has Victorian and other periods "quality" pieces for the advanced collector.
Catalog: 25¢.

Priscilla's Little Red Tole House
Box 7026
Tulsa, OK   74105
918-742-0684

Books: glass painting, rub out painting.

PRO Custom Hobbies
742 Frederick Rd.
Catonsville, MD   21228
301-788-8770

Model accessories, model castings, model construction materials, model hand tools, model paints, model power tools, model railroad equipment, model wire.
Brass locomotive list, 50¢.
Books.

Carries model railroad equipment for N, HO,HOn2, On2,On3 and O gauge.
Kits: model railroad.

Products and Systems, Inc.
P. O. Box 26362
Sacramento, CA   95826
916-362-8463

Books: restringing beads and pearls.

Prospector's Pouch
Box 112
Kennesaw, GA   30144
404-427-6481

Engraving equipment, jewelrymaking equipment, lapidary equipment, star rose quartz slabs.
Carries other world wide rocks, gems and minerals.
Write for information.

P. T. I.
P.O. Box 511, Old Chelsea Station
New York, NY   10011
212-255-1444

Nylon.
Books: time saving tips; using trace'n fit.
Transparent fabric with grid of dots for tracing, duplication, enlarging, or making patterns.

Puppeteers of America, Inc.
Box 1061
Ojai, CA   93023
805-646-2258

Organization is devoted to national puppet crafters; membership includes monthly publication, membership directory and consulting service; sponsors annual national festival with workshops, exhibits and performances throughout the country.
Organizations: puppetmaking.
Write for information.

The Puppetry Store
3500 Tyler N.E.
Minneapolis, MN   55418
No phone orders.

Books: puppetmaking, stage and costume making.
Catalog.

Purcelli's Gems
3496 Spring Circle
Decatur, GA   30032
404-289-8489

Company Listing
Purcelli's—R/C

Amber, amethyst, andalusite, aquamarine, beryls, chrysoberyl, chrysoprase, cut gemstones, diopside moonstone, garnet, jade, kornerupine, kunzite, malachite, opals, peridot, rose quartz, rubies, sapphire, tourmaline, zircon.

Pursenalities Inc.
1619 Grand Ave.
North Baldwin, NY 11510
516-223-4334
Catalog.
Kits: fabric purse, frame type bags, shoulder bags.

Putnam Co.
1001 Grand St.
Harvard, IL 60033
414-275-3505

Bonded polyester quilt batts, polyester Fiberfil stuffing, polyester filled pillow forms.
Discount: quantity purchases.
Write for information.

G. P. Putnam's Sons
200 Madison Ave.
New York, NY 10016
212-883-5500
Books: general arts & crafts series.
Contact your nearest bookstore or write above.
Write for information.

The Putter Shop
Box 66
Congers, NY 10920
914-268-2842

Boutique braids, Christmas tree ornaments, Easter decorating items, edgings, miniatures, pearls, trims.
Catalog: 70¢.
Kits.

Pylam Products, Inc.
95-10 218th St.
Queens Village, NY 11429
212-464-0860
Candle dyes.
Catalog: plus samples.

Pyronetics
10025 Shoemaker Ave.
Sante Fe Springs, CA 90670
213-941-0237
Books: metal sculpture.
Write for information.

Quilter's Newsletter
Box 394
Wheatridge, CO 80033
303-423-8442

Magazine features quilting patterns and articles on quilters and their work.
Magazines: quilting.
Subscriptions: monthly copy 50¢, 1 year $4.25.

Quilts
Box 39
Valley Park, MO 63088
314-825-2021
Quilt patterns.
Catalog: plus free patterns, 25¢.

Quilts and Other Comforts
5315 W. 38th Ave.
Denver, CO 80212
303-423-8442

Precut plastic quilt patterns, quilt patterns.
Books: quilting.
Catalog: 50¢.
Kits: pre-cut plastic patterns.

Quinn Mineral
804 E. Jefferson St.
Iowa City, IA 52240
319-337-2447

Devonian hexagonaria colony coral, Iowa Betoskey stone, lapidary supplies.
Discount: quantity purchases.
Write for information.

R/C Cars International
Box 148
South Gate, CA 90280
213-639-4474

Radio controlled boats, radio controlled cars.
Kits: airplanes.
Write for information.

R & R Ceramic Molds Inc.
P.O. Box 10127, 9 1/2 E. 39th St.
Kansas City, MO 64111
816-753-1131
    Ceramic molds.
    Catalog: $1 (refundable).

R L L Enterprise
82 Manetto Hill Mall
Plainview, NY 11803
516-681-7006
    Velvet needlepoint yarn.
    Carries velvet needlepoint yarn in 26 colors.
    Write for information.

Radio Shack
National Office
2617 W. 7th St.
Fort Worth, TX 76107
817-335-3711
    Carries fiber optic kits with variety of shapes including aurora display, moonstone display.
    Kits: fiber optic.
    Write for nearest location.
    Write for information.

Railway Express
8323 Balboa
Van Nuys, CA 91406
213-345-3220
    Model cannon, model electronic components, model railroad equipment, model railroads, model ships, model structures, model tools, model tracks, model trains.
    Books.
    Kits: metal building, model railroad, plastic building, wood buildings.
    Send SASE for list of catalogs.

Railroad Modeler
7950 Deering Ave.
Canoga Park, CA 91304
No phone orders.
    Magazine features model railroad layouts, accessories, how-to's on crafting model buildings, new product information and calendar of events throughout U. S..
    Magazines: model crafts.
    Subscriptions: monthly copy $1, 1 year $11.

A. Raimer
5544 S. E. 128th
Portland, OR 97236
503-761-4074
    Pompom dolls, pompom hat, pompom poncho, pompom purse, pompom shawls, pompom throw pillows.
    Send $1 and SASE for instructions.

Ramont's Floral Arts Studio
550 E. 1st St.
Beaumont, CA 92223
714-845-3177
    Decoupage finishes, floral craft, liquid drape, wood fibre.
    Catalog.
    Kits: flowers.

Random House Inc.
201 E. 50th St.
New York, NY 10022
212-751-2600
    Books: children's crafts, crafts anthology, crochet, dressmaking, embroidery patterns, encyclopedia of carpentry, furniture for nomads, gemstones, general arts & crafts series, knitting, leather craft, needlepoint, needlework, sewing guide, woodworking tools.
    Write for information.

Kenneth Rarick
1405 Coffman St.
Longmont, CO 80501
303-776-0116
    China painting supplies.
    Catalog: 25¢.
    Lithographed color designs on china blanks.

Rays Rock Shop
P.O. Box 514
Scappoose, OR 97056
503-543-6968
    Transistor clock movements.
    Write for information.

Raytech Industries Inc.
P.O. Box 84 Stafford Ind. Park
Stafford Springs, CT 06076
203-684-4273
    Diamond saws, grinders, lapidary laps,

lapidary supplies, lapidary tumblers, polishing machines, ultraviolet lamps.
Write for information.
Write for local distributor.

Reade Knitting Designs
3111 Whitten Dr.
Eugene, OR 97405
503-343-2363
Books: knitting and panel designs.

Real Woods
107 Trumbull St.
Elizabeth, NJ 07206
201-351-1990
Cane, carving blocks, hardware, rare woods, rush, veneers, wood, wood finishing supplies.
Catalog: plus 10 veneer samples $1.
Leaflets: cabinetmaking, veneering, wood finishing.

Reed Industries
Chloride Star Rd., Box 201
Kingman, AZ 86401
602-565-3355
Cabochon machines, custom-made lapidary equipment, grinders, saws.
Catalog.

Reeves Knotique
P.O. Box 5011
Riverside, CA 92507
714-682-7717
Macrame cords, porcelain beads, stoneware beads, stoneware planter pots, wall plaques.
Books.
Catalog: 75¢.
Discount: quantity purchases.

Reggi's Ceramic Colors
1024 Dixie Hwy.
Rossford, OH 43460
419-666-2957
Metallic rubs, molds, opaque stains, water soluble metallic paints.
Write for information.
Write for local distributor.

Henry Regnery Co.
114 W. Illinois St.
Chicago, IL 60610
312-527-3300
Books: general arts & crafts series, leather craft, needlecrafts.
Contact your nearest bookstore or write above.
Write for information.

Reichert's Fabrics
101 Nashua Rd.
E. Pepperell, MA 01437
617-433-2872
Corduroy scraps, cotton-polyester woven scraps, craft furs, leather scraps, polyester double knit scraps, quilt scraps, wool blends.
Scraps are sold by the pound.
Write for information.

Reilly & Lee Books
114 West Illinois St.
Chicago, IL 60610
312-527-3300
Books: general arts & crafts series, jewelry, leather, rug, stitchery.
Write for information.

Reisinger Net Co.
129 Druid Oak Lane
St. Simons Island, GA 31522
912-638-3522
Netting needles.
Books: making net hammocks.
Price list available.

Ren Ann Crafts
2508 E. Bijou St.
Colorado Springs, CO 80909
303-632-7308
Egg craft, miniatures.
Books: bejeweled eggs.
Catalog: $1.

Renaldy's
277 Park St.
Troy, MI 48084
313-585-3575
Brushes, ceramic tiles, china lamps, china painting supplies, glass lamps, jewelry

mountings, paints, stones, wrought iron tile frames.
Books.
Catalog: 50¢ (refundable) jewelry, 25¢.
Imported white china dinnerware, bowls, pitchers, egg and jewel boxes, coffee sets, plates, vases, picture frames.

Ju Rene Ceramic Molds
Hwy. 69
Franklin, KS   66735
316-347-4585
Ceramic molds.
Catalog: 75¢.

Reynolds Yarns Inc.
15 Oser
Hauppauge, NY   11787
516-582-9330
Books: nordic design knitting.
Club offers new knitting and crocheting patterns and fashion-of-the-month.
Club plans: crochet, knitting.
Write for information.

Carol Rice Creatives
1790 Fredna Ave.
Williamsport, PA   17701
717-323-4521
Crepe paper.
Catalog.
Kits: carnation, daisy, flower, large cabbage rose and poinsettia, poppy, rose.

Richland Ceramics Inc.
7124 Montecello Rd.
Columbia, SC   29203
803-754-6991
Chemicals, clays, kilns, potter's equipment, potter's wheels.
Write for information.

D. E. Rinck
Box 10202
New Orleans, LA   70181
504-835-3827
Cuckoo clock kit is of natural color wood with 10 in. quarterhour parts and instructions, moving bird.
Kits: cuckoo clock.
Write for information.

Robertson Studio
502 Peden Ave.
Houston, TX   77006
No phone orders.
China painting supplies.
Also carries reproductions, studies and designs.
Catalog: 25¢.
Discount: quantity purchases for teachers.

Robin & Russ Handweavers
533 North Adams St.
McMinnville, OR   97128
503-472-5760
Bobbins, clamp-on lamps, Egyptian cotton thread, electric bobbin winders, handbag frames, handmade Swiss wood beads, Icelandic lopi, inkle looms, jack looms, jute, linen thread, loom accessories, looms, shuttles, silk thread, skein winders, spinning wheels, spool racks, Swedish bobbin winders, Swiss bell pulls, threads, yardage counters, yarns.
Books: batik, bobbin lace, embroidery, knitting, macrame, spinning, vegetable and other dyeing, weaving.
Catalog.
Magazine features sample swatches with each issue and directions for multiple harness weaving.
Magazines: weaving.
Subscriptions: monthly, 1 year $5.

Keith Robinson
Rt. 1, Box 663
Florence, OR   97439
503-997-2386
Bottle cutters, jug cutter, wood boards.
Write for information.

The Roc Shop
15824 E. Main St.
La Puente, CA   91744
213-330-7625
Jewelrymaking equipment, ring mandrel.
Catalog.

Rock Mountain Farm
Box 167
Mosier, OR   97040
No phone orders.
Bantam eggshells, blue duck eggshells, blue hen eggshells, bobwhite eggshells, ca-

nary eggshells, dove eggshells, egg accessories, eggshells, finch eggshells, goose eggshells, green hen eggshells, parakeet eggshells, peafowl eggshells, pheasant eggshells, plastic pigeon eggs, quail eggshells, rhea eggshells, swan eggshells, tinamou eggshells, wood canary eggs.
All eggs are blown except quail, finch, canary.
Send SASE for information.

Rock's Lapidary Equipment
P.O. Box 10075
San Antonio, TX 78210
512-532-3814
Slab-grabber.
Slab-grabber is used to get slabs left in nub ends of stone.
Write for information.
Write for local distributor.

W. B. Roddey
P.O. Box 99
Richburg, SC 29729
803-789-5491
Cotton crochet yarn.
Catalog: plus samples.

Rohm & Haas Co.
Independence Mall-West
Philadelphia, PA 19105
215-592-3000
Acrylic in sheet form.
Books: "do-it-yourself" acrylics.
Write for local distributor.

Rombins' Nest Farm
Box 72
Fairfield, PA 17320
717-642-8409
Bead flowermaking, cast iron, cast iron brackets, cast iron candle cups, cast iron hooks, cast iron sconces, dollhouse furniture, dolls, gem polishing supplies, miniatures, needlecrafts, woodware.
Catalog: 25¢.
Kits: beaded flower.

Rose Rocks Co.
P.O. Box 1016
Moore, OK 73160
405-794-4451
Rose rocks.
"This area is the world's only known source for rose rocks of this high quality."
Catalog: 50¢.

Rosemond Hobbycraft
Box 4929
Chicago, IL 60680
No phone orders.
Adjustable hairpin lace loom, daisy winder.
Books: daisy design, hairpin lace.
Daisy winder for afghans, sweaters and stoles cuts crochet time in half.
Write for information.

Mrs. Rossi
616 E. Angeleno Ave.
Burbank, CA 91501
213-845-1130
Doll clothes crochet patterns, doll clothes knitting patterns.
Catalog: 25¢.

Rub 'N Buff
Box 68163
Indianapolis, IN 46268
317-293-5591
Electrostatic flocking, liquid metallic finishes, rub-on metallic finishes.
Kits: batik.
Write for local distributor.
Write for information.

Rug Hooker News & Views
Kennebunkport, ME 04046
207-967-3711
Magazine features rug hooking from beginners to most advanced craftsman; includes designs; patterns, dyeing, color and techniques.
Magazines: rugmaking.
Subscriptions: bimonthly $1.25, 1 year $5, Canada $6.

Rupert, Gibbon & Spider
470 Maylin St.
Pasadena, CA 91105
213-792-0600
Batik materials, blockprinting dye, permanent brush-on dyeing, textile dyes, tools.

Books: batik.
Catalog: plus color chart; $1.

The Rusty Nail
141 Carlisle St.
Hanover, PA   17331
No phone orders.
  Calico blender coverups, calico can opener coverups, calico mixer coverups, calico toaster coverups, denim tote bags, tote bags.
  Calico swatch cards 50¢.
  Kits: calico cat, calico gingerbread man, calico mobil, calico owl, calico rooster, calico santa, gingham puppy.

Mrs. W. Bradley Ryan
The Guild Collection
Box 247
Reading, MA   01867
617-944-3185
  Colonial heritage collection, Danish needlepoint, iron-on patterns, linen, linen twill, needlepoint canvas, needlepoint hardware.
  Also has pre-packaged natural and colored even-count 100% pure Belgian linen.
  Catalog: $1.
  Kits: embroidery.
  Write for local distributor.

S & W Crafts Mfg.
P.O. Box 5501
Pasadena, CA   91107
213-793-2443
  Catalog: 25¢.
  Kits: wood handicraft.

Evelyn Saft
Udall, KS   67146
316-782-3536
  Plastic molds.
  Catalog: 50¢.

St. Louis Crafts Inc.
P.O. Box 3033
St. Louis, MO   63119
314-961-7414
  Aluminum circles, brass foil, colored aluminum foils, cooking crystals, copper foil, etching supplies.

Catalog: 25¢.
Write for local distributor.

Salyer Publishing Co.
3111 N.W. 19th
Olkahoma City, OK   73107
405-943-3841
  China brushes, china enamels, china mediums, china painting supplies, decals, punchers, quill pens.
  Books: china painting.
  Kits: stencils.
  Send SASE for information.

Howard W. Sams & Co., Inc.
Subsidiary Of ITT
4300 West 62nd St.
Indianapolis, IN   46268
317-291-3100
  Books: building trades, carpentry, do-it-yourself subjects, electronic organs, electronics projects, machine shop, upholstering.
  Catalog.

Sancraft Industries
Mountainview Rd., R.D. 2
Patterson, NY   12563
No phone orders.
  Patterns.
  Books: bead crafts, burlap, crepe papers, crochet, decoupage, embroidery, felt, knitting, net, out-of-prints, papier mache, resin craft, tatting, tissue paper.
  Write for catalog information.

Sandeen's Scandinavian Gift & Card Shop
1315 White Bear Ave.
St. Paul, MN   55106
612-776-7012
  Rosemaling brushes, rosemaling paints, rosemaling supplies, woodware.
  Catalog: 25¢ (refundable).
  Kits: beginners, rosemaling.

The Sandvigs
902 North Riverside Ave.
Medford, OR   97501
503-773-3207
  Belt buckles, jewelry mountings, lapidary supplies.

Company Listing
Sandvigs—Sax

Catalog.
Write for local distributor.

Sangray Corp.
Box 2388
Pueblo, CO   81004
303–564–3408

Decoupage, transfers.
Kits: transfer process.
Write for local distributor.
Write for information.

Santa Cruz Mountain Crafts
123 Hoover Rd.
Santa Cruz, CA   95065
408–475–0941

Iron-on transfers, quilt patterns.
Catalog: 25¢.
Has iron-on transfers for embroidery, needlepoint, cloth dolls.

Santos Miniatures
P.O. Box 4062
Harrisburg, PA   17111
717–545–2949

Military miniatures, model materials, model paints, model tools.
Books.
Kits: model figure.
Send SASE for list or $3 for catalog.

Sav-On-Crafts
Box 305
Miami Shores, FL   33153
305–891–4100

Animal eyes, beadery, boutique items, calyx, cameos, candle molds, candle waxes, candlemaking supplies, chenille, craft furs, doll parts, felt, flocked fruit, floral craft, floral tape, floral wire, flower looms, furniture finishes, glassware, honeycomb ribbon, jewelry findings, jewelry mountings, jingle bells, knitting machines, limoges, macrame accessories, paints, perforated plastic shapes, ribbon, sequins, Styrofoam®, synthetic straw, velvet, white plastic ware, wire.
Books.
Catalog.
Kits: beads, candlemaking, leather craft, ornaments, shag rug.

Savin Handcrafts
P.O. Box 4251
Hamden, CT   06514
No phone orders.

Cane, weaving supplies.
Books.
Catalog.
Kits: basket weaving, caning, caning door panels, caning footstool, caning seat backs, caning seats, seat weaving.

Sax Arts & Crafts
207 N. Milwaukee St.
Milwaukee, WI   53202
414–272–4900

Alphabet stencils, American Indian crafts, art foam, art metal tools, ballpoint paints, balsa wood, basketry, batik, beadery, block-printing, brass rods, brass sheets, candle molds, candlemaking supplies, cane, canvas, carving tools, casting units, cements, ceramic glazes, ceramic supplies, chenille, copper shapes, cork, decoupage trims, dyes, engraving, etching supplies, fabrics, firing clay, glass paints, glues, hand looms, instant papier mache, jewelry findings, jewelrymaking accessories, jewelrymaking tools, kilns, lacing, lacquers, lapidary machinery, latex, leathercraft, monk's cloth, mosaic forms, mosaic stone, mosaic tiles, nickel, nonfiring clay, nonhardening clay, papers, pewter, plaster carving, plaster casting, plaster molds, plastic boxes, potter's wheels, pottery stands, prints, raffia, reed, resin craft molds, resin craft supplies, ring forms, rug backings, rug hooks, rug needles, scissors, screen process supplies, silver, silversmithing supplies, soldering tools, stencils, sterling silver sheet, stitchery, stone carving, synthetic straw, textile paints, tooling metals, tools, wax, white foam cutters, white foam shapes, wood, woodware, yarns.
Books.
Catalog: $1.
Discount: quantity purchases.
Kits: candlemaking, carving, jewelrymaking, leather craft, mosaic, plastic model, screen processing.

Scale Modeler
7950 Deering Ave.
Canoga Park, CA 91304
213-887-0550
Magazine features how-to instructions and diagrams for model airplanes, cars, miniature figures; lists new products and supply sources.
Magazines: model crafts.
Subscriptions: monthly copy $1.25, 1 year $13.

Scandinavian Rya Rugs
P.O. Box 447
Bloomfield Hills, MI 48013
313-338-1300
Danish embroidery.
Catalog: $1; 3 rya and embroidery brochures, $1.
Kits: pillow, rya rug.

Schacht Spindle Co.
1708 Walnut St.
Boulder, CO 80302
303-443-1133
Belt shuttles, boat shuttles, drop spindles, floor looms, inkle looms, looms, Navajo Indian spindles, rope making machine, table looms, tapestry beaters, tapestry looms, warping boards.
Catalog.

John & Susan Scheewe
Suzie's Tole House
1949 Weissner Dr., N.E.
Salem, OR 97302
503-393-4568
Cast iron, clock movements, decoupage, tilt top tables, tole painting, tole patterns.
Books: design, tole.
Send SASE for information.

Schiltz Goose Farm
Box P
Bancroft, IA 50517
515-885-2435
Goose eggshells.
Catalog.

Schneider's
13021 Poway Rd.
Poway, CA 92064
714-748-3719
Catalog.
Kits: gemstone.

Schober Organ Corp.
43 W. 61st St.
New York, NY 10023
212-586-7552
Catalog.
Kits: electronic organ.

Al Schoellkopf Mold Co.
2730 Lexington Ave. R.T. 42
Mansfield, OH 44904
419-884-3440
Ceramic molds.
Catalog: $1.

School Arts
50 Portland St.
Worcester, MA 01608
617-754-7201
Magazine features arts and crafts from student/teacher viewpoints; instructions on classroom crafts; lists events, exhibits and new product information.
Magazines: general arts and crafts.
Subscriptions: monthly copy $1, 1 year $8.

School Products Co.
312 E. 23rd St.
New York, NY 10010
212-674-7220
Bobbins, cards, fleece, floor looms, inkle looms, linen yarns, looms, reed, Salish looms, Scandinavian yarns, shuttles, spindles, spinning wheels, table looms, tablet looms, tapestry looms, winders.
Catalog.
Discount: quantity purchases.

Schrock's, The House of Hobbies & Crafts
4235 W. Tuscarawas St.
Canton, OH 44708
216-478-1841
Artificial flowers, crewel, decoupage, hooked rug, macrame accessories, needlepoint, pearls, plaster craft, resin craft supplies, samplers, yarns.
Catalog: $1 (refundable).
Kits: rugs-by-number.

Company Listing
Schuller—Sculpture

Jack V. Schuller, Inc.
P.O. Box 420
Park Ridge, IL 60068
312–823–7691
   Diamond compounds, diamond laps, diamond products, lapidary supplies, maple lap compound polishers.
   Kits.
   Price lists available.

Scientific Gas Products
Lakeside Office Park, North Ave.
Wakefield, MA 01880
617–245–8707
   Catalog.
   Kits: fiber optic.

Scientific Models Inc.
340 Synder Ave.
Berkeley Heights, NJ 07922
201–464–7070
   Catalog: 25¢.
   Kits: clipper model, wood ship model.
   Write for local distributor.

Scissortail Arts & Crafts
P.O. Box 1218
Oklahoma City, OK 73112
No phone orders.
   Mini-prints, Old Masters prints, prints.
   Catalog: of prints, 25¢.

Scotch House
950 Geary St.
San Francisco, CA 94109
415–776–6445
   Clan blazer emblems, embroidered family crest emblems, fabrics, tartans, wool clan tartans.
   Catalog: 15¢.

Isabel Scott Fabrics Corp.
133-36 36th Rd.
Flushing, NY 11354
212–353–8400
   Cottons, hand weaving yarns, rayons, wool.
   Write for information.

Scott Scientific Inc.
1900 East Lincoln
Fort Collins, CO 80521
303–484–4706
   Fossils, grits, mineral collections, rock collections, rock tumblers, seashells, tumbling items.
   Catalog.
   Kits: inkle loom craft, rock tumbling.

Screen Process Supplies Mfg. Co.
1199 E. 12th St.
Oakland, CA 94606
415–451–1048
   Screen process supplies, screens.
   Books.
   Kits: screen process.
   Write for information.

Charles Scribner's Sons
597 Fifth Ave.
New York, NY 10017
212–486–4070
   Books: bead craft, crochet, decoupage, needlepoint, plant and flower preserving, plant dyeing.
   Contact your nearest bookstore or write above.
   Write for information.

Sculptmetal Co.
701 Investment Bldg.
Pittsburgh, PA 15222
412–261–5734
   Sculpture supplies.
   Catalog: 25¢.
   Sculpturing medium in paste form with properties of metal.
   Write for local distributor.

Sculpture Associates Ltd.
114 E. 25th St.
New York, NY 10010
212–777–2400
   Armatures, bronze casting-pneumatic equipment, casting accessories, hard stones, kilns, modeling clay, power tools, rare woods, sculpture bases, sculpture pedestals, self-hardening clays, soft stones, stone carving tools, wax, wax melting pot, wax modeling, wood carving tools.
   Books.

112

Company Listing
Sculpture—Sewing

Catalog.
Discount: quantity purchases.

Sculpture House
38 E. 30th St.
New York, NY 10016
212-684-3445

Casting supplies, kilns, modeling clay, power tools, sculpture bases, sculpture pedestals, sculpturing metal, sculpturing stone, self-hardening clays, stone carving tools, wood carving tools.
Catalog.
Kits: sculpture.

Sculpture Services Inc.
9 E. 19th St.
New York, NY 10003
212-254-8585

Casting plastic, fiberglass, metal sculpture tools, modeling clay, modeling equipment, modeling stands, modeling wheels, moulage molding, potter's plasters, potter's wheels, pour-cold mold rubber, resins, rubber, sculpture armatures, sculpture bases, sculpture pedestals, stone carving tools, stones, wood carving tools.
Catalog.
Kits: sculpture.

Sea Novelties
Dana Point, CA 92629
No phone orders.
   Matrix plastic.
   Matrix plastic is used for reproducing the human face or any delicate object.
   Write for information.

Sears, Roebuck & Co.
National Office
925 S. Homan Ave.
Chicago, IL 60607
312-265-2500

Beadery, candle molds, candlemaking supplies, crewel, decoupage, dip film, embroidery frames, leathercraft, macrame accessories, needlecrafts, needlepoint, rug frames, straw-look crafts, yarns.
Books.
Catalog.

Kits: afghan, clock, crochet, knitting, punch hook rug, purse, toy, Christmas ornament.

Henry Seligman Co. Inc.
24 W. 25th St.
New York, NY 10010
212-243-4826

Crochet carrying bags, knitting carrying bags, knitting stands, organizer for needles and hooks, sewing stands.
Kits: needlepoint.
Write for information.

Johnny Sens of New Orleans
4000 D'Hemecourt St.
New Orleans, LA 70119
504-482-1305
   Plastic ceramic molds.
   Catalog: $1.

Sew-Its-Seams
1002 Greenleaf
Wilmette, IL 60091
312-251-4161
Catalog.
Services: needlepoint finishing.

Sewakers Industries Inc.
1619 Grand Ave.
Baldwin, NY 11510
516-333-4334

Graph paper, perforated embroidery paper.
Catalog.
Kits: interchangeable handbag.

The Sewing Bee
261 E. 7th St.
St. Paul, MN 55101
612-222-5528

Decorative trims, knit fabrics, lingerie fabrics, patterns.
Carries patterns at discount prices.
Catalog: plus swatches $1.

Sewing Products Co.
6018 Ridge Ave.
Cincinnati, OH 45213
513-351-6485

Punch needle, rug frames, rugmaking supplies, slipper soles, tote bags.
Catalog.

Company Listing
Shaker—Shuttlecraft

Shaker Workshops Inc.
Box 710, 2 Lexington Rd.
Concord, MA   01742
617-369-1790
> *Catalog: 50¢.*
> Kits: shaker artifacts, shaker furniture, wood paints, wood stains.

Sharon's Petite Sherre
149 Cervantes Rd.
Redwood City, CA   94062
415-366-6534
> Accessories, crochet animals, crochet patterns, crochet pot holders, doll advertisement papers, doll antique photographs, English decoupage prints, knitting patterns, metal frames, old fashioned doll packs, pin cushions, rugs, sock doll, Victorian design gift wrap paper.
> *Catalog: send 2 stamps.*

Robert E. Sharpton
P.O. Box 661
Miami, FL   33156
305-274-0980
> String sculpture, string sculpture patterns.
> *Catalog: $1.*

Shaw Mudge & Co.
51 Manor St.
Stamford, CT   06902
203-327-3132
> Candle scents.
> *Scents include exotic, bouquets, fruity notes, citrus and others.*
> *Write for information.*
> *Write for local distributor.*

H. Shealy
109 Walnut Ridge Rd.
Wilmington, DE   19807
302-654-0457
> *Books: doll house furniture from clothespins & cigar boxes.*

Sheru Bead Boutique Shop
49 W. 38th St.
New York, NY   10018
212-565-0766
> Beadery, beadery accessories.
> *Catalog: 50¢.*
> Kits: bead embroidery, bead-art, beaded fruits, boutique items, rings, sequin roses.
> *Specialists in huge assortments of loose mixed beads by the pound.*

Shil-La Art Gems Inc.
P.O. Box 2770, Grand Central Station
New York, NY   10017
212-581-1298
> Smoky quartz, synthetic stones.
> *Carries faceted and calibrated smoky quartz in round, oval, emerald, octagon and navette shape; and all standard sizes of cut synthetic stones.*
> *Write for information.*

Shillcraft
500 N. Calvert St.
Baltimore, MD   21202
301-539-0430
> Canvas.
> *Catalog: plus wool samples.*
> Kits: hooked rug.

Shipley's Mineral House
Gem Village
Bayfield, CO   81122
303-884-2632
> Cab heaters, casting equipment, lapidary supplies, lapidary tumblers, leather bolo cords, mountings, power tools, wax melting pot.
> *Write for information.*

Ships Unlimited
P.O. Box 32
Morton Grove, IL   60053
312-869-5188
> Model paints, model tools.
> *Catalog: $1.*
> Kits: model ship building, plastic power boats, plastic sail boats, wood power boats, wood sail boats.

Shoenail Supply
Box 2435
Pampa, TX   79065
806-665-8417
> *Books: decorative painting, needlecraft, tole.*

Shuttlecraft
P.O. Box 6041
Providence, RI   02904
401-722-5600

Textile yarns, weaving yarns.
Write for information; sample card, 50¢.

Siderod Shop
P.O. Box 1443
Huntsville, AL 35807
205-837-1990
Model scenery, model tools.
Catalog: $1 (refundable).
Kits: model railroad.

Sig Manufacturing Co., Inc.
401 S. Front St.
Montezuma, IA 50171
515-623-5154
Aircraft kits include classics, old timers, gliders, sailplanes, remote control.
Catalog: $1.
Kits: model aircraft.
Write for your local distributor.

Sign of the Arrow
9740 Clayton Rd.
St. Louis, MO 63124
314-994-0606
Accessories, canvas, needlepoint yarn, rug yarn, yarns.
Catalog: 25¢.
Kits: needlepoint.

Sign of the Times Publishing Co.
407 Gilbert Ave.
Cincinnati, OH 45202
513-421-2050
Books: alphabets and antique alphabets, gold leafing, lettering, screen printing, sign painting.
Contact your nearest bookstore or write above.
Write for information.

Silhouette Custom-Fit Pattern Co.
Box 677
Rye, NY 10580
No phone orders.
Custom-fit computerized patterns.
Pattern catalog.

Silver & Gem Shop
7047 Arkansas
Hammond, IN 46323
219-844-1395
Gold mountings, lapidary equipment, lapidary supplies, polished gemstones, silver mountings.
Write for information.

Silver Shuttle
1301 35th St. N.W.
Washington, DC 20007
202-338-3789
Hand weaving, looms, weaving supplies, yarns.
Books.
Catalog: plus samples $1..

Silvo Hardware Co.
107 Walnut St.
Philadelphia, PA 19106
215-925-4876
Hand tools, power tools.
Catalog: $1.

Simplicity Fashion Magazine
200 Madison Ave.
New York, NY 10016
212-679-3700
Magazine features newest fashion patterns, trims, notions, fabrics and ideas.
Magazines: sewing and fashion.
Subscriptions: tri-annual copy 75¢, 1 year $2, foreign $2.25.

Simplicity Home Catalog
200 Madison Ave.
New York, NY 10016
212-679-3700
Magazine features newest sewing fashions, accessories and fabrics.
Magazines: fabrics, sewing.
Subscriptions: tri-annual copy 75¢, 1 year $2.

Simplicity Young Ideas Catalog
200 Madison Ave.
New York, NY 10016
212-679-3700
Magazine features newest teen fashion patterns.
Magazines: sewing.
Subscriptions: semi-annual copy 75¢, 1 year $1.35.

Sinclair's Auto Miniatures Inc.
3831 W. 12th St.
Eric, PA 16505
814-838-2274

Company Listing
Sinclair's—Smock

Model cars, model racing cars.
Auto kits include vintage type Alfa Romeo, Bentley, MG-TC, Bugatti Royale.
Catalog: $1 (refundable).
Kits: auto delux.

Beryl Sink
808 So. Madison St.
Bloomington, IN 47401
812-332-1190

Books: crochet jewelry, frosting windows, making finger paint, making household glue, making varnish and waterproof cement, making writing ink, show for holiday decorations.
Catalog.

Sinkankas Diamond Products
P.O. Box 201
La Jolla, CA 92037
714-454-2509

Diamond compounds, synthetic diamond powders.
Catalog.
Write for local distributor.

Siphon Art Products
Durable Arts Div.
74 Hamilton Dr.
Ignacio, CA 94947
415-883-9006

Acrylic modifier, batik wax blends, cold process batik textile wax, press block print makers, water soluble leather paints, water soluble textile paints, wax medium.
Write for information.

S. Siracusa
14581 Jefferson St.
Midway City, CA 92655
714-893-7827

Crochet patterns.
Write for information.

Susan Sirkis
281 Bowman Loop
West Point, NY 10996
914-446-2029

China doll, First Ladies fashions, French fashion dolls, miniature dolls, rag dolls, wood dolls.
Books: 19th and 20th century dolls and dollmaking.
Send SASE for information.

Skil-Crafts Division
The Brown Leather Co.
Box 105
Joplin, MO 64801
417-624-4038

Accessories, adhesives, airbrushes, art paper, artist's supplies, balsa wood, beadery, boutique items, braids, carving tools, cleaners, copper enameling supplies, cork, craft knives, crepe paper, decoupage, dyes, engraving tools, etching supplies, firing clay, flocking, flowermaking, glass balls, glass gems, gold paper ornaments, hardware, jewelry findings, laces, lacing, leather tools, leathercraft, mache, magnets, metal finishing, metal tooling, miniatures, music box movements, nonfiring clay, papers, plaster casting, plaster molds, resin casting, resin craft molds, Styrofoam®, transfers, velour, woodware.
Books.
Catalog: $1 (refundable).
Kits: bead, bead loom, jewel decorated purses, leather, silk applique pictures.

Skon
53 Lambert Lane
New Rochelle, NY 10804
914-235-0797

Catalog: rya, $1; embroidery, $2 (refundable with $25 order).
Kits: Swedish rya.
Leaflets: bargello needlecraft, Swedish embroidery.

Smithers Oasis
P.O. Box 118
Kent, OH 44240
216-673-5831

Books: flower crafts.

The Smock Shop
3123 Bransford Rd.
Augusta, GA 30904
404-736-1500

Design plates, patterns.
Books: English smocking.
Write for information.

Smokey Mtn. Rock Shop
P.O. Box 6050, San Carlos Blvd.
Ft. Meyers Beach, FL 33931
813–481–4112

Findings, finished gemstones, lapidary equipment, lapidary machinery, lapidary supplies, mountings, rocks, silver, silversmithing machinery, silversmithing supplies.
Catalog.

Jane Snead Samplers
Box 4909
Philadelphia, PA 19119
215–848–1577

Frames.
Catalog: 20¢.
Kits: pin cushion, sampler.

The Sneak Box Studio
Box 55
Concord, MA 01742
No phone orders.

Paints, wood carving supplies, wood carving tools.
Books.
Catalog: $1.
Leaflets: decoy kits, decoy plans.

Solartherm Co.
P.O. Box 696
Roswell, GA 30075
404–993–0211

Casting block, casting crucibles, gold casting items, jewelrymaking supplies, silver casting items.
Catalog.

Some Place
2990 Adeline St.
Berkeley, CA 94703
415–841–6716

Lacemaking materials, lacemaking tools, rugmaking supplies, spinning supplies, spinning wheels, table looms, weaving supplies, wool rug yarn mill ends.
Books.
Catalog: plus yarn samples, 50¢.

C. W. Somers & Co.
387 Washington St.
Boston, MA 02108
617–426–6880

Casting supplies, gemstones, jewelry findings, jewelrymaking tools.
Write for information.

Elyse Sommer
Box E
Woodmere, NY 11598
516–295–0046

Collage prints, decoupage prints, edgings.
Books: bread dough, burlap, decoupage, jewelry, rock and stone crafts, sewing.
Catalog: plus samples 50¢ and SASE.

South Shore Woman's Exchange
60 South St.
Hingham, MA 02043
617–749–4384

Dollhouse miniatures.
Catalog: $1.

Doris Southard
New Hartford, IA 50660
319–983–2318

Course offers bobbin lacemaking for beginners; include 5 lessons, patterns, Danish bobbins and other supplies.
Home study courses: lacemaking.
Send SASE for information.

Southern Highlands Handicraft Guild
P.O. Box 9145
Asheville, NC 28805
704–298–7928

Books: crafts in the Southern Highlands.
Organization endeavors to conserve, develop and maintain high standards of craftsmanship in the mountain counties of the Virginias, the Carolinas, Kentucky, Tennessee, Georgia, Maryland and Alabama; provides educational and marketing programs; sponsors traveling exhibits and operates craft shops in which members' work is sold; membership includes monthly publication "Highland Highlights".
Organizations: Southern regional crafts guild.
Write for information.

Company Listing
Southern—Squadron

Southern Living Books
P.O. Box 2463
Birmingham, AL 35202
205–870–4440
Books: needlecraft, quilts.

Sparkle Studio
5701 Sheridan Rd.-27J
Chicago, IL 60660
No phone orders.
Crystal miniatures, miniature candlesticks, miniature chandeliers, miniature furniture, miniature lamps.
Catalog: send 2 stamps, or one stamp for information.
Write for many one-of-a-kind items in 1 in. to 1 ft. scale..

Spaulding & Frost Co., Inc.
Fremont, NH 03044
603–895–3372
Unfinished barrels, unfinished kegs, unfinished pails, unfinished unassembled children's furniture.
Kits.
Write for information.

Specialty Products
731 So. Brooks Rd.
Muskegon, MI 49442
616–773–3754
Candlemaking supplies, cooking crystals, copper enameling supplies, dip film, heatless glazing for ceramics, heatless glazing for metals, jewelry findings, lamp frames, plaster casting, resin craft supplies, soap craft, stained glass paints, Styrofoam®.
Books.
Catalog: $1 (refundable).

W. Spencer Inc.
446 Fore St.
Portland, ME 04111
207–773–0552
Candle dyes, candle molds, candle waxes, candle wicks, candlemaking supplies, rubber mold compound.
Catalog: 50¢.

Spencer Gifts Inc.
National Office
1601 Albany Ave.
Atlantic City, NJ 08401
609–345–3141
Carbide tipped engraving tool, felt pens, nylon thread, small weaving looms, woven labels.
Catalog.
Kits: bottle cutter, lamp wiring.
Write for nearest location.

Sperry & Son
605 Main St.
Hyannis, MA 02601
617–775–4833
Needlecraft stand, rug frames, tapestry standing frames.
Write for information.

Spincraft
P.O. Box 332
Richardson, TX 75080
214–235–0864
Carders, hand spinning, spinning wheels.
Kits: hand spinning.
Price list available.

Mildred Sprout
P.O. Box 351
Hawthorne, CA 90250
213–679–3545
Braiders, cloth cutter, hand hooks, rug braiding, rug hooking supplies, threads, wool, yarns.
Books: rugs.
Catalog: 25¢.

The Squadron Shop
23500 John Rd.
Hazel Park, MI 48030
313–548–1390
Metal tanks, model accessories, model cars, plastic tanks.
Carries Japanese and American model aircraft and imported car models.
Kits: scale model.
Write for nearest location.
Write for information.

Stackpole Books
Cameron & Kelker Sts.
Harrisburg, PA 17105
717-234-5091
> Books: gunsmithing, gunstock carving, gunstock finishing, nature crafts, Early American crafts.
> Contact your nearest bookstore or write above.
> Write for information.

Stacy Fabrics Corp.
469 Seventh Ave.
New York, NY 10018
212-239-3300
> Polyamide.
> Catalog.
> Sold by the yard, polyamide is used to fuse fabrics together without sewing; washable, dry cleanable.
> Write for local distributor.

The Stained Glass Club
P.O. Box 244
Norwood, NJ 07648
201-768-7055
> Glass tools, stained glass supplies.
> Catalog: $1; write for information.
> Club offers discounts on stained glass supplies and materials; membership includes 6 issues of "The Glass Workshop".
> Club plans: stained glass.

Standard Ceramic Supply
Box 4435
Pittsburgh, PA 15205
412-923-1655
> Ceramic glazes, ceramic supplies, ceramic tools, chemicals, clays.
> Catalog.

Standard Doll Co.
23-83 31st St
Long Island City, NY 11105
212-721-7787
> Doll accessories, doll arms, doll beads, doll clothes, doll clothes patterns, doll laces, doll making, doll music box movements, doll parts, doll sound boxes, doll voices, dollhouse furniture, dressed dolls, undressed dolls.
> Books: crafts, crochet, doll, doll clothes, knitting.
> Catalog: 25¢.
> Discount: quantity purchases.
> Kits: accessories, doll house.
> Undressed dolls include teen boy and girl, pre-teen, negro and Indian, miniature, toddler, bisque and wood manikin, bisque baby, doll clothes include teenage bridal, everyday, servicemen's uniforms, hats, panties.

Stanley Lapidary Products
503 So. Grand Ave.
Santa Ana, CA 92705
714-542-5783
> Faceting units, lapidary machinery.
> Catalog.
> Write for local distributor.

Kit Stansbury
87 Lewis St.
Phillipsburg, NJ 08865
201-859-4496
> Books: egg decorating, tree-trims.
> Write for information.

Star Diamond Industries
1421 W. 240th
Harbor City, CA 90710
213-325-9696
> Blade flanges, diamond blades, faceting units, gem grinders, gem makers, gem polishers, grinding wheels, jewelry abrasives, jewelry cement, jewelry disks, lapidary equipment, lapidary supplies, lapidary tumblers, lapidary workshops, rock picks, slab saws, trim saws, tumbling accessories, vibrating laps.
> Books.
> Catalog.
> Kits: tumbling.

Star Models
20675 Audette
Dearborn, MI 48124
No phone orders.
> Catalog: 10¢.
> Kits: narrow gauge model railroad passenger car.

Starfire Lapidary
Box 344
Orem, UT 84057
801-224-1020

Company Listing
Starfire—Stohlman

Bansanite, Brazilian quartz, lapidary supplies, tumbled stones, Utah varscite.
Write for information.

Starlite Rock Shop
3413 Starlite Dr.
Dubuque, IA 52001
319-583-4182
   Rock tumblers, tumbler ready rock.
   Write for information.

The L. S. Starrett Co.
Athol, MA 01331
617-249-3551
   Calipers, carpentry tools, jeweler's tools, miniature tools, mosaic cutters, pin vises, steel rules, thickness gauges, tile cutters.
   Catalog.

The Stearns & Foster Co.
11750 Chesterdale Rd., Bldg. 34
Cincinnati, OH 45246
513-827-0700
   Books: quilting.

Stein & Day
Scarborough House
Briarcliff Manor, NY 10510
914-762-2151
   Books: crochet, general arts & crafts series, knitting, macrame, paper puppets and toys.
   Contact your nearest bookstore or write above.
   Write for information.

Sterling Hallmark Co.
4103 Lowden Rd.
Cleveland, OH 44121
216-486-2297
   Sterling silver scrap chips.
   Carries silver scrap chips for casting, melting, silversmithing.
   Write for information.

Sterling Publishing Co. Inc.
419 Park Ave. So.
New York, NY 10016
212-532-7160
   Books: art foam, bead craft, beads macrame, burlap and felt crafts, candlemaking, general arts & crafts series, jewelrymaking, lace making, metal and wire sculpture, nail sculpture, needlepoint, paper crafts, printing, scrap crafts, stained glass, tole painting, trapunto, wood carving, wood cuts.
   Catalog.
   Contact your nearest bookstore or write above.

Stevenson Industries
P.O. Box 5302
Winston-Salem, NC 27103
919-784-9236
   Decoupage, parchment quotes.
   Catalog: $1 (refundable).

Stewart Industries
6520 N. Hoyne Ave.
Chicago, IL 60645
No phone orders.
   Blockprinting, blockprinting papers, blockprinting press, blocks, brayers, Finnish imported plywood, wood.
   Write for information.

Ken Stewart's Gem Shop
220 W. 3rd So.
Salt Lake City, UT 84101
801-355-5246
   Jewelrymaking supplies, silver strip.
   Write for information.

The Stitchery
204 Worcester Tnpk.
Wellesley Hills, MA 02181
617-237-1744
   Needlecraft supplies.
   Catalog: 25¢.
   Kits: crewel embroidery and creative stitchery, needlepoint.

Al Stohlman Leathercraft Home Study Course
Box 791
Fort Worth, TX 76101
817-335-4161
   Course offers basic leather working and carving; membership includes all supplies and tools; students complete 7 leather items; certificate earned upon completion.
   Home study courses: leathercraft.
   Write for information.

A. L. Stone Displays
353 W. 57th St.
New York, NY   10019
212–757–0868

Collector's cases, easels, electrical turntables, Formica® cabinets, holders, Lucite® cabinets, manual battery turntables, metal cabinets, pedestals, plexiglass cabinets, revolvable bases, stands, wood cabinets.
Write for information.

Stonehouse
1916 Freedom Blvd.
Freedom, CA   95019
408–722–2590

Geode cutters, lapidary supplies, lost wax casting materials, slab display racks.
Discount: quantity purchases.
Write for information.

Stop 'N Rock Shop
Tekoa, WA   99033
509–284–4696

Cut stones, faceting equipment, faceting supplies, garnet, garnet cabochons, gemstone rough material.
Write for information.

Straw Into Gold
5509 College Ave.
Oakland, CA   94618
415–654–8359

Accessories, basketry, dyes, mordants, needlecrafts, spinning, weaving supplies, wool, yarns.
Catalog: 25¢.

String Instrument Service Inc.
2300 Payne Ave., Suite 504
Cleveland, OH   44114
216–781–9427

Guitarmaking accessories, imported prefabricated guitar wood.
Write for information.

Struck Corp.
Cedarburg, WI   53012
414–377–3300
Catalog: 50¢.
Kits: build-it-yourself power hacksaw.

Studio D
657 Alma
Palo Alto, CA   94301
415–328–1840

Imported novelties, miniatures.
Catalog.

Studio Twelve
150 Baker St.
Costa Mesa, CA   92626
714–540–9495
Flower looms.
Books.
Catalog.
Kits: stitchery.
Write for local distributor.

Studio Yarn Farms Inc.
10024 14th Ave. S.W.
Seattle, WA   98146
206–763–1310

Automatic knitting machines, computerized knitting machine, sewing machines, yarns.
Books: machine knitting, pattern drafting.
Catalog: general; yarns.

Sturbridge Yankee Workshop
Dept. CH
Brimfield Tnpk.
Sturbridge, MA   01566
617–347–3356

Early American glassware, furniture stains, glass display domes, hardware, paints, unfinished early American furniture, white ironstone ware.
Books: furniture construction.
Catalog: 25¢.
Kits: antiquing, decorating.

Stylecraft of Baltimore
Div. of L. Gordon & Son Inc.
1800 Johnson St.
Baltimore, MD   21230
301–539–4547

Chess set casting compound, chess set molds.
Also has molds for historic, English imported chess sets including Lewis, Oriental Camelot style.
Kits: bottle cutter.

Company Listing
Stylecraft—Supreme

Write for information.
Write for local distributor.

Sudberry House
Wesley Ave.
Westbrook, CT   06498
203-399-9458

Bermuda bag handles, needlecraft designs.
   Kits: crewel handbags, needlepoint handbag.
   Write for information.

Sue's Custom Quilting
P. O. Box 647, 948 S. Armour
Wichita, KS   67201
316-684-5990

Quilter unit, quilting machine.
   Catalog.
   Kits: pillows, quilts.
   Services: needlepoint blocked.

Suncoast Models
Box 785
Black Mountain, NC   28711
704-669-8096

   Catalog: 35¢.
   Kits: buildings, freight cars, freight stations, metal models, model structures, plastic models, wood models.
   Write for local distributor.

Sunflower Crafts
Box 12212
Omaha, NE   68112
402-455-6026

Ceramic oval plaques, ceramic whiteware miniatures, gold finish wire easels, repousse crafts, tole painting, unpainted miniatures.
   Catalog.

Sunray Yarn House
349 Grand St.
New York, NY   10002
212-475-0062

Beadery, crochet accessories, dolls, knitting accessories, rug hooks, yarns.
   Discount: quantity purchases.
   Kits: crochet, knitting, needlepoint.

Sunset House
Sunset Bldg.
Beverly Hills, CA   90213
213-271-2700

Do-it-yourself Christmas ornaments, glass display domes, knitting rings, leather stitcher, plastic display domes, small weaving looms, woodworking tools.
   Books.
   Catalog.
   Kits: crochet ring.

Supreme Handicrafts
Box 395-CB
Sioux Falls, SD   57101
605-336-2227

Art foam, art prints, basketry, bead flowermaking, beadery, candlemaking supplies, chenille, Christmas figures, craft furs, crepe paper, decals, decoupage, dip film, doll parts, draping, fabrics, feathers, floral craft wood fibre, furniture finishes, glass paints, jewelry findings, jewels, leather packs, mache, macrame accessories, magnets, marbles, miniatures, papers, plaster casting, raffia, stains, Styrofoam®, tissue paper, woodburning.
   Catalog: 25¢.
   Kits: biblical banner.

Supreme Watch Material Co.
P.O. Box 4746
Atlanta, GA   30302
404-524-2835

Casting equipment, plating accessories, plating equipment, furnaces, jewelrymaking supplies, melting equipment, mold making equipment, polishing accessories, polishing machines, polishing tools, ring blanks, scales, soldering equipment, watchmaker's tools, wax, wax tools.
   Books.
   Carries several types wax: wax wires, sprue, sheet casting, sticky, water soluble, and all purpose, also has numerous wax tools: carvers, spatulas including electric, lost wax irons, others.
   Catalog: $1.
   Kits: tool.

Surburbia, Inc.
366 Wacouta
St. Paul, MN 55101
612-225-7873
  Gemstone polishers.
  Books: glass cutting.
  Catalog: 25¢.
  Kits: clock, stained glass, Christmas card.

Surma Book & Music Store
11 E. 7th St.
New York, NY 10003
212-477-0729
  Dyes, kistka, wax.
  Kits: Ukrainian egg decorating.
  Write for information.

E. Suydam & Co.
Box 55
Duarte, CA 91010
213-358-8736
  Catalog: building materials, 50¢; intercuban modeling, $1.50.
  Kits: HO scale model building.

Swan-Son
P.O. Box 1257
Murfeesboro, TN 37130
No phone orders.
  Candle molds, craft furs, decoupage, hobby optics, jewelry findings, pearls, plaster molds, resin craft molds, resin craft supplies, string art.
  Catalog.
  Kits: decoupage.

Swanjord Hatchery
Rt. 1
Balaton, MN 56115
507-734-5168
  Blown goose eggs, eggshells.
  Send SASE for information.

Swensons Lapidary Equipment, Inc.
10402 East Apache Trail
Apache Junction, AZ 85220
602-986-4394
  Cutting stones, faceting units, jewelrymaking accessories, jewelrymaking tools, lapidary abrasives, lapidary compounds, lapidary equipment, lapidary supplies, lapidary tools.
  Catalog.

Swest Inc.
P.O. Box 2010, 10803 Composite Dr.
Dallas, TX 75220
214-350-4011
  Casting supplies, combination power tools, findings, jeweler's supplies, jeweler's tools, jeweler's tubing, jeweler's wire, karat gold sheet, precious stones, semi-precious stones, sterling silver sheet.
  Carries power tools for stone setting, florentining, bright-cutting, stippling, carving, burnishing and engraving.
  Catalog: $1 (refundable).

Swest Inc.
118 Broadway, P.O. Box 1298
San Antonio, TX 78295
512-222-0393
  See entry above.

Swest Inc.
1725 Victory Blvd.
Glendale, CA 91201
213-246-8385
  See entry above.

Swiss Bernina, Inc.
34 So. Vine
Hinsdale, IL 60521
312-654-4136
  Sewing machines.
  Features overlocking and stretch stitches, buttonholer and tailor tacks.
  Write for local distributor.

Switched On, Ltd.
1225 W. Mitchell, Suite 221
Milwaukee, WI 53204
414-384-2458
  Catalog.
  Kits: tiffany lamp.
  Tiffany kits come in Renaissance and Gothic styles.

Sandy Symons
Main St.
Ashwood, OR 97711
503-489-3293
  Agates, friend eggs, lapidary cutting

Company Listing
Symons—Tartas

materials, Paulina red moss, pink jasper agate, priday eggs.
Write for information.

Syn-Crer Creations
Box 335
Clinton, MD 20735
301-292-9652

Amethyst, aquamarine, Australian opals, aventurine, beryls, black star sapphire, bloodstone, cabochons, cat's-eye, chrysoberyl, cut stones, diamonds, emeralds, garnet, golden sapphire, green beryl, Indian gemstones, iolite, jasper, jewelrymaking supplies, lapis lazuli, moonstone, moss agate, onyx, opal chips, precious amber, rough stones, rubies, smoky quartz, spinel, star ruby, star sapphires, Taiwan jade, tigereye, tree agates, YAG, zircon.
Catalog.
Discounts.

Tahki Imports, Limited
336 West End Ave.
New York, NY 10023
212-724-7314

Beadery, hooking yarns, knitting yarns, weaving accessories, weaving yarns, yarns.
Books.
Catalog: general; sample yarn cards, $1.

Tainter's Chick Bookshop
Temple, NH 03084
603-878-1758
Services: locates any book.
Write for specific information.

Tektos
Box 6921
Los Angeles, CA 90022
No phone orders.

Lapidary cutting materials, moldavites, Thai Moong Nong-type tektites.
Send stamp for list.

Talisman Crafts
Div. of Harrison Hoge Industries Inc.
104 Arlington
St. James, NY 11780
516-724-8900

Copper wire, gold wire, jewelrymaking supplies, silver wire.
Kits.
Write for information.

Tandy Leather Co.
1001 Foch
Fort Worth, TX 76107
817-335-4161

American Indian crafts, awls, billfold accessories, billfold parts, craft-cuts, garment leathers, key chain parts, knives, lacing, leather additives, leather carving, leather cements, leather dyes, leather linings, leathercraft, macrame beads, macrame cords, mallets, modeling tools, patterns, professional tool sets, punchers, purse hardware, snap setters, stamps, templates, tooling leather, tools.
Books.
Catalog.
Kits: belt, billfold, furniture, gun holsters, handbag, key case, saddles, watchband.
Write for nearest location.

TAP Plastic Inc.
3011 Alvarado St.
San Leandro, CA 94577
415-357-3535

Candle molds, plaster, resins, soap casting.
Catalog.
Write for local distributor.

Taplinger Publishing Co.
200 Park Ave. So.
New York, NY 10003
212-533-6110
Books: bead embroidery, children's crafts, enameling, jewelrymaking, knitting, puppet making, toys.
Contact your nearest bookstore or write above.
Write for information.

Joseph Tartas
1204 Ringwood Ave.
Haskell, NJ 07420
201-835-2368

Jewelrymaking supplies, jewelrymaking tools.

Catalog: 50¢.
Kits: beginner jewelrymaking.

Doris Taylor
715 Fontaine St.
Alexandria, VA 22302
703-836-3831
China painting supplies, pre-mixed china paints.
Books: ceramic painting, china painting.
Write for information.

Taylor Bedding Mfg. Co.
Dept. CC-1, Box 979
Taylor, TX 76574
512-352-6311
Books: quilting.

Taylor House
Bench & Perry St.
Galena, IL 61036
815-777-9114
Beadery, decoupage, die-cut papers, egg accessories, egg stands, fabric braids, findings, gold paper borders, gold paper ornaments, jewels, miniatures, pearls, satin balls, trims, velvet ribbons.
Catalog: 75¢.
Kits.

Technical Specialties International Inc.
487 Elliott W.
Seattle, WA 98119
206-282-0997
Plating equipment, enameling, jewelrymaking supplies, lost wax casting materials, lost wax casting tools, mold making equipment, power tools, silversmithing tools.
Catalog: $1.

Tepping Studio Supply Co.
3003 Salem Ave.
Dayton, OH 45406
513-274-1114
Ceramic glazes, ceramic stains, ceramic supplies, clays, enameling supplies.
Catalog: enameling 50¢; ceramics $1.

Terminal Hobby Shop
4054 N. 34 St.
Milwaukee, WI 53216
414-445-3440
Historical miniature figures, metal modeling materials, model railroad equipment, model tools, plastic modeling materials, wood modeling materials.
Kits: model railroad.
Write for information.

Terra Products
6206 W. Slanson Ave.
Culver City, CA 90230
213-398-6765
Diamond equipment, lapidary supplies.
Catalog.

Textile Crafts
Box 3216
Los Angeles, CA 90028
213-660-4887
Hooking looms, hooking yarns, looms, weaving yarns.
Magazine features hand crafted textiles and weaving; also has listing of textile craftsman who have crafts for sale.
Magazines: textiles and weaving.
Subscriptions: quarterly copy $1.50, 1 year $5.

Textile Crafts
P.O. Box 626
Pacific Grove, CA 93950
408-373-0764
Books: dyeing, general arts & crafts series, spinning, tatting, textile crafts, weaving.
Catalog: 50¢.

Thieves Market
118 A. St. N.W.
Ardmore, OK 73401
405-223-0352
Gold zodiac signs, miniatures.
Send SASE for information.

The Rev. Henry N. Thomas
4493 Thomaston Rd.
Macon, GA 31204
912-743-4277
Leaflets: making gold draped angels.

Company Listing
Thompson—Tinkler

Thomas C. Thompson
1539 Old Deerfield Rd.
Highland Park, IL   60035
312–831–2231
   Enamel colors, kilns.
   Catalog.
   Enameling kit includes kiln.
   Kits: enameling.

The Thread Shed, Inc.
307 Freeport Rd., Aspinwall
Pittsburgh, PA   15215
412–781–4990
   Accessories, embroidery, embroidery fabrics, embroidery threads.
   Books.
   Services: custom-designs.
   Write for information.

Threadneedle
7 E. Palisade Ave.
Englewood, NJ   07631
201–568–2640
   Canvas, Persian yarn, silk yarn.
   Catalog: 50¢.
   Services: custom design needlepoint.

Three Gables Homecrafts
1825 Charleston Beach
Bremerton, WA   98310
206–377–7844
   Ceramic beads.
   Catalog: plus sample bead 20¢.

3 M Company
National Office
Bldg. 224-5W, 3 M Center
St. Paul, MN   55101
612–733–1110
   Lapidary supplies, sandpaper wet or dry.
   Books: boat refinishing, furniture finishing and refinishing.
   Write for local distributor.

Thrift Mailmart
Box 1428, Dept CC
Iverness, FL   32650
904–726–3252
   Doll parts.
   Catalog: 15¢.
   Discount: quantity purchases.
   Doll faces include rabbit, monkey, cat, panda, sweetheart.
   Kits: clown doll sew.

Thumbelina Needlework Shop
1685 Copenhagen Dr.
Solvang, CA   93463
805–688–4136
   Canvas, footstool frames, threads, yarns.
   Books.
   Catalog: 50¢.
   Kits: Danish needlecraft.

Tie Clip Information
P.O. Box 2535
Hialeah, FL   33012
No phone orders.
   Books: making and tying pretied ties.

Tillalla Inc.
Box 484
New York, NY   10021
No phone orders.
   Catalog: Danish rya, & $1; Swedish embroidery, $2 refundable.
   Kits: assorted rya, Scandinavian embroidery.

Timberline Lake Rock Shop
220 N. Hiway 65, Box 188
Lincoln, MO   65338
816–547–3511
   Avalon hematite, lapidary supplies, Missouri Mozarkite stone.
   Write for information.

Times Mirror Magazine
Popular Science--Outdoor Life Book Co.
380 Madison Ave.
New York, NY   10017
212–687–3000
   Books: formulas, home improvement, mechanical movements, repairs, tools, wood finishing, woodworking, workshops.
   Write for information.

Tinkler & Co. Inc.
P.O. Box 17
Norristown, PA   19404
215–539–9198
   Cotton cord, cotton selvages, cotton yarn, jute, roving yarns, synthetic selvages.
   Catalog and samples.

Osma G. Tod Weaving & Lace Studio
319 Mendoza Ave.
Coral Gables, FL   33134
305-444-8843
   Bobbin lacemaking, bobbin winders, creels, Danish bobbins, lace prickers, linen thread, looms, patterns, weaving supplies.
   Books: bobbin lace, weaving.
   Leaflets: instructions on lace and weaving.
   Write for information.

Cheryl Todd
395 Lafayette Ave.
Westwood, NJ   07675
201-664-3350
   Kits: "Granny pin" jewelry.
   Write for information.

Tole 'N Stuff
2043 Nirvana
Eugene, OR   97401
503-345-3665
   Patterns.
   Books: decorative painting, folk art, tole.
   Catalog.

Toolkraft Corp.
Plainfield St.
Chicopee, MA   01013
413-737-3591
   Bench power tools, table saws.

Tools of the Trade
RFD
Fair Haven, VT   05743
518-269-7417
   Floor looms, harness table looms.
   Catalog.

Torrington Rock Shop
Rt. 1, Box 491
Torrington, WY   82240
307-532-5938
   Black jade, lapidary supplies, velvet black jade, Wyoming jade.
   Price list available.

Town & Country Crafts
235 Newark Pompton Tpk.
Pequannock, NJ   07440
No phone orders.
   Animal molds, beadery, bisque eggs, candle molds, candlemaking supplies, cooking crystals, decoupage, decoupage hardware, edgings, metal hand-cast miniatures, miniature ceramic figures, ornament molds, ribbon, spangles, wood panels, woodware.
   Books.
   Catalogs: 50¢; candlemaking 50¢; miniatures & eggery 50¢.
   Kits: jewelry, old inne sign.

Trader South
P.O. Box 231
Dunwoody, GA   30338
No phone orders.
   Citrine, clear quartz, faceting machines, faceting supplies, garnet, lapidary laps, lapidary supplies, Mexican opal, preforms, rose de France amethyst, rough faceting material, slabs, smoky quartz, synthetic stones, topaz, YAG.
   Catalog: 25¢; write for information.
   Club offers gemstone slabs of new and unusual variety each month goldstone, others.
   Club plans: lapidary.

Traditional Norwegian Rosemaling
1506 Lynn Ave.
Marquette, MI   49855
906-226-3931
   Norwegian rosemaling, woodware.
   Books: instructions, patterns.
   Wood decorators catalog 30¢.

Trailcraft Inc.
P.O. Box 606
Concordia, KS   66901
913-243-1313
   Catalog.
   Kits: canoe building, of wood and canvas, or molded fiberglass.

Transart
P.O. Box 9777
Kansas City, MO   64114
816-523-7748

Company Listing
Transart—Turnbull

Cake decorating designs, craft designs, iron-on transfers, leather designs, tole patterns.
Send SASE for information and free sample.

Transworld Trading Co.
565 Fifth Ave.
New York, NY 10017
212-697-8770

Amethyst, emeralds, faceted stones, garnet, opals, precious stones, rough stones, semi-precious stones, tourmaline, YAG.
Price list available.

Trask Plastics
P.O. Box 608
Yermo, CA 92398
No phone orders.

Candle molds, plaster molds, resin craft molds.
Catalog: 50¢.

Treasure Chest
87 Lewis St.
Phillipsburg, NJ 08865
201-859-4496

Magazine features ideas and techniques for egg decorating.
Magazines: eggery.
Subscriptions: quarterly copy $1.50, 1 year $5.

The Treasure Chest
P.O. Box 54, Rt. 40
Havre De Grace, MD 21078
301-939-4468

Agates, aventurine, coconut geodes, gemstone cutting material, jasper, lapidary supplies, malachite, obsidian, rainbow jasper, rhodochrosite, sagenite quartz, sodalite, tumbling stones, wonderstone.
Carries tumbling stones: Mexican agate, lavender jasper, African amethyst, grossularite garnet, other agates, obsidian, blue aventurine.
Write for information.

Treasure of the Pirates, Inc.
7125 Wisconsin Ave.
Bethesda, MD 20034
301-656-3500

Amethyst, cabochons, citrine, faceting stones, gem cutting equipment, gemstones, jewelrymaking equipment, jewelrymaking supplies, lapidary equipment, lapidary supplies, minerals, rocks, Russian synthetic blue quartz, sunstone, topaz.
Carries over 1,000 species of rocks, gems and minerals including gemstones for faceting or cabochons.
Write for information.

Tree Toys
Box 492
Hinsdale, IL 60521
312-325-4043

Quilling paper, quilling supplies.
Books: quilling.
Catalog.
Kits: quilling.

Trojan Press Inc.
310 East 18th Ave.
N. Kansas City, MO 64116
816-221-6477

Books: antique dolls, glass, sewing for dolls.
Write for brochure.

Trowbridge Crafts
Box 278, 4 E. McDonald Rd.
Prospect Heights, IL 60070
312-392-4960

Casting grain, gold sheet, gold wire, jewelrymaking tools, lapidary equipment, lapidary supplies, lost wax casting, silver jewelrymaking, sterling silver sheet, sterling silver wire.

Tumblecraft
5401 James Ave. N.
Minneapolis, MN 55430
612-560-0736

Agate cabochons, agates, garnet, glass cabochons, opal cabochons, quartz crystals, stone mixes, turquoise nuggets.
Catalog: 50¢.

Turnbull Looms
P.O. Box 4296
Mobile, AL 36604
No phone orders.

Floor looms, folding frame loom, harness looms, home built loom.

Catalog.
Kits: metal parts.

M. Turner
22 N. Craig
Lombard, IL 60148
312-627-6855
Corded magnifier.
Books: machine knitting.
Send SASE for information.

Turpen Times
Box 14341
Oklahoma City, OK 73114
405-341-9237
Magazine features original patterns for decorative painters and decoupage work; Americana in flavor.
Magazines: decoupage.
Subscriptions: bimonthly, 1 year $6.

Charles E. Tuttle Co. Inc.
26-30 S. Main St.
Rutland, VT 05701
802-773-8930
Books: furniture restoration, Chinese kites.
Contact your nearest bookstore or write above.
Write for information.

Tuxedo Yarn & Needlework
36-35 Main St.
Flushing, NY 11354
212-539-2900
Beadery, needlepoint, yarns.
Books.
Kits: macrame crewel.
Write for information.

Twenty-five Weekend Build-It Projects
229 Park Ave. South
New York, NY 10003
212-673-1300
Magazine features a variety of do-it-yourself projects, including furniture, games and toys.
Magazines: do-it-yourself projects.
Subscriptions: annual, single copy at newsstands $1.

Twin Peaks Rock Shop
Box 14, Hwy 90 West
Alpine, TX 79830
No phone orders.
Agates, bouquet slabs, lapidary material, plume slabs, steer horns.
Catalog.

Two Brothers Inc.
808 Washington
St. Louis, MO 63101
314-421-0026
Automatic needle threaders, braids, buttons, edgings, lace, rayon towels, trims, unwoven cotton, zippers.
Discount: quantity purchases.
Write for information.

Tye's
2308 N. Main St.
Dayton, OH 45405
513-277-0061
Coin rings, display cards, jewelry findings, jewelrymaking equipment, jewelrymaking supplies, minerals, stones.
Catalog.

U. C. Hobby Center
4079 Governor Dr.
San Diego, CA 92121
714-453-2363
Model decals, model paints.
Catalog: aircraft ships tanks, 70¢, wood ships, $1.50.
Kits: model aircraft, plastic ships, wood ships.

Ukrainian Gift Shop
2422 Central Ave. N.E.
Minneapolis, MN 55418
612-788-2545
Egg craft, Ukrainian items.
Catalog: egg craft supply guide.

Ultra-Violet Products, Inc.
5100 Walnut Grove Ave.
San Gabriel, CA 91778
213-285-3123
Fluorescent lamps, lapidary supplies.
Catalog.
Write for local distributor.

Company Listing
Unger—University

William Unger & Co. Inc.
230 Fifth Ave.
New York, NY 10001
212-532-0689
Books: *crocheting tops and shawls, knitting tops and shawls.*

The Unicorn
Box 645
Rockville, MD 20851
301-881-4770
Books: *applique, batik, brocade and silk velvet weaving, ceramics, colonial lighting, costume, crochet, design, doll making, dyeing, embroidery, glass, jewelrymaking, knitting, knotting, lace and tatting, lacquer painting, macrame, metalwork, netting, quilting, sewing crafts, soft toy making, spinning and weaving, suede sewing, textile printing, tie-dye, woodworking.*
Catalog: 50¢.

Unique Creations
70 S. Chapel St.
Newark, DE 19711
No phone orders.
Lampshade patterns, lampshade supplies.
Books: *lamp shades.*
Catalog: 25¢.

Unique Handicraft
30899 Roosevelt Dr.
Wickliffe, OH 44092
216-944-8881
Also has miniatures, miniature gardens and bonkei for heirloom eggcraft.
Catalog: with instructions $1.

United Abrasive Inc.
910 Brown St.
Norway, MI 49870
906-563-2591
Lapidary supplies, lapidary tools.
Catalog.
Kits: *lapidary tool.*

United Specialties Co.
P.O. Box 39
Newark, CA 94560
415-657-1887
Knitting needle holder.
Knitting needle holder keeps needles upright and has a built-in sizing gauge.
Write for information.

United States Committee for UNICEF
331 East 38th St.
New York, NY 10016
212-686-5522
Books: *making folk toys.*
Catalog.

Universal Strap Co.
P.O. Box 40
Mt. Jackson, WI 53037
414-377-5670
Straps for banding large and small ceramic molds.
Write for information.

Universal Wirecraft Jewelry Co.
Box 88
Vermillion, OH 44089
No phone orders.
Cut stones, jewelrymaking tools, pliers, solderless wire jewelrymaking, vises, wire.
Books.
Carries various wires: 14 kt. solid gold, brass, gold filled, sterling silver, others.
Price list available.

University Circle Publications and Supply Co.
11020 Magnolia Dr.
Cleveland, OH 44106
216-795-4759
Enamel sheeting, painting enamels, textile enamels, tiles.
Books: *enameling, enameling for beginners.*
Catalog.
Kits: *enameling.*

University of Minnesota Press
2037 University Ave., S.E.
Minneapolis, MN 55455
612-373-3266
Books: *sculpturing in wood, sculpturing with a torch.*

Use 'Em Up Creations
4411 Elston Ave.
Chicago, IL 60630
No phone orders.
> Catalog: 10¢.
> Leaflets: plans for quilts from nylon stockings & cotton dresses, poncho and afghans of old fashioned granny squares.

Valley Handweaving Supply
200 W. Olive
Fresno, CA 93728
209-266-0903
> Alpaca, fleece, homespun yarns, looms, mohair yarn, spinning accessories, spinning wheel parts, spinning wheels, yarns.
> Write for information.

Valspar Corp.
200 Sayre
Rockford, IL 61101
815-965-7721
> Books: antiquing, creative book, decoupage, resin craft, woodfinishing.

Van Gelder Wood Products
407 S. Main
Niles, OH 44446
216-652-8970
> Miniature chests, wood boxes, wood turnings.
> Carries wood turnings for lamps, candleholders, stands, tables..
> Services: custom work to order.
> Write for information.

Van Howe Ceramic Supply Co.
11975 E. 40th
Denver, CO 80239
303-371-4030
> Ceramic chemicals, ceramic clays, ceramic glazes, ceramic molds, ceramic supplies, ceramic tools, potter's wheels.
> Catalog: $1.

Van Nostrand Reinhold Co.
450 W. 33rd St.
New York, NY 10001
212-594-8660
> Books: balsa wood, band saws, ceramics, craft anthology, doll clothes, general arts & crafts series, jewelry repair and design, jig saws, knitting, macrame, paper and fabric decorating, pottery, preserved flowers, weaving, Peruvian designs.
> Contact your nearest bookstore or write above.
> Send SASE for information, needlepoint or general catalog.

Vermont Toy Crafts
Rt. 7
Manchester Center, VT 05263
802-362-1524
> Catalog: 25¢.
> Kits: birch doll house, wood toy.

Lillian Vernon
510 S. Fulton Ave.
Mt. Vernon, NY 10550
914-699-8881
> Acrylic felt pens, acrylic items, appliques, flower press, Lucite® mini-easels, metal mini-easels, mini-mosaic frames, patches, sewing machine monogram attachment template, studs.
> Catalog.
> Kits: basket purse, christmas ornaments, grospoint purse, mini-flower pot, needlepoint, shadow-box keepsake.

Veronica
Box 759
Groton, CT 06340
No phone orders.
> Cameo pieces, jewelry stones, unusual beads.
> Catalog: 50¢.

Veteran Leather Co., Inc.
88 University Place
New York, NY 10003
212-691-8070
> Belts, hides, leather lacings, leather scraps, leather tools.
> Catalog.
> Kits: leather.

Vicki's Patience Unlimited
804 Washington Ave.
Huntington, WV 25704
304-522-4933
> Needlepoint supplies, Persian yarn, tapestry yarn.

Company Listing
Vicki's—Wallace

Carries good quality tapestry yarn in 89 colors.
Kits: bargello, hand-painted needlepoint.
Services: made-to-order kits.
Write for information.

Victoria Gifts
12 Water St.
Bryn Mawr, PA   19010
215–525–3493
Catalog.
Kits: cross-stitch samplers, needlecraft.

The Victors
South 1709 Cedar
Spokane, WA   99203
No phone orders.
Books: gem tumbling and baroque jewelry making.
Write for local distributor.

Viking Press
625 Madison Ave.
New York, NY   10022
212–755–4330
Books: ceramics, drawing, general arts & crafts series, jewelrymaking, knitting, mosaics, painting, pottery, weaving.
Contact your nearest bookstore or write above.
Write for information.

Village Art Gallery
Box 236
Destin, FL   32541
904–837–2228
Harness lap loom, New Zealand spinning wheels.
Write for information.

Village Candle & Craft
P.O. Box 486
Marshfield, WI   54449
715–387–1155
Candle accessories, candle additives, candle dyes, candle molds, candle waxes, candleholders, candlemaking supplies, welding tools.
"Surprise assortments" of candlemaking items including samples odd lots, discontinued products catalog: 25¢.
Books: candle crafting, candle dipping, sand casting.
Kits: incense.

Village Designs
P.O. Box 159, Ryder Station
Brooklyn, NY   11234
212–531–9376
Button elevator model, fast basting tool, hem clips, sewing accessories.
Kits: perfect fitting.
Write for information.

The Village Smithy
73 Kensington Rd.
Bronxville, NY   10708
914–337–5351
Handcrafted miniature wrought iron accessories, miniature wrought iron furniture.
Catalog: $1.
Services: custom design in any scale.

Wadsworth Publishing Co., Inc.
10 Davis Drive
Belmont, CA   94002
415–592–1300
Books: crafts design, general arts & crafts series.
Contact your nearest bookstore or write above.
Write for information.

Wagner's Crafts
489 Parkway
Lawrence Park Industrial District
Broomall, PA   19008
215–543–4946
Braids, miniatures, ribbon, sequins, Styrofoam®.
Also has crafts for all holidays.
Write for information.

Mary Wales
Box 1487
San Mateo, CA   94401
415–345–8012
Books: making handbags, shoemaking.

Raymond P. Wallace
77 Orange Rd., Apt. 85
Montclair, NJ   07042
201–744–5405
Carving designs, embroidery designs, leather designs.
Send SASE for specific information.

Wallis Designs
145 Valley View Dr.
South Windsor, CT 06074
203-644-8354
> *Catalog.*
> *Kits: build-it-yourself potter's wheel.*

Walnut Hill Co.
Box 355
Huntingdon Valley, PA 19006
215-947-6613

Adhesive sprays, beeswax, candle accessories, candle dyes, candle hardeners, candle molds, candle scents, candle wicks, candlemaking supplies, decorating accessories, diamond dust, glitter, gloss spray, mold releases, pearl flakes, poof bottles, snow sprays.
> *Catalog: 25¢.*
> *Kits: candle, floater candles, pillar candles, voltive candles.*

Wm. Walthers Inc.
4050 N. 34th St.
Milwaukee, WI 53216
414-445-4060

Decals, historical miniature figures, military miniatures, model bridges, model buildings, model cements, model electrical items, model figures, model interior detail items, model paints, model parts, model power packs, model railroad accessories, model scenery, model scratch building supplies, model signals, model structures, model tools.
> *Books.*
> *Catalog: HO scale, $3; O scale, $2, decal, $1; miniatures, $2.*
> *Kits: freight car, passenger car.*
> *Write for local distributor.*

Wanda's Workshop
Arthur, IA 51431
712-367-2412
> *Patterns.*
> *Books: chenille craft, foilcraft.*
> *Information sheet available.*

Montgomery Ward & Co., Inc.
National Office
541-619 W. Chicago
Chicago, IL 60607
312-467-2000

Buckskin, chains, craft furs, engraving tools, fabrics, fur, hand tools, lapidary equipment, mirror tiles, power tools, quilting, rug frames, rug hoops, scissors, spray guns, suede, table legs, upholstery supplies, welding tools, wet look vinyl, wood carving supplies, yarns.
> *Catalog.*
> *Kits: afghan, lapidary, needlecraft.*
> *Write for nearest location.*

Ward International Inc.
P.O. Box 3628
Granada Hills, CA 91344
213-360-8683

Indo-Pacific sea shells.
> *Write for information.*

Lee Wards
National Office
1200 St. Charles Rd.
Elgin, IL 60120
312-697-3800

Artificial flowers, artificial plants, ballpoint paints, beadery, bottle cutters, boutique trims, candle molds, candlemaking supplies, cotton seamless tubing, craft furs, crewel yarn, crochet yarns, crocheting supplies, decoupage, decoupage hardware, doll parts, embroidery, embroidery blocks, embroidery threads, fabrics, feathers, flowermaking, hardanger, jewelry findings, knitting machines, knitting supplies, knitting yarns, machine yarns, macrame accessories, perforated plastic motifs, precut rug yarn, pre-quilted pieces for embroidering, quilting, quilting frames, resin craft supplies, rhinestones, rug burlap, rug canvas, rug cutters, rug frames, rug hooking supplies, rug hooks, rug yarn, sweater wheels, synthetic straw craft, threads, white foam shapes, woodware, yarn color chart, yarns.
> *Books.*
> *Catalog: general; yarn color chart, 50¢.*
> *Discount: quantity purchases.*
> *Kits: afghan, beading, boutique trim, crewel, cro-*

Company Listing
Wards—Wee

chet, decoupage purse, floral, floral memorials, hanging lamp, knitting, latch hook, macrame, punchwork, rug hooking, stitchery, window shade, wood sculpture, Christmas items.
Write for nearest location.

Lee Wards Christmas Tree Club
1200 St. Charles Rd.
Elgin, IL 60120
312-695-6000

Club offers monthly bontique ornament kits with ends, sequins, braids and other trims.
Club plans: Christmas crafts.
Write for information.

Frederick Warne & Co. Inc.
101 Fifth Ave.
New York, NY 10003
212-675-1151

Books: pottery.
Contact your nearest bookstore or write above.
Write for information.

Warp & Weft
533 North Adams St.
McMinnville, OR 97128
503-472-5760

Magazine features 4 harness weaving with sample swatches and instructions.
Magazines: weaving.
Subscriptions: 1 year $4.50 10 times yearly.

Gary H. Watson
15 Birwood Rd.
Lower Hutt, New Zealand
No phone orders.

Grease wool, hand spinning wool, washed white wool.
Write for information.

Carolyn Watson
302 Southeast Payton
Des Moines, IA 50315
515-285-1053

Precut decoupage designs.
Catalog: plus 4 samples, $1.

Watson-Guptill Publications
One Astor Plaza
New York, NY 10036
212-764-7300

Books: bookbinding, doll making, fabric printing, general arts & crafts series, jewelrymaking, macrame, miniatures, mosaics, paper sculpture, papier mache, plastics, seed collage, soft toymaking, stained glass, weaving and rug weaving.
Contact your nearest bookstore or write above.
Write for information.

Wearden's
P.O. Box 34
Escondido, CA 92025
714-747-3327

California black sea fan coral.
Carries California black sea fan coral in 3 in. to 8 in. high tree-like shapes, pliable when soaked--used for gem tree stems.
Write for information.

Weaver's Gems and Minerals
1871 Chestnut St.
Emmaus, PA 18049
215-967-2547

Carved wood mineral display stands.
Write for information.

A. C. Weber & Co., Inc.
216 North Canal St.
Chicago, IL 60606
312-346-0414

Automatic knitting machines, knitting accessories, patterns.
Also has knitting machine for making a true double knit.
Catalog: 25¢.

Wee Goodies of the Month Club
67 Pomona Ave.
Yonkers, NY 10703
914-968-7616

Club offers miniature for doll houses; no purchase obligation.
Club plans: miniatures.
Send SASE for information.

Wee 3 Sandwich Glass Jewelry
Bourne, MA 02532
617-759-4525

Sandwich glass fragments, singing colors.
Write for information.

G. Weidinger
P.O. Box 5
Cape Coral, FL 33904
813-542-8516

Agates, amethyst, Australian opals, cabochons, chrysocolla, citrine, cut stones, display stands, emeralds, Florida coral, gold filled wire, gold sheet, gold solder, goldstones, jade, jewelry findings, jewelry mountings, jewelrymaking supplies, lapidary equipment, lapidary material, lapidary supplies, lapidary tools, malachite, metallic foil labels, Mexican opal, moonstone, obsidian, polished stones, quartz, rhodochrosite, rhodonite, sterling silver sheet, sterling silver wire, synthetic stones, tigereye, turquoise, zoisite.
Catalog.
Discount: quantity purchases.

Weidinger Inc.
P.O. Box 39
Matteson, IL 60443
312-798-6336

Blades, cutting materials, gold, gold plated items, grits, jewelry findings, jewelry mountings, jewelrymaking equipment, jewelrymaking tools, polishes, sterling silver items.
Catalog.

Weisz Import Export Corp.
15 W. 47th St.
New York, NY 10036
212-582-4065

Amethyst, aquamarine, black onyx, cabochon rough material, citrine, faceted stones, garnet, quartz, rough faceting material, smoky quartz, tourmaline, YAG.
Price lists available.

Wel-Dex Mfg. Co.
Box 10776
Houston, TX 77018
713-682-5681

Arc welding supplies.
Carries arc welder outfits (welds, brazes, solders and cuts), uses standard 1/8 in. rods, 6 welding heats, heavy duty type.
Write for information.

C. R. Wells
P.O. Box 4
Eatontown, NJ 07724
201-222-8909

Chrysoprase, jasper, mixed agates, opals, slabs, wood.
Books: opal.
Carries opals in mixed colors; small, medium and large pieces.
Price list.

Western Tree Cones
1925 S. W. Brookline Dr.
Corvallis, OR 97330
No phone orders.

Candleholders, cones, seed pods, wood roses.
Carries various size and type tree cones including redwood, fir, pine, spruce, hemlock.
Catalog: 45¢.

Westwood Ceramic Supply Co.
14400 Lomitas
City of Industry, CA 91744
213-330-0631

Additives, bamboo handles, ceramic glazes, ceramic stains, ceramic supplies, clays, cork, cork disks, dry clays, glass blowing equipment, kilns, modeling tools, plaster, plaster casting, potter's tools, potter's wheels, pug mills, rattan handles, refractories, spigots, wax.
Books.
General; glass blowing.
Kits: latex rubber mold making.

Whisper Farm Furs
Box 68
Rogers, AR 72756
501-636-4361

Rabbit furs.
Carries rabbit furs in over 40 colors.
Catalog.
Kits: afghans, fur tote bags.

Whistle Stop
3745 E. Colorado
Pasadena, CA 91107
213-796-7791

Model accessories, model railroads.
Carries accessories in O, HO, N and Z scales.

Company Listing
Whistle—Wilton

Kits: model.
Send SASE for information.

Whitson's
30 D, S.W.
Miami, OK 74354
918-542-2383

Also has information on new machine applique methods and patterns.
Books: wall hangings.

Whittemore-Durgin Glass Co.
Box 2065
Hanover, MA 02339
617-871-1743

Aged documents, antique newspapers, beer labels, bottle cutters, cathedral glass, cigar tin labels, copper foil, crushed glass, flux, glass chunks, glass ornaments, glass tools, hat pins, imported glass, ironmongery, jug cutter, lampshade forms, lead came, opal glass, patterns, solder, stained glass, stained glass supplies, wine labels.
Books.
Catalog: 50¢.
Discount: quantity purchases.
Glass items include jewels, prisms, nuggets, animal eyes, zodiac transparent plaques, chandelier jewels, coffee pot tops, ruby arrows, tiffany rondels, opal glass ovals, finals, drops, balls, on wire, brooch stones, doll eyes, vault lights, pushpin heads, fish eyes, black glass noses for animals, door knobs, simulated ice cubes, oblongs, parasol ornaments, ruby semaphores, cabochons, earring stones, rosary beads, typewriter keys. Also has 9000 types of hat pins.

Wichelt Import Co.
R.R. 1
Stoddard, WI 54658
608-788-0961

Brass bell pulls, Norwegian wool yarns, pewter buttons.
Catalog: 50¢.
Kits: Norwegian embroidery, Swedish embroidery.

Wilfred Enterprises
Rt. 2, Box 273A
Englishtown, NJ 07726
201-536-9769

Ceramic bisque, ceramic eggs, miniature ceramic figures.
Kits: doll.
Leaflets: candlemaking, ceramics, dollmaking, plaster casting.
Write for information.

Williams Bros.
181 Pownee St.
San Marcos, CA 92069
714-744-3082

Model aircraft accessories, model scratch building supplies.
Catalog: 25¢.
Kits: engine pipeline parts.
Write for local distributor.

Erica Wilson Correspondence Courses
717 Madison Ave.
New York, NY 10021
212-832-7290

Catalog: $1.
Courses offer crewel, embroidery and needlepoint for beginner's and advanced; includes materials.
Home study courses: embroidery, needlepoint, offers crewel embroidery and needlepoint.

Erica Wilson Needleworks
717 Madison Ave.
New York, NY 10021
212-832-7290

Catalog: $1.
Kits: crewel, needlepoint, original designs.

Erica Wilson's Creative Needlework Society
717 Madison Ave.
New York, NY 10021
212-832-7290

Club offers exclusive needlework designs; kits may be adaptations of famous etchings or Erica Wilson design; announcements sent every 6 months.
Club plans: needlecrafts.
Write for information.

Wilton Enterprises, Inc.
833 W. 115th St.
Chicago, IL 60643
312-785-1144

Books: cake decorating.

Winona Trading Post
P. O. Box 324
Sante Fe, NM 87501
No phone orders.
   American Indian crafts, beadery, bells, bones, feathers, hides.
   Books.
   Catalog: $1.

Winston's Fabrics
P.O. Box 1205
St. Louis, MO 63188
314-421-0040
   Designer fabrics, natural fiber fabrics, pure cottons, pure linens, pure silks, pure velveteens.
   Swatches, 50¢.

Mrs. L. Winum
327 Route 52
Walden, NY 12586
914-774-7692
   Patterns.
   Leaflets: flowers, pillows, slippers, teen doll furniture, toys, wash cloth & felt square projects.
   Send SASE for information.

Sue Wise
1 Renfro Rd.
Somerset, NJ 08873
201-247-6221
   Doll patterns, toy patterns.
   Also has reprints of doll and toy patterns.
   Catalog: 10¢.

Wm. H. Wise & Co. Inc.
336 Mountain Rd.
Union City, NJ 07087
201-864-5200
   Also has shopping guide for craft information for foreign countries.
   Books: handyman's guide.
   Free brochure available.

Jack D. Wolfe Co. Inc.
724 Meeker Ave.
Brooklyn, NY 11222
212-387-3604
   Ceramic supplies, copper enameling supplies, sculpture supplies.
   Catalog: $1.

D. R. Wolfe Overglazes
4165 Barnett St.
Philadelphia, PA 19135
215-338-3963
   China blanks, china brushes, china colors, china painting supplies.
   Catalog.

Woman's Board
North Shore Country Day School
310 Green Bay Rd.
Winnetka, IL 60093
312-446-0674
   Books: needlepoint.

Woman's Day Knit & Stitch
Fawcett Bldg.
Greenwich, CT 06830
203-661-6700
   Magazine features how-to instructions for crochet, crewel, decorative accessories, knitting, needlepoint, sewing, clothes patterns.
   Magazines: needlecrafts.
   Subscriptions: quarterly copy at newsstand 95¢.

Woman's Day Knitting Book
Fawcett Bldg.
Greenwich, CT 06830
203-661-6700
   Magazine features patterns and projects clothing, decorative accessories and children's items.
   Magazines: knitting.
   Subscriptions: quarterly, single copy at newsstand 75¢.

Woman's Day Needlework Ideas
Fawcett Bldg.
Greenwich, CT 06830
203-661-6700
   Magazine features needlecraft how-to's including crewel, crochet, knitting, needlepoint, stitchery and patterns.
   Magazines: needlecrafts.
   Subscriptions: quarterly copy at newsstand 95¢.

Woman's Day 101 Sweaters to Knit and Crochet
Fawcett Bldg.
Greenwich, CT 06830
203-661-6700

Company Listing
Woman's—Wool

Magazine features 101 patterns for knitting and crocheted tops and sportswear for all ages.
Magazines: knitting and crocheting.
Subscriptions: annual copy at newsstand, 75¢.

Woman's Day Sewing & Fashion Ideas
Fawcett Bldg.
Greenwich, CT 06830
203-661-6700

Magazine features patterns, decorative items and accessories for sewing and stitchery.
Magazines: sewing.
Subscriptions: annual copy at newsstand 95¢.

Woman's How-To Book Club
44 Hillside Ave.
Manhasset, NY 10030
516-365-9696

Club offers decorating, crafts and other how-to books; monthly book bulletins sent; must buy at least one selection per year at discount.
Club plans: craft books.
Write for information.

Wonoco Yarn Co.
35 Clay St.
Brooklyn, NY 11222
212-389-1904

Acrylic yarn, angora yarn, wool yarn, yarns.
Books.
Catalog: yarn color card, 50¢.
Kits: crochet, embroidery, knitting.

The Wood Barn
1129 Nottingham
Grosse Pointe Park, MI 48230
313-822-1674

Tinware, unfinished milk cans, wood cutouts.
Books: decorative painting.
Catalog: 25¢.

Wood Projects
229 Park Ave. South
New York, NY 10003
212-673-1300

Magazine features a variety of cabinetry, furniture making and other crafts; information on wood tools and machinery, new trends and projects.
Magazines: woodworking.
Subscriptions: annual copy at newsstand $1.

Woodland Craft Designs
Box C
Hazelhurst, WI 54531
715-356-6101

Crewel embroidery designs, patterns.
Craft design list, 25¢; embroidery design list, 75

Woodshop
P.O. Box 110, Redwood Highway 101 South
Crescent City, CA 95531
707-464-6663

Carving wood, myrtlewood, redwood.
Write for information.

Woodward Ranch
16 Miles South
Alpine, TX 79830
915-364-2271

Lapidary supplies, pompoms, slabs, Texas gem carnelian, Texas moss agate, Texas plumes material.
Carries Texas moss agate in all colors.
Price list available.

Woodworker
229 Park Ave. South
New York, NY 10003
212-673-1300

Magazine features projects for the woodworker-craftsman; also has new product information, tips and tricks for woodworking and use of various tools.
Magazines: woodworking.
Subscriptions: annual copy at newsstand $1.

Wool-Art Studios Inc.
Box 1005
Weston, CT 06880
203-227-8189

Catalog: 25¢.
Kits: crewel.

Wool 'N Wick
1901 N. Morton Ave.
Morton, IL 61550
309-267-7727

Crewel, knitting yarns, needlepoint, rugs.

Company Listing
Wool—Worldwide

Books: knitting Christmas decorations.
Carries both imported and domestic knitting yarns.
Write for information.

Wool Products Ltd.
127 N. Palm Drive
Beverly Hills, CA   90210
No phone orders.
Hand carders, hand-operated wool carding machine.
Write for information.

Woolcraft Ltd.
512 West Hastings
Vancouver 2, B.C., Canada
604–681–4935
Catalog: general; A. Godkin designs, $1; painted canvases $1.
Kits: needlepoint, petitpoint.

W. Wooley & Co.
Box 29-L
Peoria, IL   61601
309–688–2270
Adhesives, candle molds, candle waxes, candle wicks, candlemaking supplies, dyes, fillers, flocking, liquid rubber, molds, paints, plaster, plaster additives, plaster craft, plaster molds, resin craft supplies, vinyl molds.
Books: making plaster and cement molds.
Catalog: 10¢; molds, $1.
Kits: candle, plaster, resin.

The Workbasket
4251 Pennsylvania Ave.
Kansas City, MO   64111
816–531–5730
Magazine features directions for crocheting, knitting and tatting.
Magazines: needlecraft.
Subscriptions: bimonthly copy 25¢, 1 year $1.50.

The Workbench
4251 Pennsylvania Ave.
Kansas City, MO   64111
816–531–5730
Magazine features woodworking, cabinetry do-it-yourself building projects and plans.
Magazines: cabinetry and woodworking.
Subscriptions: bimonthly copy 35¢, 1 year $2.

Workman Publishing Co.
231 East 51st St.
New York, NY   10022
212–421–8050
Books: general arts & crafts series, guide to crafts supplies, potpourri making, soapmaking, toymaking.
Contact your nearest bookstore or write above.
Write for information.

Workshop
Box 31
Redwood Falls, MN   56283
No phone orders.
Home study courses: Norweigian rosemaling learn-along letters.
Send stamp for information.

The Workshop
P.O. Box 158
Pittsford, NY   14534
No phone orders.
Ash splint, cane, reed, restoring materials, rush.
Catalog: 25¢ (refundable).

The World of Stitch 'N Knit
Box 709
Framingham, MA   01701
617–875–5220
Catalog: 25¢.
Kits: crewel, embroidery, needlepoint.

World Organization of China Painters
311 N.W. 19th
Oklahoma City, OK   73107
405–943–3841
Organization endeavors to enlarge and enrich the art; membership is open to students, teachers, craftsmen and interested persons; members receive publication "China Painters".
Organizations: china painting.
Write for information.

Worldwide Curio House
Box 17095
Minneapolis, MN   55417
No phone orders.
Herbs, roots.
Books.

Company Listing
Worldwide—Yarns

Catalog: 25¢.
One of the world's largest listings of herbs and roots.

William E. Wright Co.
South Street
West Warren, MA 01092
413-436-7732
Books: Christmas trims.

Wright's Rock Shop
406 Airport Rd., Hwy. 70
Hot Springs, AR 71901
501-624-6111
Arkansas minerals, cutting materials, quartz, wavellite.
Catalog.

Wrightway Quilting
2675 S. Sante Fe Dr.
Denver, CO 80223
303-778-0092
Catalog.
Services: quilt's made from customer's quilt top, quilting.

Wyco Yarn Co.
814 Greenwood Ave.
Jenkintown, PA 19046
215-884-6881
Crochet accessories, knitting accessories, yarns.
Catalog: 35¢.
Kits: crochet, handbag, knitting, needlecraft.

Yaley Enterprises
129 Sylvester Rd.
So. San Francisco, CA 94080
415-761-3428
Books: candlemaking.
Write for local distributor.

The Yarn Depot
545 Sutter St.
San Francisco, CA 94102
415-362-0501
Canvas, embroidery, looms, macrame cords, needlecraft yarn, rug craft, weaving accessories, weaving frames, weaving yarns.
Books.
Send SASE for information and samples.

The Yarn Dome
1113 E. Main St.
Greenville, OH 45331
513-548-2242
Needlecraft supplies, yarns.
Write for information.

The Yarn Nook
P.O. Box 343
Stoughton, WI 53589
608-873-3555
Bell pull hardware.
Kits: Norwegian needlecraft.
Write for information.

Yarn Primitives
P.O. Box 1013
Weston, CT 06880
203-227-7793
Yarns.
Carries handspun yarns from Greece, Ecuador, Haiti, Bolivia, India and Peru.
Catalog: plus $1.

The Yarn and Soda Shop
Glen Arbor, MI 49636
616-334-3362
Knitting supplies, matching fabrics, yarns.
Books: knitting.
Carries over 200 different yarns.
Yarn samples and refund coupons: $1.

Yarns Galore
2422 Ponce de Leon Blvd.
Coral Gables, FL 33134
305-445-0367
Catalog: 25¢.
Kits: needlepoint.

Yarns Unlimited
Box 1161, 1434 Santa Monica Mall
Santa Monica, CA 90406
213-395-3880
Canvas, embroidery hoops, frames, knitting accessories, rosette winders, rug hooks, weave-it looms, yarns.
Books.
Carries both imported and domestic yarns.
Catalog: $2 (refundable).
Kits: crochet, embroidery.

Yield House
North Conway, NH 03860
603-356-5507
  Dollhouse furniture.
  Catalog: 25¢.
  Kits: furniture.

Z-Handicrafts
Fulford, Quebec, Canada
No phone orders.
  Magazine features designing and drafting weaves; equipment, yarn and marketing information; complete list of back issues available 25¢.
  Magazines: weaving.
  Subscriptions: quarterly, single copy $1.50.

F. C. Ziegler Co.
415 E. 12th St.
Tulsa, OK 74120
918-587-4131
  Frames, mini-easels, prints.
  Catalog: 25¢.
  Kits: embroidery.

Zim's
P.O. Box 7620
Salt Lake City, UT 84107
801-262-5469
  Art foam, artificial fruits, basketry, beadery, boutique trims, burlap, candlemaking supplies, chenille, Christmas decorating items, cooking crystals, craft furs, crepe paper, decoupage, dip film, enameling, fabric paint, fabrics, feathers, felt, flowermaking, foil paper, frames, glass paints, gold leaf, jewelry findings, metal tooling, miniature animals, miniature baskets, miniatures, nylon net, paints, papers, papier mache, plaster casting, raffia, rattan, resin craft supplies, Styrofoam®, transfer pencils, velour paper, velvet, velvet tubing, wood fibre.
  Books.
  Catalog: 50¢.

Zondervan Publishing House
1415 Lake Dr. S.E.
Grand Rapids, MI 49506
616-456-5406
  Books: general arts & crafts series, handicrafts.
  Contact your nearest bookstore or write above.

CRAFT ITEM INDEX

abalone
Biship's House of Gems; M. Nowotny.
abrasive disks
Foredom Electric Co.
abrasive points
Foredom Electric Co.
accessories
Boin Arts & Crafts; Castolite; R. S. Duncan & Co.; Foam Fantasy; Knits'N That Yarn Shop; Merribee; Joan Moshimer; Sharon's Petite Sherre; Sign of the Arrow; Skil-Crafts Division; Straw Into Gold; The Thread Shed, Inc.
acetate
Dick Blick; Plaza Artists Materials, Inc.
acid dyes
Glen Black Handwoven Textiles.
acrylics
Bear Cave.
acrylic felt pens
Lillian Vernon.
acrylic in sheet form
Rohm & Haas Co.
acrylic items
Greentree Ranch Wools, Countryside Handweavers; Lillian Vernon.
acrylic modifier
Siphon Art Products.
acrylic yarn
Wonoco Yarn Co.
additives
Adhesive Products Corp.; Castolite; Westwood Ceramic Supply Co
adhesive sprays
Walnut Hill Co.
adhesives
Art Mart, Inc.; Basic Crafts Co.; Arthur Brown & Bro., Inc.; The Ducketts; Holiday Craft; Skil-Crafts Division; W. Wooley & Co.
adjustable hairpin lace loom
Rosemond Hobbycraft.
adz
Elizabeth R. King.
aerosol finishes
Carnival Arts & Crafts.
afghans
Merribee.
African trading beads
Jewelart Inc.; Jeweler's Emporium.
agate cabochons
Adris Oriental Gem & Art Corp.; Tumblecraft.
agate carnelian
Murray American Corp.
agates
Aspen Lapidary; Biship's House of Gems; Mississippi Petrified Forest; Sandy Symons; The Treasure Chest;

Craft Item Index
Agates—Animal

Tumblecraft; Twin Peaks Rock Shop; G. Weidinger.
aged documents
Whittemore-Durgin Glass Co.
aida
The Hidden Village; Needlecraft Shop Inc.
airbrushes
Badger Air-Brush Co.; Dick Blick; Arthur Brown & Bro., Inc.; Douglas & Sturgess, Inc.; Newton's Potters Supply; Plaza Artists Materials, Inc.; Skil-Crafts Division.
alcohol burners
Gilman's.
alcohol dyes
Fezandie & Sperrle, Inc.
alcohol lamps
Delco Craft Center, Inc.
alexandrite
De Lapa Mining Inc.; International Import Co.
alloyed gold
T. B. Hagstoz & Son.
alpaca
Colonial Textiles; Greentree Ranch Wools, Countryside Handweavers; The Hidden Village; KM Yarn Co.; Valley Handweaving Supply.
alpencarpet
Greentree Ranch Wools, Countryside Handweavers.
alphabet beads
Bead Game; Jewelart Inc.
alphabet stencils
Sax Arts & Crafts.
aluminum
A 'N L's Hobbicraft, Inc.
aluminum circles
St. Louis Crafts Inc.
aluminum enamels
Ceramic Coating Co.
aluminum foils
Delco Craft Center, Inc.
aluminum molds for ornamental concrete
Concrete Machinery Co.
amazonite
Murray American Corp.
amazonite baroques
Jim's Rock Shop.

amber
Purcelli's Gems.
amber agate
M. W. Jackson & Assoc.
American Indian artifacts
Dover Scientific Co.
American Indian bead corn
Crowe & Coulter.
American Indian crafts
Boin Arts & Crafts; Craft Service; Magnus Craft Materials, Inc.; Sax Arts & Crafts; Tandy Leather Co.; Winona Trading Post.
American Indian flower corn
Crowe & Coulter.
American Indian jewelry supplies
Panther International Ltd.
American Indian seed beads
Anne's Treasure Trove; The Beadcraft Corner/Beadcraft Club; Nicole Bead & Craft Co., Inc.
Americana samplers
J. L. T.; Northwest Handcraft House.
amethyst
Aspen Lapidary; Biship's House of Gems; Commercial Mineral Corp.; De Lapa Mining Inc.; Gem-O-Rama, Inc.; Inter-Ocean Trade Co.; International Import Co.; Melbourn Gem Co.; Murray American Corp.; Norlene Lapidary; M. Nowotny; Oceanside Gem Imports, Inc.; Purcelli's Gems; Syn-Crer Creations; Transworld Trading Co.; Treasure of the Pirates, Inc.; G. Weidinger; Weisz Import Export Corp.
andalusite
Commercial Mineral Corp.; De Lapa Mining Inc.; W. D. Hudson, Jr.; International Import Co.; Oceanside Gem Imports, Inc.; Purcelli's Gems.
angora yarn
Wonoco Yarn Co.
aniline dyes
Fezandie & Sperrle, Inc.
animal eyes
Sav-On-Crafts.
animal fossils
Geological Enterprises.
animal molds
Town & Country Crafts.

Craft Item Index
Antique—Australian

antique dolls
The Needle Works.
antique newspapers
Whittemore-Durgin Glass Co.
antiquing
Birchwood Casey; Carnival Arts & Crafts.
anvils
Frank Mittermeier Inc.
Apache tears
Panther International Ltd.
apatite
Norlene Lapidary.
appliques
Leman Publications; Lillian Vernon.
aquamarine
Harry Bookstone; Commercial Mineral Corp.; De Lapa Mining Inc.; Inter-Ocean Trade Co.; International Import Co.; Murray American Corp.; Norlene Lapidary; Oceanside Gem Imports, Inc.; Purcelli's Gems; Syn-Crer Creations; Weisz Import Export Corp.
arbors
Green's Rock & Lapidary Ltd.; Lindell Industries; Lortone Inc.
arc welding supplies
Wel-Dex Mfg. Co.
Arkansas minerals
Wright's Rock Shop.
armatures
Delco Craft Center, Inc.; Plaza Artists Materials, Inc.; Sculpture Associates Ltd.
art foam
Dick Blick; Boin Arts & Crafts; Cleveland Leather Co.; Craft Service; Craftsman Supply House; Delco Craft Center, Inc.; Economy Handicrafts, Inc.; Foam Fantasy; The Handcraft Supply Corp.; Holiday Handicrafts, Inc.; House of Flowers; Hazel Pearson Handi Craft; Sax Arts & Crafts; Supreme Handicrafts; Zim's.
art foam patterns
Don's Hobby Co.
art metal
American Handicrafts.
art metal tools
Sax Arts & Crafts.

art paper
Delco Craft Center, Inc.; Skil-Crafts Division.
art prints
Supreme Handicrafts.
art tape
Economy Handicrafts, Inc.
artificial flowers
Schrock's, The House of Hobbies & Crafts; Lee Wards.
artificial foliage
Boycan's Craft Supplies.
artificial fruits
Zim's.
artificial plants
Lee Wards.
artificial straw
House of Flowers.
artist portfolios
Framaway Co.
artist's dry colors
Fezandie & Sperrle, Inc.
artist's supplies
A 'N L's Hobbicraft, Inc.; Bergen Arts & Crafts, Inc.; Dick Blick; Bob's Arts & Crafts; Boin Arts & Crafts; Arthur Brown & Bro., Inc.; D. M. Campana Co.; Craft Service; Delco Craft Center, Inc.; Kraft Korner; Make It Happen Craft Studio; NASCO Arts & Crafts; Plaza Artists Materials, Inc.; Skil-Crafts Division.
asbestos tile cutters
Beno J. Gundlach Co.
ash splint
The Workshop.
ash tray inserts
Albert Constantine & Son Inc.
asphalt cutters
Beno J. Gundlach Co.
aurora borealis beads
The Beadcraft Corner/Beadcraft Club.
Australian chrysoprase
Australian Imports.
Australian gem rough
Minex Lapidary Supplies.
Australian jade
Interlectric House of Fine Australian Opals.
Australian opals
Australian Exports; Australian Imports;

Craft Item Index
Australian—Batik

Crown Gems Co.; Frank's Jewelry & Gem Shop; Gem-O-Rama, Inc.; Interlectric House of Fine Australian Opals; Walter E. Johansen; Syn-Crer Creations; G. Weidinger.

Austrian angora yarns
Folklorico.

automatic knitting machines
Brother International Corp.; Genie; Knitking; Studio Yarn Farms Inc.; A. C. Weber & Co., Inc.

automatic needle threaders
Two Brothers Inc.

avalon hematite
Timberline Lake Rock Shop.

aventurine
M. Nowotny; Syn-Crer Creations; The Treasure Chest.

aventurine balls
Edwards Jewelry Co.

awls
Hanover House Industries, Inc.; Jewelart Inc.; Tandy Leather Co.

backings for hangings
Coulter Studios.

backings for rya rugs
Coulter Studios.

backstrap (waist) loom
Robert Nelson.

bag handles
Knit Services, Inc.

ball mills
Cole Ceramics Laboratories.

ballpoint paints
Arthur Brown & Bro., Inc.; Budget Buddy Co.; The Handcrafters; Sax Arts & Crafts; Lee Wards.

balls
Diamond-Pro Unlimited.

balsa wood
Bob's Arts & Crafts; Paul K. Guillow Inc.; Sax Arts & Crafts; Skil-Crafts Division.

bamboo
Boin Arts & Crafts.

bamboo beads
The Beadcraft Corner/Beadcraft Club; Pack-O-Fun.

bamboo brushes
Plaza Artists Materials, Inc.

bamboo handles
Minnesota Clay; Paramount Ceramic Inc.; Westwood Ceramic Supply Co.

banded agate
M. W. Jackson & Assoc.

bansanite
Starfire Lapidary.

bantam eggshells
Allegra Milano; Rock Mountain Farm.

bar magnets
Maryland Magnet Co.

barrettes
J. L. T.

bargello
The Needle Works.

barite of roses
Mission Rocks.

baroques
Alessi Lapidary Supplies; Harry Bookstone.

basket tote bags
Helen Gallagher.

basketry
A 'N L's Hobbicraft, Inc.; Atlantic Upholstery Supply Co.; Bergen Arts & Crafts, Inc.; Bersted's; Boin Arts & Crafts; Cane & Basket Supply Co.; Century 21; Craft Service; Craftsman Supply House; Economy Handicrafts, Inc.; Gibsons Creations; The Hidden Village; John's Hardware & Decoupage Supplies; Magnus Craft Materials, Inc.; NASCO Arts & Crafts; Sax Arts & Crafts; Straw Into Gold; Supreme Handicrafts; Zim's.

basswood boxes
O-P Craft Co., Inc.

basswood figures
Country Woodcraft.

batik
Bergen Arts & Crafts, Inc.; Boin Arts & Crafts; Arthur Brown & Bro., Inc.; Craftool Co.; Essayons Studio, Hand Arts Center; Gemex Co.; Magic Circle Corp.; Magnus Craft Materials, Inc.; Joan Moshimer; Hazel Pearson Handi Craft; Sax Arts & Crafts.

batik dyes
Fezandie & Sperrle, Inc.; Northwest Handcraft House.

Craft Item Index
Batik—Bench

batik (instant)
Polyproducts Corp.
batik materials
Rupert, Gibbon & Spider.
batik supplies
Behnsen Silk Screen Supply Ltd.
batik tools
Glen Black Handwoven Textiles; Joan Moshimer.
batik wax
Delco Craft Center, Inc.; Hazel Pearson Handi Craft.
batik wax blends
Siphon Art Products.
bayberry wax
Barker Enterprises.
bead flowermaking
Kit Kraft; Rombins' Nest Farm; Supreme Handicrafts.
bead looms
Bead Game; Nicole Bead & Craft Co., Inc.
bead making
Bob and Carol Oliver.
bead mills
Gilman's.
bead rods
Kay Kinney -Contoured Glass.
beadery
American Handicrafts; P. S. Andrews Co.; Bead Game; The Beadcraft Corner/Beadcraft Club; Beadnik's Arts & Crafts; Bethlehem Imports; Dick Blick; Bob's Arts & Crafts; Boin Arts & Crafts; Boutique Trims; Boycan's Craft Supplies; The Craft Corner; Craft Service; Craftsman Supply House; Creative Craft House; Crowe & Coulter; Delco Craft Center, Inc.; Derby Lane Shell Center; Easy Street; Economy Handicrafts, Inc.; Feather & Flower Craft; Gemex Co.; Gibsons Creations; The Handcrafters; P. C. Herwig Co., Inc.; The Hidden Village; Holiday Craft; House of Flowers; House of Orange; Jeane's; Jewel Creations; Jewelart Inc.; Jeweler's Emporium; Jo-El's Craft Co.; Kaydee; Kaydee Craft Supplies; Kit Kraft; Knit Services, Inc.; Kraft Korner; Macrame and Weaving Supply Co.; Magnus Craft Materials, Inc.; The Mannings Creative Crafts; Mary Maxim Inc.; Modern Craft; New Products Co.; Nicole Bead & Craft Co., Inc.; Ovgem Craft Supply Co.; Hazel Pearson Handi Craft; Sav-On-Crafts; Sax Arts & Crafts; Sears, Roebuck & Co.; Sheru Bead Boutique Shop; Skil-Crafts Division; Sunray Yarn House; Supreme Handicrafts; Tahki Imports, Limited; Taylor House; Town & Country Crafts; Tuxedo Yarn & Needlework; Lee Wards; Winona Trading Post; Zim's.
beadery accessories
The Beadcraft Corner/Beadcraft Club; House of Orange; Jewelart Inc.; Nicole Bead & Craft Co., Inc.; Sheru Bead Boutique Shop.
beadery tools
Jewelart Inc.
beading wax
Nicole Bead & Craft Co., Inc.
beer labels
Whittemore-Durgin Glass Co.
beeswax
Barker Enterprises; Walnut Hill Co.
beggar beads
Adris Oriental Gem & Art Corp.
Belgian linen
Greentree Ranch Wools, Countryside Handweavers.
Belgian yarn
The Hidden Village.
bell pull hardware
The Yarn Nook.
bells
Jewelart Inc.; Jeweler's Emporium; Knit Services, Inc.; Winona Trading Post.
belt buckles
Edwards Jewelry Co.; House of York; Leathercrafters Supply Co.; Macrame and Weaving Supply Co.; The Sandvigs.
belt sanders
American Machine & Tool Co.; Covington Engineering Corp.; Gilman's; Highland Park Manufacturing.
belt shuttles
Schacht Spindle Co.
belts
The Ducketts; Veteran Leather Co., Inc.
bench power tools
Badger Air-Brush Co.; Toolkraft Corp.

Craft Item Index
Bench—Boat

bench top multiuse units
Dremel Creative Power Tools.
Bermuda bag handles
Sudberry House.
beryl zircon
International Import Co.
beryls
International Import Co.; Lochs; Oceanside Gem Imports, Inc.; Purcelli's Gems; Syn-Crer Creations.
billfold accessories
Tandy Leather Co.
billfold parts
Tandy Leather Co.
binders board
Basic Crafts Co.
bird feathers
Herter's, Inc.
ceramic bisque
Crafty Ideas; Wilfred Enterprises.
bisque eggs
Howe Studio; Town & Country Crafts.
ceramic bisque sets
Crafty Ideas.
bisqued ceramic tiles
Newton's Potters Supply.
black agate
M. W. Jackson & Assoc.
black agate nodules
Beaver Canyon Campground.
black jade
Torrington Rock Shop.
black nephrite
Gene's Rock Shop.
black onyx
Weisz Import Export Corp.
black opals
Australian Gem Trading Co.; Geode Industries; International Import Co.
black star sapphire
W. D. Hudson, Jr.; Syn-Crer Creations.
blade flanges
Star Diamond Industries.
blades
Jenkins Lapidary Equipment; Weidinger Inc.
blank greeting cards
Plaza Artists Materials, Inc.
blank gun stocks
Midland Walnut.

blank labels
Althor Products.
block bisque
Diedricks Crafts.
blockprinting
American Handicrafts; Art Mart, Inc.; Bergen Arts & Crafts, Inc.; Dick Blick; Boin Arts & Crafts; Arthur Brown & Bro., Inc.; Craft Service; Delco Craft Center, Inc.; Economy Handicrafts, Inc.; Sax Arts & Crafts; Stewart Industries.
blockprinting dye
Rupert, Gibbon & Spider.
blockprinting papers
Stewart Industries.
blockprinting press
Stewart Industries.
blocks
Stewart Industries.
bloodstone
Adris Oriental Gem & Art Corp.; Dowse's Lapidary Supply, Inc.; M. Nowotny; Panther International Ltd.; Syn-Crer Creations.
bloodstone baroques
Jim's Rock Shop.
bloodstone rough material
Gem Center, U.S.A.
blown goose eggs
Swanjord Hatchery.
blowpipes
Gilman's.
blue agate
Beaver Canyon Campground; M. W. Jackson & Assoc.
blue Australian sapphires
Crown Gems Co.
blue calcite
Panther International Ltd.
blue duck eggshells
Rock Mountain Farm.
blue fire flash moonstone
Minerals & Gems.
blue hen eggshells
Rock Mountain Farm.
blue lace agate
Libra Gems.
blue star sapphire
Gems International.
boat building supplies
M & M Hardwood.

boat shuttles
Schacht Spindle Co.
bobbin lacemaking
Osma G. Tod Weaving & Lace Studio.
bobbin winders
Frederick J. Fawcett, Inc.; Osma G. Tod Weaving & Lace Studio.
bobbins
Alfred Decker; Leclerc Corp.; Charles W. Miller; Robin & Russ Handweavers; School Products Co.
bobwhite eggshells
Rock Mountain Farm.
bolo parts
Jeweler's Emporium.
bolo tie cords
Florida Supply House, Inc.
bolo tie slides
J. W. Day Mfg. Co.; Green's Rock & Lapidary Ltd.
bolo tie tips
Florida Supply House, Inc.
bolsters
Atlantic Upholstery Supply Co.
bonded polyester quilt batts
Putnam Co.
bones
Winona Trading Post.
book cloths
Basic Crafts Co.
book presses
Basic Crafts Co.
botryoidal jade
Gene's Rock Shop.
bottle cutters
American Handicrafts; P. S. Andrews Co.; Bob's Arts & Crafts; Albert Constantine & Son Inc.; Craftsman Supply House; Delco Craft Center, Inc.; Walter Drake; Edmund Scientific Co.; Floyd Fleming; The Handcrafters; Hanover House Industries, Inc.; Kay Kinney - Contoured Glass; J. C. Penney Co., Inc.; Keith Robinson; Lee Wards; Whittemore-Durgin Glass Co.
bottle knotting looms
Gerhardt Macrame Studio.
bouquet slabs
Twin Peaks Rock Shop.
boutique braids
The Putter Shop.
boutique items
Fabulous Holiday House; Holiday Handicrafts, Inc.; Sav-On-Crafts; Skil-Crafts Division.
boutique pendants
Jewelart Inc.
boutique ribbons
Hazel Pearson Handi Craft.
boutique supplies
Gibsons Creations.
boutique trims
Lee Wards; Zim's.
braiders
Berry's of Maine; Mildred Sprout.
braiding chair seats
The Dorr Mill Store.
braiding hangings
The Dorr Mill Store.
braids
Boutique Trims; Country Crafts; Home-Sew Inc.; Knit Services, Inc.; Lace Lady; Mill Store; Hazel Pearson Handi Craft; Skil-Crafts Division; Two Brothers Inc.; Wagner's Crafts.
braids for Battenburg lace
Muriel N. Charney.
brass
T. B. Hagstoz & Son.
brass beads
Bead Game; Macrame and Weaving Supply Co.
brass bell pulls
Wichelt Import Co.
brass foil
St. Louis Crafts Inc.
brass hardware
John's Hardware & Decoupage Supplies.
brass hinges
Boutique Trims; Handcraft Originals.
brass lamp ornaments
Angelo Bros. Co.
brass rings
Flair-Craft Inc.
brass rods
Sax Arts & Crafts.
brass sheets
Sax Arts & Crafts.
brass snap closures
Leathercrafters Supply Co.
brass stands
George W. Park Seed Co., Inc.

Craft Item Index
Brayers—Cabochons

brayers
Stewart Industries.
Brazilian fire agate
Michigan Lapidary Supply Co.
Brazilian gems
Inter-Ocean Trade Co.; Oceanside Gem Imports, Inc.
Brazilian opal
Frank's Jewelry & Gem Shop.
Brazilian quartz
Starfire Lapidary.
Brazilianite
Murray American Corp.
brilliant cut diamonds
Harry Z. Kurs.
British tapestry wool
Greentree Ranch Wools, Countryside Handweavers.
British buckles
Leathercrafters Supply Co.
bronze buckles
Leathercrafters Supply Co.
bronze casting-pneumatic equipment
Sculpture Associates Ltd.
bronze model metal
T. B. Hagstoz & Son.
bronze powder
Carson & Ellis, Inc.; Peg Hall Studios.
brooches
Jeweler's Emporium.
brushes
Peg Hall Studios; Barbara Jones China House; Ohio Ceramic Supply Inc.; Plaza Artists Materials, Inc.; Renaldy's.
buck eggshells
Allegra Milano.
buckles
La Venta Corp.; Leathercrafters Supply Co.; Mac Leather Co.; Pollack's Furrier's Supply Corp.
buckskin
Montgomery Ward & Co., Inc.
bulk opals
Australian Imports.
bulky knit yarns
KeeWai Krafts.
bunka embroidery
House of Flowers.
bunting
Dick Blick.

burlap
Berry's of Maine; Bon Bazar; Cleveland Leather Co.; Craft Yarns of Rhode Island Inc.; Craftsman Supply House; Delco Craft Center, Inc.; Joan Moshimer; Zim's.
burlap rug patterns
John E. Garrett Ltd.
Burma cabochons
Crown Cultured Pearl Corp.
Burma jade (jadeite) jewelry
Crown Cultured Pearl Corp.
burrs
Foredom Electric Co.
butcher's twine
Knit Services, Inc.
butterflies
Arthur Brown & Bro., Inc.; The Collector's Cabinet; House of York; Hazel Pearson Handi Craft.
button backs
Grieger's Inc.
button elevator model
Village Designs.
buttons
Home-Sew Inc.; House of York; Lace Lady; Two Brothers Inc.
cab heaters
Shipley's Mineral House.
cabbers
Exactra-Craft Corp.
cabbing amethyst
Gems International.
cabbing rough
W. D. Hudson, Jr.
cabinet hardware
Craftsman Wood Service Co.
cable cord
Knit Services, Inc.
cabochon gemstones
International Import Co.
cabochon machines
Reed Industries.
cabochon preforms
Elvin.
cabochon rough material
Weisz Import Export Corp.
cabochons
R. C. Baker; Harry Bookstone; Craft House; Crown Cultured Pearl Corp.; Dover Scientific Co.; Ebersole Lapidary

Supply Inc.; Edwards Jewelry Co.; Gemex Co.; Gilman's; Jim's Rock Shop; Walter E. Johansen; Jim Kesterson; Minerals & Gems; Minex Lapidary Supplies; Mission Rocks; Mueller's; Murray American Corp.; Syn-Crer Creations; Treasure of the Pirates, Inc.; G. Weidinger.

cake decorating designs
Transart.

cake decorating molds
General Supplies Co.

cake decorating supplies
Cake Decorators & Craft Supplies; Maid of Scandinavia.

cake decorating tools
General Supplies Co.; Maid of Scandinavia.

cake molds
Cake Decorators & Craft Supplies.

cake tops
Cake Decorators & Craft Supplies.

calf lacing
Leathercrafters Supply Co.

calico blender coverups
The Rusty Nail.

calico can opener coverups
The Rusty Nail.

calico mixer coverups
The Rusty Nail.

calico toaster coverups
The Rusty Nail.

California black sea fan coral
Wearden's.

calipers
The L. S. Starrett Co.

calyx
Sav-On-Crafts.

camel bells
Macrame and Weaving Supply Co.

camel hair
Colonial Textiles; Macrame and Weaving Supply Co.

cameo pieces
Veronica.

cameos
Gemex Co.; Jewelart Inc.; Jeweler's Emporium; Sav-On-Crafts.

Canadian latigo
Leathercrafters Supply Co.

canary eggshells
Rock Mountain Farm.

candle accessories
Celebration Candlemaking Supplies; General Supplies Co.; House of Wood Candles; May-Wal, Inc.; Village Candle & Craft; Walnut Hill Co.

candle additives
Barker Enterprises; Candle Kitchen; Celebration Candlemaking Supplies; Doll's Candle & Craft Supplies; House of Wood Candles; May-Wal, Inc.; Natcol Crafts, Inc.; Pourette Mfg. Co.; Village Candle & Craft.

candle covers
Angelo Bros. Co.

candle dyes
Barker Enterprises; Cake Decorators & Craft Supplies; Candle Kitchen; Candle Mill Village; Candlewic Co.; Celebration Candlemaking Supplies; Craft & Candle House; Doll's Candle & Craft Supplies; May-Wal, Inc.; Natcol Crafts, Inc.; Pourette Mfg. Co.; Pylam Products, Inc.; W. Spencer Inc.; Village Candle & Craft; Walnut Hill Co.

candle hardeners
Walnut Hill Co.

candle molds
Candle Kitchen; Candle Mill Village; Candlewic Co.; Celebration Candlemaking Supplies; Craft & Candle House; Deep Flex Plastic Molds, Inc.; General Supplies Co.; House of Wood Candles; Pourette Mfg. Co.; Sav-On-Crafts; Sax Arts & Crafts; Sears, Roebuck & Co.; W. Spencer Inc.; Swan-Son; TAP Plastic Inc.; Town & Country Crafts; Trask Plastics; Village Candle & Craft; Walnut Hill Co.; Lee Wards; W. Wooley & Co.

candle paints
Bersted's.

candle scents
Barker Enterprises; Beacon Chemical Co., Inc.; Cake Decorators & Craft Supplies; Candle Kitchen; Candle Mill Village; Candlewic Co.; Craft & Candle House; Doll's Candle & Craft Supplies; May-Wal, Inc.; Natcol Crafts, Inc.; Pourette Mfg. Co.; Shaw Mudge & Co.; Walnut Hill Co.

Craft Item Index
Candle—Carpentry

candle waxes
Barker Enterprises; Cake Decorators & Craft Supplies; Candle Kitchen; Candle Mill Village; Craft Service; Doll's Candle & Craft Supplies; House of Wood Candles; Sav-On-Crafts; W. Spencer Inc.; Village Candle & Craft; W. Wooley & Co.

candle wicks
Barker Enterprises; Cake Decorators & Craft Supplies; Craft & Candle House; Doll's Candle & Craft Supplies; Pourette Mfg. Co.; W. Spencer Inc.; Walnut Hill Co.; W. Wooley & Co.

candleholders
Barker Enterprises; Village Candle & Craft; Western Tree Cones.

candlemaking supplies
American Handicrafts; P. S. Andrews Co.; Barker Enterprises; Beacon Chemical Co., Inc.; Bergen Arts & Crafts, Inc.; Bersted's; Bob's Arts & Crafts; Boin Arts & Crafts; Brown's Miniatures; Cake Decorators & Craft Supplies; Candle Kitchen; Candle Mill Village; Candlewic Co.; Celebration Candlemaking Supplies; The Craft Corner; Craftsman Supply House; Creator's Corner; Delco Craft Center, Inc.; Doll's Candle & Craft Supplies; Economy Handicrafts, Inc.; Gemex Co.; General Supplies Co.; The Handcrafters; P. C. Herwig Co., Inc.; Holiday Handicrafts, Inc.; House of Patterns; House of Wood Candles; Kaydee Craft Supplies; Kit Kraft; Magnus Craft Materials, Inc.; Make It Happen Craft Studio; May-Wal, Inc.; Natcol Crafts, Inc.; New Products Co.; Ovgem Craft Supply Co.; Hazel Pearson Handi Craft; J. C. Penney Co., Inc.; Pourette Mfg. Co.; Sav-On-Crafts; Sax Arts & Crafts; Sears, Roebuck & Co.; Specialty Products; W. Spencer Inc.; Supreme Handicrafts; Town & Country Crafts; Village Candle & Craft; Walnut Hill Co.; Lee Wards; W. Wooley & Co.; Zim's.

candy decorating tools
General Supplies Co.

candy making equipment
General Supplies Co.

candy molding
Cake Decorators & Craft Supplies.

cane
A 'N L's Hobbicraft, Inc.; Atlantic Upholstery Supply Co.; Bersted's; Cane & Basket Supply Co.; Albert Constantine & Son Inc.; Craft Service; Delco Craft Center, Inc.; The Handcrafters; Real Woods; Savin Handcrafts; Sax Arts & Crafts; The Workshop.

cane webbing
Albert Constantine & Son Inc.

canvas
Craft Yarns of Rhode Island Inc.; Crossroads; Delco Craft Center, Inc.; The Hidden Village; International Creations; Jerry S. Kaye Assoc.; Leonida Leatherdale's Embroidery Studio; Mary Maxim Inc.; Merribee; The Needlecase; Needlecraft House; Nimble Thimble; Peri's Homework; Plush Point Patterns by Marcia Podell; Sax Arts & Crafts; Shillcraft; Sign of the Arrow; Threadneedle; Thumbelina Needlework Shop; The Yarn Depot; Yarns Unlimited.

canvas panels
Framaway Co.

canvas tape
Needle-Ease.

carbide cutters
Foredom Electric Co.

carbide tipped engraving tool
Spencer Gifts Inc.

carbon tracing paper
Pins & Needles.

carders
Colonial Textiles; Spincraft.

cards
School Products Co.

carnauba wax
Barker Enterprises.

carnelian
Virgil Owens; Panther International Ltd.

carnelian agate gemballs
Anozira Jewelers.

carpentry power tools
American Machine & Tool Co.; Arco Tools Inc.

carpentry tools
Brookstone Co.; The L. S. Starrett Co.

Craft Item Index
Carpet—Cat's-eye

carpet knives
Beno J. Gundlach Co.
carpet round
Greentree Ranch Wools, Countryside Handweavers.
carpet tools
Beno J. Gundlach Co.
carpet warp
Knit Services, Inc.; The Oriental Rug Co.
carved beads
Bethlehem Imports.
carved trims
Albert Constantine & Son Inc.
carved wood mineral display stands
Weaver's Gems and Minerals.
carving blocks
Albert Constantine & Son Inc.; Real Woods.
carving designs
Raymond P. Wallace.
carving drills
Foredom Electric Co.
carving leathers
La Venta Corp.
carving tools
Art Mart, Inc.; Albert Constantine & Son Inc.; M & M Hardwood; Sax Arts & Crafts; Skil-Crafts Division.
carving wood
Art Mart, Inc.; Woodshop.
carvings
Crown Cultured Pearl Corp.
cashmere
Colonial Textiles.
cashmere yarn
The Hidden Village.
cast iron
Rombins' Nest Farm; John & Susan Scheewe.
cast iron brackets
Rombins' Nest Farm.
cast iron candle cups
Rombins' Nest Farm.
cast iron hooks
Rombins' Nest Farm.
cast iron rings
Jeweler's Emporium.
cast iron sconces
Rombins' Nest Farm.

cast metal buckles in antique finishes
Leathercrafters Supply Co.
casting accessories
Kerr Mfg. Co.; Sculpture Associates Ltd.
casting block
Solartherm Co.
casting compounds
Castolite.
casting crucibles
Solartherm Co.
casting epoxy
Bear Cave.
casting equipment
Allcraft Tool & Supply Co.; Bet-Roc Enterprises Inc.; Dick Ells Co.; Gems Galore; Shipley's Mineral House; Supreme Watch Material Co.
casting foam
Bear Cave.
casting grain
Trowbridge Crafts.
casting investment molding material
Kerr Mfg. Co.
casting items
Art Consultants.
casting plastic
Sculpture Services Inc.
casting stone
Delco Craft Center, Inc.
casting supplies
Dick Blick; Dick Ells Co.; Ettl Studios Inc.; Gems Galore; C. R. Hill Co.; J. J. Jewelcraft; Sculpture House; C. W. Somers & Co.; Swest Inc.
casting table racks
Cole Ceramics Laboratories.
casting tables
Air Capitol Molds, Inc.
casting tools
Allcraft Tool & Supply Co.
casting units
Sax Arts & Crafts.
casting waxes
Allcraft Tool & Supply Co.; Delco Craft Center, Inc.
castings
Panther International Ltd.
cat's-eye
Harry Bookstone; International Import Co.; Walter E. Johansen; Syn-Crer Creations.

Craft Item Index
Catches—Ceramic

catches
Albert Constantine & Son Inc.
cathedral glass
Artists & Craftsman Guild; Whittemore-Durgin Glass Co.
cellophane paper
Dick Blick; Arthur Brown & Bro., Inc.; Economy Handicrafts, Inc.; Plaza Artists Materials, Inc.
cements
Delco Craft Center, Inc.; Knit Services, Inc.; Leathercrafters Supply Co.; Sax Arts & Crafts.
centrifugal casting equipment
T. B. Hagstoz & Son.
ceramic armatures
Cole Ceramics Laboratories; Newton's Potters Supply.
ceramic bead trees
Cole Ceramics Laboratories.
ceramic beads
Gloria's Glass Garden; Jewelart Inc.; Macrame and Weaving Supply Co.; Three Gables Homecrafts.
ceramic chemicals
Cole Ceramics Laboratories; Van Howe Ceramic Supply Co.
ceramic clays
Paramount Ceramic Inc.; Van Howe Ceramic Supply Co.
ceramic decals
National Artcraft Supply Co.
ceramic eggs
Wilfred Enterprises.
ceramic glazes
Bergen Arts & Crafts, Inc.; Newton's Potters Supply; Paramount Ceramic Inc.; Sax Arts & Crafts; Standard Ceramic Supply; Tepping Studio Supply Co.; Van Howe Ceramic Supply Co.; Westwood Ceramic Supply Co.
ceramic greenware
Fieldwood Co.
ceramic hardware
Cole Ceramics Laboratories.
ceramic industrial hand cream
Air Capitol Molds, Inc.
ceramic kilns
A 'N L's Hobbicraft, Inc.; A. D. Alpine Inc.; Bergen Arts & Crafts, Inc.; Clay-Crafters Products; Delco Craft Center, Inc.; Newton's Potters Supply; Paragon Industries Inc.; Paramount Ceramic Inc.
ceramic molds
Air Capitol Molds, Inc.; Alberta's Molds Inc.; Anchor Mold Co.; Atlantic Mold Corp.; Clay-Crafters Products; Cramer Mold Shop; Curio Ceramic Molds; Daddy's Mold Shop; Dinky Molds; Holland Mold Inc.; Jamar-Mallory Inc.; Jane's Ceramic Molds; Mindy Molds; Ohio Ceramic Supply Inc.; R & R Ceramic Molds Inc.; Ju Rene Ceramic Molds; Al Schoellkopf Mold Co.; Van Howe Ceramic Supply Co.
ceramic oval plaques
Sunflower Crafts.
ceramic plaques
The Cellar Ceramic Shop.
ceramic power tool
Marcella's Ceramics Inc.
ceramic stains
Tepping Studio Supply Co.; Westwood Ceramic Supply Co.
ceramic stands
Newton's Potters Supply.
ceramic supplies
A 'N L's Hobbicraft, Inc.; A. D. Alpine Inc.; Art Consultants; Art Mart, Inc.; Dick Blick; Blue Grass Art & Hobby Center; Bluebird Manufacturing; Cole Ceramics Laboratories; Delco Craft Center, Inc.; Diedricks Crafts; Economy Handicrafts, Inc.; Essayons Studio, Hand Arts Center; Ettl Studios Inc.; Loretta's Ceramic Studio; Mountain Ceramic Crafts; NASCO Arts & Crafts; Newton's Potters Supply; Ohio Ceramic Supply Inc.; Paramount Ceramic Inc.; Sax Arts & Crafts; Standard Ceramic Supply; Tepping Studio Supply Co.; Van Howe Ceramic Supply Co.; Westwood Ceramic Supply Co.; Jack D. Wolfe Co. Inc.
ceramic tile cutters
Beno J. Gundlach Co.
ceramic tiles
Renaldy's.
ceramic tools
Anne Amiot; Art Consultants; Cole Ceramics Laboratories; Economy Handicrafts, Inc.; Newton's Potters Supply;

Paramount Ceramic Inc.; Standard Ceramic Supply; Van Howe Ceramic Supply Co.
ceramic whiteware miniatures
Sunflower Crafts.
ceramic wisemen
Crafty Ideas.
chains
Green's Rock & Lapidary Ltd.; Jewel Creations; Jeweler's Emporium; Montgomery Ward & Co., Inc.
chalks
American Art Clay Co. Inc.
chamois
Leathercrafters Supply Co.
chasing supplies
William Dixon Co.
Chatham emerald rough
Panther International Ltd.
cheese boards
National Artcraft Supply Co.
chemicals
Minnesota Clay; Richland Ceramics Inc.; Standard Ceramic Supply.
chenille
Dick Blick; Bob's Arts & Crafts; Craftsman Supply House; Don's Hobby Co.; House of Flowers; Hazel Pearson Handi Craft; Sav-On-Crafts; Sax Arts & Crafts; Supreme Handicrafts; Zim's.
chenille boutique trims
Delco Craft Center, Inc.
cherry blocks
Crowe & Coulter.
cherry opals
Andria Bree Gem Co.
cherry wood
Midland Walnut.
chess set casting compound
Stylecraft of Baltimore.
chess set molds
Stylecraft of Baltimore.
children's knitting patterns
Knit-O-Graf Pattern Co.
china blanks
House of Clay China Shop; D. R. Wolfe Overglazes.
china brushes
Ruth Little's Studio; Salyer Publishing Co.; D. R. Wolfe Overglazes.
china colors
D. R. Wolfe Overglazes.
china decals
D. M. Campana Co.
china decorating
Irene Goodwin.
china doll
Susan Sirkis.
china doll parts
Antique Doll Reproductions; Doll Repair Parts, Inc.
china enamels
Salyer Publishing Co.
china lamps
Renaldy's.
china mediums
Salyer Publishing Co.
china painting designs
Bell Studio; Frank Boothe; House of Clay China Shop; Barbara Jones China House; Ruth Little's Studio; J. Opal Stover Studio.
china painting supplies
Anita of Calif.; Dorothy Berryman Studio; Blue Grass Art & Hobby Center; D. M. Campana Co.; The China Cottage; Collector Studies; Gladys Galloway; Holly Studio Inc; Helen Humes Studio; Barbara Jones China House; Darlene Lewis; Ruth Little's Studio; J. Opal Stover Studio; Kenneth Rarick; Renaldy's; Robertson Studio; Salyer Publishing Co.; Doris Taylor; D. R. Wolfe Overglazes.
china silk brocades
Exotic Thai Silks.
china silks
Exotic Thai Silks.
china studies
D. M. Campana Co.
chloromelanite
Jade World/Wilderness Originals.
Christmas boutique items
Holiday Craft.
Christmas decorating items
Beadnik's Arts & Crafts; Fabulous Holiday House; Zim's.
Christmas figures
Supreme Handicrafts.
Christmas tree ornaments
The Putter Shop.

Craft Item Index
Chrysoberyl—Coin

chrysoberyl
W. D. Hudson, Jr.; International Import Co.; Oceanside Gem Imports, Inc.; Purcelli's Gems; Syn-Crer Creations.

chrysocolla
The Jewelry Mart; G. Weidinger.

chrysoprase
Walter E. Johansen; W. L. Maison Opals, Etc.; Murray American Corp.; Purcelli's Gems; C. R. Wells.

chrysoprase rough
Minex Lapidary Supplies.

cigar tin labels
Whittemore-Durgin Glass Co.

cigarette lighter mechanisms
Craft-Mark Products.

circular glaze calculator
Dial-A-Glaze.

circus model equipment
Lyman E. Cox, Scale Trains.

citrine
Commercial Mineral Corp.; De Lapa Mining Inc.; Inter-Ocean Trade Co.; International Import Co.; Norlene Lapidary; Oceanside Gem Imports, Inc.; Trader South; Treasure of the Pirates, Inc.; G. Weidinger; Weisz Import Export Corp.

Civil War prints
Lynchburg Hdwr. & General Store.

clamp-on lamps
Robin & Russ Handweavers.

clamps
Colonial Printing Ink Co.; House of Gould.

clan blazer emblems
Scotch House.

clay beads
Bead Game.

clay carts
A. D. Alpine Inc.

clay containers
Cole Ceramics Laboratories.

clay mixers
Bluebird Manufacturing.

clay molds
Kay Kinney -Contoured Glass.

clays
American Art Clay Co. Inc.; Bob's Arts & Crafts; Boin Arts & Crafts; Cole Ceramics Laboratories; Craft Service; Handcraft House; Minnesota Clay; Ohio Ceramic Supply Inc.; Plaza Artists Materials, Inc.; Richland Ceramics Inc.; Standard Ceramic Supply; Tepping Studio Supply Co.; Westwood Ceramic Supply Co.

cleaners
Leathercrafters Supply Co.; Skil-Crafts Division.

clear quartz
Beaver Canyon Campground; Commercial Mineral Corp.; Trader South.

Clearcreek jadeite
Gene's Rock Shop.

clock accessories
Craftsman Wood Service Co.; H. DeCovnick & Son; Dek-Co Manufacturing Co.

clock dial cutters
Craftsman Wood Service Co.; H. DeCovnick & Son; Dek-Co Manufacturing Co.

clock movements
Atlantic Mold Corp.; Bergen Arts & Crafts, Inc.; Craft Products; Craftsman Wood Service Co.; H. DeCovnick & Son; Diedricks Crafts; Emperor Clock Co.; Minnesota Woodworkers Supply Co.; National Artcraft Supply Co.; Newport Enterprises; Ohio Ceramic Supply Inc.; Hazel Pearson Handi Craft; Plasco; John & Susan Scheewe.

clock patterns
Craft Products.

cloth cutter
Mildred Sprout.

cloth doll patterns
Dorris Dolls.

cloth slitting machines
Frederick J. Fawcett , Inc.

coasters
J. L. T.; Marie Mitchell's Decoupage Center.

coat-of-arms needlepoint
Beard's Art Needlework Studio.

cobbler sandal supplies
Leathercrafters Supply Co.

coconut geodes
The Treasure Chest.

coin rings
Tye's.

cold enameling
Delco Craft Center, Inc.
cold process batik textile wax
Siphon Art Products.
cold water dyes
Artis, Inc.; Glen Black Handwoven Textiles; Creator's Corner; Delco Craft Center, Inc.; Knit Services, Inc.
collage prints
Elyse Sommer.
collar molds
Kay Kinney -Contoured Glass.
collector's cases
A. L. Stone Displays.
colonial heritage collection
Mrs. W. Bradley Ryan.
color parchment posters
Flair-Craft Inc.
colored aluminum foils
St. Louis Crafts Inc.
colored diamond
Industrial Diamond Tool Co. Inc.
colored metal foils
Carl Hepp Mosaic Co.
colored safety pins
Jewelart Inc.
colored sawdust
Carver Co.
combination power tools
Swest Inc.
computerized knitting machine
Brother International Corp.; Studio Yarn Farms Inc.
cones
Boycan's Craft Supplies; Diamond-Pro Unlimited; Driftwood House; Western Tree Cones.
construction paper
Folkcrafts.
cookie stamp sets
Downs.
cooking crystal molds
Hazel Pearson Handi Craft.
cooking crystals
P. S. Andrews Co.; Delco Craft Center, Inc.; Carl Hepp Mosaic Co.; New Products Co.; Hazel Pearson Handi Craft; St. Louis Crafts Inc.; Specialty Products; Town & Country Crafts; Zim's.

copper
Anchor Tool & Supply Co.; Bergen Arts & Crafts, Inc.; T. B. Hagstoz & Son.
copper craft
American Handicrafts.
copper enameling supplies
Alessi Lapidary Supplies; American Handicrafts; Ceramic Coating Co.; Essayons Studio, Hand Arts Center; Kit Kraft; Bob and Carol Oliver; Ovgem Craft Supply Co.; Skil-Crafts Division; Specialty Products; Jack D. Wolfe Co. Inc.
copper foil
Delco Craft Center, Inc.; St. Louis Crafts Inc.; Whittemore-Durgin Glass Co.
copper shapes
Sax Arts & Crafts.
copper tape
Artists & Craftsman Guild.
copper wire
Talisman Crafts.
coral
The Collector's Cabinet; The Freed Co.; International Import Co.; Max of Dallas; Panther International Ltd.
corded magnifier
M. Turner.
cording
Nature's Fibers.
cords
Dick Blick; P. C. Herwig Co., Inc.; Macrame and Weaving Supply Co.
corduroy scraps
Reichert's Fabrics.
cork
Arthur Brown & Bro., Inc.; Cleveland Leather Co.; Craft Service; Craftsman Supply House; Economy Handicrafts, Inc.; The Handcrafters; Magnus Craft Materials, Inc.; NASCO Arts & Crafts; Plaza Artists Materials, Inc.; Sax Arts & Crafts; Skil-Crafts Division; Westwood Ceramic Supply Co.
cork disks
Westwood Ceramic Supply Co.
corks
Cork Products Co. Inc.; Minnesota Clay.

Craft Item Index
Corrugated—Crinoids

corrugated paper
Dick Blick; Boin Arts & Crafts; Plaza Artists Materials, Inc.
corsage making supplies
Dorothy Biddle Service.
corundum boules
Gems Galore.
costume jewelrymaking
Jeweler's Emporium; K42 Rock Shop.
cottolin yarn
The Hidden Village.
cotton blends
Knit Services, Inc.
cotton cord
Creator's Corner; Tinkler & Co. Inc.
cotton crochet yarn
W. B. Roddey.
cotton lace
Home-Sew Inc.; National Artcraft Supply Co.
cotton patchwork quilt squares
House of Lines.
cotton ropes polished
Knit Services, Inc.
cotton seamless tubing
Lee Wards.
cotton selvages
Tinkler & Co. Inc.
cotton threads
The Mail Train.
cotton yarn
Craft Yarns of Rhode Island Inc.; Tinkler & Co. Inc.
cotton-polyester woven scraps
Reichert's Fabrics.
cottons
Contessa Yarns; Isabel Scott Fabrics Corp.
cow horn beads
Bead Game.
cowhair yarns
House of Kleen.
cowhide
Leathercrafters Supply Co.
cowing leather
Leathercrafters Supply Co.
cowry shells
Anne's Treasure Trove.
craft designs
Transart.

craft furs
Deep Flex Plastic Molds, Inc.; The Handcrafters; House of Flowers; Reichert's Fabrics; Sav-On-Crafts; Supreme Handicrafts; Swan-Son; Montgomery Ward & Co., Inc.; Lee Wards; Zim's.
craft knives
Frank Mittermeier Inc.; Skil-Crafts Division.
craft plans
Minnesota Woodworkers Supply Co.
craft sticks
Pack-O-Fun.
craft tissue
Party Bazaar.
craft-cuts
Tandy Leather Co.
crafting equipment
Allcraft Tool & Supply Co.
crazy lace agate
Dowse's Lapidary Supply, Inc.
creels
Osma G. Tod Weaving & Lace Studio.
crepe paper
Dick Blick; Boin Arts & Crafts; Cleveland Leather Co.; Koehler's Craft Outlet; Party Bazaar; Hazel Pearson Handi Craft; Carol Rice Creatives; Skil-Crafts Division; Supreme Handicrafts; Zim's.
crewel
Creativity Needlepoint; The Custom House of Needle Arts & Design; Jeane's; Jerry S. Kaye Assoc.; Merribee; Needlecraft Shop Inc.; Schrock's, The House of Hobbies & Crafts; Sears, Roebuck & Co.; Wool 'N Wick.
crewel embroidery
The Needlecase; J. C. Penney Co., Inc.
crewel embroidery design transfers
Nantucket Needleworks.
crewel embroidery designs
Woodland Craft Designs.
crewel tapestry wall hangings
General Crafts Corp.
crewel wool
The Hidden Village; Needlecraft House.
crewel yarn
Lee Wards.
crinoids
Mission Rocks.

crochet accessories
Sunray Yarn House; Wyco Yarn Co.
crochet animals
Sharon's Petite Sherre.
crochet carrying bags
Henry Seligman Co. Inc.
crochet designs for baby things
Alice Fowler Originals.
crochet doll patterns
Ruth Lukasik.
crochet jewelry
American Handicrafts.
crochet patterns
Brunswick Worsted Mills; Sharon's Petite Sherre; S. Siracusa.
crochet pot holders
Sharon's Petite Sherre.
crochet yarns
Cliveden Yarns; Merribee; Lee Wards.
crocheting supplies
Liveright; Macrame and Weaving Supply Co.; J. C. Penney Co., Inc.; Lee Wards.
crushed glass
American Handicrafts; The Handcrafters; Whittemore-Durgin Glass Co.
crystal miniatures
Sparkle Studio.
crystallized mineral specimens
Nature's Treasures.
crystallizing paint
Edmund Scientific Co.
crystals
The Fluorite Shop; Green's Rock & Lapidary Ltd.; Inter-Ocean Trade Co.; Max of Dallas.
cullets
Drykiln Design.
cultured pearls
Anozira Jewelers; Crown Cultured Pearl Corp.; Liberty Gem & Supply.
curly maple wood
Herter's, Inc.
custom crafted hand tools
King's Studio.
custom rug templates
New Products Co.
custom wood
HERE Inc.
custom-fit computerized patterns
Silhouette Custom-Fit Pattern Co.
custom-made ceramic decals
Art Decal Co.
custom-made lapidary equipment
Reed Industries.
custom-made miniatures
Custom Made Carvings & Miniatures.
custom-made needlepoint patterns
Wm. Hooper.
cut amethyst
Crown Gems Co.
cut aquamarine
Crown Gems Co.
cut chrysoprase
Interlectric House of Fine Australian Opals.
cut gemstones
Harry Bookstone; Crown Gems Co.; Gem-O-Rama, Inc.; Interlectric House of Fine Australian Opals; Lakewood Lapidary; Virgil V. Lundell; Purcelli's Gems.
cut opals
Crown Gems Co.
cut peridot
Crown Gems Co.
cut shells
Derby Lane Shell Center.
cut stones
M & M Distributors; Montana Assay Office; Stop 'N Rock Shop; Syn-Crer Creations; Universal Wirecraft Jewelry Co.; G. Weidinger.
cut turquoise
Crown Gems Co.
cutters
Arthur Brown & Bro., Inc.; Beno J. Gundlach Co.
cutting laps
Walter E. Johansen.
cutting machines
Gilman's; Heritage Hill Patterns; House of Gould; Joan Moshimer.
cutting materials
Weidinger Inc.; Wright's Rock Shop.
cutting stones
Swensons Lapidary Equipment, Inc.
cuttle bone
T. B. Hagstoz & Son.
Dacron® batting
Contemporary Quilts.

Craft Item Index
Dacron—Decoupage

Dacron® sail rigs
Folbot Corp.
daisy looms
Walter Drake.
daisy winder
Rosemond Hobbycraft.
Danish bobbins
Osma G. Tod Weaving & Lace Studio.
Danish embroidery
Scandinavian Rya Rugs.
Danish needlepoint
Mrs. W. Bradley Ryan.
Danish wool
Greentree Ranch Wools, Countryside Handweavers.
decals
America's Hobby Center Inc.; Walter Drake; Hobby Gallery; Salyer Publishing Co.; Supreme Handicrafts; Wm. Walthers Inc.
decorated tinware
Crafts Manufacturing Co.
decorating accessories
Walnut Hill Co.
decorating stains
Crafty Ideas.
decorative foil
Koehler's Craft Outlet.
decorative lamp chain
Angelo Bros. Co.
decorative mounts
Nature's Treasures.
decorative painting designs
Jean's.
decorative patterns
Bernadette Decorative Art.
decorative stamping items
Holly Studio Inc.
decorative trims
The Sewing Bee.
decoupage
A 'N L's Hobbicraft, Inc.; Adventures In Crafts; American Handicrafts; P. S. Andrews Co.; Bergen Arts & Crafts, Inc.; Boin Arts & Crafts; Carson & Ellis, Inc.; Century 21; Corner Cupboard Crafts, Inc.; Deep Flex Plastic Molds, Inc.; Dek-Co Manufacturing Co.; Gemex Co.; The Handcrafters; Harrower House of Decoupage; P. C. Herwig Co., Inc.; Holiday Handicrafts, Inc.; Jeane's; John's Hardware & Decoupage Supplies Kraft Korner; Magnus Craft Materials, Inc.; Make It Happen Craft Studio; Party Bazaar; Hazel Pearson Handi Craft; J. C. Penney Co., Inc.; Sangray Corp.; John & Susan Scheewe; Schrock's, The House of Hobbies & Crafts; Sears, Roebuck & Co.; Skil-Crafts Division; Stevenson Industries; Supreme Handicrafts; Swan-Son; Taylor House; Town & Country Crafts; Lee Wards; Zim's.
decoupage accessories
Century 21.
decoupage boxes
Dek-Co Manufacturing Co.; Harrower House of Decoupage.
decoupage brushes
John's Hardware & Decoupage Supplies.
decoupage decals
Carnival Arts & Crafts.
decoupage designs
Bell Studio; Gladys Galloway; Barbara Jones China House.
decoupage easels
Dek-Co Manufacturing Co.
decoupage finishes
Carnival Arts & Crafts; Century 21; John's Hardware & Decoupage Supplies; Marie Mitchell's Decoupage Center; Hazel Pearson Handi Craft; Ramont's Floral Arts Studio.
decoupage fixatives
Carnival Arts & Crafts.
decoupage foil papers
Harrower House of Decoupage.
decoupage frames
Dek-Co Manufacturing Co.; John's Hardware & Decoupage Supplies.
decoupage glues
Century 21.
decoupage hardware
Harrower House of Decoupage; Marie Mitchell's Decoupage Center; Town & Country Crafts; Lee Wards.
decoupage lap desks
Dek-Co Manufacturing Co.
decoupage mining prints
Ken Prag.
decoupage oil company prints
Ken Prag.

Craft Item Index
Decoupage—Diamond

decoupage plaques
The Cellar Ceramic Shop; Dek-Co Manufacturing Co.; Harrower House of Decoupage.
decoupage posters
Gary Bunting.
decoupage prints
Buck Hill Associates; Carnival Arts & Crafts; Century 21; Marie Mitchell's Decoupage Center; Old Print Center; Elyse Sommer.
decoupage purse handles
Dek-Co Manufacturing Co.
decoupage railroad prints
Ken Prag.
decoupage slat purses
Dek-Co Manufacturing Co.
decoupage stains
Century 21.
decoupage stock certificates prints
Ken Prag.
decoupage stools
Dek-Co Manufacturing Co.
decoupage tools
Harrower House of Decoupage.
decoupage trims
Sax Arts & Crafts.
deerskin
Leathercrafters Supply Co.
demagnetizer
Gilman's.
denim tote bags
The Rusty Nail.
design plates
The Smock Shop.
designer fabrics
Winston's Fabrics.
designs for baby things
Alice Fowler Originals.
devonian hexagonaria colony coral
Quinn Mineral.
diamond abrasives
The Ducketts.
diamond arbors
Gem Tool Specialties.
diamond bar wheel dressers
Gem Tec Diamond Tool Co.
diamond blades
Covington Engineering Corp.; Earth Treasures; Farmers Gem and Rock Shop; Gem Tool Specialties; Star Diamond Industries.
diamond burrs
Gem Tool Specialties.
diamond carvers
Metro Diamond Drill Co.
diamond coated files
Metro Diamond Drill Co.
diamond compounds
Walter E. Johansen; Jack V. Schuller, Inc.; Sinkankas Diamond Products.
diamond cores
Gem Tool Specialties.
diamond crystals
Commercial Mineral Corp.; Panther International Ltd.
diamond disks
Gem Tool Specialties.
diamond drills
Gem Tool Specialties; Geode Industries.
diamond dust
Holiday Craft; Walnut Hill Co.
diamond equipment
Terra Products.
diamond gem maker
Gem Tec Diamond Tool Co.
diamond impregnated core drills
Metro Diamond Drill Co.
diamond lapidaries
Gem Tool Specialties.
diamond laps
Jack V. Schuller, Inc.
diamond machines
Gem Tool Specialties.
diamond pads
Gem Tool Specialties.
diamond points
Gem Tool Specialties.
diamond powders
Aleta's Rock Shop; Gem Tool Specialties; Industrial Diamond Tool Co. Inc.; Walter E. Johansen.
diamond products
Green's Rock & Lapidary Ltd.; Highland Park Manufacturing; Jack V. Schuller, Inc.
diamond saw blades
Highland Park Manufacturing.
diamond saws
Raytech Industries Inc.

Craft Item Index
Diamond—Dollhouse

diamond tools
Gem Tec Diamond Tool Co.; Gem Tool Specialties.

diamond wheels
Diamond-Pro Unlimited; Gem Tec Diamond Tool Co.; Gem Tool Specialties.

diamonds
Biship's House of Gems; Diamond Sales Co.; H & A Mfg. Corp.; International Import Co.; The Jewelry Mart; Syn-Crer Creations.

die-cut papers
Taylor House.

die-cuts
House of Lines.

dies
Gilman's.

diffraction jewels
Edmund Scientific Co.

dimensional plastic shapes
Holiday Craft.

dinosaur bone
Dowse's Lapidary Supply, Inc.

diopside moonstone
Purcelli's Gems.

diopside star
International Import Co.

dip film
A 'N L's Hobbicraft, Inc.; American Handicrafts; Bergen Arts & Crafts, Inc.; Boin Arts & Crafts; Carson & Ellis, Inc.; Cleveland Leather Co.; Craft Service; Craftsman Supply House; Delco Craft Center, Inc.; Economy Handicrafts, Inc.; Gemex Co.; Make It Happen Craft Studio; J. C. Penney Co., Inc.; Sears, Roebuck & Co.; Specialty Products; Supreme Handicrafts; Zim's.

disk magnets
Maryland Magnet Co.

display cards
Tye's.

display domes
Hanover House Industries, Inc.

display stands
G. Weidinger.

do-it-yourself Christmas ornaments
Life-Like Products Inc.; Sunset House.

doll accessories
Doll Repair Parts, Inc.; Dollspart Supply Co., Inc.; Mark Farmer Co., Inc.; Frances La Monica; Standard Doll Co.

doll advertisement papers
Sharon's Petite Sherre.

doll antique photographs
Sharon's Petite Sherre.

doll arms
Standard Doll Co.

doll beads
Standard Doll Co.

doll bisque
Dollspart Supply Co., Inc.

doll clothes
Standard Doll Co.

doll clothes crochet patterns
Virginia Lakin; Mrs. Rossi.

doll clothes knitting patterns
Virginia Lakin; Mrs. Rossi.

doll clothes patterns
Doll Castle News; Mark Farmer Co., Inc.; Standard Doll Co.

doll laces
Standard Doll Co.

doll making
Bob's Arts & Crafts; Standard Doll Co.

doll music box movements
Standard Doll Co.

doll parts
Antique Doll Reproductions; The Beadcraft Corner/Beadcraft Club; Craftsman Supply House; Doll Repair Parts, Inc.; Dollspart Supply Co., Inc.; Hazel Pearson Handi Craft; Sav-On-Crafts; Standard Doll Co.; Supreme Handicrafts; Thrift Mailmart; Lee Wards.

doll patterns
Yvonne Brandon; Dolly Darling Inc.; Ervins; Platypus; Sue Wise.

doll repair items
Dollspart Supply Co., Inc.

doll sound boxes
Standard Doll Co.

doll stands
Downs.

doll voices
Standard Doll Co.

dollhouse accessories
Fieldwood Co.; Joen Ellen Kanze; Frances La Monica; LeMar's Decoupage Center; Miniatures by Marty.

Craft Item Index
Dollhouse—Easels

dollhouse furniture
Davault Miniature Furniture; Mark Farmer Co., Inc.; Rombins' Nest Farm; Standard Doll Co.; Yield House.
dollhouse miniatures
The Doll Cupboard; Lamonica; The Miniature Mart-The Peddler's Shop; South Shore Woman's Exchange.
dollhouse wallpaper
The Miniature Mart-The Peddler's Shop.
dolls
Rombins' Nest Farm; Sunray Yarn House.
domestic feathers
Dersh Feather & Trading Corp.; Hollywood Fancy Feather Co.
domestic hardwoods
Craftsman Wood Service Co.
dops
Walter E. Johansen; A. D. McBurney.
double stick tape
Plaza Artists Materials, Inc.
double woven cotton accessories
J. P. Fliegel Co.
dough craft
Hazel Pearson Handi Craft.
dough art mix
Natcol Crafts, Inc.
dough art patterns
Natcol Crafts, Inc.
dough art tools
Natcol Crafts, Inc.
dough doll heads
Ervins.
dove eggshells
Rock Mountain Farm.
drapery supplies
Atlantic Upholstery Supply Co.
draping
Supreme Handicrafts.
drawing paper
Bergen Arts & Crafts, Inc.
dress form
Harrison-Hoge Ind. Inc.
dressed dolls
Antique Doll Reproductions; Standard Doll Co.
dressed fur pelts
Great Central Fur Corp.

dressmakers pattern graph paper
Dorothy H. Becker.
dressmaking curves
The Needle Works.
dressmaking rulers
The Needle Works.
driftwood
Driftwood House; Dale Magnuson.
driftwood polish
Deb Products.
driftwood wax
Driftwood House.
drill attachments
Arco Tools Inc.
drill presses
American Machine & Tool Co.; Dremel Creative Power Tools.
drop spindles
Colonial Textiles; Schacht Spindle Co.
dry clays
Westwood Ceramic Supply Co.
drying cabinets
Cole Ceramics Laboratories.
drying paper
The Handcraft Supply Corp.
duck eggshells
Bowersox Eggcraft Supplies; Handcraft Originals; Hoffman Hatchery.
Dutch yarn
B & M Yarn Co.
dyes
Berry's of Maine; Castolite; Cleveland Leather Co.; Delco Craft Center, Inc.; Dharma Trading Co.; Handcraft House; The Hidden Village; House of Gould; KM Yarn Co.; Leathercrafters Supply Co.; Magnus Craft Materials, Inc.; The Niddy Noddy; Sax Arts & Crafts; Skil-Crafts Division; Straw Into Gold; Surma Book & Music Store; W. Wooley & Co.
Dylite®
Koehler's Craft Outlet.
Early American glassware
Sturbridge Yankee Workshop.
earring mountings
The Jewelry Mart.
earthenware beads
P. C. Herwig Co., Inc.
easels
Artistry In Wood; Framaway Co.; A. L. Stone Displays.

Craft Item Index
Easter—Embroidery

Easter decorating items
Fabulous Holiday House; The Putter Shop.
ecology shadow boxes
Delco Craft Center, Inc.
edgings
Boutique Trims; Creative Craft House; Lace Lady; The Putter Shop; Elyse Sommer; Town & Country Crafts; Two Brothers Inc.
egg accessories
Rock Mountain Farm; Taylor House.
egg bases
Natalie Originals Studio.
egg blowers
Kaydee.
egg craft
Boutique Trims; Crafty's Backroom; Hoffman Hatchery; Holiday Craft; Kaydee; The Miniature Mart-The Peddler's Shop; Natalie Originals Studio; Ren Ann Crafts; Ukrainian Gift Shop.
egg cutter attachment
Loosie Goosie Egg Craft Shop.
egg decorating supplies
Gail's Decorative Arts Studio.
egg hardware
Carnival Arts & Crafts.
egg marker
The Egg Shell.
egg stands
A 'N L's Hobbicraft, Inc.; Boutique Trims; Country Crafts; Gail's Decorative Arts Studio; Howe Studio; Taylor House.
eggshells
Rock Mountain Farm; Swanjord Hatchery.
Egyptian cotton thread
Robin & Russ Handweavers.
elastics
Home-Sew Inc.; Kieffer's Lingerie Fabric & Supplies.
electric bobbin winders
Robin & Russ Handweavers.
electric carver
Green's Rock & Lapidary Ltd.
electric kilns
Cole Ceramics Laboratories; Diedricks Crafts.

electric lapidary equipment
Lapidabrade Inc.
electric lehrs
A. D. Alpine Inc.
electric model motors
James Bliss & Co. Inc.
electrical parts
National Artcraft Supply Co.
electric potter's wheels
Cole Ceramics Laboratories.
electric punch rug hook
KM Yarn Co.; Needlecraft Shop Inc.
electric tools
Bear Cave.
electric tufting
The Hidden Village.
electrical turntables
A. L. Stone Displays.
electric wax spatula
Green's Rock & Lapidary Ltd.
plating accessories
C. R. Hill Co.; Supreme Watch Material Co.
plating equipment
Supreme Watch Material Co.; Technical Specialties International Inc.
electroplated mountings
J. J. Jewelcraft.
electroplating supplies
William Dixon Co.
electroplating tools
William Dixon Co.
electrostatic flocking
Rub 'N Buff.
embossed pewter buttons
Downs.
embroidered appliques
Embroideries Unlimited.
embroidered family crest emblems
Scotch House.
embroidery
The Handcrafters; The Hidden Village; Jerry S. Kaye Assoc.; Needlecraft Shop Inc.; The Thread Shed, Inc.; Lee Wards; The Yarn Depot.
embroidery blocks
Lee Wards.
embroidery charts
Needlecraft Shop Inc.

embroidery designs
House of Patterns; Raymond P. Wallace.

embroidery fabrics
Leonida Leatherdale's Embrodery Studio; Needlecraft House; The Thread Shed, Inc.

embroidery frames
Crossroads; KAY an EE Corp. of America; Mary Maxim Inc.; Merribee; Sears, Roebuck & Co.

embroidery hoops
Crossroads; KAY an EE Corp. of America; Mary Maxim Inc.; Merribee; Needlecraft House; Yarns Unlimited.

embroidery linen
Jerry S. Kaye Assoc.

embroidery materials
Easy Street.

embroidery scissors
Polly Chester Inc.

embroidery threads
Crossroads; Frederick J. Fawcett, Inc.; Folklorico; Leonida Leatherdale's Embroidery Studio; The Mail Train; Merribee; Nantucket Needleworks; Needlecraft House; The Thread Shed, Inc.; Lee Wards.

embroidery transfer patterns
Crewel Elephant.

emerald beads
Adris Oriental Gem & Art Corp.

emeralds
Adris Oriental Gem & Art Corp.; De Lapa Mining Inc.; Diamond Sales Co.; H & A Mfg. Corp.; W. D. Hudson, Jr.; International Import Co.; Murray American Corp.; Syn-Crer Creations; Transworld Trading Co.; G. Weidinger.

enamel colors
Thomas C. Thompson.

enamel sheeting
University Circle Publications and Supply Co.

enameling
A 'N L's Hobbicraft, Inc.; Allcraft Tool & Supply Co.; Art Mart, Inc.; Bergen Arts & Crafts, Inc.; Cleveland Leather Co.; Craft Service; Delco Craft Center, Inc.; Economy Handicrafts, Inc.; The Handcrafters; Kraft Korner; Magnus Craft Materials, Inc.; J. C. Penney Co., Inc.; Technical Specialties International Inc.; Zim's.

enameling kilns
A 'N L's Hobbicraft, Inc.; Bergen Arts & Crafts, Inc.; Craft Service.

enameling supplies
Anchor Tool & Supply Co.; William Dixon Co.; Tepping Studio Supply Co.

enameling tools
William Dixon Co.

enamels
C. R. Hill Co.

English decoupage prints
Sharon's Petite Sherre.

English kip
Leathercrafters Supply Co.

English war-game figures
Miniature Figurines--USA, Inc.

English yarns
R. S. Duncan & Co.

engraving
Allcraft Tool & Supply Co.; Bergen Arts & Crafts, Inc.; Craftsman Supply House; Sax Arts & Crafts.

engraving blocks
Frank Mittermeier Inc.

engraving chisels
Frank Mittermeier Inc.

engraving equipment
Prospector's Pouch.

engraving tools
Bergen Arts & Crafts, Inc.; Dremel Creative Power Tools; Beno J. Gundlach Co.; Miles Kimball; Skil-Crafts Division; Montgomery Ward & Co., Inc.

enstatite
Murray American Corp.

epidote
Panther International Ltd.

epoxy adhesives
Beacon Chemical Co., Inc.

epoxy glues
High Strength Adhesives Corp.

epoxy resins
High Strength Adhesives Corp.; Polyproducts Corp.

etching supplies
Art Mart, Inc.; Arthur Brown & Bro., Inc.; Craft Service; Craftsman Supply House; William Dixon Co.; Economy

Craft Item Index
Etching—Felt

Handicrafts, Inc.; The Handcrafters; St. Louis Crafts Inc.; Sax Arts & Crafts; Skil-Crafts Division.

etching tools
William Dixon Co.

European miniature figures
Natalie Originals Studio.

evil-eye beads
Bead Game.

exotic minerals
The Collector's Cabinet.

eye loupes
Gemological Institute of America.

fabric braids
Taylor House.

fabric dyes
Joan Moshimer.

fabric paint
Boin Arts & Crafts; House of Patterns; Zim's.

fabrics
Barnes & Blake; Crossroads; Eagle Mill; Economy Handicrafts, Inc.; Exotic Thai Silks; Heritage Hill Patterns; The Hidden Village; Homespun Fabrics; International Creations; The Mail Train; Mary Maxim Inc.; Merribee; Nantucket Needleworks; Hazel Pearson Handi Craft; Sax Arts & Crafts; Scotch House; Supreme Handicrafts; Montgomery Ward & Co., Inc.; Lee Wards; Zim's.

facet grade flourite
Beaver Canyon Campground.

facet heads
Covington Engineering Corp.

facet laps
Covington Engineering Corp.

facet preforms
Lee Lapidaries.

facet units
Lee Lapidaries.

faceted beads
The Beadcraft Corner/Beadcraft Club; Jim Kesterson.

faceted garnets
Anozira Jewelers.

faceted gemstones
De Lapa Mining Inc.; Dover Scientific Co.; International Import Co.; Minerals & Gems.

faceted stones
Biship's House of Gems; The Ducketts; Gemex Co.; Gilman's; Jim's Rock Shop; Michigan Lapidary Supply Co.; Mueller's; Transworld Trading Co.; Weisz Import Export Corp.

faceter's trim slab saw
A. D. McBurney.

faceting amethyst
Gems International.

faceting equipment
Jim's Rock Shop; Lochs; Stop 'N Rock Shop.

faceting instruments
Exactra-Craft Corp.; MDR Mfg. Co., Inc.

faceting machines
Geode Industries; Henry B. Graves Co.; Walter E. Johansen; Trader South.

faceting stones
Treasure of the Pirates, Inc.

faceting supplies
Brad's Rock Shop; The Ducketts; Walter E. Johansen; Stop 'N Rock Shop; Trader South.

faceting units
Aleta's Rock Shop; Farmers Gem and Rock Shop; Gilman's; Industrial Diamond Tool Co. Inc.; Stanley Lapidary Products; Star Diamond Industries; Swensons Lapidary Equipment, Inc.

factory cutaway fabrics
Cutaway.

fast basting tool
Village Designs.

feather craft
Craftsman Supply House; Creative Craft House.

feathers
Bead Game; Boycan's Craft Supplies; Gemex Co.; The Hidden Village; Koehler's Craft Outlet; Mangrove Feather Co., Inc.; Hazel Pearson Handi Craft; Supreme Handicrafts; Lee Wards; Winona Trading Post; Zim's.

felt
American Handicrafts; P. S. Andrews Co.; Boin Arts & Crafts; Cleveland Leather Co.; Commonwealth Felt Co.; The Craft Corner; Craft Service; Craftsman Supply House; Delco Craft Center,

Inc.; Economy Handicrafts, Inc.; The Handcrafters; Holiday Handicrafts, Inc.; House of Flowers; Magnus Craft Materials, Inc.; Mary Maxim Inc.; Merribee; Hazel Pearson Handi Craft; Sav-On-Crafts; Zim's.

felt appliques
Home-Sew Inc.

felt mill ends
Eastern Mills.

felt pens
Art Mart, Inc.; Dick Blick; Arthur Brown & Bro., Inc.; Spencer Gifts Inc.

felt remnants
Commonwealth Felt Co.; House of Lines.

felt vinyl
Dick Blick.

ferns
Arthur Brown & Bro., Inc.

fetishes heishe
Panther International Ltd.

fiber optics
Boin Arts & Crafts; Edmund Scientific Co.

fiberglass
Adhesive Products Corp.; Polyproducts Corp.; Sculpture Services Inc.

fiberglass cloth
Castolite; High Strength Adhesives Corp.; Kick-Shaw Inc.

fiberglass mat
High Strength Adhesives Corp.; Kick-Shaw Inc.

fiberglass molds
Plycrete Mold Co.

fiberglass plaques
Plycrete Mold Co.

fibers
Clems and Clems Spinning Wheels.

figure draping
Hazel Pearson Handi Craft.

filigree beads
Jewelart Inc.

filigree paper lace
P. S. Andrews Co.

filigrees
Boutique Trims; Gibsons Creations; Holiday Craft.

fillers
Adhesive Products Corp; Castolite; W. Wooley & Co.

finch eggshells
Rock Mountain Farm.

findings
The Beadcraft Corner/Beadcraft Club; Ebersole Lapidary Supply Inc.; Fabulous Holiday House; Feather & Flower Craft; Frostline; Gemex Co.; Gems Galore; Gibsons Creations; Gilman's; Gordon's; Green's Rock & Lapidary Ltd.; Grieger's Inc.; C. R. Hill Co.; House of Flowers; Jewelart Inc.; Jeweler's Emporium; Jim's Rock Shop; K42 Rock Shop; Kaydee Craft Supplies; Kit Kraft; Leathercrafters Supply Co.; Smokey Mtn. Rock Shop; Swest Inc.; Taylor House.

fine silver casting grains
H. A. Cole.

finished gemstones
Smokey Mtn. Rock Shop.

finishers
Highland Park Manufacturing.

finishing supplies
Homecraft Veneer.

Finnish imported plywood
Stewart Industries.

fire agate
Crown Gems Co.; M. Nowotny.

fire cut agate
Crown Gems Co.

fire opals
International Import Co.

firey astrilite
Walter E. Johansen.

firing clay
American Art Clay Co. Inc.; Arthur Brown & Bro., Inc.; Delco Craft Center, Inc.; Plaza Artists Materials, Inc.; Sax Arts & Crafts; Skil-Crafts Division.

firing enamel
Boin Arts & Crafts.

First Ladies fashions
Susan Sirkis.

fittings
King's Studio.

flat chenille
Greentree Ranch Wools, Countryside Handweavers.

Craft Item Index
Flat—Foil

flat laps
Gilman's.
flat plastic shapes
Holiday Craft.
flax line fiber
Frederick J. Fawcett , Inc.
flax straw (retted)
Frederick J. Fawcett , Inc.
fleece
Colonial Textiles; Greentree Ranch Wools, Countryside Handweavers; The Hidden Village; KM Yarn Co.; The Makings; The Niddy Noddy; School Products Co.; Valley Handweaving Supply.
fleece wool
KeeWai Krafts.
flexible brass settings
E. H. Ashley & Co., Inc.
flexible curve ruler
Arthur Brown & Bro., Inc.
flexible magnetic strips
Maryland Magnet Co.
flexible shaft machines
Gems Galore.
flint paper
Arthur Brown & Bro., Inc.; Plaza Artists Materials, Inc.
flocked fruit
Sav-On-Crafts.
flocking
Dick Blick; Boin Arts & Crafts; Arthur Brown & Bro., Inc.; Craft Service; Skil-Crafts Division; W. Wooley & Co.
floor hoops
KAY an EE Corp. of America.
floor looms
The Hidden Village; House of Yarn & Crafts; KAY an EE Corp. of America; Schacht Spindle Co.; School Products Co.; Tools of the Trade; Turnbull Looms.
floor tile cutters
Beno J. Gundlach Co.
floral clay
American Art Clay Co. Inc.
floral craft
Florida Supply House, Inc.; House of Flowers; Koehler's Craft Outlet; Hazel Pearson Handi Craft; Ramont's Floral Arts Studio; Sav-On-Crafts.

floral craft wood fibre
Supreme Handicrafts.
floral prints
John's Hardware & Decoupage Supplies.
floral tape
Sav-On-Crafts.
floral tools
Hazel Pearson Handi Craft.
floral wire
Sav-On-Crafts.
Florida coral
G. Weidinger.
flower arrangement supplies
Dorothy Biddle Service.
flower drying agents
Creator's Corner.
flower looms
Craftsman Supply House; Delco Craft Center, Inc.; Hanover House Industries, Inc.; Hazel Pearson Handi Craft; Sav-On-Crafts; Studio Twelve.
flower press
The Handcraft Supply Corp.; Lillian Vernon.
flower wax cutters
Doll's Candle & Craft Supplies.
flowermaking
Craft Service; Craftsman Supply House; Delco Craft Center, Inc.; Holiday Handicrafts, Inc.; Kit Kraft; Skil-Crafts Division; Lee Wards; Zim's.
flowermaking supplies
Dorothy Biddle Service; Don's Hobby Co.
fluffs feathers
Dersh Feather & Trading Corp.
fluid solder
Lox-Seal Adhesives.
fluorescent agate
M. W. Jackson & Assoc.
fluorescent lamps
Ultra-Violet Products, Inc.
fluorescent paper
Arthur Brown & Bro., Inc.
flux
Barbara Lawshe; Panther International Ltd.; Whittemore-Durgin Glass Co.
foil
Boin Arts & Crafts; Craftsman Supply House; Economy Handicrafts, Inc.; The Handcrafters; Barbara Lawshe.

Craft Item Index
Foil—Garment

foil craft
  Bob's Arts & Crafts.
foil etching
  Cleveland Leather Co.
foil paper
  Dick Blick; Gibsons Creations; Zim's.
foil prints
  Carnival Arts & Crafts.
folding floor harness looms
  Norwood Loom Co.
folding frame loom
  Robert Nelson; Turnbull Looms.
folding precision scissors
  Carter Associates.
foot-operated looms
  Kessenich Looms.
footstool frames
  Thumbelina Needlework Shop.
foreign gem rough
  Minex Lapidary Supplies.
foreign model railroad accessories
  Amro.
foreign model railroad trains
  Amro.
Formica® cabinets
  A. L. Stone Displays.
fossils
  The Collector's Cabinet; Colorado Geological Industries Inc.; Dover Scientific Co.; The Fluorite Shop; Green's Rock & Lapidary Ltd.; Scott Scientific Inc.
frames
  American Handicrafts; Crewel World; Delco Craft Center, Inc.; The Handcraft Supply Corp.; The Hidden Village; Jerry S. Kaye Assoc.; Joan Moshimer; Nantucket Needleworks; Needlecraft Shop Inc.; Jane Snead Samplers; Yarns Unlimited; F. C. Ziegler Co.; Zim's.
frames for china
  J. Opal Stover Studio.
frames for hanging tiles
  Downs.
fraternal wood emblems
  Albert Constantine & Son Inc.
French fashion dolls
  Susan Sirkis.
French yarn
  B & M Yarn Co.
friend eggs
  Sandy Symons.

fringe wool
  Greentree Ranch Wools, Countryside Handweavers.
fringes
  Home-Sew Inc.
frow
  King's Studio.
fur
  The Hidden Village; Montgomery Ward & Co., Inc.
fur trimmings
  Great Central Fur Corp.
furnaces
  Drykiln Design; Supreme Watch Material Co.
furnaces for bronze casting
  McEnglevan Heat Treating & Mfg. Inc.
furniture finishes
  American Art Clay Co. Inc.; Art Mart, Inc.; Carson & Ellis, Inc.; Albert Constantine & Son Inc.; Douglas & Sturgess, Inc.; Leathercrafters Supply Co.; Hazel Pearson Handi Craft; Plasco; Sav-On-Crafts; Supreme Handicrafts.
furniture glues
  Albert Constantine & Son Inc.
furniture hardware
  Albert Constantine & Son Inc.
furniture legs
  Atlantic Upholstery Supply Co.; Giles & Kendall Inc.
furniture lumber
  Giles & Kendall Inc.
furniture parts
  Atlantic Upholstery Supply Co.; Giles & Kendall Inc.
furniture patterns
  Davault Miniature Furniture.
furniture polishes
  Albert Constantine & Son Inc.
furniture stains
  Albert Constantine & Son Inc.; Sturbridge Yankee Workshop.
fused glass items
  Glass Creations.
ganoin ivory
  Ken Kyte.
garment leathers
  Leathercrafters Supply Co.; Tandy Leather Co.

Craft Item Index
Garnet—Geode

garnet
Biship's House of Gems; Ed Brandt Stone Co.; W. D. Hudson, Jr.; Inter-Ocean Trade Co.; International Import Co.; Jewelart Inc.; Jim's Rock Shop; Lochs; Minerals & Gems; Norlene Lapidary; Oceanside Gem Imports, Inc.; Panther International Ltd.; Purcelli's Gems; Stop 'N Rock Shop; Syn-Crer Creations; Trader South; Transworld Trading Co.; Tumblecraft; Weisz Import Export Corp.

garnet cabochons
Stop 'N Rock Shop.

gas kilns
Cole Ceramics Laboratories.

gas lehrs
A. D. Alpine Inc.

gay 90's newsprint sacks
Downs.

gem beads
Bead Game.

gem cutting equipment
Earth Treasures; Treasure of the Pirates, Inc.

gem detectors
Gemological Institute of America.

gem drills
Lindell Industries; Mohave Industries.

gem faceting supplies
Earth Treasures.

gem findings
Aleta's Rock Shop.

gem graders
Gemological Institute of America.

gem grinders
Star Diamond Industries.

gem makers
Gilman's; Green's Rock & Lapidary Ltd.; Star Diamond Industries.

gem making equipment
Allcraft Tool & Supply Co.; Craftool Co.

gem polishers
Dorothy Blake; Star Diamond Industries.

gem polishing supplies
Earth Treasures; Rombins' Nest Farm.

gem rock
Michigan Lapidary Supply Co.

gem rough material
Andria Bree Gem Co.; Crown Gems Co.; Geophile International; Ken Kyte; Murray American Corp.

gem saws
Aleta's Rock Shop.

gem scales
Gilman's; Morang Balance Co.

gem shops
Covington Engineering Corp.

gem vises
Gilman's.

gemballs
Gemex Co.

Gemmaster faceting laps
MDR Mfg. Co., Inc.

Gemmaster faceting systems
MDR Mfg. Co., Inc.

gemstone accessories
Crown Gems Co.

gemstone baroques
Jim's Rock Shop.

gemstone cutting material
The Treasure Chest.

gemstone polishers
Surburbia, Inc.

gemstone rough material
Stop 'N Rock Shop.

gemstone solutions
Crown Gems Co.

gemstone supplies
Jade World/Wilderness Originals.

gemstones
Australian Exports; Australian Imports; Bead Game; Bourget Bros. Gems & Minerals; Ed Brandt Stone Co.; Commercial Mineral Corp.; Diamond Sales Co.; Dowse's Lapidary Supply, Inc.; Geophile International; Gilman's; Green's Rock & Lapidary Ltd.; H & A Mfg. Corp.; Jewelart Inc.; J. J. Jewelcraft; Jim's Rock Shop; Walter E. Johansen; Jim Kesterson; Lakewood Lapidary; Liberty Gem & Supply; Libra Gems; Mueller's; Norlene Lapidary; M. Nowotny; Panther International Ltd; C. W. Somers & Co.; Treasure of the Pirates, Inc.

geode cutters
Stonehouse.

German goathair
Greentree Ranch Wools, Countryside Handweavers.
giant quartz
Beaver Canyon Campground.
gilding brushes
Plaza Artists Materials, Inc.
glacier green jade
Jade World/Wilderness Originals.
glass additives
Kay Kinney -Contoured Glass.
glass anchors
Glass Creations.
glass angels
Glass Creations.
glass balls
Skil-Crafts Division.
glass beads
Bead Game; The Freed Co.; Gloria's Glass Garden; P. C. Herwig Co., Inc.; Jewelart Inc.; Macrame and Weaving Supply Co.
glass blowing equipment
A. D. Alpine Inc.; Westwood Ceramic Supply Co.
glass bulbs
Floating Gem Co.
glass cabochons
Jewelart Inc.; Tumblecraft.
glass chunks
Bergen Arts & Crafts, Inc.; Whittemore-Durgin Glass Co.
glass crafts
Kay Kinney -Contoured Glass.
glass cutters
Brookstone Co.; Cookson & Thode.
glass designs
Bell Studio.
glass display domes
Downs; Flemington Cut Glass Co.; Helen Gallagher; Max of Dallas; Sturbridge Yankee Workshop; Sunset House.
glass enamels
Kay Kinney -Contoured Glass.
glass eyes
Bay Country Woodcrafters.
glass fish
Glass Creations.
glass gems
Bergen Arts & Crafts, Inc.; Delco Craft Center, Inc.; Skil-Crafts Division.

glass globs
Boin Arts & Crafts; Delco Craft Center, Inc.; Magnus Craft Materials, Inc.
glass icicles
Glass Creations.
glass intaglios
Jewelart Inc.
glass jewel pendants
Florida Supply House, Inc.
glass jewels
Jewelart Inc.; National Artcraft Supply Co.
glass ladybug
House of York.
glass lamps
Renaldy's.
glass marbles
Delco Craft Center, Inc.
glass melting furnaces
Cole Ceramics Laboratories.
glass melting tanks
A. D. Alpine Inc.
glass mold coats
Kay Kinney -Contoured Glass.
glass mosaic crosses
House of Orange.
glass mosaic pendants
House of Orange.
glass ornaments
Holiday Craft; Whittemore-Durgin Glass Co.
glass paints
Sax Arts & Crafts; Supreme Handicrafts; Zim's.
glass paperweights
Craft Service; Florida Supply House, Inc.
glass sailboats
Glass Creations.
glass scribing tools
Brookstone Co.
glass snowflakes
Glass Creations.
glass stars
Glass Creations.
glass stones
E. H. Ashley & Co., Inc.
glass tools
Mollica Stained Glass Press; The Stained Glass Club; Whittemore-Durgin Glass Co.

Craft Item Index
Glass—Gold

glass tubular beads
Bethlehem Imports.
glassware
Barker Enterprises; House of Orange; Sav-On-Crafts.
glaze formula tables
Cole Ceramics Laboratories.
glazed beads
Bead Game.
glazed ceramic tiles
Newton's Potters Supply.
glazes
Cole Ceramics Laboratories; Delco Craft Center, Inc.; Minnesota Clay; Ohio Ceramic Supply Inc.
glitter
Country Crafts; Holiday Handicrafts, Inc.; Walnut Hill Co.
glory holes
A. D. Alpine Inc.; Cole Ceramics Laboratories.
gloss spray
Walnut Hill Co.
glues
Carson & Ellis, Inc.; Cleveland Leather Co.; Craftsman Supply House; Jeweler's Emporium; Koehler's Craft Outlet; Hazel Pearson Handi Craft; Sax Arts & Crafts.
goat lacing
Leathercrafters Supply Co.
goathair
KM Yarn Co.
gold
Charbonneau's Lapidary Service; Gems Galore; Weidinger Inc.
gold braids
P. S. Andrews Co.
gold casting items
Solartherm Co.
gold casting mountings
Lapidabrade Inc.
gold coin replicas
Jewelart Inc.
gold etching
Irene Goodwin.
gold filled findings
Albert Findings, Inc.; Anozira Jewelers; Edwards Jewelry Co.; T. B. Hagstoz & Son.

gold filled mountings
J. J. Jewelcraft; Libra Gems.
gold filled wire
G. Weidinger.
gold findings
Albert Findings, Inc.; Country Crafts.
gold finish mini-easels
Jewelart Inc.
gold finish wire easels
Sunflower Crafts.
gold foil
Basic Crafts Co.
gold grain
Green's Rock & Lapidary Ltd.
gold lace borders
Harrower House of Decoupage.
gold lace frames
Harrower House of Decoupage.
gold lace ornaments
Harrower House of Decoupage.
gold leaf
P. S. Andrews Co.; Arthur Brown & Bro., Inc.; Carson & Ellis, Inc.; Peg Hall Studios; Marie Mitchell's Decoupage Center; Hazel Pearson Handi Craft; Zim's.
gold mountings
Andria Bree Gem Co.; Eric Martin Co; J. J. Jewelcraft; Silver & Gem Shop.
gold paper borders
Taylor House.
gold paper decorations
Country Crafts.
gold paper laces
Hazel Pearson Handi Craft.
gold paper ornaments
Skil-Crafts Division; Taylor House.
gold paper trims
Holiday Craft.
gold plated items
Weidinger Inc.
gold sheet
Green's Rock & Lapidary Ltd.; Trowbridge Crafts; G. Weidinger.
gold solder
G. Weidinger.
gold wire
Green's Rock & Lapidary Ltd.; Talisman Crafts; Trowbridge Crafts.
gold zodiac signs
Thieves Market.

golden beryl
  Norlene Lapidary.
golden labradorite
  Dowse's Lapidary Supply, Inc.
golden sapphire
  Syn-Crer Creations.
golden tiger's-eye
  Craft House; Libra Gems.
goldsmithing equipment
  Allcraft Tool & Supply Co.; C. R. Hill Co.; Magic Circle Corp.
goldstone balls
  Edwards Jewelry Co.
goldstones
  M. Nowotny; G. Weidinger.
goose eggshells
  Herb Allen's Hole in One; Bowersox Eggcraft Supplies; The Golden Egg; Handcraft Originals; Hoffman Hatchery; Kathryn Johnson; Loosie Goosie Egg Craft Shop; Allegra Milano; Natalie Originals Studio; Rock Mountain Farm; Schiltz Goose Farm.
goose feathers
  Mangrove Feather Co., Inc.
gourd seeds
  George W. Park Seed Co., Inc.
graded grease wool
  Midwest Wool Marketing Cooperative.
graph paper
  Sewakers Industries Inc.
grease mohair wool
  Angora Diablo.
grease wool
  The Freed Co.; Gary H. Watson.
green agate gemballs
  Anozira Jewelers.
green aventurine
  Libra Gems.
green beryl
  Inter-Ocean Trade Co.; Syn-Crer Creations.
green flourite
  Beaver Canyon Campground.
green grossular garnets
  Beaver Canyon Campground.
green hen eggshells
  Rock Mountain Farm.
green malachite
  Gem-O-Rama, Inc.
green moss
  Dowse's Lapidary Supply, Inc.
green nephrite
  Gene's Rock Shop.
green plume
  Bitterroot Lapidary Supply.
green quartz
  Commercial Mineral Corp.
green tree agates
  Dowse's Lapidary Supply, Inc.
green wing teals
  Bay Country Woodcrafters.
greeting card craft
  Arthur Brown & Bro., Inc.
grinders
  Covington Engineering Corp.; Lortone Inc.; Raytech Industries Inc.; Reed Industries.
grinding compounds
  Aleta's Rock Shop.
grinding equipment
  Brad's Rock Shop; Mohave Industries.
grinding units
  Aleta's Rock Shop.
grinding wheels
  Covington Engineering Corp.; Jenkins Lapidary Equipment; Star Diamond Industries.
grits
  Covington Engineering Corp.; Scott Scientific Inc.; Weidinger Inc.
grospoint yarn
  Peri's Homework.
grout
  F. E. Biegert Co.
grout colors
  F. E. Biegert Co.
guinea eggs
  Hoffman Hatchery.
guitarmaking accessories
  String Instrument Service Inc.
gummed paper
  Dick Blick.
hackle feathers
  Mangrove Feather Co., Inc.
hairpin lace patterns
  Kile-Gore Designs.
hammered metal supplies
  William Dixon Co.
hammered metal work tools
  William Dixon Co.

Craft Item Index
Hand—Hardware

hand bookbinding equipment
Basic Crafts Co.
hand carders
Wool Products Ltd.
hand cards
The Freed Co.; E. B. Frye & Son, Inc.
hand fabric loom
Palmloom Co.
hand grinder
Dremel Creative Power Tools.
hand hooking
The Dorr Mill Store.
hand hooks
Mildred Sprout.
hand knitting yarns
International Creations.
hand looms
Walter Drake; Harrisville Designs; Kessenich Looms; L. W. Macomber Ad-A Harness Looms; Sax Arts & Crafts.
hand loupes
Gemological Institute of America.
hand punch hooks
Needlecraft Shop Inc.
hand spinning
Spincraft.
hand spinning wool
Essayons Studio, Hand Arts Center; Gary H. Watson.
hand tools
Allcraft Tool & Supply Co.; Bear Cave; Bergen Arts & Crafts, Inc.; Boin Arts & Crafts; Brookstone Co.; Arthur Brown & Bro., Inc.; Albert Constantine & Son Inc.; Craftsman Supply House; Craftsman Wood Service Co.; Delco Craft Center, Inc.; Economy Handicrafts, Inc.; Edmund Scientific Co.; The Handcrafters; J. J. Jewelcraft; Silvo Hardware Co.; Montgomery Ward & Co., Inc.
hand weaving
Robert Ayottes' Designery; KM Yarn Co.; Silver Shuttle.
hand weaving yarns
J & H Clasgens Co.; Lily Mills Co.; Isabel Scott Fabrics Corp.
handbag frames
Mary Maxim Inc.; Merribee; Modern Needlepoint; Robin & Russ Handweavers.
handbag handles
Mary Maxim Inc.; Merribee.
handbag leather
Modern Needlepoint.
handcrafted bread dough miniatures
Hallie Copeland.
handcrafted looms
Heritage Looms.
handcrafted miniature wrought iron accessories
The Village Smithy.
handcrafted miniatures
The Doll Cupboard; Federal Smallwares; Betty Fielding; Great Brook Miniatures.
handcrafted shoes supplies
Barb's Shoe Makings.
handcrafted stoneware beads
Earthworks.
handmade Swiss wood beads
Robin & Russ Handweavers.
hand-operated wool carding machine
Kulch; Wool Products Ltd.
hand-painted miniatures
Flint FBG Imports; Great Brook Miniatures.
hand-painted needlepoint canvas
The Amber Lion; Creativity Needlepoint; Most Unusual Custom Needleworks Inc.
hand-piece accessories
Foredom Electric Co.
handspun Greek yarns
Knit Services, Inc.
handspun Mexican wool yarns
Mexiskeins.
handspun wool
KeeWai Krafts.
handspun yarns
Dharma Trading Co.; The Hidden Village; Sachiye Jones; Maytex.
hardanger
The Hidden Village; Needlecraft Shop Inc.; Lee Wards.
hard stones
Sculpture Associates Ltd.
hardtwist yarns
Maytex.
hardware
Adventures In Crafts; P. S. Andrews Co.; Bedford Lumber Co., Inc.; Carson & Ellis, Inc.; Albert Constantine & Son

Inc.; Craft Products; Dek-Co Manufacturing Co.; Giles & Kendall Inc.; Leathercrafters Supply Co.; Hazel Pearson Handi Craft; Real Woods; Skil-Crafts Division; Sturbridge Yankee Workshop.

hardware wood
Minnesota Woodworkers Supply Co.

hardwood
M & M Hardwood.

hardwood blocks
Cummings Wood Co.

harness lap loom
Village Art Gallery.

harness looms
The Pendleton Shop; Turnbull Looms.

harness table looms
Tools of the Trade.

hat pins
Hazel Pearson Handi Craft; Whittemore-Durgin Glass Co.

heart glass bulbs
Floating Gem Co.

heatless glazing for ceramics
Specialty Products.

heatless glazing for metals
Specialty Products.

heavy duty hand carders
Kulch.

hem clips
Village Designs.

herbs
Worldwide Curio House.

hertha
The Hidden Village.

hickoryite
Dowse's Lapidary Supply, Inc.

hides
Leathercrafters Supply Co.; Veteran Leather Co., Inc.; Winona Trading Post.

high-fire clays
Newton's Potters Supply.

hinges
Albert Constantine & Son Inc.; Country Crafts.

historic advertisements
Buck Hill Associates.

historic handbills
Buck Hill Associates.

historic posters
Buck Hill Associates.

historic prints
Buck Hill Associates.

historical miniature figures
Terminal Hobby Shop; Wm. Walthers Inc.

HO gauge figures
K & L Co.

HO models
Campbell Scale Models.

HO railroad accessories
Paige Enterprises.

hobby lighting
Nature's Treasures.

hobby optics
Deep Flex Plastic Molds, Inc.; SwanSon.

hobby workbench
Craft House.

holders
A. L. Stone Displays.

hollow geodes
Panther International Ltd.

home built loom
Turnbull Looms.

homespun crewel yarn
KeeWai Krafts.

homespun wool
Greentree Ranch Wools, Countryside Handweavers.

homespun yarns
Craft Yarns of Rhode Island Inc.; Valley Handweaving Supply.

honey cat's-eye
Craft House.

honeycomb
Craft Service.

honeycomb candles
Cleveland Leather Co.

honeycomb ribbon
Sav-On-Crafts.

honeycomb wax sheets
Brown's Miniatures.

Hong Kong grass
Craftsman Supply House.

hooked rug
Schrock's, The House of Hobbies & Crafts.

hooked rug patterns
Karlkraft Studio-Cheva.

hooking looms
Textile Crafts.

Craft Item Index
Hooking—Ironmongery

hooking yarns
Tahki Imports, Limited; Textile Crafts.
hoops
The Hidden Village; Jerry S. Kaye Assoc.; Nantucket Needleworks; Needlecraft Shop Inc.
horn anvils
Gilman's.
horsehair
The Hidden Village.
hot point testers
Gemological Institute of America.
huck
The Mail Train.
hutch boxes
Koehler's Craft Outlet.
Icelandic lopi
Folklorico; Robin & Russ Handweavers.
Icelandic yarn
The Hidden Village.
Idaho agates
M. W. Jackson & Assoc.
Idaho tapestry agate
Bitterroot Lapidary Supply.
illuminated number boards
Paige Enterprises.
imitation gemstones
Grieger's Inc.; Liberty Gem & Supply.
imperial chrysophrase
Gem-O-Rama, Inc.
imported beads
Bead Game.
imported canvas
The Needle Works.
imported feathers
Dersh Feather & Trading Corp.; Hollywood Fancy Feather Co.
imported glass
Whittemore-Durgin Glass Co.
imported hardwoods
Craftsman Wood Service Co.
imported novelties
Studio D.
imported prefabricated guitar wood
String Instrument Service Inc.
imported white china
D. M. Campana Co.
Indian gemstones
Syn-Crer Creations.
Indian moonstone
Biship's House of Gems.
Indian silks
Exotic Thai Silks.
Indian stones
Adris Oriental Gem & Art Corp.
Indo-Pacific sea shells
Ward International Inc.
inkle looms
Cleve-Craft E-Z Loom; Knit Services, Inc.; Lily Mills Co.; The Loom Factory; The Loomery; Morgan Inkle Loom Factory; Robin & Russ Handweavers; Schacht Spindle Co.; School Products Co.
inks
Advance Process Supply Co.; Leathercrafters Supply Co.
inlay casting wax
Green's Rock & Lapidary Ltd.
instant papier mache
The Mail Train; Sax Arts & Crafts.
instrument accessories
International Violin.
instrument bridge
HERE Inc.
instrument nut
HERE Inc.
instrument strings
HERE Inc.
instrument tuners
HERE Inc.
instrument wood
International Violin.
intaglios
Jeweler's Emporium.
interfacing
Home-Sew Inc.
iolite
Commercial Mineral Corp.; International Import Co.; Syn-Crer Creations.
Iowa Betoskey stone
Quinn Mineral.
iridescent diffraction (polyester) foil
Diffraction Co., Inc.
Irish fisherman yarn
House of Yarn & Crafts.
Irish oiled yarn
The Pirate's Cove.
iron table pedestals
Plasco.
ironmongery
Whittemore-Durgin Glass Co.

iron-on patterns
Mrs. W. Bradley Ryan.
iron-on transfers
Needlecraft Shop Inc.; Santa Cruz Mountain Crafts; Transart.
Italian glass mosaic tiles
F. E. Biegert Co.
Italian silks
Exotic Thai Silks.
ivory beads
Bead Game; Jewelart Inc.
ivory jade
Jade World/Wilderness Originals.
ivory plume
Bitterroot Lapidary Supply.
jack looms
The Pendleton Shop; Robin & Russ Handweavers.
jade
Bergsten Jade Co.; Biship's House of Gems; Crown Cultured Pearl Corp.; International Import Co.; Jade World/Wilderness Originals; Jim's Rock Shop; Virgil V. Lundell; Michigan Lapidary Supply Co.; New World Jade Co.; M. Nowotny; Purcelli's Gems; G. Weidinger.
jade baroques
Jim's Rock Shop.
jadeite
Jade World/Wilderness Originals
jamb
Beno J. Gundlach Co.
Japanese filament
Nature's Fibers.
Japanese pongee prints
Exotic Thai Silks.
Japanese silk
Exotic Thai Silks; Greentree Ranch Wools, Countryside Handweavers.
jasper
Ed Brandt Stone Co.; Syn-Crer Creations; The Treasure Chest; C. R. Wells.
jewel caps
Arlene Handley Rock Hobby Supplies.
jewel stone assortments
De Mallie Crafts.
jeweler's bronze
Anchor Tool & Supply Co.
jeweler's circles
Anchor Tool & Supply Co.

jeweler's sprue wax
Green's Rock & Lapidary Ltd.
jeweler's supplies
Swest Inc.
jeweler's tools
Anchor Tool & Supply Co.; The L. S. Starrett Co.; Swest Inc.
jeweler's tubing
Swest Inc.
jeweler's wire
Anchor Tool & Supply Co.; Swest Inc.
jewelry abrasives
Star Diamond Industries.
jewelry casting lamps
O'Brien Lapidary Equipment Co.
jewelry casting supplies
Exactra-Craft Corp.; Gemex Co.; Magic Circle Corp.; O'Brien Lapidary Equipment Co.
jewelry casting tools
O'Brien Lapidary Equipment Co.
jewelry cement
Star Diamond Industries.
jewelry chains
Bead Game.
jewelry cutting materials
Max of Dallas.
jewelry disks
Star Diamond Industries.
jewelry display cases
Liberty Gem & Supply; Max of Dallas; Nature's Treasures.
jewelry findings
Anchor Tool & Supply Co.; Art Mart, Inc.; Aspen Lapidary; Bead Game; Bob's Arts & Crafts; Boutique Trims; Boycan's Craft Supplies; Craft Service; Creative Craft House; Deep Flex Plastic Molds, Inc.; Delco Craft Center, Inc.; The Ducketts; Economy Handicrafts, Inc.; Edwards Jewelry Co.; Farmers Gem and Rock Shop; Fieldwood Co.; Florida Supply House, Inc.; Gem-O-Rama, Inc.; Handcraft Originals; Jo-El's Craft Co.; Kaydee; Jim Kesterson; Koehler's Craft Outlet; Lapidabrade Inc.; Liberty Gem & Supply; M & M Distributors; Max of Dallas; Modern Craft; Montana Assay Office; Natcol Crafts, Inc.; Hazel Pearson Handi Craft; Sav-On-Crafts; Sax Arts & Crafts; Skil-Crafts Division; C.

Craft Item Index
Jewelry—Kilns

W. Somers & Co.; Specialty Products; Supreme Handicrafts; Swan-Son; Tye's; Lee Wards; G. Weidinger; Weidinger Inc.; Zim's.

jewelry mountings
The Ducketts; Geophile International; Gilman's; K42 Rock Shop; Lapidabrade Inc.; Liberty Gem & Supply; M & M Distributors; Montana Assay Office; National Artcraft Supply Co.; Renaldy's; The Sandvigs; Sav-On-Crafts; G. Weidinger; Weidinger Inc.

jewelry patterns
Creations for the Artist.

jewelry scales
O'Brien Lapidary Equipment Co.

jewelry stones
Veronica.

jewelry workbench
Craft House.

jewelrymaking accessories
American Handicrafts; Bead Game; Bergen Arts & Crafts, Inc.; Boin Arts & Crafts; Craftsman Supply House; Essayons Studio, Hand Arts Center; Kit Kraft; National Artcraft Supply Co.; J. C. Penney Co., Inc.; Sax Arts & Crafts; Swensons Lapidary Equipment, Inc.

jewelrymaking equipment
Exactra-Craft Corp.; Grieger's Inc.; K42 Rock Shop; Prospector's Pouch; The Roc Shop; Treasure of the Pirates, Inc.; Tye's; Weidinger Inc.

jewelrymaking machinery
Jim Kesterson.

jewelrymaking supplies
ARE Creations Inc.; D. M. Campana Co.; William Dixon Co.; Gemex Co.; Geophile International; Gordon's; Green's Rock & Lapidary Ltd.; Grieger's Inc.; T. B. Hagstoz & Son; C. R. Hill Co.; Jewel Creations; Jewelart Inc.; J. J. Jewelcraft; K42 Rock Shop; Lapidabrade Inc.; Modern Craft; Panther International Ltd.; Solartherm Co.; Ken Stewart's Gem Shop; Supreme Watch Material Co.; Syn-Crer Creations; Talisman Crafts; Joseph Tartas; Technical Specialties International Inc.; Treasure of the Pirates, Inc.; Tye's; G. Weidinger.

jewelrymaking tools
Allcraft Tool & Supply Co.; Brookstone Co.; William Dixon Co.; Gems Galore; Green's Rock & Lapidary Ltd.; T. B. Hagstoz & Son; Jim Kesterson; Maroon Bells Ind. Inc.; Montana Assay Office; Sax Arts & Crafts; C. W. Somers & Co.; Swensons Lapidary Equipment, Inc.; Joseph Tartas; Trowbridge Crafts; Universal Wirecraft Jewelry Co.; Weidinger Inc.

jewels
Country Crafts; Gibsons Creations; Holiday Craft; Jeweler's Emporium; Kit Kraft; Natalie Originals Studio; Supreme Handicrafts; Taylor House.

jigsaw
Dremel Creative Power Tools.

jingle bells
Sav-On-Crafts.

joiner-planers
American Machine & Tool Co.

jug cutter
Floyd Fleming; Keith Robinson; Whittemore-Durgin Glass Co.

jute
Contessa Yarns; Creator's Corner; P. C. Herwig Co., Inc.; The Hidden Village; Knit Services, Inc.; The Loomery; Robin & Russ Handweavers; Tinkler & Co. Inc.

karakul
KM Yarn Co.

karat gold sheet
Swest Inc.

key chain parts
Tandy Leather Co.

key chains
The Beadcraft Corner/Beadcraft Club.

kiln accessories
Delco Craft Center, Inc.

kiln shelves
Cole Ceramics Laboratories.

kilns
Allcraft Tool & Supply Co.; Anchor Tool & Supply Co.; Art Consultants; Bergen Arts & Crafts, Inc.; Boin Arts & Crafts; Arthur Brown & Bro., Inc.; Handcraft House; Loretta's Ceramic Studio; Minnesota Clay; Ohio Ceramic Supply Inc.; Plaza Artists Materials,

Inc.; Richland Ceramics Inc.; Sax Arts & Crafts; Sculpture Associates Ltd.; Sculpture House; Thomas C. Thompson; Westwood Ceramic Supply Co.
Kingman turquoise
Panther International Ltd.
kistka
Surma Book & Music Store.
kitchen clock glass
C. W. Bullock.
knit fabrics
The Sewing Bee.
knitting accessories
Sunray Yarn House; A. C. Weber & Co., Inc.; Wyco Yarn Co.; Yarns Unlimited.
knitting carrying bags
Henry Seligman Co. Inc.
knitting instructions
Bea Freeman Enterprises.
knitting machines
House of Yarn & Crafts; Liveright; Sav-On-Crafts; Lee Wards.
knitting needle holder
United Specialties Co.
knitting needles
Melrose Yarn Co., Inc.
knitting patterns
Brunswick Worsted Mills; Liveright; Sharon's Petite Sherre.
knitting rings
Sunset House.
knitting stands
Henry Seligman Co. Inc.
knitting supplies
Fiber to Fabric; The Handcrafters; Merribee; Lee Wards; The Yarn and Soda Shop.
knitting worsted
R. S. Duncan & Co.
knitting yarns
J & H Clasgens Co.; Cliveden Yarns; Conlin Yarns; Filature Lemieux Inc.; The Handcrafters; House of Yarn & Crafts; Melrose Yarn Co., Inc.; Tahki Imports, Limited; Lee Wards; Wool 'N Wick.
knives
Art Mart, Inc.; Tandy Leather Co.
kornerupine
Purcelli's Gems.

kunzite
Commercial Mineral Corp.; Inter-Ocean Trade Co.; International Import Co.; Norlene Lapidary; Oceanside Gem Imports, Inc.; Purcelli's Gems.
labradorite
M. Nowotny.
lace
Lace Lady; Two Brothers Inc.
lace prickers
Osma G. Tod Weaving & Lace Studio.
lacemaking materials
Alfred Decker; Some Place.
lacemaking tools
Some Place.
lacers
House of Gould.
laces
Home-Sew Inc.; Kieffer's Lingerie Fabric & Supplies; Skil-Crafts Division.
lacing
American Handicrafts; P. S. Andrews Co.; Craft Service; Craftsman Supply House; Sax Arts & Crafts; Skil-Crafts Division; Tandy Leather Co.
lacquers
Sax Arts & Crafts.
laguna
Bonnie's Rock Shop.
lambswool
R. S. Duncan & Co.
lame cord
Knit Services, Inc.
laminating supplies
Homecraft Veneer.
lamp accessories
Angelo Bros. Co.
lamp ball ornaments
Angelo Bros. Co.
lamp bandings
Angelo Bros. Co.
lamp bases
Angelo Bros. Co.
lamp canopies
Angelo Bros. Co.
lamp filigrees
Angelo Bros. Co.
lamp finials
Angelo Bros. Co.
lamp finishes
Angelo Bros. Co.

Craft Item Index
Lamp—Lapidary

lamp frames
Specialty Products.
lamp marble bases
Angelo Bros. Co.
lamp parts
Angelo Bros. Co.; Bergen Arts & Crafts, Inc.; Albert Constantine & Son Inc.; Craftsman Wood Service Co.; Diedricks Crafts; Gyro Lamp Supply Corp.; Loretta's Ceramic Studio; Minnesota Woodworkers Supply Co.; Natcol Crafts, Inc.; National Artcraft Supply Co.; Ohio Ceramic Supply Inc.
lamp switchplates
Angelo Bros. Co.
lamp tassels
Angelo Bros. Co.
lamp wiring diagrams
Gyro Lamp Supply Corp.
lampmaking
American Handicrafts; Bob's Arts & Crafts.
lamps
Gilman's.
lampshades
Craftsman Supply House; Lightsaround, Inc.
lampshade forms
Whittemore-Durgin Glass Co.
lampshade holders
Angelo Bros. Co.
lampshade patterns
Unique Creations.
lampshade supplies
Unique Creations.
lapidary abrasives
Aspen Lapidary; Minnesota Lapidary Supply Inc.; Swensons Lapidary Equipment, Inc.
lapidary belt sanders
Great Western Equipment Co.
lapidary carving tools
Industrial Diamond Tool Co. Inc.
lapidary cleaning accessories
L & R Manufacturing Co.
lapidary combination units
Farmers Gem and Rock Shop; Great Western Equipment Co.
lapidary compounds
Industrial Diamond Tool Co. Inc.; Swensons Lapidary Equipment, Inc.
lapidary cutting materials
Bitterroot Lapidary Supply; Frank's Jewelry & Gem Shop; Gem Center, U.S.A.; Mississippi Petrified Forest; Sandy Symons; Tektos.
lapidary dressers
Industrial Diamond Tool Co. Inc.
lapidary drills
Industrial Diamond Tool Co. Inc.
lapidary equipment
Alessi Lapidary Supplies; Charbonneau's Lapidary Service; Colorado Geological Industries Inc.; Covington Engineering Corp.; Dowse's Lapidary Supply, Inc.; Earth Treasures; Ebersole Lapidary Supply Inc.; Gems Galore; Geophile International; Gilman's; Great Western Equipment Co.; Highland Park Manufacturing; Hillquist; Lee Lapidaries; Lindell Industries; Lortone Inc.; Main Service Co.; Minnesota Lapidary Supply Inc.; Prospector's Pouch; Silver & Gem Shop; Smokey Mtn. Rock Shop; Star Diamond Industries; Swensons Lapidary Equipment, Inc.; Treasure of the Pirates, Inc.; Trowbridge Crafts; Montgomery Ward & Co., Inc.; G. Weidinger
lapidary findings
Charbonneau's Lapidary Service.
lapidary grinders
Beacon; Great Western Equipment Co.
lapidary grits
Brown's Rock & Lapidary Supplies.
lapidary historical scribes
Industrial Diamond Tool Co. Inc.
lapidary laps
Brad's Rock Shop; Green's Rock & Lapidary Ltd.; Industrial Diamond Tool Co. Inc.; Lee Lapidaries; Lortone Inc.; Raytech Industries Inc.; Trader South.
lapidary machinery
Aspen Lapidary; Brad's Rock Shop; Brown's Rock & Lapidary Supplies; Farmers Gem and Rock Shop; Green's Rock & Lapidary Ltd.; Lindell Industries; Max of Dallas; A. D. McBurney; Michigan Lapidary Supply Co.; Minex Lapidary Supplies; Minnesota Lapidary Supply Inc.; Sax Arts & Crafts; Smokey

Craft Item Index
Lapidary—Lazulite

Mtn. Rock Shop; Stanley Lapidary Products.

lapidary material
Gorin's Gem Arts & Rocks; Mueller's; Twin Peaks Rock Shop; G. Weidinger.

lapidary mountings
Bonnie's Rock Shop; Mueller's.

lapidary polishing equipment
Beacon; Great Western Equipment Co.

lapidary rough material
Melbourn Gem Co.

lapidary sanders
Great Western Equipment Co.

lapidary saw blades
Industrial Diamond Tool Co. Inc.

lapidary saws
Beacon; Industrial Diamond Tool Co. Inc.; Lortone Inc.

lapidary supplies
Aleta's Rock Shop; Allcraft Tool & Supply Co.; Aspen Lapidary; Beacon; Bet-Roc Enterprises Inc.; Bonnie's Rock Shop; Brown's Rock & Lapidary Supplies; Colorado Geological Industries Inc.; Craftool Co.; Diamond-Pro Unlimited; Dover Scientific Co.; Dowse's Lapidary Supply, Inc.; Earth Treasures; Edmund Scientific Co.; Farmers Gem and Rock Shop; Gem Center, U.S.A.; Gems Galore; Gems International; Geode Industries; Geophile International; Green's Rock & Lapidary Ltd.; Industrial Diamond Tool Co. Inc.; Jenkins Lapidary Equipment; J. J. Jewelcraft; Kachina Gem Co.; Lapidabrade Inc.; Marshall's Lapidary Co., Ltd.; Metro Diamond Drill Co.; Minnesota Lapidary Supply Inc.; Mississippi Petrified Forest; Mohave Industries; Ovgem Craft Supply Co.; Virgil Owens; Quinn Mineral; Raytech Industries Inc.; The Sandvigs; Jack V. Schuller, Inc.; Shipley's Mineral House; Silver & Gem Shop; Smokey Mtn. Rock Shop; Star Diamond Industries; Starfire Lapidary; Stonehouse; Swensons Lapidary Equipment, Inc.; Terra Products; 3 M Company; Timberline Lake Rock Shop; Torrington Rock Shop; Trader South; The Treasure Chest; Treasure of the Pirates, Inc.; Trowbridge Crafts; Ultra-Violet Products, Inc.; United Abrasive Inc.; G. Weidinger; Woodward Ranch.

lapidary templates
Farmers Gem and Rock Shop.

lapidary tools
Aspen Lapidary; Charbonneau's Lapidary Service; Ebersole Lapidary Supply Inc.; Farmers Gem and Rock Shop; Minnesota Lapidary Supply Inc.; Swensons Lapidary Equipment, Inc.; United Abrasive Inc.; G. Weidinger.

lapidary tumblers
Aleta's Rock Shop; Bet-Roc Enterprises Inc.; Farmers Gem and Rock Shop; Geode Industries; Geophile International; Gilman's; Green's Rock & Lapidary Ltd.; Industrial Diamond Tool Co. Inc.; Lortone Inc.; Mohave Industries; Raytech Industries Inc.; Shipley's Mineral House; Star Diamond Industries.

lapidary ultrasonic cleaning systems
L & R Manufacturing Co.

lapidary vibrating laps
Industrial Diamond Tool Co. Inc.

lapidary wheels
Industrial Diamond Tool Co. Inc.

lapidary workshops
Star Diamond Industries.

lapis lazuli
R. C. Baker; Gem-O-Rama, Inc.; International Import Co.; Syn-Crer Creations.

latch hook rugs
Bea Freeman Enterprises; The Hidden Village.

latch hooks
Needlecraft Shop Inc.

latch rug yarns
Brunswick Worsted Mills.

latex
Sax Arts & Crafts.

lathes
American Machine & Tool Co.; Campbell Tools Co.

latigo
La Venta Corp.

lava-talc
Bitterroot Lapidary Supply.

lazulite
Commercial Mineral Corp.

Craft Item Index
Lead—Linde

lead bearing enamels
Ceramic Coating Co.
lead came
Artists & Craftsman Guild; Carl Hepp Mosaic Co.; Barbara Lawshe; Whittemore-Durgin Glass Co.
lead came soldering fluids
Carl Hepp Mosaic Co.
lead free enamels
Ceramic Coating Co.
leather
American Handicrafts; P. S. Andrews Co.; Cleveland Leather Co.; The Hidden Village; Leathercrafters Supply Co.
leather additives
Tandy Leather Co.
leather belts
Pollack's Furrier's Supply Corp.
leather bolo cords
Shipley's Mineral House.
leather buttons
Pollack's Furrier's Supply Corp.
leather carving
Tandy Leather Co.
leather cements
Tandy Leather Co.
leather designs
Transart; Raymond P. Wallace.
leather dyes
Fezandie & Sperrle, Inc.; La Venta Corp.; Mac Leather Co.; Tandy Leather Co.
leather interlinings
Pollack's Furrier's Supply Corp.
leather lacings
Anne's Treasure Trove; Knit Services, Inc.; Mac Leather Co.; Veteran Leather Co., Inc.
leather linings
Pollack's Furrier's Supply Corp.; Tandy Leather Co.
leather packs
Supreme Handicrafts.
leather padding
Pollack's Furrier's Supply Corp.
leather preservatives
Leathercrafters Supply Co.
leather rawhide lacing
Leathercrafters Supply Co.
leather scraps
Mac Leather Co.; Reichert's Fabrics; Veteran Leather Co., Inc.
leather skins
J. P. Fliegel Co.; Mac Leather Co.; Pollack's Furrier's Supply Corp.
leather stitcher
Sunset House.
leather thongs
Jewelart Inc.
leather tools
La Venta Corp.; Leathercrafters Supply Co.; Mac Leather Co.; Skil-Crafts Division; Veteran Leather Co., Inc.
leathercraft
Boin Arts & Crafts; Arthur Brown & Bro., Inc.; Craft Service; Delco Craft Center, Inc.; Economy Handicrafts, Inc.; The Handcrafters; Holiday Handicrafts, Inc.; La Venta Corp.; Magnus Craft Materials, Inc.; J. C. Penney Co., Inc.; Sax Arts & Crafts; Sears, Roebuck & Co.; Skil-Crafts Division; Tandy Leather Co.
leaves
Gail's Decorative Arts Studio.
left handed tools
The Left Hand Inc.
lehrs
Cole Ceramics Laboratories; Drykiln Design.
lichen
Holiday Craft; Life-Like Products Inc.
lifelike grass
Life-Like Products Inc.
lifelike stone
Life-Like Products Inc.
light bulbs
Angelo Bros. Co.
light stabilizer additive
Chemical Additives Co.
lighter inserts
Bergen Arts & Crafts, Inc.; National Artcraft Supply Co.
lighting supplies
Lightsaround, Inc.
limoges
Jeweler's Emporium; Sav-On-Crafts.
Linde star boules
Elvin.

Linde stars
The Jewelry Mart.
linen
Contessa Yarns; Delco Craft Center, Inc.; Greentree Ranch Wools, Countryside Handweavers; International Creations; Knit Services, Inc.; Nantucket Needleworks; Needlecraft House; Mrs. W. Bradley Ryan.
linen cord
The Hidden Village.
linen rope
Knit Services, Inc.
linen thread
Frederick J. Fawcett, Inc.; The Hidden Village; Robin & Russ Handweavers; Osma G. Tod Weaving & Lace Studio.
linen twill
Mrs. W. Bradley Ryan.
linen twine
Knit Services, Inc.
linen yarns
Coulter Studios; School Products Co.
lingerie fabrics
Kieffer's Lingerie Fabric & Supplies; The Sewing Bee.
lining papers
Harrower House of Decoupage.
linoleum knives
Beno J. Gundlach Co.
liquid cement
Lox-Seal Adhesives.
liquid drape
Ramont's Floral Arts Studio.
liquid latex (bonded bronze)
Adhesive Products Corp.
liquid metallic finishes
Rub 'N Buff.
liquid plastic casting equipment
Nationwide Plastics Co.
liquid rubber
Bersted's; W. Wooley & Co.
locks
Albert Constantine & Son Inc.
long flat glass bulbs
Floating Gem Co.
long separating zippers
Mary Maxim Inc.
loom accessories
KAY an EE Corp. of America; Robin & Russ Handweavers.

loom equipment
Lily Mills Co.
looms
Robert Ayottes' Designery; Dick Blick; Boin Arts & Crafts; Delco Craft Center, Inc.; Essayons Studio, Hand Arts Center; Frederick J. Fawcett, Inc.; Fiber to Fabric; The Fringe and Frame; Gerhardt Macrame Studio; Greentree Ranch Wools, Countryside Handweavers; Handcraft House; The Handcrafters; KM Yarn Co.; Leclerc Corp.; Leonida Leatherdale's Embroidery Studio; Lily Mills Co.; The Loomery; Magnolia Weaving; Make It Happen Craft Studio; The Makings; The Mannings Creative Crafts; The New England Craftsman; The Niddy Noddy; Northwest Handcraft House; The Oriental Rug Co.; Robin & Russ Handweavers; Schacht Spindle Co.; School Products Co.; Silver Shuttle; Textile Crafts; Osma G. Tod Weaving & Lace Studio; Valley Handweaving Supply; The Yarn Depot.
looms for handicapped
Kessenich Looms.
looper looms
Pack-O-Fun.
loopers
Pack-O-Fun.
loose diamond-cut
Industrial Diamond Tool Co. Inc.
lost wax casting
Economy Handicrafts, Inc.; Green's Rock & Lapidary Ltd.; Ovgem Craft Supply Co.; Trowbridge Crafts.
lost wax casting materials
Stonehouse; Technical Specialties International Inc.
lost wax casting tools
Technical Specialties International Inc.
lost wax jewelrymaking
Kerr Mfg. Co.
Lucite®
Arthur Brown & Bro., Inc.
Lucite® cabinets
A. L. Stone Displays.
Lucite® mini-easels
Lillian Vernon.

Craft Item Index
Lumber—Matching

lumber
Bedford Lumber Co., Inc.; Albert Constantine & Son Inc.; Midland Walnut.
lumber squares
Midland Walnut.
mache
Arthur Brown & Bro., Inc.; Cleveland Leather Co.; Craftsman Supply House; Economy Handicrafts, Inc.; The Handcrafters; Skil-Crafts Division; Supreme Handicrafts.
mache beads
Bead Game.
machine attachments
Genie.
machine yarns
Lee Wards.
machinery
J. J. Jewelcraft.
macrame accessories
American Handicrafts; Artis, Inc.; Bergen Arts & Crafts, Inc.; Bob's Arts & Crafts; Boin Arts & Crafts; The Craft Corner; Delco Craft Center, Inc.; Dharma Trading Co.; Economy Handicrafts, Inc.; Essayons Studio, Hand Arts Center; Fiber to Fabric; Gemex Co.; P. C. Herwig Co., Inc.; The Hidden Village; Jeweler's Emporium; Jo-El's Craft Co.; Kaydee Craft Supplies; Kit Kraft; Knit Services, Inc.; Kraft Korner; Macrame and Weaving Supply Co.; Magnus Craft Materials, Inc.; The Mannings Creative Crafts; Ovgem Craft Supply Co.; Hazel Pearson Handi Craft; J. C. Penney Co., Inc.; Sav-On-Crafts; Schrock's, The House of Hobbies & Crafts; Sears, Roebuck & Co.; Supreme Handicrafts; Lee Wards.
macrame beads
Tandy Leather Co.
macrame board
Knit Services, Inc.
macrame cords
Craft Yarns of Rhode Island Inc.; Delco Craft Center, Inc.; Dharma Trading Co.; Fetty-Nielsen Macrame Loom; House of Orange; Jo-El's Craft Co.; Knit Services, Inc.; Lily Mills Co.; The Mannings Creative Crafts; Reeves Knotique; Tandy Leather Co.; The Yarn Depot.
macrame pins
Knit Services, Inc.
macrame yarn
Frederick J. Fawcett, Inc.
macrocrystalline wax
Arthur Brown & Bro., Inc.
magnets
Bob's Arts & Crafts; Edmund Scientific Co.; Home-Sew Inc.; Maryland Magnet Co.; Hazel Pearson Handi Craft; Skil-Crafts Division; Supreme Handicrafts.
magnifiers
Dick Blick; Brookstone Co.; Arthur Brown & Bro., Inc.; Dover Scientific Co.; Walter Drake; Plaza Artists Materials, Inc.
magnifying glasses
Nel-King Products.
mahogany blocks
Crowe & Coulter.
malachite
M. Nowotny; Purcelli's Gems; The Treasure Chest; G. Weidinger.
mallets
Tandy Leather Co.
manual battery turntables
A. L. Stone Displays.
manual tufting
The Hidden Village.
manzanita wood
Country Crafts.
map pins
Plaza Artists Materials, Inc.
maple lap compound polishers
Jack V. Schuller, Inc.
marabou feathers
Dersh Feather & Trading Corp.; Hollywood Fancy Feather Co.
marble craft
Derby Lane Shell Center; Koehler's Craft Outlet.
marbles
Bob's Arts & Crafts; Supreme Handicrafts.
marking pencils
Art Mart, Inc.
marquetry items
Albert Constantine & Son Inc.; Homecraft Veneer.
matching fabrics
The Yarn and Soda Shop.

matrix opals
Andria Bree Gem Co.
matrix plastic
Sea Novelties.
melting equipment
Art Consultants; Supreme Watch Material Co.
mesh canvas rug patterns
John E. Garrett Ltd.
mesh cloth
Craft Yarns of Rhode Island Inc.; KM Yarn Co.; Magnus Craft Materials, Inc.
metal alloys
Magic Circle Corp.
metal boxes
Carson & Ellis, Inc.
metal cabinets
A. L. Stone Displays.
metal compounds
Delco Craft Center, Inc.
metal craft
Bergen Arts & Crafts, Inc.; Cleveland Leather Co.; Magnus Craft Materials, Inc.
metal detectors
Brown's Rock & Lapidary Supplies; Covington Engineering Corp.; Gems Galore.
metal enameling equipment
American Art Clay Co. Inc.
metal etching
Delco Craft Center, Inc.
metal finishing
Birchwood Casey; Skil-Crafts Division.
metal foil paper
Arthur Brown & Bro., Inc.
metal frames
Sharon's Petite Sherre.
metal hand-cast miniatures
Town & Country Crafts.
metal hand-painted miniatures
Brown's Miniatures.
metal miniature doll houses
Holgate & Raynolds.
metal miniature figures
K & L Co.
metal miniatures
Great Brook Miniatures; Handcraft Originals.
metal mini-easels
Helen Gallagher; Lillian Vernon.

metal modeling materials
Terminal Hobby Shop.
metal molds
Cake Decorators & Craft Supplies; Doll's Candle & Craft Supplies.
metal powders
Polyproducts Corp.
metal rings
Knit Services, Inc.
metal sconces
Carson & Ellis, Inc.
metal sculpture tools
Sculpture Services Inc.
metal squirrel
House of York.
metal stampings
Green's Rock & Lapidary Ltd.
metal stands
Max of Dallas.
metal tanks
The Squadron Shop.
metal tooling
Hazel Pearson Handi Craft; Skil-Crafts Division; Zim's.
metal trays
Carson & Ellis, Inc.; Peg Hall Studios.
metal trivets
National Artcraft Supply Co.
metal ware
Carson & Ellis, Inc.; Magnus Craft Materials, Inc.
metal working tools
Brookstone Co.
metallic beads
The Beadcraft Corner/Beadcraft Club.
metallic braids
Gibsons Creations; Knit Services, Inc.
metallic foil labels
G. Weidinger.
metallic latex paints
Plycrete Mold Co.
metallic rubs
Reggi's Ceramic Colors.
metallic sculpture compound
Economy Handicrafts, Inc.
metallic tape
Plaza Artists Materials, Inc.
metallic threads
The Hidden Village.
metallic trims
Home-Sew Inc.

Craft Item Index
Metals—Miniature

metals
Art Consultants; Boin Arts & Crafts; Campbell Tools Co.; Gems Galore; Montana Assay Office; NASCO Arts & Crafts.

Mexican agates grab bag
Gorin's Gem Arts & Rocks.

Mexican crystal
Odyssey Mineral and Fossil.

Mexican fire agate
Australian Exports; Dowse's Lapidary Supply, Inc.; Michigan Lapidary Supply Co.

Mexican heavyspun yarn
The Hidden Village.

Mexican opal
Australian Exports; Australian Imports; Crown Gems Co.; Trader South; G. Weidinger

Mexican pottery clay
American Art Clay Co. Inc.

Mexican wool
Folklorico.

mica mirrors
Kitsophrenia, Inc.

military miniatures
The Hobby Bench; Polk's Hobby Dept. Store; Santos Miniatures; Wm. Walthers Inc.

milk bottles
Dairy Service, Inc.

milk cans
Dairy Service, Inc.

mill ends
General Supplies Co.; Mill Store.

mill products
Greentree Ranch Wools, Countryside Handweavers.

mill yarns
Davidson's Old Mill Yarn.

mineral collections
Colorado Geological Industries Inc.; Scott Scientific Inc.

mineral specimens
Colorado Geological Industries Inc.; Commercial Mineral Corp.; Minex Lapidary Supplies.

minerals
Dover Scientific Co.; The Fluorite Shop; Max of Dallas; Ovgem Craft Supply Co.; Reo N. Pickens, Jr.; Treasure of the Pirates, Inc.; Tye's.

mini vacuum-vise
Miles Kimball.

miniature accessories
The House of Miniatures; Joen Ellen Kanze; Miles Kimball; The Miniature Mart-The Peddler's Shop; Mrs. Mell Prescott.

miniature angels
Holiday Craft.

miniature animals
Brown's Miniatures; Custom Made Carvings & Miniatures; Flint FBG Imports; Great Brook Miniatures; Great Central Fur Corp.; Leathercrafters Supply Co.; Zim's.

miniature antique replicas
Federal Smallwares.

miniature baskets
Zim's.

miniature bedding
Lamonica.

miniature birdhouses
Hallie Copeland.

miniature birds
Hallie Copeland.

miniature bone china animals
The Gift Shoppe.

miniature boys
Hallie Copeland.

miniature candlesticks
Sparkle Studio.

miniature ceramic animals
The Gift Shoppe.

miniature ceramic bowls
Grueny's Gift Center.

miniature ceramic figures
Grueny's Gift Center; Town & Country Crafts; Wilfred Enterprises.

miniature ceramic pitchers
Grueny's Gift Center.

miniature ceramic vases
Grueny's Gift Center

miniature chandeliers
The Miniature Mart-The Peddler's Shop; Sparkle Studio.

miniature chests
Van Gelder Wood Products.

miniature creche figures
Holiday Craft.

miniature doll accessories
  Lamonica.
miniature dolls
  Helen Gallagher; Susan Sirkis.
miniature Early American furniture
  The Enchanted Doll House.
miniature egg craft
  Country Crafts.
miniature El-Kru china
  The Miniature Mart-The Peddler's Shop.
miniature flags
  Flags Galore.
miniature flowers
  Holiday Craft.
miniature French dolls
  Grueny's Gift Center.
miniature furniture
  Barnstable Originals by H.W. Smith; Custom Made Carvings & Miniatures; Federal Smallwares; Helen Gallagher; Grueny's Gift Center; The House of Miniatures; Miles Kimball; Lamonica; The Miniature Mart-The Peddler's Shop; Mrs. Mell Prescott; Sparkle Studio.
miniature girls
  Hallie Copeland.
miniature glass
  The Miniature Mart-The Peddler's Shop.
miniature glass animals
  The Gift Shoppe.
miniature grass
  Holiday Craft.
miniature hardware
  The Miniature Mart-The Peddler's Shop.
miniature Japanese girls
  Hallie Copeland.
miniature lamps
  Lamonica; Sparkle Studio.
miniature lead figures
  Hobby Gallery.
miniature mice
  Hallie Copeland.
miniature ornaments
  The Miniature Mart-The Peddler's Shop.
miniature pewter dishes
  Downs.

miniature power tools
  Brookstone Co.; Foredom Electric Co.; Gilman's.
miniature pulls
  The Miniature Mart-The Peddler's Shop.
miniature rabbits
  Hallie Copeland.
miniature rooms accessories
  LeMar's Decoupage Center.
miniature silk pictures
  Country Crafts.
miniature silver
  The Miniature Mart-The Peddler's Shop.
miniature soldiers
  Hobby Gallery.
miniature tanks
  Coker Craft.
miniature tools
  Walter Drake; The L. S. Starrett Co.
miniature trees
  Holiday Craft.
miniature wrought iron furniture
  The Village Smithy.
miniature 19th century figures
  Flint FBG Imports.
miniatures
  A 'N L's Hobbicraft, Inc.; Bob's Arts & Crafts; Boutique Trims; Boycan's Craft Supplies; Craftsman Supply House; Creative Craft House; Custom Made Carvings & Miniatures; The Enchanted Doll House; Fabulous Holiday House; Fieldwood Co.; Grueny's Gift Center; Holiday Craft; Holiday Handicrafts, Inc.; Howe Studio; Miles Kimball; Koehler's Craft Outlet; Lamonica; Hazel Pearson Handi Craft; The Putter Shop; Ren Ann Crafts; Rombins' Nest Farm; Skil-Crafts Division; Studio D; Supreme Handicrafts; Taylor House; Thieves Market; Wagner's Crafts; Zim's.
mini-easels
  American Handicrafts; F. C. Ziegler Co.
mini molds
  Nationwide Ceramic Enterprises.
mini-mosaic frames
  Lillian Vernon.
mini-pots
  Mrs. Marilyn G. Alabran.

Craft Item Index
Mini-prints—Model

mini-prints
Scissortail Arts & Crafts.
mink
Great Central Fur Corp.
mink scraps
The Hidden Village.
miocene vertebrate fossils
C. R. Boylin.
mirror tiles
Montgomery Ward & Co., Inc.
mirrors
Edmund Scientific Co.; Party Bazaar; Hazel Pearson Handi Craft.
Missouri Mozarkite stone
Timberline Lake Rock Shop.
mixed agates
C. R. Wells.
model accessories
America's Hobby Center Inc.; Campbell Scale Models; Life-Like Products Inc.; Mars Models; Miniature Aircraft; Model Railroad Equipment Corp.; National Hobby Inc.; PRO Custom Hobbies; The Squadron Shop; Whistle Stop.
model airbrushes
Miniature Aircraft.
model aircraft accessories
Williams Bros.
model aircraft engines
Canadian Aero-Supply.
model airplanes
Vern Clements; The Hobby Bench; National Hobby Inc.; Polk's Hobby Dept. Store.
model animals
Bachmann.
model boat landings
JV Models.
model boats
National Hobby Inc.
model bridges
Campbell Scale Models; Wm. Walthers Inc.
model building materials
Northeastern Scale Models Inc.
model buildings
Wm. Walthers Inc.
model cannon
Railway Express.
model car accessories
Auto World, Inc.

model cars
Bachmann; Life-Like Products Inc.; Sinclair's Auto Miniatures Inc.; The Squadron Shop.
model castings
PRO Custom Hobbies.
model cements
Model Railroad Equipment Corp.; Wm. Walthers Inc.
model coaling dock
Campbell Scale Models.
model construction materials
PRO Custom Hobbies.
model decals
Boxcar Ken; Miniature Aircraft; U. C. Hobby Center.
model electrical items
Wm. Walthers Inc.
model electronic components
Railway Express.
model fencing
Bachmann.
model figures
Boxcar Ken; Circus Hobby Hall; Wm. Walthers Inc.
model fittings
James Bliss & Co. Inc.; Bluejacket Ship Crafters.
model forest ranger station
JV Models.
model freight depots
Campbell Scale Models.
model freight load equipment
Bachmann.
model hand tools
America's Hobby Center Inc.; PRO Custom Hobbies.
model HO cars
Auto World, Inc.
model HO railroad
The Hobby Bench; JMC.
model HON3 railroad
The Hobby Bench.
model interior detail items
Wm. Walthers Inc.
model making
Delco Craft Center, Inc.
model materials
Santos Miniatures.
model N railroad
The Hobby Bench; JMC.

Craft Item Index
Model—Modeling

model O railroad
JMC.
model ON3 railroad
The Hobby Bench.
model paints
Boxcar Ken; Hobby Gallery; Miniature Aircraft; Model Railroad Equipment Corp.; PRO Custom Hobbies; Santos Miniatures; Ships Unlimited; U. C. Hobby Center; Wm. Walthers Inc.
model parts
Wm. Walthers Inc.
model passenger depots
Campbell Scale Models.
model piping components
Plastruct.
model power packs
Wm. Walthers Inc.
model power tools
America's Hobby Center Inc.; Sal Marino Co.; PRO Custom Hobbies.
model produce docks
Campbell Scale Models.
model produce stands
JV Models.
model racing cars
Sinclair's Auto Miniatures Inc.
model railroad accessories
Bachmann; JMC; Wm. Walthers Inc.
model railroad buildings
Associated Hobby Manufacturers Inc.
model railroad car parts
Northeastern Scale Models Inc.
model railroad cars
Associated Hobby Manufacturers Inc.
model railroad equipment
Associated Hobby Manufacturers Inc.; Lyman E. Cox, Scale Trains; PRO Custom Hobbies; Railway Express; Terminal Hobby Shop.
model railroad signs
Bachmann.
model railroads
Boxcar Ken; Mars Models; National Hobby Inc.; Polk's Hobby Dept. Store; Railway Express; Whistle Stop.
model room castings
Holgate & Raynolds.
model saloons
Campbell Scale Models.
model sand house
Campbell Scale Models.
model scenery
Boxcar Ken; Campbell Scale Models; Siderod Shop; Wm. Walthers Inc.
model scratch building supplies
Model Railroad Equipment Corp.; Wm. Walthers Inc.; Williams Bros.
model ships
The Hobby Bench; Polk's Hobby Dept Store; Railway Express.
model signals
Wm. Walthers Inc.
model slot cars
Auto World, Inc.
model steam engines
James Bliss & Co. Inc.
model structures
Boxcar Ken; Railway Express; Wm. Walthers Inc.
model tools
James Bliss & Co. Inc.; Boxcar Ken; Model Railroad Equipment Corp.; National Hobby Inc.; Paige Enterprises; Railway Express; Santos Miniatures; Ships Unlimited; Siderod Shop; Terminal Hobby Shop; Wm. Walthers Inc.
model town buildings
Campbell Scale Models.
model tracks
Railway Express.
model trains
JMC; Model Railroad Equipment Corp.; Railway Express.
model trees
Bachmann.
model tressels
Campbell Scale Models.
model trucks
Bachmann.
model water tank
Campbell Scale Models.
model wire
PRO Custom Hobbies.
modeling clay
American Art Clay Co. Inc.; Douglas & Sturgess, Inc.; Economy Handicrafts, Inc.; Sculpture Associates Ltd.; Sculpture House; Sculpture Services Inc.
modeling dough clay
American Art Clay Co. Inc.

Craft Item Index
Modeling—Motors

modeling equipment
Sculpture Services Inc.
modeling stands
Sculpture Services Inc.
modeling supplies
Ettl Studios Inc.
modeling tools
Delco Craft Center, Inc.; Tandy Leather Co.; Westwood Ceramic Supply Co.
modeling wheels
Sculpture Services Inc.
modern miniatures
Miniatures by Marty.
mohair yarn
Craft Yarns of Rhode Island Inc.; The Hidden Village; House of Yarn & Crafts; Macrame and Weaving Supply Co.; Valley Handweaving Supply.
mold making equipment
Supreme Watch Material Co.; Technical Specialties International Inc.
mold materials
Polyproducts Corp.
mold patterns
Bee Basch Designs.
mold releases
Atlantic Mold Corp.; High Strength Adhesives Corp.; Walnut Hill Co.
mold stands
Gilmour Campbell.
moldavites
Tektos.
molded plaques
Albert Constantine & Son Inc.
molding compound
Natcol Crafts, Inc.
moldings
Albert Constantine & Son Inc.; Craft Products; Craftsman Wood Service Co.; M & M Hardwood; Midland Walnut; Minnesota Woodworkers Supply Co.
molds
Castolite; Plasco; Reggi's Ceramic Colors; W. Wooley & Co.
monk's cloth
The Hidden Village; KM Yarn Co.; Sax Arts & Crafts.
Montana agate rough forms
B. T. Hallam.
Montana agate slab
B. T. Hallam.

Montana moss
Bitterroot Lapidary Supply.
moonstone
International Import Co.; Syn-Crer Creations; G. Weidinger.
moonstone baroques
Jim's Rock Shop.
mordants
Straw Into Gold.
morganite
De Lapa Mining Inc.; Inter-Ocean Trade Co.; International Import Co.
mosaic beads
Bead Game; Jeweler's Emporium.
mosaic cutters
The L. S. Starrett Co.
mosaic forms
Delco Craft Center, Inc.; Sax Arts & Crafts.
mosaic jade
Jade World/Wilderness Originals.
mosaic mirrors
Carl Hepp Mosaic Co.; Nicole Bead & Craft Co., Inc.
mosaic rock
P. S. Andrews Co.
mosaic stone
Sax Arts & Crafts.
mosaic tiles
Art Mart, Inc.; Boin Arts & Crafts; Delco Craft Center, Inc.; Sax Arts & Crafts.
mosaic tools
Delco Craft Center, Inc.
mosaics
A 'N L's Hobbicraft, Inc.; Bergen Arts & Crafts, Inc.; Cleveland Leather Co.; Craft Service; Craftsman Supply House; Delco Craft Center, Inc.; Economy Handicrafts, Inc.; The Handcrafters; Carl Hepp Mosaic Co.; Magnus Craft Materials, Inc.; National Artcraft Supply Co.
moss agate
Adris Oriental Gem & Art Corp.; Ken Kyte; Mission Rocks; M. Nowotny; Syn-Crer Creations.
mother-of-pearl
Biship's House of Gems.
motors
The Ducketts.

Craft Item Index
Moulage—Needlepoint

moulage molding
Douglas & Sturgess, Inc.; Sculpture Services Inc.
mountings
Alessi Lapidary Supplies; Ebersole Lapidary Supply Inc.; Farmers Gem and Rock Shop; Gem-O-Rama, Inc.; Gemex Co.; Gems Galore; Gordon's; Green's Rock & Lapidary Ltd.; Grieger's Inc.; Jewelart Inc.; Jim's Rock Shop; Harry Z. Kurs; Shipley's Mineral House; Smokey Mtn Rock Shop.
movable eyes
Holiday Handicrafts, Inc.; Home-Sew Inc.
music box accessories
Craftsman Wood Service Co.
music box movements
Albert Constantine & Son Inc.; Craft Products; Craftsman Wood Service Co.; Minnesota Woodworkers Supply Co.; O-P Craft Co., Inc.; Skil-Crafts Division.
music boxes
Bergen Arts & Crafts, Inc.; Country Crafts; National Artcraft Supply Co.
Mylar®
Plaza Artists Materials, Inc.
myrtlewood
Woodshop.
N gauge O scale traction equipment
Mars Models.
natural cane
H. H. Perkins Co.
natural fiber fabrics
Winston's Fabrics.
natural gemstones
The Cab-N-Facet, Inc.; Grieger's Inc.
natural stone beads
Jewelart Inc.
natural yarn
The Hidden Village.
Navajo Indian loom
The Pendleton Shop.
Navajo Indian yarns
Naakai Dine-E Biye.
Navajo Indian spindles
Schacht Spindle Co.
navy cord
The Hidden Village; Knit Services, Inc.

neck rings
Jeweler's Emporium.
needlecraft designs
Donna Jean Carver; Sudberry House.
needlecraft stand
Sperry & Son.
needlecraft supplies
Fiber to Fabric; Gemex Co.; Homespun Fabrics; Kazari; Nimble Thimble; The Stitchery; The Yarn Dome.
needlecraft yarn
The Yarn Depot.
needlecrafts
Knits'N That Yarn Shop; Merribee; Rombins' Nest Farm; Sears, Roebuck & Co.; Straw Into Gold.
needlepoint
Jerry S. Kaye Assoc.; Ladies Home Journal Needle & Craft; Merribee; The Needle Works; Needlecraft Shop Inc.; J. C. Penney Co., Inc.; Schrock's, The House of Hobbies & Crafts; Sears, Roebuck & Co.; Tuxedo Yarn & Needlework; Wool 'N Wick.
needlepoint canvas
Crossroads; Needlecraft Shop Inc.; Mrs. W. Bradley Ryan.
needlepoint charts
Needlecraft Shop Inc.
needlepoint cleaner
The Needle Works.
needlepoint designs
International Creations; The Knittery.
needlepoint handbag linings
Modern Needlepoint.
needlepoint hardware
Mrs. W. Bradley Ryan.
needlepoint lace
Wm. Hooper.
needlepoint mountings
Modern Needlepoint.
needlepoint rods
Needlecraft House.
needlepoint supplies
The Knittery; Vicki's Patience Unlimited.
needlepoint templates
New Products Co.
needlepoint yarn
Frederick J. Fawcett, Inc.; House of Flowers; Kaleidoscope Needleworks;

Craft Item Index
Needlepoint—Old

Nantucket Needleworks; Sign of the Arrow.

needles
House of Gould; Jerry S. Kaye Assoc.; Knit Services, Inc.; The Mail Train; Mary Maxim Inc.; Merribee; The Needle Works; Needlecraft Shop Inc.

needleweaving cloth
Nantucket Needleworks.

needlework dolls
Donna Jean Carver.

needlework stuffed toys
Donna Jean Carver.

nephrite jade
Bergsten Jade Co.; Crown Cultured Pearl Corp.; B. T. Hallam; Jade World/Wilderness Originals.

netting needles
Reisinger Net Co.

netting patterns
Frank J. Nelson.

New York Adirondack gem garnet rough
Minerals & Gems.

New Zealand spinning wheels
Village Art Gallery.

nickel
Sax Arts & Crafts.

nickel silver
T. B. Hagstoz & Son.

nippers
F. E. Biegert Co.; Beno J. Gundlach Co.

no-fire glazes
National Craft & Hobby Co., Inc.

no-fire stone-like flakes for ceramics
Hoff House Ceramic Supplies, Inc.

noil
Nature's Fibers.

nonfiring clay
American Art Clay Co. Inc.; Arthur Brown & Bro., Inc.; Delco Craft Center, Inc.; Plaza Artists Materials, Inc.; Sax Arts & Crafts; Skil-Crafts Division.

nonfiring enamel
Boin Arts & Crafts; The Mail Train.

nonhardening clay
Arthur Brown & Bro., Inc.; Sax Arts & Crafts.

nonmetallic trims
Home-Sew Inc.

norganite
Harry Bookstone.

North American fossils
Odyssey Mineral and Fossil.

Norwegian rosemaling
Traditional Norwegian Rosemaling.

Norwegian wool yarns
Wichelt Import Co.

no-slip frame
Blank-It Corp.

notching tools
Beno J. Gundlach Co.

notions
Kieffer's Lingerie Fabric & Supplies.

nuts
Bead Game.

nylon
Charles M. Butterworth; The Hidden Village; Macrame and Weaving Supply Co.; P. T. I.

nylon blends
Knit Services, Inc.

nylon braided cord
Fetty-Nielsen Macrame Loom.

nylon dyes
Creator's Corner.

nylon lace
Home-Sew Inc.; Nucleus.

nylon net
Bob's Arts & Crafts; The Clever Crafters; Zim's.

nylon parachute cord
Knit Services, Inc.

nylon thread
Danfield Threads Inc.; Walter Drake; Spencer Gifts Inc.

O G clock glass
C. W. Bullock.

O gauge railroad accessories
Paige Enterprises.

O gauge sheets plastic embossed
Holgate & Raynolds.

obsidian
Dowse's Lapidary Supply, Inc.; The Treasure Chest; G. Weidinger.

oil paints
D. M. Campana Co.

oil soluble dyes
Fezandie & Sperrle, Inc.

oilstones
Frank Mittermeier Inc.

old barn wood picture frames
Lynchburg Hdwr. & General Store.

Craft Item Index
Old—Paints

old fashioned doll packs
Sharon's Petite Sherre.
Old Masters prints
John's Hardware & Decoupage Supplies; Scissortail Arts & Crafts.
old time circus wagons
Circus Hobby Hall.
old time whiskey labels
Lynchburg Hdwr. & General Store.
olivewood beads
Bethlehem Imports.
one stroke design
Bell Studio.
onyx
M. Nowotny; Syn-Crer Creations.
onyx balls
Edwards Jewelry Co.
opal baroques
Jim's Rock Shop.
opal cabochons
Tumblecraft.
opal carvings
Australian Imports.
opal chip cabochons
Frank's Jewelry & Gem Shop.
opal chips
Australian Exports; Minex Lapidary Supplies; Syn-Crer Creations.
opal cutting pieces
Australian Exports.
opal glass
Whittemore-Durgin Glass Co.
opal practice pieces
Australian Exports.
opal quartz
Libra Gems.
opal specimens
Australian Imports; Minex Lapidary Supplies.
opal triplets
Australian Exports; Australian Imports.
opals
Australian Gem Trading Co.; Australian Imports; De Lapa Mining Inc.; Down Under Opal; Geode Industries; H & A Mfg. Corp.; International Import Co.; W. L. Maison Opals, Etc.; Melbourn Gem Co.; Michigan Lapidary Supply Co.; Murray American Corp.; M. Nowotny; Purcelli's Gems; Transworld Trading Co.; C. R. Wells.

opaque stains
Reggi's Ceramic Colors.
Oregon agate
Lakewood Lapidary.
organic dyes
Colonial Textiles.
organizer for needles and hooks
Henry Seligman Co. Inc.
oriental prints
John's Hardware & Decoupage Supplies.
ornament molds
Town & Country Crafts.
ornamental stampings
Jeweler's Emporium.
ostrich eggs
Herb Allen's Hole in One; The Golden Egg; Kathryn Johnson; Edith Maier.
ostrich feathers
Dersh Feather & Trading Corp.; Hollywood Fancy Feather Co.
overlock sewing machines
Knitking.
paint stripers
Miles Kimball.
paint-by-number
New Products Co.
painted porcelain cabochons
Jewelart Inc.
painting enamels
University Circle Publications and Supply Co.
painting fabrics
Floquil, Inc.
painting glass
Floquil, Inc.
painting mediums
Barbara Jones China House.
painting wood
Floquil, Inc.
paints
American Decorative Arts, Inc.; Art Mart, Inc.; Boin Arts & Crafts; Boycan's Craft Supplies; Budget Buddy Co.; Carson & Ellis, Inc.; Cleveland Leather Co.; Craft Service; Craftsman Supply House; Delco Craft Center, Inc.; Floquil, Inc.; The Handcrafters; Koehler's Craft Outlet; Magnus Craft Materials, Inc.; Hazel Pearson Handi Craft; Renaldy's; Sav-On-Crafts; The Sneak Box Studio; Stur-

Craft Item Index
Paints—Pedestals

bridge Yankee Workshop; W. Wooley & Co.; Zim's.

pallettes
Koehler's Craft Outlet.

palm onions
Mission Rocks.

paper cutters
Dick Blick.

paper dip dyes
Delco Craft Center, Inc.

paper frames
Make It Happen Craft Studio.

paper grass
Life-Like Products Inc.

paper models
John Hathaway.

paper sparkle
Life-Like Products Inc.

paper strips
Artistry In Wood.

paper tole
John's Hardware & Decoupage Supplies; Make It Happen Craft Studio.

papers
Craft Service; Craftsman Supply House; Delco Craft Center, Inc.; Economy Handicrafts, Inc.; Sax Arts & Crafts; Skil-Crafts Division; Supreme Handicrafts; Zim's.

papier mache
American Handicrafts; Artis, Inc.; Bersted's; Delco Craft Center, Inc.; Plasco; Zim's.

parakeet eggshells
Rock Mountain Farm.

parchment paper
Arthur Brown & Bro., Inc.

parchment quotes
Stevenson Industries.

Parian doll heads
Antique Doll Reproductions.

passenger car drumheads
Paige Enterprises.

patches
M. B. Austin; Lillian Vernon.

patchwork techniques
Leman Publications.

pattern cards
Genie.

pattern paper
Pins & Needles.

patterns
American Handicrafts; Anne Amiot; Barbara Bannister; Berry's of Maine; Better Homes & Gardens; Carson & Ellis, Inc.; Chilton Book Co.; The Clever Crafters; Albert Constantine & Son Inc.; Craftplans; D-Carol; Davis & Co.; Dek-Co Manufacturing Co.; R. S. Duncan & Co.; Foam Fantasy; Bea Freeman Enterprises; The Ghen Studio; Gloria; The Handcrafters; House of Patterns; Kieffer's Lingerie Fabric & Supplies; Kay Kinney -Contoured Glass; The Knitting Needle; Barbara Lawshe; Thomas S. Maquire's; The Needle Works; Needlecraft House; Sancraft Industries; The Sewing Bee; The Smock Shop; Tandy Leather Co.; Osma G. Tod Weaving & Lace Studio; Tole 'N Stuff; Wanda's Workshop; A. C. Weber & Co., Inc.; Whittemore-Durgin Glass Co.; Mrs. L. Winum; Woodland Craft Designs.

Paulina red moss
Sandy Symons.

peacock feathers
Dersh Feather & Trading Corp.

peafowl eggshells
Rock Mountain Farm.

pearl flakes
Walnut Hill Co.

pearl parchment
Koehler's Craft Outlet; Hazel Pearson Handi Craft.

pearl strands
Jeweler's Emporium.

pearls
Anne's Treasure Trove; Bead Game; The Beadcraft Corner/Beadcraft Club; Deep Flex Plastic Molds, Inc.; Gilman's; Home-Sew Inc.; International Import Co.; Jewelart Inc.; Kaydee; Kit Kraft; M & M Distributors; Natalie Originals Studio; New Products Co.; The Putter Shop; Schrock's, The House of Hobbies & Crafts; Swan-Son; Taylor House.

pebble gems
Delco Craft Center, Inc.

pedestals
Hazel Pearson Handi Craft; A. L. Stone Displays.

Craft Item Index
Pee—Plaster

pee wee eggshells
 Handcraft Originals.
peg looms
 Cleve-Craft E-Z Loom.
peps
 Holiday Craft.
perfect-measurement sewing patterns for knit fabrics
 Kandel Knits, Inc.
perforated embroidery paper
 Sewakers Industries Inc.
perforated plastic motifs
 Lee Wards.
perforated plastic shapes
 Sav-On-Crafts.
perforated ribbon
 Hazel Pearson Handi Craft.
peridot
 Biship's House of Gems; Crown Gems Co.; International Import Co.; Norlene Lapidary; Purcelli's Gems.
peridot baroques
 Kachina Gem Co.
peridot faceted stones
 Kachina Gem Co.
peridot faceting material
 Kachina Gem Co.
peridot gemstones
 Kachina Gem Co.
peridot rough
 Kachina Gem Co.; Panther International Ltd.
period hardware
 Albert Constantine & Son Inc.
permanent brush-on dyeing
 Rupert, Gibbon & Spider.
Persian needlepoint yarn
 Craft Yarns of Rhode Island Inc.
Persian yarn
 Crossroads; The Hidden Village; The Needle Works; Threadneedle; Vicki's Patience Unlimited.
personalized woven labels
 L & L Stitchery; Melrose Yarn Co., Inc.; The Needle Works.
petrified wood
 Bonnie's Rock Shop; Mississippi Petrified Forest.
petrified wood stumps
 Mission Rocks.

petrified woods agate
 Ken Kyte.
pewter
 Anchor Tool & Supply Co.; T. B. Hagstoz & Son; Sax Arts & Crafts.
pewter buckles
 Leathercrafters Supply Co.
pewter buttons
 House of York; Wichelt Import Co.
pheasant eggshells
 The Golden Egg; Rock Mountain Farm.
pheasant feathers
 Dersh Feather & Trading Corp.
picture frames
 National Artcraft Supply Co.
pigeon blood agate
 Dowse's Lapidary Supply, Inc.
pillows
 The Hidden Village.
pin cushions
 Sharon's Petite Sherre.
pin vises
 The L. S. Starrett Co.
pine wood purse
 Dek-Co Manufacturing Co.
pink jasper agate
 Sandy Symons.
pins
 Home-Sew Inc.
pipes
 Drykiln Design.
planes
 King's Studio.
plans
 Minnesota Woodworkers Supply Co.
plant fossils
 Geological Enterprises.
plaques
 Plasco.
plaster
 Art Mart, Inc.; Cole Ceramics Laboratories; TAP Plastic Inc.; Westwood Ceramic Supply Co.; W. Wooley & Co.
plaster additives
 W. Wooley & Co.
plaster carving
 Sax Arts & Crafts.
plaster casting
 Bersted's; Bob's Arts & Crafts; Boin Arts & Crafts; Bric-Mold Corp.; Arthur Brown & Bro., Inc.; Craft Service;

Craft Item Index
Plaster—Plated

Craftsman Supply House; Delco Craft Center, Inc.; Douglas & Sturgess, Inc.; Kit Kraft; Hazel Pearson Handi Craft; Sax Arts & Crafts; Skil-Crafts Division; Specialty Products; Supreme Handicrafts; Westwood Ceramic Supply Co.; Zim's.

plaster ceramic molds
Bee Basch Designs.

plaster craft
Belle Craft; Cleveland Leather Co.; Schrock's, The House of Hobbies & Crafts; W. Wooley & Co.

plaster impregnated sculpture tape
American Art Clay Co. Inc.

plaster molds
Deep Flex Plastic Molds, Inc.; Delco Craft Center, Inc.; Fres-O-Lone Mold Corp.; Sax Arts & Crafts; Skil-Crafts Division; Swan-Son; Trask Plastics; W. Wooley & Co.

plaster plaques
Koehler's Craft Outlet.

plaster ware finishes
National Craft & Hobby Co., Inc.

plastic beads
Bead Game; Florida Supply House, Inc.

plastic bottle craft
House of Patterns.

plastic boxes
Althor Products; Craft Service; Florida Supply House, Inc.; Sax Arts & Crafts.

plastic candle molds
Barker Enterprises; Natcol Crafts, Inc.

plastic cane
H. H. Perkins Co.

plastic casting
Art Mart, Inc.

plastic ceramic molds
Johnny Sens of New Orleans.

plastic disks
Derby Lane Shell Center.

plastic display domes
Walter Drake; Edmund Scientific Co.; Sunset House.

plastic domes
Craftsman Supply House; O-P Craft Co., Inc.; Hazel Pearson Handi Craft.

plastic embossed HO gauge sheets
Holgate & Raynolds.

plastic foam
Boin Arts & Crafts.

plastic frames
Craftsman Supply House.

plastic heads
Hazel Pearson Handi Craft.

plastic laminate countertopping
Beno J. Gundlach Co.

plastic laminate tools
Beno J. Gundlach Co.

plastic miniatures
Handcraft Originals.

plastic model structural components
Plastruct.

plastic modeling materials
Terminal Hobby Shop.

plastic molds
Cake Decorators & Craft Supplies; Evelyn Saft.

plastic mosaic tile
Boin Arts & Crafts.

plastic objects
Diedricks Crafts.

plastic ornaments
Florida Supply House, Inc.

plastic pellets
The Handcrafters.

plastic pigeon eggs
Rock Mountain Farm.

plastic portrait balls
Downs.

plastic scale models
Minicraft Models Inc.

plastic shapes
Country Crafts; Florida Supply House, Inc.

plastic squeeze bottles
Bear Cave.

plastic tanks
The Squadron Shop.

plastic vacuum molding
Nationwide Plastics Co.

plastic wall tile cutters
Beno J. Gundlach Co.

plate (dish) frames
Downs.

plate holders
Downs.

plated gold filled mountings
Lapidabrade Inc.

plated gold findings
  Lapidabrade Inc.
platinum
  T. B. Hagstoz & Son.
plexiglass
  Economy Handicrafts, Inc.
plexiglass cabinets
  A. L. Stone Displays.
pliers
  Universal Wirecraft Jewelry Co.
plume
  Mission Rocks.
plume slabs
  Twin Peaks Rock Shop.
pods
  Driftwood House.
polariscopes
  Gemological Institute of America.
polished gemstones
  Biship's House of Gems; Gem-O-Rama, Inc.; Silver & Gem Shop.
polished stones
  Odyssey Mineral and Fossil; G. Weidinger.
polished Tampa Bay coral
  C. R. Boylin.
polishes
  Dorothy Blake; Covington Engineering Corp.; The Ducketts; Gilman's; Walter E. Johansen; Weidinger Inc.
polishing accessories
  Brad's Rock Shop; Supreme Watch Material Co.
polishing laps
  Walter E. Johansen.
polishing machines
  Allcraft Tool & Supply Co.; Raytech Industries Inc.; Supreme Watch Material Co.
polishing motor
  Gilman's.
polishing tools
  Supreme Watch Material Co.
polyamide
  Stacy Fabrics Corp.
polyester double knit scraps
  Reichert's Fabrics.
polyester Fiberfil stuffing
  Putnam Co.
polyester filled pillow forms
  Putnam Co.
polyester lace
  Home-Sew Inc.
polyester resins
  High Strength Adhesives Corp.; Polyproducts Corp.
polyurethane foam
  Adhesive Products Corp.; Art Consultants; Hanover House Industries, Inc.; High Strength Adhesives Corp.; Kick-Shaw Inc.
pompom dolls
  A. Raimer.
pompom hat
  A. Raimer.
pompom poncho
  A. Raimer.
pompom purse
  A. Raimer.
pompom shawls
  A. Raimer.
pompom throw pillows
  A. Raimer.
pompoms
  Woodward Ranch.
pompon agate
  Ken Kyte.
pontils
  Drykiln Design.
pony beads
  The Beadcraft Corner/Beadcraft Club.
poof bottles
  Walnut Hill Co.
poplar blocks
  Crowe & Coulter.
porcelain
  Holiday Craft; House of York.
porcelain beads
  Bead Game; Reeves Knotique.
porcelain findings
  Felts Manufacturing Co. Inc.
porcelain flowers
  Bergen Arts & Crafts, Inc.
porcelain in gold plated jewelry findings
  Creations for the Artist.
porcupine quills
  Easy Street.
portable loom
  Northwest Looms.
portable macrame looms
  Fetty-Nielsen Macrame Loom.

Craft Item Index
Portable—Preserved

portable plating equipment
Platers Service Co.
portraits of customer's home or pets
Beard's Art Needlework Studio.
potter's accessories
Menco Engineers Inc.
potter's equipment
Bergen Arts & Crafts, Inc.; Richland Ceramics Inc.
potter's kick wheels
Cole Ceramics Laboratories; Pacific Crafts.
potter's plasters
Sculpture Services Inc.
potter's tools
Cole Ceramics Laboratories; Westwood Ceramic Supply Co.
potter's wheels
A. D. Alpine Inc.; Bluebird Manufacturing; Arthur Brown & Bro., Inc.; Gilmour Campbell; Craftool Co.; Creative Industries; Delco Craft Center, Inc.; Diedricks Crafts; Earth Treasures; Handcraft House; Menco Engineers Inc.; Minnesota Clay; Newton's Potters Supply; Ohio Ceramic Supply Inc.; Paramount Ceramic Inc.; Plaza Artists Materials, Inc.; Richland Ceramics Inc.; Sax Arts & Crafts; Sculpture Services Inc.; Van Howe Ceramic Supply Co.; Westwood Ceramic Supply Co.
pottery stands
Sax Arts & Crafts.
pour-cold mold rubber
Sculpture Services Inc.
power accessories
Dremel Creative Power Tools.
power etching instrument
Electro Stylus Mfg. Co.
power tool attachments
Walter Drake; Hanover House Industries, Inc.
power tools
Allcraft Tool & Supply Co.; Bergen Arts & Crafts, Inc.; Boin Arts & Crafts; Brookstone Co.; Arthur Brown & Bro., Inc.; Albert Constantine & Son Inc.; Craftsman Supply House; Craftsman Wood Service Co.; Delco Craft Center, Inc.; Dremel Creative Power Tools; Economy Handicrafts, Inc.; Edmund Scientific Co.; Beno J. Gundlach Co.; The Handcrafters; Frank Mittermeier Inc.; Sculpture Associates Ltd.; Sculpture House; Shipley's Mineral House; Silvo Hardware Co.; Technical Specialties International Inc.; Montgomery Ward & Co., Inc.
precious amber
Syn-Crer Creations.
precious casting metals
Bourget Bros. Gems & Minerals; H. A. Cole.
precious metal findings
Bourget Bros. Gems & Minerals.
precious metals
Michigan Lapidary Supply Co.
precious moonstone
Jim's Rock Shop.
precious opals
International Import Co.
precious stones
International Import Co.; Swest Inc.; Transworld Trading Co.
precision glass blowing tools
Drykiln Design.
pre-Columbian beads
Bead Game.
precut decoupage designs
Carolyn Watson.
precut eggs
Herb Allen's Hole in One.
precut plastic quilt patterns
Quilts and Other Comforts.
precut rug yarn
Lee Wards.
precut wood forms
Mrs. Ruby Brandon.
preforms
Trader South.
pre-mixed china paints
Doris Taylor.
pre-quilted pieces for embroidering
Lee Wards.
pre-ringed baroques
Pacific Gemstones.
preserved butterflies
J. Alday; American Butterfly Co.; Dorothy Biddle Service.
preserved foliage
Boycan's Craft Supplies.

press block print makers
Siphon Art Products.
pressed flower craft
The Handcraft Supply Corp.
priday eggs
Sandy Symons.
primitive yarn
The Hidden Village.
printed woven edge satin labels
Helmor Label Co.
printing ceramics
Floquil, Inc.
printmaking
Delco Craft Center, Inc.
prints
Adventures In Crafts; American Handicrafts; P. S. Andrews Co.; Artistry In Wood; N. S. Braverman; Carson & Ellis, Inc.; Dek-Co Manufacturing Co.; Gemex Co.; Harrower House of Decoupage; National Wildlife Art Exchange; Old Print Center; Hazel Pearson Handi Craft; Sax Arts & Crafts; Scissortail Arts & Crafts; F. C. Ziegler Co.
procion® dyes
Dharma Trading Co.
professional jeweler's instruments
Gemological Institute of America.
professional sewing machines
General Supplies Co.
professional tool sets
Tandy Leather Co.
propane equipment
Beno J. Gundlach Co.
propellar (tri) beads
The Beadcraft Corner/Beadcraft Club.
pug mills
A. D. Alpine Inc.; Bluebird Manufacturing; Cole Ceramics Laboratories; Westwood Ceramic Supply Co.
pulleys
The Ducketts.
punch needle
Sewing Products Co.
punchers
Salyer Publishing Co.; Tandy Leather Co.
pure cottons
Winston's Fabrics.
pure linens
Winston's Fabrics.
pure silks
Winston's Fabrics.
pure velveteens
Winston's Fabrics.
purse craft
Make It Happen Craft Studio.
purse hardware
Tandy Leather Co.
purse trimmings
House of Flowers.
push pins
Plaza Artists Materials, Inc.
quail eggshells
The Golden Egg; Handcraft Originals; Rock Mountain Farm.
quartz
International Import Co.; Lochs; G. Weidinger; Weisz Import Export Corp.; Wright's Rock Shop.
quartz crystals
Tumblecraft.
quartz tops
Down Under Opal.
quick-slip pouring
Air Capitol Molds, Inc.
quickstitch yarn
Crossroads.
quill engravers
Peg Hall Studios.
quill feathers
Hollywood Fancy Feather Co.
quill pens
Salyer Publishing Co.
quill scrollers
Peg Hall Studios.
quilling paper
Folkcrafts; Leisure Services; Tree Toys.
quilling supplies
Artistry In Wood; House of Flowers; Tree Toys.
quilt designs
Aunt Martha's Studios Inc.
quilt patterns
Contemporary Quilts; Quilts; Quilts and Other Comforts; Santa Cruz Mountain Crafts.
quilt scraps
Reichert's Fabrics.
quilter unit
Sue's Custom Quilting.

Craft Item Index
Quilting—Resin

quilting
Leman Publications; Montgomery Ward & Co., Inc.; Lee Wards.

quilting frames
KAY an EE Corp. of America; Lee Wards.

quilting machine
Sue's Custom Quilting.

rabbit furs
Whisper Farm Furs.

raccoon furs
Great Central Fur Corp.

radio controlled boats
R/C Cars International.

radio controlled cars
R/C Cars International.

raffia
B & M Yarn Co.; Cleveland Leather Co.; Craftsman Supply House; Delco Craft Center, Inc.; The Handcrafters; Sax Arts & Crafts; Supreme Handicrafts; Zim's.

rag doll patterns
American Indian Portrait Dolls; Dot's Dollhouse; Betty James Originals.

rag dolls
Susan Sirkis.

rain forest jasper
Bonnie's Rock Shop.

rainbow jasper
The Treasure Chest.

rare cut gemstones
H. Obodda.

rare fine facet rough
Lochs.

rare gems
International Import Co.

rare woods
Real Woods; Sculpture Associates Ltd.

rattail
The Hidden Village.

rattan
Craftsman Supply House; Holiday Handicrafts, Inc.; Zim's.

rattan handles
Westwood Ceramic Supply Co.

rayon towels
Adhesive Products Corp.; Two Brothers Inc.

rayon yarn
Contessa Yarns; Craft Yarns of Rhode Island Inc.

rayons
Knit Services, Inc.; Isabel Scott Fabrics Corp.

ready-made baskets
Fran's Basket House.

ready-stretched canvas
Framaway Co.

ready-to-fly gliders
Paul K. Guillow Inc.

red cullet
Biship's House of Gems.

red horn coral
Bonnie's Rock Shop; Dowse's Lapidary Supply, Inc.

red jasper
Beaver Canyon Campground.

redwood
Woodshop.

reed
Bersted's; Cleveland Leather Co.; Craft Service; Craftsman Supply House; Delco Craft Center, Inc.; Sax Arts & Crafts; School Products Co.; The Workshop.

refractometers
Gemological Institute of America.

refractories
Westwood Ceramic Supply Co.

repeat glass
Arthur Brown & Bro., Inc.; Plaza Artists Materials, Inc.

replacement burners for oil lamps
Gyro Lamp Supply Corp.

replacement parts for kilns
Delco Craft Center, Inc.

repousse crafts
Sunflower Crafts.

reproduction prints
Old Print Center.

resin casting
Bob's Arts & Crafts; Arthur Brown & Bro., Inc.; Craft Service; Ovgem Craft Supply Co.; Skil-Crafts Division.

resin craft accessories
Green's Rock & Lapidary Ltd.; High Strength Adhesives Corp.; Natcol Crafts, Inc.

resin craft additives
Natcol Crafts, Inc.

Craft Item Index
Resin—Rocks

resin craft embediments
Natcol Crafts, Inc.
resin craft molds
Belle Craft; Deep Flex Plastic Molds, Inc.; Delco Craft Center, Inc.; Green's Rock & Lapidary Ltd.; Natcol Crafts, Inc.; Sax Arts & Crafts; Skil-Crafts Division; Swan-Son; Trask Plastics.
resin craft supplies
American Handicrafts; Craftsman Supply House; Deep Flex Plastic Molds, Inc.; Delco Craft Center, Inc.; Douglas & Sturgess, Inc.; Economy Handicrafts, Inc.; Green's Rock & Lapidary Ltd.; The Handcrafters; High Strength Adhesives Corp.; Holiday Handicrafts, Inc.; National Artcraft Supply Co.; J. C. Penney Co., Inc.; Sax Arts & Crafts; Schrock's, The House of Hobbies & Crafts; Specialty Products; Swan-Son; Lee Wards; W. Wooley & Co.; Zim's.
resins
Art Consultants; Bergen Arts & Crafts, Inc.; Boin Arts & Crafts; Cleveland Leather Co.; Kick-Shaw Inc.; Sculpture Services Inc.; TAP Plastic Inc.
restoring materials
The Workshop.
revolvable bases
A. L. Stone Displays.
rhea eggshells
Rock Mountain Farm.
rhinestone bandings
Gail's Decorative Arts Studio; Gibsons Creations.
rhinestone chain
Boutique Trims.
rhinestones
P. S. Andrews Co.; Boutique Trims; Derby Lane Shell Center; Florida Supply House, Inc.; Gail's Decorative Arts Studio; Gibsons Creations; Handcraft Originals; Home-Sew Inc.; Kit Kraft; National Artcraft Supply Co.; Lee Wards.
rhodium mountings
J. J. Jewelcraft.
rhodochrosite
M. Nowotny; The Treasure Chest; G. Weidinger.

rhodonite
G. Weidinger.
rhodosite
Aspen Lapidary.
ribbon
B & M Yarn Co.; Boycan's Craft Supplies; Holiday Craft; Home-Sew Inc.; House of Flowers; Koehler's Craft Outlet; Sav-On-Crafts; Town & Country Crafts; Wagner's Crafts.
ribbon straw
Koehler's Craft Outlet.
rice paper
Bergen Arts & Crafts, Inc.; Arthur Brown & Bro., Inc.; Harrower House of Decoupage; Marie Mitchell's Decoupage Center.
rickrack
Home-Sew Inc.
ring blanks
Gilman's; Supreme Watch Material Co.
ring forms
Sax Arts & Crafts.
ring mandrel
The Roc Shop.
ring mountings
The Jewelry Mart.
ring shapes
Green's Rock & Lapidary Ltd.
rocailles
The Beadcraft Corner/Beadcraft Club.
rock clamps
Lindell Industries; Mohave Industries.
rock collections
Colorado Geological Industries Inc.; Scott Scientific Inc.
rock crystal
Biship's House of Gems.
rock picks
Star Diamond Industries.
rock polishers
Arthur Brown & Bro., Inc.
rock supplies
The Fluorite Shop.
rock tumblers
Scott Scientific Inc.; Starlite Rock Shop.
rock vise
A. D. McBurney.
rocks
Aleta's Rock Shop; Charbonneau's Lapidary Service; Dover Scientific Co.;

Craft Item Index
Rocks—Rubellite

Ebersole Lapidary Supply Inc.; Max of Dallas; Smokey Mtn. Rock Shop; Treasure of the Pirates, Inc.

rods
Atlantic Upholstery Supply Co.

roll and stretch frame
Needle-Ease.

roll canvas
Framaway Co.

rondelles
The Beadcraft Corner/Beadcraft Club.

rooster designs
Geecraft.

roots
Worldwide Curio House.

rope making machine
Schacht Spindle Co.

rose de France amethyst
Trader South.

rose quartz
Biship's House of Gems; Inter-Ocean Trade Co.; M. Nowotny; Oceanside Gem Imports, Inc.; Panther International Ltd.; Purcelli's Gems.

rose rocks
Rose Rocks Co.

rosebeads
The Beadcraft Corner/Beadcraft Club.

rosebud seashell craft
Koehler's Craft Outlet.

rosemaling brushes
Sandeen's Scandinavian Gift & Card Shop.

rosemaling paints
Sandeen's Scandinavian Gift & Card Shop.

rosemaling supplies
Sandeen's Scandinavian Gift & Card Shop.

roses
Gail's Decorative Arts Studio.

rosette winders
Holiday Handicrafts, Inc.; Mary Maxim Inc.; Merribee; Yarns Unlimited.

rough amethyst
Commercial Mineral Corp.

rough aquamarine
Commercial Mineral Corp.

rough chrysoprase
Interlectric House of Fine Australian Opals.

rough citrine
Commercial Mineral Corp.

rough cuts
Inter-Ocean Trade Co.

rough cutting stones
Alessi Lapidary Supplies.

rough faceting material
Harry Bookstone; Sam Frost; W. D. Hudson, Jr.; Jim's Rock Shop; Lochs; Trader South; Weisz Import Export Corp.

rough opals
Minex Lapidary Supplies.

rough rock
Green's Rock & Lapidary Ltd.; Jim Kesterson.

rough Russian emerald
Panther International Ltd.

rough sapphires
Minex Lapidary Supplies.

rough stones
Harry Bookstone; Michigan Lapidary Supply Co.; Syn-Crer Creations; Transworld Trading Co.

rough tourmalines
Commercial Mineral Corp.

rough triplets
W. L. Maison Opals, Etc.

round chenille
Greentree Ranch Wools, Countryside Handweavers.

round cowhide lacing
Leathercrafters Supply Co.

round glass bulbs
Floating Gem Co.

roving yarns
Tinkler & Co. Inc.

rubber
Blue Grass Art & Hobby Center; Sculpture Services Inc.

rubber cushions
Atlantic Upholstery Supply Co.

rubber latex
Douglas & Sturgess, Inc.

rubber mold compound
W. Spencer Inc.

rubber molds
Doll's Candle & Craft Supplies.

rubellite
Harry Bookstone.

rubies
Adris Oriental Gem & Art Corp.; Commercial Mineral Corp.; Diamond Sales Co.; H & A Mfg. Corp.; International Import Co.; Jewelart Inc.; Norlene Lapidary; Purcelli's Gems; Syn-Crer Creations.

rub-on metallic finishes
Rub 'N Buff.

rub-on wax gilts
Carnival Arts & Crafts.

ruby cabochon rough
Gems International.

ruby in zoisite
Murray American Corp.

rug backings
Craft Yarns of Rhode Island Inc.; Sax Arts & Crafts.

rug braiding
Berry's of Maine; The Dorr Mill Store; House of Gould; Knits'N That Yarn Shop; Mildred Sprout.

rug burlap
Lee Wards.

rug canvas
Brunswick Worsted Mills; International Creations; KM Yarn Co.; Lee Wards.

rug craft
The Yarn Depot.

rug cutters
Rebecca Andrews; Lee Wards.

rug designs
International Creations.

rug filler
Knit Services, Inc.; The Oriental Rug Co.

rug frames
Rebecca Andrews; Berry's of Maine; Craft Yarns of Rhode Island Inc.; Heritage Hill Patterns; The Hidden Village; KAY an EE Corp. of America; Nantucket Needleworks; Sears, Roebuck & Co.; Sewing Products Co.; Sperry & Son; Montgomery Ward & Co., Inc.; Lee Wards.

rug hooking guns
Bea Freeman Enterprises.

rug hooking supplies
Berry's of Maine; Dick Blick; The Handcrafters; House of Gould; The Mail Train; Joan Moshimer; The Needle Works; Party Bazaar; Mildred Sprout; Lee Wards.

rug hooking tools
Berry's of Maine.

rug hooks
Rebecca Andrews; Craft Yarns of Rhode Island Inc.; Crossroads; Delco Craft Center, Inc.; John E. Garrett Ltd.; Heritage Hill Patterns; House of Gould; Mary Maxim Inc.; Merribee; Joan Moshimer; Sax Arts & Crafts; Sunray Yarn House; Lee Wards; Yarns Unlimited.

rug hoops
Montgomery Ward & Co., Inc.

rug needles
Sax Arts & Crafts.

rug patterns
Rebecca Andrews; Heirloom Rugs; Heritage Hill Patterns; The Hidden Village; House of Gould; Joan Moshimer; Needlecraft Shop Inc.

rug punch
The Hidden Village.

rug weaving accessories
Craftool Co.

rug wool
The Dorr Mill Store; R. S. Duncan & Co.; The Hidden Village; Michigan Wool Products Co.; Needlecraft House.

rug yarn
Craft Yarns of Rhode Island Inc.; Crossroads; Filature Lemieux Inc.; The Handcrafters; KeeWai Krafts; KM Yarn Co.; Mary Maxim Inc.; Merribee; Nantucket Needleworks; Nature's Fibers; Needlecraft Shop Inc.; Sign of the Arrow; Lee Wards.

rugmaking supplies
Berry's of Maine; Craft Yarns of Rhode Island Inc.; Delco Craft Center, Inc.; The Hidden Village; Loftons; Sewing Products Co.; Some Place.

rugs
Jerry S. Kaye Assoc.; Needlecraft Shop Inc.; Sharon's Petite Sherre; Wool 'N Wick.

rush
Atlantic Upholstery Supply Co.; Cane & Basket Supply Co.; Craftsman Supply House; Magnus Craft Materials, Inc.; H.

Craft Item Index
Rush—Screens

H. Perkins Co.; Real Woods; The Workshop.
Russian synthetic blue quartz
Treasure of the Pirates, Inc.
rya pillow backings
House of Kleen.
rya rug backing
House of Kleen.
rya rug yarn
House of Kleen.
rya yarn
Coulter Studios; The Hidden Village.
safety pin jewelry items
Nicole Bead & Craft Co., Inc.
safety pins
The Beadcraft Corner/Beadcraft Club; Jeweler's Emporium.
sagenite
Dowse's Lapidary Supply, Inc.
sagenite quartz
The Treasure Chest.
Salish looms
School Products Co.
salt and pepper shakers mechanisms
Albert Constantine & Son Inc.
samplers
Schrock's, The House of Hobbies & Crafts.
sand
T. B. Hagstoz & Son.
sandblasting tools
Allcraft Tool & Supply Co.
sanding bands
Foredom Electric Co.
sanding machines
Brad's Rock Shop.
sandlewood beads
Jewelart Inc.
sandpaper wet or dry
3 M Company.
sandwich glass fragments
Wee 3 Sandwich Glass Jewelry.
sapphire
Adris Oriental Gem & Art Corp.; Australian Gem Trading Co.; Commercial Mineral Corp.; Diamond Sales Co.; H & A Mfg. Corp.; W. D. Hudson, Jr.; International Import Co.; Jewelart Inc.; Norlene Lapidary; Panther International Ltd.; Purcelli's Gems.

satin balls
Taylor House.
satin yarn
Plush Point Patterns by Marcia Podell.
satnet feathers
Hollywood Fancy Feather Co.
saw blades
Foredom Electric Co.
saws
Brad's Rock Shop; Beno J. Gundlach Co.; Reed Industries.
scaleograph
Plaza Artists Materials, Inc.
scaleograph proportional slide rule
Arthur Brown & Bro., Inc.
scales
Delco Craft Center, Inc.; Supreme Watch Material Co.
Scandinavian yarns
School Products Co.
scarabs
Gilman's.
scauper
King's Studio.
scissors
Arthur Brown & Bro., Inc.; Polly Chester Inc.; Walter Drake; The Needle Works; Hazel Pearson Handi Craft; Sax Arts & Crafts; Montgomery Ward & Co., Inc.
screen fabrics
Colonial Printing Ink Co.
screen nylon
Colonial Printing Ink Co.
screen polyester
Colonial Printing Ink Co.
screen printing equipment
Advance Process Supply Co.
screen process supplies
Art Mart, Inc.; Behnsen Silk Screen Supply Ltd.; Dick Blick; Arthur Brown & Bro., Inc.; Colonial Printing Ink Co.; Delco Craft Center, Inc.; Economy Handicrafts, Inc.; Plaza Artists Materials, Inc.; Sax Arts & Crafts; Screen Process Supplies Mfg. Co.
screen silk
Colonial Printing Ink Co.
screens
Screen Process Supplies Mfg. Co.

scribers
  Beno J. Gundlach Co.
scrimshaw scribers
  Allcraft Tool & Supply Co.
sculpture armatures
  Sculpture Services Inc.
sculpture bases
  Sculpture Associates Ltd.; Sculpture House; Sculpture Services Inc.
sculpture pedestals
  Sculpture Associates Ltd.; Sculpture House; Sculpture Services Inc.
sculpture supplies
  Art Consultants; Boin Arts & Crafts; Arthur Brown & Bro., Inc.; Economy Handicrafts, Inc.; Ettl Studios Inc.; Frank Mittermeier Inc.; Sculptmetal Co.; Jack D. Wolfe Co. Inc.
sculpture tools
  Art Consultants; Arthur Brown & Bro., Inc.; Cole Ceramics Laboratories; Frank Mittermeier Inc.
sculpture wax
  Delco Craft Center, Inc.; Douglas & Sturgess, Inc.
sculpturing
  Magic Circle Corp.
sculpturing metal
  Art Mart, Inc.; Sculpture House.
sculpturing stone
  Art Mart, Inc.; Sculpture House.
seagrass
  Atlantic Upholstery Supply Co.
seam steamers
  The Needle Works.
seashells
  The Collector's Cabinet; Max of Dallas; Scott Scientific Inc.
seed beads
  House of Orange; Macrame and Weaving Supply Co.
seed pods
  Western Tree Cones.
seeds
  Bead Game; Driftwood House; Jeweler's Emporium; George W. Park Seed Co., Inc.
seine twine
  The Hidden Village; Knit Services, Inc.
self-adhesive iridescent foil jewels
  Diffraction Co., Inc.

self-hardening clays
  Boin Arts & Crafts; Economy Handicrafts, Inc.; Newton's Potters Supply; Sculpture Associates Ltd.; Sculpture House.
semi-precious cabochons
  Virgil V. Lundell.
semi-precious stones
  E. H. Ashley & Co., Inc.; International Import Co.; K42 Rock Shop; Panther International Ltd.; Swest Inc.; Transworld Trading Co.
sequins
  Boutique Trims; Home-Sew Inc.; Kit Kraft; Koehler's Craft Outlet; Sav-On-Crafts; Wagner's Crafts.
sew-and-stuff animals
  Herter's, Inc.
sew-and-stuff dolls
  Herter's, Inc.
sewing
  House of Patterns.
sewing accessories
  Eagle Mill; The Needle Works; Village Designs.
sewing awls
  Walter Drake.
sewing machine monogram attachment template
  Lillian Vernon.
sewing machines
  Studio Yarn Farms Inc.; Swiss Bernina, Inc.
sewing stands
  Henry Seligman Co. Inc.
sew-on railroad patches
  M. B. Austin.
shadowboxes
  The Handcraft Supply Corp.; O-P Craft Co., Inc.
shark's teeth
  C. R. Boylin; Florida Supply House, Inc.
shaving horses
  King's Studio.
shears
  Polly Chester Inc.; Beno J. Gundlach Co.
sheepskin
  The Booted Sheepherder Inc.
sheet metal
  T. B. Hagstoz & Son.

Craft Item Index
Sheet—Slab

sheet waxes
Green's Rock & Lapidary Ltd.

shell beads
Bead Game.

shell flowers
Handcraft Originals.

shells
Boin Arts & Crafts; Cleveland Leather Co.; Derby Lane Shell Center; Economy Handicrafts, Inc.; Florida Supply House, Inc.; Magnus Craft Materials, Inc.

Shetland
R. S. Duncan & Co.

shimmering silk jade
Jade World/Wilderness Originals.

ship models
Coker Craft.

shisha glass
Maharani Boutique.

shop tools
Albert Constantine & Son Inc.

shuttles
Heritage Looms; Leclerc Corp.; Robin & Russ Handweavers; School Products Co.

sieves
Cole Ceramics Laboratories.

silhouette designs
Geecraft.

silica gel
Artis, Inc.; Plantabbs Co.

silicon carbide
The Ducketts.

silicone rubber
High Strength Adhesives Corp.

silk
Contessa Yarns.

silk finish eggshells
Edith Maier.

silk screened fraternity and sorority crests
Mrs. G's.

silk thread
The Hidden Village; Robin & Russ Handweavers.

silk wrap ornaments
Gibsons Creations.

silk yarn
Nature's Fibers; Threadneedle.

silver
ARE Creations Inc.; The Camp Fire Co.; Charbonneau's Lapidary Service; Gems Galore; Sax Arts & Crafts; Smokey Mtn. Rock Shop.

silver casting items
Solartherm Co.

silver finish mini-easels
Jewelart Inc.

silver grain
Green's Rock & Lapidary Ltd.

silver hinges
Boutique Trims.

silver jewelrymaking
Trowbridge Crafts.

silver mountings
Andria Bree Gem Co.; Eric Martin Co; Silver & Gem Shop.

silver ring castings
The Ducketts.

silver strip
Ken Stewart's Gem Shop.

silver wire
Talisman Crafts.

silversmithing machinery
Allcraft Tool & Supply Co.; Smokey Mtn. Rock Shop.

silversmithing supplies
Anchor Tool & Supply Co.; The Camp Fire Co.; William Dixon Co.; C. R. Hill Co.; Kraft Korner; Magic Circle Corp.; Ovgem Craft Supply Co.; Sax Arts & Crafts; Smokey Mtn. Rock Shop.

silversmithing tools
Allcraft Tool & Supply Co.; The Camp Fire Co.; Charbonneau's Lapidary Service; William Dixon Co.; Technical Specialties International Inc.

singing colors
Wee 3 Sandwich Glass Jewelry.

single ply for warp
KeeWai Krafts.

sisal
Contessa Yarns; P. C. Herwig Co., Inc.

skein maker
Clems and Clems Spinning Wheels.

skein winders
Robin & Russ Handweavers.

slab display racks
Stonehouse.

slab polishers
Covington Engineering Corp.

slab saws
Covington Engineering Corp.; Gilman's;

Craft Item Index
Slab—Spinning

slab (continued)
Great Western Equipment Co.; Green's Rock & Lapidary Ltd.; Highland Park Manufacturing; Lindell Industries; Mohave Industries; Star Diamond Industries.

slab-grabber
Rock's Lapidary Equipment.

slabs
Alessi Lapidary Supplies; Trader South; C. R. Wells; Woodward Ranch.

sliding hardware
Albert Constantine & Son Inc.

slip cover supplies
Atlantic Upholstery Supply Co.

slipper soles
Sewing Products Co.

small easels
Hanover House Industries, Inc.

small mirrors
Dick Blick; Magnus Craft Materials, Inc.

small unfinished furniture
Carson & Ellis, Inc.

small weaving looms
Spencer Gifts Inc.; Sunset House.

smoky quartz
Beaver Canyon Campground; Geode Industries; International Import Co.; Libra Gems; Oceanside Gem Imports, Inc.; Shil-La Art Gems Inc.; Syn-Crer Creations; Trader South; Weisz Import Export Corp.

snap setters
Tandy Leather Co.

snow sprays
Walnut Hill Co.

snowflake obsidian
Beaver Canyon Campground; Bonnie's Rock Shop.

soap blocks
Country Woodcraft.

soap casting
TAP Plastic Inc.

soap craft
Specialty Products.

soap cutting tools
Anne Amiot.

soapmaking
Creator's Corner.

soapstone
Mission Rocks.

sock doll
Sharon's Petite Sherre.

sodalite
M. Nowotny; Panther International Ltd.; The Treasure Chest.

soft stones
Sculpture Associates Ltd.

solder
Gilman's; Carl Hepp Mosaic Co.; Barbara Lawshe; Panther International Ltd.; Whittemore-Durgin Glass Co.

soldering equipment
Supreme Watch Material Co.

soldering tools
Allcraft Tool & Supply Co.; Brookstone Co.; Delco Craft Center, Inc.; Gilman's; Frank Mittermeier Inc.; Sax Arts & Crafts.

solderless jewelry
Bob and Carol Oliver.

solderless wire jewelrymaking
Universal Wirecraft Jewelry Co.

sole leather
Leathercrafters Supply Co.

solid brass buckles
Leathercrafters Supply Co.

spangles
Town & Country Crafts.

specialty cake pans
Helen Gallagher; Maid of Scandinavia.

specimen trimmers
Nature's Treasures.

speed rivets
Leathercrafters Supply Co.

sphenes
Commercial Mineral Corp.

sphere makers
Covington Engineering Corp.

spigots
Westwood Ceramic Supply Co.

spindles
Greentree Ranch Wools, Countryside Handweavers; School Products Co.

spinel
Commercial Mineral Corp.; International Import Co.; Walter E. Johansen; Syn-Crer Creations.

spinel boules
Gems Galore.

spinning
Fiber to Fabric; The Hidden Village;

Craft Item Index
Spinning—Steatite

The Mannings Creative Crafts; Straw Into Gold.

spinning accessories
Robert Ayottes' Designery; Clems and Clems Spinning Wheels; Greentree Ranch Wools, Countryside Handweavers; Lillstina Inc.; The Makings; Valley Handweaving Supply.

spinning supplies
The Freed Co.; Midwest Wool Marketing Cooperative; Some Place.

spinning wheel parts
Valley Handweaving Supply.

spinning wheels
Cambridge Wools; Clems and Clems Spinning Wheels; Colonial Textiles; Craftool Co.; Frederick J. Fawcett, Inc.; Greentree Ranch Wools, Countryside Handweavers; The Hidden Village; Kee-Wai Krafts; Leclerc Corp.; The Makings; The Mannings Creative Crafts; Robin & Russ Handweavers; School Products Co.; Some Place; Spincraft; Valley Handweaving Supply.

spinning yarns
Cambridge Wools; Greentree Ranch Wools, Countryside Handweavers.

splash shields
Lortone Inc.

splint seat weaving
Atlantic Upholstery Supply Co.; H. H. Perkins Co.

spool racks
Robin & Russ Handweavers.

spray adhesives
Carnival Arts & Crafts.

spray booths
Cole Ceramics Laboratories.

spray guns
Montgomery Ward & Co., Inc.

spray paints
Party Bazaar; Plasco.

square gold filled wire
Frankie's Twistcraft Jewelry.

squeeze bottles
Delco Craft Center, Inc.

stained glass
American Handicrafts; Bergen Arts & Crafts, Inc.; Dick Blick; Boin Arts & Crafts; Delco Craft Center, Inc.; Economy Handicrafts, Inc.; Gemex Co.; Carl Hepp Mosaic Co.; Kraft Korner; Magnus Craft Materials, Inc.; Make It Happen Craft Studio; National Craft & Hobby Co., Inc.; New Products Co.; Whittemore-Durgin Glass Co.

stained glass paints
Art Mart, Inc.; Arthur Brown & Bro., Inc.; Delco Craft Center, Inc.; The Handcrafters; Kay Kinney -Contoured Glass; Koehler's Craft Outlet; Plaza Artists Materials, Inc.; Specialty Products.

stained glass supplies
Artists & Craftsman Guild; Blue Grass Art & Hobby Center; Craft Service; Mollica Stained Glass Press; The Stained Glass Club; Whittemore-Durgin Glass Co.

stains
Cole Ceramics Laboratories; Supreme Handicrafts.

stamped linens
Merribee.

stamps
Gilman's; Tandy Leather Co.

stands
Berry's of Maine; A. L. Stone Displays.

star
Walter E. Johansen.

star quartz
Melbourn Gem Co.

star rose quartz slabs
Prospector's Pouch.

star ruby
Adris Oriental Gem & Art Corp.; Gems International; W. D. Hudson, Jr.; Jim's Rock Shop; Melbourn Gem Co.; Michigan Lapidary Supply Co.; Syn-Crer Creations.

star sapphires
Adris Oriental Gem & Art Corp.; Syn-Crer Creations.

starched lace
Holiday Handicrafts, Inc.

stationery decorating
House of Patterns.

statuary
Jeane's.

steatite (soapstone)
Lakewood Lapidary.

steel rules
  The L. S. Starrett Co.
steer horns
  Twin Peaks Rock Shop.
stencil brushes
  American Decorative Arts, Inc.
stencil paper
  Budget Buddy Co.
stencil tools
  Budget Buddy Co.
stencils
  Budget Buddy Co.; Economy Handicrafts, Inc.; Leathercrafters Supply Co.; Thelma Sutton Martin; Sax Arts & Crafts.
sterling silver
  T. B. Hagstoz & Son; Libra Gems; Panther International Ltd.
sterling silver beads
  Jewelart Inc.
sterling silver casting grains
  H. A. Cole.
sterling silver findings
  Albert Findings, Inc.; Edwards Jewelry Co.; Lapidabrade Inc.
sterling silver items
  Weidinger Inc.
sterling silver mountings
  J. J. Jewelcraft; Lapidabrade Inc.
sterling silver scrap chips
  Sterling Hallmark Co.
sterling silver sheet
  Alessi Lapidary Supplies; Anchor Tool & Supply Co.; Green's Rock & Lapidary Ltd.; Sax Arts & Crafts; Swest Inc.; Trowbridge Crafts; G. Weidinger.
sterling silver wire
  Alessi Lapidary Supplies; Green's Rock & Lapidary Ltd.; Trowbridge Crafts; G. Weidinger.
stick looms
  Cleve-Craft E-Z Loom.
stick magnets
  Maryland Magnet Co.
sticker prints
  Downs.
sticky wax
  Green's Rock & Lapidary Ltd.
stitch-and-stuff toys
  Platypus.
stitchery
  Cottage Crafts; Ladies Home Journal Needle & Craft; Sax Arts & Crafts.
stitchery mesh (2 gauges)
  Delco Craft Center, Inc.
stock threaded plastic jars
  Parkway Plastics Inc.
stone carving
  Sax Arts & Crafts.
stone carving tools
  Frank Mittermeier Inc.; Newton's Potters Supply; Sculpture Associates Ltd.; Sculpture House; Sculpture Services Inc.
stone mixes
  Tumblecraft.
stones
  Florida Supply House, Inc.; Jeweler's Emporium; Dale Magnuson; Renaldy's; Sculpture Services Inc.; Tye's.
stoneware beads
  P. C. Herwig Co., Inc.; Knit Services, Inc.; Reeves Knotique.
stoneware planter pots
  Reeves Knotique.
storm scene jade
  Jade World/Wilderness Originals.
straps for banding large and small ceramic molds
  Universal Strap Co.
straw-look crafts
  Sears, Roebuck & Co.
stretch dress forms
  Acme Dress Form Co., Inc.
stretcher strips
  Framaway Co.
string art
  Deep Flex Plastic Molds, Inc.; Swan-Son.
string sculpture
  Robert E. Sharpton.
string sculpture patterns
  Robert E. Sharpton.
studs
  Lillian Vernon.
stuffed animals
  Magnus Craft Materials, Inc.
stuffed doll patterns
  Virginia Black Designs.
styrene
  Bear Cave.

Craft Item Index
Styrofoam—Tapestry

Styrofoam®
 Bob's Arts & Crafts; Boin Arts & Crafts; Boycan's Craft Supplies; Craft Service; Craftsman Supply House; Delco Craft Center, Inc.; Economy Handicrafts, Inc.; Foam Fantasy; Holiday Handicrafts, Inc.; Home-Sew Inc.; Koehler's Craft Outlet; Party Bazaar; Sav-On-Crafts; Skil-Crafts Division; Specialty Products; Supreme Handicrafts; Wagner's Crafts; Zim's.

Styrofoam® cutter
 Economy Handicrafts, Inc.

suede
 Leathercrafters Supply Co.; Montgomery Ward & Co., Inc.

sunstone
 Treasure of the Pirates, Inc.

surgical knives
 Brookstone Co.

surgical scissors
 Brookstone Co.

swan eggshells
 Rock Mountain Farm.

swatches
 Berry's of Maine.

sweater wheels
 Bea Freeman Enterprises; Lee Wards.

Swedish bobbin winders
 Robin & Russ Handweavers.

Swedish fishnet
 Knit Services, Inc.

Swedish looms
 Lillstina Inc.

Swiss bell pulls
 Robin & Russ Handweavers.

synthetic corundum
 Walter E. Johansen.

synthetic diamond powders
 Sinkankas Diamond Products.

synthetic faceting material
 Green's Rock & Lapidary Ltd.

synthetic raffia straw
 Artis, Inc.

synthetic sapphire
 Eric Martin Co.

synthetic selvages
 Tinkler & Co. Inc.

synthetic spinel rough
 Eric Martin Co.

synthetic stones
 Shil-La Art Gems Inc.; Trader South; G. Weidinger.

synthetic straw
 Craft Service; Make It Happen Craft Studio; Sav-On-Crafts; Sax Arts & Crafts.

synthetic straw craft
 Lee Wards.

synthetic straw loom
 Delco Craft Center, Inc.

synthetic yarn
 J & H Clasgens Co.

T'Caro material
 Paradise Rocks.

table bases
 Atlantic Upholstery Supply Co.

table hoops
 KAY an EE Corp. of America.

table legs
 Albert Constantine & Son Inc.; Montgomery Ward & Co., Inc.

table lighter inserts
 Albert Constantine & Son Inc.

table looms
 The Hidden Village; House of Yarn & Crafts; KAY an EE Corp. of America; Schacht Spindle Co.; School Products Co.; Some Place.

table saws
 Toolkraft Corp.

table size yarn winders
 KeeWai Krafts.

table top machining center
 American Edestaal Inc.

tablet looms
 School Products Co.

Taiwan jade
 Gem-O-Rama, Inc.; Jewelart Inc.; Syn-Crer Creations.

tanzanite
 Lochs.

tape
 Beadnik's Arts & Crafts; Arthur Brown & Bro., Inc.; Plaza Artists Materials, Inc.

tapestry beaters
 Schacht Spindle Co.

tapestry looms
 Schacht Spindle Co.; School Products Co.

tapestry standing frames
Sperry & Son.
tapestry threads
Needlecraft Shop Inc.
tapestry wool
Berry's of Maine; The Hidden Village; Needlecraft House; Needlecraft Shop Inc.
tapestry yarn
Coulter Studios; Craft Yarns of Rhode Island Inc.; Filature Lemieux Inc.; The Hidden Village; KeeWai Krafts; KM Yarn Co.; Vicki's Patience Unlimited.
tarred marlin cord
The Hidden Village.
tartans
Scotch House.
tatting
Mary Maxim Inc.; Merribee.
teak trays
Marie Mitchell's Decoupage Center.
teakite lamp bases
Angelo Bros. Co.
teenage doll patterns
Betty James Originals; Manlove Originals.
tektites
Geode Industries; M. Nowotny.
templates
Gilman's; Green's Rock & Lapidary Ltd.; Tandy Leather Co.
Tennessee Mt. agate
Virgil Owens.
tennis racquet covers
Peri's Homework.
teredo wood slabs
Brown's Rock & Lapidary Supplies.
Texas cutting material
Mission Rocks.
Texas gem carnelian
Woodward Ranch.
Texas moss agate
Woodward Ranch.
Texas plumes material
Woodward Ranch.
textile
Budget Buddy Co.
textile brushes
Thelma Sutton Martin.

textile crafts
The Fringe and Frame; The Niddy Noddy.
textile dyes
Rupert, Gibbon & Spider.
textile enamels
University Circle Publications and Supply Co.
textile paints
Art Mart, Inc.; Bergen Arts & Crafts, Inc.; Arthur Brown & Bro., Inc.; Craft Service; Thelma Sutton Martin; Sax Arts & Crafts.
textile stencils
Delco Craft Center, Inc.; Thelma Sutton Martin.
textile yarns
Shuttlecraft.
Thai cottons
Exotic Thai Silks.
Thai Moong Nong-type tektites
Tektos.
Thai silks
Exotic Thai Silks.
thickness gauges
The L. S. Starrett Co.
thread holders
The Needle Works.
threads
Dick Blick; Home-Sew Inc.; Leathercrafters Supply Co.; Mary Maxim Inc.; The Needlecase; Robin & Russ Handweavers; Mildred Sprout; Thumbelina Needlework Shop; Lee Wards.
three king heads
Holiday Handicrafts, Inc.
thulite
Aspen Lapidary.
tiffany glass buckles
Leathercrafters Supply Co.
tigereye
Aspen Lapidary; Biship's House of Gems; Gem-O-Rama, Inc.; Jewelart Inc.; Michigan Lapidary Supply Co.; M. Nowotny; Panther International Ltd.; Syn-Crer Creations; G. Weidinger.
tigereye balls
Edwards Jewelry Co.
tigereye baroques
Jim's Rock Shop.

Craft Item Index
Tile—Tote

tile cutters
Beno J. Gundlach Co.; The L. S. Starrett Co.
tile saws
Beno J. Gundlach Co.
tiles
Magnus Craft Materials, Inc.; University Circle Publications and Supply Co.
tilt top tables
John & Susan Scheewe.
tin basket shapes
Keller-Charles of Philadelphia.
tin boxes
Keller-Charles of Philadelphia.
tin buckets
Jamar, Inc.; Keller-Charles of Philadelphia.
tin can craft
Hazel Pearson Handi Craft.
tin candleholders
Jamar, Inc.
tin coal hods
Keller-Charles of Philadelphia.
tin mini-water cans
Jamar, Inc.
tin pitchers
Jamar, Inc.
tin sconces
Jamar, Inc.; Keller-Charles of Philadelphia.
tin storage cans
Keller-Charles of Philadelphia.
tin trays
Jamar, Inc.; Keller-Charles of Philadelphia.
tin umbrella stands
Keller-Charles of Philadelphia.
tin urns
Keller-Charles of Philadelphia.
tin wash tubs
Jamar, Inc.
tin watering cans
Keller-Charles of Philadelphia.
tinamou eggshells
Rock Mountain Farm.
tinsel sticks
Holiday Craft.
tinware
Adventures In Crafts; Country Woodcraft; Jamar, Inc.; The Wood Barn.
tiny tumbled stones
Arlene Handley Rock Hobby Supplies.
tissue beads
Holiday Handicrafts, Inc.
tissue paper
Bergen Arts & Crafts, Inc.; Dick Blick; Boin Arts & Crafts; Hazel Pearson Handi Craft; Supreme Handicrafts.
tjanting tool
Hazel Pearson Handi Craft.
tole painting
Corner Cupboard Crafts, Inc.; P. C. Herwig Co., Inc.; Kraft Korner; John & Susan Scheewe; Sunflower Crafts.
tole patterns
Bernadette Decorative Art; Decorative Designs by Dare; John & Susan Scheewe; Transart.
toleware
A 'N L's Hobbicraft, Inc.; P. S. Andrews Co.
tool handles
King's Studio.
tooling leather
Leathercrafters Supply Co.; Tandy Leather Co.
tooling metals
Sax Arts & Crafts.
tools
Allcraft Tool & Supply Co.; Basic Crafts Co.; Campbell Tools Co.; Cleveland Leather Co.; Delco Craft Center, Inc.; Homecraft Veneer; Jeweler's Emporium; Minnesota Woodworkers Supply Co.; Ohio Ceramic Supply Inc.; Plaza Artists Materials, Inc.; Rupert, Gibbon & Spider; Sax Arts & Crafts; Tandy Leather Co.
topaz
Beaver Canyon Campground; Harry Bookstone; Dowse's Lapidary Supply, Inc.; Inter-Ocean Trade Co.; International Import Co.; Lochs; Norlene Lapidary; Oceanside Gem Imports, Inc.; Trader South; Treasure of the Pirates, Inc.
tortoise-shell beads
Bead Game.
tote bags
The Rusty Nail; Sewing Products Co.

Craft Item Index
Tourmaline—Turquoise

tourmaline
Harry Bookstone; Commercial Mineral Corp.; W. D. Hudson, Jr.; International Import Co.; Jim's Rock Shop; Norlene Lapidary; Oceanside Gem Imports, Inc.; Purcelli's Gems; Transworld Trading Co.; Weisz Import Export Corp.

tourmaline XL'S
Beaver Canyon Campground.

toy patterns
Dorris Dolls; Sue Wise.

toys
House of Patterns.

tracing paper
Plaza Artists Materials, Inc.

trade beads
Bead Game.

transfer pencils
House of Gould; Merribee; Needlecraft Shop Inc.; Zim's.

transfers
Budget Buddy Co.; The Hidden Village; Jerry S. Kaye Assoc.; Sangray Corp.; Skil-Crafts Division.

transistor clock movements
Rays Rock Shop.

Transvaal jade
Beaver Canyon Campground.

treasure detectors
Covington Engineering Corp.

tree agates
Syn-Crer Creations.

tree making
Bet-Roc Enterprises Inc.

tree skirts
Gibsons Creations.

tri-beads
Don's Hobby Co.

trim saws
Brad's Rock Shop; Covington Engineering Corp.; Gilman's; Green's Rock & Lapidary Ltd.; Highland Park Manufacturing; Lindell Industries; MDR Mfg. Co., Inc.; Star Diamond Industries.

trimming tools
Polly Chester Inc.; Beno J. Gundlach Co.

trims
Adventures In Crafts; Craftsman Supply House; Eagle Mill; Fabulous Holiday House; Holiday Handicrafts, Inc.; Lace Lady; Magnus Craft Materials, Inc.; Mill Store; Hazel Pearson Handi Craft; The Putter Shop; Taylor House; Two Brothers Inc.

trunk repair parts
Dorothy Mae's Trunks.

tube agate
M. W. Jackson & Assoc.

tubular braid
Knit Services, Inc.

tubular tufting
Knit Services, Inc.

tumble polished gems
B. T. Hallam.

tumbled stone tree materials
Arlene Handley Rock Hobby Supplies.

tumbled stones
Starfire Lapidary.

tumbler ready rock
Starlite Rock Shop.

tumbling accessories
Ken Kyte; Star Diamond Industries.

tumbling items
Scott Scientific Inc.

tumbling stones
Harry Bookstone; The Treasure Chest.

turkey eggs
Mrs. Barbara Allen; Hoffman Hatchery.

turkey feathers
Dersh Feather & Trading Corp.

turkey flats feathers
Mangrove Feather Co., Inc.

turkey hip feathers
Mangrove Feather Co., Inc.

turkey marabou feathers
Mangrove Feather Co., Inc.

turned legs
Bedford Lumber Co., Inc.

turntables
Gilmour Campbell; Delco Craft Center, Inc.

turquoise
Biship's House of Gems; Crown Gems Co.; International Import Co.; Jewelart Inc.; Murray American Corp.; G. Weidinger.

turquoise nuggets
Tumblecraft.

turquoise rough
Gems International.

Craft Item Index
Turritella—Vegetable

turritella
  Mission Rocks.
tussah type yarn
  Nature's Fibers.
twilight blue jade
  Jade World/Wilderness Originals.
twill
  Needlecraft Shop Inc.
twine
  Knit Services, Inc.; Netcraft.
Ukrainian items
  Ukrainian Gift Shop.
ultrasonic cleaners
  Branson Cleaning Equipment; Crown Gems Co.; Geode Industries.
ultraviolet lamps
  Raytech Industries Inc.
ultraviolet lights
  Nature's Treasures.
unbleached cotton cord
  Kristine Eckert.
uncut diamond
  Industrial Diamond Tool Co. Inc.
undecorated tinware
  Crafts Manufacturing Co.
undecorated woodenware
  Adventures In Crafts.
undressed dolls
  Standard Doll Co.
unfinished barrels
  Spaulding & Frost Co., Inc.
unfinished basswood boxes
  Albert Constantine & Son Inc.
unfinished boxes
  Carson & Ellis, Inc.
unfinished early American furniture
  Sturbridge Yankee Workshop.
unfinished kegs
  Spaulding & Frost Co., Inc.
unfinished milk cans
  Dairy Service, Inc; The Wood Barn.
unfinished pails
  Spaulding & Frost Co., Inc.
unfinished plaques
  Albert Constantine & Son Inc.
unfinished purse boxes
  Carson & Ellis, Inc.
unfinished tinware
  Keller-Charles of Philadelphia.
unfinished unassembled children's furniture
  Spaulding & Frost Co., Inc.
unfinished woodenware
  Bernadette Decorative Art; Hoffman Hatchery.
unpainted miniatures
  Glo-Classics; Sunflower Crafts.
unpainted plaster figurines
  House of Figurines.
unusual agates
  Ken Kyte.
unusual beads
  Veronica.
unwoven cotton
  Lace Lady; Two Brothers Inc.
upholstery cleaning
  Atlantic Upholstery Supply Co.
upholstery fabrics
  General Supplies Co.
upholstery supplies
  Atlantic Upholstery Supply Co.; Minnesota Woodworkers Supply Co.; Montgomery Ward & Co., Inc.
upholstery tools
  Albert Constantine & Son Inc.; Craftsman Wood Service Co.; General Supplies Co.
urethane foam blocks
  Delco Craft Center, Inc.
used leather machinery
  La Venta Corp.
used plating equipment
  Platers Service Co.
Utah red nodules
  Beaver Canyon Campground.
Utah ribbon agate
  Bonnie's Rock Shop.
Utah varscite
  Starfire Lapidary.
utility knives
  Beno J. Gundlach Co.
vacuum casting
  Allcraft Tool & Supply Co.
vanadium steel cutters
  Foredom Electric Co.
vat dyes
  Inkodye.
vegetable dyes
  Dharma Trading Co.

velour
Skil-Crafts Division.
velour paper
Dick Blick; Hazel Pearson Handi Craft; Zim's.
velvet
Sav-On-Crafts; Zim's.
velvet black jade
Torrington Rock Shop.
velvet crepe papers
Koehler's Craft Outlet.
velvet flowers
Country Crafts.
velvet leaves
Country Crafts.
velvet needlepoint yarn
R L L Enterprise.
velvet patchwork quilt squares
House of Lines.
velvet quilt pieces
Nucleus.
velvet ribbons
Boutique Trims; Taylor House.
velvet tubing
Zim's.
veneers
Craftsman Wood Service Co.; Minnesota Woodworkers Supply Co.; Real Woods.
verdite
Aspen Lapidary.
vibrating laps
Star Diamond Industries.
Victorian design gift wrap paper
Sharon's Petite Sherre.
Victorian miniatures
Miniatures by Marty.
vinyl doll heads
The Clever Crafters.
vinyl glues
High Strength Adhesives Corp.
vinyl molds
W. Wooley & Co.
vises
Universal Wirecraft Jewelry Co.
wagon wheels
Albert Constantine & Son Inc.
wall plaques
Reeves Knotique.
walnut blocks
Crowe & Coulter.

walnut wood
Midland Walnut.
ware trucks
Cole Ceramics Laboratories.
warp cloth
KM Yarn Co.
warp yarn
Craft Yarns of Rhode Island Inc.
warping boards
Schacht Spindle Co.
washed white wool
Gary H. Watson.
Washington opalized wood
Lakewood Lapidary.
Washington wood agate
Lakewood Lapidary.
watch repair supplies
Lapidabrade Inc.
watchmaker's tools
Supreme Watch Material Co.
water-mount decals
Cerami Corner Inc.
water soluble leather paints
Siphon Art Products.
water soluble metallic paints
Reggi's Ceramic Colors.
water soluble textile paints
Siphon Art Products.
wavellite
Wright's Rock Shop.
wax
Bourget Bros. Gems & Minerals; Gilman's; Kerr Mfg. Co.; Sax Arts & Crafts; Sculpture Associates Ltd.; Supreme Watch Material Co.; Surma Book & Music Store; Westwood Ceramic Supply Co.
wax casting tools
Allcraft Tool & Supply Co.
wax cutting tools
Anne Amiot.
wax gilt
Plasco.
wax gold
Arthur Brown & Bro., Inc.
wax medium
Siphon Art Products.
wax melting pot
Sculpture Associates Ltd.; Shipley's Mineral House.

Craft Item Index
Wax—Wire

wax modeling
Sculpture Associates Ltd.
wax patterns
Exactra-Craft Corp.
wax pens
Art Consultants; Bourget Bros. Gems & Minerals.
wax ring patterns
Eric Martin Co.
wax ring stands
Bourget Bros. Gems & Minerals.
wax tools
Supreme Watch Material Co.
waxed linen
The Hidden Village.
weathered decorative boards
Dale Magnuson.
weave-it looms
Mary Maxim Inc.; Yarns Unlimited.
weaving accessories
The Fringe and Frame; Leclerc Corp.; Northwest Handcraft House; Norwood Loom Co.; The Oriental Rug Co.; Tahki Imports, Limited; The Yarn Depot.
weaving cutters
The Mannings Creative Crafts.
weaving frames
The Mannings Creative Crafts; The Yarn Depot.
weaving supplies
Boin Arts & Crafts; Craftool Co.; Essayons Studio, Hand Arts Center; Frederick J. Fawcett , Inc.; Fiber to Fabric; E. B. Frye & Son, Inc.; Handcraft House; Heritage Looms; The Hidden Village; Macrame and Weaving Supply Co.; Magnolia Weaving; The Mannings Creative Crafts; The New England Craftsman; Northwest Handcraft House; Savin Handcrafts; Silver Shuttle; Some Place; Straw Into Gold; Osma G. Tod Weaving & Lace Studio.
weaving yarns
Charles M. Butterworth; Conlin Yarns; Contessa Yarns; Cottage Crafts; Coulter Studios; Craft Yarns of Rhode Island Inc.; Frederick J. Fawcett , Inc.; Filature Lemieux Inc.; The Handcrafters; House of Kleen; House of Yarn & Crafts; Jean Malsada Inc.; The Mannings Creative Crafts; Shuttlecraft; Tahki Imports, Limited; Textile Crafts; The Yarn Depot.
wedding cake supplies
General Supplies Co.
wedging tables
Cole Ceramics Laboratories.
welding tools
Village Candle & Craft; Montgomery Ward & Co., Inc.
welding unit
Allcraft Tool & Supply Co.
western Latigo
Leathercrafters Supply Co.
wet look vinyl
Montgomery Ward & Co., Inc.
wheels
Atlantic Upholstery Supply Co.
whistles
Jewelart Inc.
white birch bark
Dale Magnuson.
white coral
Panther International Ltd.
white foam cutters
Sax Arts & Crafts.
white foam shapes
Hazel Pearson Handi Craft; Sax Arts & Crafts; Lee Wards.
white ironstone ware
Sturbridge Yankee Workshop.
white jewelry findings
Country Crafts.
white metal castings
Paige Enterprises.
white plastic ware
Sav-On-Crafts.
white YAG
Walter E. Johansen.
wiggle eyes
Delco Craft Center, Inc.
wildlife miniatures
Great Brook Miniatures.
winders
School Products Co.
wine labels
Whittemore-Durgin Glass Co.
wire
Beadnik's Arts & Crafts; Craft Service; Gilman's; T. B. Hagstoz & Son; Sav-On-Crafts; Universal Wirecraft Jewelry Co.

wire bending jig
Plaza Artists Materials, Inc.
wire jewelrymaking tools
Frankie's Twistcraft Jewelry.
wire winder tool
Netcraft.
wonderstone
The Treasure Chest.
wood
Carson & Ellis, Inc.; Glencraft Shop; Magnus Craft Materials, Inc.; NASCO Arts & Crafts; Real Woods; Sax Arts & Crafts; Stewart Industries; C. R. Wells.
wood agate
M. W. Jackson & Assoc.
wood barrels
Dairy Service, Inc.
wood beads
Bead Game; Florida Supply House, Inc.; Gloria's Glass Garden; P. C. Herwig Co., Inc.; Jewelart Inc.
wood boards
Keith Robinson.
wood bookends
Downs.
wood bowls
Midland Walnut; O-P Craft Co., Inc.
wood boxes
Artistry In Wood; Holiday Handicrafts, Inc.; Kit Kraft; Van Gelder Wood Products.
wood buckles
Knit Services, Inc.
wood buttons
O-P Craft Co., Inc.
wood cabinets
A. L. Stone Displays.
wood canary eggs
Rock Mountain Farm.
wood carving scraps
Glencraft Shop.
wood carving supplies
Dick Blick; Craft Service; Crowe & Coulter; Economy Handicrafts, Inc.; Ettl Studios Inc.; The Handcrafters; Hearth & Heather Ltd.; The Sneak Box Studio; Montgomery Ward & Co., Inc.
wood carving tools
Brookstone Co.; Arthur Brown & Bro., Inc.; Country Woodcraft; Hobbi-Carve; Frank Mittermeier Inc.; Newton's Potters Supply; Sculpture Associates Ltd.; Sculpture House; Sculpture Services Inc.; The Sneak Box Studio.
wood chests
O-P Craft Co., Inc.
wood crosses
O-P Craft Co., Inc.
wood cutouts
The Wood Barn.
wood dolls
Susan Sirkis.
wood ducks
Bay Country Woodcrafters.
wood eggs
O-P Craft Co., Inc.
wood fibre
Bob's Arts & Crafts; Boycan's Craft Supplies; Koehler's Craft Outlet; Ramont's Floral Arts Studio; Zim's.
wood finishing
Birchwood Casey.
wood finishing supplies
Minnesota Woodworkers Supply Co.; Real Woods.
wood frames
Midland Walnut; Marie Mitchell's Decoupage Center.
wood hardware
Minnesota Woodworkers Supply Co.
wood hoops
Knit Services, Inc.
wood jewelry
Artistry In Wood.
wood jewelry scraps
Glencraft Shop; Jeweler's Emporium.
wood kegs
Dairy Service, Inc.
wood lamp bases
Angelo Bros. Co.
wood legs
Midland Walnut; Minnesota Woodworkers Supply Co.
wood mallards
Bay Country Woodcrafters.
wood milk cases
Dairy Service, Inc.
wood milk kegs
Dairy Service, Inc.
wood miniatures
Handcraft Originals.

Craft Item Index
Wood—Work

wood modeling materials
Terminal Hobby Shop.
wood panels
Town & Country Crafts.
wood parts
Minnesota Woodworkers Supply Co.
wood plaques
Artistry In Wood; The Cellar Ceramic Shop; O-P Craft Co., Inc.; Party Bazaar.
wood roses
Western Tree Cones.
wood scraps
Harrison Neustadt.
wood spools
Allegra Milano.
wood tables
Marie Mitchell's Decoupage Center.
wood stains
Fezandie & Sperrle, Inc.
wood tiles
Pack-O-Fun.
wood trays
O-P Craft Co., Inc.
wood turnings
Van Gelder Wood Products.
wood veneers
Albert Constantine & Son Inc.; Homecraft Veneer; The New England Craftsman.
woodburning
Supreme Handicrafts.
wooden apple cone
Colonial Decorations.
wooden candle molds
Barker Enterprises.
wooden candle sconces
Marie Mitchell's Decoupage Center.
wooden candleholders
O-P Craft Co., Inc.
wooden clocks
Marie Mitchell's Decoupage Center.
wooden switch plates
Marie Mitchell's Decoupage Center.
wooden tatting shuttles
Alfred Decker.
woodware
P. S. Andrews Co.; Bergen Arts & Crafts, Inc.; Boin Arts & Crafts; Carson & Ellis, Inc.; Century 21; Corner Cupboard Crafts, Inc.; Country Woodcraft; Craft Service; Economy Handicrafts, Inc.; P. C. Herwig Co., Inc.; John's Hardware & Decoupage Supplies; Magnus Craft Materials, Inc.; Marie Mitchell's Decoupage Center; Rombins' Nest Farm; Sandeen's Scandinavian Gift & Card Shop; Sax Arts & Crafts; Skil-Crafts Division; Town & Country Crafts; Traditional Norwegian Rosemaling; Lee Wards.
woodworking patterns
Craft Patterns.
woodworking supplies
Minnesota Woodworkers Supply Co.
woodworking tools
American Machine & Tool Co.; Arco Tools Inc.; Brookstone Co.; Sunset House.
wool
Charles M. Butterworth; Carlbert Fabrics; Contessa Yarns; Northwest Handcraft House; Isabel Scott Fabrics Corp.; Mildred Sprout; Straw Into Gold.
wool blends
Reichert's Fabrics.
wool carders
Frederick J. Fawcett, Inc.
wool clan tartans
Scotch House.
wool dyes
Creator's Corner; Northwest Handcraft House.
wool mill ends
Carlbert Fabrics.
wool patchwork quilt square patterns
House of Lines.
wool remnant pieces
Carlbert Fabrics.
wool rug yarn mill ends
Some Place.
wool swatches
Joan Moshimer.
wool velour panels
Framaway Co.
wool yarn
J & H Clasgens Co.; Wm. Condon & Sons Ltd.; Coulter Studios; Filature Lemieux Inc.; Folklorico; Harrisville Designs; Wonoco Yarn Co.
work benches
King's Studio.

Craft Item Index
Workshop—3-D

workshop power tools
Allcraft Tool & Supply Co.; Belsaw Power Tools.

worsted yarn
Greentree Ranch Wools, Countryside Handweavers.

woven labels
Charm Woven Labels; Walter Drake; Knit-Sew Labels; Spencer Gifts Inc.

wreaths
Holiday Handicrafts, Inc.

wrought iron tile frames
Renaldy's.

Wyoming jade
Bonnie's Rock Shop; Torrington Rock Shop.

YAG
The Jewelry Mart; Walter E. Johansen; Virgil V. Lundell; Syn-Crer Creations; Trader South; Transworld Trading Co.; Weisz Import Export Corp.

yardage counters
Robin & Russ Handweavers.

yarn color chart
Lee Wards.

yarn mixture packages
Contessa Yarns.

yarn surprise boxes
Fairtex Distributing Co.

yarn winders
KAY an EE Corp. of America.

yarns
Robert Ayottes' Designery; B & M Yarn Co.; Better Homes & Gardens; Dick Blick; Craft Yarns of Rhode Island Inc.; Crossroads; Delco Craft Center, Inc.; Dharma Trading Co.; Easy Street; Essayons Studio, Hand Arts Center; Fairtex Distributing Co.; Frederick J. Fawcett, Inc.; The Fringe and Frame; John E. Garrett Ltd.; Greentree Ranch Wools, Countryside Handweavers; Handcraft House; Heritage Hill Patterns; P. C. Herwig Co., Inc.; The Hidden Village; House of Flowers; Jerry S. Kaye Assoc.; Knitking; Knitking Magazine; Macrame and Weaving Supply Co.; Magnolia Weaving; The Makings; Mary Maxim Inc.; The Needlecase; Nimble Thimble; Robin & Russ Handweavers; Sax Arts & Crafts; Schrock's, The House of Hobbies & Crafts; Sears, Roebuck & Co.; Sign of the Arrow; Silver Shuttle; Mildred Sprout; Straw Into Gold; Studio Yarn Farms Inc.; Sunray Yarn House; Tahki Imports, Limited; Thumbelina Needlework Shop; Tuxedo Yarn & Needlework; Valley Handweaving Supply; Montgomery Ward & Co., Inc.; Lee Wards; Wonoco Yarn Co.; Wyco Yarn Co.; The Yarn Dome; Yarn Primitives; The Yarn and Soda Shop; Yarns Unlimited.

yellow gold casting grains
H. A. Cole.

yellow gold earwires
The Jewelry Mart.

yellow gold mountings
J. J. Jewelcraft.

zebra stone
Aspen Lapidary.

zippers
Home-Sew Inc.; Lace Lady; Two Brothers Inc.

zircon
Commercial Mineral Corp.; W. D. Hudson, Jr.; International Import Co.; Norlene Lapidary; Purcelli's Gems; Syn-Crer Creations.

zodiac inlay emblems
Craftsman Wood Service Co.

zodiacs
Jeweler's Emporium.

zoisite
W. D. Hudson, Jr.; G. Weidinger.

14 kt gold castings
Madewell Products Inc.

18th century prints
John's Hardware & Decoupage Supplies.

$2 bills
Hanover House Industries, Inc.

2/20's handweaving worsted
Frederick J. Fawcett, Inc.

2/7 wool
Greentree Ranch Wools, Countryside Handweavers.

3-D beading
Country Crafts.

3-D flexible decoupage cut-outs
Gemex Co.

3-D plastic molds
Doll's Candle & Craft Supplies

CRAFT CATEGORY INDEX

accessories
    Boin Arts & Crafts
    Sharon's Petite Sherre
    Skil-Crafts Division
    Straw Into Gold
acrylic felt pens
    Lillian Vernon
art tape
    Economy Handicrafts, Inc.
ash tray inserts
    Albert Constantine & Son Inc.
bag handles
    Knit Services, Inc.
bar magnets
    Maryland Magnet Co.
basket tote bags
    Helen Gallagher
beadery accessories
    The Beadcraft Corner/Beadcraft Club
    House of Orange
    Jewelart Inc.
    Nicole Bead & Craft Co., Inc.
    Sheru Bead Boutique Shop
belt buckles
    Edwards Jewelry Co.
    House of York
    Leathercrafters Supply Co.
    Macrame and Weaving Supply Co.
    The Sandvigs

Bermuda bag handles
    Sudberry House
billfold accessories
    Tandy Leather Co.
billfold parts
    Tandy Leather Co.
blank labels
    Althor Products
canvas tape
    Needle-Ease
carbon tracing paper
    Pins & Needles
cigarette lighter mechanisms
    Craft-Mark Products
decorating accessories
    Walnut Hill Co.
decoupage brushes
    John's Hardware & Decoupage Supplies
decoupage glues
    Century 21
dimensional plastic shapes
    Holiday Craft
disk magnets
    Maryland Magnet Co.
display cards
    Tye's
display domes
    Hanover House Industries, Inc.

Craft Category Index
Accessories—Accessories

display stands
   G. Weidinger
double stick tape
   Plaza Artists Materials, Inc.
flexible curve ruler
   Arthur Brown & Bro., Inc.
flexible magnetic strips
   Maryland Magnet Co.
flint paper
   Arthur Brown & Bro., Inc.
   Plaza Artists Materials, Inc.
fluid solder
   Lox-Seal Adhesives
gilding brushes
   Plaza Artists Materials, Inc.
graph paper
   Sewakers Industries Inc.
gummed paper
   Dick Blick
hat pins
   Hazel Pearson Handi Craft
   Whittemore-Durgin Glass Co.
hobby workbench
   Craft House
lighter inserts
   Bergen Arts & Crafts, Inc.
   National Artcraft Supply Co.
magnets
   Bob's Arts & Crafts
   Edmund Scientific Co.
   Home-Sew Inc.
   Maryland Magnet Co.
   Hazel Pearson Handi Craft
   Skil-Crafts Division
   Supreme Handicrafts
magnifiers
   Dick Blick
   Brookstone Co.
   Arthur Brown & Bro., Inc.
   Dover Scientific Co.
   Walter Drake
   Plaza Artists Materials, Inc.
magnifying glasses
   Nel-King Products
map pins
   Plaza Artists Materials, Inc.
marking pencils
   Art Mart, Inc.
metallic foil labels
   G. Weidinger

metallic tape
   Plaza Artists Materials, Inc.
miniature accessories
   The House of Miniatures
   Joen Ellen Kanze
   Miles Kimball
   The Miniature Mart-The Peddler's Shop
   Mrs. Mell Prescott
movable eyes
   Holiday Handicrafts, Inc.
   Home-Sew Inc.
plastic boxes
   Althor Products
   Craft Service
   Florida Supply House, Inc.
   Sax Arts & Crafts
plastic laminate countertopping
   Beno J. Gundlach Co.
plastic squeeze bottles
   Bear Cave
push pins
   Plaza Artists Materials, Inc.
repeat glass
   Arthur Brown & Bro., Inc.
   Plaza Artists Materials, Inc.
safety pins
   The Beadcraft Corner/Beadcraft Club
   Jeweler's Emporium
salt and pepper shakers mechanisms
   Albert Constantine & Son Inc.
sandpaper wet or dry
   3 M Company
scissors
   Arthur Brown & Bro., Inc.
   Polly Chester Inc.
   Walter Drake
   The Needle Works
   Hazel Pearson Handi Craft
   Sax Arts & Crafts
   Montgomery Ward & Co., Inc.
squeeze bottles
   Delco Craft Center, Inc.
steel rules
   The L. S. Starrett Co.
stick magnets
   Maryland Magnet Co.
stock threaded plastic jars
   Parkway Plastics Inc.
surgical knives
   Brookstone Co.

surgical scissors
  Brookstone Co.
table lighter inserts
  Albert Constantine & Son Inc.
wax pens
  Art Consultants
  Bourget Bros. Gems & Minerals
wiggle eyes
  Delco Craft Center, Inc.
acrylics *(see Plastic crafts)*
adhesives
  Art Mart, Inc.
  Basic Crafts Co.
  Arthur Brown & Bro., Inc.
  The Ducketts
  Holiday Craft
  Skil-Crafts Division
  W. Wooley & Co.
adhesive sprays
  Walnut Hill Co.
cements
  Delco Craft Center, Inc.
  Knit Services, Inc.
  Leathercrafters Supply Co.
  Sax Arts & Crafts
decoupage glues
  Century 21
double stick tape
  Plaza Artists Materials, Inc.
epoxy adhesives
  Beacon Chemical Co., Inc.
epoxy glues
  High Strength Adhesives Corp.
epoxy resins
  High Strength Adhesives Corp.
  Polyproducts Corp.
fluid solder
  Lox-Seal Adhesives
furniture glues
  Albert Constantine & Son Inc.
glues
  Carson & Ellis, Inc.
  Cleveland Leather Co.
  Craftsman Supply House
  Jeweler's Emporium
  Koehler's Craft Outlet
  Hazel Pearson Handi Craft
  Sax Arts & Crafts
grout
  F. E. Biegert Co.

gummed paper
  Dick Blick
jewelry cement
  Star Diamond Industries
leather cements
  Tandy Leather Co.
liquid cement
  Lox-Seal Adhesives
silicone rubber
  High Strength Adhesives Corp.
spray adhesives
  Carnival Arts & Crafts
vinyl glues
  High Strength Adhesives Corp.
American Indian crafts
  Boin Arts & Crafts
  Craft Service
  Magnus Craft Materials, Inc.
  Sax Arts & Crafts
  Tandy Leather Co.
  Winona Trading Post
American Indian artifacts
  Dover Scientific Co.
American Indian bead corn
  Crowe & Coulter
American Indian flower corn
  Crowe & Coulter
American Indian jewelry supplies
  Panther International Ltd.
American Indian seed beads
  Anne's Treasure Trove
  The Beadcraft Corner/Beadcraft Club
  Nicole Bead & Craft Co., Inc.
books
  Association Press
  Cleveland Leather Co.
  Craft Course Publishers
  Dharma Trading Co.
  Naturegraph Publishers
  Popular Library Inc.
group plans
  Boin Arts & Crafts
kits
  Cleveland Leather Co.
  Crowe & Coulter
  Jewelart Inc.
animal hair *(see also Furs)*
alpaca
  Colonial Textiles
  Greentree Ranch Wools, Countryside Handweavers

Craft Category Index
Animal—Artist's

    The Hidden Village
    KM Yarn Co.
    Valley Handweaving Supply
camel hair
    Colonial Textiles
    Macrame and Weaving Supply Co.
goathair
    KM Yarn Co.
horsehair
    The Hidden Village

antiquing *(see also Furniture refinishing)*
books
    Valspar Corp.
kits
    American Handicrafts
    Sturbridge Yankee Workshop

artist's supplies
    A 'N L's Hobbicraft, Inc.
    Bergen Arts & Crafts, Inc.
    Dick Blick
    Bob's Arts & Crafts
    Boin Arts & Crafts
    Arthur Brown & Bro., Inc.
    D. M. Campana Co.
    Craft Service
    Delco Craft Center, Inc.
    Kraft Korner
    Make It Happen Craft Studio
    NASCO Arts & Crafts
    Plaza Artists Materials, Inc.
    Skil-Crafts Division
airbrushes
    Badger Air-Brush Co.
    Dick Blick
    Arthur Brown & Bro., Inc.
    Douglas & Sturgess, Inc.
    Newton's Potters Supply
    Plaza Artists Materials, Inc.
    Skil-Crafts Division
art paper
    Delco Craft Center, Inc.
    Skil-Crafts Division
art tape
    Economy Handicrafts, Inc.
artist portfolios
    Framaway Co.
artist's dry colors
    Fezandie & Sperrle, Inc.
ballpoint paints
    Arthur Brown & Bro., Inc.
    Budget Buddy Co.

    The Handcrafters
    Sax Arts & Crafts
    Lee Wards
bamboo brushes
    Plaza Artists Materials, Inc.
brayers
    Stewart Industries
bronze powder
    Carson & Ellis, Inc.
    Peg Hall Studios
brushes
    Peg Hall Studios
    Plaza Artists Materials, Inc.
calipers
    The L. S. Starrett Co.
canvas panels
    Framaway Co.
chalks
    American Art Clay Co. Inc.
cork
    Arthur Brown & Bro., Inc.
    Cleveland Leather Co.
    Craft Service
    Craftsman Supply House
    Economy Handicrafts, Inc.
    The Handcrafters
    Magnus Craft Materials, Inc.
    NASCO Arts & Crafts
    Plaza Artists Materials, Inc.
    Sax Arts & Crafts
    Skil-Crafts Division
    Westwood Ceramic Supply Co.
cork disks
    Westwood Ceramic Supply Co.
corrugated paper
    Dick Blick
    Boin Arts & Crafts
    Plaza Artists Materials, Inc.
drawing paper
    Bergen Arts & Crafts, Inc.
easels
    Framaway Co.
etching supplies
    Art Mart, Inc.
    Arthur Brown & Bro., Inc.
    Craft Service
    Craftsman Supply House
    William Dixon Co.
    Economy Handicrafts, Inc.
    The Handcrafters
    St. Louis Crafts Inc.

Craft Category Index
Artist's—Basketry

Sax Arts & Crafts
Skil-Crafts Division
etching tools
William Dixon Co.
felt pens
Art Mart, Inc.
Dick Blick
Arthur Brown & Bro., Inc.
Spencer Gifts Inc.
flexible curve ruler
Arthur Brown & Bro., Inc.
flint paper
Arthur Brown & Bro., Inc.
Plaza Artists Materials, Inc.
gilding brushes
Plaza Artists Materials, Inc.
graph paper
Sewakers Industries Inc.
inks
Advance Process Supply Co.
knives
Art Mart, Inc.
model airbrushes
Miniature Aircraft
pallettes
Koehler's Craft Outlet
power etching instrument
Electro Stylus Mfg. Co.
ready-stretched canvas
Framaway Co.
roll canvas
Framaway Co.
scaleograph
Plaza Artists Materials, Inc.
scaleograph proportional slide rule
Arthur Brown & Bro., Inc.
spray guns
Montgomery Ward & Co., Inc.
steel rules
The L. S. Starrett Co.
stencil brushes
American Decorative Arts, Inc.
stretcher strips
Framaway Co.
tape
Beadnik's Arts & Crafts
Arthur Brown & Bro., Inc.
Plaza Artists Materials, Inc.
tilt top tables
John & Susan Scheewe

tracing paper
Plaza Artists Materials, Inc.
wax pens
Art Consultants
Bourget Bros. Gems & Minerals
wool velour panels
Framaway Co.
banner making *(see wall hangings)*
bargello *(see Needlepoint)*
basketry *(see also Cane, reed, and rush working)*
A 'N L's Hobbicraft, Inc.
Atlantic Upholstery Supply Co.
Bergen Arts & Crafts, Inc.
Bersted's
Boin Arts & Crafts
Cane & Basket Supply Co.
Century 21
Craft Service
Craftsman Supply House
Economy Handicrafts, Inc.
Gibsons Creations
The Hidden Village
John's Hardware & Decoupage Supplies
Magnus Craft Materials, Inc.
NASCO Arts & Crafts
Sax Arts & Crafts
Straw Into Gold
Supreme Handicrafts
Zim's
bamboo
Boin Arts & Crafts
books
Cane & Basket Supply Co.
Dharma Trading Co.
Naturegraph Publishers
Pitman Publishing Corp.
Hong Kong grass
Craftsman Supply House
kits
Pack-O-Fun
Savin Handcrafts
ready-made baskets
Fran's Basket House
reed
Bersted's
Cleveland Leather Co.
Craft Service
Craftsman Supply House

Craft Category Index
Basketry—Beadery

    Delco Craft Center, Inc.
    Sax Arts & Crafts
batik *(see also Dyes, Wax)*
    Bergen Arts & Crafts, Inc.
    Boin Arts & Crafts
    Arthur Brown & Bro., Inc.
    Craftool Co.
    Essayons Studio, Hand Arts Center
    Gemex Co.
    Magic Circle Corp.
    Magnus Craft Materials, Inc.
    Joan Moshimer
    Hazel Pearson Handi Craft
    Sax Arts & Crafts
  accessories
    Joan Moshimer
  batik (instant)
    Polyproducts Corp.
  batik dyes
    Berry's of Maine
    Castolite
    Cleveland Leather Co.
    Delco Craft Center, Inc.
    Dharma Trading Co.
    Fezandie & Sperrle, Inc.
    Handcraft House
    The Hidden Village
    House of Gould
    KM Yarn Co.
    Leathercrafters Supply Co.
    Magnus Craft Materials, Inc.
    The Niddy Noddy
    Northwest Handcraft House
    Sax Arts & Crafts
    Skil-Crafts Division
    Straw Into Gold
    Surma Book & Music Store
    W. Wooley & Co.
  batik materials
    Rupert, Gibbon & Spider
  batik supplies
    Behnsen Silk Screen Supply Ltd.
  batik tools
    Glen Black Handwoven Textiles
    Joan Moshimer
  batik wax
    Delco Craft Center, Inc.
    Hazel Pearson Handi Craft
  batik wax blends
    Siphon Art Products

  blowpipes
    Gilman's
  books
    Book Barn
    Chilton Book Co.
    Craftool Co.
    Crafty Ideas
    Crown Publishers
    Davis Publications, Inc.
    Dye-Craft Ideas
    LeJeune, Inc.
    Parker Publishing Co., Inc.
    Robin & Russ Handweavers
    Rupert, Gibbon & Spider
    The Unicorn
  cold process batik textile wax
    Siphon Art Products
  cold water dyes
    Artis, Inc.
    Glen Black Handwoven Textiles
    Creator's Corner
    Delco Craft Center, Inc.
    Knit Services, Inc.
  fabric dyes
    Joan Moshimer
  frames
    Joan Moshimer
  kits
    Craftool Co.
    Rub 'N Buff
  magazines
    American Home Crafts
    Decorating & Craft Ideas Made Easy
    McCall's Needlework & Crafts
    McCall's Pattern Fashions
    1001 Fashion & Needlecraft Ideas
  tjanting tool
    Hazel Pearson Handi Craft
  wax
    Sax Arts & Crafts
    Surma Book & Music Store
beadery *(see also Jewelrymaking)*
    American Handicrafts
    P. S. Andrews Co.
    Bead Game
    The Beadcraft Corner/Beadcraft Club
    Beadnik's Arts & Crafts
    Bethlehem Imports
    Dick Blick
    Bob's Arts & Crafts
    Boin Arts & Crafts

Craft Category Index
Beadery—Beadery

Boutique Trims
Boycan's Craft Supplies
The Craft Corner
Craft Service
Craftsman Supply House
Creative Craft House
Crowe & Coulter
Delco Craft Center, Inc.
Derby Lane Shell Center
Easy Street
Economy Handicrafts, Inc.
Feather & Flower Craft
Gemex Co.
Gibsons Creations
The Handcrafters
P. C. Herwig Co., Inc.
The Hidden Village
Holiday Craft
House of Flowers
House of Orange
Jeane's
Jewel Creations
Jewelart Inc.
Jeweler's Emporium
Jo-El's Craft Co.
Kaydee
Kaydee Craft Supplies
Kit Kraft
Knit Services, Inc.
Kraft Korner
Macrame and Weaving Supply Co.
Magnus Craft Materials, Inc.
The Mannings Creative Crafts
Mary Maxim Inc.
Modern Craft
New Products Co.
Nicole Bead & Craft Co., Inc.
Bob and Carol Oliver
Ovgem Craft Supply Co.
Hazel Pearson Handi Craft
Sav-On-Crafts
Sax Arts & Crafts
Sears, Roebuck & Co.
Sheru Bead Boutique Shop
Skil-Crafts Division
Sunray Yarn House
Supreme Handicrafts
Tahki Imports, Limited
Taylor House
Town & Country Crafts
Tuxedo Yarn & Needlework

Lee Wards
Winona Trading Post
Zim's
African trading beads
  Jewelart Inc.
  Jeweler's Emporium
alphabet beads
  Bead Game
  Jewelart Inc.
American Indian seed beads
  Anne's Treasure Trove
  The Beadcraft Corner/Beadcraft Club
  Nicole Bead & Craft Co., Inc.
aurora borealis beads
  The Beadcraft Corner/Beadcraft Club
bamboo beads
  The Beadcraft Corner/Beadcraft Club
  Pack-O-Fun
bead flowermaking
  Kit Kraft
  Rombins' Nest Farm
  Supreme Handicrafts
bead looms
  Bead Game
  Nicole Bead & Craft Co., Inc.
bead mills
  Gilman's
bead rods
  Kay Kinney-Contoured Glass
beadery accessories
  The Beadcraft Corner/Beadcraft Club
  House of Orange
  Jewelart Inc.
  Nicole Bead & Craft Co., Inc.
  Sheru Bead Boutique Shop
beadery tools
  Jewelart Inc.
beading wax
  Nicole Bead & Craft Co., Inc.
beggar beads
  Adris Oriental Gem & Art Corp.
books
  Better Homes & Gardens Books
  Book Barn
  Charles T. Branford Co.
  Crown Publishers
  Gloria's Glass Garden
  P. C. Herwig Co., Inc.
  Museum Books Inc.
  Products and Systems, Inc.
  Sancraft Industries

Craft Category Index
Beadery—Beadery

    Charles Scribner's Sons
    Sterling Publishing Co. Inc.
    Taplinger Publishing Co.
brass beads
    Bead Game
    Macrame and Weaving Supply Co.
carved beads
    Bethlehem Imports
ceramic bead trees
    Cole Ceramics Laboratories
ceramic beads
    Gloria's Glass Garden
    Jewelart Inc.
    Macrame and Weaving Supply Co.
    Three Gables Homecrafts
chains
    Green's Rock & Lapidary Ltd.
    Jewel Creations
    Jeweler's Emporium
    Montgomery Ward & Co., Inc.
clay beads
    Bead Game
club plans
    The Beadcraft Corner/Beadcraft Club
cow horn beads
    Bead Game
earthenware beads
    P. C. Herwig Co., Inc.
emerald beads
    Adris Oriental Gem & Art Corp.
evil-eye beads
    Bead Game
faceted beads
    The Beadcraft Corner/Beadcraft Club
    Jim Kesterson
filigree beads
    Jewelart Inc.
findings
    The Beadcraft Corner/Beadcraft Club
    Feather & Flower Craft
    Gibsons Creations
    Jewelart Inc.
    Jeweler's Emporium
    Kaydee Craft Supplies
    Kit Kraft
gem beads
    Bead Game
glass beads
    Bead Game
    The Freed Co.
    Gloria's Glass Garden
    P. C. Herwig Co., Inc.
    Jewelart Inc.
    Macrame and Weaving Supply Co.
glass tubular beads
    Bethlehem Imports
glazed beads
    Bead Game
group packs
    Boin Arts & Crafts
handcrafted stoneware beads
    Earthworks
handmade Swiss wood beads
    Robin & Russ Handweavers
imported beads
    Bead Game
ivory beads
    Bead Game
    Jewelart Inc.
kits
    Alohalei Hawaii
    Beadcraft
    Bead-Weavers
    Brookhurst Hobbys
    Feather & Flower Craft
    Gemex Co.
    Gloria's Glass Garden
    Koehler's Craft Outlet
    Mary Maxim Inc.
    Nicole Bead & Craft Co., Inc.
    Bob and Carol Oliver
    Rombins' Nest Farm
    Sav-On-Crafts
    Sheru Bead Boutique Shop
    Skil-Crafts Division
    Lee Wards
mache beads
    Bead Game
macrame beads
    Tandy Leather Co.
magazines
    American Home Crafts
metallic beads
    The Beadcraft Corner/Beadcraft Club
mosaic beads
    Bead Game
    Jeweler's Emporium
natural stone beads
    Jewelart Inc.
nuts
    Bead Game

Craft Category Index
Beadery—Blockprinting

olivewood beads
  Bethlehem Imports
pearls
  Anne's Treasure Trove
  Bead Game
  The Beadcraft Corner/Beadcraft Club
  Deep Flex Plastic Molds, Inc.
  Gilman's
  Home-Sew Inc.
  International Import Co.
  Jewelart Inc.
  Kaydee
  Kit Kraft
  M & M Distributors
  Natalie Originals Studio
  New Products Co.
  The Putter Shop
  Schrock's, The House of Hobbies & Crafts
  Swan-Son
  Taylor House
plastic beads
  Bead Game
  Florida Supply House, Inc.
pony beads
  The Beadcraft Corner/Beadcraft Club
porcelain beads
  Bead Game
  Reeves Knotique
pre-Columbian beads
  Bead Game
propellar (tri) beads
  The Beadcraft Corner/Beadcraft Club
rocailles
  The Beadcraft Corner/Beadcraft Club
rondelles
  The Beadcraft Corner/Beadcraft Club
rosebeads
  The Beadcraft Corner/Beadcraft Club
sandlewood beads
  Jewelart Inc.
seed beads
  House of Orange
  Macrame and Weaving Supply Co.
self-adhesive iridescent foil jewels
  Diffraction Co., Inc.
shell beads
  Bead Game
sterling silver beads
  Jewelart Inc.
stoneware beads
  P. C. Herwig Co., Inc.
  Knit Services, Inc.
  Reeves Knotique
tissue beads
  Holiday Handicrafts, Inc.
tortoise-shell beads
  Bead Game
trade beads
  Bead Game
tri-beads
  Don's Hobby Co.
unusual beads
  Veronica
wood beads
  Bead Game
  Florida Supply House, Inc.
  Gloria's Glass Garden
  P. C. Herwig Co., Inc.
  Jewelart Inc.
3-D beading
  Country Crafts
bisque *(see Ceramics)*
blockprinting *(see also Screen processing)*
  American Handicrafts
  Art Mart, Inc.
  Bergen Arts & Crafts, Inc.
  Dick Blick
  Boin Arts & Crafts
  Arthur Brown & Bro., Inc.
  Craft Service
  Delco Craft Center, Inc.
  Economy Handicrafts, Inc.
  Sax Arts & Crafts
  Stewart Industries
blockprinting dye
  Rupert, Gibbon & Spider
blockprinting papers
  Stewart Industries
blockprinting press
  Stewart Industries
blocks
  Stewart Industries
brayers
  Stewart Industries
carving tools
  Art Mart, Inc.
  Sax Arts & Crafts

Craft Category Index
Boat—Books

boat building
  boat building supplies
    M & M Hardwood
  books
    Arco Publishing Co., Inc.
    Coward, McCann & Geoghegan
    Model Craftsman Publishing Corp.
    3 M Company
  Dacron® sail rigs
    Folbot Corp.
  kits
    Bear Cave
    Folbot Corp.
    Luger
    Ships Unlimited
    Trailcraft Inc.
  leaflets
    Popular Mechanics Press
  magazines
    Boat Builder
  ship models
    Coker Craft

books *(see also specific craft)*
    A 'N L's Hobbicraft, Inc.
    Activa Products Inc.; celluclay (instant papier mache), flower drying with silica gel, general arts & crafts series, porcelainizing fresh flowers with Ceramex.
    Adobe-Craft; making water resistant adobes.
    Adventures In Crafts; decoupage.
    Alessi Lapidary Supplies
    Allcraft Tool & Supply Co.
    Mrs. Barbara Allen; egg decorating.
    The Amber Lion; decorative patterns for tole and cutouts.
    America's Hobby Center Inc
    American Art Associates Publications, Inc.; decoupage under glass
    American Art Clay Co. Inc.; ceramic decoration, metal enameling, potter's wheel.
    American Decorative Arts, Inc.; stencils.
    American Technical Society; basic graphic arts, cabinetmaking, carpentry fundamentals, machine shop operations, masonry, metal work, metallurgy, millwork, oxyacetylene welding, plastering, sheet metal, upholstery.
    Sonie Ames
    Amherst Press; silhouettes.
    Anne Amiot
    The Amulet; jewelry wire.
    Rebecca Andrews
    Arco Publishing Co., Inc.; boats, cabinetry, carpentry, children's projects, craft anthology, furniture refinishing, general arts & crafts series, metal working, model airplanes, model car handbook, needlework, Early American furniture making.
    Art Mart, Inc.
    Artcraft
    Artis, Inc.; painting.
    Artistry In Wood
    Arts and Crafts Unlimited; greeting card patterns.
    Associated Book Sellers; general arts & crafts series.
    Association Press; clock repair, jewelrymaking, American Indian crafts.
    Theodore Audel & Co.; bricklaying, building, carpentry, masonry.
    Aunt Martha's Studios Inc.; quilt patterns.
    Australian Gem Trading Co.; gemstones of Australia.
    Robert Ayottes' Designery
    Ballantine Books, Inc.; clothing, fabric printing, general arts & crafts series, macrame, pottery, printing, sewing, tie-dye.
    Barbara Bannister; dolls, needlecrafts, quilts.
    Barker Enterprises
    A. S. Barnes and Co., Inc.; candlemaking, country crafts, decorating, general arts & crafts series, wood carving, wood crafts.
    The Beadcraft Corner/Beadcraft Club
    Beagle Mfg. Co.; leaded stain glass.
    Belle Craft
    Charles A. Bennett Co., Inc.; cabinetry, drafting, enameling, furniture making, industrial plastics, leather craft, metal working, millwork,

sheet metal, tailoring, wood turning, woodworking.
Dorothy Benson
Bruce Benziger; general arts & crafts series, machine shop, operation of woodworking machines, sheet metal, upholstery, woodturning.
Bergen Arts & Crafts, Inc.
Berry's of Maine
Bersted's
Best Foods; dye patterns and techniques, dye-craft.
Bet-Roc Enterprises Inc.; gemology, lapidary, rockhounding.
Better Homes & Gardens
Better Homes & Gardens Books; bead craft, crewel embroidery, embroidery, general arts & crafts series, needlepoint, sewing.
Dick Blick
James Bliss & Co. Inc.; ship model building.
Bob's Arts & Crafts
Boin Arts & Crafts
Vivian Bonnema
Book Barn; applique, batik, bead crafts, bird carving, blacksmithing, book binding, calligraphy, candlemaking, ceramics, crewel, crochet, decoupage, design, doll making, dyeing, embroidery, enamel, flower drying, general arts & crafts series, handweaving, jewelry, knitting, lacemaking, lapidary, leather crafts, macrame, metalwork, mosaics, needlepoint, papier mache, patchwork, printing, puppetry, rug hooking, silk screen, spinning, symmography, tie-dye, toleware, woodworking.
Bookpost; old book values.
Bovin Publishing; centrifugal or lost wax casting, jewerlymaking, silversmithing & art metal.
Boycan's Craft Supplies; advanced wood fibre, corsage designs, crocheted jewelry, foliage arrangements, marble jewelry, pine cones, plastic laminating, wood fibre, Christmas projects.
Charles T. Branford Co.; bead embroidery, canvas work, creative stitchery, crochet, doll making, embroidery from English patterns, fabric printing, general arts & crafts series, patchwork, rug making.
Brookhurst Hobbys
Brooklyn Botanic Garden; dye plants and dyeing.
Brookstone Co.; metal, woodworking.
Arthur Brown & Bro., Inc.
Budget Buddy Co.
Karen Burrus; tole designs.
Butterick Fashion Marketing Co.; sewing adjustments and alterations.
Cadillac Plastic & Chemical Co.; plastics craftsmanship.
Cake Decorators & Craft Supplies
D. M. Campana Co.
Candle Mill Village; candlemaking.
Cane & Basket Supply Co.
Carson & Ellis, Inc.
Carter Craft Doll House; doll fashions.
Castolite
Cavalier Handicrafts
Ceramics Monthly; ceramics, enameling, pottery.
Charbonneau's Lapidary Service
Chemical Publishing Co., Inc.; brickwork, inventor's reference book, technical devices handbook.
Chilton Book Co.; ceramics, cloth toys, collage, enameling, flameworking, gemcraft, general arts & crafts series, glass craft, glassforming, jewelrymaking, kiln-fired glass, knitting & crocheting, leather, metalsmithing, nature crafts, needlepoint, papier mache, plastics, polystyrene foam craft, porcelain painting, potterymaking, quilting, rug making, sandcast candles, sculpting in steel, sculpture, selling handcrafts, shellcraft, stained glass, stained glass lamps, wax sculpture, wooden toys, Christmas creations.
China Decorator; china painting.
Chrismon Committee; Chrismon monograms and symbols.
Cleveland Leather Co.; American Indian crafts.

Craft Category Index
Books—Books

The Clever Crafters; art foam, egg, net, scrap craft.
Coker Craft; ships, tanks.
Colorado Geological Industries Inc.; geological.
Albert Constantine & Son Inc.
Contemporary Quilts; beginner quilting.
Cooke Novelty Co.; cement casting, mold making, plaster casting.
Cookson & Thode; leaded stained glass designs.
The Country Craftsmen; weaving with fur.
Country Woodcraft; carving, handmade soap, wood carving patterns.
Covington Engineering Corp.; cabochons, facet cutting, gems, minerals, rocks.
Coward, McCann & Geogheagan; fiberglass boat building.
The Craft Corner
Craft Course Publishers; art foam, bead jewelry, bread dough, candlemaking, craft sticks, crepe paper flowers, decoupage, dip film, felt, figure draping, general arts & crafts series, macrame, nylon net, papier mache, resin craft, synthetic straw, tissue flowers, American Indian crafts.
Craft Service
Craftool Co.; canework, cardboard model making, glove making, lacemaking, lampshades, netting, terracotta, willow work, wood toymaking.
Crafts Yarns & Gifts
Crafts Yarns & Gifts Ltd.; safety pin jewelry, tri-bead jewelry, yarn winding.
Craftsman Circle Book Club; macrame, needlecraft, spinning, weaving.
Craftsman Supply House
Crafty Ideas; candlemaking, ceramics, decoupage, folk art painting, folk painting, glass and resin crafts, needlework, rosemaling, Christmas crafts.
Creative Craft House; selling crafts.

Creative Hands Co., Inc.
Dr. David Crespi; ceramic glazes, clay and glazes.
Crewel Elephant; patterns for embroidered clothing.
Crossroads; crewel, needlepoint.
Crown Publishers; bargello, batik, bead design, bottle cutting, candlemaking, card weaving, casting, ceramics, crewel, crochet, decoupage, dye, found materials, gem cutting, general arts & crafts series, gold and silversmithing, gold leaf, hand weaving, macrame, metal enameling, metal sculpture, model aircraft, mosaics, paper, papier mache, plastics, sculpture casting, shell crafts, stone sculpture, string art, tie-dye, tole designs, wall hanging, wood.
Mrs. Danner's Quilts; basic quiltmaking.
Margaret Davis; rugs from nylons and pantyhose.
Davis & Co.; American folk art painting.
Davis Publications, Inc.; batik dye, ceramics, clay, design, general arts & crafts series, mosaics, papier mache, puppetmaking, scrap art, screen, sculpture, stitchery, tie-dye, tissue paper, wall hangings, weaving without a loom, wire sculpture.
Marquerite P. Davison; handweaver's patterns.
Deft; decoupage.
Delco Craft Center, Inc.
Delmar Publishers; hand tools for woodworking.
T. S. Denison & Co., Inc.; paper crafts, party decorations.
Dharma Trading Co.
The Dial Press Inc.; collage, needlepoint, sand sculpturing, slate sculpturing.
Doll Repair Parts, Inc.
Doll's Candle & Craft Supplies
Dollspart Supply Co., Inc.
Dorothy Mae's Trunks; installing interiors, refinishing, repairing, restoring antique trunks.

The Dorr Mill Store
Dover Publications Inc.; basketry, furniture making, general arts & crafts series, pottery, primitive, screen printing, sculpture, wood carving, Pueblo and other American Indian design.
Dover Scientific Co.
Dowse's Lapidary Supply, Inc.; table top making.
Drake Publishers Inc.; cabinet making, carpenter's tools, china repairs and restoration, crochet, dried flower decorating, egg decorating, embroidery, fabric crafts, furnituremaking, general arts & crafts series, knitting, leather crafts, log sculpture, marquetry, masonry, mosaics, paper crafts, rag doll making, rug making, scratch board, smocking, toys and wood toys, upholstery, woodworking.
Driftwood House; crafting, driftwood.
The Ducketts
E. P. Dutton & Co., Inc.; candlemaking, classic guitar making and guitar repair, folding paper masks, general arts & crafts series, origami, puppet making, sewing.
Dye-Craft Ideas; batik, dye craft, solid color dyeing, stitch dyeing, tiedye.
East River Publications; belt-weaving, loom building.
Edmund Scientific Co.
Dick Ells Co.; lost wax jewelry casting.
Emerson Books Inc.; knotting, leather craft, mobiles, net making, paper crafts, watch and clock repair, woodworking.
The Enchanted Doll House; doll making.
Ewanna England; dimensional painting, reverso painting with foil.
Luella Ensz; patterns for tole painters.
Essayons Studio, Hand Arts Center
Eva Ann Dolls; applehead dolls.
Exact Performance; aviation, military.
Exposition Press; cornshuck crafts.
Fairtex Distributing Co.

The Family Handyman; carpentry, furniture antiquing and restoring, hand and power tools.
Fawcett Special Interest Magazines & Books; decorating, general arts & crafts series, needlework, Christmas crafts.
Mrs. C. Ference; Ukrainian Easter Eggs.
Ficket; resilvering mirrors, using sawdust 20 ways.
Flair-Craft Inc.; decoupage, tole painting.
N. Flayderman & Co.; scrimshaw.
Florida Supply House, Inc.
Follett Publishing Co.; model rocketry, taxidermy.
Fountains for the Home; ceramic fountain.
Frank's Jewelry & Gem Shop; gem.
Frankie's Twistcraft Jewelry; twistcraft jewelry.
Gager's Handicrafts
Gay World of Dolls Museum; Doll Repair.
Gemex Co.
Gemological Institute of America; gem identification, gemstone carving and cutting, ivory, jewelry design and instructions, jewelry repair, stones.
Gems & Minerals; gem cutting, jewelrymaking, lost wax casting, minerals, stone collecting, tumbling.
Gerhardt Macrame Studio; square knotting.
The Ghen Studio; came method of making stained glass medallions, copper foil stained glass medallions.
Gilman's
Glass Bottle Blowers Assn.; making useful articles for the home from glass bottles.
Glass House Studio; introducing stained glass.
Gloria's Glass Garden; beadcraft, candlemaking, macrame.
Goodhert-Willcox Co., Inc.; ceramics, industrial woodworking, metal projects, metal working, plastics, welding.

Craft Category Index
Books—Books

Irene Goodwin; gold etching.
Gordon's
Great Outdoors Publishing Co.; cast net construction, general arts & crafts series, pine cone crafts, shells.
Green's Rock & Lapidary Ltd.
Grosset & Dunlap Inc.; candlecraft, crewel, general arts & crafts series, needlepoint, quilting, sewing.
T. B. Hagstoz & Son
Peg Hall Studios; designs, metal and wood ware decorating, patterns, stenciling.
Handcraft House
The Handcrafters
Harper & Row, Publishers Inc.; crochet, general arts & crafts series, knitting, model airplanes, needlework, pile rug making, pottery.
Harrower House of Decoupage
Hearthside Press; bargello, beaded flower making, crochet, decoupage, egg decorating, general arts & crafts series, knitting, leather and fur sewing, macrame, needle made rug design, needlecraft, paper crafts, papier mache, pottery, preserved flower designs and decorating, quilting, shell craft, tole, Christmas decorations.
P. C. Herwig Co., Inc.; beadery, candlemaking, decoupage, knitting, macrame, paper, weaving.
The Hidden Village; textile handicrafts.
Elizabeth Hiddleson; crochet.
Historical Society of Early American Decoration, Inc; publishes semi-annual journal "The Decorator".
Hobby Gallery
Hobby House Press; doll collecting, dollmaking.
Holiday Handicrafts, Inc.
Cherie Hooper; candlemaking.
House of Flowers; quilling.
House of Gould
House of Yarn & Crafts
Howe Studio; designs for eggers and mini-crafts.
HTH Publishers; looms, tapestry, textiles, weaving.
Industrial Press Inc.; machine shop.
Japan Publications Trading Co.; mobiles, origami, paper aircraft, Japanese kits.
Jewelart Inc.
J. J. Jewelcraft
Walter E. Johansen
Kathryn Johnson; eggery.
Kalmbach Publishing Co.; model railroading.
Karlkraft Studio-Cheva
Kaydee
Kieffer's Lingerie Fabric & Supplies; lingerie construction.
Kay Kinney-Contoured Glass
Kit Kraft
Knitking; machine knitting.
Kodansha International, U.S.A.; Japanese ceramics.
Koehler's Craft Outlet
Lane Magazine & Book Co.; ceramics, furniture finishing, furniture upholstery, general arts & crafts series, leather, macrame, needlepoint, outdoor construction, papier mache, quilting and patchwork, woodcarving, woodworking.
Lantern Press Inc.; craft anthologies, holiday crafts, world-wide crafts.
Lapidary Journal Book Dept.; carving, cutting, flourescence, gem craft, gemology, gold and silversmithing, jewelry craft, jewelry repair, lost wax, minerals, precious and semi-precious stones, rocks, stones.
Barbara Lawshe
Leathercrafters Supply Co.; leatherworking.
Leclerc Corp.; weaving.
Lee Mountain; ceramics, rugmaking, used books silk screening.
Leisure Hour Products; coathanger items, various crafts.
Leisure Services; quilling.
LeJeune, Inc.; batik and dyeing, macrame.
Leman Publications; quilting.
Lewiscraft; crafts for children.
The Library Corner; ceramics.

Craft Category Index
Books—Books

Lily Mills Co.; needlecraft, weaving.
James F. Lincoln Arc Welding Foundation; Arc Welding.
J. B. Lippincott Co.; children's crafts, general arts & crafts series, nature crafts, Christmas decorations.
Ruth Little's Studio; flower studies.
Liveright; knitting.
Lothrop, Lee & Shephard; bread dough craft, general arts & crafts series, spoolcraft.
S. Lynds Patterns; jig saw patterns.
MAC Enterprises; refinishing and restoring antiques.
The Macmillan Publishing Co.; candlemaking, ceramics, general arts & crafts series, leather craft, paper craft, plastics.
Macrame and Weaving Supply Co.
Magic Circle Corp.; construction of wax models.
Maid of Scandinavia
The Mail Train; Swedish weaving (crewel).
Make It Happen Craft Studio
The Makings
The Mannings Creative Crafts
Margaret's Egg Craft; egg craft.
Thelma Sutton Martin; decorative painting, textile designs, tole designs.
Martin Fabrics; sewing and caring for velvet.
Maxant Button & Supply Co.; covered buttons.
Mary Maxim Inc.
McGraw-Hill Book Co.; building modern and built-in furniture, general arts & crafts series, machine metal working, making children's furniture, making children's furniture and play equipment, plywood projects, upholstered furniture making and design, woodworking and wood finishing.
David McKay Co., Inc.; general arts & crafts series, paper crafts, puppets.
McKnight Publishing Co.; general arts & crafts series, jewelrymaking, leather craft, metal working, plastics, upholstering, wood furniture making, wood laminating, woodworking.
Minex Lapidary Supplies
Miniature Figurines--USA, Inc.
Minnesota Clay
Minnesota Woodworkers Supply Co.
Marie Mitchell's Decoupage Center; crafts, decoupage, rice paper.
Frank Mittermeier Inc.
Model Craftsman Publishing Corp.; model aircraft, model railroad, model ship building.
Model Railroad Equipment Corp.
Mollica Stained Glass Press; leaded glass technique.
Mon Tricot; hairpin lace, jacquard, knitting dictionary, knitting stitches & patterns/crochet stitches & patterns, patchwork.
William Morrow & Co.; general arts & crafts series, string art.
Joan Moshimer
Mountain Ceramic Crafts; ceramic project.
Mrs. Carl F. Murray; dyeing.
Museum Books Inc.; bead crafts, candlemaking, ceramics, crochet, decoupage, enameling, general arts & crafts series, gold leafing, jewelrymaking, knitting, macrame, metal, needlecrafts, pottery, rug making, sewing, stained glass, textile, weaving, wood carving and working.
Nantucket Needleworks; needlecraft.
Natcol Crafts, Inc.
National Craft & Hobby Co., Inc.; figurine, painting.
National Hobby Inc.
Naturegraph Publishers; preserving in clear plastic, sandpainting, American Indian basket weaving.
The Needle Works; embroidery, needlepoint, quilting.
The Needlecase
Needlecraft House; needlecraft.
Needlecraft Shop Inc.
Frank J. Nelson
Nelson-Hall Co.; watch repairing.
Newton's Potters Supply

Craft Category Index
Books—Books

The Niddy Noddy
Nimble Thimble
Northwest Handcraft House
O-P Craft Co., Inc.
Bob and Carol Oliver; solderless jewelry.
Ima Ova; decorating eggs for Christmas, Easter and special occasions.
Oxford University Press; mosaics.
Pack-O-Fun
Paramount Ceramic Inc.
Parker Publishing Co., Inc.; batik, bottle items, foil etching, mobiles, nail design, paper crafts, pine cone decorating, plaster of Paris carvings, scenic oceans, sculpture, shell chimes, string printing, teaching arts and crafts, wall plaques.
Hazel Pearson Handi Craft
Penguin Books Inc.; pottery, selling crafts.
Phentex, Inc.; knitting and crochet patterns.
Pins & Needles; patternmaking and designing.
Pitman Publishing Corp.; basketry, general arts & crafts series, millinery, paper sculpture, screen process, welding.
Plasco
Plexiglas; plexiglas acrylic sheet.
Plush Point Patterns by Marcia Podell
Forrest W. Pond; gem carving tools, making.
Popular Library Inc.; bottle cutting, general arts & crafts series, American Indian crafts.
Popular Mechanics Press; furniture refinishing, upholstery.
Powell; knitting.
Praeger Publishers; craftsman's manual, general arts & crafts series.
Prentice-Hall Inc.; general arts & crafts series, industrial arts for the shop, metal working, model railroading, sculpture, seriography, textiles, woodworking for industrial arts.
Priscilla's Little Red Tole House; glass painting, rub out painting.
PRO Custom Hobbies
Products and Systems, Inc.; restringing beads and pearls.
P. T. I.; time saving tips; using trace'n fit.
The Puppetry Store; puppetmaking, stage and costume making.
G. P. Putnam's Sons; general arts & crafts series.
Pyronetics; metal sculpture.
Quilts and Other Comforts; quilting.
Railway Express
Random House Inc.; children's crafts, crafts anthology, crochet, dressmaking, embroidery patterns, encyclopedia of carpentry, furniture for nomads, gemstones, general arts & crafts series, knitting, leather craft, needlepoint, needlework, sewing guide, woodworking tools.
Reade Knitting Designs; knitting and panel designs.
Reeves Knotique
Henry Regnery Co.; general arts & crafts series, leather craft, needlecrafts.
Reilly & Lee Books; general arts & crafts series, jewelry, leather, rug, stitchery.
Reisinger Net Co.; making net hammocks.
Ren Ann Crafts; bejeweled eggs.
Renaldy's
Reynolds Yarns Inc.; nordic design knitting.
Robin & Russ Handweavers; batik, bobbin lace, embroidery, knitting, macrame, spinning, vegetable and other dyeing, weaving.
Rohm & Haas Co.; "do-it-yourself" acrylics.
Rosemond Hobbycraft; daisy design, hairpin lace.
Rupert, Gibbon & Spider; batik.
Salyer Publishing Co.; china painting.
Howard W. Sams & Co., Inc.; building trades, carpentry, do-it-yourself subjects, electronic organs, electronics projects, machine shop, upholstering.
Sancraft Industries; bead crafts, burlap, crepe papers, crochet, decoup-

Craft Category Index
Books—Books

age, embroidery, felt, knitting, net, out-of-prints, papier mache, resin craft, tatting, tissue paper.
Santos Miniatures
Sav-On-Crafts
Savin Handcrafts
Sax Arts & Crafts
John & Susan Scheewe; design, tole.
Screen Process Supplies Mfg. Co.
Charles Scribner's Sons; bead craft, crochet, decoupage, needlepoint, plant and flower preserving, plant dyeing.
Sculpture Associates Ltd.
Sears, Roebuck & Co.
H. Shealy; doll house furniture from clothespins & cigar boxes.
Shoenail Supply; decorative painting, needlecraft, tole.
Sign of the Times Publishing Co.; alphabets and antique alphabets, gold leafing, lettering, screen printing, sign painting.
Silver Shuttle
Beryl Sink; crochet jewelry, frosting windows, making finger paint, making household glue, making varnish and waterproof cement, making writing ink, show for holiday decorations.
Susan Sirkis; 19th and 20th century dolls and dollmaking.
Skil-Crafts Division
Smithers Oasis; flower crafts.
The Smock Shop; English smocking.
The Sneak Box Studio
Some Place
Elyse Sommer; bread dough, burlap, decoupage, jewelry, rock and stone crafts, sewing.
Southern Highlands Handicraft Guild; crafts in the Southern Highlands.
Southern Living Books; needlecraft, quilts.
Specialty Products
Mildred Sprout; rugs.
Stackpole Books; gunsmithing, gunstock carving, gunstock finishing, nature crafts, Early American crafts.
Standard Doll Co.; crafts, crochet, doll, doll clothes, knitting.
Kit Stansbury; egg decorating, treetrims.
Star Diamond Industries
The Stearns & Foster Co.; quilting.
Stein & Day; crochet, general arts & crafts series, knitting, macrame, paper puppets and toys.
Sterling Publishing Co. Inc.; art foam, bead craft, beads macrame, burlap and felt crafts, candlemaking, general arts & crafts series, jewelrymaking, lace making, metal and wire sculpture, nail sculpture, needlepoint, paper crafts, printing, scrap crafts, stained glass, tole painting, trapunto, wood carving, wood cuts.
Studio Twelve
Studio Yarn Farms Inc.; machine knitting, pattern drafting.
Sturbridge Yankee Workshop; furniture construction.
Sunset House
Supreme Watch Material Co.
Surburbia, Inc.; glass cutting.
Tahki Imports, Limited
Tandy Leather Co.
Taplinger Publishing Co.; bead embroidery, children's crafts, enameling, jewelrymaking, knitting, puppet making, toys.
Doris Taylor; ceramic painting, china painting.
Taylor Bedding Mfg. Co.; quilting.
Textile Crafts; dyeing, general arts & crafts series, spinning, tatting, textile crafts, weaving.
The Thread Shed, Inc.
3 M Company; boat refinishing, furniture finishing and refinishing.
Thumbelina Needlework Shop
Tie Clip Information; making and tying pretied ties.
Times Mirror Magazine; formulas, home improvement, mechanical movements, repairs, tools, wood finishing, woodworking, workshops.
Osma G. Tod Weaving & Lace Studio; bobbin lace, weaving.
Tole 'N Stuff; decorative painting, folk art, tole.

Craft Category Index
Books—Books

Town & Country Crafts
Traditional Norwegian Rosemaling; instructions, patterns.
Tree Toys; quilling.
Trojan Press Inc.; antique dolls, glass, sewing for dolls.
M. Turner; machine knitting.
Charles E. Tuttle Co. Inc.; furniture restoration, Chinese kites.
Tuxedo Yarn & Needlework
William Unger & Co. Inc.; crocheting tops and shawls, knitting tops and shawls.
The Unicorn; applique, batik, brocade and silk velvet weaving, ceramics, colonial lighting, costume, crochet, design, doll making, dyeing, embroidery, glass, jewelrymaking, knitting, knotting, lace and tatting, lacquer painting, macrame, metalwork, netting, quilting, sewing crafts, soft toy making, spinning and weaving, suede sewing, textile printing, tie-dye, woodworking.
Unique Creations; lamp shades.
United States Committee for UNICEF; making folk toys.
Universal Wirecraft Jewelry Co.
University Circle Publications and Supply Co.; enameling, enameling for beginners.
University of Minnesota Press; sculpturing in wood, sculpturing with a torch.
Valspar Corp.; antiquing, creative book, decoupage, resin craft, woodfinishing.
Van Nostrand Reinhold Co.; balsa wood, band saws, ceramics, craft anthology, doll clothes, general arts & crafts series, jewelry repair and design, jig saws, knitting, macrame, paper and fabric decorating, pottery, preserved flowers, weaving, Peruvian designs.
The Victors; gem tumbling and baroque jewelry making.
Viking Press; ceramics, drawing, general arts & crafts series, jewelrymaking, knitting, mosaics, painting, pottery, weaving.

Village Candle & Craft; candle crafting, candle dipping, sand casting.
Wadsworth Publishing Co., Inc.; crafts design, general arts & crafts series.
Mary Wales; making handbags, shoemaking.
Wm. Walthers Inc.
Wanda's Workshop; chenille craft, foilcraft.
Lee Wards
Frederick Warne & Co. Inc.; pottery.
Watson-Guptill Publications; bookbinding, doll making, fabric printing, general arts & crafts series, jewelrymaking, macrame, miniatures, mosaics, paper sculpture, papier mache, plastics, seed collage, soft toymaking, stained glass, weaving and rug weaving.
C. R. Wells; opal.
Westwood Ceramic Supply Co.
Whitson's; wall hangings.
Whittemore-Durgin Glass Co.
Wilton Enterprises, Inc.; cake decorating.
Winona Trading Post
Wm. H. Wise & Co. Inc.; handyman's guide.
Woman's Board; needlepoint.
Wonoco Yarn Co.
The Wood Barn; decorative painting.
Wool 'N Wick; knitting Christmas decorations.
W. Wooley & Co.; making plaster and cement molds.
Workman Publishing Co.; general arts & crafts series, guide to crafts supplies, potpourri making, soapmaking, toymaking.
Worldwide Curio House
William E. Wright Co.; Christmas trims.
Yaley Enterprises; candlemaking.
The Yarn Depot
The Yarn and Soda Shop; knitting.
Yarns Unlimited
Zim's
Zondervan Publishing House; general arts & crafts series, handicrafts.

bookprinting and binding
  binders board
    Basic Crafts Co.
  book cloths
    Basic Crafts Co.
  book presses
    Basic Crafts Co.
  books
    Book Barn
    Watson-Guptill Publications
  gold foil
    Basic Crafts Co.
  hand bookbinding equipment
    Basic Crafts Co.
  kits
    Craftool Co.

brass and brassware *(see also Metals, Metalware)*
  T. B. Hagstoz & Son
  brass beads
    Bead Game
    Macrame and Weaving Supply Co.
  brass bell pulls
    Wichelt Import Co.
  brass foil
    St. Louis Crafts Inc.
  brass hardware
    John's Hardware & Decoupage Supplies
  brass hinges
    Boutique Trims
    Handcraft Originals
  brass lamp ornaments
    Angelo Bros. Co.
  brass rings
    Flair-Craft Inc.
  brass rods
    Sax Arts & Crafts
  brass sheets
    Sax Arts & Crafts
  brass snap closures
    Leathercrafters Supply Co.
  brass stands
    George W. Park Seed Co., Inc.

boutique trims and notions *(see also Trims)*
  bells
    Jewelart Inc.
    Jeweler's Emporium
    Knit Services, Inc.
    Winona Trading Post

  boutique braids
    The Putter Shop
  boutique items
    Fabulous Holiday House
    Holiday Handicrafts, Inc.
    Sav-On-Crafts
    Skil-Crafts Division
  boutique pendants
    Jewelart Inc.
  boutique ribbons
    Hazel Pearson Handi Craft
  boutique supplies
    Gibsons Creations
  boutique trims
    Lee Wards
    Zim's
  braids
    Boutique Trims
    Country Crafts
    Mill Store
    Hazel Pearson Handi Craft
    Skil-Crafts Division
    Wagner's Crafts
  camel bells
    Macrame and Weaving Supply Co.
  chenille boutique trims
    Delco Craft Center, Inc.
  Christmas boutique items
    Holiday Craft
  colored safety pins
    Jewelart Inc.
  diamond dust
    Holiday Craft
    Walnut Hill Co.
  edgings
    Boutique Trims
    Creative Craft House
    Lace Lady
    The Putter Shop
    Elyse Sommer
    Town & Country Crafts
    Two Brothers Inc.
  filigrees
    Boutique Trims
    Gibsons Creations
    Holiday Craft
  findings
    Fabulous Holiday House
    Gibsons Creations
    House of Flowers
    Taylor House

Craft Category Index
Boutique—Buckles

flocking
  Dick Blick
  Boin Arts & Crafts
  Arthur Brown & Bro., Inc.
  Craft Service
  Skil-Crafts Division
  W. Wooley & Co.

fringes
  Home-Sew Inc.

gold braids
  P. S. Andrews Co.

gold lace borders
  Harrower House of Decoupage

gold lace frames
  Harrower House of Decoupage

gold lace ornaments
  Harrower House of Decoupage

gold paper borders
  Taylor House

gold paper decorations
  Country Crafts

gold paper laces
  Hazel Pearson Handi Craft

gold paper ornaments
  Skil-Crafts Division
  Taylor House

gold paper trims
  Holiday Craft

imported novelties
  Studio D

kits
  General Supplies Co.
  Sheru Bead Boutique Shop
  Lee Wards

mica mirrors
  Kitsophrenia, Inc.

pearl strands
  Jeweler's Emporium

sequins
  Boutique Trims
  Home-Sew Inc.
  Kit Kraft
  Koehler's Craft Outlet
  Sav-On-Crafts
  Wagner's Crafts

bottlecutting and decorating *(see also Glass craft)*

books
  Crown Publishers
  Glass Bottle Blowers Assn.
  Parker Publishing Co., Inc.
  Popular Library Inc.

bottle cutters
  American Handicrafts
  P. S. Andrews Co.
  Bob's Arts & Crafts
  Albert Constantine & Son Inc.
  Craftsman Supply House
  Delco Craft Center, Inc.
  Walter Drake
  Edmund Scientific Co.
  Floyd Fleming
  The Handcrafters
  Hanover House Industries, Inc.
  Kay Kinney-Contoured Glass
  J. C. Penney Co., Inc.
  Keith Robinson
  Lee Wards
  Whittemore-Durgin Glass Co.

jug cutter
  Floyd Fleming
  Keith Robinson
  Whittemore-Durgin Glass Co.

kits
  Spencer Gifts Inc.
  Stylecraft of Baltimore

milk bottles
  Dairy Service, Inc

plastic bottle craft
  House of Patterns

poof bottles
  Walnut Hill Co.

buckles
  La Venta Corp.
  Leathercrafters Supply Co.
  Mac Leather Co.
  Pollack's Furrier's Supply Corp.

belt buckles
  Edwards Jewelry Co.
  House of York
  Leathercrafters Supply Co.
  Macrame and Weaving Supply Co.
  The Sandvigs

British buckles
  Leathercrafters Supply Co.

bronze buckles
  Leathercrafters Supply Co.

cast metal buckles in antique finishes
  Leathercrafters Supply Co.

pewter buckles
  Leathercrafters Supply Co.

Craft Category Index
Buckles—Candlemaking

solid brass buckles
    Leathercrafters Supply Co.
tiffany glass buckles
    Leathercrafters Supply Co.
wood buckles
    Knit Services, Inc.

cake and cookie decorating
books
    Wilton Enterprises, Inc.
cake decorating designs
    Transart
cake decorating molds
    General Supplies Co.
cake decorating supplies
    Cake Decorators & Craft Supplies
    Maid of Scandinavia
cake decorating tools
    General Supplies Co.
    Maid of Scandinavia
cake molds
    Cake Decorators & Craft Supplies
cake tops
    Cake Decorators & Craft Supplies
cookie stamp sets
    Downs
home study courses
    Candy & Cake Institute
magazines
    Celebrate
specialty cake pans
    Helen Gallagher
    Maid of Scandinavia
wedding cake supplies
    General Supplies Co.

candlemaking *(see also Dyes, Wax)*
animal molds
    Town & Country Crafts
bayberry wax
    Barker Enterprises
beeswax
    Barker Enterprises
    Walnut Hill Co.
books
    A. S. Barnes and Co., Inc.
    Book Barn
    Candle Mill Village
    Chilton Book Co.
    Craft Course Publishers
    E. P. Dutton & Co., Inc.
    Gloria's Glass Garden
    Grosset & Dunlap Inc.
    P. C. Herwig Co., Inc.
    Cherie Hooper
    The Macmillan Publishing Co.
    Museum Books Inc.
    Sterling Publishing Co. Inc.
    Village Candle & Craft
    Yaley Enterprises
candle accessories
    Celebration Candlemaking Supplies
    General Supplies Co.
    House of Wood Candles
    May-Wal, Inc.
    Village Candle & Craft
    Walnut Hill Co.
candle additives
    Barker Enterprises
    Candle Kitchen
    Celebration Candlemaking Supplies
    Doll's Candle & Craft Supplies
    House of Wood Candles
    May-Wal, Inc.
    Natcol Crafts, Inc.
    Pourette Mfg. Co.
    Village Candle & Craft
candle covers
    Angelo Bros. Co.
candle dyes
    Barker Enterprises
    Cake Decorators & Craft Supplies
    Candle Kitchen
    Candle Mill Village
    Candlewic Co.
    Celebration Candlemaking Supplies
    Craft & Candle House
    Doll's Candle & Craft Supplies
    May-Wal, Inc.
    Natcol Crafts, Inc.
    Pourette Mfg. Co.
    Pylam Products, Inc.
    W. Spencer Inc.
    Village Candle & Craft
    Walnut Hill Co.
candle hardeners
    Walnut Hill Co.
candle molds
    Candle Kitchen
    Candle Mill Village
    Candlewic Co.
    Celebration Candlemaking Supplies
    Craft & Candle House
    Deep Flex Plastic Molds, Inc.

Craft Category Index
Candlemaking—Candlemaking

General Supplies Co.
House of Wood Candles
Pourette Mfg. Co.
Sav-On-Crafts
Sax Arts & Crafts
Sears, Roebuck & Co.
W. Spencer Inc.
Swan-Son
TAP Plastic Inc.
Town & Country Crafts
Trask Plastics
Village Candle & Craft
Walnut Hill Co.
Lee Wards
W. Wooley & Co.

candle paints
Bersted's

candle scents
Barker Enterprises
Beacon Chemical Co., Inc.
Cake Decorators & Craft Supplies
Candle Kitchen
Candle Mill Village
Candlewic Co.
Craft & Candle House
Doll's Candle & Craft Supplies
May-Wal, Inc.
Natcol Crafts, Inc.
Pourette Mfg. Co.
Shaw Mudge & Co.
Walnut Hill Co.

candle waxes
Barker Enterprises
Cake Decorators & Craft Supplies
Candle Kitchen
Candle Mill Village
Craft Service
Doll's Candle & Craft Supplies
House of Wood Candles
Sav-On-Crafts
Sax Arts & Crafts
W. Spencer Inc.
Village Candle & Craft
W. Wooley & Co.

candle wicks
Barker Enterprises
Cake Decorators & Craft Supplies
Craft & Candle House
Doll's Candle & Craft Supplies
Pourette Mfg. Co.
W. Spencer Inc.

Walnut Hill Co.
W. Wooley & Co.

candleholders
Barker Enterprises
Village Candle & Craft
Western Tree Cones

candlemaking supplies
American Handicrafts
P. S. Andrews Co.
Barker Enterprises
Beacon Chemical Co., Inc.
Bergen Arts & Crafts, Inc.
Bersted's
Bob's Arts & Crafts
Boin Arts & Crafts
Brown's Miniatures
Cake Decorators & Craft Supplies
Candle Kitchen
Candle Mill Village
Candlewic Co.
Celebration Candlemaking Supplies
The Craft Corner
Craftsman Supply House
Creator's Corner
Delco Craft Center, Inc.
Doll's Candle & Craft Supplies
Economy Handicrafts, Inc.
Gemex Co.
General Supplies Co.
The Handcrafters
P. C. Herwig Co., Inc.
Holiday Handicrafts, Inc.
House of Patterns
House of Wood Candles
Kaydee Craft Supplies
Kit Kraft
Magnus Craft Materials, Inc.
Make It Happen Craft Studio
May-Wal, Inc.
Natcol Crafts, Inc.
New Products Co.
Ovgem Craft Supply Co.
Hazel Pearson Handi Craft
J. C. Penney Co., Inc.
Pourette Mfg. Co.
Sav-On-Crafts
Sax Arts & Crafts
Sears, Roebuck & Co.
Specialty Products
W. Spencer Inc.
Supreme Handicrafts

Craft Category Index
Candlemaking—Cane

    Town & Country Crafts
    Village Candle & Craft
    Walnut Hill Co.
    Lee Wards
    W. Wooley & Co.
    Zim's
carnauba wax
    Barker Enterprises
cast iron candle cups
    Rombins' Nest Farm
cast iron sconces
    Rombins' Nest Farm
decorating accessories
    Walnut Hill Co.
flower wax cutters
    Doll's Candle & Craft Supplies
gloss spray
    Walnut Hill Co.
honeycomb
    Craft Service
honeycomb candles
    Cleveland Leather Co.
honeycomb wax sheets
    Brown's Miniatures
kits
    American Handicrafts
    Bersted's
    Columbia Candlecraft
    Craft & Candle House
    The Craft Corner
    Doll's Candle & Craft Supplies
    Helen Gallagher
    Hawthorne House, Inc.
    Herter's, Inc.
    P. C. Herwig Co., Inc.
    Koehler's Craft Outlet
    Mary Maxim Inc.
    Party Bazaar
    Sav-On-Crafts
    Sax Arts & Crafts
    Village Candle & Craft
    Walnut Hill Co.
    W. Wooley & Co.
leaflets
    Wilfred Enterprises
light stabilizer additive
    Chemical Additives Co.
magazines
    The American Candlemaker
    Decorating & Craft Ideas Made Easy
    Pourette Mfg. Co.

organizations
    International Guild of Candle Artisans
pearl flakes
    Walnut Hill Co.
plastic candle molds
    Barker Enterprises
    Natcol Crafts, Inc.
poof bottles
    Walnut Hill Co.
wax gilt
    Plasco
wax gold
    Arthur Brown & Bro., Inc.
wooden candle molds
    Barker Enterprises
wooden candleholders
    O-P Craft Co., Inc.

candy making and decorating
candy decorating tools
    General Supplies Co.
candy making equipment
    General Supplies Co.
candy molding
    Cake Decorators & Craft Supplies
home study courses
    Candle Institute
    Candy & Cake Institute

cane, reed, and rush working *(see also Basketry)*
books
    Cane & Basket Supply Co.
    Craftool Co.
    Crafty Ideas
cane
    A 'N L's Hobbicraft, Inc.
    Atlantic Upholstery Supply Co.
    Bersted's
    Cane & Basket Supply Co.
    Albert Constantine & Son Inc.
    Craft Service
    Delco Craft Center, Inc.
    The Handcrafters
    Real Woods
    Savin Handcrafts
    Sax Arts & Crafts
    The Workshop
cane webbing
    Albert Constantine & Son Inc.
kits
    Bersted's

Craft Category Index
Cane—Casting

    Albert Constantine & Son Inc.
    Craftsman Supply House
    Savin Handcrafts
natural cane
    H. H. Perkins Co.
plastic cane
    H. H. Perkins Co.
reed
    Bersted's
    Cleveland Leather Co.
    Craft Service
    Craftsman Supply House
    Delco Craft Center, Inc.
    Sax Arts & Crafts
    School Products Co.
    The Workshop

cardmaking
    Arthur Brown & Bro., Inc.
blank greeting card
    Plaza Artists Materials, Inc.
books
    Arts and Crafts Unlimited
kits
    Arts and Crafts Unlimited
    Surburbia, Inc.
stationery decorating
    House of Patterns

casting *(see also Molds)*
additives
    Castolite
books
    Cooke Novelty Co.
    Crown Publishers
casting accessories
    Castolite
    Kerr Mfg. Co.
    Sculpture Associates Ltd.
casting block
    Solartherm Co.
casting compounds
    Castolite
casting crucibles
    Solartherm Co.
casting epoxy
    Bear Cave
casting equipment
    Allcraft Tool & Supply Co.
    Bet-Roc Enterprises Inc.
    Dick Ells Co.
    Gems Galore
    Shipley's Mineral House
    Supreme Watch Material Co.
casting foam
    Bear Cave
casting grain
    Trowbridge Crafts
casting investment molding material
    Kerr Mfg. Co.
casting items
    Art Consultants
casting plastic
    Sculpture Services Inc.
casting resins
    Adhesive Products Corp.
casting supplies
    Dick Blick
    Dick Ells Co.
    Ettl Studios Inc.
    Gems Galore
    C. R. Hill Co.
    J. J. Jewelcraft
    Sculpture House
    C. W. Somers & Co.
    Swest Inc.
casting table racks
    Cole Ceramics Laboratories
casting tables
    Air Capitol Molds, Inc.
casting tools
    Allcraft Tool & Supply Co.
casting units
    Sax Arts & Crafts
casting waxes
    Allcraft Tool & Supply Co.
    Delco Craft Center, Inc.
colored sawdust
    Carver Co.
fiberglass cloth
    Castolite
    High Strength Adhesives Corp.
    Kick-Shaw Inc.
fiberglass mat
    High Strength Adhesives Corp.
    Kick-Shaw Inc.
fillers
    Adhesive Products Corp.
    Castolite
furnaces for bronze casting
    McEnglevan Heat Treating & Mfg. Inc.

Craft Category Index
Casting—Ceramics

gold casting items
   Solartherm Co.
gold casting mountings
   Lapidabrade Inc.
home study courses
   Metals Engineering Institute
jewelry casting supplies
   Exactra-Craft Corp.
   Gemex Co.
   Magic Circle Corp.
   O'Brien Lapidary Equipment Co.
jewelry casting tools
   O'Brien Lapidary Equipment Co.
kits
   Castolite
   Gilman's
   Gordon's
   Locomotive Workshop
   Michigan Lapidary Supply Co.
liquid plastic casting equipment
   Nationwide Plastics Co.
model castings
   PRO Custom Hobbies
plastic casting
   Art Mart, Inc.
precious casting metals
   Bourget Bros. Gems & Minerals
   H. A. Cole
resin casting
   Bob's Arts & Crafts
   Arthur Brown & Bro., Inc.
   Craft Service
   Ovgem Craft Supply Co.
   Skil-Crafts Division
rubber
   Blue Grass Art & Hobby Center
   Sculpture Services Inc.
rubber latex
   Douglas & Sturgess, Inc.
silver casting items
   Solartherm Co.
sterling silver
   T. B. Hagstoz & Son
   Libra Gems
   Panther International Ltd.
sterling silver casting grains
   H. A. Cole
sterling silver scrap chips
   Sterling Hallmark Co.
vacuum casting
   Allcraft Tool & Supply Co.

wax casting tools
   Allcraft Tool & Supply Co.
wax pots
   Shipley's Mineral House
carpentry
  books
   American Technical Society
   Arco Publishing Co., Inc.
   Theodore Audel & Co.
   Charles A. Bennett Co., Inc.
   Drake Publishers Inc.
   The Family Handyman
   Random House Inc.
   Howard W. Sams & Co., Inc.
  home study courses
   American School
   Lee Mountain
  jambs
   Beno J. Gundlach Co.
  joiner-planers
   American Machine & Tool Co.
  lathes
   American Machine & Tool Co.
   Campbell Tools Co.
  magazines
   The Family Handyman
cast iron ware
   Rombins' Nest Farm
   John & Susan Scheewe
  cast iron brackets
   Rombins' Nest Farm
  cast iron candle cups
   Rombins' Nest Farm
  cast iron hooks
   Rombins' Nest Farm
  cast iron rings
   Jeweler's Emporium
  cast iron sconces
   Rombins' Nest Farm
  iron table pedestals
   Plasco
  ironmongery
   Whittemore-Durgin Glass Co.
ceramics
  additives
   Westwood Ceramic Supply Co.
  ball mills
   Cole Ceramics Laboratories
  bamboo handles
   Minnesota Clay

Craft Category Index
Ceramics—Ceramics

    Paramount Ceramic Inc.
    Westwood Ceramic Supply Co.
bisque
    Crafty Ideas
    Wilfred Enterprises
bisque eggs
    Howe Studio
    Town & Country Crafts
bisqued ceramic tiles
    Newton's Potters Supply
bisque sets
    Crafty Ideas
block bisque
    Diedricks Crafts
books
    American Art Clay Co. Inc.
    Ceramics Monthly
    Chilton Book Co.
    Dr. David Crespi
    Crown Publishers
    Davis Publications, Inc.
    Fountains for the Home
    Goodhert-Willcox Co., Inc.
    Kodansha International, U.S.A.
    Lane Magazine & Book Co.
    Lee Mountain
    The Library Corner
    The Macmillan Publishing Co.
    Mountain Ceramic Crafts
    Museum Books Inc.
    Doris Taylor
    The Unicorn
    Van Nostrand Reinhold Co.
    Viking Press
brushes
    Ohio Ceramic Supply Inc.
casting supplies
    Ettl Studios Inc.
    Sculpture House
casting table racks
    Cole Ceramics Laboratories
casting tables
    Air Capitol Molds, Inc.
ceramic armatures
    Cole Ceramics Laboratories
    Newton's Potters Supply
ceramic bead trees
    Cole Ceramics Laboratories
ceramic beads
    Gloria's Glass Garden
    Jewelart Inc.

    Macrame and Weaving Supply Co.
    Three Gables Homecrafts
ceramic chemicals
    Cole Ceramics Laboratories
    Minnesota Clay
    Richland Ceramics Inc.
    Standard Ceramic Supply
    Van Howe Ceramic Supply Co.
ceramic clays
    Paramount Ceramic Inc.
    Van Howe Ceramic Supply Co.
ceramic decals
    National Artcraft Supply Co.
ceramic eggs
    Wilfred Enterprises
ceramic glazes
    Bergen Arts & Crafts, Inc.
    Cole Ceramics Laboratories
    Delco Craft Center, Inc.
    Minnesota Clay
    Newton's Potters Supply
    Ohio Ceramic Supply Inc.
    Paramount Ceramic Inc.
    Sax Arts & Crafts
    Standard Ceramic Supply
    Tepping Studio Supply Co.
    Van Howe Ceramic Supply Co.
    Westwood Ceramic Supply Co.
ceramic greenware
    Fieldwood Co.
ceramic hardware
    Cole Ceramics Laboratories
ceramic industrial hand cream
    Air Capitol Molds, Inc.
ceramic miniatures
    Town & Country Crafts
    Wilfred Enterprises
ceramic molds
    Air Capitol Molds, Inc.
    Alberta's Molds Inc.
    Anchor Mold Co.
    Atlantic Mold Corp.
    Clay-Crafters Products
    Cramer Mold Shop
    Curio Ceramic Molds
    Daddy's Mold Shop
    Dinky Molds
    Holland Mold Inc.
    Jamar-Mallory Inc.
    Jane's Ceramic Molds
    Mindy Molds

Craft Category Index
Ceramics—Ceramics

Ohio Ceramic Supply Inc.
R & R Ceramic Molds Inc.
Ju Rene Ceramic Molds
Al Schoellkopf Mold Co.
Van Howe Ceramic Supply Co.
ceramic oval plaques
   Sunflower Crafts
ceramic plaques
   The Cellar Ceramic Shop
ceramic power tool
   Marcella's Ceramics Inc.
ceramic stains
   Cole Ceramics Laboratories
   Tepping Studio Supply Co.
   Westwood Ceramic Supply Co.
ceramic stands
   Newton's Potters Supply
ceramic supplies
   A 'N L's Hobbicraft, Inc.
   A. D. Alpine Inc.
   Art Consultants
   Art Mart, Inc.
   Dick Blick
   Blue Grass Art & Hobby Center
   Bluebird Manufacturing
   Cole Ceramics Laboratories
   Delco Craft Center, Inc.
   Diedricks Crafts
   Economy Handicrafts, Inc.
   Essayons Studio, Hand Arts Center
   Ettl Studios Inc.
   Loretta's Ceramic Studio
   Mountain Ceramic Crafts
   NASCO Arts & Crafts
   Newton's Potters Supply
   Ohio Ceramic Supply Inc.
   Paramount Ceramic Inc.
   Sax Arts & Crafts
   Standard Ceramic Supply
   Tepping Studio Supply Co.
   Van Howe Ceramic Supply Co.
   Westwood Ceramic Supply Co.
   Jack D. Wolfe Co. Inc.
ceramic tile cutters
   Beno J. Gundlach Co.
ceramic tile nippers
   Beno J. Gundlach Co.
ceramic tiles
   Renaldy's
ceramic tools
   Anne Amiot

   Art Consultants
   Cole Ceramics Laboratories
   Economy Handicrafts, Inc.
   Newton's Potters Supply
   Paramount Ceramic Inc.
   Standard Ceramic Supply
   Van Howe Ceramic Supply Co.
ceramic whiteware miniatures
   Sunflower Crafts
ceramic wisemen
   Crafty Ideas
chess set casting compound
   Stylecraft of Baltimore
chess set molds
   Stylecraft of Baltimore
china blanks
   House of Clay China Shop
   D. R. Wolfe Overglazes
china lamps
   Renaldy's
circular glaze calculator
   Dial-A-Glaze
clay molds
   Kay Kinney-Contoured Glass
custom-made ceramic decals
   Art Decal Co.
decorating stains
   Crafty Ideas
doll bisque
   Dollspart Supply Co., Inc.
electric kilns
   Cole Ceramics Laboratories
   Diedricks Crafts
electric lehrs
   A. D. Alpine Inc.
firing clay
   American Art Clay Co. Inc.
   Arthur Brown & Bro., Inc.
   Delco Craft Center, Inc.
   Plaza Artists Materials, Inc.
   Sax Arts & Crafts
   Skil-Crafts Division
gas kilns
   Cole Ceramics Laboratories
glaze formula tables
   Cole Ceramics Laboratories
glazed ceramic tiles
   Newton's Potters Supply
heatless glazing for ceramics
   Specialty Products

Craft Category Index
Ceramics—Ceramics

kiln accessories
    Delco Craft Center, Inc.
kiln shelves
    Cole Ceramics Laboratories
kilns
    A 'N L's Hobbicraft, Inc.
    Allcraft Tool & Supply Co.
    A. D. Alpine Inc.
    Anchor Tool & Supply Co.
    Art Consultants
    Bergen Arts & Crafts, Inc.
    Boin Arts & Crafts
    Arthur Brown & Bro., Inc.
    Clay-Crafters Products
    Delco Craft Center, Inc.
    Handcraft House
    Loretta's Ceramic Studio
    Minnesota Clay
    Newton's Potters Supply
    Ohio Ceramic Supply Inc.
    Paragon Industries Inc.
    Paramount Ceramic Inc.
    Plaza Artists Materials, Inc.
    Richland Ceramics Inc.
    Sax Arts & Crafts
    Sculpture Associates Ltd.
    Sculpture House
    Thomas C. Thompson
    Westwood Ceramic Supply Co.
kits
    Craftool Co.
    Diedricks Crafts
leaflets
    Fountains for the Home
    Wilfred Enterprises
magazines
    Ceramics
    Ceramics Monthly
    Challenge Publications, Inc
    Popular Ceramics
metallic rubs
    Reggi's Ceramic Colors
Mexican pottery clay
    American Art Clay Co. Inc.
miniature ceramic animals
    The Gift Shoppe
miniature ceramic bowls
    Grueny's Gift Center
miniature ceramic figures
    Grueny's Gift Center

miniature ceramic pitchers
    Grueny's Gift Center
miniature ceramic vases
    Grueny's Gift Center
moulage molding
    Douglas & Sturgess, Inc.
    Sculpture Services Inc.
no-fire glazes
    National Craft & Hobby Co., Inc.
no-fire stone-like flakes for ceramics
    Hoff House Ceramic Supplies, Inc.
plaster ceramic molds
    Bee Basch Designs
plastic ceramic molds
    Johnny Sens of New Orleans
printing ceramics
    Floquil, Inc.
pug mills
    A. D. Alpine Inc.
    Bluebird Manufacturing
    Cole Ceramics Laboratories
    Westwood Ceramic Supply Co.
quick-slip pouring
    Air Capitol Molds, Inc.
rattan handles
    Westwood Ceramic Supply Co.
refractories
    Westwood Ceramic Supply Co
salt and pepper shakers mechanisms
    Albert Constantine & Son Inc
self-hardening clays
    Boin Arts & Crafts
    Economy Handicrafts, Inc.
    Newton's Potters Supply
    Sculpture Associates Ltd.
    Sculpture House
sieves
    Cole Ceramics Laboratories
spigots
    Westwood Ceramic Supply Co.
spray booths
    Cole Ceramics Laboratories
statuary
    Jeane's
straps for banding large and small ceramic molds
    Universal Strap Co.
table lighter inserts
    Albert Constantine & Son Inc.

Craft Category Index
Ceramics—China

turntables
  Gilmour Campbell
  Delco Craft Center, Inc.
ware trucks
  Cole Ceramics Laboratories
water soluble metallic paints
  Reggi's Ceramic Colors
water-mount decals
  Cerami Corner Inc.
wedging tables
  Cole Ceramics Laboratories
white ironstone ware
  Sturbridge Yankee Workshop

chenille
  Dick Blick
  Bob's Arts & Crafts
  Craftsman Supply House
  Don's Hobby Co.
  House of Flowers
  Hazel Pearson Handi Craft
  Sav-On-Crafts
  Sax Arts & Crafts
  Supreme Handicrafts
  Zim's
  chenille boutique trims
    Delco Craft Center, Inc.
  flat chenille
    Greentree Ranch Wools, Countryside Handweavers
  kits
    Koehler's Craft Outlet
  round chenille
    Greentree Ranch Wools, Countryside Handweavers

children's crafts
  books
    Lewiscraft
    J. B. Lippincott Co.
    Taplinger Publishing Co.

china painting
  books
    Chilton Book Co.
    China Decorator
    Drake Publishers Inc.
    Ruth Little's Studio
    Salyer Publishing Co.
    Doris Taylor
  brushes
    Barbara Jones China House
    Ruth Little's Studio
    Renaldy's
    Salyer Publishing Co.
    D. R. Wolfe Overglazes
  china blanks
    House of Clay China Shop
    D. R. Wolfe Overglazes
  china colors
    D. R. Wolfe Overglazes
  china decals
    D. M. Campana Co.
  china decorating
    Irene Goodwin
  china enamels
    Salyer Publishing Co.
  china lamps
    Renaldy's
  china mediums
    Salyer Publishing Co.
  china painting designs
    Bell Studio
    Frank Boothe
    House of Clay China Shop
    Barbara Jones China House
    Ruth Little's Studio
    J. Opal Stover Studio
  china painting supplies
    Anita of Calif.
    Dorothy Berryman Studio
    Blue Grass Art & Hobby Center
    D. M. Campana Co.
    The China Cottage
    Collector Studies
    Gladys Galloway
    Holly Studio Inc
    Helen Humes Studio
    Barbara Jones China House
    Darlene Lewis
    Ruth Little's Studio
    J. Opal Stover Studio
    Kenneth Rarick
    Renaldy's
    Robertson Studio
    Salyer Publishing Co.
    Doris Taylor
    D. R. Wolfe Overglazes
  china studies
    D. M. Campana Co.
  decorative stamping items
    Holly Studio Inc
  frames for china
    J. Opal Stover Studio

Craft Category Index
China—Christmas

gilding brushes
   Plaza Artists Materials, Inc.
gold etching
   Irene Goodwin
imported white china
   D. M. Campana Co.
kits
   Holly Studio Inc
leaflets
   Sonie Ames
   Brandywine Studies
limoges
   Jeweler's Emporium
   Sav-On-Crafts
magazines
   China Decorator
   China Painter
one stroke design
   Bell Studio
organizations
   World Organization of China Painters
painting mediums
   Barbara Jones China House
pre-mixed china paints
   Doris Taylor
punchers
   Salyer Publishing Co.
quill pens
   Salyer Publishing Co.

Christmas crafts *(see also Holiday decorations)*
books
   Boycan's Craft Supplies
   Chilton Book Co.
   Fawcett Special Interest Magazines & Books
   Hearthside Press
   J. B. Lippincott Co.
   Ima Ova
   Wool 'N Wick
   William E. Wright Co.
boutique items
   Fabulous Holiday House
   Holiday Handicrafts, Inc.
ceramic wisemen
   Crafty Ideas
Christmas boutique items
   Holiday Craft
Christmas decorating items
   Beadnik's Arts & Crafts
   Fabulous Holiday House
   Zim's
Christmas figures
   Supreme Handicrafts
Christmas tree ornaments
   The Putter Shop
club plans
   Lee Wards Christmas Tree Club
diamond dust
   Holiday Craft
   Walnut Hill Co.
dimensional plastic shapes
   Holiday Craft
do-it-yourself Christmas ornaments
   Life-Like Products Inc.
   Sunset House
glass ornaments
   Holiday Craft
   Whittemore-Durgin Glass Co.
glass snowflakes
   Glass Creations
glass stars
   Glass Creations
kits
   Arts and Crafts Unlimited
   Ball O' Yarn
   Country Crafts
   Gibsons Creations
   Gift Craft
   Holiday Handicrafts, Inc.
   Sears, Roebuck & Co.
   Surburbia, Inc.
   Lillian Vernon
   Lee Wards
leaflets
   Craftplans
   The Rev. Henry N. Thomas
magazines
   Crafty Ideas
   Creative Crafts Christmas Annual
miniature accessories
   The House of Miniatures
   Joen Ellen Kanze
   Miles Kimball
   The Miniature Mart-The Peddler's Shop
   Mrs. Mell Prescott
miniature angels
   Holiday Craft
miniature animals
   Brown's Miniatures

Craft Category Index
Christmas—Clay

    Custom Made Carvings & Miniatures
    Flint FBG Imports
miniature bone china animals
    The Gift Shoppe
miniature candlesticks
    Sparkle Studio
miniature ceramic animals
    The Gift Shoppe
miniature ceramic figures
    Grueny's Gift Center
miniature creche figures
    Holiday Craft
patterns
    Gloria
plastic heads
    Hazel Pearson Handi Craft
plastic portrait balls
    Downs
satin balls
    Taylor House
self-adhesive iridescent foil jewels
    Diffraction Co., Inc.
snow sprays
    Walnut Hill Co.
three king heads
    Holiday Handicrafts, Inc.
tinsel sticks
    Holiday Craft
tree skirts
    Gibsons Creations
woodworking patterns
    Craft Patterns
wreaths
    Holiday Handicrafts, Inc.

clay and clay sculpting
  books
    Dr. David Crespi
    Davis Publications, Inc.
  calipers
    The L. S. Starrett Co.
  casting items
    Art Consultants
  casting supplies
    Ettl Studios Inc.
    Sculpture House
  casting table racks
    Cole Ceramics Laboratories
  casting tables
    Air Capitol Molds, Inc.

ceramic armatures
    Cole Ceramics Laboratories
    Newton's Potters Supply
ceramic clays
    Paramount Ceramic Inc.
    Van Howe Ceramic Supply Co.
clay beads
    Bead Game
clay carts
    A. D. Alpine Inc.
clay containers
    Cole Ceramics Laboratories
clay mixers
    Bluebird Manufacturing
clay molds
    Kay Kinney-Contoured Glass
clays
    American Art Clay Co. Inc.
    Bob's Arts & Crafts
    Boin Arts & Crafts
    Cole Ceramics Laboratories
    Craft Service
    Minnesota Clay
    Ohio Ceramic Supply Inc.
    Plaza Artists Materials, Inc.
    Richland Ceramics Inc.
    Standard Ceramic Supply
    Tepping Studio Supply Co.
    Westwood Ceramic Supply Co.
collar molds
    Kay Kinney-Contoured Glass
dry clays
    Westwood Ceramic Supply Co.
firing clay
    American Art Clay Co. Inc.
    Arthur Brown & Bro., Inc.
    Delco Craft Center, Inc.
    Plaza Artists Materials, Inc.
    Sax Arts & Crafts
    Skil-Crafts Division
floral clay
    American Art Clay Co. Inc.
high-fire clays
    Newton's Potters Supply
kits
    Edmund Scientific Co.
Mexican pottery clay
    American Art Clay Co. Inc.
modeling clay
    American Art Clay Co. Inc.
    Douglas & Sturgess, Inc.

Craft Category Index
Clay—Cloth

  Economy Handicrafts, Inc.
  Sculpture Associates Ltd.
  Sculpture House
  Sculpture Services Inc.
 nonfiring clay
  American Art Clay Co. Inc.
  Arthur Brown & Bro., Inc.
  Delco Craft Center, Inc.
  Plaza Artists Materials, Inc.
  Sax Arts & Crafts
  Skil-Crafts Division
 nonhardening clay
  Arthur Brown & Bro., Inc.
  Sax Arts & Crafts
 plaster impregnated sculpture tape
  American Art Clay Co. Inc.
 pottery clays
  Handcraft House
 self-hardening clays
  Boin Arts & Crafts
  Economy Handicrafts, Inc.
  Newton's Potters Supply
  Sculpture Associates Ltd.
  Sculpture House

clockmaking
 books
  Emerson Books Inc.
 clock accessories
  Craftsman Wood Service Co.
  H. DeCovnick & Son
  Dek-Co Manufacturing Co.
 clock dial cutters
  C. W. Bullock
 clock motors
  Albert Constantine & Son Inc.
 clock movements
  Atlantic Mold Corp.
  Bergen Arts & Crafts, Inc.
  Craft Products
  Craftsman Wood Service Co.
  H. DeCovnick & Son
  Diedricks Crafts
  Emperor Clock Co.
  Minnesota Woodworkers Supply Co.
  National Artcraft Supply Co.
  Newport Enterprises
  Ohio Ceramic Supply Inc.
  Hazel Pearson Handi Craft
  Plasco
  John & Susan Scheewe

 clock patterns
  Craft Products
 hardware
  Craft Products
 kitchen clock glass
  C. W. Bullock
 kits
  C. W. Bullock
  Albert Constantine & Son Inc.
  Craft Products
  H. DeCovnick & Son
  Dek-Co Manufacturing Co.
  Emperor Clock Co.
  The Enchanted Doll House
  Gilman's
  Mason & Sullivan Co.
  Minnesota Woodworkers Supply Co.
  Newport Enterprises
  D. E. Rinck
  Sears, Roebuck & Co.
  Surburbia, Inc.
 O G clock glass
  C. W. Bullock
 transistor clock movements
  Rays Rock Shop

cloth toymaking
 books
  Chilton Book Co.
  Drake Publishers Inc.
  The Unicorn
  Watson-Guptill Publications
 kits
  The Clever Crafters
  The Rusty Nail
  Thrift Mailmart
 movable eyes
  Holiday Handicrafts, Inc.
  Home-Sew Inc.
 patterns
  D-Carol
  Davis & Co.
 plastic heads
  Hazel Pearson Handi Craft
 polyester fiberfill stuffing
  Putnam Co.
 rag doll patterns
  American Indian Portrait Dolls
  Dot's Dollhouse
  Betty James Originals
 rag dolls
  Susan Sirkis

sew-and-stuff animals
   Herter's, Inc.
sew-and-stuff dolls
   Herter's, Inc.
stitch-and-stuff toys
   Platypus
stuffed animals
   Magnus Craft Materials, Inc.
stuffed doll patterns
   Virginia Black Designs
wiggle eyes
   Delco Craft Center, Inc.

club plans *(see also specific craft)*
   Artrox Rock of the Month Club; lapidary.
   Robert Ayottes' Designery; yarns.
   The Beadcraft Corner/Beadcraft Club; beadery.
   Craftsman Circle Book Club; craft book.
   Designers Fabrics Buy-Mail; fabrics.
   Fabrics 'Round the World Inc.; fabrics.
   Fashion Fabrics Club; fabrics.
   Mary Maxim Inc.; needlecraft.
   National Handcraft Society; decorative crafts.
   Popular Science Book Club; books.
   Reynolds Yarns Inc.; crochet, knitting.
   The Stained Glass Club; stained glass.
   Trader South; lapidary.
   Lee Wards Christmas Tree Club; Christmas crafts.
   Wee Goodies of the Month Club; miniatures.
   Erica Wilson's Creative Needlework Society; needlecrafts.
   Woman's How-To Book Club; craft books.

collage
   aged documents
      Whittemore-Durgin Glass Co.
   antique newspapers
      Whittemore-Durgin Glass Co.
   beer labels
      Whittemore-Durgin Glass Co.
   books
      Chilton Book Co.
      The Dial Press Inc.
   collage prints
      Elyse Sommer

concrete casting, molding, sculpting
   aluminum molds for ornamental concrete
      Concrete Machinery Co.
   armatures
      Delco Craft Center, Inc.
      Plaza Artists Materials, Inc.
      Sculpture Associates Ltd.

cookie decorating *(see Cake decorating)*

cooking crystal craft
   books
      Chilton Book Co.
   cooking crystal molds
      Hazel Pearson Handi Craft
   cooking crystals
      P. S. Andrews Co.
      Delco Craft Center, Inc.
      Carl Hepp Mosaic Co.
      New Products Co.
      Hazel Pearson Handi Craft
      St. Louis Crafts Inc.
      Specialty Products
      Town & Country Crafts
      Zim's
   kits
      Koehler's Craft Outlet
      New Products Co.

copper *(see also Metals, Metalware)*
   Anchor Tool & Supply Co.
   Bergen Arts & Crafts, Inc.
   T. B. Hagstoz & Son
   copper craft
      American Handicrafts
   copper enameling supplies
      Alessi Lapidary Supplies
      American Handicrafts
      Ceramic Coating Co.
      Essayons Studio, Hand Arts Center
      Kit Kraft
      Bob and Carol Oliver
      Ovgem Craft Supply Co.
      Skil-Crafts Division
      Specialty Products
      Jack D. Wolfe Co. Inc.
   copper foil
      Delco Craft Center, Inc.
      St. Louis Crafts Inc.
   copper shapes
      Sax Arts & Crafts

Craft Category Index
Copper—Cord

copper wire
  Talisman Crafts
kits
  American Handicrafts
cord, thread, and rope
  butcher's twine
    Knit Services, Inc.
  cable cord
    Knit Services, Inc.
  cording
    Nature's Fibers
  cords
    Dick Blick
    P. C. Herwig Co., Inc.
    Macrame and Weaving Supply Co.
  cotton cord
    Creator's Corner
    Tinkler & Co. Inc.
  cotton threads
    The Mail Train
  cotton-ropes polished
    Knit Services, Inc.
  Egyptian cotton thread
    Robin & Russ Handweavers
  flax line fiber
    Frederick J. Fawcett, Inc.
  flax straw (retted)
    Frederick J. Fawcett, Inc.
  goat lacing
    Leathercrafters Supply Co.
  Japanese filament
    Nature's Fibers
  jute
    Contessa Yarns
    Creator's Corner
    P. C. Herwig Co., Inc.
    The Hidden Village
    Knit Services, Inc.
    The Loomery
    Robin & Russ Handweavers
    Tinkler & Co. Inc.
  kits
    Diversikit, Inc.
  lacing
    American Handicrafts
    P. S. Andrews Co.
    Craft Service
    Craftsman Supply House
    Sax Arts & Crafts
  lame cord
    Knit Services, Inc.
  leather bolo cords
    Shipley's Mineral House
  linen cord
    The Hidden Village
  linen rope
    Knit Services, Inc.
  linen thread
    Frederick J. Fawcett, Inc.
    The Hidden Village
    Robin & Russ Handweavers
    Osma G. Tod Weaving & Lace Studio
  linen twine
    Knit Services, Inc.
  macrame cords
    Craft Yarns of Rhode Island Inc.
    Delco Craft Center, Inc.
    Dharma Trading Co.
    Fetty-Nielsen Macrame Loom
    House of Orange
    Jo-El's Craft Co.
    Knit Services, Inc.
    Lily Mills Co.
    The Mannings Creative Crafts
    Reeves Knotique
    Tandy Leather Co.
    The Yarn Depot
  metallic threads
    The Hidden Village
  navy cord
    The Hidden Village
    Knit Services, Inc.
  nylon
    Macrame and Weaving Supply Co.
  nylon braided cord
    Fetty-Nielsen Macrame Loom
  nylon parachute cord
    Knit Services, Inc.
  nylon thread
    Danfield Threads Inc.
    Walter Drake
    Spencer Gifts Inc.
  rattail
    The Hidden Village
  rope making machine
    Schacht Spindle Co.
  seine twine
    The Hidden Village
    Knit Services, Inc.
  silk thread
    The Hidden Village
    Robin & Russ Handweavers

Craft Category Index
Cord—Crewel

sisal
   Contessa Yarns
   P. C. Herwig Co., Inc.
tapestry threads
   Needlecraft Shop Inc.
tarred marlin cord
   The Hidden Village
threads
   Dick Blick
   Home-Sew Inc.
   Leathercrafters Supply Co.
   Mary Maxim Inc.
   The Needlecase
   Robin & Russ Handweavers
   Mildred Sprout
   Thumbelina Needlework Shop
   Lee Wards
twine
   Knit Services, Inc.
   Netcraft
unbleached cotton cord
   Kristine Eckert

cork
   Arthur Brown & Bro., Inc.
   Cleveland Leather Co.
   Cork Products Co. Inc.
   Craft Service
   Craftsman Supply House
   Economy Handicrafts, Inc.
   The Handcrafters
   Magnus Craft Materials, Inc.
   Minnesota Clay
   NASCO Arts & Crafts
   Plaza Artists Materials, Inc.
   Sax Arts & Crafts
   Skil-Crafts Division
   Westwood Ceramic Supply Co.
cork disks
   Westwood Ceramic Supply Co.

crewel *(see also Frames, Hoops, Needlecrafts, Yarns)*
   Creativity Needlepoint
   The Custom House of Needle Arts & Design
   Jeane's
   Jerry S. Kaye Assoc.
   Merribee
   The Needlecase
   Needlecraft Shop Inc.
   J. C. Penney Co., Inc.
   Schrock's, The House of Hobbies & Crafts
   Sears, Roebuck & Co.
   Wool 'N Wick
Belgian linen
   Greentree Ranch Wools, Countryside Handweavers
books
   Better Homes & Gardens Books
   Book Barn
   Crossroads
   Crown Publishers
   Grosset & Dunlap Inc.
crewel embroidery design transfers
   Nantucket Needleworks
crewel embroidery designs
   Woodland Craft Designs
crewel tapestry wall hangings
   General Crafts Corp.
crewel wool
   The Hidden Village
floor hoops
   KAY an EE Corp. of America
home study courses
   National Standards Council of American Embroiderers
   Erica Wilson Correspondence Courses
homespun crewel yarn
   KeeWai Krafts
hoops
   The Hidden Village
   Jerry S. Kaye Assoc.
   Nantucket Needleworks
   Needlecraft Shop Inc.
kits
   Better Homes & Gardens
   Budget Buddy Co.
   Crafts Yarns & Gifts
   Crafts Yarns & Gifts Ltd.
   Crain-Harmon
   Crewel World
   James L. Douthat
   General Crafts Corp.
   Good Housekeeping
   Holmes-Corey Ltd.
   Nantucket Needleworks
   The Needle Works
   Needlecraft House
   The Stitchery
   Sudberry House
   Tuxedo Yarn & Needlework

Craft Category Index
Crewel—Crochet

    Lee Wards
    Erica Wilson Needleworks
    Wool-Art Studios Inc.
    The World of Stitch 'N Knit
linen
    Needlecraft House
magazines
    Good Housekeeping Needlecraft
    Ladies Home Journal Needlecraft
    Woman's Day Knit & Stitch
    Woman's Day Needlework Ideas
roll and stretch frame
    Needle-Ease
wool crewel
    Needlecraft House

crochet *(see also Cord, Yarns)*
afghans
    Merribee
books
    Book Barn
    Boycan's Craft Supplies
    Charles T. Branford Co.
    Chilton Book Co.
    Crown Publishers
    Drake Publishers Inc.
    Harper & Row, Publishers Inc.
    Hearthside Press
    Elizabeth Hiddleson
    Museum Books Inc.
    Phentex, Inc.
    Random House Inc.
    Rosemond Hobbycraft
    Sancraft Industries
    Charles Scribner's Sons
    Beryl Sink
    Standard Doll Co.
    Stein & Day
    William Unger & Co. Inc.
    The Unicorn
club plans
    Reynolds Yarns Inc.
corded magnifier
    M. Turner
cotton crochet yarn
    W. B. Roddey
crochet accessories
    Sunray Yarn House
    Wyco Yarn Co.
crochet animals
    Sharon's Petite Sherre

crochet carrying bags
    Henry Seligman Co. Inc.
crochet designs for baby things
    Alice Fowler Originals
crochet doll patterns
    Ruth Lukasik
crochet jewelry
    American Handicrafts
crochet patterns
    Brunswick Worsted Mills
    Sharon's Petite Sherre
    S. Siracusa
crochet pot holders
    Sharon's Petite Sherre
crochet yarns
    Cliveden Yarns
    Merribee
    Lee Wards
crocheting supplies
    Liveright
    Macrame and Weaving Supply Co.
    J. C. Penney Co., Inc.
    Lee Wards
daisy looms
    Walter Drake
daisy winder
    Rosemond Hobbycraft
doll clothes crochet patterns
    Virginia Lakin
    Mrs. Rossi
flower looms
    Craftsman Supply House
    Delco Craft Center, Inc.
    Hanover House Industries, Inc.
    Hazel Pearson Handi Craft
    Sav-On-Crafts
    Studio Twelve
kits
    Diversikit, Inc.
    Fairtex Distributing Co.
    Mary Maxim Inc.
    Melrose Yarn Co., Inc.
    Needlewoman Shop
    Sears, Roebuck & Co.
    Sunray Yarn House
    Sunset House
    Montgomery Ward & Co., Inc.
    Lee Wards
    Whisper Farm Furs
    Wonoco Yarn Co.

Craft Category Index
Crochet—Decorative

    Wyco Yarn Co.
    Yarns Unlimited
  leaflets
    Lion Brand Yarn Co.
  magazines
    Bookful of Crochet
    Good Housekeeping Needlecraft
    Ladies Home Journal Needlecraft
    McCall's Needlework & Crafts
    McCall's Pattern Fashions
    1001 Fashion & Needlecraft Ideas
    Woman's Day Knit & Stitch
    Woman's Day Needlework Ideas
    Woman's Day 101 Sweaters to Knit and Crochet
    The Workbasket
  patterns
    Gloria

decaling
  aged documents
    Whittemore-Durgin Glass Co.
  china decals
    D. M. Campana Co.
  cigar tin labels
    Whittemore-Durgin Glass Co.
  Civil War prints
    Lynchburg Hdwr. & General Store
  custom-made ceramic decals
    Art Decal Co.
  decals
    America's Hobby Center Inc.
    Walter Drake
    Hobby Gallery
    Salyer Publishing Co.
    Supreme Handicrafts
    Wm. Walthers Inc.
  decoupage decals
    Carnival Arts & Crafts
  kits
    The Farmhouse Craft Shoppe
  model decals
    Boxcar Ken
    Miniature Aircraft
    U. C. Hobby Center

decorative accessories
    Walnut Hill Co.
  adhesive sprays
    Walnut Hill Co.
  bells
    Jewelart Inc.
    Jeweler's Emporium
    Knit Services, Inc.
    Winona Trading Post
  bird feathers
    Herter's, Inc.
  boutique braids
    The Putter Shop
  boutique ribbons
    Hazel Pearson Handi Craft
  boutique trims
    Lee Wards
    Zim's
  braids
    Boutique Trims
    Country Crafts
    Home-Sew Inc.
    Knit Services, Inc.
    Lace Lady
    Mill Store
    Hazel Pearson Handi Craft
    Skil-Crafts Division
    Two Brothers Inc.
    Wagner's Crafts
  bronze powder
    Carson & Ellis, Inc.
    Peg Hall Studios
  camel bells
    Macrame and Weaving Supply Co.
  diamond dust
    Holiday Craft
    Walnut Hill Co.
  electrostatic flocking
    Rub 'N Buff
  embroidered appliques
    Embroideries Unlimited
  embroidered family crest emblems
    Scotch House
  felt appliques
    Home-Sew Inc.
  filigree paper lace
    P. S. Andrews Co.
  filigrees
    Gibsons Creations
    Holiday Craft
  flat plastic shapes
    Holiday Craft
  flocked fruit
    Sav-On-Crafts
  flocking
    Dick Blick
    Boin Arts & Crafts
    Arthur Brown & Bro., Inc.

Craft Category Index
Decorative—Decorative

    Craft Service
    Skil-Crafts Division
    W. Wooley & Co.
fluffs feathers
    Dersh Feather & Trading Corp.
foil
    Boin Arts & Crafts
    Craftsman Supply House
    Economy Handicrafts, Inc.
    The Handcrafters
    Barbara Lawshe
fringes
    Home-Sew Inc.
glass ornaments
    Holiday Craft
    Whittemore-Durgin Glass Co.
glass snowflakes
    Glass Creations
glass stars
    Glass Creations
glitter
    Country Crafts
    Holiday Handicrafts, Inc.
    Walnut Hill Co.
gloss spray
    Walnut Hill Co.
gold braids
    P. S. Andrews Co.
gold foil
    Basic Crafts Co.
gold lace borders
    Harrower House of Decoupage
gold lace frames
    Harrower House of Decoupage
gold lace ornaments
    Harrower House of Decoupage
gold leaf
    P. S. Andrews Co.
    Arthur Brown & Bro., Inc.
    Carson & Ellis, Inc.
    Peg Hall Studios
    Marie Mitchell's Decoupage Center
    Hazel Pearson Handi Craft
    Zim's
gold paper borders
    Taylor House
gold paper decorations
    Country Crafts
gold paper laces
    Hazel Pearson Handi Craft

gold paper ornaments
    Skil-Crafts Division
    Taylor House
gold paper trims
    Holiday Craft
gourd seeds
    George W. Park Seed Co., Inc.
hat pins
    Hazel Pearson Handi Craft
    Whittemore-Durgin Glass Co.
honeycomb ribbon
    Sav-On-Crafts
imported novelties
    Studio D
jingle bells
    Sav-On-Crafts
kits
    American Decorative Arts, Inc.
    Cottage Crafts
magazines
    American Home Crafts
    1001 Decorating Ideas
    1001 Fashion & Needlecraft Ideas
    Woman's Day Knit & Stitch
    Woman's Day Knitting Book
    Woman's Day Sewing & Fashion Ideas
metal stampings
    Green's Rock & Lapidary Ltd.
metallic beads
    The Beadcraft Corner/Beadcraft Club
metallic braids
    Gibsons Creations
    Knit Services, Inc.
mica mirrors
    Kitsophrenia, Inc.
mirror tiles
    Montgomery Ward & Co., Inc.
paper grass
    Life-Like Products Inc.
paper sparkle
    Life-Like Products Inc.
pearl flakes
    Walnut Hill Co.
pearl parchment
    Koehler's Craft Outlet
    Hazel Pearson Handi Craft
pearls
    Anne's Treasure Trove
    Bead Game
    The Beadcraft Corner/Beadcraft Club

Craft Category Index
Decorative—Decoupage

    Deep Flex Plastic Molds, Inc.
    Gilman's
    Home-Sew Inc.
    International Import Co.
    Jewelart Inc.
    Kaydee
    Kit Kraft
    M & M Distributors
    Natalie Originals Studio
    New Products Co.
    The Putter Shop
    Schrock's, The House of Hobbies & Crafts
    Swan-Son
    Taylor House
porcupine quills
    Easy Street
rhinestone bandings
    Gail's Decorative Arts Studio
    Gibsons Creations
rhinestone chain
    Boutique Trims
rhinestones
    P. S. Andrews Co.
    Boutique Trims
    Derby Lane Shell Center
    Florida Supply House, Inc.
    Gail's Decorative Arts Studio
    Gibsons Creations
    Handcraft Originals
    Home-Sew Inc.
    Kit Kraft
    National Artcraft Supply Co.
    Lee Wards
rub-on metallic finishes
    Rub 'N Buff
rub-on wax gilts
    Carnival Arts & Crafts
self-adhesive iridescent foil jewels
    Diffraction Co., Inc.
sequins
    Boutique Trims
    Home-Sew Inc.
    Kit Kraft
    Koehler's Craft Outlet
    Sav-On-Crafts
    Wagner's Crafts
sew-on railroad patches
    M. B. Austin
silver hinges
    Boutique Trims

small mirrors
    Dick Blick
    Magnus Craft Materials, Inc.
snow sprays
    Walnut Hill Co.
spangles
    Town & Country Crafts
sticker prints
    Downs
studs
    Lillian Vernon
three king heads
    Holiday Handicrafts, Inc.
tinsel sticks
    Holiday Craft
velvet ribbons
    Boutique Trims
    Taylor House
wax gilt
    Plasco
wax gold
    Arthur Brown & Bro., Inc.

decoupage *(see also Prints, Woodware)*
    A 'N L's Hobbicraft, Inc.
    Adventures In Crafts
    American Handicrafts
    P. S. Andrews Co.
    Bergen Arts & Crafts, Inc.
    Boin Arts & Crafts
    Carson & Ellis, Inc.
    Century 21
    Corner Cupboard Crafts, Inc.
    Deep Flex Plastic Molds, Inc.
    Dek-Co Manufacturing Co.
    Gemex Co.
    The Handcrafters
    Harrower House of Decoupage
    P. C. Herwig Co., Inc.
    Holiday Handicrafts, Inc.
    Jeane's
    John's Hardware & Decoupage Supplies
    Kraft Korner
    Magnus Craft Materials, Inc.
    Make It Happen Craft Studio
    Party Bazaar
    Hazel Pearson Handi Craft
    J. C. Penney Co., Inc.
    Sangray Corp.
    John & Susan Scheewe

Craft Category Index
Decoupage—Decoupage

    Schrock's, The House of Hobbies & Crafts
    Sears, Roebuck & Co.
    Skil-Crafts Division
    Stevenson Industries
    Supreme Handicrafts
    Swan-Son
    Taylor House
    Town & Country Crafts
    Lee Wards
    Zim's

$2 bills
    Hanover House Industries, Inc.

aerosol finishes
    Carnival Arts & Crafts

aged documents
    Whittemore-Durgin Glass Co.

antique newspapers
    Whittemore-Durgin Glass Co.

antiquing
    Carnival Arts & Crafts

art prints
    Supreme Handicrafts

beer labels
    Whittemore-Durgin Glass Co.

books
    Adventures In Crafts
    American Art Associates Publications, Inc.
    Book Barn
    Craft Course Publishers
    Crown Publishers
    Deft
    Flair-Craft Inc.
    Hearthside Press
    P. C. Herwig Co., Inc.
    Marie Mitchell's Decoupage Center
    Museum Books Inc.
    Sancraft Industries
    Elyse Sommer
    Valspar Corp.

brass hardware
    John's Hardware & Decoupage Supplies

bronze powder
    Carson & Ellis, Inc.
    Peg Hall Studios

cigar tin labels
    Whittemore-Durgin Glass Co.

Civil War prints
    Lynchburg Hdwr. & General Store

coasters
    Marie Mitchell's Decoupage Center

decoupage accessories
    Century 21

decoupage boxes
    Artistry In Wood
    Dek-Co Manufacturing Co.
    Harrower House of Decoupage
    Van Gelder Wood Products

decoupage brushes
    Peg Hall Studios
    John's Hardware & Decoupage Supplies

decoupage decals
    Carnival Arts & Crafts

decoupage designs
    Bell Studio
    Gladys Galloway
    Barbara Jones China House

decoupage easels
    Dek-Co Manufacturing Co.

decoupage finishes
    Carnival Arts & Crafts
    Century 21
    John's Hardware & Decoupage Supplies
    Marie Mitchell's Decoupage Center
    Hazel Pearson Handi Craft
    Ramont's Floral Arts Studio

decoupage fixatives
    Carnival Arts & Crafts

decoupage foil papers
    Harrower House of Decoupage

decoupage frames
    Dek-Co Manufacturing Co.
    John's Hardware & Decoupage Supplies

decoupage glues
    Century 21

decoupage hardware
    Adventures In Crafts
    Carson & Ellis, Inc.
    Dek-Co Manufacturing Co.
    Harrower House of Decoupage
    Marie Mitchell's Decoupage Center
    Hazel Pearson Handi Craft
    Town & Country Crafts
    Lee Wards

decoupage lap desks
    Dek-Co Manufacturing Co.

Craft Category Index
Decoupage—Decoupage

decoupage mining prints
   Ken Prag
decoupage oil company prints
   Ken Prag
decoupage plaques
   The Cellar Ceramic Shop
   Dek-Co Manufacturing Co.
   Harrower House of Decoupage
decoupage posters
   Gary Bunting
decoupage prints
   Buck Hill Associates
   Carnival Arts & Crafts
   Century 21
   Marie Mitchell's Decoupage Center
   Old Print Center
   Elyse Sommer
decoupage purse handles
   Dek-Co Manufacturing Co.
decoupage railroad prints
   Ken Prag
decoupage slat purses
   Dek-Co Manufacturing Co.
decoupage stains
   Century 21
decoupage stock certificates prints
   Ken Prag
decoupage stools
   Dek-Co Manufacturing Co.
decoupage tools
   Harrower House of Decoupage
decoupage trims
   Sax Arts & Crafts
doll advertisement papers
   Sharon's Petite Sherre
doll antique photographs
   Sharon's Petite Sherre
English decoupage prints
   Sharon's Petite Sherre
floral prints
   John's Hardware & Decoupage Supplies
gold lace borders
   Harrower House of Decoupage
gold lace frames
   Harrower House of Decoupage
gold lace ornaments
   Harrower House of Decoupage
gold leaf
   P. S. Andrews Co.
   Arthur Brown & Bro., Inc.
   Carson & Ellis, Inc.
   Peg Hall Studios
   Marie Mitchell's Decoupage Center
   Hazel Pearson Handi Craft
   Zim's
historic advertisements
   Buck Hill Associates
historic handbills
   Buck Hill Associates
historic posters
   Buck Hill Associates
historic prints
   Buck Hill Associates
home study courses
   Harrower House of Decoupage
kits
   Adventures In Crafts
   American Handicrafts
   Bersted's
   Cleveland Leather Co.
   Craft Kits
   Deep Flex Plastic Molds, Inc.
   Jamar, Inc.
   Marie Mitchell's Decoupage Center
   Swan-Son
   Lee Wards
magazines
   American Home Crafts
   Happy Hobbies Magazine
   1001 Decorating Ideas
   Turpen Times
Old Masters prints
   John's Hardware & Decoupage Supplies
   Scissortail Arts & Crafts
old time whiskey labels
   Lynchburg Hdwr. & General Store
parchment quotes
   Stevenson Industries
patterns
   Dek-Co Manufacturing Co.
pearl parchment
   Koehler's Craft Outlet
   Hazel Pearson Handi Craft
precut decoupage designs
   Carolyn Watson
rub-on wax gilts
   Carnival Arts & Crafts
unfinished basswood boxes
   Albert Constantine & Son Inc.

Craft Category Index
Decoupage—Designs

   unfinished boxes
      Carson & Ellis, Inc.
   unfinished milk cans
      Dairy Service, Inc
      The Wood Barn
   unfinished pails
      Spaulding & Frost Co., Inc.
   unfinished plaques
      Albert Constantine & Son Inc.
   unfinished purse boxes
      Carson & Ellis, Inc.
   Victorian design gift wrap paper
      Sharon's Petite Sherre
   wine labels
      Whittemore-Durgin Glass Co.
   wooden candle sconces
      Marie Mitchell's Decoupage Center
   wooden clocks
      Marie Mitchell's Decoupage Center
   wooden switch plates
      Marie Mitchell's Decoupage Center
   woodware
      P. S. Andrews Co.
      Bergen Arts & Crafts, Inc.
      Carson & Ellis, Inc.
      Century 21
      Corner Cupboard Crafts, Inc.
      Country Woodcraft
      Craft Service
      Economy Handicrafts, Inc.
      P. C. Herwig Co., Inc.
      John's Hardware & Decoupage Supplies
      Magnus Craft Materials, Inc.
      Marie Mitchell's Decoupage Center
      Sandeen's Scandinavian Gift & Card Shop
      Sax Arts & Crafts
      Skil-Crafts Division
      Town & Country Crafts
      Lee Wards
   3-D flexible decoupage cut-outs
      Gemex Co.

decoys
   glass eyes
      Bay Country Woodcrafters
   green wing teals
      Bay Country Woodcrafters
   kits
      Bay Country Woodcrafters
   leaflets
      The Sneak Box Studio
   paints
      The Sneak Box Studio
   wood ducks
      Bay Country Woodcrafters
   wood mallards
      Bay Country Woodcrafters

designs *(see also specific craft)*
   books
      Peg Hall Studios
      John & Susan Scheewe
   cake decorating designs
      Transart
   craft designs
      Transart
   crewel embroidery designs
      Woodland Craft Designs
   crochet designs for baby things
      Alice Fowler Originals
   decorative painting designs
      Jean's
   decoupage designs
      Bell Studio
      Gladys Galloway
      Barbara Jones China House
   design plates
      The Smock Shop
   embroidery designs
      House of Patterns
      Raymond P. Wallace
   glass designs
      Bell Studio
   kits
      Erica Wilson Needleworks
   leather designs
      Transart
      Raymond P. Wallace
   needlepoint designs
      International Creations
      The Knittery
   needlework designs
      Donna Jean Carver
      Sudberry House
   precut decoupage designs
      Carolyn Watson
   quilt designs
      Aunt Martha's Studios Inc.
   repeat glass
      Arthur Brown & Bro., Inc.
      Plaza Artists Materials, Inc.

rooster designs
  Geecraft
rug designs
  International Creations
silhouette designs
  Geecraft

diamond machinery and equipment *(see also Lapidary)*
  Gem Tool Specialties
  Terra Products
diamond abrasives
  The Ducketts
diamond arbors
  Gem Tool Specialties
diamond bar wheel dressers
  Gem Tec Diamond Tool Co.
diamond blades
  Covington Engineering Corp.
  Earth Treasures
  Farmers Gem and Rock Shop
  Gem Tool Specialties
  Star Diamond Industries
diamond burrs
  Gem Tool Specialties
diamond carvers
  Metro Diamond Drill Co.
diamond coated files
  Metro Diamond Drill Co.
diamond compounds
  Walter E. Johansen
  Jack V. Schuller, Inc.
  Sinkankas Diamond Products
diamond cores
  Gem Tool Specialties
diamond crystals
  Commercial Mineral Corp.
  Panther International Ltd.
diamond disks
  Gem Tool Specialties
diamond drills
  Gem Tool Specialties
  Geode Industries
diamond gem maker
  Gem Tec Diamond Tool Co.
diamond impregnated core drills
  Metro Diamond Drill Co.
diamond laps
  Jack V. Schuller, Inc.
diamond pads
  Gem Tool Specialties

diamond points
  Gem Tool Specialties
diamond powders
  Aleta's Rock Shop
  Gem Tool Specialties
  Industrial Diamond Tool Co. Inc.
  Walter E. Johansen
diamond products
  Green's Rock & Lapidary Ltd.
  Highland Park Manufacturing
  Jack V. Schuller, Inc.
diamond saw blades
  Highland Park Manufacturing
diamond saws
  Raytech Industries Inc.
diamond tools
  Gem Tec Diamond Tool Co.
  Gem Tool Specialties
diamond wheels
  Diamond-Pro Unlimited
  Gem Tec Diamond Tool Co.
  Gem Tool Specialties

dolls
  Rombins' Nest Farm
  Sunray Yarn House
antique dolls
  The Needle Works
books
  Eva Ann Dolls
  Hobby House Press
  Standard Doll Co.
  Trojan Press Inc.
china doll
  Susan Sirkis
china doll parts
  Antique Doll Reproductions
  Doll Repair Parts, Inc.
doll advertisement papers
  Sharon's Petite Sherre
doll bisque
  Dollspart Supply Co., Inc.
doll miniatures
  Susan Sirkis
doll repair items
  Dollspart Supply Co., Inc.
dressed dolls
  Antique Doll Reproductions
  Standard Doll Co.
First Ladies fashions
  Susan Sirkis

Craft Category Index
Dolls—Display

French fashion dolls
  Susan Sirkis
kits
  Doll Repair Parts, Inc.
  Eva Mae Doll Co.
  Mark Farmer Co., Inc.
  Gift Craft
  Thrift Mailmart
magazines
  Doll Castle News
miniature dolls
  Helen Gallagher
miniature French dolls
  Grueny's Gift Center
needlework dolls
  Donna Jean Carver
old fashioned doll packs
  Sharon's Petite Sherre
rag doll patterns
  American Indian Portrait Dolls
  Dot's Dollhouse
  Betty James Originals
rag dolls
  Susan Sirkis
sew-and-stuff dolls
  Herter's, Inc.
sock doll
  Sharon's Petite Sherre
undressed dolls
  Standard Doll Co.
wood dolls
  Susan Sirkis

dip film
  A 'N L's Hobbicraft, Inc.
  American Handicrafts
  Bergen Arts & Crafts, Inc.
  Boin Arts & Crafts
  Carson & Ellis, Inc.
  Cleveland Leather Co.
  Craft Service
  Craftsman Supply House
  Delco Craft Center, Inc.
  Economy Handicrafts, Inc.
  Gemex Co.
  • Make It Happen Craft Studio
  J. C. Penney Co., Inc.
  Sears, Roebuck & Co.
  Specialty Products
  Supreme Handicrafts
  Zim's

books
  Craft Course Publishers
kits
  American Handicrafts

display accessories
blank labels
  Althor Products
brass stands
  George W. Park Seed Co., Inc.
carved wood mineral display stands
  Weaver's Gems and Minerals
collector's cases
  A. L. Stone Displays
decorative mounts
  Nature's Treasures
display domes
  Hanover House Industries, Inc.
display stands
  G. Weidinger
easels
  Artistry In Wood
  A. L. Stone Displays
electrical turntables
  A. L. Stone Displays
fluorescent lamps
  Ultra-Violet Products, Inc
Formica® cabinets
  A. L. Stone Displays
frames for china
  J. Opal Stover Studio
frames for hanging tiles
  Downs
glass bulbs
  Floating Gem Co.
glass display domes
  Downs
  Flemington Cut Glass Co.
  Helen Gallagher
  Max of Dallas
  Sturbridge Yankee Workshop
  Sunset House
gold finish mini-easels
  Jewelart Inc.
gold finish wire easels
  Sunflower Crafts
heart glass bulbs
  Floating Gem Co.
hobby lighting
  Nature's Treasures
holders
  A. L. Stone Displays

jewelry display cases
  Liberty Gem & Supply
  Max of Dallas
  Nature's Treasures
long flat glass bulbs
  Floating Gem Co.
Lucite® cabinets
  A. L. Stone Displays
Lucite® mini-easels
  Lillian Vernon
manual battery turntables
  A. L. Stone Displays
metal stands
  Max of Dallas
mini-easels
  American Handicrafts
  F. C. Ziegler Co.
plastic boxes
  Althor Products
  Craft Service
  Florida Supply House, Inc.
  Sax Arts & Crafts
plastic display domes
  Walter Drake
  Edmund Scientific Co.
  Sunset House
plate (dish) frames
  Downs
plate holders
  Downs
plexiglass cabinets
  A. L. Stone Displays
push pins
  Plaza Artists Materials, Inc.
revolvable bases
  A. L. Stone Displays
round glass bulbs
  Floating Gem Co.
silver finish mini-easels
  Jewelart Inc.
slab display racks
  Stonehouse
small easels
  Hanover House Industries, Inc.
stands
  A. L. Stone Displays
stock threaded plastic jars
  Parkway Plastics Inc.
tree making
  Bet-Roc Enterprises Inc.

ultraviolet lamps
  Raytech Industries Inc.
ultraviolet lights
  Nature's Treasures
wax ring stands
  Bourget Bros. Gems & Minerals
wood cabinets
  A. L. Stone Displays
wrought iron tile frames
  Renaldy's
doll clothes and accessories
  Doll Repair Parts, Inc.
  Dollspart Supply Co., Inc.
  Mark Farmer Co., Inc.
  Frances La Monica
  Standard Doll Co.
books
  Carter Craft Doll House
  Standard Doll Co.
  Trojan Press Inc.
  Van Nostrand Reinhold Co.
doll advertisement papers
  Sharon's Petite Sherre
doll antique photographs
  Sharon's Petite Sherre
doll beads
  Standard Doll Co.
doll clothes crochet patterns
  Virginia Lakin
  Mrs. Rossi
doll clothes knitting patterns
  Virginia Lakin
  Mrs. Rossi
doll clothes patterns
  Doll Castle News
  Mark Farmer Co., Inc.
  Standard Doll Co.
doll laces
  Standard Doll Co.
doll patterns
  Yvonne Brandon
  Dolly Darling Inc.
  Ervins
  Platypus
  Sue Wise
doll repair items
  Dollspart Supply Co., Inc.
doll sound boxes
  Standard Doll Co.
doll stands
  Downs

Craft Category Index
Doll—Doll

doll voices
    Standard Doll Co.
First Ladies fashions
    Susan Sirkis
home study courses
    Lifetime Career Schools
kits
    Dolly Darling Inc.
    Standard Doll Co.
miniature doll accessories
    Lamonica
miniature dollhouse accessories
    The Doll Cupboard
    Lamonica
patterns
    House of Patterns

doll houses and furniture
    Davault Miniature Furniture
    Mark Farmer Co., Inc.
    Rombins' Nest Farm
    Standard Doll Co.
    Yield House
books
    H. Shealy
club plans
    Wee Goodies of the Month Club
dollhouse accessories
    The Doll Cupboard
    Fieldwood Co.
    Joen Ellen Kanze
    Frances La Monica
    Lamonica
    LeMar's Decoupage Center
    Miniatures by Marty
dollhouse wallpaper
    The Miniature Mart-The Peddler's Shop
dollhouse miniatures
    The Doll Cupboard
    The Miniature Mart-The Peddler's Shop
    South Shore Woman's Exchange
kits
    Standard Doll Co.
    Vermont Toy Crafts
    Yield House
leaflets
    Davault Miniature Furniture
magazines
    Doll Castle News

metal miniature doll houses
    Holgate & Raynolds

doll making and parts
    Antique Doll Reproductions
    The Beadcraft Corner/Beadcraft Club
    Bob's Arts & Crafts
    Craftsman Supply House
    Doll Repair Parts, Inc.
    Dollspart Supply Co., Inc.
    Hazel Pearson Handi Craft
    Sav-On-Crafts
    Standard Doll Co.
    Supreme Handicrafts
    Thrift Mailmart
    Lee Wards
books
    Book Barn
    Charles T. Branford Co.
    Chilton Book Co.
    Drake Publishers Inc.
    The Enchanted Doll House
    Gay World of Dolls Museum
    Hobby House Press
    Susan Sirkis
    Trojan Press Inc.
    The Unicorn
    Watson-Guptill Publications
china doll
    Susan Sirkis
china doll parts
    Antique Doll Reproductions
    Doll Repair Parts, Inc.
cloth doll patterns
    Dorris Dolls
crochet doll patterns
    Ruth Lukasik
doll arms
    Standard Doll Co.
doll beads
    Standard Doll Co.
doll bisque
    Dollspart Supply Co., Inc.
doll patterns
    Yvonne Brandon
    Dolly Darling Inc.
    Ervins
    Platypus
    Sue Wise
doll repair items
    Dollspart Supply Co., Inc.

Craft Category Index
Doll—Dyes

doll sound boxes
  Standard Doll Co.
doll voices
  Standard Doll Co.
dough doll heads
  Ervins
home study courses
  Jo's Doll Dressing Course
kits
  The Clever Crafters
  Ervins
  M. Knopp
  Koehler's Craft Outlet
  Wilfred Enterprises
leaflets
  Wilfred Enterprises
magazine
  Doll Castle News
  Ladies Home Journal Needlecraft
movable eyes
  Holiday Handicrafts, Inc.
  Home-Sew Inc.
parian doll heads
  Antique Doll Reproductions
plastic heads
  Hazel Pearson Handi Craft
pompom dolls
  A. Raimer
sew-and-stuff dolls
  Herter's, Inc.
stuffed doll patterns
  Virginia Black Designs
teenage doll patterns
  Betty James Originals
  Manlove Originals
undressed dolls
  Standard Doll Co.
vinyl doll heads
  The Clever Crafters
dough craft
  Hazel Pearson Handi Craft
books
  Chilton Book Co.
  Craft Course Publishers
  Lothrop, Lee & Shephard
  Elyse Sommer
dough art mix
  Natcol Crafts, Inc.
dough art patterns
  Natcol Crafts, Inc.

dough art tools
  Natcol Crafts, Inc.
dough doll heads
  Ervins
handcrafted bread dough miniatures
  Hallie Copeland
kits
  Natcol Crafts, Inc.
draping
  Supreme Handicrafts
figure draping
  Hazel Pearson Handi Craft
liquid drape
  Ramont's Floral Arts Studio
dyes and dyeing *(see also specific craft)*
  Berry's of Maine
  Castolite
  Cleveland Leather Co.
  Delco Craft Center, Inc.
  Dharma Trading Co.
  Handcraft House
  The Hidden Village
  House of Gould
  KM Yarn Co.
  Leathercrafters Supply Co.
  Magnus Craft Materials, Inc.
  The Niddy Noddy
  Sax Arts & Crafts
  Skil-Crafts Division
  Straw Into Gold
  Surma Book & Music Store
  W. Wooley & Co.
acid dyes
  Glen Black Handwoven Textiles
alcohol dyes
  Fezandie & Sperrle, Inc.
aniline dyes
  Fezandie & Sperrle, Inc.
batik dyes
  Fezandie & Sperrle, Inc.
  Northwest Handcraft House
blockprinting dye
  Rupert, Gibbon & Spider
books
  Best Foods
  Book Barn
  Brooklyn Botanic Garden
  Crown Publishers
  Dye-Craft Ideas
  LeJeune, Inc.
  Mrs. Carl F. Murray

Craft Category Index
Dyes—Ecology

    Robin & Russ Handweavers
    Textile Crafts
    The Unicorn
candle dyes
    Barker Enterprises
    Cake Decorators & Craft Supplies
    Candle Kitchen
    Candle Mill Village
    Candlewic Co.
    Celebration Candlemaking Supplies
    Craft & Candle House
    Doll's Candle & Craft Supplies
    May-Wal, Inc.
    Natcol Crafts, Inc.
    Pourette Mfg. Co.
    Pylam Products, Inc.
    W. Spencer Inc.
    Village Candle & Craft
    Walnut Hill Co.
cold water dyes
    Artis, Inc.
    Glen Black Handwoven Textiles
    Creator's Corner
    Delco Craft Center, Inc.
    Knit Services, Inc.
fabric dyes
    Joan Moshimer
kits
    Doll's Candle & Craft Supplies
leather dyes
    Fezandie & Sperrle, Inc.
    La Venta Corp.
    Mac Leather Co.
    Tandy Leather Co.
magazines
    Rug Hooker News & Views
mordants
    Straw Into Gold
nylon dyes
    Creator's Corner
oil soluble dyes
    Fezandie & Sperrle, Inc.
organic dyes
    Colonial Textiles
paper dip dyes
    Delco Craft Center, Inc.
permanent brush-on dyeing
    Rupert, Gibbon & Spider
Procion® dyes
    Dharma Trading Co.

services
    KM Yarn Co.
textile dyes
    Rupert, Gibbon & Spider
vat dyes
    Inkodye
vegetable dyes
    Dharma Trading Co.
wool dyes
    Creator's Corner
    Northwest Handcraft House
ecology crafts *(see also Nature crafts)*
    American Indian bead corn
        Crowe & Coulter
    American Indian flower corn
        Crowe & Coulter
    books
        Chilton Book Co.
        Driftwood House
        Parker Publishing Co., Inc.
    butterflies
        Arthur Brown & Bro., Inc.
        The Collector's Cabinet
        House of York
        Hazel Pearson Handi Craft
    ecology shadow boxes
        Delco Craft Center, Inc.
    ferns
        Arthur Brown & Bro., Inc.
    gourd seeds
        George W. Park Seed Co., Inc.
    herbs
        Worldwide Curio House
    hutch boxes
        Koehler's Craft Outlet
    kits
        Anne's Treasure Trove
        Driftwood House
    leaves
        Gail's Decorative Arts Studio
    lichen
        Holiday Craft
        Life-Like Products Inc.
    lifelike grass
        Life-Like Products Inc.
    lifelike stone
        Life-Like Products Inc.
    magazines
        Good Housekeeping Needlecraft
    miniature glass animals
        The Gift Shoppe

Craft Category Index
Ecology—Eggery

miniature grass
   Holiday Craft
miocene vertebrate fossils
   C. R. Boylin
North American fossils
   Odyssey Mineral and Fossil
petrified wood
   Bonnie's Rock Shop
   Mississippi Petrified Forest
petrified wood stumps
   Mission Rocks
plant fossils
   Geological Enterprises
pods
   Driftwood House
preserved butterflies
   J. Alday
   American Butterfly Co.
   Dorothy Biddle Service
preserved foliage
   Boycan's Craft Supplies
roots
   Worldwide Curio House
seashells
   The Collector's Cabinet
   Max of Dallas
   Scott Scientific Inc.
seed pods
   Western Tree Cones
seeds
   Bead Game
   Driftwood House
   Jeweler's Emporium
   George W. Park Seed Co., Inc.
shadowboxes
   The Handcraft Supply Corp.
weathered decorative boards
   Dale Magnuson

eggery and egg decorating *(see also Boutique trims, Miniatures)*
   Boutique Trims
   Crafty's Backroom
   Hoffman Hatchery
   Holiday Craft
   Kaydee
   The Miniature Mart-The Peddler's Shop
   Natalie Originals Studio
   Ren Ann Crafts
   Ukrainian Gift Shop

bantam eggshells
   Allegra Milano
   Rock Mountain Farm
bisque eggs
   Howe Studio
   Town & Country Crafts
blown goose eggs
   Swanjord Hatchery
blue duck eggshells
   Rock Mountain Farm
blue hen eggshells
   Rock Mountain Farm
bobwhite eggshells
   Rock Mountain Farm
books
   Mrs. Barbara Allen
   The Clever Crafters
   Drake Publishers Inc.
   Mrs. C. Ference
   Hearthside Press
   Howe Studio
   Kathryn Johnson
   Margaret's Egg Craft
   Ima Ova
   Ren Ann Crafts
   Kit Stansbury
brass hinges
   Boutique Trims
   Handcraft Originals
buck eggshells
   Allegra Milano
canary eggshells
   Rock Mountain Farm
ceramic eggs
   Wilfred Enterprises
dove eggshells
   Rock Mountain Farm
duck eggshells
   Bowersox Eggcraft Supplies
   Handcraft Originals
   Hoffman Hatchery
egg accessories
   Rock Mountain Farm
   Taylor House
egg bases
   Natalie Originals Studio
egg blowers
   Kaydee
egg cutter attachment
   Loosie Goosie Egg Craft Shop

Craft Category Index
Eggery—Eggery

egg decorating supplies
   Gail's Decorative Arts Studio
egg hardware
   Carnival Arts & Crafts
egg marker
   The Egg Shell
egg stands
   A 'N L's Hobbicraft, Inc.
   Boutique Trims
   Country Crafts
   Gail's Decorative Arts Studio
   Howe Studio
   Taylor House
eggshells
   Rock Mountain Farm
   Swanjord Hatchery
filigrees
   Boutique Trims
   Holiday Craft
finch eggshells
   Rock Mountain Farm
goose eggshells
   Herb Allen's Hole in One
   Bowersox Eggcraft Supplies
   The Golden Egg
   Handcraft Originals
   Hoffman Hatchery
   Kathryn Johnson
   Loosie Goosie Egg Craft Shop
   Allegra Milano
   Natalie Originals Studio
   Rock Mountain Farm
   Schiltz Goose Farm
green-hen eggshells
   Rock Mountain Farm
guinea eggs
   Hoffman Hatchery
hinges
   Country Crafts
kistka
   Surma Book & Music Store
kits
   Country Crafts
   Surma Book & Music Store
leaflets
   Evelyn Downing
magazines
   Egg Album
   Portfolio of Egg Artistry
   Treasure Chest

miniatures egg craft
   Country Crafts
newspapers
   The Eggs-Aminer
ostrich eggs
   Herb Allen's Hole in One
   The Golden Egg
   Kathryn Johnson
   Edith Maier
parakeet eggshells
   Rock Mountain Farm
peafowl eggshells
   Rock Mountain Farm
pee wee eggshells
   Handcraft Originals
pheasant eggshells
   The Golden Egg
   Rock Mountain Farm
plastic pigeon eggs
   Rock Mountain Farm
plastic portrait balls
   Downs
precut eggs
   Herb Allen's Hole in One
priday eggs
   Sandy Symons
quail eggshells
   The Golden Egg
   Handcraft Originals
   Rock Mountain Farm
rhea eggshells
   Rock Mountain Farm
silk finish eggshells
   Edith Maier
swan eggshells
   Rock Mountain Farm
tinamou eggshells
   Rock Mountain Farm
turkey eggs
   Mrs. Barbara Allen
   Hoffman Hatchery
Ukrainian items
   Ukrainian Gift Shop
wax
   Surma Book & Music Store
wood canary eggs
   Rock Mountain Farm
wood eggs
   O-P Craft Co., Inc.

Craft Category Index
Electrical—Embroidery

electrical crafts
  lamp wiring diagrams
    Gyro Lamp Supply Corp.
  lighting supplies
    Lightsaround, Inc.
electric tools and equipment
  burrs
    Foredom Electric Co.
  carpentry power tools
    American Machine & Tool Co.
    Arco Tools Inc.
  carving drills
    Foredom Electric Co.
  electric bobbin winders
    Robin & Russ Handweavers
  electric carver
    Green's Rock & Lapidary Ltd.
  electric kilns
    Cole Ceramics Laboratories
    Diedricks Crafts
  electric lapidary equipment
    Lapidabrade Inc.
  electric lehrs
    A. D. Alpine Inc.
  electric model motors
    James Bliss & Co. Inc.
  electric potter's wheels
    Cole Ceramics Laboratories
  electric punch rug hook
    KM Yarn Co.
    Needlecraft Shop Inc.
  electric tufting
    The Hidden Village
  electric wax spatula
    Green's Rock & Lapidary Ltd.
  flexible shaft machines
    Gems Galore
embroidery *(see also Frames, Hoops, Needlecrafts, Yarns)*
    The Needlecase
    J. C. Penney Co., Inc.
  accessories
    The Thread Shed, Inc.
  Americana samplers
    J. L. T.
    Northwest Handcraft House
  Belgian linen
    Greentree Ranch Wools, Countryside Handweavers
  books
    Better Homes & Gardens Books
    Book Barn
    Charles T. Branford Co.
    Crewel Elephant
    Drake Publishers Inc.
    The Needle Works
    Random House Inc.
    Robin & Russ Handweavers
    Sancraft Industries
    The Unicorn
  bunka embroidery
    House of Flowers
  corded magnifier
    M. Turner
  crewel embroidery design transfers
    Nantucket Needleworks
  crewel embroidery designs
    Woodland Craft Designs
  Danish embroidery
    Scandinavian Rya Rugs
  embroidered appliques
    Embroideries Unlimited
  embroidered family crest emblems
    Scotch House
  embroidery blocks
    Lee Wards
  embroidery charts
    Needlecraft Shop Inc.
  embroidery designs
    House of Patterns
    Raymond P. Wallace
  embroidery fabrics
    Leonida Leatherdale's Embroidery Studio
    Needlecraft House
    The Thread Shed, Inc.
  embroidery frames
    Crossroads
    KAY an EE Corp. of America
    Mary Maxim Inc.
    Merribee
    Sears, Roebuck & Co.
  embroidery hoops
    Crossroads
    The Hidden Village
    KAY an EE Corp. of America
    Jerry S. Kaye Assoc.
    Mary Maxim Inc.
    Merribee
    Nantucket Needleworks
    Needlecraft House

Craft Category Index
Embroidery—Enameling

    Needlecraft Shop Inc.
    Yarns Unlimited
embroidery linen
    Jerry S. Kaye Assoc.
    Needlecraft House
embroidery materials
    Easy Street
embroidery scissors
    Polly Chester Inc.
embroidery threads
    Crossroads
    Frederick J. Fawcett , Inc.
    Folklorico
    Leonida Leatherdale's Embroidery Studio
    The Mail Train
    Merribee
    Nantucket Needleworks
    Needlecraft House
    The Thread Shed, Inc.
    Lee Wards
embroidery transfer patterns
    Crewel Elephant
floor hoops
    KAY an EE Corp. of America
home study courses
    National Standards Council of American Embroiderers
kits
    Barnes & Blake
    Berry's of Maine
    The Corner Shop
    Crossroads
    The Custom House of Needle Arts & Design
    James A. Gardner
    Good Housekeeping
    Guild of Strawberry Banks Inc.
    Heritage Hill Patterns
    Historic House
    Holmes-Corey Ltd.
    House of Stitches
    Needlecraft House
    Needlewoman Shop
    Needles 'N Hoops
    Mrs. W. Bradley Ryan
    Jane Snead Samplers
    The Stitchery
    Tillalla Inc.
    Victoria Gifts
    Wichelt Import Co.
    Wonoco Yarn Co.
    The World of Stitch 'N Knit
    Yarns Unlimited
    F. C. Ziegler Co.
leaflets
    Skon
magazines
    Ladies Home Journal Needlecraft
    McCall's Pattern Fashions
organizations
    National Standards Council of American Embroiderers
perforated embroidery paper
    Sewakers Industries Inc.
pre-quilted pieces for embroidering
    Lee Wards
roll and stretch frame
    Needle -Ease

enamels *(see also finishes, Paints, stains)*
    C. R. Hill Co.
    University Circle Publications and Supply Co.
aluminum enamels
    Ceramic Coating Co.
books
    Book Barn
enamel colors
    Thomas C. Thompson
firing enamel
    Boin Arts & Crafts
glass enamels
    Kay Kinney -Contoured Glass
lead bearing enamels
    Ceramic Coating Co.
lead free enamels
    Ceramic Coating Co.

enameling *(see also Copper)*
    A 'N L's Hobbicraft, Inc.
    Allcraft Tool & Supply Co.
    Art Mart, Inc.
    Bergen Arts & Crafts, Inc.
    Cleveland Leather Co.
    Craft Service
    Delco Craft Center, Inc.
    Economy Handicrafts, Inc.
    The Handcrafters
    Kraft Korner
    Magnus Craft Materials, Inc.
    J. C. Penney Co., Inc.

Craft Category Index
Enameling—Etching

Technical Specialties International Inc.
Zim's
books
American Art Clay Co. Inc.
Charles A. Bennett Co., Inc.
Ceramics Monthly
Chilton Book Co.
Museum Books Inc.
Taplinger Publishing Co.
University Circle Publications and Supply Co.
cold enameling
Delco Craft Center, Inc.
copper
Anchor Tool & Supply Co.
Bergen Arts & Crafts, Inc.
T. B. Hagstoz & Son
copper enameling supplies
Alessi Lapidary Supplies
American Handicrafts
Ceramic Coating Co.
Essayons Studio, Hand Arts Center
Kit Kraft
Bob and Carol Oliver
Ovgem Craft Supply Co.
Skil-Crafts Division
Specialty Products
Jack D. Wolfe Co. Inc.
copper shapes
Sax Arts & Crafts
enamel colors
Thomas C. Thompson
enamel sheeting
University Circle Publications and Supply Co.
enameling kilns
A 'N L's Hobbicraft, Inc.
Bergen Arts & Crafts, Inc.
Craft Service
enameling supplies
Anchor Tool & Supply Co.
William Dixon Co.
Tepping Studio Supply Co.
enameling tools
William Dixon Co.
firing enamel
Boin Arts & Crafts
glass enamels
Kay Kinney-Contoured Glass

heatless glazing for metals
Specialty Products
kits
Thomas C. Thompson
University Circle Publications and Supply Co.
metal enameling equipment
American Art Clay Co. Inc.
nonfiring enamel
Boin Arts & Crafts
The Mail Train
engraving
Allcraft Tool & Supply Co.
Bergen Arts & Crafts, Inc.
Craftsman Supply House
Sax Arts & Crafts
carbide tipped engraving tool
Spencer Gifts Inc.
engraving blocks
Frank Mittermeier Inc.
engraving chisels
Frank Mittermeier Inc.
engraving equipment
Prospector's Pouch
engraving tools
Bergen Arts & Crafts, Inc.
Dremel Creative Power Tools
Beno J. Gundlach Co.
Miles Kimball
Skil-Crafts Division
Montgomery Ward & Co., Inc.
scauper
King's Studio
etching
books
Irene Goodwin
etching supplies
Art Mart, Inc.
Arthur Brown & Bro., Inc.
Craft Service
Craftsman Supply House
William Dixon Co.
Economy Handicrafts, Inc.
The Handcrafters
St. Louis Crafts Inc.
Sax Arts & Crafts
Skil-Crafts Division
etching tools
William Dixon Co.
foil etching
Cleveland Leather Co.

Craft Category Index
Etching—Fabrics

   glass scribing tools
      Brookstone Co.
   gold etching
      Irene Goodwin
   kits
      Craftool Co.
   metal etching
      Delco Craft Center, Inc.

fabric painting and printing
    Boin Arts & Crafts
    Floquil, Inc.
    House of Patterns
    Zim's
   books
      Ballantine Books, Inc.
      Charles T. Branford Co.
      Van Nostrand Reinhold Co.
      Watson-Guptill Publications
   fabric dyes
      Joan Moshimer
   kits
      Edmund Scientific Co.
   repeat glass
      Arthur Brown & Bro., Inc.
      Plaza Artists Materials, Inc.
   water soluble textile paints
      Siphon Art Products

fabrics
    Barnes & Blake
    Crossroads
    Eagle Mill
    Economy Handicrafts, Inc.
    Exotic Thai Silks
    Heritage Hill Patterns
    The Hidden Village
    Homespun Fabrics
    International Creations
    The Mail Train
    Mary Maxim Inc.
    Merribee
    Nantucket Needleworks
    Hazel Pearson Handi Craft
    Sax Arts & Crafts
    Scotch House
    Supreme Handicrafts
    Montgomery Ward & Co., Inc.
    Lee Wards
    Zim's
   aida
      The Hidden Village
      Needlecraft Shop Inc.
   Belgian linen
      Greentree Ranch Wools, Countryside Handweavers
   bonded polyester quilt batts
      Putnam Co.
   book cloths
      Basic Crafts Co.
   books
      Drake Publishers Inc.
      Martin Fabrics
   bunting
      Dick Blick
   burlap
      Berry's of Maine
      Bon Bazar
      Cleveland Leather Co.
      Craft Yarns of Rhode Island Inc.
      Craftsman Supply House
      Delco Craft Center, Inc.
      Joan Moshimer
      Zim's
   calico blender coverups
      The Rusty Nail
   calico can opener coverups
      The Rusty Nail
   calico mixer coverups
      The Rusty Nail
   calico toaster coverups
      The Rusty Nail
   canvas
      Craft Yarns of Rhode Island Inc.
      Delco Craft Center, Inc.
   cements
      Knit Services, Inc.
   chamois
      Leathercrafters Supply Co.
   China silk brocades
      Exotic Thai Silks
   China silks
      Exotic Thai Silks
   club plans
      Designers Fabrics Buy-Mail
      Fabrics 'Round the World Inc.
      Fashion Fabrics Club
   corduroy scraps
      Reichert's Fabrics
   cotton blends
      Knit Services, Inc.
   cotton selvages
      Tinkler & Co. Inc.

Craft Category Index
Fabrics—Fabrics

cotton-polyester woven scraps
  Reichert's Fabrics
cottons
  Contessa Yarns
  Isabel Scott Fabrics Corp.
craft furs
  Deep Flex Plastic Molds, Inc.
  The Handcrafters
  House of Flowers
  Reichert's Fabrics
  Sav-On-Crafts
  Supreme Handicrafts
  Swan-Son
  Montgomery Ward & Co., Inc.
  Lee Wards
  Zim's
Dacron® batting
  Contemporary Quilts
Dacron® sail rigs
  Folbot Corp.
designer fabrics
  Winston's Fabrics
die-cuts
  House of Lines
double woven cotton accessories
  J. P. Fliegel Co.
embroidery fabrics
  Leonida Leatherdale's Embroidery Studio
  Needlecraft House
  The Thread Shed, Inc.
embroidery linen
  Jerry S. Kaye Assoc.
factory cutaway fabrics
  Cutaway
felt
  American Handicrafts
  P. S. Andrews Co.
  Boin Arts & Crafts
  Cleveland Leather Co.
  Commonwealth Felt Co.
  The Craft Corner
  Craft Service
  Craftsman Supply House
  Delco Craft Center, Inc.
  Economy Handicrafts, Inc.
  The Handcrafters
  Holiday Handicrafts, Inc.
  House of Flowers
  Magnus Craft Materials, Inc.
  Mary Maxim Inc.
  Merribee
  Hazel Pearson Handi Craft
  Sav-On-Crafts
  Zim's
felt mill ends
  Eastern Mills
felt remnants
  Commonwealth Felt Co.
  House of Lines
felt vinyl
  Dick Blick
hardanger
  The Hidden Village
  Needlecraft Shop Inc.
  Lee Wards
hertha
  The Hidden Village
home study courses
  Fabricon Co.
huck
  The Mail Train
imported canvas
  The Needle Works
Indian silks
  Exotic Thai Silks
interfacing
  Home-Sew Inc.
Italian silks
  Exotic Thai Silks
Japanese pongee prints
  Exotic Thai Silks
Japanese silk
  Exotic Thai Silks
  Greentree Ranch Wools, Countryside Handweavers
kits
  Bear Cave
knit fabrics
  The Sewing Bee
linen
  Contessa Yarns
  Delco Craft Center, Inc.
  Greentree Ranch Wools, Countryside Handweavers
  International Creations
  Knit Services, Inc.
  Nantucket Needleworks
  Needlecraft House
  Mrs. W. Bradley Ryan
linen twill
  Mrs. W. Bradley Ryan

Craft Category Index
Fabrics—Fabrics

lingerie fabrics
   Kieffer's Lingerie Fabric & Supplies
   The Sewing Bee
magazines
   Ladies Home Journal Needlecraft
   Simplicity Fashion Magazine
   Simplicity Home Catalog
matching fabrics
   The Yarn and Soda Shop
mesh cloth
   Craft Yarns of Rhode Island Inc.
   KM Yarn Co.
   Magnus Craft Materials, Inc.
Mexican wool
   Folklorico
mill ends
   General Supplies Co.
   Mill Store
mill products
   Greentree Ranch Wools, Countryside Handweavers
monk's cloth
   The Hidden Village
   KM Yarn Co.
   Sax Arts & Crafts
natural fiber fabrics
   Winston's Fabrics
needleweaving cloth
   Nantucket Needleworks
nylon
   Charles M. Butterworth
   The Hidden Village
   P. T. I.
nylon blends
   Knit Services, Inc.
nylon net
   Bob's Arts & Crafts
   The Clever Crafters
   Zim's
polyester double knit scraps
   Reichert's Fabrics
pure cottons
   Winston's Fabrics
pure linens
   Winston's Fabrics
pure silks
   Winston's Fabrics
pure velveteens
   Winston's Fabrics
quilt scraps
   Reichert's Fabrics

rayon towels
   Two Brothers Inc.
rayons
   Knit Services, Inc.
   Isabel Scott Fabrics Corp.
rug burlap
   Lee Wards
rug canvas
   Brunswick Worsted Mills
   International Creations
   KM Yarn Co.
   Lee Wards
screen fabrics
   Colonial Printing Ink Co.
silk
   Contessa Yarns
swatches
   Berry's of Maine
Swedish fishnet
   Knit Services, Inc.
synthetic selvages
   Tinkler & Co. Inc.
tartans
   Scotch House
Thai cottons
   Exotic Thai Silks
Thai silks
   Exotic Thai Silks
twill
   Needlecraft Shop Inc.
unwoven cotton
   Lace Lady
   Two Brothers Inc.
upholstery fabrics
   General Supplies Co.
velour
   Skil-Crafts Division
velvet
   Sav-On-Crafts
   Zim's
velvet patchwork quilt squares
   House of Lines
velvet quilt pieces
   Nucleus
wet look vinyl
   Montgomery Ward & Co., Inc.
wool
   Charles M. Butterworth
   Carlbert Fabrics
   Isabel Scott Fabrics Corp.

Craft Category Index
Fabrics—Felt

wool blends
    Reichert's Fabrics
wool clan tartans
    Scotch House
wool mill ends
    Carlbert Fabrics
wool patchwork quilt square patterns
    House of Lines
wool remnant pieces
    Carlbert Fabrics
wool swatches
    Joan Moshimer

fake furs *(see Furs and craft furs)*

feathers and feather crafts
    Bead Game
    Boycan's Craft Supplies
    Craftsman Supply House
    Creative Craft House
    Gemex Co.
    The Hidden Village
    Koehler's Craft Outlet
    Mangrove Feather Co., Inc.
    Hazel Pearson Handi Craft
    Supreme Handicrafts
    Lee Wards
    Winona Trading Post
    Zim's
bird feathers
    Herter's, Inc.
domestic feathers
    Dersh Feather & Trading Corp.
    Hollywood Fancy Feather Co.
fluffs feathers
    Dersh Feather & Trading Corp.
goose feathers
    Mangrove Feather Co., Inc.
hackle feathers
    Mangrove Feather Co., Inc.
imported feathers
    Dersh Feather & Trading Corp.
    Hollywood Fancy Feather Co.
marabou feathers
    Dersh Feather & Trading Corp.
    Hollywood Fancy Feather Co.
ostrich feathers
    Dersh Feather & Trading Corp.
    Hollywood Fancy Feather Co.
peacock feathers
    Dersh Feather & Trading Corp.
pheasant feathers
    Dersh Feather & Trading Corp.
quill engravers
    Peg Hall Studios
quill feathers
    Hollywood Fancy Feather Co.
quill pens
    Salyer Publishing Co.
quill scrollers
    Peg Hall Studios
satnets feathers
    Hollywood Fancy Feather Co.
turkey feathers
    Dersh Feather & Trading Corp.
turkey flats feathers
    Mangrove Feather Co., Inc.
turkey hip feathers
    Mangrove Feather Co., Inc.
turkey marabou feathers
    Mangrove Feather Co., Inc.

felt crafts
books
    Craft Course Publishers
    Sancraft Industries
felt
    American Handicrafts
    P. S. Andrews Co.
    Boin Arts & Crafts
    Cleveland Leather Co.
    Commonwealth Felt Co.
    The Craft Corner
    Craft Service
    Craftsman Supply House
    Delco Craft Center, Inc.
    Economy Handicrafts, Inc.
    The Handcrafters
    Holiday Handicrafts, Inc.
    House of Flowers
    Magnus Craft Materials, Inc.
    Mary Maxim Inc.
    Merribee
    Hazel Pearson Handi Craft
    Sav-On-Crafts
    Zim's
felt appliques
    Home-Sew Inc.
felt mill ends
    Eastern Mills
felt remnants
    Commonwealth Felt Co.
    House of Lines
felt vinyl
    Dick Blick

Craft Category Index
Felt—Flowermaking

    kits
        The Craft Corner
fiber optics
    Boin Arts & Crafts
    Edmund Scientific Co.
    hobby optics
        Deep Flex Plastic Molds, Inc.
        Swan-Son
    kits
        Radio Shack
        Scientific Gas Products
finishes *(see also Antiquing, Enamels, Paints, Stains)*
    antiquing
        Birchwood Casey
    decoupage finishes
        Carnival Arts & Crafts
        Century 21
        John's Hardware & Decoupage Supplies
        Marie Mitchell's Decoupage Center
        Hazel Pearson Handi Craft
        Ramont's Floral Arts Studio
    driftwood polish
        Deb Products
    lacquers
        Sax Arts & Crafts
    liquid metallic finishes
        Rub 'N Buff
flower arranging, drying, preserving, pressing *(see also Nature crafts)*
    artificial flowers
        Schrock's, The House of Hobbies & Crafts
        Lee Wards
    artificial foliage
        Boycan's Craft Supplies
    artificial fruits
        Zim's
    artificial plants
        Lee Wards
    artificial straw
        House of Flowers
    books
        Activa Products Inc.
        Book Barn
        Drake Publishers Inc.
        Hearthside Press
        Van Nostrand Reinhold Co.
    corsage making supplies
        Dorothy Biddle Service
    drying paper
        The Handcraft Supply Corp.
    ferns
        Arthur Brown & Bro., Inc.
    flocked fruit
        Sav-On-Crafts
    floral clay
        American Art Clay Co. Inc.
    floral craft
        Florida Supply House, Inc.
        House of Flowers
        Koehler's Craft Outlet
        Hazel Pearson Handi Craft
        Ramont's Floral Arts Studio
        Sav-On-Crafts
    floral craft wood fibre
        Supreme Handicrafts
    floral tape
        Sav-On-Crafts
    floral tools
        Hazel Pearson Handi Craft
    floral wire
        Sav-On-Crafts
    flower arrangement supplies
        Dorothy Biddle Service
    flower drying agents
        Creator's Corner
    flower press
        The Handcraft Supply Corp.
        Lillian Vernon
    frames
        The Handcraft Supply Corp.
    home study courses
        Lifetime Career Schools
    kits
        Antoine's
    leaves
        Gail's Decorative Arts Studio
    lichen
        Holiday Craft
    lifelike grass
        Life-Like Products Inc.
    preserved foliage
        Boycan's Craft Supplies
    pressed flower craft
        The Handcraft Supply Corp.
    silica gel
        Artis, Inc.
        Plantabbs Co.
flowermaking
    Craft Service

Craft Category Index
Flowermaking—Foamcraft

    Craftsman Supply House
    Delco Craft Center, Inc.
    Holiday Handicrafts, Inc.
    Kit Kraft
    Skil-Crafts Division
    Lee Wards
    Zim's
bead flowermaking
    Kit Kraft
    Rombins' Nest Farm
    Supreme Handicrafts
books
    Boycan's Craft Supplies
    Craft Course Publishers
    Hearthside Press
    Smithers Oasis
calyx
    Sav-On-Crafts
corsage making supplies
    Dorothy Biddle Service
dip film
    A 'N L's Hobbicraft, Inc.
    American Handicrafts
    Bergen Arts & Crafts, Inc.
    Boin Arts & Crafts
    Carson & Ellis, Inc.
    Cleveland Leather Co.
    Craft Service
    Craftsman Supply House
    Delco Craft Center, Inc.
    Economy Handicrafts, Inc.
    Gemex Co.
    Make It Happen Craft Studio
    J. C. Penney Co., Inc.
    Sears, Roebuck & Co.
    Specialty Products
    Supreme Handicrafts
    Zim's
floral clay
    American Art Clay Co. Inc.
floral craft
    Florida Supply House, Inc.
    House of Flowers
    Koehler's Craft Outlet
    Hazel Pearson Handi Craft
    Ramont's Floral Arts Studio
    Sav-On-Crafts
floral craft wood fibre
    Supreme Handicrafts
floral tape
    Sav-On-Crafts

floral tools
    Hazel Pearson Handi Craft
floral wire
    Sav-On-Crafts
flower looms
    Craftsman Supply House
    Delco Craft Center, Inc.
    Hanover House Industries, Inc.
    Hazel Pearson Handi Craft
    Sav-On-Crafts
    Studio Twelve
flowermaking supplies
    Dorothy Biddle Service
    Don's Hobby Co.
kits
    Beadnik's Arts & Crafts
    Don's Hobby Co.
    Economy Handicrafts, Inc.
    Gemex Co.
    Nicole Bead & Craft Co., Inc.
    Ramont's Floral Arts Studio
    Carol Rice Creatives
    Rombins' Nest Farm
leaflets
    Mrs. L. Winum
miniature flowers
    Holiday Craft
peps
    Holiday Craft
porcelain flowers
    Bergen Arts & Crafts, Inc.
pressed flower craft
    The Handcraft Supply Corp.
shell flowers
    Handcraft Originals
velvet flowers
    Country Crafts
velvet leaves
    Country Crafts
wood fibre
    Bob's Arts & Crafts
    Boycan's Craft Supplies
    Koehler's Craft Outlet
    Ramont's Floral Arts Studio
    Zim's
foamcraft
accessories
    Foam Fantasy
art foam
    Dick Blick
    Boin Arts & Crafts

Craft Category Index
Foamcraft—Foils

    Cleveland Leather Co.
    Craft Service
    Craftsman Supply House
    Delco Craft Center, Inc.
    Economy Handicrafts, Inc.
    Foam Fantasy
    The Handcraft Supply Corp.
    Holiday Handicrafts, Inc.
    House of Flowers
    Hazel Pearson Handi Craft
    Sax Arts & Crafts
    Supreme Handicrafts
    Zim's
art foam patterns
    Don's Hobby Co.
books
    Chilton Book Co.
    The Clever Crafters
    Craft Course Publishers
    Sterling Publishing Co. Inc.
Dylite®
    Koehler's Craft Outlet
electric tools
    Bear Cave
kits
    Holiday Handicrafts, Inc.
    Koehler's Craft Outlet
plastic foam
    Boin Arts & Crafts
polyurethane foam
    Adhesive Products Corp.
    Art Consultants
    Hanover House Industries, Inc.
    High Strength Adhesives Corp.
    Kick-Shaw Inc.
Styrofoam®
    Bob's Arts & Crafts
    Boin Arts & Crafts
    Boycan's Craft Supplies
    Craft Service
    Craftsman Supply House
    Delco Craft Center, Inc.
    Economy Handicrafts, Inc.
    Foam Fantasy
    Holiday Handicrafts, Inc.
    Home-Sew Inc.
    Koehler's Craft Outlet
    Party Bazaar
    Sav-On-Crafts
    Skil-Crafts Division
    Specialty Products
    Supreme Handicrafts
    Wagner's Crafts
    Zim's
Styrofoam® cutter
    Economy Handicrafts, Inc.
urethane foam blocks
    Delco Craft Center, Inc.
white foam cutters
    Sax Arts & Crafts
woodworking patterns
    Craft Patterns

foils and foil craft
    Bob's Arts & Crafts
    Boin Arts & Crafts
    Craftsman Supply House
    Economy Handicrafts, Inc.
    The Handcrafters
    Barbara Lawshe
aluminum foils
    Delco Craft Center, Inc.
books
    Parker Publishing Co., Inc.
    Wanda's Workshop
brass foil
    St. Louis Crafts Inc.
colored aluminum foils
    St. Louis Crafts Inc.
colored metal foils
    Carl Hepp Mosaic Co.
copper foil
    Delco Craft Center, Inc.
    St. Louis Crafts Inc.
decorative foil
    Koehler's Craft Outlet
decoupage foil papers
    Harrower House of Decoupage
foil etching
    Cleveland Leather Co.
foil paper
    Dick Blick
    Gibsons Creations
    Zim's
foil prints
    Carnival Arts & Crafts
gold foil
    Basic Crafts Co.
iridescent diffraction (polyester) foil
    Diffraction Co., Inc.
kits
    Midwest Mail Service

Craft Category Index
Foils—Furniture

metal foil paper
  Arthur Brown & Bro., Inc.
metallic foil labels
  G. Weidinger

frames
  American Handicrafts
  Crewel World
  Delco Craft Center, Inc.
  The Handcraft Supply Corp.
  The Hidden Village
  Jerry S. Kaye Assoc.
  Joan Moshimer
  Nantucket Needleworks
  Needlecraft Shop Inc.
  Jane Snead Samplers
  Yarns Unlimited
  F. C. Ziegler Co.
  Zim's
  metal frames
    Sharon's Petite Sherre
  mini-mosaic frames
    Lillian Vernon
  no-slip frame
    Blank-It Corp.
  old barn wood picture frames
    Lynchburg Hdwr. & General Store
  paper frames
    Make It Happen Craft Studio
  picture frames
    National Artcraft Supply Co.
  plastic frames
    Craftsman Supply House
  plate (dish) frames
    Downs

furniture making *(see also Finishes, Hardware, Wood)*
  books
    Arco Publishing Co., Inc.
    Charles A. Bennett Co., Inc.
    Chilton Book Co.
    Dorothy Mae's Trunks
    Dowse's Lapidary Supply, Inc.
    Drake Publishers Inc.
    McGraw-Hill Book Co.
    McKnight Publishing Co.
    Random House Inc.
    Sturbridge Yankee Workshop
  braiding chair seats
    The Dorr Mill Store
  cabinet hardware
    Craftsman Wood Service Co.
  carved trims
    Albert Constantine & Son Inc.
  finishing supplies
    Homecraft Veneer
  furniture finishes
    American Art Clay Co. Inc.
    Art Mart, Inc.
    Carson & Ellis, Inc.
    Albert Constantine & Son Inc.
    Douglas & Sturgess, Inc.
    Leathercrafters Supply Co.
    Hazel Pearson Handi Craft
    Plasco
    Sav-On-Crafts
    Supreme Handicrafts
  furniture glues
    Albert Constantine & Son Inc.
  furniture hardware
    Albert Constantine & Son Inc.
  furniture legs
    Atlantic Upholstery Supply Co.
    Giles & Kendall Inc.
  furniture lumber
    Giles & Kendall Inc.
  furniture parts
    Atlantic Upholstery Supply Co.
    Giles & Kendall Inc.
  furniture patterns
    Davault Miniature Furniture
  furniture polishes
    Albert Constantine & Son Inc.
  furniture stains
    Albert Constantine & Son Inc.
    Sturbridge Yankee Workshop
  hardware
    Bedford Lumber Co., Inc.
    Albert Constantine & Son Inc.
    Giles & Kendall Inc.
    Real Woods
    Sturbridge Yankee Workshop
  home study courses
    Modern Upholstery Institute
  iron table pedestals
    Plasco
  kits
    Bedford Lumber Co., Inc.
    Classic Crafts
    Cohasset Colonials
    Shaker Workshops Inc.
    Tandy Leather Co.

Craft Category Index
Furniture—Furniture

leaflets
   Furniture Designs
   Old South Patterns
   Mrs. L. Winum
magazines
   The Family Handyman
   1001 Decorating Ideas
   Twenty-five Weekend Build-It Projects
services
   The Village Smithy
table bases
   Atlantic Upholstery Supply Co.
table legs
   Albert Constantine & Son Inc.
   Montgomery Ward & Co., Inc.
turned legs
   Bedford Lumber Co., Inc.
wagon wheels
   Albert Constantine & Son Inc.
wood finishing
   Birchwood Casey
wood finishing supplies
   Minnesota Woodworkers Supply Co.
   Real Woods
wood frames
   Midland Walnut
   Marie Mitchell's Decoupage Center
wood legs
   Midland Walnut
   Minnesota Woodworkers Supply Co.

furniture refinishing and restoring *(see also Antiquing, Cane, Finishes)*

antiquing
   Birchwood Casey
ash splint
   The Workshop
books
   Arco Publishing Co., Inc.
   Chilton Book Co.
   Crown Publishers
   Dorothy Mae's Trunks
   The Family Handyman
   Lane Magazine & Book Co.
   MAC Enterprises
   Popular Mechanics Press
   3 M Company
   Charles E. Tuttle Co. Inc.
braiding chair seats
   The Dorr Mill Store
cabinet hardware
   Craftsman Wood Service Co.
cane
   A 'N L's Hobbicraft, Inc.
   Atlantic Upholstery Supply Co.
   Bersted's
   Cane & Basket Supply Co.
   Albert Constantine & Son Inc.
   Craft Service
   Delco Craft Center, Inc.
   The Handcrafters
   Real Woods
   Savin Handcrafts
   Sax Arts & Crafts
   The Workshop
cane webbing
   Albert Constantine & Son Inc.
carved trims
   Albert Constantine & Son Inc.
finishing supplies
   Homecraft Veneer
furniture finishes
   American Art Clay Co. Inc.
   Art Mart, Inc.
   Carson & Ellis, Inc.
   Albert Constantine & Son Inc.
   Douglas & Sturgess, Inc.
   Leathercrafters Supply Co.
   Hazel Pearson Handi Craft
   Plasco
   Sav-On-Crafts
   Supreme Handicrafts
furniture glues
   Albert Constantine & Son Inc.
furniture hardware
   Albert Constantine & Son Inc.
furniture legs
   Atlantic Upholstery Supply Co.
   Giles & Kendall Inc.
furniture lumber
   Giles & Kendall Inc.
furniture parts
   Atlantic Upholstery Supply Co.
   Giles & Kendall Inc.
furniture polishes
   Albert Constantine & Son Inc.
furniture stains
   Albert Constantine & Son Inc.
   Sturbridge Yankee Workshop
kits
   Albert Constantine & Son Inc.

Sav-On-Crafts
Savin Handcrafts
laminating supplies
   Homecraft Veneer
magazines
   1001 Decorating Ideas
   1001 How-To Ideas
metal finishing
   Birchwood Casey
   Skil-Crafts Division
paint stripers
   Miles Kimball
period hardware
   Albert Constantine & Son Inc.
plastic cane
   H. H. Perkins Co.
plastic laminate countertopping
   Beno J. Gundlach Co.
reed
   The Workshop
restoring materials
   The Workshop
splint seat weaving
   Atlantic Upholstery Supply Co.
   H. H. Perkins Co.
table bases
   Atlantic Upholstery Supply Co.
table legs
   Albert Constantine & Son Inc.
   Montgomery Ward & Co., Inc.
templates
   Tandy Leather Co.
trunk repair parts
   Dorothy Mae's Trunks
veneers
   Craftsman Wood Service Co.
   Minnesota Woodworkers Supply Co.
   Real Woods
wheels
   Atlantic Upholstery Supply Co.
wood finishing
   Birchwood Casey
wood finishing supplies
   Minnesota Woodworkers Supply Co.
   Real Woods

furs and craft furs *(see also Animal hair)*
books
   The Country Craftsmen
   Hearthside Press
craft furs
   Deep Flex Plastic Molds, Inc.
   The Handcrafters
   House of Flowers
   Reichert's Fabrics
   Sav-On-Crafts
   Supreme Handicrafts
   Swan-Son
   Montgomery Ward & Co., Inc.
   Lee Wards
   Zim's
dressed fur pelts
   Great Central Fur Corp.
furs
   The Hidden Village
   Montgomery Ward & Co., Inc.
fur trimmings
   Great Central Fur Corp.
kits
   Audria's
   Koehler's Craft Outlet
   Whisper Farm Furs
mink
   Great Central Fur Corp.
mink scraps
   The Hidden Village
rabbit furs
   Whisper Farm Furs
raccoon furs
   Great Central Fur Corp.
sheepskin
   The Booted Sheepherder Inc.

gemcraft *(see also Lapidary)*
adhesives
   The Ducketts
black opals
   Australian Gem Trading Co.
   Geode Industries
   International Import Co.
black star sapphire
   W. D. Hudson, Jr.
   Syn-Crer Creations
bloodstone
   Adris Oriental Gem & Art Corp.
   Dowse's Lapidary Supply, Inc.
   M. Nowotny
   Panther International Ltd.
   Syn-Crer Creations
blue agate
   Beaver Canyon Campground
   M. W. Jackson & Assoc.
blue Australian sapphires
   Crown Gems Co.

Craft Category Index
Gemcraft—Gemcraft

blue fire flash moonstone
   Minerals & Gems
blue lace agate
   Libra Gems
blue star sapphire
   Gems International
botryoidal jade
   Gene's Rock Shop
Brazilian fire agate
   Michigan Lapidary Supply Co.
Brazilian gems
   Inter-Ocean Trade Co.
   Oceanside Gem Imports, Inc.
Brazilian opal
   Frank's Jewelry & Gem Shop
Brazilian quartz
   Starfire Lapidary
brilliant cut diamonds
   Harry Z. Kurs
bulk opals
   Australian Imports
cabbing amethyst
   Gems International
cabochon gemstones
   International Import Co.
carnelian agate gemballs
   Anozira Jewelers
diamond abrasives
   The Ducketts
diamond arbors
   Gem Tool Specialties
diamond bar wheel dressers
   Gem Tec Diamond Tool Co.
diamond blades
   Covington Engineering Corp.
   Earth Treasures
   Farmers Gem and Rock Shop
   Gem Tool Specialties
   Star Diamond Industries
diamond burrs
   Gem Tool Specialties
diamond carvers
   Metro Diamond Drill Co.
diamond coated files
   Metro Diamond Drill Co.
diamond compounds
   Walter E. Johansen
   Jack V. Schuller, Inc.
   Sinkankas Diamond Products
diamond cores
   Gem Tool Specialties

diamond crystals
   Commercial Mineral Corp.
   Panther International Ltd.
diamond disks
   Gem Tool Specialties
diamond drills
   Gem Tool Specialties
   Geode Industries
diamond equipment
   Terra Products
diamond gem maker
   Gem Tec Diamond Tool Co.
diamond impregnated core drills
   Metro Diamond Drill Co.
diamond lapidaries
   Gem Tool Specialties
diamond laps
   Jack V. Schuller, Inc.
diamond machines
   Gem Tool Specialties
diamond pads
   Gem Tool Specialties
diamond points
   Gem Tool Specialties
diamond powders
   Aleta's Rock Shop
   Gem Tool Specialties
   Industrial Diamond Tool Co. Inc.
   Walter E. Johansen
diamond products
   Green's Rock & Lapidary Ltd.
   Highland Park Manufacturing
   Jack V. Schuller, Inc.
diamond saw blades
   Highland Park Manufacturing
diamond saws
   Raytech Industries Inc.
diamond tools
   Gem Tec Diamond Tool Co.
   Gem Tool Specialties
diamond wheels
   Diamond-Pro Unlimited
   Gem Tec Diamond Tool Co.
   Gem Tool Specialties
diamonds
   Biship's House of Gems
   Diamond Sales Co.
   H & A Mfg. Corp.
   International Import Co.
   The Jewelry Mart
   Syn-Crer Creations

dies
    Gilman's
diffraction jewels
    Edmund Scientific Co.
dops
    Walter E. Johansen
    A. D. McBurney
gem beads
    Bead Game
gem cutting equipment
    Earth Treasures
    Treasure of the Pirates, Inc.
gem detectors
    Gemological Institute of America
gem drills
    Lindell Industries
    Mohave Industries
gem faceting supplies
    Earth Treasures
gem findings
    Aleta's Rock Shop
gem graders
    Gemological Institute of America
gem grinders
    Star Diamond Industries
gem making
    Allcraft Tool & Supply Co.
gem making equipment
    Craftool Co.
    Gilman's
    Green's Rock & Lapidary Ltd.
    Star Diamond Industries
gem polishers
    Dorothy Blake
    Star Diamond Industries
gem polishing supplies
    Earth Treasures
    Rombins' Nest Farm
gem rock
    Michigan Lapidary Supply Co.
gem rough material
    Andria Bree Gem Co.
    Crown Gems Co.
    Geophile International
    Ken Kyte
    Murray American Corp.
gem saws
    Aleta's Rock Shop
gem scales
    Gilman's
    Morang Balance Co.

gem shops
    Covington Engineering Corp.
gem vises
    Gilman's
gemballs
    Gemex Co.
Gemmaster faceting laps
    MDR Mfg. Co., Inc.
Gemmaster faceting systems
    MDR Mfg. Co., Inc.
gemstone accessories
    Crown Gems Co.
gemstone baroques
    Jim's Rock Shop
gemstone cutting material
    The Treasure Chest
gemstone polishers
    Surburbia, Inc.
gemstone rough material
    Stop 'N Rock Shop
gemstone solutions
    Crown Gems Co.
gemstone supplies
    Jade World/Wilderness Originals
gemstones
    Australian Exports
    Australian Imports
    Bead Game
    Bourget Bros. Gems & Minerals
    Commercial Mineral Corp.
    Diamond Sales Co.
    Dowse's Lapidary Supply, Inc.
    Geophile International
    Gilman's
    Green's Rock & Lapidary Ltd.
    H & A Mfg. Corp.
    Jewelart Inc.
    J. J. Jewelcraft
    Jim Kesterson
    Lakewood Lapidary
    Liberty Gem & Supply
    Libra Gems
    Norlene Lapidary
    M. Nowotny
    Panther International Ltd.
    C. W. Somers & Co.
    Treasure of the Pirates, Inc.
glass bulbs
    Floating Gem Co.
glass gems
    Bergen Arts & Crafts, Inc.

Craft Category Index
Gemcraft—Glass

    Delco Craft Center, Inc.
    Skil-Crafts Division
hand loupes
    Gemological Institute of America
heart glass bulbs
    Floating Gem Co.
long flat glass bulbs
    Floating Gem Co.
round glass bulbs
    Floating Gem Co.
zircon
    Commercial Mineral Corp.
    W. D. Hudson, Jr.
    International Import Co.
    Norlene Lapidary
    Purcelli's Gems
    Syn-Crer Creations

glass
ash tray inserts
    Albert Constantine & Son Inc.
cathedral glass
    Artists & Craftsman Guild
    Whittemore-Durgin Glass Co.
Early American glassware
    Sturbridge Yankee Workshop
electric lehrs
    A. D. Alpine Inc.
furnaces
    Drykiln Design
fused glass items
    Glass Creations
glass additives
    Kay Kinney-Contoured Glass
glass anchors
    Glass Creations
glass angels
    Glass Creations
glass balls
    Skil-Crafts Division
glass beads
    Bead Game
    The Freed Co.
    Gloria's Glass Garden
    P. C. Herwig Co., Inc.
    Jewelart Inc.
    Macrame and Weaving Supply Co.
glass bulbs
    Floating Gem Co.
glass chunks
    Bergen Arts & Crafts, Inc.
    Whittemore-Durgin Glass Co.

glass designs
    Bell Studio
glass display domes
    Downs
    Flemington Cut Glass Co.
    Helen Gallagher
    Max of Dallas
    Sturbridge Yankee Workshop
    Sunset House
glass fish
    Glass Creations
glass globs
    Boin Arts & Crafts
    Delco Craft Center, Inc.
    Magnus Craft Materials, Inc.
glass icicles
    Glass Creations
glass intaglios
    Jewelart Inc.
glass ladybug
    House of York
glass marbles
    Delco Craft Center, Inc.
glass mosaic crosses
    House of Orange
glass mosaic pendants
    House of Orange
glass ornaments
    Holiday Craft
    Whittemore-Durgin Glass Co.
glass paperweights
    Craft Service
    Florida Supply House, Inc.
glass sailboats
    Glass Creations
glass snowflakes
    Glass Creations
glass stars
    Glass Creations
glass supplies
    Blue Grass Art & Hobby Center
    Craft Service
    Mollica Stained Glass Press
    Whittemore-Durgin Glass Co.
glass tools
    The Stained Glass Club
    Whittemore-Durgin Glass Co.
glassware
    Barker Enterprises
    House of Orange
    Sav-On-Crafts

heart glass bulbs
    Floating Gem Co.
long flat glass bulbs
    Floating Gem Co.
round glass bulbs
    Floating Gem Co.
sandwich glass fragments
    Wee 3 Sandwich Glass Jewelry

glass blowing *(see also Machinery, Tools)*
  cullets
    Drykiln Design
  electric lehrs
    A. D. Alpine Inc.
  furnaces
    Drykiln Design
  gas lehrs
    A. D. Alpine Inc.
  glass blowing equipment
    A. D. Alpine Inc.
    Westwood Ceramic Supply Co.
  glass melting furnaces
    Cole Ceramics Laboratories
  glass melting tanks
    A. D. Alpine Inc.
  glory holes
    A. D. Alpine Inc.
    Cole Ceramics Laboratories
  pipes
    Drykiln Design
  pontils
    Drykiln Design
  precision glass blowing tools
    Drykiln Design

glass crafts *(see also Bottlecutting)*
    Kay Kinney-Contoured Glass
  books
    Chilton Book Co.
    Priscilla's Little Red Tole House
    Surburbia, Inc.
    Trojan Press Inc.
    The Unicorn
  bottle cutters
    American Handicrafts
    P. S. Andrews Co.
    Bob's Arts & Crafts
    Craftsman Supply House
    Delco Craft Center, Inc.
    Walter Drake
    Edmund Scientific Co.
    Floyd Fleming

    The Handcrafters
    Hanover House Industries, Inc.
    Kay Kinney-Contoured Glass
    J. C. Penney Co., Inc.
    Keith Robinson
    Lee Wards
    Whittemore-Durgin Glass Co.
  carbide cutters
    Foredom Electric Co.
  cathedral glass
    Artists & Craftsman Guild
    Whittemore-Durgin Glass Co.
  collar molds
    Kay Kinney-Contoured Glass
  crushed glass
    American Handicrafts
    The Handcrafters
    Whittemore-Durgin Glass Co.
  cullets
    Drykiln Design
  electric lehrs
    A. D. Alpine Inc.
  fused glass items
    Glass Creations
  gas kilns
    Cole Ceramics Laboratories
  gas lehrs
    A. D. Alpine Inc.
  glass additives
    Kay Kinney-Contoured Glass
  glass anchors
    Glass Creations
  glass angels
    Glass Creations
  glass balls
    Skil-Crafts Division
  glass beads
    Bead Game
    The Freed Co.
    Gloria's Glass Garden
    P. C. Herwig Co., Inc.
    Jewelart Inc.
    Macrame and Weaving Supply Co.
  glass cabochons
    Jewelart Inc.
    Tumblecraft
  glass chunks
    Bergen Arts & Crafts, Inc.
    Whittemore-Durgin Glass Co.

Craft Category Index
Glass—Glass

glass cutters
  Brookstone Co.
  Cookson & Thode
glass designs
  Bell Studio
glass display domes
  Downs
  Flemington Cut Glass Co.
  Helen Gallagher
  Max of Dallas
  Sturbridge Yankee Workshop
  Sunset House
glass enamels
  Kay Kinney -Contoured Glass
glass fish
  Glass Creations
glass gems
  Bergen Arts & Crafts, Inc.
  Delco Craft Center, Inc.
  Skil-Crafts Division
glass globs
  Boin Arts & Crafts
  Delco Craft Center, Inc.
  Magnus Craft Materials, Inc.
glass icicles
  Glass Creations
glass intaglios
  Jewelart Inc.
glass jewel pendants
  Florida Supply House, Inc.
glass jewels
  Jewelart Inc.
  National Artcraft Supply Co.
glass ladybug
  House of York
glass marbles
  Bob's Arts & Crafts
  Delco Craft Center, Inc.
  Supreme Handicrafts
glass melting furnaces
  Cole Ceramics Laboratories
glass melting tanks
  A. D. Alpine Inc.
glass mold coats
  Kay Kinney -Contoured Glass
glass mosaic crosses
  House of Orange
glass mosaic pendants
  House of Orange

glass ornaments
  Holiday Craft
  Whittemore-Durgin Glass Co.
glass paints
  Sax Arts & Crafts
  Supreme Handicrafts
  Zim's
glass paperweights
  Craft Service
  Florida Supply House, Inc.
glass sailboats
  Glass Creations
glass scribing tools
  Brookstone Co.
glass snowflakes
  Glass Creations
glass stars
  Glass Creations
glass stones
  E. H. Ashley & Co., Inc.
glass supplies
  Blue Grass Art & Hobby Center
  Craft Service
  Mollica Stained Glass Press
  Whittemore-Durgin Glass Co.
glass tools
  The Stained Glass Club
  Whittemore-Durgin Glass Co.
glass tubular beads
  Bethlehem Imports
glass-bottle cutter
  Albert Constantine & Son Inc.
imported glass
  Whittemore-Durgin Glass Co.
kits
  Edmund Scientific Co.
lehrs
  Cole Ceramics Laboratories
  Drykiln Design
magazines
  Glass Art Magazine
marble craft
  Derby Lane Shell Center
  Koehler's Craft Outlet
milk bottles
  Dairy Service, Inc
miniature glass
  The Miniature Mart-The Peddler's Shop
miniature glass animals
  The Gift Shoppe

Craft Category Index
Glass—Gold

painting glass
   Floquil, Inc.
sandwich glass fragments
   Wee 3 Sandwich Glass Jewelry
shisha glass
   Maharani Boutique
singing colors
   Wee 3 Sandwich Glass Jewelry

glass stain *(see also Stains)*
  glass paints
   Sax Arts & Crafts
   Supreme Handicrafts
   Zim's
  glass stain paint
   Arthur Brown & Bro., Inc.
   The Handcrafters
   Kay Kinney -Contoured Glass
   Koehler's Craft Outlet
   Plaza Artists Materials, Inc.
  singing colors
   Wee 3 Sandwich Glass Jewelry

glazes and glaze application
  airbrushes
   Newton's Potters Supply
  books
   Dr. David Crespi
  brushes
   Ohio Ceramic Supply Inc.
  ceramic chemicals
   Cole Ceramics Laboratories
   Van Howe Ceramic Supply Co.
  ceramic glazes
   Bergen Arts & Crafts, Inc.
   Newton's Potters Supply
   Paramount Ceramic Inc.
   Sax Arts & Crafts
   Standard Ceramic Supply
   Tepping Studio Supply Co.
   Van Howe Ceramic Supply Co.
   Westwood Ceramic Supply Co.
  glaze formula tables
   Cole Ceramics Laboratories
  glazes
   Cole Ceramics Laboratories
   Delco Craft Center, Inc.
   Minnesota Clay
   Ohio Ceramic Supply Inc.
  heatless glazing for ceramics
   Specialty Products
  no-fire glazes
   National Craft & Hobby Co., Inc.

stains
   Cole Ceramics Laboratories
glues *(see Adhesives)*
gold
   Charbonneau's Lapidary Service
   Gems Galore
   Weidinger Inc.
  alloyed gold
   T. B. Hagstoz & Son
  gold casting items
   Solartherm Co.
  gold casting mountings
   Lapidabrade Inc.
  gold coin replicas
   Jewelart Inc.
  gold etching
   Irene Goodwin
  gold filled findings
   Albert Findings, Inc.
   Anozira Jewelers
   Edwards Jewelry Co.
   T. B. Hagstoz & Son
  gold filled mountings
   J. J. Jewelcraft
   Libra Gems
  gold filled wire
   G. Weidinger
  gold findings
   Albert Findings, Inc.
   Country Crafts
  gold grain
   Green's Rock & Lapidary Ltd.
  gold leaf
   P. S. Andrews Co.
   Arthur Brown & Bro., Inc.
   Carson & Ellis, Inc.
   Peg Hall Studios
   Marie Mitchell's Decoupage Center
   Hazel Pearson Handi Craft
   Zim's
  gold mountings
   Andria Bree Gem Co.
   Eric Martin Co
   J. J. Jewelcraft
   Silver & Gem Shop
  gold plated items
   Weidinger Inc.
  gold sheet
   Green's Rock & Lapidary Ltd.
   Trowbridge Crafts
   G. Weidinger

Craft Category Index
Gold—Handbag

gold solder
   G. Weidinger
gold wire
   Green's Rock & Lapidary Ltd.
   Talisman Crafts
   Trowbridge Crafts
gold zodiac signs
   Thieves Market
goldsmithing equipment
   Allcraft Tool & Supply Co.
   C. R. Hill Co.
   Magic Circle Corp.
yellow gold earwires
   The Jewelry Mart
yellow gold mountings
   J. J. Jewelcraft

gold leafing, gilding, foiling
   books
      Museum Books Inc.
      Sign of the Times Publishing Co.
   gilding brushes
      Plaza Artists Materials, Inc.
   gold foil
      Basic Crafts Co.
   gold leaf
      P. S. Andrews Co.
      Arthur Brown & Bro., Inc.
      Carson & Ellis, Inc.
      Peg Hall Studios
      Marie Mitchell's Decoupage Center
      Hazel Pearson Handi Craft
      Zim's

goldsmithing
   books
      Crown Publishers
      Lapidary Journal Book Dept.
   gold
      Charbonneau's Lapidary Service
      Gems Galore
      Weidinger Inc.
   gold sheet
      Green's Rock & Lapidary Ltd.
      Trowbridge Crafts
      G. Weidinger
   goldsmithing equipment
      Allcraft Tool & Supply Co.
      C. R. Hill Co.
      Magic Circle Corp.
   horn anvils
      Gilman's

   leaflets
      Miniature Aircraft

greeting cards *(see Cardmaking)*

group packs *(see also specific craft)*
   American Handicrafts
   Boin Arts & Crafts; beads, games, leather, paper, toys, American Indian crafts.
   Cavalier Handicrafts
   Creative Hands Co., Inc.
   Delco Craft Center, Inc.
   Gager's Handicrafts

handbag making
   bag handles
      Knit Services, Inc.
   basket tote bags
      Helen Gallagher
   Bermuda bag handles
      Sudberry House
   books
      Chilton Book Co.
      Mary Wales
   decoupage purse handles
      Dek-Co Manufacturing Co.
   decoupage slat purses
      Dek-Co Manufacturing Co.
   denim tote bags
      The Rusty Nail
   gay 90's newsprint sacks
      Downs
   handbag frames
      Mary Maxim Inc.
      Merribee
      Modern Needlepoint
      Robin & Russ Handweavers
   handbag handles
      Mary Maxim Inc.
      Merribee
   handbag leather
      Modern Needlepoint
   kits
      Beard's Art Needlework Studio
      Diversikit, Inc.
      General Crafts Corp.
      Libby's Needlepoint
      Magic Needle
      The Needle Works
      Pursenalities Inc.
      Sears, Roebuck & Co.
      Sewakers Industries Inc.
      Skil-Crafts Division

Craft Category Index
Handbag—Holiday

    Sudberry House
    Tandy Leather Co.
    Lillian Vernon
    Wyco Yarn Co.
needlepoint handbag linings
    Modern Needlepoint
pine wood purse
    Dek-Co Manufacturing Co.
purse craft
    Make It Happen Craft Studio
purse hardware
    Tandy Leather Co.
purse trimmings
    House of Flowers
tote bags
    The Rusty Nail
    Sewing Products Co.
unfinished purse boxes
    Carson & Ellis, Inc.

hardware
    Adventures In Crafts
    P. S. Andrews Co.
    Bedford Lumber Co., Inc.
    Carson & Ellis, Inc.
    Albert Constantine & Son Inc.
    Craft Products
    Dek-Co Manufacturing Co.
    Giles & Kendall Inc.
    Leathercrafters Supply Co.
    Hazel Pearson Handi Craft
    Real Woods
    Skil-Crafts Division
    Sturbridge Yankee Workshop
bell pull hardware
    The Yarn Nook
brass bell pulls
    Wichelt Import Co.
brass hardware
    John's Hardware & Decoupage Supplies
brass hinges
    Boutique Trims
    Handcraft Originals
brass lamp ornaments
    Angelo Bros. Co.
cabinet hardware
    Craftsman Wood Service Co.
ceramic hardware
    Cole Ceramics Laboratories
decoupage hardware
    Harrower House of Decoupage
    Marie Mitchell's Decoupage Center
    Town & Country Crafts
    Lee Wards
egg hardware
    Carnival Arts & Crafts
furniture hardware
    Albert Constantine & Son Inc.
hinges
    Albert Constantine & Son Inc.
ironmongery
    Whittemore-Durgin Glass Co.
locks
    Albert Constantine & Son Inc.
needlepoint hardware
    Mrs. W. Bradley Ryan
period hardware
    Albert Constantine & Son Inc.
purse hardware
    Tandy Leather Co.
sliding hardware
    Albert Constantine & Son Inc.
wood hardware
    Minnesota Woodworkers Supply Co.

hand tools *(see Tools)*

holiday decorations and ornaments *(see also Christmas crafts, Ornament making)*
books
    Lantern Press Inc.
    Ima Ova
    Beryl Sink
boutique items
    Fabulous Holiday House
    Holiday Handicrafts, Inc.
ceramic wisemen
    Crafty Ideas
Christmas boutique items
    Holiday Craft
Christmas decorating items
    Beadnik's Arts & Crafts
    Fabulous Holiday House
    Zim's
Christmas figures
    Supreme Handicrafts
Christmas tree ornaments
    The Putter Shop
diamond dust
    Holiday Craft
    Walnut Hill Co.
dimensional plastic shapes
    Holiday Craft

Craft Category Index
Holiday—Home

do-it-yourself Christmas ornaments
   Life-Like Products Inc.
   Sunset House
Easter decorating items
   Fabulous Holiday House
   The Putter Shop
glass ornaments
   Holiday Craft
   Whittemore-Durgin Glass Co.
glass snowflakes
   Glass Creations
glass stars
   Glass Creations
kits
   Gibsons Creations
miniature accessories
   The House of Miniatures
   Joen Ellen Kanze
   Miles Kimball
   The Miniature Mart-The Peddler's Shop
   Mrs. Mell Prescott
miniature animals
   Brown's Miniatures
   Custom Made Carvings & Miniatures
   Flint FBG Imports
miniature ceramic figures
   Grueny's Gift Center
plastic heads
   Hazel Pearson Handi Craft
plastic ornaments
   Florida Supply House, Inc.
plastic portrait balls
   Downs
satin balls
   Taylor House
self-adhesive iridescent foil jewels
   Diffraction Co., Inc.
snow sprays
   Walnut Hill Co.
three king heads
   Holiday Handicrafts, Inc.
tinsel sticks
   Holiday Craft
trims
   Fabulous Holiday House
   Holiday Handicrafts, Inc.
woodworking patterns
   Craft Patterns
wreaths
   Holiday Handicrafts, Inc.

home study courses *(see also specific craft)*
American School; blacksmith, carpentry, cement masonry, graphic arts, machine shop, masonry, metallurgy, sheet metal, sheet metal working, upholstery, welding, woodworking.
Auto Upholstery Institute; upholstering.
Brother International Corp.; machine knitting.
The Camp Fire Co.; silversmithing.
Candle Institute; candlemaking.
Candy & Cake Institute; cake decorating, candy making.
Chicago School of Interior Decoration; interior decorating.
Custom Drapery Institute; drapery making.
Fabricon Co.; mending fabrics.
Gemological Institute of America; lapidary.
Harrower House of Decoupage; decoupage.
International Correspondence Schools; interior design.
Jo's Doll Dressing Course; doll clothes.
Lee Mountain; carpentry, needlecrafts.
Lifetime Career Schools; decorative arts and crafts, doll craft, flower arranging, modern dressmaking.
Magic Circle Corp.; jewelry casting and sculpting.
Metals Engineering Institute; metal working, welding.
Modern Upholstery Institute; furniture upholstering.
Nantucket School of Needlery; needlecrafts.
National School of Dress Design; sewing.
National Standards Council of American Embroiderers; embroidery.
National Weavers Training School; weaving.
Doris Southard; lacemaking.
Al Stohlman Leathercraft Home Study Course; leathercraft.

Erica Wilson Correspondence
Courses; embroidery, needlepoint,
offers crewel embroidery and needlepoint.
Workshop; Norwegian rosemaling
learn-along letters.

hoops
The Hidden Village
Jerry S. Kaye Assoc.
Nantucket Needleworks
Needlecraft Shop Inc.
floor hoops
KAY an EE Corp. of America
table hoops
KAY an EE Corp. of America

jewelry findings and mountings
brooches
Jeweler's Emporium
catches
Albert Constantine & Son Inc.
coin rings
Tye's
colored safety pins
Jewelart Inc.
earring mountings
The Jewelry Mart
filigrees
Boutique Trims
flexible brass settings
E. H. Ashley & Co., Inc.
gold casting items
Solartherm Co.
gold casting mountings
Lapidabrade Inc.
gold filled findings
Albert Findings, Inc.
Anozira Jewelers
Edwards Jewelry Co.
T. B. Hagstoz & Son
gold filled mountings
J. J. Jewelcraft
Libra Gems
gold filled wire
G. Weidinger
gold findings
Albert Findings, Inc.
gold mountings
Andria Bree Gem Co.
Eric Martin Co
J. J. Jewelcraft
Silver & Gem Shop

gold plated items
Weidinger Inc.
jewel caps
Arlene Handley Rock Hobby Supplies
jeweler's circles
Anchor Tool & Supply Co.
jewelry chains
Bead Game
Green's Rock & Lapidary Ltd.
Jewel Creations
Jeweler's Emporium
Montgomery Ward & Co., Inc.
jewelry findings
Anchor Tool & Supply Co.
Art Mart, Inc.
Aspen Lapidary
Bead Game
The Beadcraft Corner/Beadcraft Club
Bob's Arts & Crafts
Boutique Trims
Boycan's Craft Supplies
Charbonneau's Lapidary Service
Craft Service
Creative Craft House
Deep Flex Plastic Molds, Inc.
Delco Craft Center, Inc.
The Ducketts
Economy Handicrafts, Inc.
Edwards Jewelry Co.
Farmers Gem and Rock Shop
Fieldwood Co.
Florida Supply House, Inc.
Gem-O-Rama, Inc.
Gemex Co.
Gems Galore
Gilman's
Gordon's
Green's Rock & Lapidary Ltd.
Grieger's Inc.
Handcraft Originals
C. R. Hill Co.
Jewelart Inc.
Jeweler's Emporium
Jim's Rock Shop
Jo-El's Craft Co.
K42 Rock Shop
Kaydee
Jim Kesterson
Kit Kraft
Koehler's Craft Outlet
Lapidabrade Inc.

Craft Category Index
Jewelry—Jewelry

Liberty Gem & Supply
M & M Distributors
Max of Dallas
Modern Craft
Montana Assay Office
Natcol Crafts, Inc.
Hazel Pearson Handi Craft
Sav-On-Crafts
Sax Arts & Crafts
Skil-Crafts Division
C. W. Somers & Co.
Specialty Products
Supreme Handicrafts
Swan-Son
Swest Inc.
Tye's
Lee Wards
G. Weidinger
Weidinger Inc.
Zim's

jewelry mountings
Alessi Lapidary Supplies
Bonnie's Rock Shop
The Ducketts
Ebersole Lapidary Supply Inc.
Farmers Gem and Rock Shop
Gem-O-Rama, Inc.
Gemex Co.
Gems Galore
Geophile International
Gilman's
Gordon's
Green's Rock & Lapidary Ltd.
Grieger's Inc.
Jewelart Inc.
Jim's Rock Shop
K42 Rock Shop
Harry Z. Kurs
Lapidabrade Inc.
Liberty Gem & Supply
M & M Distributors
Montana Assay Office
Mueller's
National Artcraft Supply Co.
Renaldy's
The Sandvigs
Sav-On-Crafts
Shipley's Mineral House
Smokey Mtn. Rock Shop
G. Weidinger
Weidinger Inc.

jewelrymaking accessories
American Handicrafts
Bead Game
Bergen Arts & Crafts, Inc.
Boin Arts & Crafts
Craftsman Supply House
Essayons Studio, Hand Arts Center
Kit Kraft
National Artcraft Supply Co.
J. C. Penney Co., Inc.
Sax Arts & Crafts
Swensons Lapidary Equipment, Inc.

karat gold sheet
Swest Inc.

key chains
The Beadcraft Corner/Beadcraft Club

metal rings
Knit Services, Inc.

plated gold filled mountings
Lapidabrade Inc.

plated gold findings
Lapidabrade Inc.

porcelain findings
Felts Manufacturing Co. Inc.

porcelain in gold plated jewelry findings
Creations for the Artist

precious metal findings
Bourget Bros. Gems & Minerals

rhinestone chain
Boutique Trims

rhodium mountings
J. J. Jewelcraft

safety pin jewelry items
Nicole Bead & Craft Co., Inc.

silver mountings
Andria Bree Gem Co.
Eric Martin Co
Silver & Gem Shop

sterling silver findings
Albert Findings, Inc.
Edwards Jewelry Co.
Lapidabrade Inc.

sterling silver mountings
J. J. Jewelcraft
Lapidabrade Inc.

white jewelry findings
Country Crafts

wire metal
T. B. Hagstoz & Son

yellow gold earwires
The Jewelry Mart

Craft Category Index
Jewelry—Jewelrymaking

yellow gold mountings
    J. J. Jewelcraft

jewelrymaking *(see also Lapidary)*
  adhesives
    The Ducketts
  American Indian jewelry supplies
    Panther International Ltd.
  awls
    Jewelart Inc.
  bamboo beads
    The Beadcraft Corner/Beadcraft Club
    Pack-O-Fun
  blades
    Weidinger Inc.
  books
    The Amulet
    Association Press
    Book Barn
    Bovin Publishing
    Boycan's Craft Supplies
    Chilton Book Co.
    Craft Course Publishers
    Craftool Co.
    Crafts Yarns & Gifts Ltd.
    Crafty Ideas
    Dick Ells Co.
    Frankie's Twistcraft Jewelry
    Gemological Institute of America
    Gems & Minerals
    Lapidary Journal Book Dept.
    McKnight Publishing Co.
    Museum Books Inc.
    Bob and Carol Oliver
    Reilly & Lee Books
    Beryl Sink
    Elyse Sommer
    Sterling Publishing Co. Inc.
    Taplinger Publishing Co.
    The Unicorn
    Van Nostrand Reinhold Co.
    The Victors
    Viking Press
    Watson-Guptill Publications
  boutique pendants
    Jewelart Inc.
  brooches
    Jeweler's Emporium
  Burma jade (jadeite) jewelry
    Crown Cultured Pearl Corp.
  cameos
    Gemex Co.
    Jewelart Inc.
    Jeweler's Emporium
    Sav-On-Crafts
    Veronica
  casting accessories
    Kerr Mfg. Co.
  casting block
    Solartherm Co.
  casting crucibles
    Solartherm Co.
  casting equipment
    Allcraft Tool & Supply Co.
    Bet-Roc Enterprises Inc.
    Dick Ells Co.
    Gems Galore
    Shipley's Mineral House
    Supreme Watch Material Co.
  casting grain
    Trowbridge Crafts
  casting investment molding material
    Kerr Mfg. Co.
  casting supplies
    Dick Blick
    Dick Ells Co.
    Gems Galore
    C. R. Hill Co.
    J. J. Jewelcraft
    C. W. Somers & Co.
    Swest Inc.
  casting tools
    Allcraft Tool & Supply Co.
  casting units
    Sax Arts & Crafts
  casting waxes
    Allcraft Tool & Supply Co.
    Delco Craft Center, Inc.
  castings
    Panther International Ltd.
  catches
    Albert Constantine & Son Inc.
  centrifugal casting equipment
    T. B. Hagstoz & Son
  chains
    Green's Rock & Lapidary Ltd.
    Jewel Creations
    Jeweler's Emporium
    Montgomery Ward & Co., Inc.
  chasing supplies
    William Dixon Co.
  coin rings
    Tye's

Craft Category Index
Jewelrymaking—Jewelrymaking

colored safety pins
    Jewelart Inc.
combination power tools
    Swest Inc.
complete faceting machines
    Henry B. Graves Co.
copper
    Anchor Tool & Supply Co.
    Bergen Arts & Crafts, Inc.
    T. B. Hagstoz & Son
copper shapes
    Sax Arts & Crafts
copper wire
    Talisman Crafts
coral
    The Collector's Cabinet
    The Freed Co.
    International Import Co.
    Max of Dallas
    Panther International Ltd.
costume jewelrymaking
    Jeweler's Emporium
    K42 Rock Shop
crochet jewelry
    American Handicrafts
cutting materials
    Weidinger Inc.
cuttle bone
    T. B. Hagstoz & Son
earring mountings
    The Jewelry Mart
electric carver
    Green's Rock & Lapidary Ltd.
electric wax spatula
    Green's Rock & Lapidary Ltd.
electroplated mountings
    J. J. Jewelcraft
electroplating accessories
    C. R. Hill Co.
    Supreme Watch Material Co.
electroplating equipment
    Supreme Watch Material Co.
    Technical Specialties International Inc.
electroplating supplies
    William Dixon Co.
electroplating tools
    William Dixon Co.
enamels
    C. R. Hill Co.

engravers
    Beno J. Gundlach Co.
    Skil-Crafts Division
faceted beads
    The Beadcraft Corner/Beadcraft Club
    Jim Kesterson
faceted garnets
    Anozira Jewelers
faceted gemstones
    De Lapa Mining Inc.
    Dover Scientific Co.
    International Import Co.
    Minerals & Gems
faceted stones
    Biship's House of Gems
    The Ducketts
    Gemex Co.
    Gilman's
    Jim's Rock Shop
    Michigan Lapidary Supply Co.
    Mueller's
    Transworld Trading Co.
    Weisz Import Export Corp.
filigree beads
    Jewelart Inc.
filigrees
    Boutique Trims
findings
    The Beadcraft Corner/Beadcraft Club
    Gemex Co.
    Gems Galore
    Gilman's
    Gordon's
    Green's Rock & Lapidary Ltd.
    Grieger's Inc.
    C. R. Hill Co.
    Jewelart Inc.
    Jeweler's Emporium
    Jim's Rock Shop
    K42 Rock Shop
    Kit Kraft
    Swest Inc.
fine silver casting grains
    H. A. Cole
finished gemstones
    Smokey Mtn. Rock Shop
flexible brass settings
    E. H. Ashley & Co., Inc.
flexible shaft machines
    Gems Galore

Craft Category Index
Jewelrymaking—Jewelrymaking

furnaces
   Supreme Watch Material Co.
glass jewel pendants
   Florida Supply House, Inc.
glass jewels
   Jewelart Inc.
   National Artcraft Supply Co.
glass mosaic crosses
   House of Orange
glass mosaic pendants
   House of Orange
glass stones
   E. H. Ashley & Co., Inc.
glass tubular beads
   Bethlehem Imports
glazed beads
   Bead Game
glues
   Jeweler's Emporium
gold
   Charbonneau's Lapidary Service
   Gems Galore
   Weidinger Inc.
gold casting items
   Solartherm Co.
gold casting mountings
   Lapidabrade Inc.
gold coin replicas
   Jewelart Inc.
gold filled findings
   Albert Findings, Inc.
   Anozira Jewelers
   Edwards Jewelry Co.
   T. B. Hagstoz & Son
gold filled mountings
   J. J. Jewelcraft
   Libra Gems
gold filled wire
   G. Weidinger
gold findings
   Albert Findings, Inc.
gold grain
   Green's Rock & Lapidary Ltd.
gold mountings
   Andria Bree Gem Co.
   Eric Martin Co
   J. J. Jewelcraft
   Silver & Gem Shop
gold plated items
   Weidinger Inc.

gold sheet
   Green's Rock & Lapidary Ltd.
   Trowbridge Crafts
   G. Weidinger
gold solder
   G. Weidinger
gold wire
   Green's Rock & Lapidary Ltd.
   Talisman Crafts
   Trowbridge Crafts
gold zodiac signs
   Thieves Market
hammered metal supplies
   William Dixon Co.
hammered metal work tools
   William Dixon Co.
hand loupes
   Gemological Institute of America
hand tools
   J. J. Jewelcraft
handcrafted stoneware beads
   Earthworks
handmade Swiss wood beads
   Robin & Russ Handweavers
home study courses
   Gemological Institute of America
   Magic Circle Corp.
horn anvils
   Gilman's
hot point testers
   Gemological Institute of America
jewel caps
   Arlene Handley Rock Hobby Supplies
jewel stone assortments
   De Mallie Crafts
jeweler's bronze
   Anchor Tool & Supply Co.
jeweler's circles
   Anchor Tool & Supply Co.
jeweler's sprue wax
   Green's Rock & Lapidary Ltd.
jeweler's supplies
   Swest Inc.
jeweler's tools
   Anchor Tool & Supply Co.
   The L. S. Starrett Co.
   Swest Inc.
jeweler's tubing
   Swest Inc.

Craft Category Index
Jewelrymaking—Jewelrymaking

jeweler's wire
   Anchor Tool & Supply Co.
   Swest Inc.
jewelry abrasives
   Star Diamond Industries
jewelry casting lamps
   O'Brien Lapidary Equipment Co.
jewelry casting supplies
   Exactra-Craft Corp.
   Gemex Co.
   Magic Circle Corp.
   O'Brien Lapidary Equipment Co.
jewelry casting tools
   O'Brien Lapidary Equipment Co.
jewelry cement
   Star Diamond Industries
jewelry chains
   Bead Game
jewelry cutting materials
   Max of Dallas
jewelry disks
   Star Diamond Industries
jewelry display cases
   Liberty Gem & Supply
   Max of Dallas
   Nature's Treasures
jewelry patterns
   Creations for the Artist
jewelry scales
   O'Brien Lapidary Equipment Co.
jewelry stones
   Veronica
jewelry workbench
   Craft House
jewelrymaking accessories
   American Handicrafts
   Bead Game
   Bergen Arts & Crafts, Inc.
   Boin Arts & Crafts
   Craftsman Supply House
   Essayons Studio, Hand Arts Center
   Kit Kraft
   National Artcraft Supply Co.
   J. C. Penney Co., Inc.
   Sax Arts & Crafts
   Swensons Lapidary Equipment, Inc.
jewelrymaking equipment
   Exactra-Craft Corp.
   Grieger's Inc.
   K42 Rock Shop
   Prospector's Pouch
   The Roc Shop
   Treasure of the Pirates, Inc.
   Tye's
   Weidinger Inc.
jewelrymaking machinery
   Jim Kesterson
jewelrymaking supplies
   ARE Creations Inc.
   D. M. Campana Co.
   William Dixon Co.
   Gemex Co.
   Geophile International
   Gordon's
   Green's Rock & Lapidary Ltd.
   Grieger's Inc.
   T. B. Hagstoz & Son
   C. R. Hill Co.
   Jewel Creations
   Jewelart Inc.
   J. J. Jewelcraft
   K42 Rock Shop
   Lapidabrade Inc.
   Modern Craft
   Panther International Ltd.
   Solartherm Co.
   Ken Stewart's Gem Shop
   Supreme Watch Material Co.
   Syn-Crer Creations
   Talisman Crafts
   Joseph Tartas
   Technical Specialties International Inc.
   Treasure of the Pirates, Inc.
   Tye's
   G. Weidinger
jewelrymaking tools
   Allcraft Tool & Supply Co.
   Brookstone Co.
   William Dixon Co.
   Gems Galore
   Green's Rock & Lapidary Ltd.
   T. B. Hagstoz & Son
   Jim Kesterson
   Maroon Bells Ind. Inc.
   Montana Assay Office
   Sax Arts & Crafts
   C. W. Somers & Co.
   Swensons Lapidary Equipment, Inc.
   Joseph Tartas
   Trowbridge Crafts

Craft Category Index
Jewelrymaking—Jewelrymaking

    Universal Wirecraft Jewelry Co.
    Weidinger Inc.
key chains
    The Beadcraft Corner/Beadcraft Club
kits
    Alohalei Hawaii
    E. H. Ashley & Co., Inc.
    B & J Star Co.
    Bead-Weavers
    Bet-Roc Enterprises Inc.
    Nadja Bolio
    Corrado Cutlery Inc.
    Craftool Co.
    Elvin
    Gemex Co.
    Gilman's
    Holiday Handicrafts, Inc.
    Jans Jewels
    Jewelart Inc.
    Michigan Lapidary Supply Co.
    Bob and Carol Oliver
    Sax Arts & Crafts
    Sheru Bead Boutique Shop
    Joseph Tartas
    Cheryl Todd
    Town & Country Crafts
limoges
    Jeweler's Emporium
    Sav-On-Crafts
lost wax jewelrymaking
    Kerr Mfg. Co.
magazines
    American Home Crafts
    Gems & Minerals
    Lapidary Journal Book Dept.
    McCall's Needlework & Crafts
melting equipment
    Supreme Watch Material Co.
metal stampings
    Green's Rock & Lapidary Ltd.
neck rings
    Jeweler's Emporium
pearl strands
    Jeweler's Emporium
pearls
    Anne's Treasure Trove
    Bead Game
    The Beadcraft Corner/Beadcraft Club
    Deep Flex Plastic Molds, Inc.
    Gilman's
    Home-Sew Inc.

    International Import Co.
    Jewelart Inc.
    Kaydee
    Kit Kraft
    M & M Distributors
    Natalie Originals Studio
    New Products Co.
    The Putter Shop
    Schrock's, The House of Hobbies & Crafts
    Swan-Son
    Taylor House
pewter
    Anchor Tool & Supply Co.
    T. B. Hagstoz & Son
    Sax Arts & Crafts
plated gold filled mountings
    Lapidabrade Inc.
plated gold findings
    Lapidabrade Inc.
platinum
    T. B. Hagstoz & Son
polariscopes
    Gemological Institute of America
polished gemstones
    Biship's House of Gems
    Gem-O-Rama, Inc.
    Silver & Gem Shop
portable plating equipment
    Platers Service Co.
professional jeweler's instruments
    Gemological Institute of America
refractometers
    Gemological Institute of America
rhinestone bandings
    Gail's Decorative Arts Studio
    Gibsons Creations
rhinestone chain
    Boutique Trims
rhinestones
    P. S. Andrews Co.
    Boutique Trims
    Derby Lane Shell Center
    Florida Supply House, Inc.
    Gail's Decorative Arts Studio
    Gibsons Creations
    Handcraft Originals
    Home-Sew Inc.
    Kit Kraft
    National Artcraft Supply Co.
    Lee Wards

Craft Category Index
Jewelrymaking—Jewelrymaking

ring blanks
  Gilman's
  Supreme Watch Material Co.
ring forms
  Sax Arts & Crafts
ring mountings
  The Jewelry Mart
ring shapes
  Green's Rock & Lapidary Ltd.
rocailles
  The Beadcraft Corner/Beadcraft Club
rondelles
  The Beadcraft Corner/Beadcraft Club
safety pin jewelry items
  Nicole Bead & Craft Co., Inc.
scauper
  King's Studio
services
  Eric Martin Co
shark's teeth
  C. R. Boylin
  Florida Supply House, Inc.
silicon carbide
  The Ducketts
silver casting items
  Solartherm Co.
silver jewelrymaking
  Trowbridge Crafts
silver mountings
  Andria Bree Gem Co.
  Eric Martin Co
  Silver & Gem Shop
silver ring castings
  The Ducketts
silver strip
  Ken Stewart's Gem Shop
silver wire
  Talisman Crafts
slabs
  Alessi Lapidary Supplies
  Trader South
  C. R. Wells
  Woodward Ranch
solder
  Gilman's
  Panther International Ltd.
soldering equipment
  Supreme Watch Material Co.
solderless jewelry
  Bob and Carol Oliver

solderless wire jewelrymaking
  Universal Wirecraft Jewelry Co.
splash shields
  Lortone Inc.
square gold filled wire
  Frankie's Twistcraft Jewelry
steer horns
  Twin Peaks Rock Shop
sterling silver
  T. B. Hagstoz & Son
  Libra Gems
  Panther International Ltd.
sterling silver findings
  Albert Findings, Inc.
  Edwards Jewelry Co.
  Lapidabrade Inc.
sterling silver items
  Weidinger Inc.
sterling silver mountings
  J. J. Jewelcraft
  Lapidabrade Inc.
sterling silver sheet
  Alessi Lapidary Supplies
  Anchor Tool & Supply Co.
  Green's Rock & Lapidary Ltd.
  Sax Arts & Crafts
  Swest Inc.
  Trowbridge Crafts
  G. Weidinger
sterling silver wire
  Alessi Lapidary Supplies
  Green's Rock & Lapidary Ltd.
  Trowbridge Crafts
  G. Weidinger
stone mixes
  Tumblecraft
stones
  Florida Supply House, Inc.
  Jeweler's Emporium
  Tye's
teredo wood slabs
  Brown's Rock & Lapidary Supplies
ultrasonic cleaners
  Branson Cleaning Equipment
  Crown Gems Co.
  Geode Industries
vacuum casting
  Allcraft Tool & Supply Co.
vibrating laps
  Star Diamond Industries

Craft Category Index
Jewelrymaking—Kits

vises
    Universal Wirecraft Jewelry Co.
wavellite
    Wright's Rock Shop
wax
    Bourget Bros. Gems & Minerals
    Gilman's
    Kerr Mfg. Co.
    Supreme Watch Material Co.
wax pots
    Shipley's Mineral House
wax ring patterns
    Eric Martin Co
whistles
    Jewelart Inc.
white metal castings
    Paige Enterprises
wire
    Universal Wirecraft Jewelry Co.
wire jewelrymaking tools
    Frankie's Twistcraft Jewelry
wire metal
    T. B. Hagstoz & Son
wood beads
    Bead Game
    Florida Supply House, Inc.
    Gloria's Glass Garden
    P. C. Herwig Co., Inc.
    Jewelart Inc.
wood crosses
    O-P Craft Co., Inc.
wood jewelry
    Artistry In Wood
wood jewelry scraps
    Glencraft Shop
    Jeweler's Emporium
yellow gold casting grains
    H. A. Cole
yellow gold earwires
    The Jewelry Mart
yellow gold mountings
    J. J. Jewelcraft
zodiacs
    Jeweler's Emporium
14 kt gold castings
    Madewell Products Inc.

kilns
    Allcraft Tool & Supply Co.
    Anchor Tool & Supply Co.
    Art Consultants
    Bergen Arts & Crafts, Inc.
    Boin Arts & Crafts
    Arthur Brown & Bro., Inc.
    Handcraft House
    Loretta's Ceramic Studio
    Minnesota Clay
    Ohio Ceramic Supply Inc.
    Plaza Artists Materials, Inc.
    Richland Ceramics Inc.
    Sax Arts & Crafts
    Sculpture Associates Ltd.
    Sculpture House
    Thomas C. Thompson
    Westwood Ceramic Supply Co.
ceramic kilns
    A 'N L's Hobbicraft, Inc.
    A. D. Alpine Inc.
    Bergen Arts & Crafts, Inc.
    Clay-Crafters Products
    Delco Craft Center, Inc.
    Newton's Potters Supply
    Paragon Industries Inc.
    Paramount Ceramic Inc.
enameling kilns
    A 'N L's Hobbicraft, Inc.
    Bergen Arts & Crafts, Inc.
    Craft Service
gas kilns
    Cole Ceramics Laboratories
kiln accessories
    Delco Craft Center, Inc.
kiln shelves
    Cole Ceramics Laboratories
kits
    Diedricks Crafts
refractories
    Westwood Ceramic Supply Co.
replacement parts for kilns
    Delco Craft Center, Inc.

kitemaking
books
    Charles E. Tuttle Co. Inc.

kits *(see also specific craft)*
    A 'N L's Hobbicraft, Inc.; leather.
    Advance Process Supply Co.; screen printing.
    Adventures In Crafts; decoupage.
    Alohalei Hawaii; bead lei necklace.
    America's Hobby Center Inc.; model aircraft, wood ship model ship.
    American Decorative Arts, Inc.; home decorating stencils.

Craft Category Index
Kits—Kits

American Handicrafts; antiquing, candlemaking, copper, decoupage, dip film, lamps, leather, resin, string, tooling.
American Machine & Tool Co.; wood shaper.
Angelo Bros. Co.; lamp adapters, lamp converters, lamp shade, make-a-lamp, swag lamp, wired converter.
Anne's Treasure Trove; pits, seeds, tropical seeds.
Antique Doll Reproductions
Antoine's; processing-your-own rose petals.
Archer's Hobby World; British railroad model.
Argosy Products; gem picture, gem tree.
Artistry In Wood; filigree ornament.
Artists & Craftsman Guild; stained glass.
Arts and Crafts Unlimited; birthday cards, note cards, Christmas cards.
Ashford Handicrafts Ltd.; spinning wheels.
E. H. Ashley & Co., Inc.; do-it-yourself, neckchains.
Associated Hobby Manufacturers Inc.
Audria's; craft dog fur.
Australian Exports
Auto World, Inc.; model car.
B & J Star Co.; linde star jewelry.
Bachmann; building lighting, model animals, model birds, model dogs, model planes, model ships, model tanks.
Ball O' Yarn; knitting poncho, mitten, Christmas bell.
Barnes & Blake; embroidery, needlepoint.
Baxwood Crafters; lamp, with wood bases.
Bay Country Woodcrafters; wood duck decoy.
Beadcraft; flower bead.
Beadnik's Arts & Crafts; beaded flower.
Bead-Weavers; necklace beadweaving.
Bear Cave; acrylic restoring and creating finishes, birdhouse, boats, patchwork, sewing, wood boxes.
Beard's Art Needlework Studio; monogrammed handbags, needlepoint.
Bedford Lumber Co., Inc.; furniture making.
Berry's of Maine; embroidery, needlepoint.
Bersted's; candlemaking, decoupage, reed.
Bet-Roc Enterprises Inc.; jewelrymaking.
Better Homes & Gardens; crewel, sampler.
James Bliss & Co. Inc.; ship model.
Bluejacket Ship Crafters; ship model.
Boin Arts & Crafts; sculpture.
Nadja Bolio; key holder, wood jewelry.
The Booted Sheepherder Inc.; jackets, sheepskin.
Brookhurst Hobbys; scale models.
Brunswick Worsted Mills; latch rug, needlepoint.
Budget Buddy Co.; crewel, needlepoint.
C. W. Bullock; clock.
Cake Decorators & Craft Supplies; soap making.
Campbell Scale Models; model railroad trackside.
Canadian Aero-Supply; model aircraft.
Carter Associates; old fashioned monkey sock.
Castolite; casting.
Cavalier Handicrafts; leather craft, screen process.
Champs Creative Materials Center; "China" gloss floral arrangements, metal art sculpture.
Classic Crafts; furniture.
Clems and Clems Spinning Wheels; distaff for ashford wheel.
Cleveland Leather Co.; decoupage, leather, wood, wood ware, American Indian crafts.
The Clever Crafters; sewing doll.
Cohasset Colonials; furniture.

Cole Ceramics Laboratories; potter's wheels.

Columbia Candlecraft; candlemaking, cascading candles, foliating candles.

Albert Constantine & Son Inc.; chair caning, clocks, guitar making, marquetry, ship model, veneer, Appalachian dulcimer.

Contemporary Quilts; crib quilts.

Continental Hobbies Inc.; aircraft, imported model, military vehicles, trains.

Corner Cupboard Crafts, Inc.; string art.

The Corner Shop; embroidery, felt needle art, needlepoint.

Corrado Cutlery Inc.; jewelry repair, tool pack.

Cottage Crafts; tote bags, velvet mushrooms, velvet strawberries.

Country Crafts; boutique, egg, Christmas ornament.

Country Woodcraft; wood carving.

Covington Engineering Corp.; build-your-own equipment.

Craft & Candle House; candlemaking starter.

The Craft Corner; candlemaking, felt, macrame, nylon net, papier mache.

Craft Kits; decoupage.

Craft Products; wood clock.

Craftint Manufacturing Co.; screen process starter.

Craftool Co.; batik, book binding, ceramics, etching, graphic arts, jewelrymaking, lapidary, papermaking, sculpture, stone carving, weaving, wood carving, woodworking.

Crafts Yarns & Gifts; crewel, needlepoint, Southwestern scenes designs.

Crafts Yarns & Gifts Ltd.; crewel in Southwestern theme designs.

Craftsman Supply House; leather, rush.

Craftsman Wood Service Co.; musical instruments, pictures, woodworking.

Craigle Studios; metal sculpture.

Crain-Harmon; astrological, crewel, designs, needlepoint, African.

Create Your Own, Inc.; patchwork, patchwork aprons, patchwork crib quilts, patchwork pillows, patchwork place mats, patchwork tote bags.

Creations by Julianna; stain glass.

Creative Hands Co., Inc.; leather craft, screen process.

Creative Metalcraft; wrought iron craft.

Creative Murals, Inc.; mural, paint-by-number.

Creative Spoolcraft; heirloom ornaments from spools.

Creativity Needlepoint; latch hooking, needlepoint.

Crewel World; crewel.

Crossroads; embroidery, needlepoint, Scandinavian rya.

Crowe & Coulter; fingerweaving, American Indian designs.

The Custom House of Needle Arts & Design; embroidery.

D. M. C. Corporation; tapestry.

H. DeCovnick & Son; grandfather clocks, grandmother clocks.

Deep Flex Plastic Molds, Inc.; decoupage.

Dek-Co Manufacturing Co.; clock.

Delco Craft Center, Inc.; leather craft, screen process.

Determined Productions, Inc.; needlepoint, quickpoint, Joan Walsh Anglund designs.

Diedricks Crafts; ceramic kilns.

Diffraction Co., Inc.

Dildine's Arts & Crafts; general.

Distlefink Designs; patchwork pillow, patchwork quilt.

Diversikit, Inc.; crochet jute, hats, shoulder bags, suede leather purse.

Doll Repair Parts, Inc.; doll repair.

Doll's Candle & Craft Supplies; candle wax dye.

Dolly Darling Inc.; "Teen doll" clothing.

Don's Hobby Co.; flower making.

Dot's Dollhouse

Craft Category Index
Kits—Kits

James L. Douthat; coat-of-arms, crewel, needlepoint, painting.
Driftwood House; driftwood.
The Ducketts; tumbler.
Dulcimer; dulcimer, musical instrument.
Earth Treasures; lapidary.
Economy Handicrafts, Inc.; paper flower, sculpture, wood ware.
Edmund Scientific Co.; clay modeling, crystal growing, glass painting, lighting, sculpture, transfer process (print-to-cloth), wax sculpture.
Elvin; simulated diamond jewelry.
Emberugs; rya.
Emperor Clock Co.; grandfather clock.
The Enchanted Doll House; clock, macrame.
Ervins; granny dolls.
Eva Mae Doll Co.; china doll.
Exact Performance; aircraft, domestic plastic model, figures, imported plastic model, ships.
Fairtex Distributing Co.; knitting and crochet.
Family Circle Kits; needlecraft.
Fantastic Fit Products; "fit and sew".
Mark Farmer Co., Inc.; doll.
The Farmhouse Craft Shoppe; "decaling".
Feather & Flower Craft; bead, doll key chain.
Fetty-Nielsen Macrame Loom; loom.
J. P. Fliegel Co.; leather glove.
Floquil, Inc.
Folbot Corp.; paddle boat.
Fotocut Lab; photo-etching.
Frank's Jewelry & Gem Shop; cabochons making.
Franzen Gifts; rug braiding.
Frostline; children's jackets, hunter's gear, parkas, ponchos, rain pants, sewing, ski apparel, sleeping bag.
Gager's Handicrafts; leather craft, screen process.
Helen Gallagher; candlemaking, needlecraft.
James A. Gardner; embroidery.
Gem Tool Specialties
Gemex Co.; bead flower, crochet jewelry, jewelry, leather beads, metal decor, needlepoint, pottery, stained glass, string art, weaving.
General Crafts Corp.; by-number handbag, crewel, mosaic wall plaque.
General Supplies Co.; seasonal trim, upholstery, vinyl repair.
Gibsons Creations; holiday ornament.
Gift Craft; dolls, macrame, nature crafts, needlecraft, planters, trivets, Christmas decorations, Christmas ornaments.
Giles & Kendall Inc.; unfinished wood furniture making.
Gilliom Mfg. Co.; build-your-own power tool.
Gilman's; grandfather clock, hand jewelry casting, polishing, sand casting.
Glass Creations; mobile.
Glass House Studio; leaded stained glass.
Gloria's Glass Garden; venetian glass bead.
Good Housekeeping; crewel, embroidery, needlecraft, needlepoint.
Gordon's; metal casting.
Green's Rock & Lapidary Ltd.; tumbling.
Guild of Strawberry Banks Inc.; sampler.
Paul K. Guillow Inc.; balsa model aircraft.
Harrisville Designs; handlooms.
John Hathaway; paper model aeroplanes, paper model castles, paper model chateaus, paper model churches, paper model miniature rooms, paper model moon rover, paper model palaces, paper model ships, paper model towns, paper model trains, paper model villages, paper model European buildings, paper model U.S. western 1883's mining town.
Hawthorne House, Inc.; soapmaking and candlemaking.
The Hen House; needlepoint.
Carl Hepp Mosaic Co.; tiffany shade.
HERE Inc.; musical instrument.

Craft Category Index
Kits—Kits

Heritage Hill Patterns; embroidery, needlepoint.
Herter's, Inc.; candlemaking, fishing, gunstock finishing, lamp, lure and rod, ships, taxidermy.
P. C. Herwig Co., Inc.; candlemaking, macrame.
High Strength Adhesives Corp.; marble resin craft, resin crafts.
Alexandra Hill Needlepoint Studios Ltd.; needlepoint.
Historic House; cross stitch, sampler.
Hobby Gallery; model.
Holgate & Raynolds; HO structure.
Holiday Handicrafts, Inc.; art foam, crochet jewelry, ornament, three kings.
Holly Studio Inc; china painting.
Holmes-Corey Ltd.; coat-of-arms, crewel embroidery.
Home-Sew Inc.; soap decorating.
House of Flowers; needlecraft.
House of Gould; braiding.
House of Lines
House of Stitches; linen, sampler.
Inkle Looms; old English style inkle loom.
International Creations; Icelandic sweater.
J. L. T.; belt, needlepoint, pillow, tote bag.
Jamar, Inc.; decoupage tin bucket.
Jans Jewels; jewelry making.
Jeane's
Jenkins Lapidary Equipment; "build-it-yourself saw", saw, slab saw.
Jesop Co.
Jewelart Inc.; jewelry, American Indian jewelry.
JMC; plastic building.
JV Models; metal castings, model dairy barn, wood castings.
Kaleidoscope Needleworks; needlepoint.
Kalico Kits; needlepoint.
Kaydee
Jerry S. Kaye Assoc.; miniature needlepoint.
Kazari; punch needlecraft.
Miles Kimball; needlecraft.
Kitsophrenia, Inc.; shisha "mirror".

Knit Services, Inc.; belt.
Knits 'N That Yarn Shop; rug hooking.
M. Knopp; doll head for antique replica china & porcelain dolls.
Koehler's Craft Outlet; art foam, beads, candlemaking, chenille, cooking crystals, craft fur, flower dip doll, pearls.
Krick Kits; needlepoint.
Ladies Home Journal Needle & Craft; needlecraft.
Barbara Lawshe; stained glass.
The Left Hand Inc.; geodesic dome model, omnistar (geodesic).
Leisure Services; quilling.
Libby's Needlepoint; handbag, needlepoint.
Life-Like Products Inc.; historic sailing ships, model airplane, model motorcycles, model ship building, model steamboats, prehistoric man and animal anatomy, HO scale buildings.
Locomotive Workshop; aluminum casting, brass diesel locomotive, brass railroad car.
Loftons; latch hook rug, stitchery.
The Loom Factory; floor loom.
Edna Looney Originals; applique, bottle covers, calendars, needlecraft wall hangings.
Luger; boat.
Lynchburg Hdwr. & General Store; whittling.
Magic Circle Corp.; stone setting.
Magic Needle; needlepoint, patchwork purse kit.
Magnus Craft Materials, Inc.; stencil, wood.
Make It Happen Craft Studio
Man-Pak, Inc.; "interior construction" items, canvas coat fronts, jackets women's, man's jackets, man's regular and delux pants, non-roll waistbands, sewing, shoulder pads, undercollar.
Sal Marino Co.; model accessories, model buildings, model railroad trains, structure.
Mars Models; HO scale building.

Craft Category Index
Kits—Kits

Mason & Sullivan Co.; clock.
Mary Maxim Inc.; candlemaking, crochet, knitting, latch hook rug, paper pottery, wood birdhouse, Indian bead loom.
Jean McIntosh Ltd.; needlecraft.
Melrose Yarn Co., Inc.; afghan.
Merribee; knitting, tapestry rugs.
Michigan Lapidary Supply Co.; jewelry casting.
Michigan Wool Products Co.; rug braiding.
Midwest Mail Service; foil craft tape.
Miniature Aircraft; balsa model airplane, plastic model airplane.
Minnesota Woodworkers Supply Co.; clock.
Marie Mitchell's Decoupage Center; decoupage.
Model Die Casting Inc.; plastic model railroad.
Model Railroad Equipment Corp.; model railroading.
Mohave Industries; saw.
Joan Moshimer; rug.
Most Unusual Custom Needleworks Inc.; needlepoint.
Nantucket Needleworks; needlepoint crewel.
Natcol Crafts, Inc.; dough art.
National Craft & Hobby Co., Inc.; painting, paints, stained glass.
National Hobby Inc.; model airplane, model boats, model railroads.
Nautique Arts; macrame.
The Needle Works; crewel, handbag, needlepoint, quilting.
Needlecraft House; bargello, crewel, embroidery, needlepoint.
Needlewoman Shop; crochet, embroidery, knitting, needlepoint, rugmaking, toymaking.
Needles 'N Hoops; needlecraft, sampler.
Frank J. Nelson; netting.
Netcraft; net making.
The New England Craftsman; wood inlay (marquetry).
New England Village Crafts; stained glass.
New Products Co.; cooking crystals.

Newport Enterprises; clock.
Nicole Bead & Craft Co., Inc.; beaded flower, carpetbag.
Bob and Carol Oliver; beading, jewelry, macrame, 12 kt. gold filled square wire.
Open Door Co.; geometric thread design.
Oxford Crafts; model historic buildings, model lighthouses, model planes, model ships, English and American card model.
Pack-O-Fun; basket, leathercraft, tissue picture, wood.
Paige Enterprises; freight and passenger car, structure, trackside detailing way, HO structure.
Paragon Needlecraft; needlecraft.
Party Bazaar; candlemaking.
Patterns for Pennies, Inc.; instruction for perfectly fitting garments.
Hazel Pearson Handi Craft; floral, macrame, synthetic straw.
J. C. Penney Co., Inc.
Peri's Homework; belt and bag, needlepoint, quickpoint.
Pins & Needles; patchwork.
Pioneer Crafts; stitchery flower pillow.
Plastruct; railroad.
Plaza Artists Materials, Inc.; screen processing.
Plush Point Patterns by Marcia Podell; satin needlepoint.
Port Lobster Co.; authentic oak lobster trap.
PRO Custom Hobbies; model railroad.
Pursenalities Inc.; fabric purse, frame type bags, shoulder bags.
The Putter Shop
Quilts and Other Comforts; pre-cut plastic patterns.
R/C Cars International; airplanes.
Radio Shack; fiber optic.
Railway Express; metal building, model railroad, plastic building, wood buildings.
Ramont's Floral Arts Studio; flowers.
Carol Rice Creatives; carnation, daisy,

flower, large cabbage rose and poinsettia, poppy, rose.
D. E. Rinck; cuckoo clock.
Rombins' Nest Farm; beaded flower.
Rub 'N Buff; batik.
The Rusty Nail; calico cat, calico gingerbread man, calico mobil, calico owl, calico rooster, calico santa, gingham puppy.
Mrs. W. Bradley Ryan; embroidery.
S & W Crafts Mfg.; wood handicraft.
Salyer Publishing Co.; stencils.
Sandeen's Scandinavian Gift & Card Shop; beginners, rosemaling.
Sangray Corp.; transfer process.
Santos Miniatures; model figure.
Sav-On-Crafts; beads, candlemaking, leather craft, ornaments, shag rug.
Savin Handcrafts; basket weaving, caning, caning door panels, caning footstool, caning seat backs, caning seats, seat weaving.
Sax Arts & Crafts; candlemaking, carving, jewelrymaking, leather craft, mosaic, plastic model, screen processing.
Scandinavian Rya Rugs; pillow, rya rug.
Schneider's; gemstone.
Schober Organ Corp.; electronic organ.
Schrock's, The House of Hobbies & Crafts; rugs-by-number.
Jack V. Schuller, Inc.
Scientific Gas Products; fiber optic.
Scientific Models Inc.; clipper model, wood ship model.
Scott Scientific Inc.; inkle loom craft, rock tumbling.
Screen Process Supplies Mfg. Co.; screen process.
Sculpture House; sculpture.
Sculpture Services Inc.; sculpture.
Sears, Roebuck & Co.; afghan, clock, crochet, knitting, punch hook rug, purse, toy, Christmas ornament.
Henry Seligman Co. Inc.; needlepoint.
Sewakers Industries Inc.; interchangeable handbag.
Shaker Workshops Inc.; shaker artifacts, shaker furniture, wood paints, wood stains.
Sheru Bead Boutique Shop; bead embroidery, bead-art, beaded fruits, boutique items, rings, sequin roses.
Shillcraft; hooked rug.
Ships Unlimited; model ship building, plastic power boats, plastic sail boats, wood power boats, wood sail boats.
Siderod Shop; model railroad.
Sig Manufacturing Co., Inc.; model aircraft.
Sign of the Arrow; needlepoint.
Sinclair's Auto Miniatures Inc.; auto delux.
Skil-Crafts Division; bead, bead loom, jewel decorated purses, leather, silk applique pictures.
Skon; Swedish rya.
Jane Snead Samplers; pin cushion, sampler.
Spaulding & Frost Co., Inc.
Spencer Gifts Inc.; bottle cutter, lamp wiring.
Spincraft; hand spinning.
The Squadron Shop; scale model.
Standard Doll Co.; accessories, doll house.
Star Diamond Industries; tumbling.
Star Models; narrow gauge model railroad passenger car
The Stitchery; crewel embroidery and creative stitchery, needlepoint.
Struck Corp.; build-it-yourself power hacksaw.
Studio Twelve; stitchery.
Sturbridge Yankee Workshop; antiquing, decorating.
Stylecraft of Baltimore; bottle cutter.
Sudberry House; crewel handbags, needlepoint handbag.
Sue's Custom Quilting; pillows, quilts.
Suncoast Models; buildings, freight cars, freight stations, metal models, model structures, plastic models, wood models.
Sunray Yarn House; crochet, knitting, needlepoint.
Sunset House; crochet ring.

Craft Category Index
Kits—Knitting

Supreme Watch Material Co.; tool.
Supreme Handicrafts; biblical banner.
Surburbia, Inc.; clock, stained glass, Christmas card.
Surma Book & Music Store; Ukrainian egg decorating.
E. Suydam & Co.; HO scale model building.
Swan-Son; decoupage.
Switched On, Ltd.; tiffany lamp.
Talisman Crafts
Tandy Leather Co.; belt, billfold, furniture, gun holsters, handbag, key case, saddles, watchband.
Joseph Tartas; beginner jewelrymaking.
Taylor House
Terminal Hobby Shop; model railroad.
Thomas C. Thompson; enameling.
Thrift Mailmart; clown doll sew.
Thumbelina Needlework Shop; Danish needlecraft.
Tillalla Inc.; assorted rya, Scandinavian embroidery.
Cheryl Todd; "Granny pin" jewelry.
Town & Country Crafts; jewelry, old inne sign.
Trailcraft Inc.; canoe building, of wood and canvas, or molded fiberglass.
Tree Toys; quilling.
Turnbull Looms; metal parts.
Tuxedo Yarn & Needlework; macrame crewel.
U. C. Hobby Center; model aircraft, plastic ships, wood ships.
United Abrasive Inc.; lapidary tool.
University Circle Publications and Supply Co.; enameling.
Vermont Toy Crafts; birch doll house, wood toy.
Lillian Vernon; basket purse, Christmas ornaments, grospoint purse, mini-flower pot, needlepoint, shadow-box keepsake.
Veteran Leather Co., Inc.; leather.
Vicki's Patience Unlimited; bargello, hand-painted needlepoint.
Victoria Gifts; cross-stitch samplers, needlecraft.
Village Candle & Craft; incense.
Village Designs; perfect fitting.
Wallis Designs; build-it-yourself potter's wheel.
Walnut Hill Co.; candle, floater candles, pillar candles, voltive candles.
Wm. Walthers Inc.; freight car, passenger car.
Montgomery Ward & Co., Inc.; afghan, lapidary, needlecraft.
Lee Wards; afghan, beading, boutique trim, crewel, crochet, decoupage purse, floral, floral memorials, hanging lamp, knitting, latch hook, macrame, punchwork, rug hooking, stitchery, window shade, wood sculpture, Christmas items.
Westwood Ceramic Supply Co.; latex rubber mold making.
Whisper Farm Furs; afghans, fur tote bags.
Whistle Stop; model.
Wichelt Import Co.; Norwegian embroidery, Swedish embroidery.
Wilfred Enterprises; doll.
Williams Bros.; engine pipeline parts.
Erica Wilson Needleworks; crewel, needlepoint, original designs.
Wonoco Yarn Co.; crochet, embroidery, knitting.
Wool-Art Studios Inc.; crewel.
Woolcraft Ltd.; needlepoint, petitpoint.
W. Wooley & Co.; candle, plaster, resin.
The World of Stitch 'N Knit; crewel, embroidery, needlepoint.
Wyco Yarn Co.; crochet, handbag, knitting, needlecraft.
The Yarn Nook; Norwegian needlecraft.
Yarns Galore; needlepoint.
Yarns Unlimited; crochet, embroidery.
Yield House; furniture.
F. C. Ziegler Co.; embroidery.

knitting *(see also Yarns)*
accessories
    R. S. Duncan & Co.
afghans
    Merribee

automatic knitting machines
  Brother International Corp.
  Genie
  Knitking
  Studio Yarn Farms Inc.
  A. C. Weber & Co., Inc.
books
  Book Barn
  Chilton Book Co.
  Drake Publishers Inc.
  Harper & Row, Publishers Inc.
  Hearthside Press
  P. C. Herwig Co., Inc.
  Knitking
  Liveright
  Mon Tricot
  Museum Books Inc.
  Phentex, Inc.
  Powell
  Random House Inc.
  Reade Knitting Designs
  Reynolds Yarns Inc.
  Robin & Russ Handweavers
  Sancraft Industries
  Standard Doll Co.
  Stein & Day
  Studio Yarn Farms Inc.
  Taplinger Publishing Co.
  M. Turner
  William Unger & Co. Inc.
  The Unicorn
  Van Nostrand Reinhold Co.
  Viking Press
  Wool 'N Wick
  The Yarn and Soda Shop
children's knitting patterns
  Knit-O-Graf Pattern Co.
club plans
  Reynolds Yarns Inc.
computerized knitting machine
  Brother International Corp.
  Studio Yarn Farms Inc.
corded magnifier
  M. Turner
doll clothes knitting patterns
  Virginia Lakin
  Mrs. Rossi
hand knitting yarns
  International Creations
home study courses
  Brother International Corp.

kits
  Fairtex Distributing Co.
  Paul K. Guillow Inc.
  International Creations
  Mary Maxim Inc.
  Melrose Yarn Co., Inc.
  Merribee
  Needlewoman Shop
  Sears, Roebuck & Co.
  Sunray Yarn House
  Montgomery Ward & Co., Inc.
  Lee Wards
  Whisper Farm Furs
  Wonoco Yarn Co.
  Wyco Yarn Co.
knitting accessories
  Sunray Yarn House
  A. C. Weber & Co., Inc.
  Wyco Yarn Co.
  Yarns Unlimited
knitting carrying bags
  Henry Seligman Co. Inc.
knitting instructions
  Bea Freeman Enterprises
knitting machines
  House of Yarn & Crafts
  Liveright
  Sav-On-Crafts
  Lee Wards
knitting needle holder
  United Specialties Co.
knitting needles
  Melrose Yarn Co., Inc.
knitting patterns
  Brunswick Worsted Mills
  Liveright
  Sharon's Petite Sherre
knitting rings
  Sunset House
knitting stands
  Henry Seligman Co. Inc.
knitting supplies
  Fiber to Fabric
  The Handcrafters
  Merribee
  Lee Wards
  The Yarn and Soda Shop
knitting worsted
  R. S. Duncan & Co.
knitting yarns
  J & H Clasgens Co.

Craft Category Index
Knitting—Lace

    Cliveden Yarns
    Conlin Yarns
    Filature Lemieux Inc.
    The Handcrafters
    House of Yarn & Crafts
    Melrose Yarn Co., Inc.
    Tahki Imports, Limited
    Lee Wards
    Wool 'N Wick
magazines
    Good Housekeeping Needlecraft
    Knitking Magazine
    Ladies Home Journal Needlecraft
    McCall's Needlework & Crafts
    McCall's Pattern Fashions
    1001 Fashion & Needlecraft Ideas
    Woman's Day Knit & Stitch
    Woman's Day Needlework Ideas
    Woman's Day 101 Sweaters to Knit and Crochet
    The Workbasket
newspapers
    House of Yarn & Crafts
pattern cards
    Genie
patterns
    R. S. Duncan & Co.
    Bea Freeman Enterprises
    Gloria
sweater wheels
    Bea Freeman Enterprises
    Lee Wards

lace making, netting, tatting
  adjustable hairpin lace loom
    Rosemond Hobbycraft
  bobbin lacemaking
    Osma G. Tod Weaving & Lace Studio
  bobbin winders
    Frederick J. Fawcett, Inc.
    Osma G. Tod Weaving & Lace Studio
  bobbins
    Alfred Decker
  books
    Book Barn
    Craftool Co.
    Crafty Ideas
    Robin & Russ Handweavers
    Rosemond Hobbycraft
    Sancraft Industries
    Sterling Publishing Co. Inc.
    Textile Crafts
    Osma G. Tod Weaving & Lace Studio
    The Unicorn
  braids for Battenburg lace
    Muriel N. Charney
  cotton lace
    Home-Sew Inc.
    National Artcraft Supply Co.
  Danish bobbins
    Osma G. Tod Weaving & Lace Studio
  gold lace borders
    Harrower House of Decoupage
  gold lace frames
    Harrower House of Decoupage
  gold lace ornaments
    Harrower House of Decoupage
  hairpin lace patterns
    Kile-Gore Designs
  home study courses
    Doris Southard
  kits
    Frank J. Nelson
  lace
    Lace Lady
    Two Brothers Inc.
  lace prickers
    Osma G. Tod Weaving & Lace Studio
  lacemaking materials
    Alfred Decker
    Some Place
  lacemaking tools
    Some Place
  lacers
    House of Gould
  laces
    Home-Sew Inc.
    Kieffer's Lingerie Fabric & Supplies
    Skil-Crafts Division
  leaflets
    Mrs. Frieda Koudelka
    Osma G. Tod Weaving & Lace Studio
  magazines
    The Workbasket
  netting needles
    Reisinger Net Co.
  netting patterns
    Frank J. Nelson
  nylon lace
    Home-Sew Inc.
    Nucleus
  organizations
    International Old Lacers

Craft Category Index
Lace—Lampshade

polyester lace
   Home-Sew Inc.
starched lace
   Holiday Handicrafts, Inc.
tatting
   Mary Maxim Inc.
   Merribee
wooden tatting shuttles
   Alfred Decker

lampmaking and accessories
   American Handicrafts
   Angelo Bros. Co.
   Bob's Arts & Crafts
alcohol lamps
   Delco Craft Center, Inc.
books
   Chilton Book Co.
   Craftool Co.
   Crafty Ideas
brass lamp ornaments
   Angelo Bros. Co.
china lamps
   Renaldy's
clamp-on lamps
   Robin & Russ Handweavers
decorative lamp chain
   Angelo Bros. Co.
electrical parts
   National Artcraft Supply Co.
glass lamps
   Renaldy's
kits
   American Handicrafts
   Angelo Bros. Co.
   Baxwood Crafters
   Carl Hepp Mosaic Co.
   Herter's, Inc.
   Spencer Gifts Inc.
   Switched On, Ltd.
   Lee Wards
lamp ball ornaments
   Angelo Bros. Co.
lamp bandings
   Angelo Bros. Co.
lamp bases
   Angelo Bros. Co.
lamp canopies
   Angelo Bros. Co.
lamp filigrees
   Angelo Bros. Co.
lamp finials
   Angelo Bros. Co.
lamp finishes
   Angelo Bros. Co.
lamp frames
   Specialty Products
lamp marble bases
   Angelo Bros. Co.
lamp parts
   Angelo Bros. Co.
   Bergen Arts & Crafts, Inc.
   Albert Constantine & Son Inc.
   Craftsman Wood Service Co.
   Diedricks Crafts
   Gyro Lamp Supply Corp.
   Loretta's Ceramic Studio
   Minnesota Woodworkers Supply Co.
   Natcol Crafts, Inc.
   National Artcraft Supply Co.
   Ohio Ceramic Supply Inc.
lamp switchplates
   Angelo Bros. Co.
lamp tassels
   Angelo Bros. Co.
lamp wiring diagrams
   Gyro Lamp Supply Corp.
lamps
   Gilman's
lampshade holders
   Angelo Bros. Co.
lampshade patterns
   Unique Creations
lampshade supplies
   Unique Creations
lampshades
   Craftsman Supply House
   Lightsaround, Inc.
light bulbs
   Angelo Bros. Co.
lighting supplies
   Lightsaround, Inc.
replacement burners for oil lamps
   Gyro Lamp Supply Corp.
teakite lamp bases
   Angelo Bros. Co.
wood lamp bases
   Angelo Bros. Co.

lampshade making
books
   Unique Creations

Craft Category Index
Lampshade—Lapidary

lampshade forms
  Whittemore-Durgin Glass Co.
lampshade holders
  Angelo Bros. Co.
lampshade patterns
  Unique Creations
lampshade supplies
  Unique Creations
lampshades
  Craftsman Supply House
  Lightsaround, Inc.

lapidary
abrasive disks
  Foredom Electric Co.
abrasive points
  Foredom Electric Co.
adhesives
  The Ducketts
agate cabochons
  Adris Oriental Gem & Art Corp.
  Tumblecraft
agate carnelian
  Murray American Corp.
agates
  Aspen Lapidary
  Biship's House of Gems
  Mississippi Petrified Forest
  Sandy Symons
  The Treasure Chest
  Tumblecraft
  Twin Peaks Rock Shop
  G. Weidinger
alcohol burners
  Gilman's
alexandrite
  De Lapa Mining Inc.
  International Import Co.
amazonite
  Murray American Corp.
amazonite baroques
  Jim's Rock Shop
amber
  Purcelli's Gems
amber agate
  M. W. Jackson & Assoc.
amethyst
  Aspen Lapidary
  Biship's House of Gems
  Commercial Mineral Corp.
  De Lapa Mining Inc.
  Gem-O-Rama, Inc.
  Inter-Ocean Trade Co.
  International Import Co.
  Melbourn Gem Co.
  Murray American Corp.
  Norlene Lapidary
  M. Nowotny
  Oceanside Gem Imports, Inc.
  Purcelli's Gems
  Syn-Crer Creations
  Transworld Trading Co.
  Treasure of the Pirates, Inc.
  G. Weidinger
  Weisz Import Export Corp.
andalusite
  Commercial Mineral Corp.
  De Lapa Mining Inc.
  W. D. Hudson, Jr.
  International Import Co.
  Oceanside Gem Imports, Inc.
  Purcelli's Gems
apache tears
  Panther International Ltd.
apatite
  Norlene Lapidary
aquamarine
  Harry Bookstone
  Commercial Mineral Corp.
  De Lapa Mining Inc.
  Inter-Ocean Trade Co.
  International Import Co.
  Murray American Corp.
  Norlene Lapidary
  Oceanside Gem Imports, Inc.
  Purcelli's Gems
  Syn-Crer Creations
  Weisz Import Export Corp.
arbors
  Green's Rock & Lapidary Ltd.
  Lindell Industries
  Lortone Inc.
Arkansas minerals
  Wright's Rock Shop
aurora borealis beads
  The Beadcraft Corner/Beadcraft Club
Australian chrysoprase
  Australian Imports
Australian gem rough
  Minex Lapidary Supplies
Australian jade
  Interlectric House of Fine Australian Opals

Australian opals
  Australian Exports
  Australian Imports
  Crown Gems Co.
  Frank's Jewelry & Gem Shop
  Gem-O-Rama, Inc.
  Interlectric House of Fine Australian Opals
  Walter E. Johansen
  Syn-Crer Creations
  G. Weidinger
avalon hematite
  Timberline Lake Rock Shop
aventurine
  M. Nowotny
  Syn-Crer Creations
  The Treasure Chest
aventurine balls
  Edwards Jewelry Co.
balls
  Diamond-Pro Unlimited
banded agate
  M. W. Jackson & Assoc.
bansanite
  Starfire Lapidary
barite of roses
  Mission Rocks
baroques
  Alessi Lapidary Supplies
  Harry Bookstone
belts
  The Ducketts
beryl zircon
  International Import Co.
beryls
  International Import Co.
  Lochs
  Oceanside Gem Imports, Inc.
  Purcelli's Gems
  Syn-Crer Creations
black agate
  M. W. Jackson & Assoc.
black agate nodules
  Beaver Canyon Campground
black jade
  Torrington Rock Shop
black nephrite
  Gene's Rock Shop
black onyx
  Weisz Import Export Corp.

black opals
  Australian Gem Trading Co.
  Geode Industries
  International Import Co.
black star sapphire
  W. D. Hudson, Jr.
  Syn-Crer Creations
blade flanges
  Star Diamond Industries
blades
  Jenkins Lapidary Equipment
  Weidinger Inc.
bloodstone
  Adris Oriental Gem & Art Corp.
  Dowse's Lapidary Supply, Inc.
  M. Nowotny
  Panther International Ltd.
  Syn-Crer Creations
bloodstone baroques
  Jim's Rock Shop
bloodstone rough material
  Gem Center, U.S.A.
blue agate
  Beaver Canyon Campground
  M. W. Jackson & Assoc.
blue Australian sapphires
  Crown Gems Co.
blue calcite
  Panther International Ltd.
blue fire flash moonstone
  Minerals & Gems
blue lace agate
  Libra Gems
blue star sapphire
  Gems International
books
  Australian Gem Trading Co.
  Bet-Roc Enterprises Inc.
  Book Barn
  Chilton Book Co.
  Covington Engineering Corp.
  Craftool Co.
  Crafty Ideas
  Crown Publishers
  Frank's Jewelry & Gem Shop
  Gemological Institute of America
  Gems & Minerals
  Lapidary Journal Book Dept.
  Random House Inc.
  The Victors
  C. R. Wells

Craft Category Index
Lapidary—Lapidary

botryoidal jade
   Gene's Rock Shop
bouquet slabs
   Twin Peaks Rock Shop
Brazilian fire agate
   Michigan Lapidary Supply Co.
Brazilian gems
   Inter-Ocean Trade Co.
   Oceanside Gem Imports, Inc.
Brazilian opal
   Frank's Jewelry & Gem Shop
Brazilian quartz
   Starfire Lapidary
brazilianite
   Murray American Corp.
brilliant cut diamonds
   Harry Z. Kurs
bulk opals
   Australian Imports
Burma cabochons
   Crown Cultured Pearl Corp.
cab heaters
   Shipley's Mineral House
cabbers
   Exactra-Craft Corp.
cabbing amethyst
   Gems International
cabbing rough
   W. D. Hudson, Jr.
cabochon gemstones
   International Import Co.
cabochon machines
   Reed Industries
cabochon preforms
   Elvin
cabochon rough material
   Weisz Import Export Corp.
cabochons
   R. C. Baker
   Harry Bookstone
   Craft House
   Crown Cultured Pearl Corp.
   Dover Scientific Co.
   Ebersole Lapidary Supply Inc.
   Edwards Jewelry Co.
   Gemex Co.
   Gilman's
   Jim's Rock Shop
   Walter E. Johansen
   Jim Kesterson
   Minerals & Gems
   Minex Lapidary Supplies
   Mission Rocks
   Mueller's
   Murray American Corp.
   Syn-Crer Creations
   Treasure of the Pirates, Inc.
   G. Weidinger
California black sea fan coral
   Wearden's
carnelian
   Virgil Owens
   Panther International Ltd.
carnelian agate gemballs
   Anozira Jewelers
carved wood mineral display stands
   Weaver's Gems and Minerals
casting block
   Solartherm Co.
casting crucibles
   Solartherm Co.
cat's-eye
   Harry Bookstone
   International Import Co.
   Walter E. Johansen
   Syn-Crer Creations
chatham emerald rough
   Panther International Ltd.
cherry opals
   Andria Bree Gem Co.
chloromelanite
   Jade World/Wilderness Originals
chrysoberyl
   W. D. Hudson, Jr.
   International Import Co.
   Oceanside Gem Imports, Inc.
   Purcelli's Gems
   Syn-Crer Creations
chrysocolla
   The Jewelry Mart
   G. Weidinger
chrysoprase
   Walter E. Johansen
   W. L. Maison Opals, Etc.
   Murray American Corp.
   Purcelli's Gems
   C. R. Wells
chrysoprase rough
   Minex Lapidary Supplies
citrine
   Commercial Mineral Corp.
   De Lapa Mining Inc.

Inter-Ocean Trade Co.
International Import Co.
Norlene Lapidary
Oceanside Gem Imports, Inc.
Trader South
Treasure of the Pirates, Inc.
G. Weidinger
Weisz Import Export Corp.

clear quartz
Beaver Canyon Campground
Commercial Mineral Corp.
Trader South

clearcreek jadeite
Gene's Rock Shop

club plans
Artrox Rock of the Month Club
Trader South

coconut geodes
The Treasure Chest

colored diamond
Industrial Diamond Tool Co. Inc.

cones
Diamond-Pro Unlimited

coral
The Collector's Cabinet
The Freed Co.
International Import Co.
Max of Dallas
Panther International Ltd.

corundum boules
Gems Galore

crazy lace agate
Dowse's Lapidary Supply, Inc.

crinoids
Mission Rocks

crystallized mineral specimens
Nature's Treasures

crystals
The Fluorite Shop
Green's Rock & Lapidary Ltd.
Inter-Ocean Trade Co.
Max of Dallas

cultured pearls
Anozira Jewelers
Crown Cultured Pearl Corp.
Liberty Gem & Supply

custom-made lapidary equipment
Reed Industries

cut amethyst
Crown Gems Co.

cut aquamarine
Crown Gems Co.

cut chrysoprase
Interlectric House of Fine Australian Opals

cut gemstones
Harry Bookstone
Crown Gems Co.
Gem-O-Rama, Inc.
Interlectric House of Fine Australian Opals
Lakewood Lapidary
Virgil V. Lundell
Purcelli's Gems

cut opals
Crown Gems Co.

cut peridot
Crown Gems Co.

cut stones
M & M Distributors
Montana Assay Office
Stop 'N Rock Shop
Syn-Crer Creations
Universal Wirecraft Jewelry Co.
G. Weidinger

cut turquoise
Crown Gems Co.

cutting laps
Walter E. Johansen

cutting machines
Gilman's

cutting stones
Swensons Lapidary Equipment, Inc.

cuttle bone
T. B. Hagstoz & Son

decorative mounts
Nature's Treasures

demagnetizer
Gilman's

devonian hexagonaria colony coral
Quinn Mineral

diamond abrasives
The Ducketts

diamond arbors
Gem Tool Specialties

diamond bar wheel dressers
Gem Tec Diamond Tool Co.

diamond blades
Covington Engineering Corp.
Earth Treasures
Farmers Gem and Rock Shop

Craft Category Index
Lapidary—Lapidary

    Gem Tool Specialties
    Star Diamond Industries
diamond burrs
    Gem Tool Specialties
diamond carvers
    Metro Diamond Drill Co.
diamond coated files
    Metro Diamond Drill Co.
diamond compounds
    Walter E. Johansen
    Jack V. Schuller, Inc.
    Sinkankas Diamond Products
diamond cores
    Gem Tool Specialties
diamond crystals
    Commercial Mineral Corp.
    Panther International Ltd.
diamond disks
    Gem Tool Specialties
diamond drills
    Gem Tool Specialties
    Geode Industries
diamond equipment
    Terra Products
diamond gem maker
    Gem Tec Diamond Tool Co.
diamond impregnated core drills
    Metro Diamond Drill Co.
diamond lapidaries
    Gem Tool Specialties
diamond laps
    Jack V. Schuller, Inc.
diamond machines
    Gem Tool Specialties
diamond pads
    Gem Tool Specialties
diamond points
    Gem Tool Specialties
diamond powders
    Aleta's Rock Shop
    Gem Tool Specialties
    Industrial Diamond Tool Co. Inc.
    Walter E. Johansen
diamond products
    Green's Rock & Lapidary Ltd.
    Highland Park Manufacturing
    Jack V. Schuller, Inc.
diamond saw blades
    Highland Park Manufacturing
diamond saws
    Raytech Industries Inc.

diamond tools
    Gem Tec Diamond Tool Co.
    Gem Tool Specialties
diamond wheels
    Diamond-Pro Unlimited
    Gem Tec Diamond Tool Co.
    Gem Tool Specialties
diamonds
    Biship's House of Gems
    Diamond Sales Co.
    H & A Mfg. Corp.
    International Import Co.
    The Jewelry Mart
    Syn-Crer Creations
dies
    Gilman's
diffraction jewels
    Edmund Scientific Co.
dinosaur bone
    Dowse's Lapidary Supply, Inc.
diopside moonstone
    Purcelli's Gems
diopside star
    International Import Co.
dops
    Walter E. Johansen
    A. D. McBurney
electric carver
    Green's Rock & Lapidary Ltd.
electric wax spatula
    Green's Rock & Lapidary Ltd.
electrical lapidary equipment
    Lapidabrade Inc.
emeralds
    Adris Oriental Gem & Art Corp.
    De Lapa Mining Inc.
    Diamond Sales Co.
    H & A Mfg. Corp.
    W. D. Hudson, Jr.
    International Import Co.
    Murray American Corp.
    Syn-Crer Creations
    Transworld Trading Co.
    G. Weidinger
enstatite
    Murray American Corp.
epidote
    Panther International Ltd.
exotic minerals
    The Collector's Cabinet

eye loupes
  Gemological Institute of America
facet grade fluorite
  Beaver Canyon Campground
facet heads
  Covington Engineering Corp.
facet laps
  Covington Engineering Corp.
facet preforms
  Lee Lapidaries
facet units
  Lee Lapidaries
faceted garnets
  Anozira Jewelers
faceted gemstones
  De Lapa Mining Inc.
  Dover Scientific Co.
  International Import Co.
  Minerals & Gems
faceted stones
  Biship's House of Gems
  The Ducketts
  Gemex Co.
  Gilman's
  Jim's Rock Shop
  Michigan Lapidary Supply Co.
  Mueller's
  Transworld Trading Co.
  Weisz Import Export Corp.
faceter's trim slab saw
  A. D. McBurney
faceting amethyst
  Gems International
faceting equipment
  Jim's Rock Shop
  Lochs
  Stop 'N Rock Shop
faceting instruments
  Exactra-Craft Corp.
  MDR Mfg. Co., Inc.
faceting machines
  Geode Industries
  Henry B. Graves Co.
  Walter E. Johansen
  Trader South
faceting stones
  Treasure of the Pirates, Inc.
faceting supplies
  Brad's Rock Shop
  The Ducketts
  Walter E. Johansen
  Stop 'N Rock Shop
  Trader South
faceting units
  Aleta's Rock Shop
  Farmers Gem and Rock Shop
  Gilman's
  Industrial Diamond Tool Co. Inc.
  Stanley Lapidary Products
  Star Diamond Industries
  Swensons Lapidary Equipment, Inc.
fetishes heishe
  Panther International Ltd.
fine silver casting grains
  H. A. Cole
finished gemstones
  Smokey Mtn. Rock Shop
finishers
  Highland Park Manufacturing
fire agate
  Crown Gems Co.
  M. Nowotny
fire cut agate
  Crown Gems Co.
fire opals
  International Import Co.
firey astrilite
  Walter E. Johansen
flat laps
  Gilman's
flexible shaft machines
  Gems Galore
Florida coral
  G. Weidinger
fluorescent agate
  M. W. Jackson & Assoc.
foreign gem rough
  Minex Lapidary Supplies
friend eggs
  Sandy Symons
ganoin ivory
  Ken Kyte
garnet
  Biship's House of Gems
  Ed Brandt Stone Co.
  W. D. Hudson, Jr.
  Inter-Ocean Trade Co.
  International Import Co.
  Jewelart Inc.
  Jim's Rock Shop
  Lochs
  Minerals & Gems

Craft Category Index
Lapidary—Lapidary

Norlene Lapidary
Oceanside Gem Imports, Inc.
Panther International Ltd.
Purcelli's Gems
Stop 'N Rock Shop
Syn-Crer Creations
Trader South
Transworld Trading Co.
Tumblecraft
Weisz Import Export Corp.
garnet cabochons
    Stop 'N Rock Shop
gem beads
    Bead Game
gem cutting equipment
    Earth Treasures
    Treasure of the Pirates, Inc.
gem detectors
    Gemological Institute of America
gem drills
    Lindell Industries
    Mohave Industries
gem faceting supplies
    Earth Treasures
gem findings
    Aleta's Rock Shop
gem graders
    Gemological Institute of America
gem grinders
    Star Diamond Industries
gem makers
    Gilman's
    Green's Rock & Lapidary Ltd.
    Star Diamond Industries
gem making
    Allcraft Tool & Supply Co.
gem polishers
    Dorothy Blake
    Star Diamond Industries
gem polishing supplies
    Earth Treasures
    Rombins' Nest Farm
gem rock
    Michigan Lapidary Supply Co.
gem rough material
    Andria Bree Gem Co.
    Crown Gems Co.
    Geophile International
    Ken Kyte
    Murray American Corp.

gem saws
    Aleta's Rock Shop
gem scales
    Gilman's
    Morang Balance Co.
gem shops
    Covington Engineering Corp.
gem vises
    Gilman's
gemballs
    Gemex Co.
Gemmaster faceting laps
    MDR Mfg. Co., Inc.
gemstone accessories
    Crown Gems Co.
gemstone baroques
    Jim's Rock Shop
gemstone cutting material
    The Treasure Chest
gemstone polishers
    Surburbia, Inc.
gemstone rough material
    Stop 'N Rock Shop
gemstone solutions
    Crown Gems Co.
gemstone supplies
    Jade World/Wilderness Originals
gemstones
    Australian Exports
    Australian Imports
    Bead Game
    Bourget Bros. Gems & Minerals
    Ed Brandt Stone Co.
    Commercial Mineral Corp.
    Diamond Sales Co.
    Dowse's Lapidary Supply, Inc.
    Geophile International
    Gilman's
    Green's Rock & Lapidary Ltd.
    H & A Mfg. Corp.
    Jewelart Inc.
    J. J. Jewelcraft
    Jim's Rock Shop
    Walter E. Johansen
    Jim Kesterson
    Lakewood Lapidary
    Liberty Gem & Supply
    Libra Gems
    Mueller's
    Norlene Lapidary
    M. Nowotny

Craft Category Index
Lapidary—Lapidary

Panther International Ltd.
C. W. Somers & Co.
Treasure of the Pirates, Inc.
geode cutters
    Stonehouse
giant quartz
    Beaver Canyon Campground
glacier green jade
    Jade World/Wilderness Originals
glass cabochons
    Jewelart Inc.
    Tumblecraft
glass gems
    Bergen Arts & Crafts, Inc.
    Delco Craft Center, Inc.
    Skil-Crafts Division
golden beryl
    Norlene Lapidary
golden labradorite
    Dowse's Lapidary Supply, Inc.
golden sapphire
    Syn-Crer Creations
golden tiger's-eye
    Craft House
    Libra Gems
goldstone balls
    Edwards Jewelry Co.
goldstones
    M. Nowotny
    G. Weidinger
green agate gemballs
    Anozira Jewelers
green aventurine
    Libra Gems
green beryl
    Inter-Ocean Trade Co.
    Syn-Crer Creations
green fluorite
    Beaver Canyon Campground
green grossular garnets
    Beaver Canyon Campground
green malachite
    Gem-O-Rama, Inc.
green moss
    Dowse's Lapidary Supply, Inc.
green nephrite
    Gene's Rock Shop
green plume
    Bitterroot Lapidary Supply
green quartz
    Commercial Mineral Corp.

green tree agates
    Dowse's Lapidary Supply, Inc.
grinding compounds
    Aleta's Rock Shop
grinding equipment
    Brad's Rock Shop
    Mohave Industries
grinding units
    Aleta's Rock Shop
grinding wheels
    Covington Engineering Corp.
    Jenkins Lapidary Equipment
    Star Diamond Industries
hickoryite
    Dowse's Lapidary Supply, Inc.
hollow geodes
    Panther International Ltd.
home study courses
    Gemological Institute of America
honey cat's-eye
    Craft House
Idaho agates
    M. W. Jackson & Assoc.
Idaho tapestry agate
    Bitterroot Lapidary Supply
imitation gemstones
    Grieger's Inc.
    Liberty Gem & Supply
imperial chrysophrase
    Gem-O-Rama, Inc.
Indian gemstones
    Syn-Crer Creations
Indian moonstone
    Biship's House of Gems
Indian stones
    Adris Oriental Gem & Art Corp.
intaglios
    Jeweler's Emporium
iolite
    Commercial Mineral Corp.
    International Import Co.
    Syn-Crer Creations
Iowa Betoskey stone
    Quinn Mineral
ivory jade
    Jade World/Wilderness Originals
ivory plume
    Bitterroot Lapidary Supply
jade
    Bergsten Jade Co.
    Biship's House of Gems

Craft Category Index
Lapidary—Lapidary

    Crown Cultured Pearl Corp.
    International Import Co.
    Jade World/Wilderness Originals
    Jim's Rock Shop
    Virgil V. Lundell
    Michigan Lapidary Supply Co.
    New World Jade Co.
    M. Nowotny
    Purcelli's Gems
    G. Weidinger
jade baroques
    Jim's Rock Shop
jadeite
    Jade World/Wilderness Originals
jasper
    Ed Brandt Stone Co.
    Syn-Crer Creations
    The Treasure Chest
    C. R. Wells
jewel stone assortments
    De Mallie Crafts
jewelry stones
    Veronica
jewels
    Country Crafts
    Gibsons Creations
    Holiday Craft
    Jeweler's Emporium
    Kit Kraft
    Natalie Originals Studio
    Supreme Handicrafts
    Taylor House
kits
    Australian Exports
    Covington Engineering Corp.
    Craftool Co.
    Earth Treasures
    Frank's Jewelry & Gem Shop
    Green's Rock & Lapidary Ltd.
    Koehler's Craft Outlet
    Magic Circle Corp.
    Schneider's
    Scott Scientific Inc.
    Star Diamond Industries
    United Abrasive Inc.
    Montgomery Ward & Co., Inc.
Kingman turquoise
    Panther International Ltd.
kornerupine
    Purcelli's Gems

kunzite
    Commercial Mineral Corp.
    Inter-Ocean Trade Co.
    International Import Co.
    Norlene Lapidary
    Oceanside Gem Imports, Inc.
    Purcelli's Gems
labradorite
    M. Nowotny
laguna
    Bonnie's Rock Shop
lapidary abrasives
    Aspen Lapidary
    Minnesota Lapidary Supply Inc.
    Swensons Lapidary Equipment, Inc.
lapidary belt sanders
    Great Western Equipment Co.
lapidary carving tools
    Industrial Diamond Tool Co. Inc.
lapidary cleaning accessories
    L & R Manufacturing Co.
lapidary combination units
    Farmers Gem and Rock Shop
    Great Western Equipment Co.
lapidary compounds
    Industrial Diamond Tool Co. Inc.
    Swensons Lapidary Equipment, Inc.
lapidary cutting materials
    Bitterroot Lapidary Supply
    Frank's Jewelry & Gem Shop
    Gem Center, U.S.A.
    Mississippi Petrified Forest
    Sandy Symons
    Tektos
    Wright's Rock Shop
lapidary dressers
    Industrial Diamond Tool Co. Inc.
lapidary drills
    Industrial Diamond Tool Co. Inc.
lapidary equipment
    Alessi Lapidary Supplies
    Charbonneau's Lapidary Service
    Colorado Geological Industries Inc.
    Covington Engineering Corp.
    Dowse's Lapidary Supply, Inc.
    Earth Treasures
    Ebersole Lapidary Supply Inc.
    Gems Galore
    Geophile International
    Gilman's
    Great Western Equipment Co.

Craft Category Index
Lapidary—Lapidary

Highland Park Manufacturing
Hillquist
Lee Lapidaries
Lindell Industries
Lortone Inc.
Main Service Co.
Minnesota Lapidary Supply Inc.
Prospector's Pouch
Silver & Gem Shop
Smokey Mtn. Rock Shop
Star Diamond Industries
Swensons Lapidary Equipment, Inc.
Treasure of the Pirates, Inc.
Trowbridge Crafts
Montgomery Ward & Co., Inc.
G. Weidinger
lapidary findings
   Charbonneau's Lapidary Service
   Ebersole Lapidary Supply Inc.
   Gilman's
   Jewelart Inc.
   Jim's Rock Shop
   Smokey Mtn. Rock Shop
lapidary grinders
   Beacon
   Covington Engineering Corp.
   Great Western Equipment Co.
   Lortone Inc.
   Raytech Industries Inc.
   Reed Industries
lapidary grits
   Brown's Rock & Lapidary Supplies
   Covington Engineering Corp.
   Scott Scientific Inc.
   Weidinger Inc.
lapidary historical scribes
   Industrial Diamond Tool Co. Inc.
lapidary laps
   Brad's Rock Shop
   Green's Rock & Lapidary Ltd.
   Industrial Diamond Tool Co. Inc.
   Lee Lapidaries
   Lortone Inc.
   Raytech Industries Inc.
   Trader South
lapidary machinery
   Aspen Lapidary
   Brad's Rock Shop
   Brown's Rock & Lapidary Supplies
   The Ducketts
   Farmers Gem and Rock Shop

   Green's Rock & Lapidary Ltd.
   Lindell Industries
   Max of Dallas
   A. D. McBurney
   Michigan Lapidary Supply Co.
   Minex Lapidary Supplies
   Minnesota Lapidary Supply Inc.
   Sax Arts & Crafts
   Smokey Mtn. Rock Shop
   Stanley Lapidary Products
lapidary material
   Gorin's Gem Arts & Rocks
   Mueller's
   Twin Peaks Rock Shop
   G. Weidinger
lapidary mountings
   Bonnie's Rock Shop
   Mueller's
lapidary polishing equipment
   Beacon
   Great Western Equipment Co.
lapidary rough material
   Melbourn Gem Co.
lapidary sanders
   Great Western Equipment Co.
lapidary saw blades
   Industrial Diamond Tool Co. Inc.
lapidary saws
   Beacon
   Brad's Rock Shop
   Industrial Diamond Tool Co. Inc.
   Lortone Inc.
   Reed Industries
lapidary supplies
   Aleta's Rock Shop
   Allcraft Tool & Supply Co.
   Aspen Lapidary
   Beacon
   Bet-Roc Enterprises Inc.
   Bonnie's Rock Shop
   Brown's Rock & Lapidary Supplies
   Colorado Geological Industries Inc.
   Craftool Co.
   Diamond-Pro Unlimited
   Dover Scientific Co.
   Dowse's Lapidary Supply, Inc.
   Earth Treasures
   Edmund Scientific Co.
   Farmers Gem and Rock Shop
   Gem Center, U.S.A.
   Gems Galore

Craft Category Index
Lapidary—Lapidary

Gems International
Geode Industries
Geophile International
Green's Rock & Lapidary Ltd.
Industrial Diamond Tool Co. Inc.
Jenkins Lapidary Equipment
J. J. Jewelcraft
Kachina Gem Co.
Lapidabrade Inc.
Marshall's Lapidary Co., Ltd.
Metro Diamond Drill Co.
Minnesota Lapidary Supply Inc.
Mississippi Petrified Forest
Mohave Industries
Ovgem Craft Supply Co.
Virgil Owens
Quinn Mineral
Raytech Industries Inc.
The Sandvigs
Jack V. Schuller, Inc.
Shipley's Mineral House
Silver & Gem Shop
Smokey Mtn. Rock Shop
Star Diamond Industries
Starfire Lapidary
Stonehouse
Swensons Lapidary Equipment, Inc.
Terra Products
3 M Company
Timberline Lake Rock Shop
Torrington Rock Shop
Trader South
The Treasure Chest
Treasure of the Pirates, Inc.
Trowbridge Crafts
Ultra-Violet Products, Inc.
United Abrasive Inc.
G. Weidinger
Woodward Ranch

lapidary templates
   Farmers Gem and Rock Shop

lapidary tools
   Aspen Lapidary
   Charbonneau's Lapidary Service
   Ebersole Lapidary Supply Inc.
   Farmers Gem and Rock Shop
   Minnesota Lapidary Supply Inc.
   Swensons Lapidary Equipment, Inc.
   United Abrasive Inc.
   G. Weidinger

lapidary tumblers
   Aleta's Rock Shop
   Bet-Roc Enterprises Inc.
   Farmers Gem and Rock Shop
   Geode Industries
   Geophile International
   Gilman's
   Green's Rock & Lapidary Ltd.
   Industrial Diamond Tool Co. Inc.
   Lortone Inc.
   Mohave Industries
   Raytech Industries Inc.
   Shipley's Mineral House
   Star Diamond Industries

lapidary ultrasonic cleaning systems
   L & R Manufacturing Co.

lapidary vibrating laps
   Industrial Diamond Tool Co. Inc.

lapidary wheels
   Industrial Diamond Tool Co. Inc.

lapidary workshops
   Star Diamond Industries

lapis lazuli
   R. C. Baker
   Gem-O-Rama, Inc.
   International Import Co.
   Syn-Crer Creations

lava-talc
   Bitterroot Lapidary Supply

lazulite
   Commercial Mineral Corp.

leaflets
   Craftplans

Linde star boules
   Elvin

Linde stars
   The Jewelry Mart

loose diamond-cut
   Industrial Diamond Tool Co. Inc.

magazines
   Gems & Minerals
   Lapidary Journal Book Dept.

malachite
   M. Nowotny
   Purcelli's Gems
   The Treasure Chest
   G. Weidinger

maple lap compound polishers
   Jack V. Schuller, Inc.

master faceting systems
   MDR Mfg. Co., Inc.

matrix opals
   Andria Bree Gem Co.
metal alloys
   Magic Circle Corp.
metal detectors
   Brown's Rock & Lapidary Supplies
   Covington Engineering Corp.
   Gems Galore
Mexican agates grab bag
   Gorin's Gem Arts & Rocks
Mexican crystal
   Odyssey Mineral and Fossil
Mexican fire agate
   Australian Exports
   Dowse's Lapidary Supply, Inc.
   Michigan Lapidary Supply Co.
Mexican opal
   Australian Exports
   Australian Imports
   Crown Gems Co.
   Trader South
   G. Weidinger
mineral collections
   Colorado Geological Industries Inc.
   Scott Scientific Inc.
mineral specimens
   Colorado Geological Industries Inc.
   Commercial Mineral Corp.
   Minex Lapidary Supplies
minerals
   Dover Scientific Co.
   The Fluorite Shop
   Max of Dallas
   Ovgem Craft Supply Co.
   Reo N. Pickens, Jr.
   Treasure of the Pirates, Inc.
   Tye's
Missouri mozarkite stone
   Timberline Lake Rock Shop
mixed agates
   C. R. Wells
moldavites
   Tektos
Montana agate rough forms
   B. T. Hallam
Montana agate slab
   B. T. Hallam
Montana moss
   Bitterroot Lapidary Supply
moonstone
   International Import Co.
   Syn-Crer Creations
   G. Weidinger
moonstone baroques
   Jim's Rock Shop
morganite
   De Lapa Mining Inc.
   Inter-Ocean Trade Co.
   International Import Co.
mosaic jade
   Jade World/Wilderness Originals
mosaic rock
   P. S. Andrews Co.
mosaic stone
   Sax Arts & Crafts
moss agate
   Adris Oriental Gem & Art Corp.
   Ken Kyte
   Mission Rocks
   M. Nowotny
   Syn-Crer Creations
mother-of-pearl
   Biship's House of Gems
natural gemstones
   The Cab-N-Facet, Inc.
   Grieger's Inc.
nephrite jade
   Bergsten Jade Co.
   Crown Cultured Pearl Corp.
   B. T. Hallam
   Jade World/Wilderness Originals
New York Adirondack gem garnet rough
   Minerals & Gems
norganite
   Harry Bookstone
obsidian
   Dowse's Lapidary Supply, Inc.
   The Treasure Chest
   G. Weidinger
oilstones
   Frank Mittermeier Inc.
onyx
   M. Nowotny
   Syn-Crer Creations
onyx balls
   Edwards Jewelry Co.
opal baroques
   Jim's Rock Shop
opal cabochons
   Tumblecraft
opal carvings
   Australian Imports

Craft Category Index
Lapidary—Lapidary

opal chip cabochons
   Frank's Jewelry & Gem Shop
opal chips
   Australian Exports
   Minex Lapidary Supplies
   Syn-Crer Creations
opal cutting pieces
   Australian Exports
opal glass
   Whittemore-Durgin Glass Co.
opal practice pieces
   Australian Exports
opal quartz
   Libra Gems
opal specimens
   Australian Imports
   Minex Lapidary Supplies
opal triplets
   Australian Exports
   Australian Imports
opals
   Australian Gem Trading Co.
   Australian Imports
   De Lapa Mining Inc.
   Down Under Opal
   Geode Industries
   H & A Mfg. Corp.
   International Import Co.
   W. L. Maison Opals, Etc.
   Melbourn Gem Co.
   Michigan Lapidary Supply Co.
   Murray American Corp.
   M. Nowotny
   Purcelli's Gems
   Transworld Trading Co.
   C. R. Wells
Oregon agate
   Lakewood Lapidary
painted porcelain cabochons
   Jewelart Inc.
palm onions
   Mission Rocks
paulina red moss
   Sandy Symons
pebble gems
   Delco Craft Center, Inc.
peridot
   Biship's House of Gems
   Crown Gems Co.
   International Import Co.
   Norlene Lapidary
   Purcelli's Gems
peridot baroques
   Kachina Gem Co.
peridot faceted stones
   Kachina Gem Co.
peridot faceting material
   Kachina Gem Co.
peridot gemstones
   Kachina Gem Co.
peridot rough
   Kachina Gem Co.
   Panther International Ltd.
petrified woods agate
   Ken Kyte
pigeon blood agate
   Dowse's Lapidary Supply, Inc.
pink jasper agate
   Sandy Symons
plume
   Mission Rocks
plume slabs
   Twin Peaks Rock Shop
polariscopes
   Gemological Institute of America
polished gemstones
   Biship's House of Gems
   Gem-O-Rama, Inc.
   Silver & Gem Shop
polished stones
   Odyssey Mineral and Fossil
   G. Weidinger
polished Tampa Bay coral
   C. R. Boylin
polishers
   Raytech Industries Inc.
polishes
   Covington Engineering Corp.
   The Ducketts
   Walter E. Johansen
   Weidinger Inc.
polishing accessories
   Brad's Rock Shop
   Supreme Watch Material Co.
polishing compounds
   Dorothy Blake
   Gilman's
polishing laps
   Walter E. Johansen

polishing machines
   Allcraft Tool & Supply Co.
   Supreme Watch Material Co.
polishing motor
   Gilman's
polishing tools
   Supreme Watch Material Co.
pompon agate
   Ken Kyte
pre-ringed baroques
   Pacific Gemstones
precious amber
   Syn-Crer Creations
precious metals
   Michigan Lapidary Supply Co.
precious moonstone
   Jim's Rock Shop
precious opals
   International Import Co.
precious stones
   International Import Co.
   Swest Inc.
   Transworld Trading Co.
preforms
   Trader South
pulleys
   The Ducketts
quartz
   International Import Co.
   Lochs
   G. Weidinger
   Weisz Import Export Corp.
   Wright's Rock Shop
quartz crystals
   Tumblecraft
quartz tops
   Down Under Opal
rain forest jasper
   Bonnie's Rock Shop
rainbow jasper
   The Treasure Chest
rare cut gemstones
   H. Obodda
rare fine facet rough
   Lochs
rare gems
   International Import Co.
red cullet
   Biship's House of Gems

red horn coral
   Bonnie's Rock Shop
   Dowse's Lapidary Supply, Inc.
red jasper
   Beaver Canyon Campground
rhodochrosite
   M. Nowotny
   The Treasure Chest
   G. Weidinger
rhodonite
   G. Weidinger
rhodosite
   Aspen Lapidary
ring blanks
   Gilman's
   Supreme Watch Material Co.
ring forms
   Sax Arts & Crafts
ring shapes
   Green's Rock & Lapidary Ltd.
rock clamps
   Lindell Industries
   Mohave Industries
rock collections
   Colorado Geological Industries Inc.
   Scott Scientific Inc.
rock crystal
   Biship's House of Gems
rock picks
   Star Diamond Industries
rock polishers
   Arthur Brown & Bro., Inc.
rock supplies
   The Fluorite Shop
rock tumblers
   Scott Scientific Inc.
   Starlite Rock Shop
rock vise
   A. D. McBurney
rocks
   Aleta's Rock Shop
   Charbonneau's Lapidary Service
   Dover Scientific Co.
   Ebersole Lapidary Supply Inc.
   Max of Dallas
   Smokey Mtn. Rock Shop
   Treasure of the Pirates, Inc.
rose de France amethyst
   Trader South
rose quartz
   Biship's House of Gems

Craft Category Index
Lapidary—Lapidary

    Inter-Ocean Trade Co.
    M. Nowotny
    Oceanside Gem Imports, Inc.
    Panther International Ltd.
    Purcelli's Gems
rose rocks
    Rose Rocks Co.
rough amethyst
    Commercial Mineral Corp.
rough aquamarine
    Commercial Mineral Corp.
rough chrysoprase
    Interlectric House of Fine Australian Opals
rough citrine
    Commercial Mineral Corp.
rough cuts
    Inter-Ocean Trade Co.
rough cutting stones
    Alessi Lapidary Supplies
rough faceting material
    Harry Bookstone
    Sam Frost
    W. D. Hudson, Jr.
    Jim's Rock Shop
    Lochs
    Trader South
    Weisz Import Export Corp.
rough opals
    Minex Lapidary Supplies
rough rock
    Green's Rock & Lapidary Ltd.
    Jim Kesterson
rough Russian emerald
    Panther International Ltd.
rough sapphires
    Minex Lapidary Supplies
rough stones
    Harry Bookstone
    Michigan Lapidary Supply Co.
    Syn-Crer Creations
    Transworld Trading Co.
rough tourmalines
    Commercial Mineral Corp.
rough triplets
    W. L. Maison Opals, Etc.
rubellite
    Harry Bookstone
rubies
    Adris Oriental Gem & Art Corp.
    Commercial Mineral Corp.
    Diamond Sales Co.
    H & A Mfg. Corp.
    International Import Co.
    Jewelart Inc.
    Norlene Lapidary
    Purcelli's Gems
    Syn-Crer Creations
ruby cabochon rough
    Gems International
ruby in zoisite
    Murray American Corp.
Russian synthetic blue quartz
    Treasure of the Pirates, Inc.
sagenite
    Dowse's Lapidary Supply, Inc.
sagenite quartz
    The Treasure Chest
sand
    T. B. Hagstoz & Son
sapphire
    Adris Oriental Gem & Art Corp.
    Australian Gem Trading Co.
    Commercial Mineral Corp.
    Diamond Sales Co.
    H & A Mfg. Corp.
    W. D. Hudson, Jr.
    International Import Co.
    Jewelart Inc.
    Norlene Lapidary
    Panther International Ltd.
    Purcelli's Gems
scales
    Supreme Watch Material Co.
scarabs
    Gilman's
semi-precious cabochons
    Virgil V. Lundell
semi-precious stones
    E. H. Ashley & Co., Inc.
    International Import Co.
    K42 Rock Shop
    Panther International Ltd.
    Swest Inc.
    Transworld Trading Co.
services
    International Import Co.
    Harry Z. Kurs
    Main Service Co.
    Norlene Lapidary
shimmering silk jade
    Jade World/Wilderness Originals

Craft Category Index
Lapidary—Lapidary

silicon carbide
  The Ducketts
silver grain
  Green's Rock & Lapidary Ltd.
slab polishers
  Covington Engineering Corp.
slab saws
  Covington Engineering Corp.
  Gilman's
  Great Western Equipment Co.
  Green's Rock & Lapidary Ltd.
  Highland Park Manufacturing
  Lindell Industries
  Mohave Industries
  Star Diamond Industries
slab-grabber
  Rock's Lapidary Equipment
smoky quartz
  Beaver Canyon Campground
  Geode Industries
  International Import Co.
  Libra Gems
  Oceanside Gem Imports, Inc.
  Shil-La Art Gems Inc.
  Syn-Crer Creations
  Trader South
  Weisz Import Export Corp.
snowflake obsidian
  Beaver Canyon Campground
  Bonnie's Rock Shop
soapstone
  Mission Rocks
sodalite
  M. Nowotny
  Panther International Ltd.
  The Treasure Chest
sphenes
  Commercial Mineral Corp.
spinel
  Commercial Mineral Corp.
  International Import Co.
  Walter E. Johansen
  Syn-Crer Creations
spinel boules
  Gems Galore
splash shields
  Lortone Inc.
stamps
  Gilman's
star
  Walter E. Johansen

star quartz
  Melbourn Gem Co.
star rose quartz slabs
  Prospector's Pouch
star ruby
  Adris Oriental Gem & Art Corp.
  Gems International
  W. D. Hudson, Jr.
  Jim's Rock Shop
  Melbourn Gem Co.
  Michigan Lapidary Supply Co.
  Syn-Crer Creations
star sapphires
  Adris Oriental Gem & Art Corp.
  Syn-Crer Creations
steatite (soapstone)
  Lakewood Lapidary
sterling silver wire
  Alessi Lapidary Supplies
  Green's Rock & Lapidary Ltd.
  Trowbridge Crafts
  G. Weidinger
stone mixes
  Tumblecraft
stones
  Florida Supply House, Inc.
  Jeweler's Emporium
  Tye's
storm scene jade
  Jade World/Wilderness Originals
sunstone
  Treasure of the Pirates, Inc.
synthetic corundum
  Walter E. Johansen
synthetic diamond powders
  Sinkankas Diamond Products
synthetic faceting material
  Green's Rock & Lapidary Ltd.
synthetic sapphire
  Eric Martin Co
synthetic spinel rough
  Eric Martin Co
synthetic stones
  Shil-La Art Gems Inc.
  Trader South
  G. Weidinger
T'Caro material
  Paradise Rocks
Taiwan jade
  Gem-O-Rama, Inc.

Craft Category Index
Lapidary—Lapidary

    Jewelart Inc.
    Syn-Crer Creations
tanzanite
    Lochs
tektites
    Geode Industries
    M. Nowotny
templates
    Gilman's
    Green's Rock & Lapidary Ltd.
Tennessee Mt. agate
    Virgil Owens
Texas cutting material
    Mission Rocks
Texas gem carnelian
    Woodward Ranch
Texas moss agate
    Woodward Ranch
Texas plumes material
    Woodward Ranch
Thai Moong Nong-type tektites
    Tektos
thulite
    Aspen Lapidary
tigereye
    Aspen Lapidary
    Biship's House of Gems
    Gem-O-Rama, Inc.
    Jewelart Inc.
    Michigan Lapidary Supply Co.
    M. Nowotny
    Panther International Ltd.
    Syn-Crer Creations
    G. Weidinger
tigereye balls
    Edwards Jewelry Co.
tigereye baroques
    Jim's Rock Shop
tiny tumbled stones
    Arlene Handley Rock Hobby Supplies
topaz
    Beaver Canyon Campground
    Harry Bookstone
    Dowse's Lapidary Supply, Inc.
    Inter-Ocean Trade Co.
    International Import Co
    Lochs
    Norlene Lapidary
    Oceanside Gem Imports Inc
    Trader South
    Treasure of the Pirates, Inc.

tourmaline
    Harry Bookstone
    Commercial Mineral Corp.
    W. D. Hudson, Jr.
    International Import Co.
    Jim's Rock Shop
    Norlene Lapidary
    Oceanside Gem Imports, Inc.
    Purcelli's Gems
    Transworld Trading Co.
    Weisz Import Export Corp.
tourmaline XL's
    Beaver Canyon Campground
Transvaal jade
    Beaver Canyon Campground
tree agates
    Syn-Crer Creations
tube agate
    M. W. Jackson & Assoc.
tumble polished gems
    B. T. Hallam
tumbled stone tree materials
    Arlene Handley Rock Hobby Supplies
tumbled stones
    Starfire Lapidary
tumbler ready rock
    Starlite Rock Shop
tumbling accessories
    Ken Kyte
    Star Diamond Industries
tumbling items
    Scott Scientific Inc.
tumbling stones
    Harry Bookstone
    The Treasure Chest
turquoise
    Biship's House of Gems
    Crown Gems Co.
    International Import Co.
    Jewelart Inc.
    Murray American Corp.
    G. Weidinger
turquoise nuggets
    Tumblecraft
turquoise rough
    Gems International
turritella
    Mission Rocks
twilight blue jade
    Jade World/Wilderness Originals

Craft Category Index
Lapidary—Leaflets

uncut diamond
   Industrial Diamond Tool Co. Inc.
unusual agates
   Ken Kyte
Utah red nodules
   Beaver Canyon Campground
Utah ribbon agate
   Bonnie's Rock Shop
Utah varscite
   Starfire Lapidary
velvet black jade
   Torrington Rock Shop
verdite
   Aspen Lapidary
Washington opalized wood
   Lakewood Lapidary
Washington wood agate
   Lakewood Lapidary
white coral
   Panther International Ltd.
white YAG
   Walter E. Johansen
wonderstone
   The Treasure Chest
wood agate
   M. W. Jackson & Assoc.
Wyoming jade
   Bonnie's Rock Shop
   Torrington Rock Shop
YAG
   The Jewelry Mart
   Walter E. Johansen
   Virgil V. Lundell
   Syn-Crer Creations
   Trader South
   Transworld Trading Co.
   Weisz Import Export Corp.
zebra stone
   Aspen Lapidary
zircon
   Commercial Mineral Corp.
   W. D. Hudson, Jr.
   International Import Co.
   Norlene Lapidary
   Purcelli's Gems
   Syn-Crer Creations
zoisite
   W. D. Hudson, Jr.
   G. Weidinger

leaflets *(see also specific craft)*
   Sonie Ames; china painting.
   Bingaman Plans; plans for making wooden lanterns.
   James Bliss & Co. Inc.; model ship building.
   Bluejacket Ship Crafters; model ship building.
   Brandywine Studies; china painting.
   Cleveland Model & Supply Co.; plans for model aircraft.
   Coker Craft; plans for model military railway equipment.
   Craftplans; action windmills, bars, birdhouses and feeders, fireplaces, flocking, garages, gem cutting, jigsaw projects, lawn novelties, looms, mirror silvering, mosaic designs, nursery pinups, old English letters, plating baby shoes, spinning wheels, unusual alphabets, weathervanes, wire figures, wood lathe projects, work benches, Christmas decorations, Stradivarius violin.
   Davault Miniature Furniture; patterns for modern & period doll house furniture.
   Evelyn Downing; eggery.
   Fountains for the Home; ceramic fountains.
   Furniture Designs; furniture making.
   Gerhardt Macrame Studio; build-it-yourself looms.
   Jesop Co.; wax crafts.
   M. Koehler; oriental colored lacquers & gold leaf methods.
   Mrs. Frieda Koudelka; tatting.
   Lion Brand Yarn Co.; crochet granny vest and cap.
   LTA Products; plans for model dirigible building.
   The Mannings Creative Crafts
   Thomas S. Maquire's; instructions and designs for crafts.
   Miniature Aircraft; plans for models.
   Model Craftsman Publishing Corp.; model leaflets, plans for model trains.
   Sid Morgan; plans for building model aircraft.
   Margaret Newman; hand weaving, instructions in weaving.

Craft Category Index
Leaflets—Leathercraft

Old South Patterns; plans of Early American furniture.
Popular Mechanics Press; aircushions vechicle plans, billiard table plans, boat plans, houseboat plans, model ship plans, sailboat plans, travel trailer plans, two-man submarine plans.
Real Woods; cabinetmaking, veneering, wood finishing.
Skon; bargello needlecraft, Swedish embroidery.
The Sneak Box Studio; decoy kits, decoy plans.
The Rev. Henry N. Thomas; making gold draped angels.
Osma G. Tod Weaving & Lace Studio; instructions on lace and weaving.
Use 'Em Up Creations; plans for quilts from nylon stockings & cotton dresses, poncho and afghans of old fashioned granny squares.
Wilfred Enterprises; candlemaking, ceramics, dollmaking, plaster casting.
Mrs. L. Winum; flowers, pillows, slippers, teen doll furniture, toys, wash cloth & felt square projects.

leathercraft
Boin Arts & Crafts
Arthur Brown & Bro., Inc.
Craft Service
Delco Craft Center, Inc.
Economy Handicrafts, Inc.
The Handcrafters
Holiday Handicrafts, Inc.
La Venta Corp.
Magnus Craft Materials, Inc.
J. C. Penney Co., Inc.
Sax Arts & Crafts
Sears, Roebuck & Co.
Skil-Crafts Division
Tandy Leather Co.

adhesives
Skil-Crafts Division

aniline dyes
Fezandie & Sperrle, Inc.

awls
Tandy Leather Co.

belt buckles
Edwards Jewelry Co.
House of York
Leathercrafters Supply Co.
Macrame and Weaving Supply Co.
The Sandvigs

belts
Veteran Leather Co., Inc.

billfold accessories
Tandy Leather Co.

billfold parts
Tandy Leather Co.

books
Book Barn
Chilton Book Co.
Drake Publishers Inc.
Emerson Books Inc.
Hearthside Press
Lane Magazine & Book Co.
Leathercrafters Supply Co.
The Macmillan Publishing Co.
McKnight Publishing Co.
Random House Inc.
Henry Regnery Co.
Reilly & Lee Books

brass snap closures
Leathercrafters Supply Co.

British buckles
Leathercrafters Supply Co.

bronze buckles
Leathercrafters Supply Co.

buckles
La Venta Corp.
Leathercrafters Supply Co.
Mac Leather Co.
Pollack's Furrier's Supply Corp

buckskin
Montgomery Ward & Co., Inc.

calf lacing
Leathercrafters Supply Co.

Canadian latigo
Leathercrafters Supply Co.

carving leathers
La Venta Corp.

carving tools
Sax Arts & Crafts

cast metal buckles in antique finishes
Leathercrafters Supply Co.

chamois
Leathercrafters Supply Co.

Craft Category Index
Leathercraft—Leathercraft

cleaners
  Leathercrafters Supply Co.
  Skil-Crafts Division
cobbler sandal supplies
  Leathercrafters Supply Co.
cowhide
  Leathercrafters Supply Co.
cowing leather
  Leathercrafters Supply Co.
craft-cuts
  Tandy Leather Co.
deerskin
  Leathercrafters Supply Co.
double woven cotton accessories
  J. P. Fliegel Co.
dressed fur pelts
  Great Central Fur Corp.
English kip
  Leathercrafters Supply Co.
findings
  Leathercrafters Supply Co.
garment leathers
  Leathercrafters Supply Co.
  Tandy Leather Co.
goat lacing
  Leathercrafters Supply Co.
group packs
  Boin Arts & Crafts
hand crafted shoes supplies
  Barb's Shoe Makings
handbag leather
  Modern Needlepoint
hardware
  Leathercrafters Supply Co.
hides
  Leathercrafters Supply Co.
  Veteran Leather Co., Inc.
  Winona Trading Post
home study courses
  Al Stohlman Leathercraft Home Study Course
inks
  Leathercrafters Supply Co.
key chain parts
  Tandy Leather Co.
kits
  A 'N L's Hobbicraft, Inc.
  American Handicrafts
  The Booted Sheepherder Inc.
  Cavalier Handicrafts
  Cleveland Leather Co.
  Craftsman Supply House
  Creative Hands Co., Inc.
  Delco Craft Center, Inc.
  J. P. Fliegel Co.
  Gager's Handicrafts
  Pack-O-Fun
  Sax Arts & Crafts
  Skil-Crafts Division
  Tandy Leather Co.
  Veteran Leather Co., Inc.
knives
  Tandy Leather Co.
latigo
  La Venta Corp.
leather
  American Handicrafts
  P. S. Andrews Co.
  Cleveland Leather Co.
  The Hidden Village
  Leathercrafters Supply Co.
leather additives
  Tandy Leather Co.
leather belts
  Pollack's Furrier's Supply Corp.
leather bolo cords
  Shipley's Mineral House
leather buttons
  Pollack's Furrier's Supply Corp.
leather carving
  Tandy Leather Co.
leather cements
  Leathercrafters Supply Co.
  Tandy Leather Co.
leather designs
  Transart
  Raymond P. Wallace
leather dyes
  Fezandie & Sperrle, Inc.
  La Venta Corp.
  Mac Leather Co.
  Tandy Leather Co.
leather interlinings
  Pollack's Furrier's Supply Corp.
leather lacings
  P. S. Andrews Co.
  Anne's Treasure Trove
  Craft Service
  Knit Services, Inc.
  Mac Leather Co.
  Skil-Crafts Division

Craft Category Index
Leathercraft—Looms

    Tandy Leather Co.
    Veteran Leather Co., Inc.
leather linings
    Pollack's Furrier's Supply Corp.
    Tandy Leather Co.
leather packs
    Supreme Handicrafts
leather padding
    Pollack's Furrier's Supply Corp.
leather preservatives
    Leathercrafters Supply Co.
leather rawhide lacing
    Leathercrafters Supply Co.
leather scraps
    Mac Leather Co.
    Reichert's Fabrics
    Veteran Leather Co., Inc.
leather skins
    J. P. Fliegel Co.
    Mac Leather Co.
    Pollack's Furrier's Supply Corp.
leather stitcher
    Sunset House
leather thongs
    Jewelart Inc.
leather tools
    La Venta Corp.
    Leathercrafters Supply Co.
    Mac Leather Co.
    Skil-Crafts Division
    Veteran Leather Co., Inc.
magazines
    Challenge Publications, Inc
    Make It With Leather
    1001 Fashion & Needlecraft Ideas
mallets
    Tandy Leather Co.
paints
    Cleveland Leather Co.
pewter buckles
    Leathercrafters Supply Co.
punchers
    Tandy Leather Co.
round cowhide lacing
    Leathercrafters Supply Co.
services
    The Hidden Village
snap setters
    Tandy Leather Co.
sole leather
    Leathercrafters Supply Co.

speed rivets
    Leathercrafters Supply Co.
stamps
    Tandy Leather Co.
stencils
    Leathercrafters Supply Co.
suede
    Leathercrafters Supply Co.
    Montgomery Ward & Co., Inc.
tooling leather
    Leathercrafters Supply Co.
    Tandy Leather Co.
used leather machinery
    La Venta Corp.
water soluble leather paints
    Siphon Art Products
Western latigo
    Leathercrafters Supply Co.

looms
    Robert Ayottes' Designery
    Dick Blick
    Boin Arts & Crafts
    Delco Craft Center, Inc.
    Essayons Studio, Hand Arts Center
    Frederick J. Fawcett, Inc.
    Fiber to Fabric
    The Fringe and Frame
    Gerhardt Macrame Studio
    Greentree Ranch Wools, Countryside
      Handweavers
    Handcraft House
    The Handcrafters
    KM Yarn Co.
    Leclerc Corp.
    Leonida Leatherdale's Embroidery
      Studio
    Lily Mills Co.
    The Loomery
    Magnolia Weaving
    Make It Happen Craft Studio
    The Makings
    The Mannings Creative Crafts
    The New England Craftsman
    The Niddy Noddy
    Northwest Handcraft House
    The Oriental Rug Co.
    Robin & Russ Handweavers
    Schacht Spindle Co.
    School Products Co.
    Silver Shuttle
    Textile Crafts

Osma G. Tod Weaving & Lace Studio
Valley Handweaving Supply
The Yarn Depot
adjustable hairpin lace loom
Rosemond Hobbycraft
backstrap (waist) loom
Robert Nelson
bead looms
Bead Game
Nicole Bead & Craft Co., Inc.
books
East River Publications
HTH Publishers
bottle knotting looms
Gerhardt Macrame Studio
daisy looms
Walter Drake
floor looms
The Hidden Village
House of Yarn & Crafts
KAY an EE Corp. of America
Schacht Spindle Co.
School Products Co.
Tools of the Trade
Turnbull Looms
flower looms
Craftsman Supply House
Delco Craft Center, Inc.
Hanover House Industries, Inc.
Hazel Pearson Handi Craft
Sav-On-Crafts
Studio Twelve
folding floor harness looms
Norwood Loom Co.
folding frame loom
Robert Nelson
Turnbull Looms
foot-operated looms
Kessenich Looms
hand fabric loom
Palmloom Co.
hand looms
Walter Drake
Harrisville Designs
Kessenich Looms
L. W. Macomber Ad-A Harness Looms
Sax Arts & Crafts
handcrafted looms
Heritage Looms

harness lap loom
Village Art Gallery
harness looms
The Pendleton Shop
Turnbull Looms
harness table looms
Tools of the Trade
home built loom
Turnbull Looms
hooking looms
Textile Crafts
inkle looms
Cleve-Craft E-Z Loom
Knit Services, Inc.
Lily Mills Co.
The Loom Factory
The Loomery
Morgan Inkle Loom Factory
Robin & Russ Handweavers
Schacht Spindle Co.
School Products Co.
jack looms
The Pendleton Shop
Robin & Russ Handweavers
kits
Fetty-Nielsen Macrame Loom
Harrisville Designs
Inkle Looms
The Loom Factory
Mary Maxim Inc.
Scott Scientific Inc.
Turnbull Looms
leaflets
Craftplans
Gerhardt Macrame Studio
loom accessories
KAY an EE Corp. of America
Robin & Russ Handweavers
loom equipment
Lily Mills Co.
looms for handicapped
Kessenich Looms
looper looms
Pack-O-Fun
magazines
The Looming Arts
Navajo Indian loom
The Pendleton Shop
peg looms
Cleve-Craft E-Z Loom

Craft Category Index
Looms—Machinery

portable loom
  Northwest Looms
portable macrame looms
  Fetty-Nielsen Macrame Loom
rosette winders
  Holiday Handicrafts, Inc.
  Mary Maxim Inc.
  Merribee
  Yarns Unlimited
Salish looms
  School Products Co.
shuttles
  Heritage Looms
  Leclerc Corp.
  Robin & Russ Handweavers
  School Products Co.
small weaving looms
  Spencer Gifts Inc.
  Sunset House
stick looms
  Cleve-Craft E-Z Loom
Swedish looms
  Lillstina Inc.
synthetic straw loom
  Delco Craft Center, Inc.
table looms
  The Hidden Village
  House of Yarn & Crafts
  KAY an EE Corp. of America
  Schacht Spindle Co.
  School Products Co.
  Some Place
tablet looms
  School Products Co.
tapestry looms
  Schacht Spindle Co.
  School Products Co.
weave-it looms
  Mary Maxim Inc.
  Yarns Unlimited

lost wax casting *(see also Jewelrymaking, Metal sculpture)*
  Economy Handicrafts, Inc.
  Green's Rock & Lapidary Ltd.
  Ovgem Craft Supply Co.
  Stonehouse
  Technical Specialties International Inc.
  Trowbridge Crafts
blowpipes
  Gilman's
books
  Bovin Publishing
  Dick Ells Co.
  Lapidary Journal Book Dept.
casting waxes
  Allcraft Tool & Supply Co.
  Bourget Bros. Gems & Minerals
  Delco Craft Center, Inc.
  Gilman's
  Kerr Mfg. Co.
  Sculpture Associates Ltd.
  Supreme Watch Material Co.
lost wax casting tools
  Technical Specialties International Inc.
lost wax jewelrymaking
  Kerr Mfg. Co.
wax pots
  Shipley's Mineral House

machinery and equipment *(see also specific craft)*
alcohol burners
  Gilman's
anvils
  Frank Mittermeier Inc.
automatic knitting machines
  Brother International Corp.
  Genie
  Knitking
  Studio Yarn Farms Inc.
  A. C. Weber & Co., Inc.
belt sanders
  American Machine & Tool Co.
  Covington Engineering Corp.
  Gilman's
  Highland Park Manufacturing
bench power tools
  Badger Air-Brush Co.
  Toolkraft Corp.
bench top multiuse units
  Dremel Creative Power Tools
blade flanges
  Star Diamond Industries
blockprinting press
  Stewart Industries
book presses
  Basic Crafts Co.
books
  Bruce Benziger
  Gloria's Glass Garden

Industrial Press Inc.
Howard W. Sams & Co., Inc.
braiders
   Berry's of Maine
   Mildred Sprout
bronze casting-pneumatic equipment
   Sculpture Associates Ltd.
cabochon machines
   Reed Industries
candy making equipment
   General Supplies Co.
centrifugal casting equipment
   T. B. Hagstoz & Son
ceramic kilns
   A 'N L's Hobbicraft, Inc.
   A. D. Alpine Inc.
   Bergen Arts & Crafts, Inc.
   Clay-Crafters Products
   Delco Craft Center, Inc.
   Newton's Potters Supply
   Paragon Industries Inc.
   Paramount Ceramic Inc.
cigarette lighter mechanisms
   Craft-Mark Products
cloth slitting machines
   Frederick J. Fawcett , Inc.
combination power tools
   Swest Inc.
complete faceting machines
   Henry B. Graves Co.
computerized knitting machine
   Brother International Corp.
   Studio Yarn Farms Inc.
crafting equipment
   Allcraft Tool & Supply Co.
custom-made lapidary equipment
   Reed Industries
cutting laps
   Walter E. Johansen
cutting machines
   Gilman's
   Heritage Hill Patterns
   House of Gould
   Joan Moshimer
diamond arbors
   Gem Tool Specialties
diamond bar wheel dressers
   Gem Tec Diamond Tool Co.
diamond blades
   Covington Engineering Corp.
   Earth Treasures

   Farmers Gem and Rock Shop
   Gem Tool Specialties
   Star Diamond Industries
diamond burrs
   Gem Tool Specialties
diamond cores
   Gem Tool Specialties
diamond drills
   Gem Tool Specialties
   Geode Industries
diamond equipment
   Terra Products
diamond gem maker
   Gem Tec Diamond Tool Co.
diamond impregnated core drills
   Metro Diamond Drill Co.
diamond lapidaries
   Gem Tool Specialties
diamond laps
   Jack V. Schuller, Inc.
diamond machines
   Gem Tool Specialties
diamond pads
   Gem Tool Specialties
diamond points
   Gem Tool Specialties
diamond saw blades
   Highland Park Manufacturing
diamond saws
   Raytech Industries Inc.
diamond wheels
   Diamond-Pro Unlimited
   Gem Tec Diamond Tool Co.
   Gem Tool Specialties
drill attachments
   Arco Tools Inc.
drill presses
   American Machine & Tool Co.
   Dremel Creative Power Tools
electric model motors
   James Bliss & Co. Inc.
electric potter's wheels
   Cole Ceramics Laboratories
enameling kilns
   A 'N L's Hobbicraft, Inc.
   Bergen Arts & Crafts, Inc.
   Craft Service
engraving blocks
   Frank Mittermeier Inc.
faceter's trim slab saw
   A. D. McBurney

Craft Category Index
Machinery—Machinery

faceting equipment
   Jim's Rock Shop
   Lochs
   Stop 'N Rock Shop

faceting machines
   Geode Industries
   Walter E. Johansen
   Trader South

flexible shaft machines
   Gems Galore

floor hoops
   KAY an EE Corp. of America

floor looms
   The Hidden Village
   House of Yarn & Crafts
   KAY an EE Corp. of America
   Schacht Spindle Co.
   School Products Co.
   Tools of the Trade
   Turnbull Looms

furnaces
   Drykiln Design

furnaces for bronze casting
   McEnglevan Heat Treating & Mfg. Inc.

gem cutting equipment
   Earth Treasures
   Treasure of the Pirates, Inc.

gem detectors
   Gemological Institute of America

gem drills
   Lindell Industries
   Mohave Industries

gem grinders
   Star Diamond Industries

gem making equipment
   Craftool Co.

gem polishers
   Dorothy Blake
   Star Diamond Industries

gemmaster faceting laps
   MDR Mfg. Co., Inc.

glass blowing equipment
   A. D. Alpine Inc.
   Westwood Ceramic Supply Co.

glass melting furnaces
   Cole Ceramics Laboratories

glass melting tanks
   A. D. Alpine Inc.

grinding equipment
   Brad's Rock Shop
   Mohave Industries

grinding units
   Aleta's Rock Shop

grinding wheels
   Covington Engineering Corp.
   Jenkins Lapidary Equipment
   Star Diamond Industries

hand bookbinding equipment
   Basic Crafts Co.

hobby workbench
   Craft House

horn anvils
   Gilman's

jewelry workbench
   Craft House

jewelrymaking equipment
   Exactra-Craft Corp.
   Grieger's Inc.
   K42 Rock Shop
   Prospector's Pouch
   The Roc Shop
   Treasure of the Pirates, Inc.
   Tye's
   Weidinger Inc.

jewelrymaking machinery
   Jim Kesterson

jig saw
   Dremel Creative Power Tools

kiln shelves
   Cole Ceramics Laboratories

kilns
   Allcraft Tool & Supply Co.
   Anchor Tool & Supply Co.
   Art Consultants
   Bergen Arts & Crafts, Inc.
   Boin Arts & Crafts
   Arthur Brown & Bro., Inc.
   Handcraft House
   Loretta's Ceramic Studio
   Minnesota Clay
   Ohio Ceramic Supply Inc.
   Plaza Artists Materials, Inc.
   Richland Ceramics Inc.
   Sax Arts & Crafts
   Sculpture Associates Ltd.
   Sculpture House
   Thomas C. Thompson
   Westwood Ceramic Supply Co.

Craft Category Index
Machinery—Machinery

kits
  Gilliom Mfg. Co.
  Jenkins Lapidary Equipment
  Struck Corp.
knitting machines
  House of Yarn & Crafts
  Liveright
  Lee Wards
lapidary belt sanders
  Great Western Equipment Co.
lapidary combination units
  Farmers Gem and Rock Shop
  Great Western Equipment Co.
lapidary equipment
  Alessi Lapidary Supplies
  Charbonneau's Lapidary Service
  Colorado Geological Industries Inc.
  Covington Engineering Corp.
  Dowse's Lapidary Supply, Inc.
  Earth Treasures
  Ebersole Lapidary Supply Inc.
  Gems Galore
  Geophile International
  Gilman's
  Great Western Equipment Co.
  Highland Park Manufacturing
  Hillquist
  Lee Lapidaries
  Lindell Industries
  Lortone Inc.
  Main Service Co.
  Minnesota Lapidary Supply Inc.
  Prospector's Pouch
  Silver & Gem Shop
  Smokey Mtn. Rock Shop
  Star Diamond Industries
  Swensons Lapidary Equipment, Inc.
  Treasure of the Pirates, Inc.
  Trowbridge Crafts
  Montgomery Ward & Co., Inc.
  G. Weidinger
lapidary grinders
  Beacon
  Great Western Equipment Co.
lapidary laps
  Industrial Diamond Tool Co. Inc.
lapidary machinery
  Aspen Lapidary
  Brad's Rock Shop
  Brown's Rock & Lapidary Supplies
  Farmers Gem and Rock Shop
  Green's Rock & Lapidary Ltd.
  Lindell Industries
  Max of Dallas
  A. D. McBurney
  Michigan Lapidary Supply Co.
  Minex Lapidary Supplies
  Minnesota Lapidary Supply Inc.
  Sax Arts & Crafts
  Smokey Mtn. Rock Shop
  Stanley Lapidary Products
lapidary polishing equipment
  Beacon
  Great Western Equipment Co.
lapidary sanders
  Great Western Equipment Co.
lapidary saw blades
  Industrial Diamond Tool Co. Inc.
lapidary saws
  Beacon
  Industrial Diamond Tool Co. Inc.
  Lortone Inc.
lapidary tumblers
  Farmers Gem and Rock Shop
lapidary ultrasonic cleaning systems
  L & R Manufacturing Co.
lapidary vibrating laps
  Industrial Diamond Tool Co. Inc.
lapidary wheels
  Industrial Diamond Tool Co. Inc.
lapidary workshops
  Star Diamond Industries
lathes
  American Machine & Tool Co.
  Campbell Tools Co.
machine attachments
  Genie
machinery
  J. J. Jewelcraft
magazines
  Good Housekeeping Needlecraft
melting equipment
  Art Consultants
  Supreme Watch Material Co.
metal enameling equipment
  American Art Clay Co. Inc.
mini vacuum-vise
  Miles Kimball
mold making equipment
  Supreme Watch Material Co.
  Technical Specialties International Inc.

Craft Category Index
Machinery—Machinery

motors
   The Ducketts
overlock sewing machines
   Knitking
pin vises
   The L. S. Starrett Co.
polariscopes
   Gemological Institute of America
polishing machines
   Allcraft Tool & Supply Co.
   Supreme Watch Material Co.
polishing motor
   Gilman's
portable plating equipment
   Platers Service Co.
potter's equipment
   Bergen Arts & Crafts, Inc.
   Richland Ceramics Inc.
potter's kick wheels
   Cole Ceramics Laboratories
   Pacific Crafts
potter's wheels
   A. D. Alpine Inc.
   Bluebird Manufacturing
   Arthur Brown & Bro., Inc.
   Gilmour Campbell
   Craftool Co.
   Creative Industries
   Delco Craft Center, Inc.
   Diedricks Crafts
   Earth Treasures
   Handcraft House
   Menco Engineers Inc.
   Minnesota Clay
   Newton's Potters Supply
   Ohio Ceramic Supply Inc.
   Paramount Ceramic Inc.
   Plaza Artists Materials, Inc
   Richland Ceramics Inc.
   Sax Arts & Crafts
   Sculpture Services Inc.
   Van Howe Ceramic Supply Co.
   Westwood Ceramic Supply Co.
professional jeweler's instruments
   Gemological Institute of America
professional sewing machines
   General Supplies Co.
propane equipment
   Beno J. Gundlach Co
pug mills
   A. D. Alpine Inc.
   Bluebird Manufacturing
   Cole Ceramics Laboratories
   Westwood Ceramic Supply Co.
quilter unit
   Sue's Custom Quilting
quilting machine
   Sue's Custom Quilting
refractometers
   Gemological Institute of America
ring mandrel
   The Roc Shop
rope making machine
   Schacht Spindle Co.
sanding bands
   Foredom Electric Co.
sanding machines
   Brad's Rock Shop
sandpaper wet or dry
   3 M Company
scales
   Delco Craft Center, Inc.
   Supreme Watch Material Co.
sewing machines
   Studio Yarn Farms Inc.
   Swiss Bernina, Inc.
shaving horses
   King's Studio
silversmithing machinery
   Allcraft Tool & Supply Co.
   Smokey Mtn. Rock Shop
sphere makers
   Covington Engineering Corp.
table saws
   Toolkraft Corp.
table top machining center
   American Edestaal Inc.
tilt top tables
   John & Susan Scheewe
treasure detectors
   Covington Engineering Corp.
trim saws
   Brad's Rock Shop
   Covington Engineering Corp.
   Gilman's
   Green's Rock & Lapidary Ltd.
   Highland Park Manufacturing
   Lindell Industries
   MDR Mfg. Co., Inc.
   Star Diamond Industries
tumbling machines
   Geophile International

Craft Category Index
Machinery—Macrame

used leather machinery
   La Venta Corp.
used plating equipment
   Platers Service Co.
welding unit
   Allcraft Tool & Supply Co.
work benches
   King's Studio
workshop power tools
   Allcraft Tool & Supply Co.
   Belsaw Power Tools

macrame (see also Cord, Yarns)
  books
   Ballantine Books, Inc.
   Book Barn
   Craft Course Publishers
   Craftsman Circle Book Club
   Crown Publishers
   Gerhardt Macrame Studio
   Hearthside Press
   P. C. Herwig Co., Inc.
   Lane Magazine & Book Co.
   LeJeune, Inc.
   Museum Books Inc.
   Robin & Russ Handweavers
   Stein & Day
   Sterling Publishing Co. Inc.
   The Unicorn
   Van Nostrand Reinhold Co.
   Watson-Guptill Publications
  bottle knotting looms
   Gerhardt Macrame Studio
  cotton cord
   Creator's Corner
   Tinkler & Co. Inc.
  cotton crochet yarn
   W. B. Roddey
  cotton-ropes polished
   Knit Services, Inc.
  cow horn beads
   Bead Game
  jute
   Contessa Yarns
   Creator's Corner
   P. C. Herwig Co., Inc.
   The Hidden Village
   Knit Services, Inc.
   The Loomery
   Robin & Russ Handweavers
   Tinkler & Co. Inc.

  kits
   The Craft Corner
   The Enchanted Doll House
   Gift Craft
   P. C. Herwig Co., Inc.
   Nautique Arts
   Bob and Carol Oliver
   Hazel Pearson Handi Craft
   Tuxedo Yarn & Needlework
   Lee Wards
  macrame accessories
   American Handicrafts
   Artis, Inc.
   Bergen Arts & Crafts, Inc.
   Bob's Arts & Crafts
   Boin Arts & Crafts
   The Craft Corner
   Delco Craft Center, Inc.
   Dharma Trading Co.
   Economy Handicrafts, Inc.
   Essayons Studio, Hand Arts Center
   Fiber to Fabric
   Gemex Co.
   P. C. Herwig Co., Inc.
   The Hidden Village
   Jeweler's Emporium
   Jo-El's Craft Co.
   Kaydee Craft Supplies
   Kit Kraft
   Knit Services, Inc.
   Kraft Korner
   Macrame and Weaving Supply Co.
   Magnus Craft Materials, Inc.
   The Mannings Creative Crafts
   Ovgem Craft Supply Co.
   Hazel Pearson Handi Craft
   J. C. Penney Co., Inc.
   Sav-On-Crafts
   Schrock's, The House of Hobbies & Crafts
   Sears, Roebuck & Co.
   Supreme Handicrafts
   Lee Wards
  macrame beads
   Tandy Leather Co.
  macrame board
   Knit Services, Inc.
  macrame cords
   Dick Blick
   Craft Yarns of Rhode Island Inc.
   Delco Craft Center, Inc.

Craft Category Index
Macrame—Magazines

    Dharma Trading Co.
    Fetty-Nielsen Macrame Loom
    P. C. Herwig Co., Inc.
    House of Orange
    Jo-El's Craft Co.
    Knit Services, Inc.
    Lily Mills Co.
    Macrame and Weaving Supply Co.
    The Mannings Creative Crafts
    Reeves Knotique
    Tandy Leather Co.
    The Yarn Depot
macrame pins
    Knit Services, Inc.
macrame yarn
    Frederick J. Fawcett , Inc.
magazines
    American Home Crafts
    Challenge Publications, Inc
    McCall's Needlework & Crafts
portable macrame looms
    Fetty-Nielsen Macrame Loom
rattail
    The Hidden Village
seine twine
    The Hidden Village
    Knit Services, Inc.
sisal
    Contessa Yarns
    P. C. Herwig Co., Inc.

magazines *(see also specific craft)*
    The American Candlemaker; candlemaking.
    American Home Crafts; batik, beadcraft, decorative accessories, decoupage, jewelry making, macrame, needlecraft.
    Artisan Crafts; general arts and crafts.
    Artweek; general arts and crafts.
    Auto Modeler; modeling.
    Boat Builder; boat building, features boat building projects, information on building materials and tools.
    Bookful of Crochet; crochet patterns.
    Butterick Home Catalog; sewing fashions.
    Carstens Publications; modeling.
    Celebrate; cake & food decorating.
    Ceramics; ceramics.
    Ceramics Monthly; ceramics.
    Challenge Publications, Inc; ceramics, foil, leather craft, macrame, needlepoint, resin, wood.
    China Decorator; china decorating.
    China Painter; china painting.
    Countrywide Crafts; general arts and crafts.
    Craft/Midwest; general arts and crafts.
    Crafty Ideas; general arts and crafts.
    Creative Crafts; general arts and crafts.
    Creative Crafts Christmas Annual; Christmas crafts.
    Decorating & Craft Ideas Made Easy; general arts and crafts.
    Design Magazine; general arts and crafts.
    Doll Castle News; dolls and dollhouses.
    Egg Album; eggery.
    The Family Handyman; how-to household projects.
    Flying Models; aircraft models.
    Gems & Minerals
    Glass Art Magazine; glass crafts.
    The Glass Workshop; stained glass crafts.
    Good Housekeeping Needlecraft; needlecrafts.
    Handweaver & Craftsman; weaving.
    Happy Hobbies Magazine; features instructions and patterns for quilting, quilting, stationery decorating, textile painting, tole.
    Journal of Contemporary Metalcraft, Casting, Related Arts; metal crafts.
    Knitking Magazine; machine knitting.
    Ladies Home Journal Needlecraft; needlecraft.
    Lapidary Journal Book Dept.; lapidary.
    The Looming Arts; 4 harness & multiharness looms.
    Make It With Leather; leathercraft.
    McCall's Needlework & Crafts; needlecrafts.
    McCall's Pattern Fashions; sewing fashions.
    McCall's You-Do-It Home Decorating; decorating ideas.
    Mon Tricot; needlecrafts.

Craft Category Index
Magazines—Metals

National Calendar of Indoor-Outdoor Art Fairs; calendar of crafts and arts.
National Sculpture Review; sculpting.
O Scale Railroading; features articles and diagrams, for O scale and ten-plate models, instructions for railroad layouts, kits, models.
1001 Decorating Ideas; interior decorating.
1001 Fashion & Needlecraft Ideas; needlecrafts.
1001 How-To Ideas; home decorating.
Pack-O-Fun; general arts and crafts.
Popular Ceramics; ceramics.
Portfolio of Egg Artistry; eggery.
Pourette Mfg. Co.; candlemaking.
Quilter's Newsletter; quilting.
Railroad Modeler; model crafts.
Robin & Russ Handweavers; weaving.
Rug Hooker News & Views; rugmaking.
Scale Modeler; model crafts.
School Arts; general arts and crafts.
Simplicity Fashion Magazine; sewing and fashion.
Simplicity Home Catalog; fabrics, sewing.
Simplicity Young Ideas Catalog; sewing.
Textile Crafts; textiles and weaving.
Treasure Chest; eggery.
Turpen Times; decoupage.
Twenty-five Weekend Build-It Projects; do-it-yourself projects.
Warp & Weft; weaving.
Woman's Day Knit & Stitch; needlecrafts.
Woman's Day Knitting Book; knitting.
Woman's Day Needlework Ideas; needlecrafts.
Woman's Day 101 Sweaters to Knit and Crochet; knitting and crocheting.
Woman's Day Sewing & Fashion Ideas; sewing.
Wood Projects; woodworking.
Woodworker; woodworking.
The Workbasket; needlecraft.
The Workbench; cabinetry and woodworking.
Z-Handicrafts; weaving.

magnets
  Bob's Arts & Crafts
  Edmund Scientific Co.
  Home-Sew Inc.
  Maryland Magnet Co.
  Hazel Pearson Handi Craft
  Skil-Crafts Division
  Supreme Handicrafts
bar magnets
  Maryland Magnet Co.
disk magnets
  Maryland Magnet Co.
flexible magnetic strips
  Maryland Magnet Co.
stick magnets
  Maryland Magnet Co.

marquetry *(see also Wood, Woodworking)*
  Albert Constantine & Son Inc.
  Homecraft Veneer
books
  Drake Publishers Inc.
kits
  Albert Constantine & Son Inc.
  The New England Craftsman
organizations
  The Marquetry Society of America

metals *(see also specific metal)*
  Art Consultants
  Boin Arts & Crafts
  Campbell Tools Co.
  Gems Galore
  Montana Assay Office
  NASCO Arts & Crafts
alloyed gold
  T. B. Hagstoz & Son
aluminum
  A 'N L's Hobbicraft, Inc.
art metal
  American Handicrafts
art metal tools
  Sax Arts & Crafts
bronze model metal
  T. B. Hagstoz & Son
gold
  Charbonneau's Lapidary Service
  Gems Galore
  Weidinger Inc.

Craft Category Index
Metals—Metal

kits
  Creative Metalcraft
nickel
  Sax Arts & Crafts
nickel silver
  T. B. Hagstoz & Son
pewter
  Anchor Tool & Supply Co.
  T. B. Hagstoz & Son
  Sax Arts & Crafts
platinum
  T. B. Hagstoz & Son
precious casting metals
  Bourget Bros. Gems & Minerals
  H. A. Cole
precious metals
  Michigan Lapidary Supply Co.
sheet metal
  T. B. Hagstoz & Son

metal sculpture
armatures
  Delco Craft Center, Inc.
  Plaza Artists Materials, Inc.
  Sculpture Associates Ltd.
books
  Chilton Book Co.
  Pyronetics
  Sterling Publishing Co. Inc.
bronze casting-pneumatic equipment
  Sculpture Associates Ltd.
bronze model metal
  T. B. Hagstoz & Son
casting accessories
  Sculpture Associates Ltd.
casting items
  Art Consultants
casting supplies
  Sculpture House
fluid solder
  Lox-Seal Adhesives
flux
  Barbara Lawshe
  Panther International Ltd.
  Whittemore-Durgin Glass Co.
furnaces for bronze casting
  McEnglevan Heat Treating & Mfg. Inc.
kits
  Champs Creative Materials Center
  Craigle Studios

metal modeling materials
  Terminal Hobby Shop
metallic sculpture compound
  Economy Handicrafts, Inc.
sculpture metal
  Art Mart, Inc.
  Sculpture House

metalware *(see also specific metal)*
  Carson & Ellis, Inc.
  Magnus Craft Materials, Inc.
aluminum circles
  St. Louis Crafts Inc.
art metal
  American Handicrafts
art metal tools
  Sax Arts & Crafts
brass
  T. B. Hagstoz & Son
brass rings
  Flair-Craft Inc.
brass rods
  Sax Arts & Crafts
brass sheets
  Sax Arts & Crafts
metal boxes
  Carson & Ellis, Inc.
metal cabinets
  A. L. Stone Displays
metal frames
  Sharon's Petite Sherre
metal mini-easels
  Helen Gallagher
  Lillian Vernon
metal sconces
  Carson & Ellis, Inc.
metal squirrel
  House of York
metal stands
  Max of Dallas
metal tanks
  The Squadron Shop
metal trays
  Carson & Ellis, Inc.
  Peg Hall Studios
metal trivets
  National Artcraft Supply Co.
milk cans
  Dairy Service, Inc

metal working *(see also Metals)*
aluminum
  A 'N L's Hobbicraft, Inc.

Craft Category Index
Metal—Miniatures

books
   American Technical Society
   Arco Publishing Co., Inc.
   Charles A. Bennett Co., Inc.
   Book Barn
   Brookstone Co.
   Chilton Book Co.
   Goodhert-Willcox Co., Inc.
   McKnight Publishing Co.
   Museum Books Inc.
   Pitman Publishing Corp.
   Prentice-Hall Inc.
   The Unicorn

fluid solder
   Lox-Seal Adhesives

flux
   Barbara Lawshe
   Panther International Ltd.
   Whittemore-Durgin Glass Co.

hammered metal supplies
   William Dixon Co.

hammered metal work tools
   William Dixon Co.

heatless glazing for metals
   Specialty Products

home study courses
   American School
   Metals Engineering Institute

horn anvils
   Gilman's

magazines
   Journal of Contemporary Metalcraft, Casting, Related Arts
   McCall's Needlework & Crafts

metal alloys
   Magic Circle Corp.

metal compounds
   Delco Craft Center, Inc.

metal craft
   Bergen Arts & Crafts, Inc.
   Cleveland Leather Co.
   Magnus Craft Materials, Inc.

metal detectors
   Brown's Rock & Lapidary Supplies
   Covington Engineering Corp.
   Gems Galore

metal etching
   Delco Craft Center, Inc.

metal finishing
   Birchwood Casey
   Skil-Crafts Division

metal mini-easels
   Helen Gallagher
   Lillian Vernon

metal modeling materials
   Terminal Hobby Shop

metal molds
   Cake Decorators & Craft Supplies
   Doll's Candle & Craft Supplies

metal powders
   Polyproducts Corp.

metal rings
   Knit Services, Inc.

metal sculpture tools
   Sculpture Services Inc.

metal tooling
   Hazel Pearson Handi Craft
   Skil-Crafts Division
   Zim's

metal working tools
   Brookstone Co.

repousse crafts
   Sunflower Crafts

scribers
   Beno J. Gundlach Co.

sheet metal
   T. B. Hagstoz & Son

tooling metals
   Sax Arts & Crafts

turntables
   Gilmour Campbell
   Delco Craft Center, Inc.

miniatures
   A 'N L's Hobbicraft, Inc.
   Bob's Arts & Crafts
   Boutique Trims
   Boycan's Craft Supplies
   Craftsman Supply House
   Creative Craft House
   Custom Made Carvings & Miniatures
   The Enchanted Doll House
   Fabulous Holiday House
   Fieldwood Co.
   Grueny's Gift Center
   Holiday Craft
   Holiday Handicrafts, Inc.
   Howe Studio
   Miles Kimball
   Koehler's Craft Outlet
   Lamonica
   Hazel Pearson Handi Craft
   The Putter Shop

Craft Category Index
Miniatures—Miniatures

    Ren Ann Crafts
    Rombins' Nest Farm
    Skil-Crafts Division
    Studio D
    Supreme Handicrafts
    Taylor House
    Thieves Market
    Wagner's Crafts
    Zim's
animal eyes
    Sav-On-Crafts
balsa wood
    Bob's Arts & Crafts
    Paul K. Guillow Inc.
    Sax Arts & Crafts
    Skil-Crafts Division
books
    Watson-Guptill Publications
boutique items
    Fabulous Holiday House
    Holiday Handicrafts, Inc.
brass hinges
    Boutique Trims
    Handcraft Originals
button elevator model
    Village Designs
ceramic whiteware miniatures
    Sunflower Crafts
circus model equipment
    Lyman E. Cox, Scale Trains
club plans
    Wee Goodies of the Month Club
crystal miniatures
    Sparkle Studio
custom-made miniatures
    Custom Made Carvings & Miniatures
dollhouse accessories
    Fieldwood Co.
    Joen Ellen Kanze
    Frances La Monica
    LeMar's Decoupage Center
    Miniatures by Marty
dollhouse furniture
    Davault Miniature Furniture
    Mark Farmer Co., Inc.
    Rombins' Nest Farm
    Standard Doll Co.
    Yield House
dollhouse wallpaper
    The Miniature Mart-The Peddler's Shop

dollhouse miniatures
    The Doll Cupboard
    Lamonica
    The Miniature Mart-The Peddler's Shop
    South Shore Woman's Exchange
gold findings
    Country Crafts
gold finish mini-easels
    Jewelart Inc.
gold finish wire easels
    Sunflower Crafts
hand-painted miniatures
    Flint FBG Imports
    Great Brook Miniatures
handcrafted bread dough miniatures
    Hallie Copeland
handcrafted miniature wrought iron accessories
    The Village Smithy
handcrafted miniatures
    The Doll Cupboard
    Federal Smallwares
    Betty Fielding
    Great Brook Miniatures
hinges
    Country Crafts
historical miniature figures
    Terminal Hobby Shop
    Wm. Walthers Inc.
imported novelties
    Studio D
kits
    Cottage Crafts
metal hand-cast miniatures
    Town & Country Crafts
metal hand-painted miniatures
    Brown's Miniatures
metal mini-easels
    Helen Gallagher
    Lillian Vernon
metal miniature doll houses
    Holgate & Raynolds
metal miniature figures
    K & L Co.
metal miniatures
    Great Brook Miniatures
    Handcraft Originals
military miniatures
    The Hobby Bench
    Polk's Hobby Dept. Store

Craft Category Index
Miniatures—Miniatures

    Santos Miniatures
    Wm. Walthers Inc.
mini-easels
    American Handicrafts
mini-mosaic frames
    Lillian Vernon
mini-pots
    Mrs. Marilyn G. Alabran
mini-prints
    Scissortail Arts & Crafts
miniature accessories
    The House of Miniatures
    Joen Ellen Kanze
    Miles Kimball
    The Miniature Mart-The Peddler's Shop
    Mrs. Mell Prescott
miniature angels
    Holiday Craft
miniature animals
    Brown's Miniatures
    Custom Made Carvings & Miniatures
    Flint FBG Imports
    Great Brook Miniatures
    Great Central Fur Corp.
    Leathercrafters Supply Co.
    Zim's
miniature antique replicas
    Federal Smallwares
miniature baskets
    Zim's
miniature bedding
    Lamonica
miniature birdhouses
    Hallie Copeland
miniature bone china animals
    The Gift Shoppe
miniature boys
    Hallie Copeland
miniature candlesticks
    Sparkle Studio
miniature ceramic animals
    The Gift Shoppe
miniature ceramic bowls
    Grueny's Gift Center
miniature ceramic figures
    Grueny's Gift Center
    Town & Country Crafts
    Wilfred Enterprises
miniature ceramic pitchers
    Grueny's Gift Center
miniature ceramic vases
    Grueny's Gift Center
miniature chandeliers
    The Miniature Mart-The Peddler's Shop
    Sparkle Studio
miniature chests
    Van Gelder Wood Products
miniature creche figures
    Holiday Craft
miniature doll accessories
    Lamonica
miniature dolls
    Helen Gallagher
    Susan Sirkis
miniature Early American furniture
    The Enchanted Doll House
miniature easels
    F. C. Ziegler Co.
miniature egg craft
    Country Crafts
miniature El-Kru china
    The Miniature Mart-The Peddler's Shop
miniature flags
    Flags Galore
miniature flowers
    Holiday Craft
miniature French dolls
    Grueny's Gift Center
miniature furniture
    Barnstable Originals by H.W. Smith
    Custom Made Carvings & Miniatures
    Federal Smallwares
    Helen Gallagher
    Grueny's Gift Center
    The House of Miniatures
    Miles Kimball
    Lamonica
    The Miniature Mart-The Peddler's Shop
    Mrs. Mell Prescott
    Sparkle Studio
miniature girls
    Hallie Copeland
miniature glass
    The Miniature Mart-The Peddler's Shop
miniature glass animals
    The Gift Shoppe

Craft Category Index
Miniatures—Model

miniature grass
   Holiday Craft
miniature hardware
   The Miniature Mart-The Peddler's Shop
miniature Japanese girls
   Hallie Copeland
miniature lamps
   Lamonica
   Sparkle Studio
miniature lead figures
   Hobby Gallery
miniature mice
   Hallie Copeland
miniature ornaments
   The Miniature Mart-The Peddler's Shop
miniature pewter dishes
   Downs
miniature power tools
   Brookstone Co.
   Foredom Electric Co.
   Gilman's
miniature pulls
   The Miniature Mart-The Peddler's Shop
miniature rabbits
   Hallie Copeland
miniature rooms accessories
   LeMar's Decoupage Center
miniature silk pictures
   Country Crafts
miniature silver
   The Miniature Mart-The Peddler's Shop
miniature soldiers
   Hobby Gallery
miniature tanks
   Coker Craft
miniature tools
   Walter Drake
   The L. S. Starrett Co.
miniature trees
   Holiday Craft
miniature wrought iron furniture
   The Village Smithy
miniature 19th century figures
   Flint FBG Imports
model figures
   Boxcar Ken
   Circus Hobby Hall
   Wm. Walthers Inc.
modern miniatures
   Miniatures by Marty
old time circus wagons
   Circus Hobby Hall
plastic miniatures
   Handcraft Originals
unpainted miniatures
   Glo-Classics
   Sunflower Crafts
Victorian miniatures
   Miniatures by Marty
wildlife miniatures
   Great Brook Miniatures
wood miniatures
   Handcraft Originals

mirrors
   Edmund Scientific Co.
   Party Bazaar
   Hazel Pearson Handi Craft
kits
   Kitsophrenia, Inc.
mica mirrors
   Kitsophrenia, Inc.
mirror tiles
   Montgomery Ward & Co., Inc.

mobiles
books
   Emerson Books Inc.
   Japan Publications Trading Co.
   Parker Publishing Co., Inc.
kits
   Glass Creations

model crafts
balsa wood
   Bob's Arts & Crafts
   Paul K. Guillow Inc.
   Sax Arts & Crafts
   Skil-Crafts Division
books
   America's Hobby Center Inc.
   Arco Publishing Co., Inc.
   James Bliss & Co. Inc.
   Chilton Book Co.
   Coker Craft
   Crown Publishers
   Follett Publishing Co.
   Harper & Row, Publishers Inc.
   Kalmbach Publishing Co.
   Model Craftsman Publishing Corp.

Model Railroad Equipment Corp.
Prentice-Hall Inc.
bronze model metal
    T. B. Hagstoz & Son
button elevator model
    Village Designs
circus model equipment
    Lyman E. Cox, Scale Trains
electric model motors
    James Bliss & Co. Inc.
English war-game figures
    Miniature Figurines--USA, Inc.
European miniature figures
    Natalie Originals Studio
foreign model railroad accessories
    Amro
foreign model railroad trains
    Amro
HO gauge figures
    K & L Co.
HO models
    Campbell Scale Models
HO railroad accessories
    Paige Enterprises
illuminated number boards
    Paige Enterprises
kits
    America's Hobby Center Inc.
    Archer's Hobby World
    Associated Hobby Manufacturers Inc.
    Auto World, Inc.
    James Bliss & Co. Inc.
    Bluejacket Ship Crafters
    Campbell Scale Models
    Canadian Aero-Supply
    Albert Constantine & Son Inc.
    Continental Hobbies Inc.
    Exact Performance
    John Hathaway
    Herter's, Inc.
    Hobby Gallery
    Holgate & Raynolds
    JMC
    JV Models
    Life-Like Products Inc.
    Locomotive Workshop
    Sal Marino Co.
    Mars Models
    Miniature Aircraft
    Model Die Casting Inc.
    Model Railroad Equipment Corp.
    National Hobby Inc.
    Oxford Crafts
    Paige Enterprises
    Plastruct
    PRO Custom Hobbies
    R/C Cars International
    Railway Express
    Santos Miniatures
    Sax Arts & Crafts
    Scientific Models Inc.
    Ships Unlimited
    Siderod Shop
    Sig Manufacturing Co., Inc.
    Sinclair's Auto Miniatures Inc.
    The Squadron Shop
    Star Models
    Suncoast Models
    E. Suydam & Co.
    Terminal Hobby Shop
    U. C. Hobby Center
    Wm. Walthers Inc.
    Whistle Stop
    Williams Bros.
leaflets
    Bluejacket Ship Crafters
    Cleveland Model & Supply Co.
    Coker Craft
    LTA Products
    Miniature Aircraft
    Model Craftsman Publishing Corp.
    Sid Morgan
    Popular Mechanics Press
lifelike grass
    Life-Like Products Inc.
lifelike stone
    Life-Like Products Inc.
magazines
    Auto Modeler
    Carstens Publications
    Flying Models
    O Scale Railroading
    Railroad Modeler
    Scale Modeler
metal miniature figures
    K & L Co.
metal tanks
    The Squadron Shop
military miniatures
    The Hobby Bench
    Polk's Hobby Dept. Store

Craft Category Index
Model—Model

    Santos Miniatures
    Wm. Walthers Inc.
miniature accessories
    The House of Miniatures
    Joen Ellen Kanze
    Miles Kimball
    The Miniature Mart-The Peddler's Shop
    Mrs. Mell Prescott
miniature animals
    Brown's Miniatures
    Custom Made Carvings & Miniatures
    Flint FBG Imports
miniature antique replicas
    Federal Smallwares
miniature baskets
    Zim's
miniature bedding
    Lamonica
miniature birdhouses
    Hallie Copeland
miniature bone china animals
    The Gift Shoppe
miniature boys
    Hallie Copeland
miniature candlesticks
    Sparkle Studio
miniature ceramic animals
    The Gift Shoppe
miniature ceramic bowls
    Grueny's Gift Center
miniature ceramic figures
    Grueny's Gift Center
miniature ceramic pitchers
    Grueny's Gift Center
miniature ceramic vases
    Grueny's Gift Center
miniature chandeliers
    The Miniature Mart-The Peddler's Shop
    Sparkle Studio
miniature chests
    Van Gelder Wood Products
miniature creche figures
    Holiday Craft
miniature dolls
    Helen Gallagher
miniature Early American furniture
    The Enchanted Doll House
miniature easels
    F. C. Ziegler Co.

miniature el-kru china
    The Miniature Mart-The Peddler's Shop
miniature flags
    Flags Galore
miniature flowers
    Holiday Craft
miniature French dolls
    Grueny's Gift Center
miniature furniture
    Barnstable Originals by H.W. Smith
    Custom Made Carvings & Miniatures
    Federal Smallwares
    Helen Gallagher
    Grueny's Gift Center
    The House of Miniatures
    Miles Kimball
    Lamonica
    The Miniature Mart-The Peddler's Shop
    Mrs. Mell Prescott
    Sparkle Studio
miniature girls
    Hallie Copeland
miniature glass
    The Miniature Mart-The Peddler's Shop
miniature glass animals
    The Gift Shoppe
miniature grass
    Holiday Craft
miniature hardware
    The Miniature Mart-The Peddler's Shop
miniature Japanese girls
    Hallie Copeland
miniature lamps
    Lamonica
    Sparkle Studio
miniature lead figures
    Hobby Gallery
miniature mice
    Hallie Copeland
miniature ornaments
    The Miniature Mart-The Peddler's Shop
miniature pewter dishes
    Downs
miniature power tools
    Brookstone Co.

Craft Category Index
Model—Model

Foredom Electric Co.
Gilman's
miniature pulls
  The Miniature Mart-The Peddler's Shop
miniature rabbits
  Hallie Copeland
miniature rooms accessories
  LeMar's Decoupage Center
miniature silk pictures
  Country Crafts
miniature silver
  The Miniature Mart-The Peddler's Shop
miniature soldiers
  Hobby Gallery
miniature tanks
  Coker Craft
miniature tools
  Walter Drake
  The L. S. Starrett Co.
miniature trees
  Holiday Craft
miniature wrought iron furniture
  The Village Smithy
miniature 19th century figures
  Flint FBG Imports
miniatures
  A 'N L's Hobbicraft, Inc.
  Bob's Arts & Crafts
  Boutique Trims
  Boycan's Craft Supplies
  Craftsman Supply House
  Creative Craft House
  Custom Made Carvings & Miniatures
  The Enchanted Doll House
  Fabulous Holiday House
  Fieldwood Co.
  Grueny's Gift Center
  Holiday Craft
  Holiday Handicrafts, Inc.
  Howe Studio
  Miles Kimball
  Koehler's Craft Outlet
  Lamonica
  Hazel Pearson Handi Craft
  The Putter Shop
  Ren Ann Crafts
  Rombins' Nest Farm
  Skil-Crafts Division
  Studio D

  Supreme Handicrafts
  Taylor House
  Thieves Market
  Wagner's Crafts
  Zim's
model scratch building supplies
  Model Railroad Equipment Corp.
  Wm. Walthers Inc.
  Williams Bros.
model accessories
  America's Hobby Center Inc.
  Campbell Scale Models
  Life-Like Products Inc.
  Mars Models
  Miniature Aircraft
  Model Railroad Equipment Corp.
  National Hobby Inc.
  PRO Custom Hobbies
  The Squadron Shop
  Whistle Stop
model airbrushes
  Miniature Aircraft
model aircraft accessories
  Williams Bros.
model aircraft engines
  Canadian Aero-Supply
model airplanes
  Vern Clements
  The Hobby Bench
  National Hobby Inc.
  Polk's Hobby Dept. Store
model animals
  Bachmann
model boat landings
  JV Models
model boats
  National Hobby Inc.
model bridges
  Campbell Scale Models
  Wm. Walthers Inc.
model building materials
  Northeastern Scale Models Inc.
model buildings
  Wm. Walthers Inc.
model cannon
  Railway Express
model car accessories
  Auto World, Inc.
model cars
  Bachmann
  Life-Like Products Inc.

Craft Category Index
Model—Model

    Sinclair's Auto Miniatures Inc.
    The Squadron Shop
model castings
    PRO Custom Hobbies
model cements
    Model Railroad Equipment Corp.
    Wm. Walthers Inc.
model coaling dock
    Campbell Scale Models
model construction materials
    PRO Custom Hobbies
model decals
    Boxcar Ken
    Miniature Aircraft
    U. C. Hobby Center
model electrical items
    Wm. Walthers Inc.
model electronic components
    Railway Express
model fencing
    Bachmann
model figures
    Boxcar Ken
    Circus Hobby Hall
    Wm. Walthers Inc.
model fittings
    James Bliss & Co. Inc.
    Bluejacket Ship Crafters
model forest ranger station
    JV Models
model freight depots
    Campbell Scale Models
model freight load equipment
    Bachmann
model hand tools
    America's Hobby Center Inc.
    PRO Custom Hobbies
model HO cars
    Auto World, Inc.
model HO railroad
    The Hobby Bench
    JMC
model HON3 railroad
    The Hobby Bench
model interior detail items
    Wm. Walthers Inc.
model making
    Delco Craft Center, Inc.
model materials
    Santos Miniatures

model N railroad
    The Hobby Bench
    JMC
model O railroad
    JMC
model ON3 railroad
    The Hobby Bench
model paints
    Boxcar Ken
    Hobby Gallery
    Miniature Aircraft
    Model Railroad Equipment Corp.
    PRO Custom Hobbies
    Santos Miniatures
    Ships Unlimited
    U. C. Hobby Center
    Wm. Walthers Inc.
model parts
    Wm. Walthers Inc.
model passenger depots
    Campbell Scale Models
model piping components
    Plastruct
model power packs
    Wm. Walthers Inc.
model power tools
    America's Hobby Center Inc.
    Sal Marino Co.
    PRO Custom Hobbies
model produce docks
    Campbell Scale Models
model produce stands
    JV Models
model racing cars
    Sinclair's Auto Miniatures Inc.
model railroad accessories
    Bachmann
    JMC
    Wm. Walthers Inc.
model railroad buildings
    Associated Hobby Manufacturers Inc.
model railroad car parts
    Northeastern Scale Models Inc.
model railroad cars
    Associated Hobby Manufacturers Inc.
model railroad equipment
    Associated Hobby Manufacturers Inc.
    Lyman E. Cox, Scale Trains
    PRO Custom Hobbies
    Railway Express
    Terminal Hobby Shop

model railroad signs
  Bachmann
model railroads
  Boxcar Ken
  Mars Models
  National Hobby Inc.
  Polk's Hobby Dept. Store
  Railway Express
  Whistle Stop
model room castings
  Holgate & Raynolds
model saloons
  Campbell Scale Models
model sand house
  Campbell Scale Models
model scenery
  Boxcar Ken
  Campbell Scale Models
  Siderod Shop
  Wm. Walthers Inc.
model ships
  The Hobby Bench
  Polk's Hobby Dept. Store
  Railway Express
model signals
  Wm. Walthers Inc.
model slot cars
  Auto World, Inc.
model steam engines
  James Bliss & Co. Inc.
model structures
  Boxcar Ken
  Railway Express
  Wm. Walthers Inc.
model tools
  James Bliss & Co. Inc.
  Boxcar Ken
  Model Railroad Equipment Corp.
  National Hobby Inc.
  Paige Enterprises
  Railway Express
  Santos Miniatures
  Ships Unlimited
  Siderod Shop
  Terminal Hobby Shop
  Wm. Walthers Inc.
model town buildings
  Campbell Scale Models
model tracks
  Railway Express

model trains
  JMC
  Model Railroad Equipment Corp.
  Railway Express
model trees
  Bachmann
model tressels
  Campbell Scale Models
model trucks
  Bachmann
model water tank
  Campbell Scale Models
model wire
  PRO Custom Hobbies
N gauge O scale traction equipment
  Mars Models
O gauge railroad accessories
  Paige Enterprises
O gauge sheets plastic embossed
  Holgate & Raynolds
old time circus wagons
  Circus Hobby Hall
paper models
  John Hathaway
passenger car drumheads
  Paige Enterprises
plastic embossed ho gauge sheets
  Holgate & Raynolds
plastic model structural components
  Plastruct
plastic modeling materials
  Terminal Hobby Shop
plastic scale models
  Minicraft Models Inc.
plastic tanks
  The Squadron Shop
radio controlled boats
  R/C Cars International
radio controlled cars
  R/C Cars International
ready-to-fly gliders
  Paul K. Guillow Inc.
ship models
  Coker Craft
modeling crafts
  modeling clay
    American Art Clay Co. Inc.
    Douglas & Sturgess, Inc.
    Economy Handicrafts, Inc.
    Sculpture Associates Ltd.

Craft Category Index
Modeling—Molds

    Sculpture House
    Sculpture Services Inc.
modeling equipment
    Sculpture Services Inc.
modeling stands
    Sculpture Services Inc.
modeling supplies
    Ettl Studios Inc.
modeling tools
    Delco Craft Center, Inc.
    Tandy Leather Co.
    Westwood Ceramic Supply Co.
modeling wheels
    Sculpture Services Inc.
plastic modeling materials
    Terminal Hobby Shop
wood modeling materials
    Terminal Hobby Shop

molds and mold making *(see also Casting)*
    Castolite
    Plasco
    Reggi's Ceramic Colors
    W. Wooley & Co.
aluminum molds for ornamental concrete
    Concrete Machinery Co.
animal molds
    Town & Country Crafts
books
    Cooke Novelty Co.
    W. Wooley & Co.
cake decorating molds
    General Supplies Co.
cake molds
    Cake Decorators & Craft Supplies
candle molds
    Candle Kitchen
    Candle Mill Village
    Candlewic Co.
    Celebration Candlemaking Supplies
    Craft & Candle House
    Deep Flex Plastic Molds, Inc.
    General Supplies Co.
    House of Wood Candles
    Pourette Mfg. Co.
    Sav-On-Crafts
    Sax Arts & Crafts
    Sears, Roebuck & Co.
    W. Spencer Inc.
    Swan-Son
    TAP Plastic Inc.
    Town & Country Crafts
    Trask Plastics
    Village Candle & Craft
    Walnut Hill Co.
    Lee Wards
    W. Wooley & Co.
candy molding
    Cake Decorators & Craft Supplies
ceramic molds
    Air Capitol Molds, Inc.
    Alberta's Molds Inc.
    Anchor Mold Co.
    Atlantic Mold Corp.
    Clay-Crafters Products
    Cramer Mold Shop
    Curio Ceramic Molds
    Daddy's Mold Shop
    Dinky Molds
    Holland Mold Inc.
    Jamar-Mallory Inc.
    Jane's Ceramic Molds
    Mindy Molds
    Ohio Ceramic Supply Inc.
    R & R Ceramic Molds Inc.
    Ju Rene Ceramic Molds
    Al Schoellkopf Mold Co.
    Van Howe Ceramic Supply Co.
chess set molds
    Stylecraft of Baltimore
clay molds
    Kay Kinney-Contoured Glass
collar molds
    Kay Kinney-Contoured Glass
cooking crystal molds
    Hazel Pearson Handi Craft
fiberglass cloth
    Castolite
    High Strength Adhesives Corp.
    Kick-Shaw Inc.
fiberglass mat
    High Strength Adhesives Corp.
    Kick-Shaw Inc.
fiberglass molds
    Plycrete Mold Co.
fillers
    Adhesive Products Corp.
    Castolite
    W. Wooley & Co.
glass mold coats
    Kay Kinney-Contoured Glass

Craft Category Index
Molds—Mosaics

kits
   Westwood Ceramic Supply Co.
liquid rubber
   Bersted's
   W. Wooley & Co.
metal molds
   Cake Decorators & Craft Supplies
   Doll's Candle & Craft Supplies
mini molds
   Nationwide Ceramic Enterprises
mold making equipment
   Supreme Watch Material Co.
   Technical Specialties International Inc.
mold materials
   Polyproducts Corp.
mold patterns
   Bee Basch Designs
mold releases
   Atlantic Mold Corp.
   High Strength Adhesives Corp.
   Walnut Hill Co.
mold stands
   Gilmour Campbell
molded plaques
   Albert Constantine & Son Inc.
molding compound
   Natcol Crafts, Inc.
moulage molding
   Douglas & Sturgess, Inc.
   Sculpture Services Inc.
ornament molds
   Town & Country Crafts
plaster ceramic molds
   Bee Basch Designs
plaster molds
   Deep Flex Plastic Molds, Inc.
   Delco Craft Center, Inc.
   Fres-O-Lone Mold Corp.
   Sax Arts & Crafts
   Skil-Crafts Division
   Swan-Son
   Trask Plastics
   W. Wooley & Co.
plastic candle molds
   Barker Enterprises
   Natcol Crafts, Inc.
plastic ceramic molds
   Johnny Sens of New Orleans

plastic molds
   Cake Decorators & Craft Supplies
   Evelyn Saft
plastic vacuum molding
   Nationwide Plastics Co.
pour-cold mold rubber
   Sculpture Services Inc.
resin molds
   Belle Craft
   Deep Flex Plastic Molds, Inc.
   Delco Craft Center, Inc.
   Green's Rock & Lapidary Ltd.
   Natcol Crafts, Inc.
   Sax Arts & Crafts
   Skil-Crafts Division
   Swan-Son
   Trask Plastics
rubber
   Blue Grass Art & Hobby Center
   Sculpture Services Inc.
rubber latex
   Douglas & Sturgess, Inc.
rubber mold compound
   W. Spencer Inc.
rubber molds
   Doll's Candle & Craft Supplies
straps for banding large and small ceramic molds
   Universal Strap Co.
vinyl molds
   W. Wooley & Co.
wooden candle molds
   Barker Enterprises
3-D plastic molds
   Basic Crafts Co.
   Doll's Candle & Craft Supplies

mosaics *(see also Tiles)*
   A 'N L's Hobbicraft, Inc.
   Bergen Arts & Crafts, Inc.
   Cleveland Leather Co.
   Craft Service
   Craftsman Supply House
   Delco Craft Center, Inc.
   Economy Handicrafts, Inc.
   The Handcrafters
   Carl Hepp Mosaic Co.
   Magnus Craft Materials, Inc.
   National Artcraft Supply Co.
bisqued ceramic tiles
   Newton's Potters Supply

Craft Category Index
Mosaics—Nature

books
  Book Barn
  Crown Publishers
  Davis Publications, Inc.
  Drake Publishers Inc.
  Oxford University Press
  Viking Press
  Watson-Guptill Publications
ceramic tile cutters
  Beno J. Gundlach Co.
ceramic tiles
  Renaldy's
grout
  F. E. Biegert Co.
grout colors
  F. E. Biegert Co.
Italian glass mosaic tiles
  F. E. Biegert Co.
kits
  General Crafts Corp.
  Sax Arts & Crafts
leaflets
  Craftplans
mini-mosaic frames
  Lillian Vernon
mosaic beads
  Bead Game
  Jeweler's Emporium
mosaic cutters
  The L. S. Starrett Co.
mosaic forms
  Delco Craft Center, Inc.
  Sax Arts & Crafts
mosaic mirrors
  Carl Hepp Mosaic Co.
  Nicole Bead & Craft Co., Inc.
mosaic tiles
  Art Mart, Inc.
  Boin Arts & Crafts
  Delco Craft Center, Inc.
  Sax Arts & Crafts
mosaic tools
  Delco Craft Center, Inc.
nippers
  F. E. Biegert Co.
  Beno J. Gundlach Co.
plastic mosaic tile
  Boin Arts & Crafts
music boxes and movements
  doll music box movements
    Standard Doll Co.
  music box accessories
    Craftsman Wood Service Co.
  music box movements
    Albert Constantine & Son Inc.
    Craft Products
    Craftsman Wood Service Co.
    Minnesota Woodworkers Supply Co.
    O-P Craft Co., Inc.
    Skil-Crafts Division
  music boxes
    Bergen Arts & Crafts, Inc.
    Country Crafts
    National Artcraft Supply Co.
musical instrument crafting *(see also Wood)*
  books
    Chilton Book Co.
    E. P. Dutton & Co., Inc.
  guitarmaking accessories
    String Instrument Service Inc.
  imported prefabricated guitar wood
    String Instrument Service Inc.
  instrument accessories
    International Violin
  instrument bridge
    HERE Inc.
  instrument nut
    HERE Inc.
  instrument strings
    HERE Inc.
  instrument tuners
    HERE Inc.
  instrument wood
    International Violin
  kits
    Albert Constantine & Son Inc.
    Craftsman Wood Service Co.
    Dulcimer
    HERE Inc.
    Schober Organ Corp.
  leaflets
    Craftplans
nail sculpture
  kits
    Bachmann
natural dyes *(see Dyes)*
nature crafts *(see also Ecology crafts)*
  American Indian bead corn
    Crowe & Coulter
  American Indian flower corn
    Crowe & Coulter

animal fossils
   Geological Enterprises
artificial flowers
   Schrock's, The House of Hobbies & Crafts
   Lee Wards
artificial foliage
   Boycan's Craft Supplies
artificial fruits
   Zim's
artificial plants
   Lee Wards
artificial straw
   House of Flowers
bones
   Winona Trading Post
books
   Boycan's Craft Supplies
   Chilton Book Co.
   Driftwood House
   Great Outdoors Publishing Co.
   J. B. Lippincott Co.
   Parker Publishing Co., Inc.
   Stackpole Books
   Watson-Guptill Publications
butterflies
   Arthur Brown & Bro., Inc.
   The Collector's Cabinet
   House of York
   Hazel Pearson Handi Craft
cones
   Boycan's Craft Supplies
   Driftwood House
   Western Tree Cones
corsage making supplies
   Dorothy Biddle Service
cut shells
   Derby Lane Shell Center
driftwood
   Driftwood House
   Dale Magnuson
driftwood polish
   Deb Products
driftwood wax
   Driftwood House
ferns
   Arthur Brown & Bro., Inc.
fossils
   The Collector's Cabinet
   Colorado Geological Industries Inc.
   Dover Scientific Co.
   The Fluorite Shop
   Green's Rock & Lapidary Ltd.
   Scott Scientific Inc.
gourd seeds
   George W. Park Seed Co., Inc.
herbs
   Worldwide Curio House
hutch boxes
   Koehler's Craft Outlet
kits
   Anne's Treasure Trove
   Driftwood House
   Gift Craft
leaves
   Gail's Decorative Arts Studio
lichen
   Holiday Craft
   Life-Like Products Inc.
lifelike grass
   Life-Like Products Inc.
lifelike stone
   Life-Like Products Inc.
miniature animals
   Brown's Miniatures
   Custom Made Carvings & Miniatures
   Flint FBG Imports
miniature birdhouses
   Hallie Copeland
miniature bone china animals
   The Gift Shoppe
miniature ceramic animals
   The Gift Shoppe
miniature glass animals
   The Gift Shoppe
miniature grass
   Holiday Craft
miocene vertebrate fossils
   C. R. Boylin
North American fossils
   Odyssey Mineral and Fossil
paper grass
   Life-Like Products Inc.
petrified wood
   Bonnie's Rock Shop
   Mississippi Petrified Forest
petrified wood stumps
   Mission Rocks
plant fossils
   Geological Enterprises
pods
   Driftwood House

Craft Category Index
Nature—Needlecrafts

preserved butterflies
  J. Alday
  American Butterfly Co.
  Dorothy Biddle Service
preserved foliage
  Boycan's Craft Supplies
roots
  Worldwide Curio House
seed beads
  House of Orange
  Macrame and Weaving Supply Co.
seed pods
  Western Tree Cones
seeds
  Bead Game
  Driftwood House
  Jeweler's Emporium
  George W. Park Seed Co., Inc.
shadowboxes
  The Handcraft Supply Corp.
shark's teeth
  C. R. Boylin
  Florida Supply House, Inc.
specimen trimmers
  Nature's Treasures
stones
  Florida Supply House, Inc.
  Dale Magnuson
weathered decorative boards
  Dale Magnuson
white birch bark
  Dale Magnuson

needlecrafts *(see also specific craft)*
  Knits'N That Yarn Shop
  Merribee
  Rombins' Nest Farm
  Sears, Roebuck & Co.
  Straw Into Gold
accessories
  Knits'N That Yarn Shop
  Merribee
  Sign of the Arrow
afghans
  Merribee
Americana samplers
  J. L. T.
  Northwest Handcraft House
appliques
  Leman Publications
  Lillian Vernon

automatic needle threaders
  Two Brothers Inc.
barrettes
  J. L. T.
bell pull hardware
  The Yarn Nook
Bermuda bag handles
  Sudberry House
books
  Arco Publishing Co., Inc.
  Barbara Bannister
  Charles T. Branford Co.
  Craftsman Circle Book Club
  Davis Publications, Inc.
  Fawcett Special Interest Magazines & Books
  Harper & Row, Publishers Inc.
  Hearthside Press
  Lily Mills Co.
  Mary Maxim Inc.
  Museum Books Inc.
  Nantucket Needleworks
  Needlecraft House
  Random House Inc.
  Henry Regnery Co.
  Reilly & Lee Books
  Shoenail Supply
  Southern Living Books
brass bell pulls
  Wichelt Import Co.
bunka embroidery
  House of Flowers
canvas
  Craft Yarns of Rhode Island Inc.
  Crossroads
  Delco Craft Center, Inc.
  The Hidden Village
  International Creations
  Jerry S. Kaye Assoc.
  Leonida Leatherdale's Embroidery Studio
  Mary Maxim Inc.
  Merribee
  The Needlecase
  Needlecraft House
  Nimble Thimble
  Peri's Homework
  Plush Point Patterns by Marcia Podell
  Sax Arts & Crafts
  Shillcraft
  Sign of the Arrow

Craft Category Index
Needlecrafts—Needlecrafts

Threadneedle
Thumbelina Needlework Shop
The Yarn Depot
Yarns Unlimited
canvas tape
   Needle-Ease
club plans
   Erica Wilson's Creative Needlework Society
daisy winder
   Rosemond Hobbycraft
electric tufting
   The Hidden Village
embroidery blocks
   Lee Wards
embroidery designs
   House of Patterns
   Raymond P. Wallace
embroidery fabrics
   Leonida Leatherdale's Embroidery Studio
   Needlecraft House
   The Thread Shed, Inc.
embroidery frames
   Crossroads
   KAY an EE Corp. of America
   Mary Maxim Inc.
   Merribee
   Sears, Roebuck & Co.
embroidery hoops
   Crossroads
   KAY an EE Corp. of America
   Mary Maxim Inc.
   Merribee
   Needlecraft House
   Yarns Unlimited
embroidery linen
   Jerry S. Kaye Assoc.
embroidery materials
   Easy Street
embroidery scissors
   Polly Chester Inc.
embroidery threads
   Crossroads
   Frederick J. Fawcett, Inc.
   Folklorico
   Leonida Leatherdale's Embroidery Studio
   The Mail Train
   Merribee
   Nantucket Needleworks

   Needlecraft House
   The Thread Shed, Inc.
   Lee Wards
embroidery transfer patterns
   Crewel Elephant
floor hoops
   KAY an EE Corp. of America
footstool frames
   Thumbelina Needlework Shop
frames
   Crewel World
   The Hidden Village
   Jerry S. Kaye Assoc.
   Joan Moshimer
   Nantucket Needleworks
   Needlecraft Shop Inc.
   Jane Snead Samplers
   Yarns Unlimited
   F. C. Ziegler Co.
grospoint yarn
   Peri's Homework
hand-painted needlepoint canvas
   The Amber Lion
   Creativity Needlepoint
   Most Unusual Custom Needleworks Inc.
home study courses
   Lee Mountain
   Nantucket School of Needlery
   National Standards Council of American Embroiderers
   Erica Wilson Correspondence Courses
hoops
   The Hidden Village
   Jerry S. Kaye Assoc.
   Nantucket Needleworks
   Needlecraft Shop Inc.
hot iron transfers
   Needlecraft Shop Inc.
   Transart
imported canvas
   The Needle Works
iron-on patterns
   Mrs. W. Bradley Ryan
kits
   Ball O' Yarn
   Better Homes & Gardens
   The Corner Shop
   Family Circle Kits
   Helen Gallagher
   Gift Craft

Craft Category Index
Needlecrafts—Needlecrafts

    Good Housekeeping
    House of Flowers
    Kazari
    Miles Kimball
    Ladies Home Journal Needle & Craft
    Loftons
    Edna Looney Originals
    Jean McIntosh Ltd.
    Needles 'N Hoops
    Paragon Needlecraft
    Pioneer Crafts
    Scandinavian Rya Rugs
    The Stitchery
    Studio Twelve
    Sue's Custom Quilting
    Thumbelina Needlework Shop
    Victoria Gifts
    Montgomery Ward & Co., Inc.
    Lee Wards
    Wyco Yarn Co.
    The Yarn Nook
leaflets
    Mrs. L. Winum
linen
    Delco Craft Center, Inc.
    International Creations
    Knit Services, Inc.
    Nantucket Needleworks
    Needlecraft House
    Mrs. W. Bradley Ryan
magazines
    American Home Crafts
    Good Housekeeping Needlecraft
    McCall's Needlework & Crafts
    Mon Tricot
    1001 Fashion & Needlecraft Ideas
    Woman's Day Knit & Stitch
    Woman's Day Needlework Ideas
    Woman's Day Sewing & Fashion Ideas
manual tufting
    The Hidden Village
needlecraft designs
    Donna Jean Carver
    Sudberry House
needlecraft stand
    Sperry & Son
needlecraft supplies
    Fiber to Fabric
    Gemex Co.
    Homespun Fabrics
    Kazari
    Nimble Thimble
    The Stitchery
    The Yarn Dome
needlecraft yarn
    The Yarn Depot
needlepoint
    Jerry S. Kaye Assoc.
    Ladies Home Journal Needle & Craft
    Merribee
    The Needle Works
    Needlecraft Shop Inc.
    J. C. Penney Co., Inc.
    Schrock's, The House of Hobbies & Crafts
    Sears, Roebuck & Co.
    Tuxedo Yarn & Needlework
    Wool 'N Wick
needlepoint canvas
    Crossroads
    Needlecraft Shop Inc.
    Mrs. W. Bradley Ryan
needlepoint charts
    Needlecraft Shop Inc.
needlepoint cleaner
    The Needle Works
needlepoint designs
    International Creations
    The Knittery
needlepoint handbag linings
    Modern Needlepoint
needlepoint hardware
    Mrs. W. Bradley Ryan
needlepoint lace
    Wm. Hooper
needlepoint mountings
    Modern Needlepoint
needlepoint rods
    Needlecraft House
needlepoint supplies
    The Knittery
    Vicki's Patience Unlimited
needlepoint templates
    New Products Co.
needles
    House of Gould
    Jerry S. Kaye Assoc.
    Knit Services, Inc.
    The Mail Train
    Mary Maxim Inc.
    Merribee

Craft Category Index
Needlecrafts—Needlepoint

The Needle Works
Needlecraft Shop Inc.
needleweaving cloth
Nantucket Needleworks
needlework dolls
Donna Jean Carver
needlework stuffed toys
Donna Jean Carver
netting needles
Reisinger Net Co.
organizations
Embroiderer's Guild of America Inc.
personalized woven labels
L & L Stitchery
Melrose Yarn Co., Inc.
The Needle Works
pillows
The Hidden Village
pin cushions
Sharon's Petite Sherre
polyester filled pillow forms
Putnam Co.
pre-quilted pieces for embroidering
Lee Wards
printed woven edge satin labels
Helmor Label Co.
punch needle
Sewing Products Co.
rayon yarn
Contessa Yarns
Craft Yarns of Rhode Island Inc.
roll and stretch frame
Needle-Ease
rosette winders
Holiday Handicrafts, Inc.
Mary Maxim Inc.
Merribee
Yarns Unlimited
roving yarns
Tinkler & Co. Inc.
rubber cushions
Atlantic Upholstery Supply Co.
rya pillow backings
House of Kleen
samplers
Schrock's, The House of Hobbies & Crafts
services
The Custom House of Needle Arts & Design
The Thread Shed, Inc.

stamped linens
Merribee
stitchery
Cottage Crafts
Ladies Home Journal Needle & Craft
Sax Arts & Crafts
stitchery mesh (2 gauges)
Delco Craft Center, Inc.
Swiss bell pulls
Robin & Russ Handweavers
tennis racquet covers
Peri's Homework
thread holders
The Needle Works
wood hoops
Knit Services, Inc.
woven labels
Charm Woven Labels
Walter Drake
Knit-Sew Labels
Spencer Gifts Inc.
yardage counters
Robin & Russ Handweavers

needlepoint (see also Frames, Hoops, Needlecrafts, Yarns)
Jerry S. Kaye Assoc.
Ladies Home Journal Needle & Craft
Merribee
The Needle Works
Needlecraft Shop Inc.
J. C. Penney Co., Inc.
Schrock's, The House of Hobbies & Crafts
Sears, Roebuck & Co.
Tuxedo Yarn & Needlework
Wool 'N Wick
bargello
The Needle Works
barrettes
J. L. T.
books
Better Homes & Gardens Books
Book Barn
Chilton Book Co.
Crossroads
Crown Publishers
The Dial Press Inc.
Grosset & Dunlap Inc.
Lane Magazine & Book Co.
The Needle Works
Random House Inc.

Craft Category Index
Needlepoint—Needlepoint

    Sterling Publishing Co. Inc.
    Woman's Board
coasters
    J. L. T.
coat-of-arms needlepoint
    Beard's Art Needlework Studio
Colonial heritage collection
    Mrs. W. Bradley Ryan
corded magnifier
    M. Turner
custom-made needlepoint patterns
    Wm. Hooper
Danish needlepoint
    Mrs. W. Bradley Ryan
floor hoops
    KAY an EE Corp. of America
grospoint yarn
    Peri's Homework
hand-painted needlepoint canvas
    The Amber Lion
    Creativity Needlepoint
    Most Unusual Custom Needleworks Inc.
home study courses
    Erica Wilson Correspondence Courses
hoops
    The Hidden Village
    Jerry S. Kaye Assoc.
    Nantucket Needleworks
    Needlecraft Shop Inc.
kits
    Barnes & Blake
    Beard's Art Needlework Studio
    Berry's of Maine
    Brunswick Worsted Mills
    Budget Buddy Co.
    The Corner Shop
    Crafts Yarns & Gifts
    Crain-Harmon
    Creativity Needlepoint
    Crossroads
    Determined Productions, Inc.
    James L. Douthat
    Gemex Co.
    Good Housekeeping
    The Hen House
    Heritage Hill Patterns
    Alexandra Hill Needlepoint Studios Ltd.
    J. L. T.
    Kaleidoscope Needleworks
    Kalico Kits
    Jerry S. Kaye Assoc.
    Krick Kits
    Libby's Needlepoint
    Magic Needle
    Most Unusual Custom Needleworks Inc.
    Nantucket Needleworks
    The Needle Works
    Needlecraft House
    Needlewoman Shop
    Peri's Homework
    Plush Point Patterns by Marcia Podell
    Henry Seligman Co. Inc.
    Sign of the Arrow
    Sudberry House
    Sunray Yarn House
    Lillian Vernon
    Vicki's Patience Unlimited
    Erica Wilson Needleworks
    Woolcraft Ltd.
    The World of Stitch 'N Knit
    Yarns Galore
leaflets
    Skon
linen
    Needlecraft House
magazines
    Challenge Publications, Inc
    Ladies Home Journal Needlecraft
    McCall's Needlework & Crafts
    McCall's Pattern Fashions
    Woman's Day Knit & Stitch
    Woman's Day Needlework Ideas
needlepoint canvas
    Crossroads
    Needlecraft Shop Inc.
    Mrs. W. Bradley Ryan
needlepoint charts
    Needlecraft Shop Inc.
needlepoint cleaner
    The Needle Works
needlepoint designs
    International Creations
    The Knittery
needlepoint handbag linings
    Modern Needlepoint
needlepoint hardware
    Mrs. W. Bradley Ryan
needlepoint lace
    Wm. Hooper

Craft Category Index
Needlepoint—Painting

needlepoint mountings
  Modern Needlepoint
needlepoint rods
  Needlecraft House
needlepoint supplies
  The Knittery
  Vicki's Patience Unlimited
needlepoint templates
  New Products Co.
needlepoint yarn
  Frederick J. Fawcett, Inc.
  House of Flowers
  Kaleidoscope Needleworks
  Nantucket Needleworks
  Sign of the Arrow
portraits of customer's home or pets
  Beard's Art Needlework Studio
roll and stretch frame
  Needle-Ease
services
  Elvette Handbag Co.
  The Hidden Village
  Most Unusual Custom Needleworks Inc.
  The Needlecase
  Sue's Custom Quilting
  Threadneedle
  Vicki's Patience Unlimited

netting *(see Lace making)*

newspapers *(see also specific craft)*
  The Eggs-Aminer; eggery.
  House of Yarn & Crafts; for machine knitters.

organizations *(see also specific craft)*
  American Crafts Council; general arts and crafts.
  Artisan Crafts; general arts and crafts.
  Embroiderer's Guild of America Inc.; embroidery.
  Handweavers Guild of America, Inc.; weaving.
  Historical Society of Early American Decoration, Inc; Early American decor.
  International Guild of Candle Artisans; candlemaking.
  International Old Lacers; lace making, tatting.
  International Wood Collectors Society; wood and woodworking.
  The Marquetry Society of America; marquetry.
  National Art Worker's Community; general arts and crafts.
  National Carvers Museum; wood carving.
  National Quilting Association; quilting.
  National Standards Council of American Embroiderers; embroidery.
  Puppeteers of America, Inc.; puppet-making.
  Southern Highlands Handicraft Guild; Southern regional crafts guild.
  World Organization of China Painters; china painting.

ornament making *(see also Boutique trims, Christmas crafts, Holiday)*
club plans
  Lee Wards Christmas Tree Club
kits
  Artistry In Wood
  Gift Craft
  Holiday Handicrafts, Inc.
  Sav-On-Crafts
ornament molds
  Town & Country Crafts
ornamental stampings
  Jeweler's Emporium
silk wrap ornaments
  Gibsons Creations

painting
books
  Artis, Inc.
  Ewanna England
  Thelma Sutton Martin
  Priscilla's Little Red Tole House
  Shoenail Supply
  Tole 'N Stuff
  The Unicorn
  Viking Press
  The Wood Barn
decorative painting designs
  Jean's
decorative patterns
  Bernadette Decorative Art
kits
  Creative Murals, Inc.
  James L. Douthat
paint-by-number
  New Products Co.

Craft Category Index
Painting—Paints

   wool velour panels
     Framaway Co.
paints *(see also Enamels, Finishes, Stains)*
     American Decorative Arts, Inc.
     Art Mart, Inc.
     Boin Arts & Crafts
     Boycan's Craft Supplies
     Budget Buddy Co.
     Carson & Ellis, Inc.
     Cleveland Leather Co.
     Craft Service
     Craftsman Supply House
     Delco Craft Center, Inc.
     Floquil, Inc.
     The Handcrafters
     Koehler's Craft Outlet
     Magnus Craft Materials, Inc.
     Hazel Pearson Handi Craft
     Renaldy's
     Sav-On-Crafts
     The Sneak Box Studio
     Sturbridge Yankee Workshop
     W. Wooley & Co.
     Zim's
   ballpoint paints
     Arthur Brown & Bro., Inc.
     Budget Buddy Co.
     The Handcrafters
     Sax Arts & Crafts
     Lee Wards
   books
     Davis & Co.
     National Craft & Hobby Co., Inc.
   candle paints
     Bersted's
   china colors
     D. R. Wolfe Overglazes
   china enamels
     Salyer Publishing Co.
   china painting supplies
     Anita of Calif.
     Dorothy Berryman Studio
     Blue Grass Art & Hobby Center
     D. M. Campana Co.
     The China Cottage
     Collector Studies
     Gladys Galloway
     Holly Studio Inc
     Helen Humes Studio
     Barbara Jones China House
     Darlene Lewis
     Ruth Little's Studio
     J. Opal Stover Studio
     Kenneth Rarick
     Renaldy's
     Robertson Studio
     Salyer Publishing Co.
     Doris Taylor
     D. R. Wolfe Overglazes
   crystallizing paint
     Edmund Scientific Co.
   fabric paint
     Boin Arts & Crafts
     House of Patterns
     Zim's
   furniture stains
     Albert Constantine & Son Inc.
     Sturbridge Yankee Workshop
   glass paints
     Sax Arts & Crafts
     Supreme Handicrafts
     Zim's
   glass stain paint
     Arthur Brown & Bro., Inc.
     The Handcrafters
     Kay Kinney-Contoured Glass
     Koehler's Craft Outlet
     Plaza Artists Materials, Inc.
   kits
     National Craft & Hobby Co., Inc.
   latex
     Sax Arts & Crafts
   lead bearing enamels
     Ceramic Coating Co.
   liquid latex (bonded bronze)
     Adhesive Products Corp.
   metallic latex paints
     Plycrete Mold Co.
   model paints
     Boxcar Ken
     Hobby Gallery
     Miniature Aircraft
     Model Railroad Equipment Corp.
     PRO Custom Hobbies
     Santos Miniatures
     Ships Unlimited
     U. C. Hobby Center
     Wm. Walthers Inc.
   oil paints
     D. M. Campana Co.

Craft Category Index
Paints—Paper

painting enamels
    University Circle Publications and Supply Co.
painting fabrics
    Floquil, Inc
painting glass
    Floquil, Inc.
painting wood
    Floquil, Inc.
pre-mixed china paints
    Doris Taylor
rosemaling paints
    Sandeen's Scandinavian Gift & Card Shop
spray paints
    Party Bazaar
    Plasco
stained glass paints
    Art Mart, Inc.
    Delco Craft Center, Inc.
    Specialty Products
textile enamels
    University Circle Publications and Supply Co.
textile paints
    Art Mart, Inc.
    Bergen Arts & Crafts, Inc.
    Arthur Brown & Bro., Inc.
    Craft Service
    Thelma Sutton Martin
    Sax Arts & Crafts
water soluble leather paints
    Siphon Art Products
water soluble metallic paints
    Reggi's Ceramic Colors
water soluble textile paints
    Siphon Art Products

paper and paper crafts
    Craft Service
    Craftsman Supply House
    Delco Craft Center, Inc.
    Economy Handicrafts, Inc.
    Sax Arts & Crafts
    Skil-Crafts Division
    Supreme Handicrafts
    Zim's
art paper
    Delco Craft Center, Inc.
    Skil-Crafts Division
blockprinting papers
    Stewart Industries

books
    Davis Publications, Inc.
    T. S. Denison & Co., Inc.
    Drake Publishers Inc.
    E. P. Dutton & Co., Inc.
    Emerson Books Inc.
    Hearthside Press
    P. C. Herwig Co., Inc.
    Japan Publications Trading Co.
    The Macmillan Publishing Co.
    David McKay Co., Inc.
    Marie Mitchell's Decoupage Center
    Parker Publishing Co., Inc.
    Pitman Publishing Corp.
    Sancraft Industries
    Stein & Day
    Sterling Publishing Co. Inc.
    Van Nostrand Reinhold Co.
    Watson-Guptill Publications
carbon tracing paper
    Pins & Needles
cellophane paper
    Dick Blick
    Arthur Brown & Bro., Inc.
    Economy Handicrafts, Inc.
    Plaza Artists Materials, Inc.
color parchment posters
    Flair-Craft Inc.
construction paper
    Folkcrafts
corrugated paper
    Dick Blick
    Boin Arts & Crafts
    Plaza Artists Materials, Inc.
craft tissue
    Party Bazaar
crepe paper
    Dick Blick
    Boin Arts & Crafts
    Cleveland Leather Co.
    Koehler's Craft Outlet
    Party Bazaar
    Hazel Pearson Handi Craft
    Carol Rice Creatives
    Skil-Crafts Division
    Supreme Handicrafts
    Zim's
die-cut papers
    Taylor House
drawing paper
    Bergen Arts & Crafts, Inc.

Craft Category Index
Paper—Papier

dressmakers pattern graph paper
   Dorothy H. Becker
flint paper
   Arthur Brown & Bro., Inc.
   Plaza Artists Materials, Inc.
fluorescent paper
   Arthur Brown & Bro., Inc.
foil paper
   Dick Blick
   Gibsons Creations
   Zim's
gold paper borders
   Taylor House
gold paper decorations
   Country Crafts
gold paper laces
   Hazel Pearson Handi Craft
gold paper ornaments
   Skil-Crafts Division
   Taylor House
gold paper trims
   Holiday Craft
graph paper
   Sewakers Industries Inc.
group packs
   Boin Arts & Crafts
gummed paper
   Dick Blick
kits
   Craftool Co.
   John Hathaway
   Mary Maxim Inc.
   Pack-O-Fun
linen
   Contessa Yarns
   Greentree Ranch Wools, Countryside Handweavers
lining papers
   Harrower House of Decoupage
metal foil paper
   Arthur Brown & Bro., Inc.
paper cutters
   Dick Blick
paper frames
   Make It Happen Craft Studio
paper models
   John Hathaway
paper sparkle
   Life-Like Products Inc.
paper strips
   Artistry In Wood

paper tole
   John's Hardware & Decoupage Supplies
   Make It Happen Craft Studio
parchment paper
   Arthur Brown & Bro., Inc.
pattern paper
   Pins & Needles
pearl parchment
   Koehler's Craft Outlet
   Hazel Pearson Handi Craft
quilling paper
   Folkcrafts
   Leisure Services
   Tree Toys
rice paper
   Bergen Arts & Crafts, Inc.
   Arthur Brown & Bro., Inc.
   Harrower House of Decoupage
   Marie Mitchell's Decoupage Center
stencil paper
   Budget Buddy Co.
tissue paper
   Bergen Arts & Crafts, Inc.
   Dick Blick
   Boin Arts & Crafts
   Hazel Pearson Handi Craft
   Supreme Handicrafts
tracing paper
   Plaza Artists Materials, Inc.
velour paper
   Dick Blick
   Hazel Pearson Handi Craft
   Zim's
velvet crepe papers
   Koehler's Craft Outlet

papier mache
   American Handicrafts
   Artis, Inc.
   Bersted's
   Delco Craft Center, Inc.
   Plasco
   Zim's
books
   Activa Products Inc.
   Book Barn
   Chilton Book Co.
   Craft Course Publishers
   Crown Publishers
   Davis Publications, Inc.
   Lane Magazine & Book Co.

Sancraft Industries
Watson-Guptill Publications
instant papier mache
The Mail Train
Sax Arts & Crafts
kits
The Craft Corner
Mary Maxim Inc.
mache
Arthur Brown & Bro., Inc.
Cleveland Leather Co.
Craftsman Supply House
Economy Handicrafts, Inc.
The Handcrafters
Skil-Crafts Division
Supreme Handicrafts
mache beads
Bead Game
magazines
McCall's Needlework & Crafts
patterns, plans, and charts *(see also specific craft)*
books
The Amber Lion
Marquerite P. Davison
Peg Hall Studios
S. Lynds Patterns
Phentex, Inc.
Quilts and Other Comforts
Studio Yarn Farms Inc.
Traditional Norwegian Rosemaling
burlap rug patterns
John E. Garrett Ltd.
children's knitting patterns
Knit-O-Graf Pattern Co.
clock patterns
Craft Products
cloth doll patterns
Dorris Dolls
craft plans
Minnesota Woodworkers Supply Co.
crochet doll patterns
Ruth Lukasik
crochet patterns
Brunswick Worsted Mills
Sharon's Petite Sherre
S. Siracusa
custom-fit computerized patterns
Silhouette Custom-Fit Pattern Co.
custom-made needlepoint patterns
Wm. Hooper

decorative patterns
Bernadette Decorative Art
doll clothes crochet patterns
Virginia Lakin
Mrs. Rossi
doll clothes knitting patterns
Virginia Lakin
Mrs. Rossi
doll clothes patterns
Doll Castle News
Mark Farmer Co., Inc.
Standard Doll Co.
doll patterns
Yvonne Brandon
Dolly Darling Inc.
Ervins
Platypus
Sue Wise
dough art patterns
Natcol Crafts, Inc.
embroidery transfer patterns
Crewel Elephant
furniture patterns
Davault Miniature Furniture
hairpin lace patterns
Kile-Gore Designs
hooked rug patterns
Karlkraft Studio-Cheva
iron-on patterns
Mrs. W. Bradley Ryan
jewelry patterns
Creations for the Artist
kits
Quilts and Other Comforts
knitting patterns
Brunswick Worsted Mills
Liveright
Sharon's Petite Sherre
lampshade patterns
Unique Creations
leaflets
Old South Patterns
magazines
Make It With Leather
1001 Fashion & Needlecraft Ideas
1001 How-To Ideas
Woman's Day Knit & Stitch
Woman's Day Needlework Ideas
Woman's Day 101 Sweaters to Knit and Crochet

Craft Category Index
Patterns—Patterns

    Woman's Day Sewing & Fashion Ideas
    The Workbench
mesh canvas rug patterns
    John E. Garrett Ltd.
mold patterns
    Bee Basch Designs
needlepoint charts
    Needlecraft Shop Inc.
needlepoint templates
    New Products Co.
needlework designs
    Donna Jean Carver
    Sudberry House
netting patterns
    Frank J. Nelson
pattern cards
    Genie
patterns
    American Handicrafts
    Anne Amiot
    Barbara Bannister
    Berry's of Maine
    Better Homes & Gardens
    Carson & Ellis, Inc.
    Chilton Book Co.
    The Clever Crafters
    Albert Constantine & Son Inc.
    Craftplans
    D-Carol
    Davis & Co.
    Dek-Co Manufacturing Co.
    R. S. Duncan & Co.
    Foam Fantasy
    Bea Freeman Enterprises
    The Ghen Studio
    Gloria
    The Handcrafters
    House of Patterns
    Kieffer's Lingerie Fabric & Supplies
    Kay Kinney-Contoured Glass
    The Knitting Needle
    Barbara Lawshe
    Thomas S. Maquire's
    The Needle Works
    Needlecraft House
    Sancraft Industries
    The Sewing Bee
    The Smock Shop
    Tandy Leather Co.
    Osma G. Tod Weaving & Lace Studio
    Tole 'N Stuff
    Wanda's Workshop
    A. C. Weber & Co., Inc.
    Whittemore-Durgin Glass Co.
    Mrs. L. Winum
    Woodland Craft Designs
perfect-measurement sewing patterns for knit fabrics
    Kandel Knits, Inc.
perforated embroidery paper
    Sewakers Industries Inc.
plans
    Minnesota Woodworkers Supply Co.
pompom dolls
    A. Raimer
precut plastic quilt patterns
    Quilts and Other Comforts
quilt patterns
    Contemporary Quilts
    Quilts
    Quilts and Other Comforts
    Santa Cruz Mountain Crafts
rag doll patterns
    American Indian Portrait Dolls
    Dot's Dollhouse
    Betty James Originals
rug patterns
    Rebecca Andrews
    Heirloom Rugs
    Heritage Hill Patterns
    The Hidden Village
    House of Gould
    Joan Moshimer
    Needlecraft Shop Inc.
string sculpture patterns
    Robert E. Sharpton
stuffed doll patterns
    Virginia Black Designs
teenage doll patterns
    Betty James Originals
    Manlove Originals
tole patterns
    Bernadette Decorative Art
    Decorative Designs by Dare
    John & Susan Scheewe
    Transart
toy patterns
    Dorris Dolls
    Sue Wise
wax patterns
    Exactra-Craft Corp.

wax ring patterns
   Eric Martin Co
woodworking patterns
   Craft Patterns
picture framing
 old barn wood picture frames
   Lynchburg Hdwr. & General Store
 picture frames
   National Artcraft Supply Co.
plaster craft *(see also Casting, Molds)*
   Belle Craft
   Cleveland Leather Co.
   Schrock's, The House of Hobbies & Crafts
   W. Wooley & Co.
 armatures
   Delco Craft Center, Inc.
   Plaza Artists Materials, Inc.
   Sculpture Associates Ltd.
 chess set casting compound
   Stylecraft of Baltimore
 chess set molds
   Stylecraft of Baltimore
 kits
   W. Wooley & Co.
 magazines
   McCall's Needlework & Crafts
 plaster
   Art Mart, Inc.
   Cole Ceramics Laboratories
   TAP Plastic Inc.
   Westwood Ceramic Supply Co.
   W. Wooley & Co.
 plaster additives
   W. Wooley & Co.
 plaster carving
   Sax Arts & Crafts
 plaster casting
   Bersted's
   Bob's Arts & Crafts
   Boin Arts & Crafts
   Bric-Mold Corp.
   Arthur Brown & Bro., Inc.
   Craft Service
   Craftsman Supply House
   Delco Craft Center, Inc.
   Douglas & Sturgess, Inc.
   Kit Kraft
   Hazel Pearson Handi Craft
   Sax Arts & Crafts
   Skil-Crafts Division

   Specialty Products
   Supreme Handicrafts
   Westwood Ceramic Supply Co.
   Zim's
 plaster ceramic molds
   Bee Basch Designs
 plaster molds
   Deep Flex Plastic Molds, Inc.
   Delco Craft Center, Inc.
   Fres-O-Lone Mold Corp.
   Sax Arts & Crafts
   Skil-Crafts Division
   Swan-Son
   Trask Plastics
   W. Wooley & Co.
 plaster plaques
   Koehler's Craft Outlet
 plaster ware finishes
   National Craft & Hobby Co., Inc.
 statuary
   Jeane's
 unpainted plaster figurines
   House of Figurines
plastic crafts
 acetate
   Dick Blick
   Plaza Artists Materials, Inc.
 acrylic in sheet form
   Rohm & Haas Co.
 acrylic items
   Greentree Ranch Wools, Countryside Handweavers
   Lillian Vernon
 acrylic modifier
   Siphon Art Products
 acrylics
   Bear Cave
 art foam
   Dick Blick
   Boin Arts & Crafts
   Cleveland Leather Co.
   Craft Service
   Craftsman Supply House
   Delco Craft Center, Inc.
   Economy Handicrafts, Inc.
   Foam Fantasy
   The Handcraft Supply Corp.
   Holiday Handicrafts, Inc.
   House of Flowers
   Hazel Pearson Handi Craft
   Sax Arts & Crafts

Craft Category Index
Plastic—Plaques

    Supreme Handicrafts
    Zim's
art foam patterns
    Don's Hobby Co.
books
    Charles A. Bennett Co., Inc.
    Cadillac Plastic & Chemical Co.
    Chilton Book Co.
    Crown Publishers
    Goodhert-Willcox Co., Inc.
    The Macmillan Publishing Co.
    McKnight Publishing Co.
    Rohm & Haas Co.
    Watson-Guptill Publications
casting plastic
    Sculpture Services Inc.
dimensional plastic shapes
    Holiday Craft
dip film
    A 'N L's Hobbicraft, Inc.
    American Handicrafts
    Bergen Arts & Crafts, Inc.
    Boin Arts & Crafts
    Carson & Ellis, Inc.
    Cleveland Leather Co.
    Craft Service
    Craftsman Supply House
    Delco Craft Center, Inc.
    Economy Handicrafts, Inc.
    Gemex Co.
    Make It Happen Craft Studio
    J. C. Penney Co., Inc.
    Sears, Roebuck & Co.
    Specialty Products
    Supreme Handicrafts
    Zim's
Dylite®
    Koehler's Craft Outlet
electric tools
    Bear Cave
fiber optics
    Boin Arts & Crafts
    Edmund Scientific Co.
fiberglass
    Adhesive Products Corp.
    Polyproducts Corp.
fiberglass cloth
    Castolite
    High Strength Adhesives Corp.
    Kick-Shaw Inc.

fiberglass mat
    High Strength Adhesives Corp.
    Kick-Shaw Inc.
fillers
    Adhesive Products Corp.
    Castolite
flat plastic shapes
    Holiday Craft
liquid plastic casting equipment
    Nationwide Plastics Co.
Lucite®
    Arthur Brown & Bro., Inc.
Lucite® cabinets
    A. L. Stone Displays
Lucite® mini-easels
    Lillian Vernon
matrix plastic
    Sea Novelties
Mylar®
    Plaza Artists Materials, Inc.
perforated plastic motifs
    Lee Wards
perforated plastic shapes
    Sav-On-Crafts
plastic disks
    Derby Lane Shell Center
plastic objects
    Diedricks Crafts
plastic pellets
    The Handcrafters
plastic portrait balls
    Downs
plastic shapes
    Country Crafts
    Florida Supply House, Inc.
plastic vacuum molding
    Nationwide Plastics Co.
plexiglass
    Economy Handicrafts, Inc.
styrene
    Bear Cave
white plastic ware
    Sav-On-Crafts
plaques *(see also Decoupage, Woodware)*
    Plasco
books
    Parker Publishing Co., Inc.
ceramic oval plaques
    Sunflower Crafts

Craft Category Index
Plaques—Pottery

ceramic plaques
    The Cellar Ceramic Shop
decoupage plaques
    The Cellar Ceramic Shop
    Dek-Co Manufacturing Co.
    Harrower House of Decoupage
fiberglass plaques
    Plycrete Mold Co.
fraternal wood emblems
    Albert Constantine & Son Inc.
molded plaques
    Albert Constantine & Son Inc.
plaster plaques
    Koehler's Craft Outlet
unfinished plaques
    Albert Constantine & Son Inc.
wall plaques
    Reeves Knotique
wood plaques
    Artistry In Wood
    The Cellar Ceramic Shop
    O-P Craft Co., Inc.
    Party Bazaar

porcelain *(see also China painting)*
    Holiday Craft
    House of York
books
    Chilton Book Co.
painted porcelain cabochons
    Jewelart Inc.
porcelain beads
    Bead Game
    Reeves Knotique
porcelain findings
    Felts Manufacturing Co. Inc.
porcelain flowers
    Bergen Arts & Crafts, Inc.
porcelain in gold plated jewelry findings
    Creations for the Artist

pottery making
airbrushes
    Newton's Potters Supply
ball mills
    Cole Ceramics Laboratories
bamboo handles
    Minnesota Clay
    Paramount Ceramic Inc.
    Westwood Ceramic Supply Co.
books
    Ballantine Books, Inc.
    Ceramics Monthly
    Chilton Book Co.
    Dharma Trading Co.
    Harper & Row, Publishers Inc.
    Hearthside Press
    Museum Books Inc.
    Penguin Books Inc.
    Van Nostrand Reinhold Co.
    Viking Press
    Frederick Warne & Co. Inc.
brushes
    Ohio Ceramic Supply Inc.
casting supplies
    Ettl Studios Inc.
    Sculpture House
casting table racks
    Cole Ceramics Laboratories
casting tables
    Air Capitol Molds, Inc.
ceramic chemicals
    Cole Ceramics Laboratories
    Van Howe Ceramic Supply Co.
ceramic clays
    Paramount Ceramic Inc.
    Van Howe Ceramic Supply Co.
ceramic glazes
    Bergen Arts & Crafts, Inc.
    Newton's Potters Supply
    Paramount Ceramic Inc.
    Sax Arts & Crafts
    Standard Ceramic Supply
    Tepping Studio Supply Co.
    Van Howe Ceramic Supply Co.
    Westwood Ceramic Supply Co.
ceramic hardware
    Cole Ceramics Laboratories
ceramic kilns
    A 'N L's Hobbicraft, Inc.
    A. D. Alpine Inc.
    Bergen Arts & Crafts, Inc.
    Clay-Crafters Products
    Delco Craft Center, Inc.
    Newton's Potters Supply
    Paragon Industries Inc.
    Paramount Ceramic Inc.
ceramic stands
    Newton's Potters Supply
ceramic supplies
    A 'N L's Hobbicraft, Inc.
    A. D. Alpine Inc.
    Art Consultants
    Art Mart, Inc.

Craft Category Index
Pottery—Pottery

    Dick Blick
    Blue Grass Art & Hobby Center
    Bluebird Manufacturing
    Cole Ceramics Laboratories
    Delco Craft Center, Inc.
    Diedricks Crafts
    Economy Handicrafts, Inc.
    Essayons Studio, Hand Arts Center
    Ettl Studios Inc.
    Loretta's Ceramic Studio
    Mountain Ceramic Crafts
    NASCO Arts & Crafts
    Newton's Potters Supply
    Ohio Ceramic Supply Inc.
    Paramount Ceramic Inc.
    Sax Arts & Crafts
    Standard Ceramic Supply
    Tepping Studio Supply Co.
    Van Howe Ceramic Supply Co.
    Westwood Ceramic Supply Co.
    Jack D. Wolfe Co. Inc.

ceramic tools
    Anne Amiot
    Art Consultants
    Cole Ceramics Laboratories
    Economy Handicrafts, Inc.
    Newton's Potters Supply
    Paramount Ceramic Inc.
    Standard Ceramic Supply
    Van Howe Ceramic Supply Co.

chemicals
    Minnesota Clay
    Richland Ceramics Inc.
    Standard Ceramic Supply

circular glaze calculator
    Dial-A-Glaze

clay carts
    A. D. Alpine Inc.

clay containers
    Cole Ceramics Laboratories

clay mixers
    Bluebird Manufacturing

clay molds
    Kay Kinney-Contoured Glass

clays
    American Art Clay Co. Inc.
    Bob's Arts & Crafts
    Boin Arts & Crafts
    Cole Ceramics Laboratories
    Craft Service
    Handcraft House
    Minnesota Clay
    Ohio Ceramic Supply Inc.
    Plaza Artists Materials, Inc.
    Richland Ceramics Inc.
    Standard Ceramic Supply
    Tepping Studio Supply Co.
    Westwood Ceramic Supply Co.

dry clays
    Westwood Ceramic Supply Co.

drying cabinets
    Cole Ceramics Laboratories

electric kilns
    Cole Ceramics Laboratories
    Diedricks Crafts

electric lehrs
    A. D. Alpine Inc.

electric potter's wheels
    Cole Ceramics Laboratories

fiberglass
    Sculpture Services Inc.

firing clay
    American Art Clay Co. Inc.
    Arthur Brown & Bro., Inc.
    Delco Craft Center, Inc.
    Plaza Artists Materials, Inc.
    Sax Arts & Crafts
    Skil-Crafts Division

gas kilns
    Cole Ceramics Laboratories

glaze formula tables
    Cole Ceramics Laboratories

glazes
    Cole Ceramics Laboratories
    Delco Craft Center, Inc.
    Minnesota Clay
    Ohio Ceramic Supply Inc.

high-fire clays
    Newton's Potters Supply

kiln accessories
    Delco Craft Center, Inc.

kiln shelves
    Cole Ceramics Laboratories

kilns
    Allcraft Tool & Supply Co.
    Anchor Tool & Supply Co.
    Art Consultants
    Bergen Arts & Crafts, Inc.
    Boin Arts & Crafts
    Arthur Brown & Bro., Inc.
    Handcraft House
    Loretta's Ceramic Studio

Craft Category Index
Pottery—Printmaking

    Minnesota Clay
    Ohio Ceramic Supply Inc.
    Plaza Artists Materials, Inc.
    Richland Ceramics Inc.
    Sax Arts & Crafts
    Sculpture Associates Ltd.
    Sculpture House
    Thomas C. Thompson
    Westwood Ceramic Supply Co.
kits
    Cole Ceramics Laboratories
    Gemex Co.
    Mary Maxim Inc.
    Wallis Designs
magazines
    Ceramics Monthly
Mexican pottery clay
    American Art Clay Co. Inc.
potter's accessories
    Menco Engineers Inc.
potter's equipment
    Bergen Arts & Crafts, Inc.
    Richland Ceramics Inc.
potter's kick wheels
    Cole Ceramics Laboratories
    Pacific Crafts
potter's plasters
    Sculpture Services Inc.
potter's tools
    Cole Ceramics Laboratories
    Westwood Ceramic Supply Co.
potter's wheels
    A. D. Alpine Inc.
    Bluebird Manufacturing
    Arthur Brown & Bro., Inc.
    Gilmour Campbell
    Craftool Co.
    Creative Industries
    Delco Craft Center, Inc.
    Diedricks Crafts
    Earth Treasures
    Handcraft House
    Menco Engineers Inc.
    Minnesota Clay
    Newton's Potters Supply
    Ohio Ceramic Supply Inc.
    Paramount Ceramic Inc.
    Plaza Artists Materials, Inc.
    Richland Ceramics Inc.
    Sax Arts & Crafts
    Sculpture Services Inc.

    Van Howe Ceramic Supply Co.
    Westwood Ceramic Supply Co.
pottery stands
    Sax Arts & Crafts
pug mills
    A. D. Alpine Inc.
    Bluebird Manufacturing
    Cole Ceramics Laboratories
    Westwood Ceramic Supply Co.
quick-slip pouring
    Air Capitol Molds, Inc.
rattan handles
    Westwood Ceramic Supply Co.
refractories
    Westwood Ceramic Supply Co.
self-hardening clays
    Boin Arts & Crafts
    Economy Handicrafts, Inc.
    Newton's Potters Supply
    Sculpture Associates Ltd.
    Sculpture House
stains
    Cole Ceramics Laboratories
white ironstone ware
    Sturbridge Yankee Workshop
posters
color parchment posters
    Flair-Craft Inc.
decoupage posters
    Gary Bunting
historic posters
    Buck Hill Associates
power tools *(see tools)*
printmaking *(see also Screen processing)*
    Delco Craft Center, Inc.
blockprinting
    American Handicrafts
    Art Mart, Inc.
    Bergen Arts & Crafts, Inc.
    Dick Blick
    Boin Arts & Crafts
    Arthur Brown & Bro., Inc.
    Craft Service
    Delco Craft Center, Inc.
    Economy Handicrafts, Inc.
    Sax Arts & Crafts
    Stewart Industries
blockprinting dye
    Rupert, Gibbon & Spider
blockprinting papers
    Stewart Industries

Craft Category Index
Printmaking—Prints

blockprinting press
    Stewart Industries
blocks
    Stewart Industries
books
    Ballantine Books, Inc.
    Book Barn
brayers
    Stewart Industries
carving tools
    Art Mart, Inc.
    Sax Arts & Crafts
clamps
    Colonial Printing Ink Co.
inks
    Advance Process Supply Co.
press block print makers
    Siphon Art Products

prints
    Adventures In Crafts
    American Handicrafts
    P. S. Andrews Co.
    Artistry In Wood
    N. S. Braverman
    Carson & Ellis, Inc.
    Dek-Co Manufacturing Co.
    Gemex Co.
    Harrower House of Decoupage
    National Wildlife Art Exchange
    Old Print Center
    Hazel Pearson Handi Craft
    Sax Arts & Crafts
    Scissortail Arts & Crafts
    F. C. Ziegler Co.

$2 bills
    Hanover House Industries, Inc.
aged documents
    Whittemore-Durgin Glass Co.
antique newspapers
    Whittemore-Durgin Glass Co.
art prints
    Supreme Handicrafts
beer labels
    Whittemore-Durgin Glass Co.
cigar tin labels
    Whittemore-Durgin Glass Co.
Civil War prints
    Lynchburg Hdwr. & General Store
collage prints
    Elyse Sommer
decoupage mining prints
    Ken Prag
decoupage oil company prints
    Ken Prag
decoupage posters
    Gary Bunting
decoupage prints
    Buck Hill Associates
    Carnival Arts & Crafts
    Century 21
    Marie Mitchell's Decoupage Center
    Old Print Center
    Elyse Sommer
decoupage railroad prints
    Ken Prag
decoupage stock certificates prints
    Ken Prag
doll advertisement papers
    Sharon's Petite Sherre
doll antique photographs
    Sharon's Petite Sherre
English decoupage prints
    Sharon's Petite Sherre
floral prints
    John's Hardware & Decoupage Supplies
foil prints
    Carnival Arts & Crafts
historic advertisements
    Buck Hill Associates
historic handbills
    Buck Hill Associates
historic posters
    Buck Hill Associates
historic prints
    Buck Hill Associates
mini-prints
    Scissortail Arts & Crafts
Old Masters prints
    John's Hardware & Decoupage Supplies
    Scissortail Arts & Crafts
old time whiskey labels
    Lynchburg Hdwr. & General Store
Oriental prints
    John's Hardware & Decoupage Supplies
parchment quotes
    Stevenson Industries
precut decoupage designs
    Carolyn Watson

Craft Category Index
Prints—Quilting

reproduction prints
  Old Print Center
Victorian design gift wrap paper
  Sharon's Petite Sherre
wine labels
  Whittemore-Durgin Glass Co.
18th century prints
  John's Hardware & Decoupage Supplies

puppetmaking
books
  Book Barn
  Davis Publications, Inc.
  E. P. Dutton & Co., Inc.
  David McKay Co., Inc.
  The Puppetry Store
  Stein & Day
  Taplinger Publishing Co.
magazines
  Ladies Home Journal Needlecraft
organizations
  Puppeteers of America, Inc.
plastic heads
  Hazel Pearson Handi Craft
wiggle eyes
  Delco Craft Center, Inc.

quilling
books
  House of Flowers
  Leisure Services
  Tree Toys
kits
  Leisure Services
  Tree Toys
quilling paper
  Folkcrafts
  Leisure Services
  Tree Toys
quilling supplies
  Artistry In Wood
  House of Flowers
  Tree Toys

quilting *(see also Fabrics, Sewing)*
  Leman Publications
  Montgomery Ward & Co., Inc.
  Lee Wards
appliques
  Leman Publications
  Lillian Vernon
bonded polyester quilt batts
  Putnam Co.
books
  Aunt Martha's Studios Inc.
  Barbara Bannister
  Book Barn
  Charles T. Branford Co.
  Chilton Book Co.
  Contemporary Quilts
  Mrs. Danner's Quilts
  Grosset & Dunlap Inc.
  Hearthside Press
  Lane Magazine & Book Co.
  Leman Publications
  Mon Tricot
  The Needle Works
  Quilts and Other Comforts
  Southern Living Books
  The Stearns & Foster Co.
  Taylor Bedding Mfg. Co.
  The Unicorn
corduroy scraps
  Reichert's Fabrics
cotton patchwork quilt squares
  House of Lines
Dacron® batting
  Contemporary Quilts
kits
  Bear Cave
  Contemporary Quilts
  Create Your Own, Inc.
  Distlefink Designs
  Edna Looney Originals
  The Needle Works
  Pins & Needles
  Quilts and Other Comforts
  Sue's Custom Quilting
leaflets
  Use 'Em Up Creations
magazines
  Happy Hobbies Magazine
  Quilter's Newsletter
organizations
  National Quilting Association
patchwork techniques
  Leman Publications
patterns
  House of Patterns
precut plastic quilt patterns
  Quilts and Other Comforts
quilt designs
  Aunt Martha's Studios Inc.

Craft Category Index
Quilting—Ribbon

quilt patterns
  Contemporary Quilts
  Quilts
  Quilts and Other Comforts
  Santa Cruz Mountain Crafts
quilt scraps
  Reichert's Fabrics
quilter unit
  Sue's Custom Quilting
quilting frames
  KAY an EE Corp. of America
  Lee Wards
quilting machine
  Sue's Custom Quilting
services
  Wrightway Quilting
velvet patchwork quilt squares
  House of Lines
velvet quilt pieces
  Nucleus
wool patchwork quilt square patterns
  House of Lines

resin craft
  $2 bills
    Hanover House Industries, Inc.
  additives
    Adhesive Products Corp.
    Natcol Crafts, Inc.
  books
    Craft Course Publishers
    Sancraft Industries
    Valspar Corp.
  colored sawdust
    Carver Co.
  epoxy resins
    High Strength Adhesives Corp.
    Polyproducts Corp.
  kits
    American Handicrafts
    High Strength Adhesives Corp.
    W. Wooley & Co.
  polyester resins
    High Strength Adhesives Corp.
    Polyproducts Corp.
  resin casting
    Bob's Arts & Crafts
    Arthur Brown & Bro., Inc.
    Craft Service
    Ovgem Craft Supply Co.
    Skil-Crafts Division
  resin craft accessories
    Green's Rock & Lapidary Ltd.
    High Strength Adhesives Corp.
    Natcol Crafts, Inc.
  resin craft embediments
    Natcol Crafts, Inc.
  resin craft molds
    Belle Craft
    Deep Flex Plastic Molds, Inc.
    Delco Craft Center, Inc.
    Green's Rock & Lapidary Ltd.
    Natcol Crafts, Inc.
    Sax Arts & Crafts
    Skil-Crafts Division
    Swan-Son
    Trask Plastics
  resin craft supplies
    American Handicrafts
    Craftsman Supply House
    Deep Flex Plastic Molds, Inc.
    Delco Craft Center, Inc.
    Douglas & Sturgess, Inc.
    Economy Handicrafts, Inc.
    Green's Rock & Lapidary Ltd.
    The Handcrafters
    High Strength Adhesives Corp.
    Holiday Handicrafts, Inc.
    National Artcraft Supply Co.
    J. C. Penney Co., Inc.
    Sax Arts & Crafts
    Schrock's, The House of Hobbies & Crafts
    Specialty Products
    Swan-Son
    Lee Wards
    W. Wooley & Co.
    Zim's
  resins
    Adhesive Products Corp.
    Art Consultants
    Bergen Arts & Crafts, Inc.
    Boin Arts & Crafts
    Cleveland Leather Co.
    Kick-Shaw Inc.
    Sculpture Services Inc.
    TAP Plastic Inc.

ribbon craft *(see also Trims)*
  boutique ribbons
    Hazel Pearson Handi Craft
  honeycomb ribbon
    Sav-On-Crafts

perforated ribbon
   Hazel Pearson Handi Craft
ribbon
   B & M Yarn Co.
   Boycan's Craft Supplies
   Holiday Craft
   Home-Sew Inc.
   House of Flowers
   Koehler's Craft Outlet
   Sav-On-Crafts
   Town & Country Crafts
   Wagner's Crafts
ribbon straw
   Koehler's Craft Outlet
velvet ribbons
   Boutique Trims
   Taylor House

rock, stone, and pebble craft *(see lapidary, nature crafts)*

rope *(see Cord)*

rosemaling
  home study courses
   Workshop
  kits
   Sandeen's Scandinavian Gift & Card Shop
  Norwegian rosemaling
   Traditional Norwegian Rosemaling
  rosemaling brushes
   Sandeen's Scandinavian Gift & Card Shop
  rosemaling paints
   Sandeen's Scandinavian Gift & Card Shop
  rosemaling supplies
   Sandeen's Scandinavian Gift & Card Shop
  woodware
   Sandeen's Scandinavian Gift & Card Shop

rugmaking *(see also Frames, Yarns)*
   Berry's of Maine
   Craft Yarns of Rhode Island Inc.
   Delco Craft Center, Inc.
   The Hidden Village
   Loftons
   Sewing Products Co.
   Some Place
   The Yarn Depot
  accessories
   Knits'N That Yarn Shop
   Joan Moshimer
   Sign of the Arrow
  backings for rya rugs
   Coulter Studios
  books
   Book Barn
   Charles T. Branford Co.
   Chilton Book Co.
   Margaret Davis
   Drake Publishers Inc.
   Harper & Row, Publishers Inc
   Hearthside Press
   Lee Mountain
   Museum Books Inc.
   Reilly & Lee Books
   Mildred Sprout
   Watson-Guptill Publications
  braiders
   Berry's of Maine
   Mildred Sprout
  burlap rug patterns
   John E. Garrett Ltd.
  carpet warp
   Knit Services, Inc.
   The Oriental Rug Co.
  clamps
   House of Gould
  custom rug templates
   New Products Co.
  cutting machines
   Heritage Hill Patterns
   House of Gould
   Joan Moshimer
  electric punch rug hook
   KM Yarn Co.
   Needlecraft Shop Inc.
  folding floor harness looms
   Norwood Loom Co.
  folding frame loom
   Robert Nelson
   Turnbull Looms
  foot-operated looms
   Kessenich Looms
  hand hooking
   The Dorr Mill Store
  hand hooks
   Mildred Sprout
  hand punch hooks
   Needlecraft Shop Inc.

Craft Category Index
Rugmaking—Rugmaking

hooked rug
   Schrock's, The House of Hobbies & Crafts

hooked rug patterns
   Karlkraft Studio-Cheva

hooking looms
   Textile Crafts

hooking yarns
   Tahki Imports, Limited
   Textile Crafts

kits
   Brunswick Worsted Mills
   Creativity Needlepoint
   Crossroads
   Emberugs
   Franzen Gifts
   Knits'N That Yarn Shop
   Loftons
   Mary Maxim Inc.
   Merribee
   Michigan Wool Products Co.
   Joan Moshimer
   Needlewoman Shop
   Sav-On-Crafts
   Scandinavian Rya Rugs
   Schrock's, The House of Hobbies & Crafts
   Sears, Roebuck & Co.
   Shillcraft
   Skon
   Tillalla Inc.
   Lee Wards

latch hook rugs
   Bea Freeman Enterprises
   The Hidden Village

latch hooks
   Needlecraft Shop Inc.

latch rug yarns
   Brunswick Worsted Mills

magazines
   Rug Hooker News & Views

mesh canvas rug patterns
   John E. Garrett Ltd.

precut rug yarn
   Lee Wards

punch needle
   Sewing Products Co.

rug backings
   Craft Yarns of Rhode Island Inc.
   Sax Arts & Crafts

rug braiding
   Berry's of Maine
   The Dorr Mill Store
   House of Gould
   Knits'N That Yarn Shop
   Mildred Sprout

rug burlap
   Lee Wards

rug canvas
   Brunswick Worsted Mills
   International Creations
   KM Yarn Co.
   Shillcraft
   Sign of the Arrow
   Lee Wards
   The Yarn Depot

rug cutters
   Rebecca Andrews
   Lee Wards

rug designs
   International Creations

rug filler
   Knit Services, Inc.
   The Oriental Rug Co.

rug frames
   Rebecca Andrews
   Berry's of Maine
   Craft Yarns of Rhode Island Inc.
   Heritage Hill Patterns
   The Hidden Village
   KAY an EE Corp. of America
   Nantucket Needleworks
   Needlecraft Shop Inc.
   Sears, Roebuck & Co.
   Sewing Products Co.
   Sperry & Son
   Montgomery Ward & Co., Inc.
   Lee Wards

rug hooking guns
   Bea Freeman Enterprises

rug hooking tools
   Berry's of Maine

rug hooks
   Rebecca Andrews
   Craft Yarns of Rhode Island Inc.
   Crossroads
   Delco Craft Center, Inc.
   John E. Garrett Ltd.
   Heritage Hill Patterns
   House of Gould
   Mary Maxim Inc.

Craft Category Index
Rugmaking—Screen

    Merribee
    Joan Moshimer
    Sax Arts & Crafts
    Sunray Yarn House
    Lee Wards
    Yarns Unlimited
rug hoops
    Montgomery Ward & Co., Inc.
rug needles
    Sax Arts & Crafts
rug patterns
    Rebecca Andrews
    R. S. Duncan & Co.
    Bea Freeman Enterprises
    Heirloom Rugs
    Heritage Hill Patterns
    The Hidden Village
    House of Gould
    Joan Moshimer
    Needlecraft Shop Inc.
rug punch
    The Hidden Village
rug weaving accessories
    Craftool Co.
rug wool
    The Dorr Mill Store
    R. S. Duncan & Co.
    The Hidden Village
    Michigan Wool Products Co.
    Needlecraft House
rug yarn
    Craft Yarns of Rhode Island Inc.
    Crossroads
    Filature Lemieux Inc.
    The Handcrafters
    KeeWai Krafts
    KM Yarn Co.
    Mary Maxim Inc.
    Merribee
    Nantucket Needleworks
    Nature's Fibers
    Needlecraft Shop Inc.
    Sign of the Arrow
    Lee Wards
rugs
    Jerry S. Kaye Assoc.
    Needlecraft Shop Inc.
    Sharon's Petite Sherre
    Wool 'N Wick
rya rug backing
    House of Kleen
rya rug yarn
    House of Kleen
stands
    Berry's of Maine
wool rug yarn mill ends
    Some Place

rush working *(see also Cane, reed, and rush working)*
rush
    Atlantic Upholstery Supply Co.
    Cane & Basket Supply Co.
    Craftsman Supply House
    Magnus Craft Materials, Inc.
    H. H. Perkins Co.
    Real Woods
    The Workshop

sand crafts
books
    Village Candle & Craft
kits
    Gilman's
sand
    T. B. Hagstoz & Son

screen processing *(see also Blockprinting)*
    Art Mart, Inc.
    Behnsen Silk Screen Supply Ltd.
    Dick Blick
    Arthur Brown & Bro., Inc.
    Colonial Printing Ink Co.
    Delco Craft Center, Inc.
    Economy Handicrafts, Inc.
    Plaza Artists Materials, Inc.
    Sax Arts & Crafts
    Screen Process Supplies Mfg. Co.
books
    Book Barn
    Dharma Trading Co.
    Lee Mountain
    Naturegraph Publishers
    Pitman Publishing Corp.
    Sign of the Times Publishing Co.
inks
    Advance Process Supply Co.
kits
    Advance Process Supply Co.
    Cavalier Handicrafts
    Craftint Manufacturing Co.
    Creative Hands Co., Inc.
    Delco Craft Center, Inc.
    Gager's Handicrafts

Craft Category Index
Screen—Services

Plaza Artists Materials, Inc.
Sax Arts & Crafts
Screen Process Supplies Mfg. Co.
screen nylon
    Colonial Printing Ink Co.
screen polyester
    Colonial Printing Ink Co.
screen printing equipment
    Advance Process Supply Co.
screen silk
    Colonial Printing Ink Co.
screens
    Screen Process Supplies Mfg. Co.

scrimshaw
  books
    N. Flayderman & Co.
  scrimshaw scribers
    Allcraft Tool & Supply Co.

sculpturing *(see also specific medium)*
  Magic Circle Corp.
  armatures
    Delco Craft Center, Inc.
    Plaza Artists Materials, Inc.
    Sculpture Associates Ltd.
    Sculpture Services Inc.
  books
    Chilton Book Co.
    Craftool Co.
    Crafty Ideas
    Crown Publishers
    Davis Publications, Inc.
    Dharma Trading Co.
    The Dial Press Inc.
    Drake Publishers Inc.
    Parker Publishing Co., Inc.
    Prentice-Hall Inc.
  kits
    Boin Arts & Crafts
    Craftool Co.
    Economy Handicrafts, Inc.
    Edmund Scientific Co.
    Sculpture House
    Sculpture Services Inc.
  magazines
    National Sculpture Review
  sculpture bases
    Sculpture Associates Ltd.
    Sculpture House
    Sculpture Services Inc.
  sculpture metal
    Art Mart, Inc.
  sculpture pedestals
    Sculpture Associates Ltd.
    Sculpture House
    Sculpture Services Inc.
  sculpture supplies
    Art Consultants
    Boin Arts & Crafts
    Arthur Brown & Bro., Inc.
    Economy Handicrafts, Inc.
    Ettl Studios Inc.
    Frank Mittermeier Inc.
    Sculptmetal Co.
    Jack D. Wolfe Co. Inc.
  sculpture tools
    Art Consultants
    Arthur Brown & Bro., Inc.
    Cole Ceramics Laboratories
    Frank Mittermeier Inc.
  sculpture wax
    Delco Craft Center, Inc.
    Douglas & Sturgess, Inc.

services *(see also specific craft)*
  Artcraft; out-of-print book search.
  Book Barn; information on craft courses, teachers and suppliers (particularly in Connecticut).
  Bookpost; appraisals by mail, free out-of-print book search.
  Country Woodcraft; spinning wheels and wood carvings.
  The Custom House of Needle Arts & Design; needlework blocking, mounting and framing.
  Elvette Handbag Co.; needlepoint and petitpoint handbag mounting.
  Eric Martin Co; custom faceting and jewelry design.
  The Hidden Village; custom design, needlepoint.
  International Bookfinders, Inc.; out-of-print books search.
  International Import Co.; lapidary.
  KM Yarn Co.; dyeing.
  Harry Z. Kurs; setting and sizing diamonds.
  Main Service Co.; lapidary equipment.
  Most Unusual Custom Needleworks Inc.; custom painting.
  The Needlecase; custom designing.
  Norlene Lapidary; lapidary.

Craft Category Index
Services—Sewing

Out of Print Bookfinder; book search out-of-print.
Sew-Its-Seams; needlepoint finishing.
Sue's Custom Quilting; needlepoint blocked.
Tainter's Chick Bookshop; locates any book.
The Thread Shed, Inc.; custom-designs.
Threadneedle; custom design needlepoint.
Van Gelder Wood Products; custom work to order.
Vicki's Patience Unlimited; made-to-order kits.
The Village Smithy; custom design in any scale.
Wrightway Quilting; quilt's made from customer's quilt top, quilting.

sewing *(see also Cord, Fabrics)*
    Eagle Mill
    House of Patterns
    The Needle Works
    Village Designs
  appliques
    Leman Publications
    Lillian Vernon
  books
    Ballantine Books, Inc.
    Better Homes & Gardens Books
    Butterick Fashion Marketing Co.
    Crewel Elephant
    E. P. Dutton & Co., Inc.
    Grosset & Dunlap Inc.
    Kieffer's Lingerie Fabric & Supplies
    Martin Fabrics
    Mon Tricot
    Museum Books Inc.
    P. T. I.
    Random House Inc.
    The Smock Shop
    Elyse Sommer
    The Unicorn
  calico blender coverups
    The Rusty Nail
  calico can opener coverups
    The Rusty Nail
  calico mixer coverups
    The Rusty Nail
  calico toaster coverups
    The Rusty Nail

cloth cutter
    Mildred Sprout
cloth slitting machines
    Frederick J. Fawcett, Inc.
club plans
    Designers Fabrics Buy-Mail
corded magnifier
    M. Turner
corduroy scraps
    Reichert's Fabrics
cotton blends
    Knit Services, Inc.
cotton cord
    Creator's Corner
    Tinkler & Co. Inc.
cotton patchwork quilt squares
    House of Lines
cotton seamless tubing
    Lee Wards
cotton selvages
    Tinkler & Co. Inc.
cotton-polyester woven scraps
    Reichert's Fabrics
cottons
    Contessa Yarns
    Isabel Scott Fabrics Corp.
fast basting tool
    Village Designs
felt
    American Handicrafts
    P. S. Andrews Co.
    Boin Arts & Crafts
    Cleveland Leather Co.
    Commonwealth Felt Co.
    The Craft Corner
    Craft Service
    Craftsman Supply House
    Delco Craft Center, Inc.
    Economy Handicrafts, Inc.
    The Handcrafters
    Holiday Handicrafts, Inc.
    House of Flowers
    Magnus Craft Materials, Inc.
    Mary Maxim Inc.
    Merribee
    Hazel Pearson Handi Craft
    Sav-On-Crafts
    Zim's
hem clips
    Village Designs

Craft Category Index
Sewing—Sewing

home study courses
   Lifetime Career Schools
   National School of Dress Design
   National Weavers Training School
interfacing
   Home-Sew Inc.
kits
   Bear Cave
   Fantastic Fit Products
   Frostline
   Knit Services, Inc.
   Man-Pak, Inc.
   Patterns for Pennies, Inc.
   Village Designs
leather garment
   Tandy Leather Co.
magazines
   Butterick Home Catalog
   Ladies Home Journal Needlecraft
   McCall's Pattern Fashions
   1001 Decorating Ideas
   1001 Fashion & Needlecraft Ideas
   Simplicity Fashion Magazine
   Simplicity Home Catalog
   Woman's Day Knit & Stitch
   Woman's Day Knitting Book
   Woman's Day 101 Sweaters to Knit and Crochet
   Woman's Day Sewing & Fashion Ideas
mill ends
   General Supplies Co.
   Mill Store
nylon blends
   Knit Services, Inc.
overlock sewing machines
   Knitking
perfect-measurement sewing patterns for knit fabrics
   Kandel Knits, Inc.
pin cushions
   Sharon's Petite Sherre
polyamide
   Stacy Fabrics Corp.
pompom dolls
   A. Raimer
pompom hat
   A. Raimer
pompom poncho
   A. Raimer
pompom purse
   A. Raimer
pompom shawls
   A. Raimer
pompom throw pillows
   A. Raimer
professional sewing machines
   General Supplies Co.
rya pillow backings
   House of Kleen
sewing awls
   Walter Drake
sewing machine monogram attachment template
   Lillian Vernon
sewing machines
   Studio Yarn Farms Inc.
   Swiss Bernina, Inc.
shears
   Polly Chester Inc.
   Beno J. Gundlach Co.
slip cover supplies
   Atlantic Upholstery Supply Co.
stitch-and-stuff toys
   Platypus
stretch dress forms
   Acme Dress Form Co., Inc.
synthetic selvages
   Tinkler & Co. Inc.
wool clan tartans
   Scotch House
zippers
   Home-Sew Inc.
   Lace Lady
   Two Brothers Inc.

sewing accessories *(see also Trims)*
   Eagle Mill
   The Needle Works
   Village Designs
automatic needle threaders
   Two Brothers Inc.
bobbins
   Charles W. Miller
books
   Maxant Button & Supply Co.
brass snap closures
   Leathercrafters Supply Co.
British buckles
   Leathercrafters Supply Co.
bronze buckles
   Leathercrafters Supply Co.

Craft Category Index
Sewing—Sewing

buckles
    La Venta Corp.
    Leathercrafters Supply Co.
    Mac Leather Co.
    Pollack's Furrier's Supply Corp.
button backs
    Grieger's Inc.
buttons
    Home-Sew Inc.
    House of York
    Lace Lady
    Two Brothers Inc.
clan blazer emblems
    Scotch House
cloth cutter
    Mildred Sprout
cloth slitting machines
    Frederick J. Fawcett , Inc.
cotton threads
    The Mail Train
custom-fit computerized patterns
    Silhouette Custom-Fit Pattern Co.
decorative trims
    The Sewing Bee
designs for baby things
    Alice Fowler Originals
double woven cotton accessories
    J. P. Fliegel Co.
drapery supplies
    Atlantic Upholstery Supply Co.
dress form
    Harrison-Hoge Ind. Inc.
dressmakers pattern graph paper
    Dorothy H. Becker
dressmaking curves
    The Needle Works
dressmaking rulers
    The Needle Works
edgings
    Boutique Trims
    Creative Craft House
    Lace Lady
    The Putter Shop
    Elyse Sommer
    Town & Country Crafts
    Two Brothers Inc.
elastics
    Home-Sew Inc.
    Kieffer's Lingerie Fabric & Supplies
electric tufting
    The Hidden Village

embroidered appliques
    Embroideries Unlimited
embroidered family crest emblems
    Scotch House
fabric braids
    Taylor House
felt appliques
    Home-Sew Inc.
findings
    Frostline
flax line fiber
    Frederick J. Fawcett, Inc.
hem clips
    Village Designs
home study courses
    Fabricon Co.
kits
    Fantastic Fit Products
lace
    Lace Lady
    Two Brothers Inc.
lacing
    American Handicrafts
    P. S. Andrews Co.
    Craft Service
    Craftsman Supply House
    Sax Arts & Crafts
    Skil-Crafts Division
    Tandy Leather Co.
long separating zippers
    Mary Maxim Inc.
magazines
    Good Housekeeping Needlecraft
    Simplicity Fashion Magazine
    Simplicity Home Catalog
manual tufting
    The Hidden Village
metallic braids
    Gibsons Creations
    Knit Services, Inc.
metallic trims
    Home-Sew Inc.
needles
    House of Gould
    Jerry S. Kaye Assoc.
    Knit Services, Inc.
    The Mail Train
    Mary Maxim Inc.
    Merribee
    The Needle Works
    Needlecraft Shop Inc.

Craft Category Index
Sewing—Shellcraft

organizer for needles and hooks
   Henry Seligman Co. Inc.
patches
   M. B. Austin
   Lillian Vernon
pearl strands
   Jeweler's Emporium
perfect-measurement sewing patterns for knit fabrics
   Kandel Knits, Inc.
personalized woven labels
   L & L Stitchery
   Melrose Yarn Co., Inc.
   The Needle Works
pewter buckles
   Leathercrafters Supply Co.
pewter buttons
   House of York
   Wichelt Import Co.
pillows
   The Hidden Village
pins
   Home-Sew Inc.
polyamide
   Stacy Fabrics Corp.
polyester fiberfill stuffing
   Putnam Co.
polyester filled pillow forms
   Putnam Co.
polyester lace
   Home-Sew Inc.
pompoms
   Woodward Ranch
printed woven edge satin labels
   Helmor Label Co.
rickrack
   Home-Sew Inc.
rosette winders
   Holiday Handicrafts, Inc.
   Mary Maxim Inc.
   Merribee
   Yarns Unlimited
round cowhide lacing
   Leathercrafters Supply Co.
rubber cushions
   Atlantic Upholstery Supply Co.
seam steamers
   The Needle Works
sew-on railroad patches
   M. B. Austin

sewing awls
   Walter Drake
sewing machine monogram attachment template
   Lillian Vernon
shears
   Polly Chester Inc.
   Beno J. Gundlach Co.
silk screened fraternity and sorority crests
   Mrs. G's
smocking design plates
   The Smock Shop
stretch dress forms
   Acme Dress Form Co., Inc.
Swiss bell pulls
   Robin & Russ Handweavers
thread holders
   The Needle Works
trims
   Eagle Mill
velvet tubing
   Zim's
wood buckles
   Knit Services, Inc.
wood buttons
   O-P Craft Co., Inc.
woven labels
   Charm Woven Labels
   Walter Drake
   Knit-Sew Labels
   Spencer Gifts Inc.

shellcraft
   Boin Arts & Crafts
   Cleveland Leather Co.
   The Collector's Cabinet
   Derby Lane Shell Center
   Economy Handicrafts, Inc.
   Florida Supply House, Inc.
   Magnus Craft Materials, Inc.
   Max of Dallas
   Scott Scientific Inc.
abalone
   Biship's House of Gems
   M. Nowotny
books
   Chilton Book Co.
   Crown Publishers
   Great Outdoors Publishing Co.
   Hearthside Press
   Parker Publishing Co., Inc.
California black sea fan coral
   Wearden's

Craft Category Index
Shellcraft—Soap

coral
  The Collector's Cabinet
  The Freed Co.
  International Import Co.
  Max of Dallas
  Panther International Ltd.
cowry shells
  Anne's Treasure Trove
cut shells
  Derby Lane Shell Center
devonian hexagonaria colony coral
  Quinn Mineral
Florida coral
  G. Weidinger
Indo-Pacific sea shells
  Ward International Inc.
polished Tampa Bay coral
  C. R. Boylin
red horn coral
  Bonnie's Rock Shop
  Dowse's Lapidary Supply, Inc.
rosebud seashell craft
  Koehler's Craft Outlet
shark's teeth
  C. R. Boylin
  Florida Supply House, Inc.
shell flowers
  Handcraft Originals

shoemaking *(see also Leathercraft)*
books
  Mary Wales
cobbler sandal supplies
  Leathercrafters Supply Co.
hand crafted shoes supplies
  Barb's Shoe Makings
slipper soles
  Sewing Products Co.

silk screening *(see also Screen processing)*
clamps
  Colonial Printing Ink Co.
silk screened fraternity and sorority crests
  Mrs. G's

silver
  ARE Creations Inc.
  The Camp Fire Co.
  Charbonneau's Lapidary Service
  Gems Galore
  Sax Arts & Crafts
  Smokey Mtn. Rock Shop

fine silver casting grains
  H. A. Cole
sterling silver
  T. B. Hagstoz & Son
  Libra Gems
  Panther International Ltd.
sterling silver scrap chips
  Sterling Hallmark Co.
sterling silver sheet
  Alessi Lapidary Supplies
  Anchor Tool & Supply Co.
  Green's Rock & Lapidary Ltd.
  Sax Arts & Crafts
  Swest Inc.
  Trowbridge Crafts
  G. Weidinger

silversmithing
books
  Bovin Publishing
  Crown Publishers
  Lapidary Journal Book Dept.
home study courses
  The Camp Fire Co.
horn anvils
  Gilman's
silversmithing machinery
  Allcraft Tool & Supply Co.
  Smokey Mtn. Rock Shop
silversmithing supplies
  Anchor Tool & Supply Co.
  The Camp Fire Co.
  William Dixon Co.
  C. R. Hill Co.
  Kraft Korner
  Magic Circle Corp.
  Ovgem Craft Supply Co.
  Sax Arts & Crafts
  Smokey Mtn. Rock Shop
silversmithing tools
  Allcraft Tool & Supply Co.
  The Camp Fire Co.
  Charbonneau's Lapidary Service
  William Dixon Co.
  Technical Specialties International Inc.
sterling silver scrap chips
  Sterling Hallmark Co.

smocking *(see sewing accessories)*

soap crafts
  Specialty Products

Craft Category Index
Soap—Spinning

books
  Country Woodcraft
  Workman Publishing Co.
kits
  Cake Decorators & Craft Supplies
  Hawthorne House, Inc.
  Home-Sew Inc.
soap blocks
  Country Woodcraft
soap casting
  TAP Plastic Inc.
soap cutting tools
  Anne Amiot
soapmaking
  Creator's Corner

spinning *(see also Wool, Wool processing)*
  Fiber to Fabric
  The Hidden Village
  The Mannings Creative Crafts
  Straw Into Gold
belt shuttles
  Schacht Spindle Co.
boat shuttles
  Schacht Spindle Co.
bobbins
  Leclerc Corp.
  School Products Co.
books
  Craftsman Circle Book Club
  Robin & Russ Handweavers
  Textile Crafts
  The Unicorn
carders
  Colonial Textiles
  Spincraft
club plans
  Robert Ayottes' Designery
creels
  Osma G. Tod Weaving & Lace Studio
drop spindles
  Colonial Textiles
  Schacht Spindle Co.
fibers
  Clems and Clems Spinning Wheels
fleece
  Colonial Textiles
  Greentree Ranch Wools, Countryside Handweavers
  The Hidden Village
  KM Yarn Co.
  The Makings
  The Niddy Noddy
  School Products Co.
  Valley Handweaving Supply
fleece wool
  KeeWai Krafts
graded grease wool
  Midwest Wool Marketing Cooperative
grease mohair wool
  Angora Diablo
grease wool
  The Freed Co.
hand spinning
  Spincraft
hand-operated wool carding machine
  Kulch
  Wool Products Ltd.
kits
  Spincraft
Navajo Indian spindles
  Schacht Spindle Co.
spindles
  Greentree Ranch Wools, Countryside Handweavers
  School Products Co.
spinning accessories
  Robert Ayottes' Designery
  Clems and Clems Spinning Wheels
  Greentree Ranch Wools, Countryside Handweavers
  Lillstina Inc.
  The Makings
  Valley Handweaving Supply
spinning supplies
  The Freed Co.
  Midwest Wool Marketing Cooperative
  Some Place
spinning yarns
  Cambridge Wools
  Greentree Ranch Wools, Countryside Handweavers
spool racks
  Robin & Russ Handweavers
winders
  School Products Co.

spinning wheels
  Cambridge Wools
  Clems and Clems Spinning Wheels
  Colonial Textiles

Craftool Co.
Frederick J. Fawcett, Inc.
Greentree Ranch Wools, Countryside Handweavers
The Hidden Village
KeeWai Krafts
Leclerc Corp.
The Makings
The Mannings Creative Crafts
Robin & Russ Handweavers
School Products Co.
Some Place
Spincraft
Valley Handweaving Supply
kits
   Ashford Handicrafts Ltd.
   Clems and Clems Spinning Wheels
New Zealand spinning wheels
   Village Art Gallery
skein maker
   Clems and Clems Spinning Wheels
skein winders
   Robin & Russ Handweavers
spinning wheel parts
   Valley Handweaving Supply

stains *(see also Enamels, Finishes, Paints)*
   Cole Ceramics Laboratories
   Supreme Handicrafts
ceramic stains
   Tepping Studio Supply Co.
   Westwood Ceramic Supply Co.
decorating stains
   Crafty Ideas
decoupage stains
   Century 21
opaque stains
   Reggi's Ceramic Colors
wood stains
   Fezandie & Sperrle, Inc.

stained glass craft
   American Handicrafts
   Bergen Arts & Crafts, Inc.
   Dick Blick
   Boin Arts & Crafts
   Delco Craft Center, Inc.
   Economy Handicrafts, Inc.
   Gemex Co.
   Carl Hepp Mosaic Co.
   Kraft Korner
   Magnus Craft Materials, Inc.
   Make It Happen Craft Studio
   National Craft & Hobby Co., Inc.
   New Products Co.
   Whittemore-Durgin Glass Co.
books
   Beagle Mfg. Co.
   Chilton Book Co.
   Cookson & Thode
   The Ghen Studio
   Glass House Studio
   Mollica Stained Glass Press
   Museum Books Inc.
   Sterling Publishing Co. Inc.
   Watson-Guptill Publications
carbide cutters
   Foredom Electric Co.
cathedral glass
   Artists & Craftsman Guild
   Whittemore-Durgin Glass Co.
club plans
   The Stained Glass Club
copper foil
   Whittemore-Durgin Glass Co.
copper tape
   Artists & Craftsman Guild
fluid solder
   Lox-Seal Adhesives
flux
   Barbara Lawshe
   Panther International Ltd.
   Whittemore-Durgin Glass Co.
glass cutters
   Brookstone Co.
   Cookson & Thode
glass globs
   Boin Arts & Crafts
   Delco Craft Center, Inc.
   Magnus Craft Materials, Inc.
glass tools
   Mollica Stained Glass Press
   The Stained Glass Club
   Whittemore-Durgin Glass Co.
imported glass
   Whittemore-Durgin Glass Co.
kits
   Artists & Craftsman Guild
   Creations by Julianna
   Gemex Co.
   Glass House Studio
   Barbara Lawshe
   National Craft & Hobby Co., Inc.

Craft Category Index
Stained—Straw

    New England Village Crafts
    Surburbia, Inc.
lead came
    Artists & Craftsman Guild
    Carl Hepp Mosaic Co.
    Barbara Lawshe
    Whittemore-Durgin Glass Co.
lead came soldering fluids
    Carl Hepp Mosaic Co.
magazines
    Glass Art Magazine
    The Glass Workshop
patterns
    Chilton Book Co.
sandwich glass fragments
    Wee 3 Sandwich Glass Jewelry
solder
    Carl Hepp Mosaic Co.
    Barbara Lawshe
    Whittemore-Durgin Glass Co.
stained glass paints
    Art Mart, Inc.
    Arthur Brown & Bro., Inc.
    Delco Craft Center, Inc.
    The Handcrafters
    Kay Kinney -Contoured Glass
    Koehler's Craft Outlet
    Plaza Artists Materials, Inc.
    Specialty Products
stained glass supplies
    Artists & Craftsman Guild
    Blue Grass Art & Hobby Center
    Craft Service
    Mollica Stained Glass Press
    The Stained Glass Club
    Whittemore-Durgin Glass Co.

stenciling
alphabet stencils
    Sax Arts & Crafts
books
    American Decorative Arts, Inc.
kits
    American Decorative Arts, Inc.
    Peg Hall Studios
    Magnus Craft Materials, Inc.
    Salyer Publishing Co.
stencil brushes
    American Decorative Arts, Inc.
stencil paper
    Budget Buddy Co.

stencil tools
    Budget Buddy Co.
stencils
    Budget Buddy Co.
    Economy Handicrafts, Inc.
    Leathercrafters Supply Co.
    Thelma Sutton Martin
    Sax Arts & Crafts

stone sculpturing and carving
    Sax Arts & Crafts
books
    Craftool Co.
    Crafty Ideas
    Crown Publishers
casting stone
    Delco Craft Center, Inc.
hard stones
    Sculpture Associates Ltd.
kits
    Craftool Co.
sculpturing stone
    Art Mart, Inc.
    Sculpture House
    Sculpture Services Inc.
soft stones
    Sculpture Associates Ltd.
steatite (soapstone)
    Lakewood Lapidary
stone carving tools
    Frank Mittermeier Inc.
    Newton's Potters Supply
    Sculpture Associates Ltd.
    Sculpture House
    Sculpture Services Inc.

stoneware
stoneware beads
    P. C. Herwig Co., Inc.
    Knit Services, Inc.
    Reeves Knotique
stoneware planter pots
    Reeves Knotique

straw and raffia crafts
artificial straw
    House of Flowers
flax straw (retted)
    Frederick J. Fawcett, Inc.
Hong Kong grass
    Craftsman Supply House
kits
    Hazel Pearson Handi Craft

raffia
    B & M Yarn Co.
    Cleveland Leather Co.
    Craftsman Supply House
    Delco Craft Center, Inc.
    The Handcrafters
    Sax Arts & Crafts
    Supreme Handicrafts
    Zim's

rattan
    Craftsman Supply House
    Holiday Handicrafts, Inc.
    Zim's

ribbon straw
    Koehler's Craft Outlet

straw-look crafts
    Sears, Roebuck & Co.

synthetic raffia straw
    Artis, Inc.

synthetic straw
    Craft Service
    Make It Happen Craft Studio
    Sav-On-Crafts
    Sax Arts & Crafts
    Lee Wards

synthetic straw loom
    Delco Craft Center, Inc.

string art
    Deep Flex Plastic Molds, Inc.
    Swan-Son

books
    Chilton Book Co.
    Crown Publishers
    William Morrow & Co.

kits
    American Handicrafts
    Corner Cupboard Crafts, Inc.
    Gemex Co.

string sculpture
    Robert E. Sharpton

string sculpture patterns
    Robert E. Sharpton

subscriptions
    The American Candlemaker; monthly copy 50¢, 1 year $3.50.
    American Home Crafts; semi-annually at newsstand, $1.25.
    Artisan Crafts; quarterly copy $1.50, 1 year $5, foreign $6.
    Artweek; single copy 35¢, 45 times yearly, 1 year $8.
    Auto Modeler; quarterly copy $1.25.
    Boat Builder; tri-annual copy at $1.
    Bookful of Crochet; bimonthly copy $1.
    Butterick Home Catalog; single copy 60¢, quarterly, 1 year $2.40, foreign $3.
    Carstens Publications; monthly copy 60¢, 1 year $6, foreign $7.
    Celebrate; bimonthly.
    Ceramics; monthly, copy 75¢, 1 year $7.50.
    Ceramics Monthly; monthly, 1 year $6.
    Challenge Publications, Inc; monthly copy $1, 1 year $11.
    China Decorator; monthly.
    China Painter; bimonthly, 1 year $5.50; foreign $6.50.
    Countrywide Crafts; bimonthly, copy at newstand $1.
    Craft/Midwest; quarterly, copy $1.25; 1 year $4.
    Crafty Ideas; quarterly, 1 year, $4.
    Creative Crafts; single copy 60¢, 8 times yearly, 12 issues $6; foreign $7.
    Creative Crafts Christmas Annual; annual copy 75¢.
    Decorating & Craft Ideas Made Easy; single copy 75¢, 10 times yearly, 1 year $6, foreign $7.50.
    Design Magazine; bimonthly, 1 year $7, Canada and foreign $7.50.
    Doll Castle News; bimonthly, copy 60¢, 1 year $3.50.
    Egg Album; quarterly, copy $1.50; 1 year $5.
    The Eggs-Aminer; quarterly, 1 year $10.
    The Family Handyman; 75¢ a copy, 9 times yearly, 1 year $5.75, foreign $6.75.
    Flying Models; monthly copy 60¢, 1 year $6, foreign $7.
    Gems & Minerals; monthly copy 50¢, 1 year $4.75.
    Glass Art Magazine; bimonthly copy $3, 1 year $15, foreign $16.
    The Glass Workshop; bimonthly, 1 year $4.

Craft Category Index
Subscriptions—Subscriptions

Good Housekeeping Needlecraft; semi-annual copy at newsstand, $1.

Handweaver & Craftsman; bimonthly copy $1.75, 1 year $8.

Happy Hobbies Magazine; bimonthly, copy 50¢.

Journal of Contemporary Metalcraft, Casting, Related Arts; quarterly copy $1.50; 1 year $5.50.

Knitking Magazine; bimonthly, 1 year $7.

Ladies Home Journal Needlecraft; semi-annual copy $1.25, 3 years $7.50.

Lapidary Journal Book Dept.; monthly copy 60¢, 1 year $5.75, foreign $6.25.

The Looming Arts; bimonthly, multi-harness issues $5 & $6.50, foreign $6 and $7.50.

Make It With Leather; bimonthly copy $1, 1 year $4.95, foreign $5.45.

McCall's Needlework & Crafts; semi-annual copy $1.50, 2 years $6, Canada $7.

McCall's Pattern Fashions; tri-annual copy $1, 1 year $1.80, foreign $2.10.

McCall's You-Do-It Home Decorating; tri-annual $1.

Mon Tricot; 6 times yearly, 1 year $6.

National Calendar of Indoor-Outdoor Art Fairs; quarterly 1 year $7.

National Sculpture Review; quarterly copy $1.25, 1 year $4, foreign $5.

O Scale Railroading; monthly, sample copy 60¢, 1 year $6.

1001 Decorating Ideas; quarterly 75¢, 1 year $3, Canada $3.50, foreign, $4.

1001 Fashion & Needlecraft Ideas; semi-annual 75¢, 1 year $3, Canada $3.50, foreign $4.

1001 How-To Ideas; semi-annual copy at newsstand $1.

Pack-O-Fun; 10 times yearly, 1 year $5, foreign $6.

Popular Ceramics; monthly copy 75¢, 1 year $7.50.

Portfolio of Egg Artistry; bimonthly, 1 year $31.50.

Pourette Mfg. Co.; monthly, 1 year $2.

Quilter's Newsletter; monthly copy 50¢, 1 year $4.25.

Railroad Modeler; monthly copy $1, 1 year $11.

Robin & Russ Handweavers; monthly, 1 year $5.

Rug Hooker News & Views; bimonthly $1.25, 1 year $5, Canada $6.

Scale Modeler; monthly copy $1.25, 1 year $13.

School Arts; monthly copy $1, 1 year $8.

Simplicity Fashion Magazine; tri-annual copy 75¢, 1 year $2, foreign $2.25.

Simplicity Home Catalog; tri-annual copy 75¢, 1 year $2.

Simplicity Young Ideas Catalog; semi-annual copy 75¢, 1 year $1.35.

Textile Crafts; quarterly copy $1.50, 1 year $5.

Treasure Chest; quarterly copy $1.50, 1 year $5.

Turpen Times; bimonthly, 1 year $6.

Twenty-five Weekend Build-It Projects; annual, single copy at newsstands $1.

Warp & Weft; 1 year $4.50 10 times yearly.

Woman's Day Knit & Stitch; quarterly copy at newsstand 95¢.

Woman's Day Knitting Book; quarterly, single copy at newsstand 75¢.

Woman's Day Needlework Ideas; quarterly copy at newsstand 95¢.

Woman's Day 101 Sweaters to Knit and Crochet; annual copy at newsstand, 75¢.

Woman's Day Sewing & Fashion Ideas; annual copy at newstand 95¢.

Wood Projects; annual copy at newsstand $1.

Woodworker; annual copy at newsstand $1.

The Workbasket; bimonthly copy 25¢, 1 year $1.50.
The Workbench; bimonthly copy 35¢, 1 year $2.
Z-Handicrafts; quarterly, single copy $1.50.

tapestry making
  books
    HTH Publishers
  crewel tapestry wall hangings
    General Crafts Corp.
  kits
    D. M. C. Corporation
  tapestry beaters
    Schacht Spindle Co.
  tapestry looms
    Schacht Spindle Co.
    School Products Co.
  tapestry standing frames
    Sperry & Son
  tapestry threads
    Needlecraft Shop Inc.
  tapestry wool
    Berry's of Maine
    The Hidden Village
    Needlecraft House
    Needlecraft Shop Inc.

tatting *(see Lace making)*

textile crafts
    Budget Buddy Co.
    The Fringe and Frame
    The Niddy Noddy
  books
    The Hidden Village
    HTH Publishers
    Thelma Sutton Martin
    Museum Books Inc.
    Prentice-Hall Inc.
    Textile Crafts
    The Unicorn
  magazines
    Happy Hobbies Magazine
    Textile Crafts
  repeat glass
    Arthur Brown & Bro., Inc.
    Plaza Artists Materials, Inc.
  textile brushes
    Thelma Sutton Martin
  textile dyes
    Rupert, Gibbon & Spider

  textile enamels
    University Circle Publications and Supply Co.
  textile paints
    Art Mart, Inc.
    Bergen Arts & Crafts, Inc.
    Arthur Brown & Bro., Inc.
    Craft Service
    Thelma Sutton Martin
    Sax Arts & Crafts
  textile stencils
    Delco Craft Center, Inc.
    Thelma Sutton Martin
  textile yarns
    Shuttlecraft
  water soluble textile paints
    Siphon Art Products

thread *(see Cord)*

tie-dye *(see also Dyes)*
  books
    Ballantine Books, Inc.
    Book Barn
    Davis Publications, Inc
    Dye-Craft Ideas
    The Unicorn
  dyes
    Berry's of Maine
    Castolite
    Cleveland Leather Co.
    Delco Craft Center, Inc.
    Dharma Trading Co.
    Handcraft House
    The Hidden Village
    House of Gould
    KM Yarn Co.
    Leathercrafters Supply Co.
    Magnus Craft Materials, Inc.
    Joan Moshimer
    The Niddy Noddy
    Sax Arts & Crafts
    Skil-Crafts Division
    Straw Into Gold
    Surma Book & Music Store
    W. Wooley & Co.

tie making
  bolo parts
    Jeweler's Emporium
  bolo tie cords
    Florida Supply House, Inc.

Craft Category Index
Tie—Tiles

   bolo tie slides
      J. W. Day Mfg. Co.
      Green's Rock & Lapidary Ltd.
   bolo tie tips
      Florida Supply House, Inc.
   books
      Tie Clip Information

tiles and tilemaking *(see also Mosaics)*
      Magnus Craft Materials, Inc.
      University Circle Publications and Supply Co.
   asbestos tile cutters
      Beno J. Gundlach Co.
   bisqued ceramic tiles
      Newton's Potters Supply
   books
      Crown Publishers
   ceramic tile cutters
      Beno J. Gundlach Co.
   ceramic tiles
      Renaldy's
   floor tile cutters
      Beno J. Gundlach Co.
   frames for hanging tiles
      Downs
   glazed ceramic tiles
      Newton's Potters Supply
   Italian glass mosaic tiles
      F. E. Biegert Co.
   mirror tiles
      Montgomery Ward & Co., Inc.
   mosaic cutters
      The L. S. Starrett Co.
   mosaic tiles
      Art Mart, Inc.
      Boin Arts & Crafts
      Delco Craft Center, Inc.
      Sax Arts & Crafts
   nippers
      F. E. Biegert Co.
      Beno J. Gundlach Co.
   plastic mosaic tile
      Boin Arts & Crafts
   plastic wall tile cutters
      Beno J. Gundlach Co.
   tile cutters
      Beno J. Gundlach Co.
      The L. S. Starrett Co.
   tile saws
      Beno J. Gundlach Co.

   wood tiles
      Pack-O-Fun
   wrought iron tile frames
      Renaldy's

tincraft
   decorated tinware
      Crafts Manufacturing Co.
   tin can craft
      Hazel Pearson Handi Craft

tinware
      Adventures In Crafts
      Country Woodcraft
      Jamar, Inc.
      The Wood Barn
   milk cans
      Dairy Service, Inc
   tin basket shapes
      Keller-Charles of Philadelphia
   tin boxes
      Keller-Charles of Philadelphia
   tin buckets
      Jamar, Inc.
      Keller-Charles of Philadelphia
   tin candleholders
      Jamar, Inc
   tin coal hods
      Keller-Charles of Philadelphia
   tin mini-water cans
      Jamar, Inc.
   tin pitchers
      Jamar, Inc.
   tin sconces
      Jamar, Inc.
      Keller-Charles of Philadelphia
   tin storage cans
      Keller-Charles of Philadelphia
   tin trays
      Jamar, Inc.
      Keller-Charles of Philadelphia
   tin umbrella stands
      Keller-Charles of Philadelphia
   tin urns
      Keller-Charles of Philadelphia
   tin wash tubs
      Jamar, Inc.
   tin watering cans
      Keller-Charles of Philadelphia
   undecorated tinware
      Crafts Manufacturing Co.
   unfinished tinware
      Keller-Charles of Philadelphia

tole art
books
The Amber Lion
Book Barn
Karen Burrus
Crown Publishers
Luella Ensz
Hearthside Press
Thelma Sutton Martin
John & Susan Scheewe
Shoenail Supply
Sterling Publishing Co. Inc.
Tole 'N Stuff
bronze powder
Carson & Ellis, Inc.
Peg Hall Studios
brushes
Peg Hall Studios
decorated tinware
Crafts Manufacturing Co.
magazines
Decorating & Craft Ideas Made Easy
Happy Hobbies Magazine
milk cans
Dairy Service, Inc
paper tole
John's Hardware & Decoupage Supplies
Make It Happen Craft Studio
tole painting
Corner Cupboard Crafts, Inc.
P. C. Herwig Co., Inc.
Kraft Korner
John & Susan Scheewe
Sunflower Crafts
tole patterns
Bernadette Decorative Art
Decorative Designs by Dare
John & Susan Scheewe
Transart
toleware
A 'N L's Hobbicraft, Inc.
P. S. Andrews Co.
unfinished milk cans
Dairy Service, Inc
The Wood Barn
unfinished pails
Spaulding & Frost Co., Inc.

tools
Allcraft Tool & Supply Co.
Basic Crafts Co.
Campbell Tools Co.
Cleveland Leather Co.
Delco Craft Center, Inc.
Homecraft Veneer
Jeweler's Emporium
Minnesota Woodworkers Supply Co.
Ohio Ceramic Supply Inc.
Plaza Artists Materials, Inc.
Rupert, Gibbon & Spider
Sax Arts & Crafts
Tandy Leather Co.
adz
Elizabeth R. King
airbrushes
Badger Air-Brush Co.
Dick Blick
Arthur Brown & Bro., Inc.
Douglas & Sturgess, Inc.
Newton's Potters Supply
Plaza Artists Materials, Inc.
Skil-Crafts Division
anvils
Frank Mittermeier Inc.
art metal tools
Sax Arts & Crafts
asbestos tile cutters
Beno J. Gundlach Co.
asphalt cutters
Beno J. Gundlach Co.
awls
Hanover House Industries, Inc.
Jewelart Inc.
Tandy Leather Co.
batik tools
Glen Black Handwoven Textiles
Joan Moshimer
beadery tools
Jewelart Inc.
belt sanders
American Machine & Tool Co.
Covington Engineering Corp.
Gilman's
Highland Park Manufacturing
bench power tools
Badger Air-Brush Co.
Toolkraft Corp.
bench top multiuse units
Dremel Creative Power Tools
blade flanges
Star Diamond Industries

Craft Category Index
Tools—Tools

blades
   Jenkins Lapidary Equipment
   Weidinger Inc.
blowpipes
   Gilman's
books
   The Family Handyman
   Flair-Craft Inc.
   Goodhert-Willcox Co., Inc.
   Van Nostrand Reinhold Co.
bottle cutters
   American Handicrafts
   P. S. Andrews Co.
   Bob's Arts & Crafts
   Albert Constantine & Son Inc.
   Craftsman Supply House
   Delco Craft Center, Inc.
   Walter Drake
   Edmund Scientific Co.
   Floyd Fleming
   The Handcrafters
   Hanover House Industries, Inc.
   Kay Kinney-Contoured Glass
   J. C. Penney Co., Inc.
   Keith Robinson
   Lee Wards
   Whittemore-Durgin Glass Co.
brayers
   Stewart Industries
burrs
   Foredom Electric Co.
cake decorating tools
   General Supplies Co.
   Maid of Scandinavia
calipers
   The L. S. Starrett Co.
candy decorating tools
   General Supplies Co.
carbide cutters
   Foredom Electric Co.
carbide tipped engraving tool
   Spencer Gifts Inc.
carpentry power tools
   American Machine & Tool Co.
   Arco Tools Inc.
carpentry tools
   Brookstone Co.
   The L. S. Starrett Co.
carpet knives
   Beno J. Gundlach Co.

carpet tools
   Beno J. Gundlach Co.
carving drills
   Foredom Electric Co.
carving tools
   Art Mart, Inc.
   Albert Constantine & Son Inc.
   M & M Hardwood
   Sax Arts & Crafts
   Skil-Crafts Division
ceramic power tool
   Marcella's Ceramics Inc.
ceramic tile cutters
   Beno J. Gundlach Co.
ceramic tools
   Anne Amiot
   Art Consultants
   Cole Ceramics Laboratories
   Economy Handicrafts, Inc.
   Newton's Potters Supply
   Paramount Ceramic Inc.
   Standard Ceramic Supply
   Van Howe Ceramic Supply Co.
clamps
   Colonial Printing Ink Co.
   House of Gould
cloth cutter
   Mildred Sprout
craft knives
   Frank Mittermeier Inc.
   Skil-Crafts Division
craft sticks
   Pack-O-Fun
custom crafted hand tools
   King's Studio
cutters
   Arthur Brown & Bro., Inc.
   Beno J. Gundlach Co.
decoupage tools
   Harrower House of Decoupage
diamond arbors
   Gem Tool Specialties
diamond blades
   Covington Engineering Corp.
   Earth Treasures
   Farmers Gem and Rock Shop
   Gem Tool Specialties
   Star Diamond Industries
diamond burrs
   Gem Tool Specialties

Craft Category Index
Tools—Tools

diamond carvers
   Metro Diamond Drill Co.
diamond coated files
   Metro Diamond Drill Co.
diamond cores
   Gem Tool Specialties
diamond disks
   Gem Tool Specialties
diamond drills
   Gem Tool Specialties
   Geode Industries
diamond impregnated core drills
   Metro Diamond Drill Co.
diamond points
   Gem Tool Specialties
diamond saw blades
   Highland Park Manufacturing
diamond saws
   Raytech Industries Inc.
diamond tools
   Gem Tec Diamond Tool Co.
   Gem Tool Specialties
dops
   Walter E. Johansen
   A. D. McBurney
dough art tools
   Natcol Crafts, Inc.
drill attachments
   Arco Tools Inc.
drill presses
   American Machine & Tool Co.
   Dremel Creative Power Tools
egg cutter attachment
   Loosie Goosie Egg Craft Shop
electric carver
   Green's Rock & Lapidary Ltd.
electric punch rug hook
   KM Yarn Co.
   Needlecraft Shop Inc.
electroplating tools
   William Dixon Co.
embroidery scissors
   Polly Chester Inc.
enameling tools
   William Dixon Co.
engraving chisels
   Frank Mittermeier Inc.
engraving tools
   Bergen Arts & Crafts, Inc.
   Dremel Creative Power Tools
   Beno J. Gundlach Co.
   Miles Kimball
   Skil-Crafts Division
   Montgomery Ward & Co., Inc.
etching tools
   William Dixon Co.
faceting instruments
   Exactra-Craft Corp.
   MDR Mfg. Co., Inc.
fast basting tool
   Village Designs
flexible curve ruler
   Arthur Brown & Bro., Inc.
floor tile cutters
   Beno J. Gundlach Co.
floral tools
   Hazel Pearson Handi Craft
folding precision scissors
   Carter Associates
frow
   King's Studio
gem grinders
   Star Diamond Industries
gem saws
   Aleta's Rock Shop
gem scales
   Gilman's
   Morang Balance Co.
gem vises
   Gilman's
geode cutters
   Stonehouse
glass cutters
   Brookstone Co.
   Cookson & Thode
glass scribing tools
   Brookstone Co.
glass tools
   The Stained Glass Club
   Whittemore-Durgin Glass Co.
hammered metal work tools
   William Dixon Co.
hand grinder
   Dremel Creative Power Tools
hand tools
   Allcraft Tool & Supply Co.
   Bear Cave
   Bergen Arts & Crafts, Inc.
   Boin Arts & Crafts
   Brookstone Co.
   Arthur Brown & Bro., Inc.
   Albert Constantine & Son Inc.

Craft Category Index
Tools—Tools

    Craftsman Supply House
    Craftsman Wood Service Co.
    Delco Craft Center, Inc.
    Economy Handicrafts, Inc.
    Edmund Scientific Co.
    The Handcrafters
    J. J. Jewelcraft
    Silvo Hardware Co.
    Montgomery Ward & Co., Inc.

jeweler's tools
    Anchor Tool & Supply Co.
    The L. S. Starrett Co.
    Swest Inc.

jewelry casting tools
    O'Brien Lapidary Equipment Co.

jewelrymaking tools
    Allcraft Tool & Supply Co.
    Brookstone Co.
    William Dixon Co.
    Gems Galore
    Green's Rock & Lapidary Ltd.
    T. B. Hagstoz & Son
    Jim Kesterson
    Maroon Bells Ind. Inc.
    Montana Assay Office
    Sax Arts & Crafts
    C. W. Somers & Co.
    Swensons Lapidary Equipment, Inc.
    Joseph Tartas
    Trowbridge Crafts
    Universal Wirecraft Jewelry Co.
    Weidinger Inc.

jig saw
    Dremel Creative Power Tools

joiner-planers
    American Machine & Tool Co.

jug cutter
    Floyd Fleming
    Keith Robinson
    Whittemore-Durgin Glass Co.

kits
    American Machine & Tool Co.
    Corrado Cutlery Inc.
    Gilliom Mfg. Co.
    Mohave Industries
    Supreme Watch Material Co.
    United Abrasive Inc.

knives
    Art Mart, Inc.
    Tandy Leather Co.

lacemaking tools
    Some Place

lapidary belt sanders
    Great Western Equipment Co.

lapidary carving tools
    Industrial Diamond Tool Co. Inc.

lapidary drills
    Industrial Diamond Tool Co. Inc.

lapidary saw blades
    Industrial Diamond Tool Co. Inc.

lapidary saws
    Beacon
    Industrial Diamond Tool Co. Inc.
    Lortone Inc.

lapidary tools
    Aspen Lapidary
    Charbonneau's Lapidary Service
    Ebersole Lapidary Supply Inc.
    Farmers Gem and Rock Shop
    Minnesota Lapidary Supply Inc.
    Swensons Lapidary Equipment, Inc.
    United Abrasive Inc.
    G. Weidinger

lathes
    American Machine & Tool Co.
    Campbell Tools Co.

leaded glass tools
    Mollica Stained Glass Press

leather stitcher
    Sunset House

leather thongs
    Jewelart Inc.

leather tools
    La Venta Corp.
    Leathercrafters Supply Co.
    Mac Leather Co.
    Skil-Crafts Division
    Veteran Leather Co., Inc.

left handed tools
    The Left Hand Inc.

linoleum knives
    Beno J. Gundlach Co.

lost wax casting tools
    Technical Specialties International Inc.

magazines
    Woodworker

mallets
    Tandy Leather Co.

metal sculpture tools
    Sculpture Services Inc.

Craft Category Index
Tools—Tools

metal working tools
  Brookstone Co.
model tools
  James Bliss & Co. Inc.
  Boxcar Ken
  Model Railroad Equipment Corp.
  National Hobby Inc.
  Paige Enterprises
  Railway Express
  Santos Miniatures
  Ships Unlimited
  Siderod Shop
  Terminal Hobby Shop
  Wm. Walthers Inc.
modeling tools
  Delco Craft Center, Inc.
  Tandy Leather Co.
  Westwood Ceramic Supply Co.
modeling wheels
  Sculpture Services Inc.
mosaic cutters
  The L. S. Starrett Co.
mosaic tools
  Delco Craft Center, Inc.
nippers
  F. E. Biegert Co.
  Beno J. Gundlach Co.
notching tools
  Beno J. Gundlach Co.
paper cutters
  Dick Blick
planes
  King's Studio
plastic laminate tools
  Beno J. Gundlach Co.
plastic wall tile cutters
  Beno J. Gundlach Co.
pliers
  Universal Wirecraft Jewelry Co.
polishing tools
  Supreme Watch Material Co.
potter's tools
  Cole Ceramics Laboratories
  Westwood Ceramic Supply Co.
power accessories
  Dremel Creative Power Tools
power etching instrument
  Electro Stylus Mfg. Co.
power tool attachments
  Walter Drake
  Hanover House Industries, Inc.

power tools
  Allcraft Tool & Supply Co.
  Bergen Arts & Crafts, Inc.
  Boin Arts & Crafts
  Brookstone Co.
  Arthur Brown & Bro., Inc.
  Albert Constantine & Son Inc.
  Craftsman Supply House
  Craftsman Wood Service Co.
  Delco Craft Center, Inc.
  Dremel Creative Power Tools
  Economy Handicrafts, Inc.
  Edmund Scientific Co.
  Beno J. Gundlach Co.
  The Handcrafters
  Frank Mittermeier Inc.
  Sculpture Associates Ltd.
  Sculpture House
  Shipley's Mineral House
  Silvo Hardware Co.
  Technical Specialties International Inc.
  Montgomery Ward & Co., Inc.
precision glass blowing tools
  Drykiln Design
professional jeweler's instruments
  Gemological Institute of America
professional tool sets
  Tandy Leather Co.
repeat glass
  Arthur Brown & Bro., Inc.
  Plaza Artists Materials, Inc.
rock picks
  Star Diamond Industries
rock polishers
  Arthur Brown & Bro., Inc.
rock tumblers
  Scott Scientific Inc.
  Starlite Rock Shop
rock vise
  A. D. McBurney
rug hooking tools
  Berry's of Maine
sandblasting tools
  Allcraft Tool & Supply Co.
saw blades
  Foredom Electric Co.
saws
  Brad's Rock Shop
  Beno J. Gundlach Co.
  Reed Industries

Craft Category Index
Tools—Tools

scauper
  King's Studio
scissors
  Arthur Brown & Bro., Inc.
  Polly Chester Inc.
  Walter Drake
  The Needle Works
  Hazel Pearson Handi Craft
  Sax Arts & Crafts
  Montgomery Ward & Co., Inc.
scribers
  Beno J. Gundlach Co.
sculpture tools
  Art Consultants
  Arthur Brown & Bro., Inc.
  Cole Ceramics Laboratories
  Frank Mittermeier Inc.
sewing awls
  Walter Drake
shop tools
  Albert Constantine & Son Inc.
silversmithing tools
  Allcraft Tool & Supply Co.
  The Camp Fire Co.
  Charbonneau's Lapidary Service
  William Dixon Co.
  Technical Specialties International Inc.
soap cutting tools
  Anne Amiot
soldering tools
  Allcraft Tool & Supply Co.
  Brookstone Co.
  Delco Craft Center, Inc.
  Gilman's
  Frank Mittermeier Inc.
  Sax Arts & Crafts
specimen trimmers
  Nature's Treasures
sphere makers
  Covington Engineering Corp.
spray guns
  Montgomery Ward & Co., Inc.
steel rules
  The L. S. Starrett Co.
stencil tools
  Budget Buddy Co.
stone carving tools
  Frank Mittermeier Inc.
  Newton's Potters Supply
  Sculpture Associates Ltd.

  Sculpture House
  Sculpture Services Inc.
surgical knives
  Brookstone Co.
surgical scissors
  Brookstone Co.
thickness gauges
  The L. S. Starrett Co.
tile cutters
  Beno J. Gundlach Co.
  The L. S. Starrett Co.
tile saws
  Beno J. Gundlach Co.
tjanting tool
  Hazel Pearson Handi Craft
tool handles
  King's Studio
trim saws
  Brad's Rock Shop
  Covington Engineering Corp.
  Gilman's
  Green's Rock & Lapidary Ltd.
  Highland Park Manufacturing
  Lindell Industries
  MDR Mfg. Co., Inc.
  Star Diamond Industries
trimming tools
  Polly Chester Inc.
  Beno J. Gundlach Co.
upholstery tools
  Albert Constantine & Son Inc.
  Craftsman Wood Service Co.
  General Supplies Co.
utility knives
  Beno J. Gundlach Co.
vanadium steel cutters
  Foredom Electric Co.
wax casting tools
  Allcraft Tool & Supply Co.
wax cutting tools
  Anne Amiot
wax tools
  Supreme Watch Material Co.
welding tools
  Village Candle & Craft
  Montgomery Ward & Co., Inc.
wire bending jig
  Plaza Artists Materials, Inc.
wire jewelrymaking tools
  Frankie's Twistcraft Jewelry

wire winder tool
  Netcraft
wood carving tools
  Brookstone Co.
  Arthur Brown & Bro., Inc.
  Country Woodcraft
  Hobbi-Carve
  Frank Mittermeier Inc.
  Newton's Potters Supply
  Sculpture Associates Ltd.
  Sculpture House
  Sculpture Services Inc.
  The Sneak Box Studio
woodburning
  Supreme Handicrafts
woodworking tools
  American Machine & Tool Co.
  Arco Tools Inc.
  Brookstone Co.
  Sunset House
workshop power tools
  Allcraft Tool & Supply Co.
  Belsaw Power Tools

toymaking
  books
    Chilton Book Co.
    Craftool Co.
    Crafty Ideas
    Drake Publishers Inc.
    Stein & Day
    Taplinger Publishing Co.
    United States Committee for UNICEF
    Workman Publishing Co.
  crochet animals
    Sharon's Petite Sherre
  doll making
    Bob's Arts & Crafts
    Standard Doll Co.
  kits
    Needlewoman Shop
    Sears, Roebuck & Co.
    Vermont Toy Crafts
  leaflets
    Mrs. L. Winum
  magazines
    Twenty-five Weekend Build-It Projects
  needlework stuffed toys
    Donna Jean Carver
  plastic heads
    Hazel Pearson Handi Craft

  sew-and-stuff animals
    Herter's, Inc.
  sew-and-stuff dolls
    Herter's, Inc.
  toy patterns
    Dorris Dolls
    Sue Wise
  toys
    House of Patterns
  wiggle eyes
    Delco Craft Center, Inc.

transfers
  Budget Buddy Co.
  The Hidden Village
  Jerry S. Kaye Assoc.
  Sangray Corp.
  Skil-Crafts Division
  crewel embroidery design transfers
    Nantucket Needleworks
  iron-on transfers
    Needlecraft Shop Inc.
    Santa Cruz Mountain Crafts
    Transart
  kits
    Sangray Corp.
  transfer pencils
    House of Gould
    Merribee
    Needlecraft Shop Inc.
    Zim's

trims and notions *(see also Boutique trims)*
  Adventures In Crafts
  Craftsman Supply House
  Eagle Mill
  Fabulous Holiday House
  Holiday Handicrafts, Inc.
  Kieffer's Lingerie Fabric & Supplies
  Lace Lady
  Magnus Craft Materials, Inc.
  Mill Store
  Hazel Pearson Handi Craft
  The Putter Shop
  Taylor House
  Two Brothers Inc.
  appliques
    Leman Publications
    Lillian Vernon
  bells
    Jewelart Inc.
    Jeweler's Emporium

Craft Category Index
Trims—Trims

Knit Services, Inc.
Winona Trading Post
boutique braids
    The Putter Shop
braids
    Home-Sew Inc.
    Knit Services, Inc.
    Lace Lady
    Mill Store
    Two Brothers Inc.
braids for Battenburg lace
    Muriel N. Charney
button backs
    Grieger's Inc.
buttons
    Home-Sew Inc.
    House of York
    Lace Lady
    Two Brothers Inc.
camel bells
    Macrame and Weaving Supply Co.
chains
    Green's Rock & Lapidary Ltd.
    Jewel Creations
    Jeweler's Emporium
    Montgomery Ward & Co., Inc.
chenille
    Dick Blick
    Bob's Arts & Crafts
    Craftsman Supply House
    Don's Hobby Co.
    House of Flowers
    Hazel Pearson Handi Craft
    Sav-On-Crafts
    Sax Arts & Crafts
    Supreme Handicrafts
    Zim's
chenille boutique trims
    Delco Craft Center, Inc.
Christmas boutique items
    Holiday Craft
cording
    Nature's Fibers
cotton cord
    Creator's Corner
    Tinkler & Co. Inc.
cotton lace
    Home-Sew Inc.
    National Artcraft Supply Co.
cotton seamless tubing
    Lee Wards

decorative trims
    The Sewing Bee
decoupage trims
    Sax Arts & Crafts
diamond dust
    Holiday Craft
    Walnut Hill Co.
die-cut papers
    Taylor House
edgings
    Boutique Trims
    Creative Craft House
    Lace Lady
    The Putter Shop
    Elyse Sommer
    Town & Country Crafts
    Two Brothers Inc.
embroidered appliques
    Embroideries Unlimited
embroidered family crest emblems
    Scotch House
fabric braids
    Taylor House
filigree paper lace
    P. S. Andrews Co.
findings
    House of Flowers
    Taylor House
flat chenille
    Greentree Ranch Wools, Countryside Handweavers
flat plastic shapes
    Holiday Craft
flocking
    Dick Blick
    Boin Arts & Crafts
    Arthur Brown & Bro., Inc.
    Craft Service
    Skil-Crafts Division
    W. Wooley & Co.
fringes
    Home-Sew Inc.
fur trimmings
    Great Central Fur Corp.
glitter
    Country Crafts
    Holiday Handicrafts, Inc.
    Walnut Hill Co.
gold braids
    P. S. Andrews Co.

gold lace borders
   Harrower House of Decoupage
gold lace frames
   Harrower House of Decoupage
gold lace ornaments
   Harrower House of Decoupage
gold paper borders
   Taylor House
gold paper decorations
   Country Crafts
gold paper laces
   Hazel Pearson Handi Craft
gold paper ornaments
   Skil-Crafts Division
   Taylor House
gold paper trims
   Holiday Craft
honeycomb ribbon
   Sav-On-Crafts
jingle bells
   Sav-On-Crafts
kits
   General Supplies Co.
lace
   Lace Lady
   Two Brothers Inc.
lacing
   American Handicrafts
   P. S. Andrews Co.
   Craft Service
   Craftsman Supply House
   Sax Arts & Crafts
   Skil-Crafts Division
   Tandy Leather Co.
leather buttons
   Pollack's Furrier's Supply Corp.
metallic braids
   Gibsons Creations
   Knit Services, Inc.
metallic threads
   The Hidden Village
metallic trims
   Home-Sew Inc.
mica mirrors
   Kitsophrenia, Inc.
nonmetallic trims
   Home-Sew Inc.
nylon braided cord
   Fetty-Nielsen Macrame Loom

nylon lace
   Home-Sew Inc.
   Nucleus
pearl strands
   Jeweler's Emporium
pearls
   Anne's Treasure Trove
   Bead Game
   The Beadcraft Corner/Beadcraft Club
   Deep Flex Plastic Molds, Inc.
   Gilman's
   Home-Sew Inc.
   International Import Co.
   Jewelart Inc.
   Kaydee
   Kit Kraft
   M & M Distributors
   Natalie Originals Studio
   New Products Co.
   The Putter Shop
   Schrock's, The House of Hobbies & Crafts
   Swan-Son
   Taylor House
perforated ribbon
   Hazel Pearson Handi Craft
pewter buttons
   House of York
   Wichelt Import Co.
polyester lace
   Home-Sew Inc.
pompoms
   Woodward Ranch
purse trimmings
   House of Flowers
rhinestone bandings
   Gail's Decorative Arts Studio
   Gibsons Creations
rhinestone chain
   Boutique Trims
rhinestones
   P. S. Andrews Co.
   Boutique Trims
   Derby Lane Shell Center
   Florida Supply House, Inc.
   Gail's Decorative Arts Studio
   Gibsons Creations
   Handcraft Originals
   Home-Sew Inc.
   Kit Kraft

Craft Category Index
Trims—Upholstering

National Artcraft Supply Co.
Lee Wards
ribbon
B & M Yarn Co.
Boycan's Craft Supplies
Holiday Craft
Home-Sew Inc.
House of Flowers
Koehler's Craft Outlet
Sav-On-Crafts
Town & Country Crafts
Wagner's Crafts
rickrack
Home-Sew Inc.
rug braiding
Berry's of Maine
The Dorr Mill Store
House of Gould
Knits'N That Yarn Shop
Mildred Sprout
sequins
Boutique Trims
Home-Sew Inc.
Kit Kraft
Koehler's Craft Outlet
Sav-On-Crafts
Wagner's Crafts
tubular braid
Knit Services, Inc.
tubular tufting
Knit Services, Inc.
velvet flowers
Country Crafts
velvet leaves
Country Crafts
velvet ribbons
Boutique Trims
Taylor House
velvet tubing
Zim's

unfinished furniture and accessories
decoupage lap desks
Dek-Co Manufacturing Co.
decoupage stools
Dek-Co Manufacturing Co.
furniture finishes
American Art Clay Co. Inc.
Art Mart, Inc.
Carson & Ellis, Inc.
Albert Constantine & Son Inc.
Douglas & Sturgess, Inc.
Leathercrafters Supply Co.
Hazel Pearson Handi Craft
Plasco
Sav-On-Crafts
Supreme Handicrafts
furniture polishes
Albert Constantine & Son Inc.
furniture stains
Albert Constantine & Son Inc.
Sturbridge Yankee Workshop
kits
Giles & Kendall Inc.
small unfinished furniture
Carson & Ellis, Inc.
unfinished barrels
Spaulding & Frost Co., Inc.
unfinished Early American furniture
Sturbridge Yankee Workshop
unfinished kegs
Spaulding & Frost Co. Inc
unfinished milk cans
Dairy Service, Inc
The Wood Barn
unfinished pails
Spaulding & Frost Co., Inc.
unfinished unassembled children's furniture
Spaulding & Frost Co., Inc.

upholstering
bolsters
Atlantic Upholstery Supply Co.
books
American Technical Society
Bruce Benziger
Lane Magazine & Book Co.
McGraw-Hill Book Co.
McKnight Publishing Co.
Popular Mechanics Press
Howard W. Sams & Co., Inc.
cording
Nature's Fibers
cotton seamless tubing
Lee Wards
home study courses
American School
Auto Upholstery Institute
Custom Drapery Institute
Modern Upholstery Institute
kits
General Supplies Co.
pillows
The Hidden Village

Craft Category Index
Upholstering—Wax

polyester Fiberfil® stuffing
   Putnam Co.
polyester filled pillow forms
   Putnam Co.
rods
   Atlantic Upholstery Supply Co.
rubber cushions
   Atlantic Upholstery Supply Co.
seagrass
   Atlantic Upholstery Supply Co.
slip cover supplies
   Atlantic Upholstery Supply Co.
upholstery cleaning
   Atlantic Upholstery Supply Co.
upholstery fabrics
   General Supplies Co.
upholstery supplies
   Atlantic Upholstery Supply Co.
   Minnesota Woodworkers Supply Co.
   Montgomery Ward & Co., Inc.
upholstery tools
   Albert Constantine & Son Inc.
   Craftsman Wood Service Co.
   General Supplies Co.
velvet tubing
   Zim's
wet look vinyl
   Montgomery Ward & Co., Inc.

wall hangings
backings for hangings
   Coulter Studios
books
   Crown Publishers
   Whitson's
braiding hangings
   The Dorr Mill Store
bunting
   Dick Blick
crewel tapestry wall hangings
   General Crafts Corp.
fraternal wood emblems
   Albert Constantine & Son Inc.
kits
   Edna Looney Originals
   Supreme Handicrafts

watchmaking and repairing
books
   Emerson Books Inc.
   Nelson-Hall Co.
hand loupes
   Gemological Institute of America
watch repair supplies
   Lapidabrade Inc.
watchmaker's tools
   Supreme Watch Material Co.

wax
   Bourget Bros. Gems & Minerals
   Gilman's
   Kerr Mfg. Co.
   Sax Arts & Crafts
   Sculpture Associates Ltd.
   Supreme Watch Material Co.
   Surma Book & Music Store
   Westwood Ceramic Supply Co.
batik wax
   Delco Craft Center, Inc.
   Hazel Pearson Handi Craft
batik wax blends
   Siphon Art Products
bayberry wax
   Barker Enterprises
beading wax
   Nicole Bead & Craft Co., Inc.
beeswax
   Barker Enterprises
   Walnut Hill Co.
candle waxes
   Barker Enterprises
   Cake Decorators & Craft Supplies
   Candle Kitchen
   Candle Mill Village
   Craft Service
   Doll's Candle & Craft Supplies
   House of Wood Candles
   Sav-On-Crafts
   W. Spencer Inc.
   Village Candle & Craft
   W. Wooley & Co.
carnauba wax
   Barker Enterprises
casting waxes
   Allcraft Tool & Supply Co.
   Delco Craft Center, Inc.
cold process batik textile wax
   Siphon Art Products
driftwood wax
   Driftwood House
flower wax cutters
   Doll's Candle & Craft Supplies
honeycomb
   Craft Service

Craft Category Index
Wax—Weaving

honeycomb candles
  Cleveland Leather Co.
honeycomb wax sheets
  Brown's Miniatures
inlay casting wax
  Green's Rock & Lapidary Ltd.
jeweler's sprue wax
  Green's Rock & Lapidary Ltd.
leaflets
  Jesop Co.
macrocrystalline wax
  Arthur Brown & Bro., Inc.
sculpture wax
  Delco Craft Center, Inc.
  Douglas & Sturgess, Inc.
sheet waxes
  Green's Rock & Lapidary Ltd.
sticky wax
  Green's Rock & Lapidary Ltd.
wax casting tools
  Allcraft Tool & Supply Co.
wax cutting tools
  Anne Amiot
wax gilt
  Plasco
wax gold
  Arthur Brown & Bro., Inc.
wax medium
  Siphon Art Products
wax melting pot
  Sculpture Associates Ltd.
  Shipley's Mineral House
wax patterns
  Exactra-Craft Corp.
wax tools
  Supreme Watch Material Co.

wax sculpting
  books
    Magic Circle Corp.
  flower wax cutters
    Doll's Candle & Craft Supplies
  sculpture wax
    Delco Craft Center, Inc.
    Douglas & Sturgess, Inc.
    Sculpture Associates Ltd.
  wax melting pot
    Sculpture Associates Ltd.
  wax modeling
    Sculpture Associates Ltd.

weaving *(see also Looms, Yarns)*
  backstrap (waist) loom
    Robert Nelson
  belt shuttles
    Schacht Spindle Co.
  boat shuttles
    Schacht Spindle Co.
  bobbin winders
    Frederick J. Fawcett, Inc.
    Osma G. Tod Weaving & Lace Studio
  bobbins
    Leclerc Corp.
    Robin & Russ Handweavers
    School Products Co.
  books
    Book Barn
    The Country Craftsmen
    Craftool Co.
    Craftsman Circle Book Club
    Crafty Ideas
    Crown Publishers
    Davis Publications, Inc.
    Marquerite P. Davison
    Delmar Publishers
    East River Publications
    P. C. Herwig Co., Inc.
    HTH Publishers
    Leclerc Corp.
    Lily Mills Co.
    The Mail Train
    Museum Books Inc.
    Robin & Russ Handweavers
    Textile Crafts
    Osma G. Tod Weaving & Lace Studio
    The Unicorn
    Van Nostrand Reinhold Co.
    Viking Press
    Watson-Guptill Publications
  cards
    School Products Co.
  carpet warp
    Knit Services, Inc.
    The Oriental Rug Co.
  club plans
    Robert Ayottes' Designery
  cords
    Dick Blick
    P. C. Herwig Co., Inc.
    Macrame and Weaving Supply Co.
  cottolin yarn
    The Hidden Village

Craft Category Index
Weaving—Weaving

cotton yarn
  Craft Yarns of Rhode Island Inc.
  Tinkler & Co. Inc.

cotton ropes polished
  Knit Services, Inc.

cowhair yarns
  House of Kleen

creels
  Osma G. Tod Weaving & Lace Studio

Egyptian cotton thread
  Robin & Russ Handweavers

electric bobbin winders
  Robin & Russ Handweavers

floor looms
  The Hidden Village
  House of Yarn & Crafts
  KAY an EE Corp. of America
  Schacht Spindle Co.
  School Products Co.
  Tools of the Trade
  Turnbull Looms

folding floor harness looms
  Norwood Loom Co.

folding frame loom
  Robert Nelson
  Turnbull Looms

foot-operated looms
  Kessenich Looms

hand cards
  The Freed Co.
  E. B. Frye & Son, Inc.

hand fabric loom
  Palmloom Co.

hand looms
  Walter Drake
  Harrisville Designs
  Kessenich Looms
  L. W. Macomber Ad-A Harness Looms
  Sax Arts & Crafts

hand weaving
  Robert Ayottes' Designery
  KM Yarn Co.
  Silver Shuttle

hand weaving yarns
  J & H Clasgens Co.
  Lily Mills Co.
  Isabel Scott Fabrics Corp.

harness lap loom
  Village Art Gallery

harness looms
  The Pendleton Shop
  Turnbull Looms

home built loom
  Turnbull Looms

home study courses
  National Weavers Training School

inkle looms
  Cleve-Craft E-Z Loom
  Knit Services, Inc.
  Lily Mills Co.
  The Loom Factory
  The Loomery
  Morgan Inkle Loom Factory
  Robin & Russ Handweavers
  Schacht Spindle Co.
  School Products Co.

kits
  Craftool Co.
  Crowe & Coulter
  Gemex Co.

leaflets
  Margaret Newman
  Osma G. Tod Weaving & Lace Studio

loom accessories
  KAY an EE Corp. of America
  Robin & Russ Handweavers

loom equipment
  Lily Mills Co.

looper looms
  Pack-O-Fun

loopers
  Pack-O-Fun

magazines
  Handweaver & Craftsman
  The Looming Arts
  Robin & Russ Handweavers
  Textile Crafts
  Warp & Weft
  Z-Handicrafts

organizations
  Handweavers Guild of America, Inc.

reed
  School Products Co.

shuttles
  Heritage Looms
  Leclerc Corp.
  Robin & Russ Handweavers
  School Products Co.

single ply for warp
  KeeWai Krafts

Craft Category Index
Weaving—Wire

skein maker
   Clems and Clems Spinning Wheels
skein winders
   Robin & Russ Handweavers
small weaving looms
   Spencer Gifts Inc.
   Sunset House
spool racks
   Robin & Russ Handweavers
Swedish bobbin winders
   Robin & Russ Handweavers
table size yarn winders
   KeeWai Krafts
warp cloth
   KM Yarn Co.
warping boards
   Schacht Spindle Co.
weave-it looms
   Mary Maxim Inc.
   Yarns Unlimited
weaving accessories
   The Fringe and Frame
   Leclerc Corp.
   Northwest Handcraft House
   Norwood Loom Co.
   The Oriental Rug Co.
   Tahki Imports, Limited
   The Yarn Depot
weaving cutters
   The Mannings Creative Crafts
weaving frames
   The Hidden Village
   The Mannings Creative Crafts
   The Yarn Depot
weaving looms
   Delco Craft Center, Inc.
   Frederick J. Fawcett , Inc.
   KM Yarn Co.
   Leclerc Corp.
   Lily Mills Co.
   The Loomery
   The Mannings Creative Crafts
   The New England Craftsman
   Textile Crafts
   The Yarn Depot
weaving supplies
   Boin Arts & Crafts
   Craftool Co.
   Essayons Studio, Hand Arts Center
   Frederick J. Fawcett , Inc.
   Fiber to Fabric
   E. B. Frye & Son, Inc.
   Handcraft House
   Heritage Looms
   The Hidden Village
   Macrame and Weaving Supply Co.
   Magnolia Weaving
   The Mannings Creative Crafts
   The New England Craftsman
   Northwest Handcraft House
   Savin Handcrafts
   Silver Shuttle
   Some Place
   Straw Into Gold
   Osma G. Tod Weaving & Lace Studio
weaving yarns
   Charles M. Butterworth
   Conlin Yarns
   Contessa Yarns
   Cottage Crafts
   Coulter Studios
   Craft Yarns of Rhode Island Inc.
   Frederick J. Fawcett, Inc.
   Filature Lemieux Inc.
   The Handcrafters
   House of Kleen
   House of Yarn & Crafts
   Jean Malsada Inc.
   The Mannings Creative Crafts
   Shuttlecraft
   Tahki Imports, Limited
   Textile Crafts
   The Yarn Depot
winders
   School Products Co.
yarn winders
   KAY an EE Corp. of America
2/20's handweaving worsted
   Frederick J. Fawcett , Inc.

welding
arc welding supplies
   Wel-Dex Mfg. Co.
books
   American Technical Society
   James F. Lincoln Arc Welding Foundation
home study courses
   American School
   Metals Engineering Institute

wire
   Beadnik's Arts & Crafts
   Craft Service

Gilman's
T. B. Hagstoz & Son
Sav-On-Crafts
Universal Wirecraft Jewelry Co.
copper wire
  Talisman Crafts
gold filled wire
  G. Weidinger
gold wire
  Green's Rock & Lapidary Ltd.
  Talisman Crafts
  Trowbridge Crafts
silver wire
  Talisman Crafts
square gold filled wire
  Frankie's Twistcraft Jewelry
sterling silver wire
  Alessi Lapidary Supplies
  Green's Rock & Lapidary Ltd.
  Trowbridge Crafts
  G. Weidinger
wire bending jig
  Plaza Artists Materials, Inc.
wire winder tool
  Netcraft

wood
Carson & Ellis, Inc.
Glencraft Shop
Magnus Craft Materials, Inc.
NASCO Arts & Crafts
Real Woods
Sax Arts & Crafts
Stewart Industries
C. R. Wells
balsa wood
  Bob's Arts & Crafts
  Paul K. Guillow Inc.
  Sax Arts & Crafts
  Skil-Crafts Division
bamboo
  Boin Arts & Crafts
books
  Crown Publishers
carving wood
  Woodshop
carvings
  Crown Cultured Pearl Corp.
cherry blocks
  Crowe & Coulter
cherry wood
  Midland Walnut

curly maple wood
  Herter's, Inc.
custom wood
  HERE Inc.
domestic hardwoods
  Craftsman Wood Service Co.
driftwood
  Driftwood House
  Dale Magnuson
Finnish imported plywood
  Stewart Industries
hardwood
  M & M Hardwood
hardwood blocks
  Cummings Wood Co.
imported hardwoods
  Craftsman Wood Service Co.
instrument wood
  International Violin
kits
  Cleveland Leather Co.
  Albert Constantine & Son Inc.
lumber
  Bedford Lumber Co., Inc.
  Albert Constantine & Son Inc.
  Midland Walnut
lumber squares
  Midland Walnut
magazines
  Challenge Publications, Inc
mahogany blocks
  Crowe & Coulter
manzanita wood
  Country Crafts
myrtlewood
  Woodshop
organizations
  International Wood Collectors Society
poplar blocks
  Crowe & Coulter
precut wood forms
  Mrs. Ruby Brandon
rare woods
  Real Woods
  Sculpture Associates Ltd.
redwood
  Woodshop
teredo wood slabs
  Brown's Rock & Lapidary Supplies
walnut blocks
  Crowe & Coulter

Craft Category Index
Wood—Woodworking

walnut wood
   Midland Walnut
wood fibre
   Bob's Arts & Crafts
   Boycan's Craft Supplies
   Koehler's Craft Outlet
   Ramont's Floral Arts Studio
   Zim's
wood jewelry scraps
   Glencraft Shop
   Jeweler's Emporium
wood panels
   Town & Country Crafts
wood parts
   Minnesota Woodworkers Supply Co.
wood scraps
   Harrison Neustadt
wood veneers
   Albert Constantine & Son Inc.
   Homecraft Veneer
   The New England Craftsman

woodworking
   Skil-Crafts Division
   Supreme Handicrafts
adz
   Elizabeth R. King
belt sanders
   American Machine & Tool Co.
   Covington Engineering Corp.
   Gilman's
   Highland Park Manufacturing
boat building supplies
   M & M Hardwood
books
   American Technical Society
   Charles A. Bennett Co., Inc.
   Bruce Benziger
   Book Barn
   Brookstone Co.
   Craftool Co.
   Crafty Ideas
   Drake Publishers Inc.
   Emerson Books Inc.
   Goodhert-Willcox Co., Inc.
   Lane Magazine & Book Co.
   S. Lynds Patterns
   McGraw-Hill Book Co.
   McKnight Publishing Co.
   Museum Books Inc.
   Prentice-Hall Inc.
   Random House Inc.
   Times Mirror Magazine
   The Unicorn
   Valspar Corp.
carpentry tools
   Brookstone Co.
   The L. S. Starrett Co.
carved trims
   Albert Constantine & Son Inc.
carving designs
   Raymond P. Wallace
carving drills
   Foredom Electric Co.
carving supplies
   Economy Handicrafts, Inc.
   Ettl Studios Inc.
craft plans
   Minnesota Woodworkers Supply Co.
driftwood polish
   Deb Products
driftwood wax
   Driftwood House
drill attachments
   Arco Tools Inc.
drill presses
   American Machine & Tool Co.
   Dremel Creative Power Tools
finishing supplies
   Homecraft Veneer
fittings
   King's Studio
frow
   King's Studio
furniture lumber
   Giles & Kendall Inc.
hand tools
   Albert Constantine & Son Inc.
   Craftsman Wood Service Co.
hardware
   Albert Constantine & Son Inc.
   Real Woods
hinges
   Albert Constantine & Son Inc.
home study courses
   American School
imported prefabricated guitar wood
   String Instrument Service Inc.
kits
   Craftool Co.
   Craftsman Wood Service Co.
   Magnus Craft Materials, Inc.
   Mary Maxim Inc.

Craft Category Index
Woodworking—Wood

    Pack-O-Fun
    S & W Crafts Mfg.
    Shaker Workshops Inc.
    Trailcraft Inc.
laminating supplies
    Homecraft Veneer
leaflets
    Craftplans
    Real Woods
magazines
    Wood Projects
    Woodworker
    The Workbench
moldings
    Albert Constantine & Son Inc.
    Craft Products
    Craftsman Wood Service Co.
    M & M Hardwood
    Midland Walnut
    Minnesota Woodworkers Supply Co.
organizations
    International Wood Collectors Society
plans
    Minnesota Woodworkers Supply Co.
salt and pepper shakers mechanisms
    Albert Constantine & Son Inc.
saws
    Beno J. Gundlach Co.
scribers
    Beno J. Gundlach Co.
services
    Van Gelder Wood Products
shaving horses
    King's Studio
wood finishing
    Birchwood Casey
wood finishing supplies
    Minnesota Woodworkers Supply Co.
    Real Woods
wood lamp bases
    Angelo Bros. Co.
wood legs
    Midland Walnut
    Minnesota Woodworkers Supply Co.
wood modeling materials
    Terminal Hobby Shop
wood stains
    Fezandie & Sperrle, Inc.
wood turnings
    Van Gelder Wood Products

woodburning
    Supreme Handicrafts
woodworking patterns
    Craft Patterns
woodworking supplies
    Minnesota Woodworkers Supply Co.
woodworking tools
    American Machine & Tool Co.
    Arco Tools Inc.
    Brookstone Co.
    Sunset House
zodiac inlay emblems
    Craftsman Wood Service Co.

wood carving and sculpting
adz
    Elizabeth R. King
balsa wood
    Bob's Arts & Crafts
    Paul K. Guillow Inc.
    Sax Arts & Crafts
    Skil-Crafts Division
basswood figures
    Country Woodcraft
blank gun stocks
    Midland Walnut
books
    A. S. Barnes and Co., Inc.
    Country Woodcraft
    Craftool Co.
    Crafty Ideas
    Dharma Trading Co.
    Lane Magazine & Book Co.
    Museum Books Inc.
    Sterling Publishing Co. Inc.
    University of Minnesota Press
carving designs
    Raymond P. Wallace
carving drills
    Foredom Electric Co.
carving wood
    Art Mart, Inc.
    Woodshop
frow
    King's Studio
green wing teals
    Bay Country Woodcrafters
hand tools
    Albert Constantine & Son Inc.
    Craftsman Wood Service Co.
kits
    Country Woodcraft

Craft Category Index
Wood—Woodware

    Craftool Co.
    Lynchburg Hdwr. & General Store
    Lee Wards
organizations
    National Carvers Museum
paints
    The Sneak Box Studio
wood carving scraps
    Glencraft Shop
wood carving supplies
    Dick Blick
    Craft Service
    Crowe & Coulter
    Crown Cultured Pearl Corp.
    Economy Handicrafts, Inc.
    Ettl Studios Inc.
    The Handcrafters
    Hearth & Heather Ltd.
    The Sneak Box Studio
    Montgomery Ward & Co., Inc.
wood carving tools
    Brookstone Co.
    Arthur Brown & Bro., Inc.
    Albert Constantine & Son Inc.
    Country Woodcraft
    Hobbi-Carve
    M & M Hardwood
    Frank Mittermeier Inc.
    Newton's Potters Supply
    Sax Arts & Crafts
    Sculpture Associates Ltd.
    Sculpture House
    Sculpture Services Inc.
    Skil-Crafts Division
    The Sneak Box Studio
wood ducks
    Bay Country Woodcrafters
wood mallards
    Bay Country Woodcrafters

woodware
    P. S. Andrews Co.
    Bergen Arts & Crafts, Inc.
    Boin Arts & Crafts
    Carson & Ellis, Inc.
    Century 21
    Corner Cupboard Crafts, Inc.
    Country Woodcraft
    Craft Service
    Economy Handicrafts, Inc.
    P. C. Herwig Co., Inc.
    John's Hardware & Decoupage Supplies
    Magnus Craft Materials, Inc.
    Marie Mitchell's Decoupage Center
    Rombins' Nest Farm
    Sandeen's Scandinavian Gift & Card Shop
    Sax Arts & Crafts
    Skil-Crafts Division
    Town & Country Crafts
    Traditional Norwegian Rosemaling
    Lee Wards
basswood boxes
    O-P Craft Co., Inc.
basswood figures
    Country Woodcraft
carved wood mineral display stands
    Weaver's Gems and Minerals
cheese boards
    National Artcraft Supply Co.
decoupage boxes
    Dek-Co Manufacturing Co.
    Harrower House of Decoupage
decoupage plaques
    The Cellar Ceramic Shop
    Dek-Co Manufacturing Co.
    Harrower House of Decoupage
ecology shadow boxes
    Delco Craft Center, Inc.
fraternal wood emblems
    Albert Constantine & Son Inc.
handmade Swiss wood beads
    Robin & Russ Handweavers
hutch boxes
    Koehler's Craft Outlet
kits
    Bear Cave
    Cleveland Leather Co.
    Economy Handicrafts, Inc.
moldings
    Albert Constantine & Son Inc.
    Craft Products
    Craftsman Wood Service Co.
    M & M Hardwood
    Midland Walnut
    Minnesota Woodworkers Supply Co.
painting wood
    Floquil, Inc.
salt and pepper shakers mechanisms
    Albert Constantine & Son Inc.

shadowboxes
   The Handcraft Supply Corp.
   O-P Craft Co., Inc.
table lighter inserts
   Albert Constantine & Son Inc.
teak trays
   Marie Mitchell's Decoupage Center
undecorated woodenware
   Adventures In Crafts
unfinished basswood boxes
   Albert Constantine & Son Inc.
unfinished boxes
   Carson & Ellis, Inc.
unfinished plaques
   Albert Constantine & Son Inc.
unfinished purse boxes
   Carson & Ellis, Inc.
unfinished woodenware
   Bernadette Decorative Art
   Hoffman Hatchery
wood barrels
   Dairy Service, Inc.
wood boards
   Keith Robinson
wood bookends
   Downs
wood bowls
   Midland Walnut
   O-P Craft Co., Inc.
wood boxes
   Artistry In Wood
   Holiday Handicrafts, Inc.
   Kit Kraft
   Van Gelder Wood Products
wood buckles
   Knit Services, Inc.
wood buttons
   O-P Craft Co., Inc.
wood canary eggs
   Rock Mountain Farm
wood chests
   O-P Craft Co., Inc.
wood crosses
   O-P Craft Co., Inc.
wood cutouts
   The Wood Barn
wood dolls
   Susan Sirkis
wood eggs
   O-P Craft Co., Inc.

wood frames
   Midland Walnut
   Marie Mitchell's Decoupage Center
wood hardware
   Minnesota Woodworkers Supply Co.
wood hoops
   Knit Services, Inc.
wood jewelry
   Artistry In Wood
wood kegs
   Dairy Service, Inc.
wood lamp bases
   Angelo Bros. Co.
wood legs
   Midland Walnut
   Minnesota Woodworkers Supply Co.
wood milk cases
   Dairy Service, Inc.
wood milk kegs
   Dairy Service, Inc.
wood miniatures
   Handcraft Originals
wood plaques
   Artistry In Wood
   The Cellar Ceramic Shop
   O-P Craft Co., Inc.
   Party Bazaar
wood roses
   Western Tree Cones
wood spools
   Allegra Milano
wood tables
   Marie Mitchell's Decoupage Center
wood tiles
   Pack-O-Fun
wood trays
   O-P Craft Co., Inc.
wooden apple cone
   Colonial Decorations
wooden candle molds
   Barker Enterprises
wooden candle sconces
   Marie Mitchell's Decoupage Center
wooden candleholders
   O-P Craft Co., Inc.
wooden clocks
   Marie Mitchell's Decoupage Center
wool
   Charles M. Butterworth
   Carlbert Fabrics
   Isabel Scott Fabrics Corp.

Craft Category Index
Wool—Yarns

alpaca
  Colonial Textiles
  Greentree Ranch Wools, Countryside Handweavers
  The Hidden Village
  KM Yarn Co.
  Valley Handweaving Supply

alpencarpet
  Greentree Ranch Wools, Countryside Handweavers

cashmere
  Colonial Textiles

fleece
  Colonial Textiles
  Greentree Ranch Wools, Countryside Handweavers
  The Hidden Village
  KM Yarn Co.
  The Makings
  The Niddy Noddy
  School Products Co.
  Valley Handweaving Supply

graded grease wool
  Midwest Wool Marketing Cooperative

grease mohair wool
  Angora Diablo

grease wool
  The Freed Co.
  Gary H. Watson

hand spinning wool
  Essayons Studio, Hand Arts Center
  Gary H. Watson

handspun wool
  KeeWai Krafts

homespun wool
  Greentree Ranch Wools, Countryside Handweavers

karakul
  KM Yarn Co.

lambswool
  R. S. Duncan & Co.

mill products
  Greentree Ranch Wools, Countryside Handweavers

washed white wool
  Gary H. Watson

wool mill ends
  Carlbert Fabrics

2/7 wool
  Greentree Ranch Wools, Countryside Handweavers

wool processing
carders
  Colonial Textiles
  Spincraft
  Wool Products Ltd.

hand cards
  The Freed Co.
  E. B. Frye & Son, Inc.

hand spinning
  Spincraft

hand spinning wool
  Essayons Studio, Hand Arts Center
  Gary H. Watson

hand-operated wool carding machine
  Kulch
  Wool Products Ltd.

heavy duty hand carders
  Kulch

noil
  Nature's Fibers

spindles
  Greentree Ranch Wools, Countryside Handweavers
  School Products Co.

wool carders
  Frederick J. Fawcett, Inc.

wool dyes
  Creator's Corner
  Northwest Handcraft House

yarns
  Robert Ayottes' Designery
  B & M Yarn Co.
  Better Homes & Gardens
  Dick Blick
  Craft Yarns of Rhode Island Inc.
  Crossroads
  Delco Craft Center, Inc.
  Dharma Trading Co.
  Easy Street
  Essayons Studio, Hand Arts Center
  Fairtex Distributing Co.
  Frederick J. Fawcett , Inc.
  The Fringe and Frame
  John E. Garrett Ltd.
  Greentree Ranch Wools, Countryside Handweavers
  Handcraft House
  Heritage Hill Patterns

P. C. Herwig Co., Inc.
The Hidden Village
House of Flowers
Jerry S. Kaye Assoc.
Knitking
Knitking Magazine
Macrame and Weaving Supply Co.
Magnolia Weaving
The Makings
Mary Maxim Inc.
The Needlecase
Nimble Thimble
Robin & Russ Handweavers
Sax Arts & Crafts
Schrock's, The House of Hobbies & Crafts
Sears, Roebuck & Co.
Sign of the Arrow
Silver Shuttle
Mildred Sprout
Straw Into Gold
Studio Yarn Farms Inc.
Sunray Yarn House
Tahki Imports, Limited
Thumbelina Needlework Shop
Tuxedo Yarn & Needlework
Valley Handweaving Supply
Montgomery Ward & Co., Inc.
Lee Wards
Wonoco Yarn Co.
Wyco Yarn Co.
The Yarn Dome
Yarn Primitives
The Yarn and Soda Shop
Yarns Unlimited

acrylic yarn
   Wonoco Yarn Co.

alpencarpet
   Greentree Ranch Wools, Countryside Handweavers

angora yarn
   Wonoco Yarn Co.

Austrian angora yarns
   Folklorico

Belgian yarn
   The Hidden Village

British tapestry wool
   Greentree Ranch Wools, Countryside Handweavers

bulky knit yarns
   KeeWai Krafts

carpet round
   Greentree Ranch Wools, Countryside Handweavers

cashmere yarn
   The Hidden Village

cottolin yarn
   The Hidden Village

cotton crochet yarn
   W. B. Roddey

cotton yarn
   Craft Yarns of Rhode Island Inc.
   Tinkler & Co. Inc.

cowhair yarns
   House of Kleen

crewel wool
   The Hidden Village
   Needlecraft House

crewel yarn
   Lee Wards

crochet yarns
   Cliveden Yarns
   Merribee
   Lee Wards

Danish wool
   Greentree Ranch Wools, Countryside Handweavers

Dutch yarn
   B & M Yarn Co.

English yarns
   R. S. Duncan & Co.

fleece wool
   KeeWai Krafts

French yarn
   B & M Yarn Co.

fringe wool
   Greentree Ranch Wools, Countryside Handweavers

German goathair
   Greentree Ranch Wools, Countryside Handweavers

grospoint yarn
   Peri's Homework

hand knitting yarns
   International Creations

handspun Greek yarns
   Knit Services, Inc.

handspun Mexican wool yarns
   Mexiskeins

handspun wool
   KeeWai Krafts

Craft Category Index
Yarns—Yarns

handspun yarns
    Dharma Trading Co.
    The Hidden Village
    Sachiye Jones
    Maytex
homespun crewel yarn
    KeeWai Krafts
homespun wool
    Greentree Ranch Wools, Countryside Handweavers
homespun yarns
    Craft Yarns of Rhode Island Inc.
    Valley Handweaving Supply
hooking yarns
    Tahki Imports, Limited
    Textile Crafts
Icelandic lopi
    Folklorico
    Robin & Russ Handweavers
Icelandic yarn
    The Hidden Village
Irish fisherman yarn
    House of Yarn & Crafts
Irish oiled yarn
    The Pirate's Cove
knitting worsted
    R. S. Duncan & Co.
knitting yarns
    J & H Clasgens Co.
    Cliveden Yarns
    Conlin Yarns
    Filature Lemieux Inc.
    The Handcrafters
    House of Yarn & Crafts
    Melrose Yarn Co., Inc.
    Tahki Imports, Limited
    Lee Wards
    Wool 'N Wick
lambswool
    R. S. Duncan & Co.
latch rug yarns
    Brunswick Worsted Mills
linen yarns
    Coulter Studios
    School Products Co.
machine yarns
    Lee Wards
macrame yarn
    Frederick J. Fawcett, Inc.
Mexican heavyspun yarn
    The Hidden Village

mill yarns
    Davidson's Old Mill Yarn
mohair yarn
    Craft Yarns of Rhode Island Inc.
    The Hidden Village
    House of Yarn & Crafts
    Macrame and Weaving Supply Co.
    Valley Handweaving Supply
natural yarn
    The Hidden Village
Navajo Indian yarns
    Naakai Dine-E Biye
needlecraft yarn
    The Yarn Depot
needlepoint yarn
    Frederick J. Fawcett, Inc.
    House of Flowers
    Kaleidoscope Needleworks
    Nantucket Needleworks
    Sign of the Arrow
Norwegian wool yarns
    Wichelt Import Co.
Persian needlepoint yarn
    Craft Yarns of Rhode Island Inc.
Persian yarn
    Crossroads
    The Hidden Village
    The Needle Works
    Threadneedle
    Vicki's Patience Unlimited
precut rug yarn
    Lee Wards
primitive yarn
    The Hidden Village
quickstitch yarn
    Crossroads
rayon yarn
    Contessa Yarns
    Craft Yarns of Rhode Island Inc.
roving yarns
    Tinkler & Co. Inc.
rug wool
    The Dorr Mill Store
    R. S. Duncan & Co.
    The Hidden Village
rug yarn
    Craft Yarns of Rhode Island Inc.
    Crossroads
    Filature Lemieux Inc.
    The Handcrafters
    KeeWai Krafts

Craft Category Index
Yarns—Yarns

    KM Yarn Co.
    Mary Maxim Inc.
    Merribee
    Nantucket Needleworks
    Nature's Fibers
    Needlecraft Shop Inc.
    Sign of the Arrow
    Lee Wards
rya rug yarn
    House of Kleen
rya yarn
    Coulter Studios
    The Hidden Village
satin yarn
    Plush Point Patterns by Marcia Podell
Scandinavian yarns
    School Products Co.
shetland
    R. S. Duncan & Co.
silk yarn
    Nature's Fibers
    Threadneedle
spinning yarns
    Cambridge Wools
    Greentree Ranch Wools, Countryside Handweavers
synthetic yarn
    J & H Clasgens Co.
tapestry yarn
    Coulter Studios
    Craft Yarns of Rhode Island Inc.
    Filature Lemieux Inc.
    The Hidden Village
    KeeWai Krafts
    KM Yarn Co.
    Vicki's Patience Unlimited
textile yarns
    Shuttlecraft
tussah type yarn
    Nature's Fibers
velvet needlepoint yarn
    R L L Enterprise
warp yarn
    Craft Yarns of Rhode Island Inc.
waxed linen
    The Hidden Village
weaving yarns
    Charles M. Butterworth
    Conlin Yarns
    Contessa Yarns
    Cottage Crafts
    Coulter Studios
    Craft Yarns of Rhode Island Inc.
    Frederick J. Fawcett, Inc.
    Filature Lemieux Inc.
    The Handcrafters
    House of Kleen
    House of Yarn & Crafts
    Jean Malsada Inc.
    The Mannings Creative Crafts
    Shuttlecraft
    Tahki Imports, Limited
    Textile Crafts
    The Yarn Depot
wool rug yarn mill ends
    Some Place
wool yarn
    J & H Clasgens Co.
    Wm. Condon & Sons Ltd.
    Contessa Yarns
    Coulter Studios
    Filature Lemieux Inc.
    Folklorico
    Harrisville Designs
    Northwest Handcraft House
    Mildred Sprout
    Straw Into Gold
    Wonoco Yarn Co.
worsted yarn
    Greentree Ranch Wools, Countryside Handweavers
yarn color chart
    Lee Wards
yarn mixture packages
    Contessa Yarns
yarn surprise boxes
    Fairtex Distributing Co.
2/20's handweaving worsted
    Frederick J. Fawcett, Inc.

GEOGRAPHICAL INDEX

Alabama
  Darlene Lewis, Birmingham
  Southern Living Books, Birmingham
  Classic Crafts, Fairhope
  Emperor Clock Co., Fairhope
  Jeane's, Fairhope
  Bet-Roc Enterprises Inc., Huntsville
  Giles & Kendall Inc., Huntsville
  Siderod Shop, Huntsville
  Turnbull Looms, Mobile
  Lee Mountain, Pisgah
  Framaway Co., Roanoke

Arizona
  Swensons Lapidary Equipment, Inc., Apache Junction
  Mohave Industries, Kingman
  Reed Industries, Kingman
  Howe Studio, Lake Havasu City
  Farmers Gem and Rock Shop, Phoenix
  Mueller's, Phoenix
  Panther International Ltd., Scottsdale
  The Looming Arts, Sedona
  The Pendleton Shop, Sedona
  Kachina Gem Co., Tempe
  Anozira Jewelers, Tucson
  R. C. Baker, Tucson

Arkansas
  Bowersox Eggcraft Supplies, Diamond City
  Wright's Rock Shop, Hot Springs
  Grueny's Gift Center, Little Rock
  Whisper Farm Furs, Rogers
  Rebecca Andrews, Walnut Ridge

California
  H. DeCovnick & Son, Alamo
  Gem Tool Specialties, Alhambra
  Eric Martin Co, Anderson
  Nimble Thimble, Aptos
  Cleve-Craft E-Z Loom, Arcadia
  Cerami Corner Inc., Azusa
  Ramont's Floral Arts Studio, Beaumont
  Australian Exports, Bellflower
  Wadsworth Publishing Co., Inc., Belmont
  Dharma Trading Co., Berkeley
  The Makings, Berkeley
  Mollica Stained Glass Press, Berkeley
  Some Place, Berkeley
  Bruce Benziger, Beverly Hills
  Kulch, Beverly Hills
  Sunset House, Beverly Hills
  Wool Products Ltd., Beverly Hills
  Gem Tec Diamond Tool Co., Buena Park
  Crossroads, Burbank
  Helen Humes Studio, Burbank
  Newport Enterprises, Burbank
  Bob and Carol Oliver, Burbank
  Mrs. Rossi, Burbank
  Open Door Co., Campbell

Geographical Index
California—California

Auto Modeler, Canoga Park
Challenge Publications, Inc., Canoga Park
Railroad Modeler, Canoga Park
Scale Modeler, Canoga Park
Mrs. Barbara Allen, Canyon Country
Griegers/B & M, Carlsbad
Adobe-Craft, Castro Valley
Bergsten Jade Co., Castro Valley
National Weavers Training School, Century City
Great Western Equipment Co., Chula Vista
Westwood Ceramic Supply Co., City of Industry
The Hidden Village, Claremont
Genie, Compton
Forrest W. Pond, Corona
Studio Twelve, Costa Mesa
Woodshop, Crescent City
Homespun Fabrics, Culver City
Terra Products, Culver City
Sea Novelties, Dana Point
Angora Diablo, Danville
Dial-A-Glaze, Davenport
E. Suydam & Co., Duarte
Andria Bree Gem Co., El Cajon
Beagle Mfg. Co., El Monte
A. D. Alpine Inc., El Segundo
Wearden's, Escondido
General Supplies Co., Fallbrook
Stonehouse, Freedom
Ceramics, Fresno
Lindell Industries, Fresno
Valley Handweaving Supply, Fresno
Brookhurst Hobbys, Garden Grove
Eva Ann Dolls, Garden Grove
Exactra-Craft Corp., Garden Grove
Kitsophrenia, Inc., Glendale
A. D. McBurney, Glendale
Swest Inc., Glendale
The Hobby Bench, Glendora
Pacific Gemstones, Granada Hills
Ward International Inc., Granada Hills
The Gift Shoppe, Hacienda Heights
Craftool Co., Harbor City
Star Diamond Industries, Harbor City
Highland Park Manufacturing, Hawthorne
Model Die Casting Inc., Hawthorne
Nature's Treasures, Hawthorne
Ken Prag, Hawthorne
Mildred Sprout, Hawthorne
Naturegraph Publishers, Healdsburg
O'Brien Lapidary Equipment Co., Hollywood
Siphon Art Products, Ignacio
Jamar-Mallory Inc., Inglewood
House of Lines, Kentfield
Sinkankas Diamond Products, La Jolla
Creative Industries, La Mesa
The Roc Shop, La Puente
Kay Kinney-Contoured Glass, Laguna Beach
Anita of Calif., Lakeview Terrace
Bookpost, Leucadia
Art Decal Co., Long Beach
Gordon's, Long Beach
Bead Game, Los Angeles
Dorothy Blake, Los Angeles
Bourget Bros. Gems & Minerals, Los Angeles
Cane & Basket Supply Co., Los Angeles
China Decorator, Los Angeles
Collector Studies, Los Angeles
Dick Ells Co., Los Angeles
Exotic Thai Silks, Los Angeles
Gemological Institute of America, Los Angeles
Hollywood Fancy Feather Co., Los Angeles
J. J. Jewelcraft, Los Angeles
Jeweler's Emporium, Los Angeles
Knitking, Los Angeles
Knitking Magazine, Los Angeles
Lifetime Career Schools, Los Angeles
MDR Mfg. Co., Inc., Los Angeles
Metro Diamond Drill Co., Los Angeles
Nationwide Plastics Co., Los Angeles
Plastruct, Los Angeles
Platers Service Co., Los Angeles
Popular Ceramics, Los Angeles
Tektos, Los Angeles
Textile Crafts, Los Angeles
J. Alday, Lucern Valley
Lane Magazine & Book Co., Menlo Park
Gems & Minerals, Mentone
S. Siracusa, Midway City
Alberta's Molds Inc., Monrovia
Heritage Looms, Monrovia

Diamond-Pro Unlimited, Monterey Park
Walter E. Johansen, Morgan Hill
Gems Galore, Mountain View
United Specialties Co., Newark
Gems International, No. Hollywood
M & M Hardwood, No. Hollywood
Gene's Rock Shop, Oakdale
Artweek, Oakland
H. A. Cole, Oakland
Drykiln Design, Oakland
Glass Art Magazine, Oakland
Inkodye, Oakland
Madewell Products Inc., Oakland
Screen Process Supplies Mfg. Co., Oakland
Straw Into Gold, Oakland
Puppeteers of America, Inc., Ojai
Archer's Hobby World, Orange
Auto Upholstery Institute, Orange
Custom Drapery Institute, Orange
Doll's Candle & Craft Supplies, Orange
Modern Upholstery Institute, Orange
The American Candlemaker, Pacific Grove
Textile Crafts, Pacific Grove
International Bookfinders, Inc., Pacific Palisades
Folklorico, Palo Alto
Cherie Hooper, Palo Alto
Studio D, Palo Alto
J. L. T., Palos Verdes Estate
JV Models, Panorama City
Sonie Ames, Paradise
Rupert, Gibbon & Spider, Pasadena
S & W Crafts Mfg., Pasadena
Whistle Stop, Pasadena
Grieger's Inc., Pasadena
Clems and Clems Spinning Wheels, Pinole
Mark Farmer Co., Inc., Point Richmond
Schneider's, Poway
Covington Engineering Corp., Redlands
Natcol Crafts, Inc., Redlands
Sharon's Petite Sherre, Redwood City
Jade World/Wilderness Originals, Redwood Valley
Reeves Knotique, Riverside
Craft Course Publishers, Rosemead
Hazel Pearson Handi Craft, Rosemead
Yvonne Brandon, Sacramento

Lyman E. Cox, Scale Trains, Sacramento
Products and Systems, Inc., Sacramento
W. L. Maison Opals, Etc., Salinas
Herb Allen's Hole in One, San Diego
Australian Imports, San Diego
Bethlehem Imports, San Diego
Lapidary Journal Book Dept., San Diego
U. C. Hobby Center, San Diego
Activa Products Inc., San Francisco
Bead-Weavers, San Francisco
Glen Black Handwoven Textiles, San Francisco
Determined Productions, Inc., San Francisco
Douglas & Sturgess, Inc., San Francisco
Japan Publications Trading Co., San Francisco
The Knittery, San Francisco
The Miniature Mart-The Peddler's Shop, San Francisco
Scotch House, San Francisco
The Yarn Depot, San Francisco
Ultra-Violet Products, Inc., San Gabriel
TAP Plastic Inc., San Leandro
Gemex Co., San Marcos
Williams Bros., San Marcos
M. B. Austin, San Mateo
Jans Jewels, San Mateo
Mary Wales, San Mateo
Eva Mae Doll Co., San Pablo
James A. Gardner, San Pedro
John Hathaway, San Pedro
HTH Publishers, Santa Ana
Stanley Lapidary Products, Santa Ana
Hallie Copeland, Santa Barbara
Creative Craft House, Santa Barbara
Hobby Gallery, Santa Clara
Santa Cruz Mountain Crafts, Santa Cruz
Bourget Bros. Gems & Minerals, Santa Monica
Gloria's Glass Garden, Santa Monica
Jo-El's Craft Co., Santa Monica
Kalico Kits, Santa Monica
Yarns Unlimited, Santa Monica
Pyronetics, Sante Fe Springs
The Eggs-Aminer, Saugus
Out of Print Bookfinder, Seaside
Crown Gems Co., Sherman Oaks
Needlecraft Shop Inc., Sherman Oaks
Yaley Enterprises, So. San Francisco

Geographical Index
California—Connecticut

Thumbelina Needlework Shop, Solvang
R/C Cars International, South Gate
Virginia Black Designs, Studio City
Kit Kraft, Studio City
LeJeune, Inc., Sunnyvale
Menco Engineers Inc., Tarzana
Artis, Inc., Temple City
Candle Institute, Torrance
Candy & Cake Institute, Torrance
Deft, Torrance
Minicraft Models Inc., Torrance
Campbell Scale Models, Tustin
Elizabeth Hiddleson, Vallejo
Creative Murals, Inc., Van Nuys
Jewelart Inc., Van Nuys
Jerry S. Kaye Assoc., Van Nuys
Railway Express, Van Nuys
Fantastic Fit Products, Walnut Creek
Leclerc West, West Sacramento
Boxcar Ken, Whittier
Floating Gem Co., Woodland Hills
Trask Plastics, Yermo

Colorado

Shipley's Mineral House, Bayfield
The Family Handyman, Boulder
Frostline, Boulder
Schacht Spindle Co., Boulder
Walter Drake, Colorado Springs
Electro Stylus Mfg. Co., Colorado Springs
Alice Fowler Originals, Colorado Springs
The Knitting Needle, Colorado Springs
Ren Ann Crafts, Colorado Springs
Aspen Lapidary, Denver
Colorado Geological Industries Inc., Denver
Cookson & Thode, Denver
Maroon Bells Ind. Inc., Denver
Quilts and Other Comforts, Denver
Van Howe Ceramic Supply Co., Denver
Wrightway Quilting, Denver
National Camera Inc., Englewood
The Clever Crafters, Estes Park
International Guild of Candle Artisans, Fort Collins
Scott Scientific Inc., Fort Collins
Bluebird Manufacturing, Ft. Collins
Kenneth Rarick, Longmont
Greentree Ranch Wools, Countryside Handweavers, Loveland
Virginia Lakin, Loveland
Bob's Arts & Crafts, Northglenn
Sangray Corp., Pueblo
Crewel Elephant, Silverton
Leman Publications, Wheatridge
Quilter's Newsletter, Wheatridge
Edwards Jewelry Co., Whitewater

Connecticut

Book Barn, Avon
Foredom Electric Co., Bethel
Associated Book Sellers, Bridgeport
Dr. David Crespi, Cheshire
Dye-Craft Ideas, Coventry
Historical Society of Early American Decoration, Inc., Darien
Cummings Wood Co., East Hartford
Colonial Textiles, East Lyme
Butterick Home Catalog, Greenwich
Ettl Studios Inc., Greenwich
Woman's Day Knit & Stitch, Greenwich
Woman's Day Knitting Book, Greenwich
Woman's Day Needlework Ideas, Greenwich
Woman's Day 101 Sweaters to Knit and Crochet, Greenwich
Woman's Day Sewing & Fashion Ideas, Greenwich
Veronica, Groton
Morgan Inkle Loom Factory, Guilford
East River Publications, Hamden
Savin Handcrafts, Hamden
Contessa Yarns, Lebanon
H. H. Perkins Co., New Haven
N. Flayderman & Co., New Milford
Cottage Crafts, Pomfret Center
Cole Ceramics Laboratories, Sharon
Branson Cleaning Equipment, Shelton
Bluejacket Ship Crafters, So. Norwalk
Wallis Designs, South Windsor
Raytech Industries Inc., Stafford Springs
Shaw Mudge & Co., Stamford
Mrs. Mell Prescott, Warrenville
Handweavers Guild of America, Inc., West Hartford
Needle-Ease, West Hartford
Sudberry House, Westbrook
Wool-Art Studios Inc., Weston
Yarn Primitives, Weston
Heritage Hill Patterns, Westport

Geographical Index
Connecticut—Illinois

Danfield Threads Inc., Winsted
Holiday Handicrafts, Inc., Winsted

Delaware
Unique Creations, Newark
Brandywine Studies, Wilmington
Paige Enterprises, Wilmington
H. Shealy, Wilmington

Florida
Florida Supply House, Inc., Bradenton
Handcraft Originals, Cape Coral
G. Weidinger, Cape Coral
Modern Craft, Clearwater
Margaret Newman, Clearwater
Circus Hobby Hall, Coral Gables
Osma G. Tod Weaving & Lace Studio, Coral Gables
Yarns Galore, Coral Gables
The Collector's Cabinet, Dania
Henry B. Graves Co., Delray Beach
Village Art Gallery, Destin
Bee Basch Designs, Englewood
Kaydee, Fort Myers
Smokey Mtn. Rock Shop, Ft. Meyers Beach
Kaydee Craft Supplies, Ft. Myers Beach
Pins & Needles, Hialeah
Tie Clip Information, Hialeah
Creativity Needlepoint, Hollywood
Feather & Flower Craft, Hollywood
Phentex, Inc., Hollywood
Thrift Mailmart, Iverness
The Library Corner, Marathon
Holmes-Corey Ltd., Marco Island
Nationwide Ceramic Enterprises, Melbourne
Diamond Sales Co., Miami
Dolly Darling Inc., Miami
Gail's Decorative Arts Studio, Miami
Gyro Lamp Supply Corp., Miami
House of Gould, Miami
Robert E. Sharpton, Miami
Sav-On-Crafts, Miami Shores
Manlove Originals, New Smyrna
C. R. Boylin, No. St. Petersburg
Anne Fitch's Handicrafts, Okeechobee
Inkle Looms, Panama City
Dorris Dolls, Riviera Beach
Kile-Gore Designs, Sarasota
Derby Lane Shell Center, St. Petersburg
Great Outdoors Publishing Co., St. Petersburg
House of Flowers, St. Petersburg
Harrison Neustadt, Sunrise
National Wildlife Art Exchange, Vero Beach
Craft House, West Palm Beach

Georgia
Jean Malsada Inc., Atlanta
Norlene Lapidary, Atlanta
Supreme Watch Material Co., Atlanta
The Beadcraft Corner/Beadcraft Club, Augusta
The Craft Corner, Augusta
The Smock Shop, Augusta
H & A Mfg. Corp., Avondale Estates
House of Stitches, Bainbridge
Purcelli's Gems, Decatur
Trader South, Dunwoody
Argosy Products, Gainesville
Prospector's Pouch, Kennesaw
Corner Cupboard Crafts, Inc., Lilburn
The Rev. Henry N. Thomas, Macon
Loosie Goosie Egg Craft Shop, Rome
Solartherm Co., Roswell
Reisinger Net Co., St. Simons Island
W. D. Hudson, Jr., Stone Mt.
International Import Co., Stone Mt.

Hawaii
Alohalei Hawaii, Honolulu
Anne's Treasure Trove, Honolulu

Idaho
Vern Clements, Caldwell
Ed Brandt Stone Co., Nampa
M. W. Jackson & Assoc., Pocatello

Illinois
Beno J. Gundlach Co., Belleville
Hawthorne House, Inc., Bloomington
McKnight Publishing Co., Bloomington
Advance Process Supply Co., Chicago
American School, Chicago
American Technical Society, Chicago
Celebrate, Chicago
Corrado Cutlery Inc., Chicago
Craftsman Wood Service Co., Chicago
Earthworks, Chicago
Fabricon Co., Chicago
Follett Publishing Co., Chicago
Gibsons Creations, Chicago
Helmor Label Co., Chicago
High Strength Adhesives Corp., Chicago
Jesop Co., Chicago

Geographical Index
Illinois—Iowa

JMC, Chicago
Harry Z. Kurs, Chicago
J. C. Larson Co., Chicago
Ruth Lukasik, Chicago
Macrame and Weaving Supply Co., Chicago
Maxant Button & Supply Co., Chicago
National Carvers Museum, Chicago
Nelson-Hall Co., Chicago
Henry Regnery Co., Chicago
Reilly & Lee Books, Chicago
Rosemond Hobbycraft, Chicago
Sears, Roebuck & Co., Chicago
Sparkle Studio, Chicago
Stewart Industries, Chicago
Use 'Em Up Creations, Chicago
Montgomery Ward & Co., Inc., Chicago
A. C. Weber & Co., Inc., Chicago
Wilton Enterprises, Inc., Chicago
Artistry In Wood, Columbia
McEnglevan Heat Treating & Mfg. Inc., Danville
Ball O' Yarn, Decatur
Lee Wards, Elgin
Lee Wards Christmas Tree Club, Elgin
Craft Patterns, Elmhurst
Craft Products, Elmhurst
Designers Fabrics Buy-Mail, Evanston
Downs, Evanston
Furniture Designs, Evanston
Holgate & Raynolds, Evanston
Franzen Gifts, Flanagan
Badger Air-Brush Co., Franklin Park
Taylor House, Galena
Dick Blick, Galesburg
Earth Treasures, Galesburg
Putnam Co., Harvard
M. Koehler, Harwood Heights
Thomas C. Thompson, Highland Park
Carnival Arts & Crafts, Hinsdale
Swiss Bernina, Inc., Hinsdale
Tree Toys, Hinsdale
LeMar's Decoupage Center, La Grange
Liberty Gem & Supply, Liberty
M. Turner, Lombard
The Needlecase, Long Grove
Weidinger Inc., Matteson
Bersted's, Monmouth
Wool 'N Wick, Morton
Ships Unlimited, Morton Grove
D. M. Campana Co., Mundelein
Chicago School of Interior Decoration, Mundelein
National School of Dress Design, Mundelein
Craigle Studios, Niles
Craft/Midwest, Northbrook
Pack-O-Fun, Park Ridge
Jack V. Schuller, Inc., Park Ridge
Charles A. Bennett Co., Inc., Peoria
Helen Gallagher, Peoria
W. Wooley & Co., Peoria
Trowbridge Crafts, Prospect Heights
Hearth & Heather Ltd., Richton Park
Gerhardt Macrame Studio, Rock Island
Dot's Dollhouse, Rockford
Valspar Corp., Rockford
Goodhert-Willcox Co., Inc., South Holland
Alessi Lapidary Supplies, Villa Park
Reo N. Pickens, Jr., Waukegan
Sew-Its-Seams, Wilmette
Magic Needle, Winnetka
Woman's Board, Winnetka
Castolite, Woodstock

Indiana
La Venta Corp., Bloomington
Beryl Sink, Bloomington
Dairy Service, Inc., Bluffton
Midwest Mail Service, Elkhart
Clay-Crafters Products, Evansville
The Fluorite Shop, Evansville
National Calendar of Indoor-Outdoor Art Fairs, Ft. Wayne
Dildine's Arts & Crafts, Hammond
Silver & Gem Shop, Hammond
American Art Clay Co. Inc., Indianapolis
Theodore Audel & Co., Indianapolis
Design Magazine, Indianapolis
Felts Manufacturing Co. Inc., Indianapolis
Miniature Aircraft, Indianapolis
O Scale Railroading, Indianapolis
Rub 'N Buff, Indianapolis
Howard W. Sams & Co., Inc., Indianapolis
M. Knopp, Marion
Decorative Designs by Dare, Munster
Craft & Candle House, Terre Haute

Iowa
Wanda's Workshop, Arthur

Schiltz Goose Farm, Bancroft
Blue Grass Art & Hobby Center, Blue Grass
Industrial Diamond Tool Co. Inc., Cedar Rapids
Davault Miniature Furniture, Creston
Better Homes & Gardens, Des Moines
Better Homes & Gardens Books, Des Moines
Gift Craft, Des Moines
National Handcraft Society, Des Moines
Carolyn Watson, Des Moines
House of Figurines, Dubuque
Starlite Rock Shop, Dubuque
Quinn Mineral, Iowa City
Edith Maier, Mapleton
Sig Manufacturing Co., Inc., Montezuma
Doris Southard, New Hartford
Geode Industries, New London

Kansas
Happy Hobbies Magazine, Cherryvale
Thelma Sutton Martin, Cherryvale
Trailcraft Inc., Concordia
Mrs. Danner's Quilts, Emporia
Ju Rene Ceramic Molds, Franklin
Luella Ensz, Inman
K42 Rock Shop, Isabel
McCall's Needlework & Crafts, Manhattan
McCall's Pattern Fashions, Manhattan
McCall's You-Do-It Home Decorating, Manhattan
Dorothy Benson, Prairie Village
Midwest Wool Marketing Cooperative, S. Hutchinson
Evelyn Saft, Udall
Air Capitol Molds, Inc., Wichita
Ebersole Lapidary Supply Inc., Wichita
Elizabeth R. King, Wichita
Sue's Custom Quilting, Wichita

Kentucky
Folkcrafts, Bowling Green
Baxwood Crafters, Lexington
Beard's Art Needlework Studio, Lexington
Ceramic Coating Co., Newport
Mrs. Ruby Brandon, Paducah

Louisiana
Carter Associates, New Iberia
D. E. Rinck, New Orleans
Johnny Sens of New Orleans, New Orleans

Maine
Nadja Bolio, Buckfield
Barnstable Originals by H.W. Smith, Camden
Allegra Milano, Guilford
Port Lobster Co., Kennebunk
Joan Moshimer, Kennebunkport
Rug Hooker News & Views, Kennebunkport
Carlbert Fabrics, Portland
W. Spencer Inc., Portland
Ficket, Whitneyville
Berry's of Maine, Yarmouth

Maryland
Artcraft, Baldwin
American Butterfly Co., Baltimore
General Crafts Corp., Baltimore
International Violin, Baltimore
Life-Like Products Inc., Baltimore
Penguin Books Inc., Baltimore
Shillcraft, Baltimore
Stylecraft of Baltimore, Baltimore
American Art Associates Publications, Inc., Bethesda
Treasure of the Pirates, Inc., Bethesda
PRO Custom Hobbies, Catonsville
Syn-Crer Creations, Clinton
National Quilting Association, Greenbelt
The Treasure Chest, Havre De Grace
Carter Craft Doll House, Hyattsville
Plantabbs Co., Lutherville-Timonium
The Golden Egg, Millersville
Maryland Magnet Co., Randallstown
Diffraction Co., Inc., Riderwood
Hobby House Press, Riverdale
The Unicorn, Rockville
Betty James Originals, Severna Park
Dulcimer, Simpsonville

Massachusetts
The L. S. Starrett Co., Athol
The Ghen Studio, Beverly
Commonwealth Felt Co., Boston
Frederick J. Fawcett, Inc., Boston
C. W. Somers & Co., Boston
Wee 3 Sandwich Glass Jewelry, Bourne
Gem-O-Rama, Inc., Braintree
Eastern Mills, Chelsea
Easy Street, Chester

Geographical Index
Massachusetts—Michigan

Toolkraft Corp., Chicopee
Cohasset Colonials, Cohasset
Shaker Workshops Inc., Concord
The Sneak Box Studio, Concord
James Bliss & Co. Inc., Dedham
Powell, E. Pepperell
Reichert's Fabrics, E. Pepperell
Mrs. Marilyn G. Alabran, Framingham
Margaret's Egg Craft, Framingham
The World of Stitch 'N Knit, Framingham
Whittemore-Durgin Glass Co., Hanover
South Shore Woman's Exchange, Hingham
Knit-Sew Labels, Hopedale
Sperry & Son, Hyannis
International Old Lacers, Ludlow
Crafts Manufacturing Co., Lunenburg
L. W. Macomber Ad-A Harness Looms, Lynn
Bergen Arts & Crafts, Inc., Marblehead
Northeastern Scale Models Inc., Methuen
Nantucket Needleworks, Nantucket
Nantucket School of Needlery, Nantucket Island
Lashette Co., Inc., Natick
S. Lynds Patterns, Natick
Charles T. Branford Co., Newton Centre
Mason & Sullivan Co., Osterville
Carver Co., Plympton
Mrs. W. Bradley Ryan, Reading
Gloria, Saugus
Peg Hall Studios, Scituate
Sturbridge Yankee Workshop, Sturbridge
The Custom House of Needle Arts & Design, W. Townsend
Paul K. Guillow Inc., Wakefield
Scientific Gas Products, Wakefield
The Stitchery, Wellesley Hills
Newton's Potters Supply, West Newton
Bear Cave, West Roxbury
Needlecraft House, West Townsend
William E. Wright Co., West Warren
New England Village Crafts, Weymouth
Davis Publications, Inc., Worcester
School Arts, Worcester

Michigan
Barbara Bannister, Alanson
Norwood Loom Co., Baldwin
Sid Morgan, Belleville
Michigan Wool Products Co., Benton Harbor
C. R. Hill Co., Berkley
Scandinavian Rya Rugs, Bloomfield Hills
Libby's Needlepoint, Brighton
Gladys Galloway, Caro
Anne Amiot, Dearborn
Star Models, Dearborn
Cadillac Plastic & Chemical Co., Detroit
Gilmour Campbell, Detroit
KM Yarn Co., Detroit
Michigan Lapidary Supply Co., Detroit
Marie Mitchell's Decoupage Center, Detroit
Polyproducts Corp., Detroit
Davidson's Old Mill Yarn, Eaton Rapids
Plycrete Mold Co., Elk Rapids
Brad's Rock Shop, Ferndale (Detroit)
The Yarn and Soda Shop, Glen Arbor
Aleta's Rock Shop, Grand Rapids
Zondervan Publishing House, Grand Rapids
The Wood Barn, Grosse Pointe Park
The Squadron Shop, Hazel Park
Miniatures by Marty, Holland
Delco Craft Center, Inc., Madison Heights
Traditional Norwegian Rosemaling, Marquette
Specialty Products, Muskegon
Creations by Julianna, New Buffalo
United Abrasive Inc., Norway
Celebration Candlemaking Supplies, Pentwater
Mary Maxim Inc., Port Huron
Kerr Mfg. Co., Romulus
Flint FBG Imports, Royal Oak
Foam Fantasy, Saginaw
Mrs. C. Ference, Saline
Knits'N That Yarn Shop, Saline
Boutique Trims, So. Lyon
The Egg Shell, South Lyon
Morang Balance Co., St. Clair Shores
International Wood Collectors Society, Trenton
Renaldy's, Troy
Beadcraft, Warren

Minnesota
The Handcraft Supply Corp., Minneapolis
Swanjord Hatchery, Balaton
Minnesota Clay, Bloomington
Geecraft, Blue Earth
Luger, Burnsville
Birchwood Casey, Eden Prairie
Paramount Ceramic Inc., Fairmont
Don's Hobby Co., Mankato
Country Woodcraft, Maple Plain
P. C. Herwig Co., Inc., Milaca
Arts and Crafts Unlimited, Minneapolis
T. S. Denison & Co., Inc., Minneapolis
Gager's Handicrafts, Minneapolis
HERE Inc., Minneapolis
Kieffer's Lingerie Fabric & Supplies, Minneapolis
Knit-O-Graf Pattern Co., Minneapolis
Maid of Scandinavia, Minneapolis
Minnesota Lapidary Supply Inc., Minneapolis
National Craft & Hobby Co., Inc., Minneapolis
The Puppetry Store, Minneapolis
Tumblecraft, Minneapolis
Ukrainian Gift Shop, Minneapolis
University of Minnesota Press, Minneapolis
Worldwide Curio House, Minneapolis
Brown's Rock & Lapidary Supplies, Moorhead
Donna Jean Carver, New London
Vivian Bonnema, Prinsburg
Koehler's Craft Outlet, Proctor
Workshop, Redwood Falls
Craftplans, Rogers
Minnesota Woodworkers Supply Co., Rogers
Beacon, Rothsay
Glass House Studio, St. Paul
Hobbi-Carve, St. Paul
Sandeen's Scandinavian Gift & Card Shop, St. Paul
The Sewing Bee, St. Paul
Surburbia, Inc., St. Paul
3 M Company, St. Paul
Herter's, Inc., Waseca

Mississippi
Mississippi Petrified Forest, Flora
C. W. Bullock, Jackson
Mrs. G's, Starkville

Missouri
The Doll Cupboard, Branson
Gary Bunting, Cape Girardeau
Ima Ova, Holland
Antoine's, Independence
Skil-Crafts Division, Joplin
Aunt Martha's Studios Inc., Kansas City
Belsaw Power Tools, Kansas City
Budget Buddy Co., Kansas City
Ervins, Kansas City
Leisure Services, Kansas City
Lox-Seal Adhesives, Kansas City
Nel-King Products, Kansas City
R & R Ceramic Molds Inc., Kansas City
Transart, Kansas City
The Workbasket, Kansas City
The Workbench, Kansas City
Flair-Craft Inc., Kimberling City
Timberline Lake Rock Shop, Lincoln
Antique Doll Reproductions, Milo
Trojan Press Inc., N. Kansas City
The Camp Fire Co., Raymore
Artisan Crafts, Reeds Spring
Midland Walnut, Savannah
P. S. Andrews Co., St. Charles
Gilliom Mfg. Co., St. Charles
Art Mart, Inc., St. Louis
Essayons Studio, Hand Arts Center, St. Louis
Frank's Jewelry & Gem Shop, St. Louis
Carl Hepp Mosaic Co., St. Louis
Kazari, St. Louis
Krick Kits, St. Louis
Lace Lady, St. Louis
St. Louis Crafts Inc., St. Louis
Sign of the Arrow, St. Louis
Two Brothers Inc., St. Louis
Winston's Fabrics, St. Louis
Bookful of Crochet, Valley Park
House of Patterns, Valley Park
Quilts, Valley Park
Paradise Rocks, Warsaw
Cutaway, Weaubleau

Montana
B. T. Hallam, Billings
Bitterroot Lapidary Supply, Missoula
Mexiskeins, Missoula

Nebraska
Charles W. Miller, Alliance
Sunflower Crafts, Omaha

Geographical Index
New Hampshire—New York

New Hampshire
  Robert Ayottes' Designery, Center Sandwich
  The Booted Sheepherder Inc., Francestown
  Spaulding & Frost Co., Inc., Fremont
  The Dorr Mill Store, Guild
  Harrisville Designs, Harrisville
  Great Brook Miniatures, Jackson
  Robert Nelson, Newport
  Yield House, North Conway
  Brookstone Co., Peterborough
  Guild of Strawberry Banks Inc., Portsmouth
  Karlkraft Studio-Cheva, S. Merrimack
  House of Yarn & Crafts, Seabrook
  Tainter's Chick Bookshop, Temple
  E. B. Frye & Son, Inc., Wilton

New Jersey
  Continental Hobbies Inc., Adelphia
  Spencer Gifts Inc., Atlantic City
  Crafty's Backroom, Augusta
  Edmund Scientific Co., Barrington
  Scientific Models Inc., Berkeley Heights
  Exact Performance, Bloomfield
  William Dixon Co., Carlstadt
  Anchor Tool & Supply Co., Chatham
  Murray American Corp., Chatham
  LTA Products, Closter
  A. S. Barnes and Co., Inc., Cranbury
  Artists & Craftsman Guild, Cranford
  Candle Kitchen, Cranford
  Colonial Printing Ink Co., E. Rutherford
  C. R. Wells, Eatontown
  D. M. C. Corporation, Elizabeth
  Real Woods, Elizabeth
  Threadneedle, Englewood
  Best Foods, Englewood Cliffs
  Prentice-Hall Inc., Englewood Cliffs
  Locomotive Workshop, Englishtown
  Wilfred Enterprises, Englishtown
  Flemington Cut Glass Co., Flemington
  Barbara Lawshe, Franklin Lakes
  Atlantic Upholstery Supply Co., Hackensack
  Joseph Tartas, Haskell
  Fieldwood Co., Ho-Ho-Kus
  L & R Manufacturing Co., Kearny
  Augusta Malle, Lakewood
  New Products Co., Maple Shade
  Create Your Own, Inc., Medham
  Harrower House of Decoupage, Milford
  Jim Kesterson, Millville
  Raymond P. Wallace, Montclair
  Boin Arts & Crafts, Morristown
  Elvin, Mountainside
  Jewel Creations, Newark
  Carstens Publications, Newton
  Creative Crafts, Newton
  Creative Crafts Christmas Annual, Newton
  Flying Models, Newton
  Model Craftsman Publishing Corp., Newton
  The Glass Workshop, Norwood
  The Stained Glass Club, Norwood
  Town & Country Crafts, Pequannock
  Egg Album, Phillipsburg
  Kit Stansbury, Phillipsburg
  Treasure Chest, Phillipsburg
  Parkway Plastics Inc., Piscataway
  MAC Enterprises, Plainfield
  Creations for the Artist, Princeton
  Fres-O-Lone Mold Corp., Princeton
  Loretta's Ceramic Studio, Scotch Plains
  H. Obodda, Short Hills
  Sue Wise, Somerset
  Holiday Craft, Sparta
  Fran's Basket House, Succasunna
  Family Circle Kits, Teaneck
  Good Housekeeping, Teaneck
  American Edestaal Inc., Tenafly
  Atlantic Mold Corp., Trenton
  Daddy's Mold Shop, Trenton
  Holland Mold Inc., Trenton
  Wm. H. Wise & Co. Inc., Union City
  Creative Metalcraft, W. Caldwell
  Doll Castle News, Washington
  B & J Star Co., Westfield
  Cheryl Todd, Westwood
  Fabulous Holiday House, Whitehouse Station

New Mexico
  Crafts Yarns & Gifts, Albuquerque
  Crafts Yarns & Gifts Ltd., Albuquerque
  The Freed Co., Albuquerque
  The House of Miniatures, Santa Fe
  Winona Trading Post, Sante Fe

New York
  Delmar Publishers, Albany
  Minerals & Gems, Albany
  Geophile International, Appalachin

Geographical Index
New York—New York

Sewakers Industries Inc., Baldwin
The Pirate's Cove, Bayport
Bric-Mold Corp., Bethpage
Lillstina Inc., Binghamton
Stein & Day, Briarcliff Manor
Adhesive Products Corp., Bronx
Albert Constantine & Son Inc., Bronx
The Marquetry Society of America, Bronx
Frank Mittermeier Inc., Bronx
Paragon Needlecraft, Bronx
The Village Smithy, Bronxville
Acme Dress Form Co., Inc., Brooklyn
Althor Products, Brooklyn
Dorothy H. Becker, Brooklyn
Brooklyn Botanic Garden, Brooklyn
Glo-Classics, Brooklyn
Melrose Yarn Co., Inc., Brooklyn
The Needle Works, Brooklyn
Village Designs, Brooklyn
Jack D. Wolfe Co. Inc., Brooklyn
Wonoco Yarn Co., Brooklyn
Emerson Books Inc., Buchanan
Brown's Miniatures, Cambridge
D-Carol, Canandiagua
Dinky Molds, Central Valley
Chestnut Hill Studio, Ltd., Churchville
Floquil, Inc., Cobleskill
The Putter Shop, Congers
Oxford Crafts, Cortland
The Niddy Noddy, Croton-On-Hudson
The New England Craftsman, Elnora
The Family Handyman, Farmingdale
Chemical Additives Co., Farmingville
Isabel Scott Fabrics Corp., Flushing
Tuxedo Yarn & Needlework, Flushing
Bovin Publishing, Forest Hills
Patterns for Pennies, Inc., Franklin Square
J. P. Fliegel Co., Gloversville
Fashion Fabrics Club, Great Neck
Hearthside Press, Great Neck
International Creations, Great Neck
Polly Chester Inc., Hartsdale
Reynolds Yarns Inc., Hauppauge
Dorothy Biddle Service, Hawthorne
Champs Creative Materials Center, Hempstead
Allcraft Tool & Supply Co., Hicksville
Most Unusual Custom Needleworks Inc., Huntington

Exposition Press, Jericho
Buck Hill Associates, Johnsburg
Sam Frost, Lake George
Peri's Homework, Larchmont
Embroideries Unlimited, Long Beach
Dollspart Supply Co., Inc., Long Island City
Dover Scientific Co., Long Island City
Standard Doll Co., Long Island City
Popular Science Book Club, Manhasset
Woman's How-To Book Club, Manhasset
Country Crafts, Maybrook
Main Service Co., Monroe
Lantern Press Inc., Mt. Vernon
Lillian Vernon, Mt. Vernon
The Jewelry Mart, Munnsville
Beadnik's Arts & Crafts, New Rochelle
Skon, New Rochelle
Adris Oriental Gem & Art Corp., New York
Adventures In Crafts, New York
Albert Findings, Inc., New York
America's Hobby Center Inc., New York
American Crafts Council, New York
American Home Crafts, New York
Arco Publishing Co., Inc., New York
Arco Tools Inc., New York
Art Consultants, New York
Association Press, New York
B & M Yarn Co., New York
Ballantine Books, Inc., New York
Barnes & Blake, New York
Basic Crafts Co., New York
Beacon Chemical Co., Inc., New York
Boat Builder, New York
Bon Bazar, New York
Harry Bookstone, New York
Brother International Corp., New York
Arthur Brown & Bro., Inc., New York
Chemical Publishing Co., Inc., New York
The Collector's Cabinet, New York
Commercial Mineral Corp., New York
Cork Products Co. Inc., New York
Coulter Studios, New York
Countrywide Crafts, New York
Coward, McCann & Geogheagan, New York
Craftsman Circle Book Club, New York

Geographical Index
New York—New York

Crain-Harmon, New York
Crown Cultured Pearl Corp., New York
Crown Publishers, New York
Dersh Feather & Trading Corp., New York
The Dial Press Inc., New York
Distlefink Designs, New York
Dover Publications Inc., New York
Drake Publishers Inc., New York
E. P. Dutton & Co., Inc., New York
Embroiderer's Guild of America Inc., New York
Fabrics 'Round the World Inc., New York
Fairtex Distributing Co., New York
Fawcett Special Interest Magazines & Books, New York
Federal Smallwares, New York
Fezandie & Sperrle, Inc., New York
Good Housekeeping Needlecraft, New York
Grosset & Dunlap Inc., New York
Handweaver & Craftsman, New York
Harper & Row, Publishers Inc., New York
Alexandra Hill Needlepoint Studios Ltd., New York
Industrial Press Inc., New York
Inter-Ocean Trade Co., New York
KAY an EE Corp. of America, New York
Kodansha International, U.S.A., New York
L & L Stitchery, New York
Ladies Home Journal Needle & Craft, New York
Ladies Home Journal Needlecraft, New York
Leathercrafters Supply Co., New York
The Left Hand Inc., New York
Lion Brand Yarn Co., New York
Liveright, New York
Lothrop, Lee & Shephard, New York
Mac Leather Co., New York
The Macmillan Publishing Co., New York
Magnus Craft Materials, Inc., New York
Mangrove Feather Co., Inc., New York
Martin Fabrics, New York
McGraw-Hill Book Co., New York
David McKay Co., Inc., New York
Model Railroad Equipment Corp., New York
Modern Needlepoint, New York
Mon Tricot, New York
William Morrow & Co., New York
Museum Books Inc., New York
National Art Worker's Community, New York
National Sculpture Review, New York
Nautique Arts, New York
Nelco Sewing Machine Co. Inc., New York
Old Print Center, New York
1001 Decorating Ideas, New York
1001 Fashion & Needlecraft Ideas, New York
1001 How-To Ideas, New York
Oxford University Press, New York
Palmloom Co., New York
Party Bazaar, New York
Pitman Publishing Corp., New York
Platypus, New York
Plaza Artists Materials, Inc., New York
Plush Point Patterns by Marcia Podell, New York
Polk's Hobby Dept. Store, New York
Pollack's Furrier's Supply Corp., New York
Popular Library Inc., New York
Popular Mechanics Press, New York
Praeger Publishers, New York
P. T. I., New York
G. P. Putnam's Sons, New York
Random House Inc., New York
Schober Organ Corp., New York
School Products Co., New York
Charles Scribner's Sons, New York
Sculpture Associates Ltd., New York
Sculpture House, New York
Sculpture Services Inc., New York
Henry Seligman Co. Inc., New York
Sheru Bead Boutique Shop, New York
Shil-La Art Gems Inc., New York
Simplicity Fashion Magazine, New York
Simplicity Home Catalog, New York
Simplicity Young Ideas Catalog, New York
Stacy Fabrics Corp., New York
Sterling Publishing Co. Inc., New York
A. L. Stone Displays, New York
Sunray Yarn House, New York

Surma Book & Music Store, New York
Tahki Imports, Limited, New York
Taplinger Publishing Co., New York
Tillalla Inc., New York
Times Mirror Magazine, New York
Transworld Trading Co., New York
Twenty-five Weekend Build-It Projects, New York
William Unger & Co. Inc., New York
United States Committee for UNICEF, New York
Van Nostrand Reinhold Co., New York
Veteran Leather Co., Inc., New York
Viking Press, New York
Frederick Warne & Co. Inc., New York
Watson-Guptill Publications, New York
Weisz Import Export Corp., New York
Erica Wilson Correspondence Courses, New York
Erica Wilson Needleworks, New York
Erica Wilson's Creative Needlework Society, New York
Wood Projects, New York
Woodworker, New York
Workman Publishing Co., New York
Pursenalities Inc., North Baldwin
Joen Ellen Kanze, North White Plains
Oceanside Gem Imports, Inc., Oceanside
Nucleus, Ossining
Sancraft Industries, Patterson
Creative Spoolcraft, Pearl River
The Workshop, Pittsford
R L L Enterprise, Plainview
Leclerc Corp., Plattsburg
Phentex, Inc., Plattsburg
Pylam Products, Inc., Queens Village
Hoff House Ceramic Supplies, Inc., Rochelle Park
Muriel N. Charney, Rochester
Craft Service, Rochester
Natalie Originals Studio, Rochester
Silhouette Custom-Fit Pattern Co., Rye
Craftsman Supply House, Scottsville
Harrison-Hoge Ind. Inc., St. James
Talisman Crafts, St. James
Sal Marino Co., Staten Island
Craft-Mark Products, Syosset
Emberugs, Syosset
Mrs. L. Winum, Walden
Lightsaround, Inc., Wantagh
De Mallie Crafts, Webster

Parker Publishing Co., Inc., West Nyack
Susan Sirkis, West Point
Elyse Sommer, Woodmere
Economy Handicrafts, Inc., Woodside
Nature's Fibers, Woodstock
Frances La Monica, Yonkers
Lamonica, Yonkers
Wee Goodies of the Month Club, Yonkers

North Carolina
A 'N L's Hobbicraft, Inc., Asheville
Ken Kyte, Asheville
Southern Highlands Handicraft Guild, Asheville
Suncoast Models, Black Mountain
Old South Patterns, Charlotte
Crowe & Coulter, Cherokee
Concrete Machinery Co., Hickory
Blank-It Corp., Monroe
Lily Mills Co., Shelby
Jamar, Inc., Winston-Salem
Stevenson Industries, Winston-Salem

Ohio
National Artcraft Supply Co., Beechwood
Mountain Ceramic Crafts, Bethesda
Cake Decorators & Craft Supplies, Blacklick
Schrock's, The House of Hobbies & Crafts, Canton
Sewing Products Co., Cincinnati
Sign of the Times Publishing Co., Cincinnati
The Stearns & Foster Co., Cincinnati
N. S. Braverman, Cleveland
Cleveland Leather Co., Cleveland
Cleveland Model & Supply Co., Cleveland
Craftint Manufacturing Co., Cleveland
Doll Repair Parts, Inc., Cleveland
Immerman's Crafts, Cleveland
Kraft Korner, Cleveland
Lee Lapidaries, Cleveland
James F. Lincoln Arc Welding Foundation, Cleveland
National Hobby Inc., Cleveland
Sterling Hallmark Co., Cleveland
String Instrument Service Inc., Cleveland
University Circle Publications and Supply Co., Cleveland

Geographical Index
Ohio—Pennsylvania

Ceramics Monthly, Columbus
Historic House, Columbus
Knit Services, Inc., Columbus
The Macrame Studio, Columbus
Kristine Eckert, Dayton
Tepping Studio Supply Co., Dayton
Tye's, Dayton
Cramer Mold Shop, Fostoria
The Yarn Dome, Greenville
Ohio Ceramic Supply Inc., Kent
Smithers Oasis, Kent
The Oriental Rug Co., Lima
Jim's Rock Shop, Louisville
Al Schoellkopf Mold Co., Mansfield
Mrs. Frieda Koudelka, Medina
Metals Engineering Institute, Metals Park
Betty Fielding, Mogadore
J & H Clasgens Co., New Richmond
Van Gelder Wood Products, Niles
Mars Models, Northfield
Old Time Shop, Poland
Reggi's Ceramic Colors, Rossford
O-P Craft Co., Inc., Sandusky
The Cab-N-Facet, Inc., Springfield
Campbell Tools Co., Springfield
Anchor Mold Co., Tipp City
Kaleidoscope Needleworks, Toledo
Netcraft, Toledo
Universal Wirecraft Jewelry Co., Vermillion
Unique Handicraft, Wickliffe
Century 21, Youngstown

Oklahoma
Geological Enterprises, Ardmore
Thieves Market, Ardmore
Belle Craft, Guthrie
Whitson's, Miami
Rose Rocks Co., Moore
The Hen House, Muskogee
China Painter, Oklahoma City
House of Clay China Shop, Oklahoma City
Jean's, Oklahoma City
Scissortail Arts & Crafts, Oklahoma City
Turpen Times, Oklahoma City
World Organization of China Painters, Oklahoma City
Salyer Publishing Co., Olkahoma City
J. Opal Stover Studio, Seminole
Ewanna England, Tulsa
Guitar Center, Tulsa
K & L Co., Tulsa
Priscilla's Little Red Tole House, Tulsa
F. C. Ziegler Co., Tulsa
The Corner Shop, Wewoka
Edna Looney Originals, Wewoka

Oregon
Karen Burrus, Albany
Sandy Symons, Ashwood
Western Tree Cones, Corvallis
Reade Knitting Designs, Eugene
Tole 'N Stuff, Eugene
Keith Robinson, Florence
Driftwood House, Harbor
Frankie's Twistcraft Jewelry, La Pine
The Loom Factory, Marcola
Robin & Russ Handweavers, McMinnville
Warp & Weft, McMinnville
The Ducketts, Medford
The Sandvigs, Medford
Cooke Novelty Co., Milwaukee
Sachiye Jones, Monroe
Rock Mountain Farm, Mosier
Gay World of Dolls Museum, Oregon City
Bernadette Decorative Art, Portland
Frank Boothe, Portland
Charm Woven Labels, Portland
Wm. Hooper, Portland
Jenkins Lapidary Equipment, Portland
Kandel Knits, Inc., Portland
Loftons, Portland
George Marshall, Portland
Mill Ends Store, Portland
Montana Assay Office, Portland
A. Raimer, Portland
John & Susan Scheewe, Salem
Rays Rock Shop, Scappoose

Pennsylvania
Needles 'N Hoops, Abington
House of Wood Candles, Allentown
Butterick Fashion Marketing Co., Altoona
Home-Sew Inc., Bethlehem
Portfolio of Egg Artistry, Bethlehem
Make It Happen Craft Studio, Broomall
Wagner's Crafts, Broomall
Bea Freeman Enterprises, Bryn Mawr
Victoria Gifts, Bryn Mawr

Geographical Index
Pennsylvania—Tennessee

Columbia Candlecraft, Catasauqua
Lochs, Center Valley
House of York, Doylestown
The Mannings Creative Crafts, East Berlin
Kathryn Johnson, Easton
Weaver's Gems and Minerals, Emmaus
Sinclair's Auto Miniatures Inc., Erie
Rombins' Nest Farm, Fairfield
Leisure Hour Products, Freeland
Hoffman Hatchery, Gratz
Hanover House Industries, Inc., Hanover
The Rusty Nail, Hanover
Santos Miniatures, Harrisburg
Stackpole Books, Harrisburg
Lapidabrade Inc., Havertown
Gilman's, Hellertown
Crewel World, Huntingdon Valley
Walnut Hill Co., Huntingdon Valley
Glass Creations, Huntingdon Valley
Wyco Yarn Co., Jenkintown
Bingaman Plans, Langhorne
Homecraft Veneer, Latrobe
Cottage Crafts, Malvern
Pioneer Crafts, Malvern
The Cellar Ceramic Shop, Mechanicsburg
English's Model Railroad Supply, Montoursville
Amro, New Oxford
Tinkler & Co. Inc., Norristown
Angelo Bros. Co., Philadelphia
Associated Hobby Manufacturers Inc., Philadelphia
Bachmann, Philadelphia
Charles M. Butterworth, Philadelphia
Cliveden Yarns, Philadelphia
Conlin Yarns, Philadelphia
Diversikit, Inc., Philadelphia
Glass Bottle Blowers Assn., Philadelphia
T. B. Hagstoz & Son, Philadelphia
Keller-Charles of Philadelphia, Philadelphia
J. B. Lippincott Co., Philadelphia
Mindy Molds, Philadelphia
Nicole Bead & Craft Co., Inc., Philadelphia
Odyssey Mineral and Fossil, Philadelphia
Plexiglas, Philadelphia
Rohm & Haas Co., Philadelphia
Silvo Hardware Co., Philadelphia
Jane Snead Samplers, Philadelphia
D. R. Wolfe Overglazes, Philadelphia
Creative Hands Co., Inc., Pittsburgh
The Fringe and Frame, Pittsburgh
National Standards Council of American Embroiderers, Pittsburgh
Sculptmetal Co., Pittsburgh
Standard Ceramic Supply, Pittsburgh
The Thread Shed, Inc., Pittsburgh
King's Studio, Quakertown
Chilton Book Co., Radnor
American Machine & Tool Co., Royersford
Auto World, Inc., Scranton
International Correspondence Schools, Scranton
Boycan's Craft Supplies, Sharon
Marquerite P. Davison, Swarthmore
Candlewic Co., Warrington
Mill Store, Williamsport
Carol Rice Creatives, Williamsport

Rhode Island
Craft Yarns of Rhode Island Inc., Harrisville
House of Kleen, Hope Valley
E. H. Ashley & Co., Inc., Providence
Shuttlecraft, Providence
Heirloom Rugs, Rumford
Carson & Ellis, Inc., Warwick

South Carolina
Coker Craft, Charleston
Folbot Corp., Charleston
Richland Ceramics Inc., Columbia
George W. Park Seed Co., Inc., Greenwood
Brunswick Worsted Mills, Pickens
W. B. Roddey, Richburg

South Dakota
American Indian Portrait Dolls, Armour
Supreme Handicrafts, Sioux Falls

Tennessee
Jo's Doll Dressing Course, Bristol
Kick-Shaw Inc., Cattanooga
Davis & Co., Concord
Colonial Decorations, Knoxville
Lynchburg Hdwr. & General Store, Lynchburg
Contemporary Quilts, Memphis
Flags Galore, Memphis

Geographical Index
Tennessee—Washington

Swan-Son, Murfeesboro
James L. Douthat, Pikeville
Bedford Lumber Co., Inc., Shelbyville
Virgil Owens, Tullahoma

Texas
Twin Peaks Rock Shop, Alpine
Woodward Ranch, Alpine
Plasco, Alvord
Dek-Co Manufacturing Co., Amarillo
Jane's Ceramic Molds, Athens
J. W. Day Mfg. Co., Austin
De Lapa Mining Inc., Corpus Christi
F. E. Biegert Co., Dallas
Biship's House of Gems, Dallas
Curio Ceramic Molds, Dallas
Eagle Mill, Dallas
Max of Dallas, Dallas
Miniature Figurines--USA, Inc., Dallas
Paragon Industries Inc., Dallas
Swest Inc., Dallas
Artrox Rock of the Month Club, El Paso
Gem Center, U.S.A., El Paso
Gorin's Gem Arts & Rocks, El Paso
Maytex, El Paso
American Handicrafts, Fort Worth
Audria's, Fort Worth
Decorating & Craft Ideas Made Easy, Fort Worth
Make It With Leather, Fort Worth
Merribee, Fort Worth
Radio Shack, Fort Worth
Al Stohlman Leathercraft Home Study Course, Fort Worth
Tandy Leather Co., Fort Worth
Mrs. Carl F. Murray, Friendswood
Deep Flex Plastic Molds, Inc., Ft. Worth
Melbourn Gem Co., Ft. Worth
The Amber Lion, Fulton
Craft Kits, Houston
The Farmhouse Craft Shoppe, Houston
The Mail Train, Houston
Man-Pak, Inc., Houston
Robertson Studio, Houston
Wel-Dex Mfg. Co., Houston
Barbara Jones China House, Longview
Irene Goodwin, Lubbock
Ruth Little's Studio, Lubbock
Shoenail Supply, Pampa
Spincraft, Richardson
Margaret Davis, San Angelo

Mission Rocks, San Angelo
Virgil V. Lundell, San Antonio
M. Nowotny, San Antonio
Rock's Lapidary Equipment, San Antonio
Swest Inc., San Antonio
Dorothy Mae's Trunks, Spearman
Taylor Bedding Mfg. Co., Taylor

Utah
Beaver Canyon Campground, Beaver
Bonnie's Rock Shop, Brigham
Naakai Dine-E Biye, Mexican Hat
Starfire Lapidary, Orem
Dowse's Lapidary Supply, Inc., Salt Lake City
Frank J. Nelson, Salt Lake City
Ken Stewart's Gem Shop, Salt Lake City
Zim's, Salt Lake City

Vermont
American Decorative Arts, Inc., Dorset
Candle Mill Village, East Arlington
Tools of the Trade, Fair Haven
The Enchanted Doll House, Manchester Center
Vermont Toy Crafts, Manchester Center
ARE Creations Inc., Plainfield
Charles E. Tuttle Co. Inc., Rutland
KeeWai Krafts, Wells River

Virginia
Doris Taylor, Alexandria
Fountains for the Home, Arlington
Chrismon Committee, Danville
Holly Studio Inc, Kilmarnock
Bay Country Woodcrafters, Oak Hall
Cavalier Handicrafts, Richmond
Evelyn Downing, Richmond
Dorothy Berryman Studio, Virginia Beach

Washington
The Country Craftsmen, Bainbridge Island
Northwest Looms, Bainbridge Island
Barb's Shoe Makings, Bellevue
Three Gables Homecrafts, Bremerton
Alfred Decker, Camas
M & M Distributors, Everett
Floyd Fleming, Federal Way
Pacific Crafts, Fenndale
Fiber to Fabric, Kirkland

Geographical Index
Washington—Foreign

Glencraft Shop, Poulsbo
Barker Enterprises, Seattle
Bell Studio, Seattle
Deb Products, Seattle
Down Under Opal, Seattle
Fetty-Nielsen Macrame Loom, Seattle
Hillquist, Seattle
Journal of Contemporary Metalcraft, Casting, Related Arts, Seattle
The Loomery, Seattle
Lortone Inc., Seattle
Magic Circle Corp., Seattle
Magnolia Weaving, Seattle
Pourette Mfg. Co., Seattle
Studio Yarn Farms Inc., Seattle
Technical Specialties International Inc., Seattle
Custom Made Carvings & Miniatures, Spokane
Thomas S. Maquire's, Spokane
The Victors, Spokane
Lakewood Lapidary, Tacoma
Stop 'N Rock Shop, Tekoa
Arlene Handley Rock Hobby Supplies, Vancouver
May-Wal, Inc., Vancouver

Washington, DC
Silver Shuttle, DC

West Virginia
Vicki's Patience Unlimited, Huntington

Wisconsin
Amherst Press, Amherst
Marcella's Ceramics Inc., Beloit
Struck Corp., Cedarburg
Crafty Ideas, Evansville
Diedricks Crafts, Evansville
NASCO Arts & Crafts, Ft. Atkinson
Woodland Craft Designs, Hazelhurst
Village Candle & Craft, Marshfield
Great Central Fur Corp., Milwaukee
Kalmbach Publishing Co., Milwaukee
J. C. Penney Co., Inc., Milwaukee
Sax Arts & Crafts, Milwaukee
Switched On, Ltd., Milwaukee
Terminal Hobby Shop, Milwaukee
Wm. Walthers Inc., Milwaukee
Universal Strap Co., Mt. Jackson
Miles Kimball, Oshkosh
Dremel Creative Power Tools, Racine
Wichelt Import Co., Stoddard
The Yarn Nook, Stoughton
The Handcrafters, Waupun
Kessenich Looms, Wauwatosa
Dale Magnuson, Winter

Wyoming
The China Cottage, Casper
Torrington Rock Shop, Torrington

Foreign
Cambridge Wools, Auckland, New Zealand
R. S. Duncan & Co., Bradford, BD150P, West Yorkshire, England
Charbonneau's Lapidary Service, Calgary, Alberta, Canada
Green's Rock & Lapidary Ltd., Calgary, Alberta T2E 2S2, Canada
Green Bay Exploration & Mining Co. Ltd., Chilliwack, B.C., Canada
Z-Handicrafts, Fulford, Quebec, Canada
Libra Gems, Goderich, Ontario, Canada
Nilus Leclerc Inc., L'Islet, Quebec, Canada
Maharani Boutique, London W1, England
Needlewoman Shop, London, WIR6BA, England
Gary H. Watson, Lower Hutt, New Zealand
Minex Lapidary Supplies, Melbourne 3000, Australia
Australian Gem Trading Co., Melbourne, Australia 3000
Handcraft House, North Vancouver, B.C., Canada
Northwest Handcraft House, North Vancouver, B.C., Canada
John E. Garrett Ltd., Nova Scotia, Canada
Ovgem Craft Supply Co., Ottawa, Canada K2POB8
Wm. Condon & Sons Ltd., P.E. Island, Canada
Phentex, Inc., Quebec, Canada
Ashford Handicrafts Ltd., Rakaia, Canterbury, New Zealand
The Amulet, Scarborough, Ontario, Canada
Filature Lemieux Inc., St. Ephrem De Beauce, Quebec, Canada
Canadian Aero-Supply, Toronto Canada
Lewiscraft, Toronto M5V 1J3, Canada

Geographical Index
Foreign—Foreign

Fotocut Lab, Toronto Ontario M6H 2Y8, Canada
Behnsen Silk Screen Supply Ltd., Vancouver 2, B.C., Canada
Woolcraft Ltd., Vancouver 2, B.C., Canada
New World Jade Co., Vancouver 9, B.C., Canada
Creator's Corner, Vancouver, B.C., Canada
Marshall's Lapidary Co., Ltd., Vancouver, B.C., Canada
Interlectric House of Fine Australian Opals, Victoria, Australia
House of Orange, Victoria, B.C. Canada
John's Hardware & Decoupage Supplies, Windsor 19, Ontario, Canada
Jean McIntosh Ltd., Winnipeg 10, Manitoba, Canada
Leonida Leatherdale's Embroidery Studio, Winnipeg, Manitoba R3C 2C3, Canada
Elvette Handbag Co., Winnipeg, R3B1K9, Canada